WORLD
BROADCASTING
SYSTEMS

WADSWORTH SERIES IN MASS COMMUNICATION

Rebecca Hayden, Senior Editor

GENERAL

The New Communications by Frederick Williams

Mediamerica: Form, Content, and Consequence of Mass Communication, 3d, by Edward Jay Whetmore

The Interplay of Influence: Mass Media & Their Publics in News, Advertising, Politics by Kathleen Hall Jamieson and Karlyn Kohrs Campbell

Mass Communication and Everyday Life: A Perspective on Theory and Effects by Dennis K. Davis and Stanley J. Baran

Mass Media Research: An Introduction by Roger D. Wimmer and Joseph R. Dominick

The Internship Experience by Lynne Schafer Gross

TELECOMMUNICATIONS

Stay Tuned: A Concise History of American Broadcasting by Christopher H. Sterling and John M. Kittross

Writing for Television and Radio, 4th, by Robert L. Hilliard

Communicating Effectively on Television by Evan Blythin and Larry A. Samovar

World Broadcasting Systems: A Comparative Analysis by Sydney W. Head

Broadcast/Cable Programming: Strategies and Practices, 2d, by Susan Tyler Eastman, Sydney W. Head, and Lewis Klein

Advertising in the Broadcast and Cable Media, 2d, by Elizabeth J. Heighton and Don R. Cunningham

Strategies in Broadcast and Cable Promotion by Susan Tyler Eastman and Robert A. Klein

Modern Radio Station Practices, 2d, by Joseph S. Johnson and Kenneth K. Jones

The Magic Medium: An Introduction to Radio in America by Edward Jay Whetmore

Audio in Media by Stanley R. Alten

Television Production Handbook, 4th, by Herbert Zettl

Sight–Sound–Motion: Applied Media Aesthetics by Herbert Zettl

Electronic Cinematography: Achieving Photographic Control over the Video Image by Harry Mathias and Richard Patterson

JOURNALISM

Media Writing: News for the Mass Media by Doug Newsom and James A. Wollert

Excellence in College Journalism by Wayne Overbeck and Thomas M. Pasqua

When Words Collide: A Journalist's Guide to Grammar & Style by Lauren Kessler and Duncan McDonald

News Editing in the '80s: Text and Exercises by William L. Rivers

Reporting Public Affairs: Problems and Solutions by Ronald P. Lovell

Newswriting for the Electronic Media: Principles, Examples, Applications by Daniel E. Garvey and William L. Rivers

Free-Lancer and Staff Writer: Newspaper Features and Magazine Articles, 3d, by William L. Rivers and Shelley Smolkin

Magazine Editing in the '80s: Text and Exercises by William L. Rivers

This is PR: The Realities of Public Relations, 3d, by Doug Newsom and Alan Scott

Writing in Public Relations Practice: Form and Style by Doug Newsom and Tom Siegfried

Creative Strategy in Advertising, 2d, by A. Jerome Jewler

WORLD BROADCASTING SYSTEMS
A Comparative Analysis

SYDNEY W. HEAD
University of Miami

Wadsworth Publishing Company
Belmont, California
A Division of Wadsworth, Inc.

ACKNOWLEDGMENTS Quotations are reprinted with permission from the following sources. **Billboard Publications, Inc.:** an excerpt from J.M. Frost, ed., *World Radio TV Handbook*, 1983. **Columbia University Press:** excerpts from Jeremy Tunstall, *The Media Are American*, ©1977 Columbia University Press. **Commonwealth Broadcasting Association:** excerpts from *Combroad 27, 35, 46, 49, 50, 51, 53, 54, 56, 57, 59.* **David and Charles:** excerpts from Anthony Smith, *British Broadcasting*, 1974. **EBU Review:** an excerpt from George Ridoux, "Audiovisual Communications in France, Stage Two," *EBU Review*, November 1982. **Her Majesty's Stationery Office:** excerpts from *Report of the Committee on the Future of Broadcasting* (Annan Report), 1977. **Independent Broadcasting Authority:** excerpts from *Television and Radio, 1983.* **International Institute of Communications:** excerpts from *InterMedia 7-5, 10-2, 10-3, 10-4/5, 11-3, 11-4/5.* **Zhang Li:** excerpts from "Unpublished and Unofficial Paper Summarizing Chinese Mass Media Facts," 1983. **The Macmillan Press Ltd.:** excerpts from Anthony Smith, *Television and Political Life*, 1979. **National Book Trust, India:** excerpts from Mehra Masani, *Broadcasting and the People*, 1976. **A.D. Peters & Co. Ltd.:** excerpts from J.C.W. Reith, *Into the Wind*, 1949. **Praeger:** excerpts from Roland S. Homet, *Politics, Cultures and Communication*, 1979; Ellen P. Mickiewicz, *Media and the Russian Public*, 1981; and Donald R. Browne, *International Radio Broadcasting*, 1982. **Sage Publications, Inc.:** excerpts from Thomas L. McPhail, *Electronic Colonialism*, 1981. **Temple University Press:** excerpts from Douglas A. Boyd, *Broadcasting in the Arab World*, 1982; Julian Hale, *Radio Power*, 1975; and John A. Lent, *Broadcasting in Asia and the Pacific*, 1978. **UNESCO:** excerpts from *Many Voices, One World*, ©1980 UNESCO. **University of Illinois Press:** excerpts from Anthony Smith, *The Shadow in the Cave*, 1973. **University of Minnesota Press:** excerpts from Burton Paulu, *Radio and Television Broadcasting in Eastern Europe*, 1974; and Burton Paulu, *Television and Radio in the United Kingdom*, 1981.

Senior Editor: Rebecca Hayden
Production Editor: Jane Townsend
Managing Designer: Paula Shuhert
Designer: Arianne Dickinson
Copy Editor: Russell Fuller
Print Buyer: Barbara Britton

Printed in the United States of America
1 2 3 4 5 6 7 8 9 10——89 88 87 86 85

ISBN 0-534-04734-3

Library of Congress Cataloging in Publication Data
Head, Sydney W.
  World broadcasting systems.

  Includes index.
  1. Broadcasting.   I. Title.
HE8689.4.H43   1985   384.54   84-21019
ISBN 0-534-04734-3

FOREWORD

I first began thinking seriously about comparative broadcasting systems upon going to Africa in 1960, heading a team of advisers for the Sudan Broadcasting System. Realizing that it would never do to advise merely imitating American programming and production methods, I felt compelled to examine the fundamental nature of broadcasting, asking myself how best to adapt it to the service of Sudanese culture. What attributes of broadcasting, I asked, rise above the political, economic, geographic, and cultural settings in which a particular system operates? Thus I acquired the habit of thinking about the attributes of broadcasting in comparative terms, an outlook that stood me in good stead when teaching and advising in a dozen different settings in the course of ten years in Africa. Among other things, during that decade I served as a consultant on UNESCO's first conference on educational broadcasting in Africa (Moshi, 1961) and as a member of the official United States observer delegation to the UNESCO Meeting of Experts on the Development of Information Media in Africa (Paris, 1962).

Soon after returning to the United States and joining Temple University in 1970, I began teaching a course in comparative broadcasting. Like most teachers of the subject, I found the lack of a textbook and the paucity of reference materials frustrating. This frustration gave me the impetus to propose the comparative regional surveys of broadcasting that I edit for the Temple University Press. They started with my own volume on Africa (1974) and have gone on to John Lent's on Asia and the Pacific (1978) and Douglas Boyd's on the Arab World (1982). A volume on Latin America is in preparation. At Temple I also taught a summer seminar in British and Commonwealth Broadcasting in London and spent a season at the University of Ghana as a Fulbright professor of broadcasting.

By the time I retired from Temple in 1980, much more literature on individual systems had become available, but still no comprehensive textbook on comparative broadcasting had emerged. When I began teaching part time at the University of Miami shortly after leaving Temple, I felt at last equipped with both the background and the time, as well as a suitable academic footing, to attempt to fill the textbook gap.

Upon once more scanning the existing books, I felt convinced that a world survey based on piling up descriptions of individual systems, one upon another, would bore and confuse students with masses of repetitive data. The task called for a more probing, analytical technique of comparison, such as the approaches taken on a limited scale by Burton Paulu in his study of Western European systems (1967), by Katz and Wedell in their report on Third World systems (1977), and by Donald Browne in his analysis of external services (1982).

Instead of describing typical systems in their entirety (which the student can study individually with the help of the annual *World Radio TV Handbook* and other existing literature), I decided to organize the text on the basis of the common problems faced by *all* systems. Every system, no matter what its setting, must deal with the basic, universal demands and dilemmas of the medium. The inherent attributes of broadcasting itself, interacting with the circumstances of a particular national setting, leave policymakers and managers with relatively few options in deciding how to finance, regulate, deploy, organize, manage, afford access to, and program their systems. Focusing on these options, which I dubbed the "problem-solving" approach, gives the student a few key questions to ask about each system, enabling a relatively easy yet meaningful comparative analysis. Moreover, students can, after making due allowances for the limitations imposed by a particular national setting, critically appraise a system by comparing reality with the ideal possibilities implied by broadcasting's attributes.

The problem-solving approach, though presumably easier for the student, did not make things easier for the writer. Surveying the entire world of broadcasting is at best a daunting task; indeed, during the course of the writing, it seemed at times downright impossible. One of the many people I consulted in the course of the writing, an Englishman working in France, remarked that it took him four years of residence there to understand French broadcasting.* Fortunately, not every system is as intricate as the French. But one cannot travel everywhere to make personal observations; even if one could, it would be

---

*Garratt, 1981: 36.

so as to absorb the nuances of every system. Of necessity, one relies heavily on experts on various specialties and on various parts of the world. I am grateful not only to previous writers and editors whose works I have read and liberally quoted but also to friends, acquaintances, and even total strangers who gave time generously to answer enquiries. Their counsel saved me from many errors. Doubtless I have made others, notwithstanding their aid, for which they of course cannot be held responsible.

Especially heartfelt thanks must go to Claude-Jean Bertrand of the University of Paris and Donald R. Browne of the University of Minnesota. International scholars of exceptionally wide experience, they read every chapter, sometimes in several different versions, making innumerable corrections and comments that saved me from many a blunder and led to invaluable improvements.

Apologizing in advance for any names inadvertently overlooked, I must also thank those who read and commented on particular sections of the manuscript, supplied specific facts, or gave more general advice. They include George Beebe, World Press Freedom Committee; William R. Berry, State University of New York, Geneseo; Douglas Boyd, University of Delaware; Aggrey Brown, University of the West Indies; Bernard Bumpus, formerly of the BBC External Services; Bruce Cook, David C. Cook Foundation; Karen Dajani, USIA/Yaounde; M. R. Dua, Indian Institute of Mass Communication; H. J. Duncan, South African Broadcasting Corporation; Desmond Fisher, formerly of Radio Telefis Eirann; Isola Folorunso, Federal Radio Corporation of Nigeria; Arthur Garratt, consultant and contributor to *Professional Video*; Arve Granlund, Norwegian Broadcasting Authority; K. Kyoon Hur, late of the University of Texas at Austin; Kenneth K. Jones, San Diego State University; Donald Le Duc, University of Wisconsin; John Lent, Temple University; Zhang Li, Institute of Journalism, Beijing; Elizabeth Mahan, Yale University; Henry Mayer, University of Sydney, Australia; Nikos Metallinos, Concordia University, Canada; John Nichols, Pennsylvania State University; Burton Paulu, University of Minnesota; Kuldip R. Rampal, Central Missouri State University; Jeff Rushton, Federation of Australian Radio Broadcasters; Girgis Salama, Plateau Television, Jos, Nigeria; Lemuel Schofield, University of Miami; Pedro Simoncini, Canal 5, Rosario, Argentina; Alvin Snyder, USIA, Washington; Christopher Sterling, George Washington University; Joseph Straubhaar, Michigan State University; Izumi Tadokoro, Nihon Shinbun Kyokai, Tokyo; Alexander Toogood, Temple University; Frank Ugboajah, University of Lagos, Nigeria; Kees Van der Haak, NOS, Netherlands; and James W. Welke, University of Wyoming. Finally, my thanks to Peter B. Orlik, Central Michigan University, for preparation of the accompanying instructor's manual.

Closer to home, my wife heroically overcame computerphobia to help with word processing, patiently endured the hardest editing chores, and gave much needed moral support. I greatly appreciated the assistance of David Gordon and Mitchell Shapiro, respectively Communication Department chairperson at University of Miami and coordinator of the department's Telecommunication Area; their backing gave me an essential academic base. Among other advantages, my appointment at Miami as Research Professor enabled me to try out some of the book's concepts in seminars on comparative broadcasting.

Coral Gables, Florida
January 1985

CONTENTS

Contents

Contents

MOTIVES AND METHODS OF COMPARATIVE BROADCASTING STUDIES

V irtually all the world's 216 sovereign nations and dependent territories have their own broadcasting systems.* All have much in common, yet each has its unique features. Why should anyone be interested in studying all these systems? How can one best be compared with another? These are the key questions addressed in this chapter.

1 ▪ 1   GOALS OF COMPARATIVE STUDIES

Though installed in widely varying social settings and differing enormously in their scope and complexity, the 200-plus national and territorial broadcasting systems share the same electromagnetic spectrum, in accordance with (or sometimes in defiance of) common international regulations. They deliver essentially similar (sometimes even identical) packets of entertainment, information, education, and inspiration, organized into similar daily program schedules. Thanks to satellite relays, the entire world can sometimes tune in simultaneously to the same broadcast event. Soon (if not even as you read this page) listeners and viewers in some parts of the world will have the option of bypassing their own national systems to pick up programs from foreign countries beamed down to their antennas from direct broadcast satellites. Of course, spillover signals from domestic stations in neighboring countries, as well as purposeful transborder transmissions from external services, already come from foreign sources. Thus broadcasting has an inherently international character.

---

*Of the 216 systems, 37 are in dependent territories. This enumeration is based on listings in the 38th edition of the *World Radio TV Handbook* (hereinafter referred to as *WRTH*, 1984).

Paradoxically, though, each national system, has a unique quality. A country's broadcasting system mirrors national character, expressing a particular political philosophy and cultural identity. "National character" in this context refers not only to traits native to a particular country but also to adopted or imposed traits. A powerful neighbor influences broadcasting in adjoining countries. Colonies inherited the broadcasting structures and hardware of their rulers; after gaining independence, former colonies modified these inheritances, but vestiges tend to endure, embedded in the new structures. All Communist systems have underlying similarities, yet each has its own traits.* Dozens of systems all over the world bear traces of the British Broadcasting Corporation's influence, yet none comes near to duplicating the British model. As Anthony Smith, a leading British student of comparative broadcasting, put it, "Every society has to reinvent broadcasting in its own image, as a means for containing or suppressing the geographical, political, spiritual and social dilemmas which broadcasting entails" (Smith, 1973: 50).

Among other things, comparative studies explore this paradoxical contrast between broadcasting as a universal, international medium and broadcasting as a uniquely national medium. Comparative analysis seeks to identify and explain both the similarities and the differences. Going beyond simply listing such similarities and contrasts, comparative analysis explores the dynamic processes that brought them about. Thus the goal is to analyze not only broadcasting systems as such but also the character of the nations and territories they serve.

In devising and developing their systems, nations have always taken a comparative approach, looking toward other countries' solutions to common broadcasting problems, hoping both to avoid the mistakes and to benefit from the successes of others. Soon after 1920, when radio broadcasting began as a regular service in the United States, foreign officials and entrepreneurs began visiting America to learn firsthand how its phenomenally fast-growing system worked. "The American experience," wrote a British observer in 1924, "provided a valuable lesson. It showed the dangers which might result in a diversely populated country of a small area like [the United Kingdom] if the go-as-you-please methods of the United States were copied" (quoted in Briggs, 1961: 67). In 1977 the Annan Committee wrote a report on the future of British broadcasting, preliminary to Parliament's consideration of renewal terms for existing licenses in the United Kingdom. The committee took testimony from a great variety of British citizens and also studied the current broadcasting situation in a dozen other countries. Committee members even personally visited Canada, Israel, France, New Zealand, West Germany, and the United States.[1]

---

*Writing of broadcasting in the East European Communist nations, Paulu emphasizes "their separateness and their individuality" (1974: 5).

Starting in the late 1960s, government bodies as well as academic researchers began doing more formal and wide-ranging comparative studies than had been usual up to then. New social problems and rapidly evolving technology began posing difficult decisions for political leaders, legislators, and administrators. The general public also became involved when voters had to choose among candidates with opposing ideas about national communication policies. Though such issues have not been high on the agendas of party platforms in the United States, they often become leading topics of political debate in other democracies. Parties take sides on such issues as whether broadcasting stations should be open to private ownership; on what terms, if at all, advertising should be permitted; and how cable television should be regulated.

Students of broadcasting—not only academics but also bureaucrats and politicians—find comparative studies valuable for deepening their understanding of the medium and sharpening critical tools. Analyzing alternative solutions to common problems and appraising their results affords the broad perspective needed for making informed judgments about the present status and future prospects of any national system. Students of communication theory also find comparative studies of interest for their role in generating hypotheses about the underlying nature of mass communication.

1 ▪ 2   PROBLEM-SOLVING ORIENTATION

Rather than using the more common country-by-country approach, this book takes what might be called a "problem-by-problem" approach to comparative analysis. The former results in a great deal of repetition because broadcasting systems have so many similarities. By the time one reads about the board of directors of the tenth broadcasting service, one begins to lose interest in boards of directors. This book shifts the emphasis from *particular systems* to *universal problems*—fundamental questions arising initially when any national authority decides to start up a broadcasting system and continuing to crop up in the course of its development. This approach involves examining the *range of solutions* that nations have adopted when faced with the problems common to all systems.

For example, when a country plans to install a broadcasting system, it must decide how to pay the costs. It might choose direct government subsidy from general tax revenues, advertising revenue from commercialized services, license fees assessed for the use of receiving sets, or a combination of these and still other sources of funds. All systems share the common problem of having to find adequate and reliable financial support, and all must choose from a limited number of feasible sources. Nations solve the problem of finance within the framework of their own economic, political, and cultural natures. The funding source or combination of sources that a country chooses profoundly influences the nature of its broadcasting services.

In short, the method used in this book consists of first identifying common problems; second, looking at the range of solutions that have been adopted in practice; and, finally, suggesting which solutions seem to work best in terms of getting the most out of the intrinsic potentials of broadcasting.

Attributes of Broadcasting

What are the "universal problems" and "intrinsic potentials" referred to above? One can identify them by sorting out the special attributes of broadcasting—its unique characteristics as both a technology and a social force. Each primary attribute of the medium gives rise to various secondary characteristics or potentialities; these in turn imply optional structures and methods of organizing, programming, and producing. I have isolated for discussion seven basic attributes that seem to have special relevancy in comparing systems.

Before discussing them, I must warn the reader that another observer might characterize these attributes in different ways, discuss them in another order, identify either more or fewer of them. In other words, the choices may seem somewhat arbitrary and subjective. Readers will have no difficulty in finding overlaps and contradictions among the seven attributes discussed below. Nor will every policymaker and broadcaster consciously exploit these potentials in practice—those closest to the trees often have difficulty in seeing the forest. But even when misused or underused, broadcasting has a wonderful resiliency. In monopolistic situations, where consumers have no opportunity to choose among fully competitive domestic services, they continue to tune in to programs for which they may have little respect and in which they may have little confidence. Given the opportunity to choose alternatives, however, people lose no time in patronizing services that satisfy urges ignored by their domestic stations.

The seven attributes include broadcasting's ubiquity, immediacy, voracity, flexibility, voluntariness, interference proneness, and its potential as a means for social control.

Ubiquity. Broadcasting has a unique ability to instantaneously surmount both natural and artificial barriers, both physical and human obstacles to communication. Among other things, this means that, within a given transmitter's service area, it costs no more to reach an audience of a million than an audience of one—assuming, of course, that the audience members voluntarily defray part of the cost by purchasing and operating their own receivers. Equally important, from the psychological and social point of view, broadcasting's ability to enter directly into the home, once a receiver has been installed, has significant implications as to types of programs and standards of production that people in any particular society will accept. No other medium can reach out to such a wide range of persons in varied environments under such diverse conditions. Broadcasting can appeal to people of all ages in all places, to people of all classes, educated or not. And it achieves this coverage with remarkable economy if efficiently used.

Immediacy. Broadcasting also has the unique attribute of being potentially always *there*, immediately on tap whenever needed. Other media arrive at their destinations intermittently and in discrete packages: the morning paper arrives once a day, the magazine appears in the mailbox once a week or month, and movie theaters offer only a limited number of daily showings. Broadcast programming, however, enters the home or other personal environment minute by minute, continuously unfolding, even as life itself. This immediacy allows broadcasting to synchronize its services with the lives of its audiences, providing timely programs to fit the needs or moods of each phase of the daily life cycle; also, broadcasting can transmit the sounds and sights of reality directly from the scenes of action. To take full advantage of this attribute, appropriate broadcast services must be continuously available.

Voracity. Its continuousness gives broadcasting a voracious appetite. No other medium consumes material so relentlessly and in such quantity. Even a truncated television schedule of only four hours a day (not unusually short in Third World countries) demands nearly three thousand half hours of program material per year. Such demands impose heavy economic and creative burdens, impossible for small systems to sustain without outside help. The medium's technology thus encourages the shared use of program resources in order to draw on a wide range of creative resources and bring the cost per viewer down. In practice, this results in national and international distribution of programs by means of networks and syndication, both of which have the effect of spreading program costs over large numbers of consumers. Such necessary sharing contributes to the international character of the medium.

Flexibility. Transmitters can cover areas of varied sizes and shapes, according to each system's needs. Moreover, they can be interconnected to form regional, national, or international networks. A transmitter that serves as a local or regional outlet can become an outlet for national network programs by the flip of a control-room switch. This flexibility has important implications for national broadcasting policies. For example, using network affiliates as mere repeaters of centrally produced programs gains in efficiency but sacrifices the potential for variety and increased audience satisfaction that regionalized and localized programming can bring.

Voluntariness. Broadcasting relies on audiences to tune in of their own free choice. Of course, reading books and newspapers and going to the movies also involve voluntary acts. But voluntariness in broadcasting goes a step further: it asks audience members to make a *capital investment* in the hardware of the system by purchasing receivers. True, group listening and viewing over facilities provided by governments do exist. During the Cultural Revolution under Chairman Mao, China evolved the use of public loudspeakers to a greater degree than any other society. Public facilities still operate, but after the fall of Mao, the new Chinese leaders repudiated excessive use of the ubiquitous public loudspeakers. Despite such exceptions, individual or family reception in a home setting, rather than group reception in a community setting, can be considered the characteristic mode of broadcast reception.

The need for services capable of motivating nearly everyone in a nation to invest voluntarily in receivers and bear the cost of operation has a powerful influence on the nature of programming. Materials must be chosen, produced, and scheduled with the realization constantly in the forefront that audience members may tune to another station or turn off the set at the slightest whim.

The public's investment in the medium also engenders a possessive attitude among audience members. Because they own part of the system, they feel a sense of entitlement that they do not feel about newspapers, magazines, or films. Politicians and bureaucrats violate what audiences consider their rights at their peril.

Interference Proneness. Stations can interfere with each other and can also be affected by interference from other sources of electromagnetic energy. This susceptibility makes government regulation of technical aspects of operation essential. Inasmuch as radio signals ignore borders, it also means that such regulation must extend across national boundaries—hence international regulation of technical matters. The need to intervene for physical reasons makes it easy for governments to take the next step—intervening for social and political reasons.

Interference also creates scarcity by limiting the number of stations able to transmit in a particular vicinity or the number of satellites able to occupy a given segment of the orbit. Technological and regulatory improvements have eased the scarcity problem but have not (though some claim otherwise) eliminated it, for reasons explored in Section 5.1.

Potential for Social Control. All these attributes acting in concert give broadcasting the further attribute of exercising social control more compellingly than any other medium. Broadcasting even challenges such primary agents of socialization as the family and school. Just how great the impacts will be under given circumstances and in what directions they will move people remain debatable. It is enough, however, that governments *perceive* broadcasting as being able to exert social control. They regard it as potentially too powerful to be left unregulated.

That governments regulate broadcasting adds to the sense of possessiveness that set ownership confers. People feel more entitled to receive satisfaction from the system when they perceive it as either a government or a quasi-government service; they also feel more entitled to resort to extralegal means of satisfaction if the government falls short of expectations.

Standard of Evaluation

The problem-solving approach to comparative analysis used in this book assumes that each country will have uniquely adapted broadcasting to suit its own needs. Does this mean that everything is relative, and that no standards exist by which to judge a national broadcasting system? Not all adaptations will have met with equal success. We can assess a particular adaptation by using as a yardstick the *ideal potentials* of broadcasting, as modified by the human and physical limitations of a given national situation.

Broadcasting's ideal potentials can be deduced from the attributes previously outlined. For example, because it needs no physical transmission conduit (an aspect of "ubiquity"), broadcasting can surmount barriers of distance and isolation. Does a given country take advantage of this attribute by doing all it can, within its inherent physical, fiscal, and political limitations, to reach its entire population? A government that spends large sums on transmission facilities and then puts up such roadblocks to reception as high import tariffs on receivers defeats its own purpose.

We can hypothesize a set of goals toward which an ideal broadcasting system would strive. Even the best systems will doubtless fall short of the ideal, but we should be able to identify conspicuous shortfalls and determine whether they arise from deficiencies in natural resources, mismanagement, or other causes.

Using the treatment of news as an example, we may ask whether a system's news services take full advantage of the relevant attributes of the medium: Is news made available with all possible speed and realism? Or is it delivered tardily, without exploiting the medium's unique ability to recreate events as they actually happened? Exploring a system's failure to live up to the medium's potential leads us to look for reasons. Do shortcomings arise from deliberate policy, bad management, lack of training, inadequate facilities, imperfect understanding of the medium, insufficient funds, or still other causes? Are they remediable or unavoidable failures?

Utopian Broadcasting

Utopia, as the best of all possible worlds, would pose no problems for broadcasting. Utopia would have no awkward mountainous areas to make signal coverage difficult, no enclaves of militant linguistic minorities with separatist demands to complicate the funding and scheduling of broadcasting services, no shortage of funds to limit the number of transmitters the system could furnish or the number of receivers the public could buy.

But what would ideal broadcasting service be like in a country with a more or less average complement of geographic, economic, cultural, and political problems? Keeping in mind the seven attributes previously outlined, I will sketch in a few of the critically significant subjects that should be explored. The subjects discussed below in fact preview the topics that form the heart of this book.

Ownership. Who owns the national facilities of broadcasting largely determines the kind of system that emerges. Ideal ownership is pluralistic rather than monolithic. Operators of monolithic systems, lacking the spur of competition, tend to become lazy, careless, and unresponsive to audience interests. Pluralistic systems, driven by more than a single motive (usually the motives of public service and profit), tend to be livelier, more creative, and more satisfying to audiences. For reasons of politics, economics, or both, not every system can afford the luxury of pluralism.

Access. Communication freedom means the liberty to be not only on the receiving end but on the sending end as well. An ideal system gives access to broadcasting facilities for varied ideas, groups, and individuals. Local and regional outlets, by definition, permit access of a type not feasible on national networks.

Law and Regulation. Ideal broadcasting laws enable adoption of a regulatory framework that minimizes technical interference, imposes accountability, ensures fairness, protects cultural autonomy, prevents abuses of public confidence, and protects children and other groups liable to exploitation. Laws are explicit enough to forestall arbitrary regulation by overzealous administrators or despotic officials.

Financial Support. Broadcasters ideally have sufficient insulation from the sources of funding to use the medium effectively. The payer should not call every tune because audiences need many different pipers. Ruled by many masters, broadcasters must have enough autonomy to serve the competing claims of the different sectors of society and of the state.

Facilities. Proper deployment of transmission facilities enables universal coverage at local, regional, and national levels, using an appropriate mix of signal types. Adequate reception facilities maximize opportunities to participate. Relays interconnect outlets into national and regional networks. Cable and satellite facilities are employed to the extent needed for efficient coverage and a varied choice of programs. Facilities exist for training technical, program, and administrative personnel.

Programs. Relevant national, regional, and local programs are always available, suited to varying levels of taste and types of audiences. The mix of entertainment, information, education, and inspiration in programming gives audiences both what they want and what they need. Production takes advantage of broadcasting's immediacy and its ability to transmit the sights and sounds of real events. Imported materials enhance the program diet without overwhelming the national culture. National programs set a standard without overwhelming minority regional and local cultures.

Audience Research. Quantitative and qualitative research analyzes both programs and audiences. Policymakers, programmers, and producers use the results of research constructively, treating broadcasting as a two-way rather than a one-way medium.

External Services. To the extent that the nation's role in the world requires it to engage in broadcast diplomacy, the system includes an external service. To maximize its effectiveness, such a service attains the credibility that comes from confidence in the evenhandedness of its treatment of political issues and the factuality of its news.

This book prefaces discussion of these topics with an introductory survey of the worlds of broadcasting in terms of major geopolitical divisions. I conclude the book with a review of the current world debate on the free flow of information and the demands of the Third World for a new disposition of communication resources.

1 ▪ 3 FRAMES OF REFERENCE

Technological Determinism

The problem-solving orientation assumes that broadcasting has universal attributes arising from the medium's technology and that each country comes to terms with these attributes when it adapts the medium to its own needs. The theory that the physical nature of a technology determines its human consequences is known as *technological determinism*. According to the authors of a widely used introduction to theories of mass communication, "Most media theorists would accept the proposition that the technological characteristics of a mass medium may be one of many factors that should be taken into account" in assessing mass media effects (De Fleur & Ball-Rokeach, 1975: 201). I go beyond "may" in the case of broadcasting, asserting that its technology *does* affect the form and content of its program output and hence its ultimate impact on people. But I agree that technology is not the only factor. Complex three-way interactions occur among (1) the universal attributes of broadcasting as a technology, (2) the universal attributes of human beings as communicators and receivers of communications, and (3) the specific political, cultural, and economic attributes of any given society.

An example: broadcasting finds the soap opera an ideal format for conserving program resources. Relatively cheap and easy to produce, these serial dramas minimize consumption of new materials in consecutive episodes yet can have a universal appeal, serving as a vehicle for expressing basic human interest themes. For these reasons (not merely imitation of the United States), soap operas occur throughout much of the world of broadcasting. They fit the needs of both the medium and its audiences. Details of soap opera content and style differ from one country to another, in keeping with cultural differentiation, but broadcasting itself makes the format universal.

A second example: because of its immediacy, its ability to leap over barriers of distance and illiteracy, its realism, and other attributes, broadcasting serves ideally as a news medium. Accordingly, all broadcasting systems offer news, in similar formats and schedules, as major components of their programming menus. Of course, universal use of news cannot be ascribed solely to the technological aptness of broadcasting for the job of delivering it. People's interest in news developed long before broadcasting, but broadcasting happens to be ideally equipped technologically to serve that interest. Technology causes broadcast news to be gathered, processed, scheduled, and presented in similar ways throughout the world. Almost anywhere in the world, you can see and hear a recognizable prime-time evening news segment. Differences among people and their cultures cause differences in their judgments as to what constitutes news and what social functions they expect news to perform. These social differences affect the ways in which different peoples exploit the common technology. Each national system uses (or abuses) news, and each does so in its own characteristic way; yet all systems schedule it in similar ways.

Perspective. Current U.S. practice serves as the point of departure for each topic of comparison, because most readers will probably be familiar with American broadcasting. This choice of a starting point, however, does not imply that the U.S. system should be viewed as an ideal model.

The available literature on foreign systems, whether in book or periodical form, covers the regions of the world very unevenly, at least in the English language. Thus we have ample material on the larger systems of Europe and North America but not on their smaller systems or on those of South America, Asia, and Africa. Inevitably, the present book reflects the uneven geographical coverage of the literature, though I have tried to be as evenhanded as possible.

You will find a great many references to the British system. Ready availability of authentic information may have played a role in this emphasis, but I have also deliberately stressed comparisons between the British and American systems because they afford an instructive contrast. Despite the close historical and cultural ties between the two countries, their broadcasting systems differ strikingly, thus serving as an apt example of my central thesis. Britain also deserves particular attention because its model has been so widely admired and imitated. Moreover, during the days when the sun never set on the British

Empire, British Broadcasting Corporation personnel carried the BBC philosophy to colonies and Commonwealth nations in every corner of the world. This influence is not a thing of the past. Through the Commonwealth Broadcasting Association, headquartered at the BBC main office in London, that influence still reaches some fifty systems, from Antigua to Zimbabwe. Moreover, the BBC External Services are generally conceded to be the best in the world.

Scope of Book

Broadcasting. In this book, I focus primarily on broadcasting as defined in U.S. law, that is, "dissemination of radio communications intended to be received by the public, directly or indirectly by the intermediary of relay stations."[2]

The term *radio* in the above definition refers to the electromagnetic radiations used by both sound ("radio") and vision ("television"). Thus *broadcasting* embraces both radio and television; when the term is used here without qualification, it means either or both media. This is not to deny that differences between the two can be significant. But underlying the differences are identical technical, legal, economic, organizational, and psychological foundations that justify treating the two as a single medium whenever their differences do not come to the forefront.

System. The term *system* refers to *all* the legal broadcasting services in a given country or territory. Thus the United States system includes not only the commercial networks, their affiliates, and the independent commercial stations but also their noncommercial counterparts and such government-run external services as the Voice of America. Many different types of *services* may operate within the framework of a single national system.

Cable Television. Under the above definition, cable television is not broadcasting, because it relies on a form of wire (that is, cable) rather than radio for dissemination. Nevertheless, I have treated cable television here because of its intimate linkages with and effects upon broadcasting.

Relays. Mention of relay stations in the definition means that consideration must be given to the methods of distributing broadcasting—the cable, microwave, and satellite interconnection facilities that form part of the *infrastructure* that supports broadcasting operations.

SUMMARY

The comparative study of broadcasting systems has value because of their interdependence and the features they share in common. The impact of such technological innovations as satellites and cable television adds urgency to the need for comparative studies. Rather than taking a country-by-country approach, I organize comparative study of the world's more than two hundred broadcasting systems in terms of the universal problems and potentials common to all of them. These universals can be deduced from the intrinsic nature of the medium, which has certain unique attributes that define its possibilities, and national systems can be judged by the degree to which they live up to these potentials.

NOTES

[1]Great Britain, 1977: 5.

[2]47 USC 103 (o).

CHAPTER 2

THE WORLDS OF BROADCASTING

T his chapter presents a broad historical and geopolitical overview of the several worlds of broadcasting and introduces examples of systems typical of each of those worlds. Historically, the two world wars marked important turning points in the medium's development. They hastened technological improvements but delayed applications to civilian services. Sound broadcasting surged forward after World War I, in the 1920s, while vision broadcasting began its big push following World War II, in the late 1940s. A third era began in the 1970s with practical applications of satellites and expanded uses of cable television.

The status of broadcasting systems varies in accordance with the political environments in which they operate. One can divide these environments roughly in terms of the First World (Western, democratic), Second World (Communist, authoritarian), and Third World (developing, nonaligned).* Far from exact, these categories must accommodate many exceptions. Australia, Israel, Japan, and New Zealand, though not western geographically, fall politically within "the West." The Soviet Union, despite advanced achievements in armaments and communications, falls within the Third World according to some experts. For our purposes, however, the tripartite division works fairly well, because broadcasting differs in characteristic ways from one world to the other.

---

*The nonaligned Third World consists of countries that are neutral or ostensibly neutral in the rivalry between the non-Communist (First World) and Communist (Second World) nations. Also referred to as less developed countries (LDCs), the Third World consists of approximately 120 nations, representing about two thirds of the world's population and area. Most of them were former colonies, many of which did not achieve independence until after World War II.

2▪1 ORIGINS

The idea of using electromagnetic energy to communicate through space without the aid of wires, a natural outgrowth of nineteenth-century scientific thinking, occurred to many investigators in many places at about the same time. Italian inventor Guglielmo Marconi, widely credited with the invention of radio, took out his original patent of 1896 in England, where Sir Oliver Lodge already had some claims on such a device. Edouard Branly pioneered in France, as did Alexander Popov in Russia. In fact, the Russians observe May 7 as Radio Day, claiming Popov's 1895 demonstration as the true beginning of radio.* These and other pioneers all owed a vital debt to Scottish scientist James Maxwell, who earlier in the century developed the theory of electromagnetic energy, as well as to German physicist Heinrich Hertz, who proved the theory in laboratory experiments. Thus radio had an international character from its very inception.

The ferment of innovation continued through the first two decades of the twentieth century, with numerous and widely scattered experiments aimed at transmitting sound (the earliest practical uses of wireless having been applied to the telegraph rather than the telephone). These experiments in sound transmission led to the establishment of the first regularly licensed and scheduled radio broadcast services in 1919 and 1920.

Sound Radio

The Dutch and Canadians anticipated the rest of the world by one year, starting radio broadcast services in 1919.† The United States followed in the fall of 1920 with the opening of KDKA in Pittsburgh. Popov began broadcasts in a laboratory setting in the same year, but regular broadcasting in the USSR dates from 1922.

During the 1920s, radio broadcasting operations started in some 40 countries—not only in the leading industrialized nations but also in Afghanistan, Argentina, Australia, China, Cuba, Egypt, and the Philippines. By the 1960s, nearly every nation and dependency had radio. The only exceptions were very small, remote places such as the Cayman Island group, a British dependency in the Caribbean with a combined population of 17,500, which inaugurated radio in 1977.[1]

Vision Radio

Experimenters began trying to send radio pictures almost as early as they tried to transmit sound. But before the 1930s, the technological

---

*Paulu reviews the evidence, concluding that it fails to "establish either Marconi or Popov indisputably as the inventor of radio communication, although the case for Marconi is stronger" (1974: 31).

†Smith, 1973: 269; Shea, 1981: 120. Marconi himself set up the Canadian station in Montreal.

groundwork had not yet been laid. By then vision radio experiments began in many countries. No individual can be singled out as *the* inventor of television.

The First 50 Services. The first regular television service made available to the public, a low-definition system, began in Berlin in 1935. But the service generally conceded as the first to use modern, high-definition standards, that of the British Broadcasting Corporation, started regular public telecasting in 1936.*

The Soviets followed in 1938, but the United States delayed public sale of receivers until it achieved somewhat higher picture standards, which it did in 1941. The U.S. black-and-white picture standards adopted at that time remain the same today, but both the British and the Russians upgraded their standards after World War II.

During the war, progress toward mass distribution of television receivers came to a halt. The Soviets resumed telecasting in 1945, followed by the British and Americans in 1946. However, several years went by before manufacturers overcame wartime shortages to enable the worldwide stampede into television that occurred in the 1950s. During that decade, 50 countries inaugurated television.†

Extension to the Third World. By 1983, three quarters of the world's nations and dependent territories had television. Only 45 had no television of their own, mostly tiny islands and such lesser-developed African countries as the Central African Republic, Mali, and Mauritania. Bhutan and its neighbor Nepal were the only South Asian countries without television.

Considering television costs and the demands it makes on electrical power and programming capacity, it may seem strange that most of the Third World has installed it. Many a country too poor to feed itself has nevertheless built its own television service. Television came upon the scene when many developing countries were newly or imminently independent, and the lure of the medium proved irresistible. Third World leaders seemed to see opening a national television service as a rite of passage into true nationhood, much like starting a national airline. Their predominantly rural populations, lacking both the income and the electrical power for television, could not benefit from transmitters confined to the capital city and perhaps one or two other major population centers. Nor could the money be found for adequate programming. But national pride demanded that visiting heads of state and

---

*The German system used 180-lines-per-frame picture definition, the British 421 lines. The most common contemporary standards are 625 lines (British) and 525 lines (U.S.).

†The number could be slightly higher. Authorities differ as to the exact starting dates for some services because of ambiguity as to when irregular experimental telecasts merged into formally scheduled services.

other foreign dignitaries should be able to receive television in their guest villas and hotel suites.

Manufacturers in the major industrial countries, on the prowl for new markets, ingeniously capitalized on the ceremonial public occasions that television so effectively heightens. When Ethiopian Emperor Haile Selassie persuaded the newly formed Organization of African Unity to hold its first meeting in his capital in 1963, an enterprising European manufacturer supplied a closed-circuit television system at Africa Hall, site of the historic meeting. Local dignitaries, visiting entourages, and the press followed the proceedings on monitors in the public rooms.

Impressed with the success of this demonstration, the emperor soon thereafter ordered installation of a regular television station in Addis Ababa, the opening to be timed with the imperial birthday—always an event for national celebration during his reign. Thomson Television International (TTI), a British firm, won the contract to install and manage the system. Somehow TTI managed to get the station on the air within six months, just in time for the royal birthday. Thus in 1964, a country with one of the world's lowest per capita incomes, one where people often die of famine, acquired television. Its radio system remained woefully inadequate, and 20 years later, Ethiopia still had fewer than fifty thousand television sets to serve a population of some 30 million.

In Senegal pressure for television came not from the political leader but from a small segment of the elite in Dakar. A tiny experimental television station, designed exclusively for educational programs, had been installed in 1965 with United Nations and French government aid. After five years of struggle, it closed down for lack of funds. Two years later, the Senegalese reactivated the station so that cosmopolitans in Dakar could watch the 1972 Olympic Games (receivable in Senegal because of a recently installed INTELSAT satellite ground station).*

> President Senghor came under intense pressure from the elite in Dakar and from the French television equipment manufacturer Thomson-CFS to reintroduce television broadcasting for the period of the games. Thomson-CFS even undertook to install a system free of charge on a trial basis and to supply a number of receiving sets for community reception. . . . The elite of Dakar ordered sets by air freight, and [the French domestic television system] supplied free programs and films to fill in the gaps between sporting events. After the games it was impossible to close down television broadcasts because of pressure on the government from those who had bought sets. (Katz & Wedell, 1977: 87)

Thailand introduced color to enhance television coverage of the Miss Thailand contest and Uganda did the same for an Organization of African Unity meeting. In 1968, when Mexico hosted the Olympic

---

*INTELSAT, the international consortium that provides intercontinental satellite relays for television and other communications, is described in Section 2.5.

Games, a private company built a microwave system connecting Mexico City with the U.S. microwave network, and the government installed a satellite ground station near the capital. These new facilities, later expanded by the government, had a profound impact on the subsequent development of Mexican broadcasting.[2]

Countries neighboring on television-equipped territories sometimes felt compelled to operate their own service to counteract spillover signals from abroad. Moreover, even beyond the reach of spillover reception, improvements in technology whet the appetites of would-be television audiences. The government of Belize, a former British Central American colony bordering on Guatemala, though more concerned about improving the banana crop than about introducing television, has been bombarded with public demands stimulated by the availability of videotape cassettes. An enterprising merchant installed a satellite earth station so that he could record pirated programs to sell on videotape. Another made a deal with a Miami shop to supply him with pirated videocassettes of movies and television shows. The Belize merchant rented them out for five dollars an evening.[3] In the West Indian Cayman Islands, which did not even have their own radio broadcasting until 1977, private clubs have satellite receiving antennas and machines for playing back videotapes.[4]

This kind of improvisation goes on in many parts of the world. If small countries could restrain their appetites for national symbols, they might be able to avoid the expense of installing their own television transmission facilities, relying instead on regionally distributed direct-broadcast satellite services and videocassettes. Local production facilities could ship or relay locally originated material to the regional satellite uplink for broadcasting back to the originating country.* Another option could be to set up a national videotape center to record materials on tape and duplicate them on cassettes. This very solution was suggested by officials in Fiji, an independent Pacific island group with a population of under a million. The government, under strong pressure to install a national television system, commissioned a study by the Asia-Pacific Institute for Broadcasting. The study indicated that the startup costs alone for regular television would amount to $80 million—more than a quarter of Fiji's entire national budget.[5]

The best-known Third World leader to hold out against the lure of television is President Julius Nyerere of Tanzania. Zanzibar, an offshore island loosely federated with Tanzania, installed its own television system in 1974. The island lies so close to the mainland that high antennas in the Tanzanian capital, Dar Es Salaam, can pick up its signal. Tanzanian residents living near the borders of Kenya and Uganda can also

---

*Certain international religious stations have successfully employed "feeder studios" to supply locally produced radio programs for transmission back to the originating countries via international short-wave transmitters (Robertson, 1974: 207).

receive telecasts from those countries. By 1982 Tanzania had some four thousand sets, and Parliament wanted to authorize mainland television despite Nyerere's opposition. Nyerere argued that Tanzania needed an efficient radio broadcasting system far more than it needed an inefficient television system. His view prevailed, and Parliament shelved the proposal.[6]

The suggestions offered above are not meant to imply that television should be an exclusive preserve of the more advanced countries. However, developing nations might weigh the costs and prospective benefits of television against prospective penalties, considering whether less costly, more appropriate technology might be employed.

Persuasive arguments overcame Sri Lanka's initial resistance to television. An island off the southern tip of India, formerly the British crown colony of Ceylon, Sri Lanka has been self-governing since 1931 and independent since 1948. Although an agricultural, village-oriented society, it has the highest literacy rate in Asia after Japan. Despite having a relatively well-developed communications infrastructure, Sri Lanka resisted the siren call for several years, turning down foreign offers of assistance. Television, said the government in a policy statement, "cannot be contemplated at a time when foreign exchange is scarce even for essential foodstuffs." Moreover, it would be "all the more indefensible at the present time since it would be a luxury of the rich" (de Silva & Siriwardene, 1977: 39).

Nevertheless, in 1977 Sri Lanka began planning for television. According to an official of the ministry responsible for communication, the protelevision arguments rested to some degree on the fact that the nation had recently recovered from mismanagement under radical left-wing political leadership and from disruptive racial and religious rivalries. He pointed out that in Third World countries, "The political leadership has to take the initiative in persuading people to go beyond the confines of their village, tribe, caste, religion or community. . . . Good communications [have], in the Third World, become necessary for political survival" (Amunugama, 1981: 265).

Other arguments of the Sri Lanka official were:

- The need for "a dramatic symbol of the 'openness' of the new society as against the earlier restricted intellectual and cultural life" under left-wing authoritarianism

- The potential benefits to education, which Sri Lankans esteem, as indicated by their high literacy level

- The potential for overcoming language barriers among the ethnic groups of the country

- Improvement in the quality of village life

- A favorable geography for television coverage (the island has a compact shape, with a high, centrally located mountain from which signals could reach all parts of the country)

In 1978 a private operator won permission to open a small station in the capital, Colombo, relying entirely on recorded material. As testimony to the latent demand for television, instead of the five thousand sets consultants predicted would be sold in the first year, the actual sales amounted to forty-five thousand. Nevertheless, the private owners soon ran out of funds, and the government took over the station, keeping it on the air. Meanwhile, Japan offered to supply Sri Lanka with equipment and technical training for a national television service. Canada and Germany gave program training, and the United States helped by lending a naval helicopter to hoist the main antenna to the top of its tower on Mount Pidurutalagala. The new national service opened in 1982.[7]

2 ■ 2 FIRST WORLD

Under the rubric "First World" I include North America, Western Europe, Australia, New Zealand, Israel, and Japan. Though geographically dispersed, these nations share a broadly similar political philosophy and correspondingly similar broadcasting systems.

North America

Despite the dominant position of U.S. broadcasting in North America, Canada strives to maintain a distinctive system of its own, resisting the powerful influence from across its 4,000-mile U.S. border. American influence began with spillover signals from south of the border and was later augmented with cable delivery of American programs. Canadian broadcast policy, dating back to the first systematic study in 1929, has been preoccupied with strategies for maintaining a distinctive Canadian culture, despite inroads from its overwhelming neighbor. As a complicating factor, Canada must broadcast in both English and French. The goal is to make both languages available in all parts of the country, even though 80 percent of the French-speaking Canadians are concentrated in Quebec province.

Canadian broadcasting includes both publicly and privately owned facilities. Commercial stations, unlike their U.S. advertising-supported counterparts, can and often do serve as affiliates of the public networks. This anomaly reflects the fact that Canadian networking has historically been mainly a government responsibility because of the need to reach vast, thinly populated, commercially unviable areas of the country. Second only to the USSR in land area, Canada has only about 24 million people, most of them concentrated along the U.S.-Canadian border.

Western Europe

The 27 countries of Western Europe constitute the most densely covered broadcasting area of the world, with only 6 percent of the world's population but 19 percent of its broadcast receivers, all crowded into only about 3 percent of the land area. This concentration means that the domestic broadcast bands teem with conflicting signals. Each country must make do with a very limited supply of channels for its own services while competing with spillover programs from neighboring countries.

In general, after the first tentative trials of the 1920s and early 1930s, European countries settled into the view that broadcasting should be regarded as a public service, supported by license fees on receiving sets, free of advertising, and organized on a national network basis rather than on a local station basis. The coming of television with its high costs, however, compelled European nations to supplement license fees with advertising revenue. Moreover, members of the business community and segments of the general public pressed their governments to allow broadcast advertising. Insistent audience demands in the late 1960s also led to more varied programs and growing attention first to regional and then to local services. Expanding cable systems and satellite relays began to impact on European systems in the late 1970s and early 1980s, severely testing the older monopolistic, highly centralized structures of the past.

Other First World Nations

Australia. An island-continent about the size of the United States, Australia has a very uneven population distribution because much of its area consists of forbidding deserts. Most of its people live in the southeast corner of the continent, concentrated in the large cities. Historically, Australians have felt a sense of isolation that profoundly affected their national character. Descendants of remote western Europe (Sydney is ten thousand miles from London), they are surrounded by alien cultures. For reasons of both geography and history, therefore, broadcasting has a special significance for Australians. It has overcome "the tyranny of distance," linking them both to each other and to their European roots. Broadcasting has assumed major responsibility as a primary conservator of Western culture: government-supported networks, under the Australian Broadcasting Corporation (ABC), maintain six symphony orchestras and several other major musical groups and hire more Australian writers than any other employer.

Australia's uneven population distribution makes it uneconomical for commercial broadcasters to cover the vast, thinly populated "outback." The ABC has the responsibility of serving these regions through its national networks, both radio and television. It operates noncommercially, financed by government grants. There are almost as many private commercial stations as government stations. Originally the former were expected to be locally oriented and to a large extent private radio has retained that character; the economics of television, however, encouraged the formation of private national networks, though they do not have the highly structured character of U.S. networks.

Contemporary Australia has taken on a distinct melting pot character. It has experienced a great influx of immigrants, especially since World War II, coming not only from Europe but also from the Middle East, Latin America, and Asia. An indigenous minority also survives, remnants of the aborigines who lived on the continent before the Europeans started permanent settlements in the late eighteenth century with the founding of British penal colonies. A second government-operated, noncommercial service, the Special Broadcasting Service (SBS), serves minorities in many foreign languages, both in radio and television. A fourth sector consists of some 50 radio stations in the Public Broadcasting Service, licensed to community groups and universities. These stations, though not fully commercial, may give credit to commercial underwriters, somewhat in the manner of U.S. public broadcasters.

New Zealand. Like Australia, New Zealand is an outpost of Western civilization isolated in an alien ocean. Westward across the Tasman Sea some eight hundred miles away lies Australia; in other directions the South Pacific stretches for thousands of miles, broken only by tiny atolls. Yet the two Commonwealth nations differ markedly: "Australia is a brash, emerging power; New Zealand, a tranquil, agrarian state" (Toogood, 1978a: 288). The latter's two main islands taken together are about the size of California. Because of its isolation, relatively small size, and rugged mountainous terrain, New Zealand depends even more heavily on broadcasting than does Australia. From broadcasting, wrote the chairman of the Broadcasting Corporation of New Zealand (BCNZ), "New Zealanders asked—and for the most part obtained—just about all their common social, cultural, and entertainment needs as a nation" (Cross, 1982: 12).

New Zealand adopted the BBC model in 1932 but, unlike Britain, retained its original corporate monopoly nearly intact into the 1980s. Until 1984 the BCNZ operated all the nation's television stations and most of its radio stations. The demand for greater private access to the medium, a political hot potato, finally resulted in government approval of plans for a third, independent television network in 1984.

Israel. The Palestine Broadcasting Service, set up by the British under its mandate in 1936, along with clandestine services run by Jewish Zionist groups during the battle for independence, became the nucleus of the Israeli broadcasting system in 1948. Both Arabs and Jews had fought a preindependence clandestine radio war. Operators of the Jewish Haganah clandestine station in Jerusalem escaped detection by choosing a neighborhood for its transmitter that had no electric power supply. "Current was supplied by a wire stretched from house to house from a nearby hospital. The Haganah's order for its concealment was: 'Hang out more undershirts.' The housewives along its route had all been asked to keep it covered with laundry" (Collins & La Pierre, 1972: 119).

Modern Israeli radio comprises six services, five civilian, and one military. Program A, the Home Service, broadcasts in Hebrew, English, and French, offering special programs for immigrants. Programs B and C are commercial services, Program D is in Arabic. An all-music service, added in 1983, broadcasts classical music 19 hours a day, designed in part to give employment to Israeli musicians. The Defense Forces operate *Galei Zahal*, a network of seven AM and one FM transmitters operating 24 hours a day.

Israel put off television for many years as too frivolous to justify the burden it would impose on the nation's limited resources. Protelevision forces within Israel prevailed when the Six-Day War of 1967 dramatized the urgent need to counteract spillover video programming from neighboring Arab countries, which used the medium to stir up Arabs living within Israel. The Israelis launched their own television service during the following year.*

Japan. An unusually homogeneous society, culturally and linguistically, Japan has a rich artistic heritage that lends itself readily to television. Moreover, the Japanese have a strong sense of national identity and self-worth. Japan's broadcasting system testifies to the universality of the medium's intrinsic nature. As Anthony Smith put it, "Although Japanese culture is strikingly different in its traditional content from that of any western country the genres of television have somehow found a way to impose their nature and needs upon it" (1973: 262).

Sound radio started in Japan in 1925 with three private stations, but within a year, the government forced them to combine into a public corporation. According to Smith, the Japanese "consciously and quite proudly used the BBC as its model" (p. 255). From the beginning, NHK (*Nippon Hoso Kyokai*), or Japanese Broadcasting Corporation, relied on receiving set license fees for its funding.

Japan's defeat in World War II interrupted the development of broadcasting, which had, of course, been taken over as a military propaganda organ during the war. General Douglas MacArthur, supreme commander of the Allied Powers, revived the NHK as an independent public corporation. In 1950 a new broadcasting law allowed private commercial broadcasting to compete with NHK. Commercial broadcasters operate on a more local basis than the NHK, which assumes responsibility for national networking, as do the public corporations in Britain, Canada, and Australia. NHK radio facilities exceed those of the 124 privately owned companies, but each service has about equal numbers of television stations.

---

*Though Israel delayed starting general television until 1968, educational television had been initiated in 1966 after long and careful planning, with Rothschild Foundation funding and U.S. technical advice.

Eastern Europe

Political leaders of the Union of Soviet Socialist Republics (USSR) and other East European Communist nations have always taken broadcasting very seriously. Indeed, even before radio broadcasting began, Lenin followed the development of radiotelegraphy with intense interest, using it in 1918 in the struggle to generate support in western Europe for the Russian Revolution.* In 1920, he wrote of the role he expected broadcasting to play in the USSR:

> The matter is of gigantic importance (a newspaper without paper and without wires, for with a loudspeaker and with the receiver which [a Russian scientist] has developed in such a way that we will easily get hundreds of receivers, all Russia will hear a newspaper read in Moscow). (Quoted in Guback & Hill, 1972: 16, emphasis in original)

It took two more years, but in August of 1922 the "newspaper without wires" went on the air from Moscow. At a time when the most advanced U.S. stations used only 500 watts of power, the Moscow station used 12,000 watts. This achievement seems the more remarkable because of the acute shortages of money and basic necessities in the postrevolution chaos. In fact, the authorities spurred on the radio experimenters with extra food rations.

For both economic and political reasons, the USSR invested heavily in *wired radio*, the audio forerunner of cable television. To this day, about half of the radio-equipped households in the USSR get radio service from loudspeaker boxes in their homes (discussed in Section 8.5). Another distinctive feature of USSR broadcasting has been the country's pioneering use of space satellites to relay television programs to the far ends of its vast territory. Dozens of domestic satellites in the *Molniya* series have been launched, starting with the world's first such satellite in 1965.

National networks in the USSR must span 11 different time zones and serve more than 60 different language groups. Considering the enormity of this task, it is not surprising that the Russians still lag behind North America and Western Europe in the number of radio and television sets relative to population. In North America there are 1.5 persons per television set, in Western Europe, 2.8, and in the USSR plus the East European Communist group, 3.4.[8]

---

*Use of wireless telegraphy to muster support for a revolution occurred even earlier, when Irish nationalists occupied the Dublin General Post Office during the 1916 Easter Uprising. They seized the nearby wireless telegraphy school and while under siege sent out bulletins in Morse code, using a jerry-rigged ship's radio (Fisher, 1978: xv).

China

With the downfall of the Gang of Four and the abandonment of Mao's Cultural Revolution, Western media scholars began flocking to Beijing and other centers to learn about its new media revolution. As one visitor observed:

> In China, communications and society are matched to a greater degree than anywhere else. Truly, communications is society. . . . In China today, the main medium of communications is not broadcasting or newspapers or the cinema, but the [Chinese Communist party]. The main resources of communications are not wavelengths or printing presses but party members (about 38 million people, some 4 percent of the population). The cadres' main tools are not TV programs but discussions. (Howkins, 1982b: 4–5)

Nevertheless, the Chinese government had long recognized broadcasting as an indispensable tool in governing its vast population; it therefore developed nearly universal radio coverage. Two thirds of China's receivers, however, consist of loudspeakers wired to local headends equipped with receivers and small studios. All radio "broadcasting" at the local level in fact came by wire until the 1980s, with over-the-air transmitters reserved for larger-scale coverage. During the Cultural Revolution, more than 90 percent of the rural production teams, each consisting of about 30 families, received constant instructions and exhortations from the speaker boxes.[9] Loudspeakers blared everywhere—"in village squares, school playgrounds, marketplaces, rice paddies, factories, mines, communal mess halls, dormitories, households, and even on treetops and telephone poles" (Chu, 1978: 27). The post-Mao government cut back on the intrusiveness of wired radio. Indeed, in 1983 China adopted a new policy of installing over-the-air stations at the city and county levels.[10]

The Chinese wired-radio headends have simple studio facilities from which teams varying in size from 2 to 20 persons can originate local closed-circuit programs. They devote about a third of the time to this material, which may include local news, music, and messages about meetings, farm production achievements, and so on. During the rest of the time, they relay regional or central programming coming to the headend by radio. The wired-radio service plays an important social role:

> It serves as a family cinema, as Chinese peasants enjoy operas and other theatrical performances. It serves as a school for farming skills, other basic knowledge, and political education. Announcements of time for planting, seeding, harvesting, meetings, coming storms, praise and criticism, lost and found, etc., are all there on the air. For many peasants it serves as a timepiece because of its regularity in programming. (Li, 1983)

Chinese television started belatedly in 1958, with help from the USSR. Almost at once, the new service received a setback when the two countries broke off relations and Russian advisors went home. During the 1960s, the Cultural Revolution closed down television activities almost entirely. Programming during that period consisted of endlessly repeated excerpts from Mao's *Little Red Book* and of the eight revolutionary operas approved for broadcast by Mao's wife, Chiang Ching. The end of this period of stagnation and repression brought exchanges of information, technology, and programs with the West. Bob Hope produced a special there in 1979, "The Road to China," and in the same year China bought its first syndicated U.S. series, *The Man from Atlantis*.[*]

Initiation of advertising, a bourgeois activity banned completely during the Cultural Revolution, symbolized the new spirit in China. The first televised sports event with commercials occurred in the fall of 1979, when Marlboros, Seven-Up, and other advertisers bought spots in a tennis match program featuring Bjorn Borg and John Alexander.[11]

By 1983, China Central Television (CCT) felt secure enough to contract with CBS International to take 64 hours of U.S. network programming in the course of a year. This was CCT's first such foreign commitment. CBS presold five minutes of advertising within each hour, dividing the proceeds with CCT.[12]

2 ▪ 4 THIRD WORLD

Broadcasting came to the Third World as an import from more advanced countries, bringing with it not only hardware but methods of using the hardware. As Table 2.1 shows, the British model influenced more countries than any other, closely followed by the U.S. and French models. A few countries, such as Iran and Thailand, adopted hybrid models. As the authors of a Third World broadcasting study put it, transfer of a broadcasting model from a developed to a developing country brings with it

> *norms, unwritten rules, styles of production, values, professional codes and expectations, beliefs, and attitudes. . . . They are transferred directly through training, socialization, and expectation, and indirectly as functions of the importation of structures, technologies, and content of broadcasting that originate in the advanced industrial nations. (Katz & Wedell, 1977: 67–68)*

Latin America

General. Several colonial traditions influenced the Latin American countries—British, Danish, Dutch, French, Spanish, and Portuguese. Although Spanish control vanished long before broadcasting emerged, its influence lingers on in social structures and language. That shared heritage turns most of Central and South America into a huge common market for television programs.

---

[*]Reportedly, this choice had no profound ideological significance; the Chinese, short of funds, chose one of the least expensive series offered by syndicators (Butterfield, 1982: 398).

TABLE 2 ■ 1 MODELS FOR THIRD WORLD SYSTEMS

Model Systems	Number of Countries Using Model
Great Britain	26
United States	21
France	21
Belgium	3
Spain	1
New Zealand	1
Netherlands	1
Hybrids	17
Total	91

SOURCE: Based on data in Table A.5 of Elihu Katz & George Wedell, Broadcasting in the Third World: Promise and Performance (Harvard University Press, Cambridge, MA, 1977).

Stimulated by the U.S. example and wooed by U.S. business interests, Latin Americans became Third World broadcasting pioneers. By 1925 Argentina, Brazil, Chile, Costa Rica, Cuba, Mexico, and Peru all had radio stations. Lax government controls enabled repair shop owners and other small entrepreneurs to start up their own stations without meeting exacting technical and program standards. Stations grew like weeds. Later, as networks emerged, broadcasting became a favorite investment of powerful mercantile families. Television accelerated this centralizing tendency. Station ownership conferred social prestige and political power.

U.S. investments in Latin America started with radio and accelerated with television. However, both local owners and U.S. investors badly misjudged the commercial potentialities of television in these Third World environments.

Before television was introduced the development of small-scale local radio broadcasting had proved itself to be profitable, as demonstrated by the great proliferation of stations. The small scale of operations ensured that costs remained low, with the expenditure being fully covered by local advertising, which also provided moderate profits. The introduction of television radically altered this pattern. The vast majority of the population was economically inactive . . . and thus the market was limited and the number of potential set-owners was low. (Katz & Wedell, 1977: 72)

Deterioration of services and frequent bankruptcies of private television companies, along with increasing resentment against foreign domination, caused most Latin American governments to reconsider their free-and-easy attitude toward broadcast regulation. Some expropriated private broadcast holdings, while others placed stringent limits on ownership. Purely commercial incentives, governments discovered, resulted in concentration of broadcasting facilities in the major cities to the neglect of rural areas where most of their people lived. In the 1970s, mixed government/private systems became the general rule in Latin America, with governments assuming responsibility for educational and cultural programming and for serving otherwise neglected rural areas. By 1983 Latin America had some 68 major television stations (not counting small repeaters). Governments owned and operated 43 percent of them, private commercial companies the rest.[13]

Brazil. Of the 19 Latin American countries surveyed for the breakdown given above, Brazil easily rates as the most dynamic, expanding market. Only slightly smaller than the United States, Brazil ranks second in the world in number of radio stations. The great majority of them belong to private companies, as do four of Brazil's five television networks. One of them, *Rede Globo*, said to be the fifth largest network in the world, exports programs to both Europe and the United States.

Even so, many parts of Brazil's 23 states and 4 territories long remained underserved by commercial stations. In 1967 the government began constructing a national microwave grid to relay programs to transmitters in the most distant settlements. It also started a government television network to supplement commercial station coverage. A decade later, Brazil pioneered in the domestic use of the INTELSAT space relay facilities,* building receive-only earth stations throughout the provinces to feed satellite signals to provincial transmitters. In 1982 it announced plans for its own domestic satellite system, to be completed in 1985.

Cuba. Cuba offers the most extreme case among Latin nations of the shift from minimal government control to complete government domination. Prior to the 1959 Castro revolution, Cuban broadcasting had been the most freewheeling private commercial system in the hemisphere. Goar Mestre, an entrepreneur of great flair and imagination, built a network in the early 1950s that covered the island, making Cuba "the first country in the world where television was available to the entire population" (Dizard, 1966: 52). Cuban broadcasting during this period became notorious for its freewheeling commercialism. Mestre invented the "radio clock" station, a 24-hour sequence of 1-minute miniprograms, each containing 30 seconds of news, 25 seconds of commercials, and a time check played against a background of clock-like "ticks," one per second.† This format, still in use under Castro, enables scheduling more than a thousand commercials a day. As to

---

*INTELSAT began leasing circuits to individual countries for relay of signals within their own territories in 1975 (see Section 2.5).

†WRTH lists it as *Radio Reloj,* a 5-kw. AM station located near Havana (1984: 290–291).

BRAZIL

television, a news correspondent wrote in 1959, "Cuban commercials have some originality but are merciless in their devastation of the viewer's nervous system. Lengthy, repetitious, noisy and often in bad taste, they blare out a spiel that would make even a Madison Avenue man shudder" (Friedman, 1959).

Castro took over the broadcasting system in 1959, converting it into a government system modeled on that of the USSR (Mestre fled to Argentina, where he started a new career as a producer).

Gone were the frenetic commercials. Castro turned one of the two television networks over to education; the other is "heavily weighted toward news and political events and commentary" (Nichols, 1982c: 268).

Caribbean

The British dominated the early development of broadcasting in 14 of the 26 islands and island groups of the Caribbean region. The French have two dependencies, Guadeloupe and Martinique, whose radio and television services come from *Radiodiffusion Française d'Outre-Mer*, the French overseas provider. The Dutch have four islands in the Netherlands Antilles (Aruba, Bonaire, Curaçao, and St. Maartens) whose privately owned facilities broadcast in Papiamento, Dutch, and English. Haiti uses French and Creole, and the Dominican Republic, Spanish.

Jamaica will serve as an example of the British West Indies. Largest of the group, about the size of Connecticut, it lies 90 miles south of Cuba. After more than a century of Spanish and three centuries of British rule, Jamaica became independent in 1962. Private British interests started radio in 1939, but the colonial government took over the station in 1940. During the next decade, its schedule expanded from two to four hours daily, using mostly transcribed materials from the British Broadcasting Corporation. In 1949 Rediffusion, Ltd., a London firm with broadcasting and wired-radio interests in a number of British colonies, bought the Jamaican station and transformed it into a commercial operation along American lines.

With attainment of internal autonomy in 1953, the Jamaican government wanted a broadcasting outlet of its own. It obtained recommendations from a Canadian expert (like many emergent Commonwealth nations, Jamaica avoided going to the fountainhead, the BBC, for advice but nevertheless stayed within the Commonwealth family). Following the Canadian's advice, the government set up a public broadcasting corporation to compete with Rediffusion's Radio Jamaica. The Jamaica Broadcasting Corporation (JBC) went on the air with radio in 1959 and television in 1963. In accordance with the Canadian consultant's advice,

JAMAICA

the corporation was supposed to be funded by a combination of government grants and advertising income. At the time of authorization, the Jamaican premier said in a budget speech, "The best thinking people all over the world suggest that you cannot have a first-class broadcasting service which relies on commercial revenue" (quoted in Whylie, 1975: 14). Over the years, however, the Jamaican government failed to provide its share of the funds. The Jamaica Labor party, voted into power in 1980, promised to appoint an independent commission to make recommendations on "cleaning up" the media. In the meantime, the new government notified JBC that it would have to become self-supporting within three years.

In 1983 JBC had five medium-wave and seven FM radio transmitters, a single television originating transmitter, and seven television repeater stations (the island, though small, has mountainous terrain requiring such repeaters). The private Radio Jamaica has four medium-wave and four FM radio transmitters but no television. In terms of power, the two radio services are about equal, but in 1982 the private company attracted 68 percent of the audience,* reflecting the lack of credibility that government services often experience.

The Middle East

Most of the 18 broadcasting systems of the Middle East grew out of a colonial past but have been powerfully influenced by the common Arabic language and Muslim religion that most of them share, by the riches poured out by oil wells, and by the intense rivalries and hatreds of the region that feed on broadcast propaganda.

Most striking perhaps is Saudi Arabia, now equipped with first-class facilities but at first prevented from broadcasting at all by its ultraconservative Muslim religious leaders, the *ulema*. The kingdom's founder, Ibn Saud, won over the *ulema* in the 1920s with a two-way demonstration transmission between Mecca and his headquarters in Riyadh. The program consisted of readings by the *ulema* from the Holy Quran; because the devil cannot read the Quran, this demonstration proved to the *ulema's* satisfaction that radio was not the devil's work.

Television presented a still more touchy issue, for the Quran forbids making images of living beings. Even after Ibn Saud persuaded the

---

*Based on private information about a Radio Jamaica survey.

ulema to allow still photography (needed for national defense), they held out against the moving pictures of television, which posed the added threat of potential Westernization of the austere Saudi culture. But King Faisal (son of Ibn Saud and third in succession) considered television an essential tool to help combat propaganda from neighboring countries and to assist in national development. Built with American advice and assistance, Saudi Arabian television went on the air in 1965.

There followed one of the strangest episodes in television history. Prince Khalid, a member of the royal family, led a protest march against the station in Riyadh. Under circumstances never fully explained, after the crowd had been dispersed, someone shot Khalid to death. Nearly a decade later, Khalid's brother avenged his death by assassinating King Faisal.*

Of course the Arabs are not alone in religious fanaticism. The Israeli Broadcasting Authority had to contend with an extremist orthodox Jewish sect that opposed television in all its forms. The authority also had difficulty in deflecting the demands of those who wanted to close down broadcasting on Friday nights because of the orthodox rule against working on the Sabbath (sunset Friday to nightfall Saturday). Broadcasting in Israel does cease entirely for the 24 hours of Yom Kippur, the most sacred occasion in the Jewish religious calendar.

Asia

Within the 27 broadcasting systems of Asia can be found the widest possible variations, from the sophisticated system of Japan to the almost nonexistent system of Bhutan, from the gigantic size of China (with nearly a fourth of the entire world's population) to Christmas Island, an Australian territory of about 3,000 inhabitants. The latter has an unusual broadcasting arrangement: its low-power AM station, on the air 24 hours a day, offers programs only 16 hours (rebroadcasting materials from Australia, the BBC, and Singapore). During the nonbroadcast hours, the transmitter gives out marine and aviation information.

India. Broadcasting came to most of Asia under colonial auspices. John Reith, director-general of the BBC, urged the colonial government of India, Britain's largest colony, to start broadcasting: "A great opportunity had been lost in India," wrote Reith. "In 1924 I had tried to get the India Office to take the potentialities of broadcasting seriously; next year wrote to the Viceroy. Without effect; in 1926 a commercial company was started" (Reith, 1949: 113). The commercial company had little success and Indian broadcasting languished.

As in many colonies, however, official interest in broadcasting suddenly came alive when officials realized the imminence of World War II.

---

*See Boyd, 1982: 120–130, for details about the introduction of broadcasting to Saudi Arabia.

That threat presented colonial administrators with tremendous new public communication demands. In 1935 the viceroy asked for help, and the BBC sent Lionel Fielden, one of its senior producers, to India as the first director of government-sponsored broadcasting. Fielden originated the present title of the radio service, All India Radio (AIR), selected he said to avoid a name "tainted with officialdom."*

India became independent in 1947, but Indian broadcasting reflects Fielden's influence to this day. An Indian former deputy director-general of AIR, upon retiring after 30 years of service, wrote a book critical of India's failure to effectively harness broadcasting to serve contemporary national needs.

> All India Radio got its name, its present administrative structure and its present programme pattern between 1937 and 1940 when India was part of the British Empire. It came into being under imperial auspices . . . but after three decades during which vast political, economic and social changes have taken place in the world and in India, the only change in AIR is an increase in the number of its installations. . . . The question arises whether the insignificant impact of broadcasting on Indian life is not due to restricted growth made inevitable by an outdated organisation. (Masani, 1976: 1–2)

On the other hand, much good came about when the colonial government took the BBC's advice and made broadcasting a federal rather than a provincial function in the India Act of 1935, which established a federal system of government in India. Had it not been for that decision in favor of a unified radio system, India's fiercely competitive language groups would doubtless have created a babel of discordant voices. AIR, however, "has played a laudable role in keeping the country emotionally united" (Awasthy, 1978: 199). This is not to say that AIR represses linguistic diversity: it broadcasts not only in the 16 official languages but also in another 91 of India's nearly 2,000 tongues.

Despite the original intention of keeping government at arm's length, after independence, AIR became ever more deeply entangled in bureaucratic red tape, suffering from "a top-heavy officialdom, too much paper work, slowness of decision, unwillingness to admit shortcomings, a casual attitude to listeners, lack of flexibility in staffing and budgeting and therefore in planning programmes" (Masani, 1976: 161).

Although some of its stations provide a commercial service, called *Vividh Bharata* (Section 7.3), AIR does not pursue sales with great vigor. In fact one commentator remarked that AIR was "perhaps the least market-oriented national radio service ever operated in a sizeable nation" (Tunstall, 1977: 121).

India initially regarded television with skepticism, but a combination of skilled salesmanship by the Indian branch of the Dutch Philips

---

*Krishnatray, 1981. Fielden's autobiography, *The Natural Bent* (1960), contains details of early Indian broadcasting.

Company, a UNESCO grant, and U.S. government assistance finally persuaded the government to experiment with an educational service. A huge, multilingual, village-dominated society like India seemed an ideal subject for such a trial. From 1959 to 1965 Indian television continued the experiment, but then the camel of entertainment slipped its nose into the tent and soon dominated the service.

Television started under AIR, but in 1976 achieved a separate identity within the same ministry under the name *Doordarshan* ("distance view"). After a slow start, *Doordarshan* began rapid expansion in 1984, aiming at 80 percent coverage of the population. Meanwhile, AIR too expanded, reaching 90 percent of the population.

Thailand. The Kingdom of Thailand offers a contrasting example, an Asian country never colonized and a television pioneer. What Thailand's broadcasting system lacks in Western orderliness it makes up in vitality and sheer fun. "By common consent of observers and participants in Thailand," remarked the authors of a study of Third World systems, "it was the Thai fascination with gimmickry and the traditional value of *sanook* (fun)" that led Thailand to pioneer both in radio in 1931 and television in 1954 (Katz & Wedell, 1977: 11). Thai broadcasting is usually described by foreign observers as "chaotic"—with some justification, considering that there is no coordination of channel assignments or technical standardization. No one seems to know how many stations there are, partly because some of them change call letters and channels within the course of a single day.

The central government grants concessions to operate stations to various arms of the government, such as the air force, navy, army, public relations department, police department, universities, and the royal household. These agencies often turn operation of their concessions over to private entrepreneurs to run at a profit, with net revenues shared between the agency and the private operator. Schedules are unpredictable and programs eclectic, drawing both from traditional Thai culture and from various foreign syndicators. "The disorganization, sloppiness, and lack of punctuality may be maddening to some," remarked one sympathetic Western observer, "but it also indicates a freedom, implying the possibility for experimentation and development" (Scandlen, 1978: 141–142).

Africa

African broadcasting on the whole started later and advanced more slowly than Asian broadcasting because of differences in their colonial pasts, in the suitability of their cultures for television, and in their degree of urbanization.[14] With more than 50 systems (including those of the offshore islands and the northern tier of Arab states bordering on the Mediterranean, often treated as part of the Near East), Africa has the largest number of broadcasting entities of any region. Colonial powers, primarily France and Britain, introduced nearly all of them. True to the principle of national adaptation of broadcasting, British and French colonial broadcasting differed markedly:

> France tended to use radio primarily as a means of disseminating French culture. . . . Britain was more inclined toward localizing the medium and encouraging it to help preserve local culture; she used it to inform, to train, and at times to distract her African subjects: "Boredom leads to discontent, and there is a very real need for some means of bringing wholesome amusement to the African." (Gibbons, 1974: 108)

The French tended to centralize broadcasting, installing regional stations to serve several colonies with a common signal and relying heavily on programming originated in France itself.

The Ghana Broadcasting Corporation (GBC) will serve as an example of the systems that evolved from the British colonial tradition. Ghana is a small country (at least by African standards) on the west coast of Africa, famed as the first colony on that coast to achieve independence. A colonial governor with an unusual passion for radio introduced broadcasting to the Gold Coast (as Ghana was then called) in 1940. He had initiated wired radio in the Falkland Islands in 1929.* On being posted to the Gold Coast in 1934, he built a similar wired system. Later, the imminence of World War II persuaded the Colonial Office to give him the funds to initiate regular broadcasting as well.

Originally, of course, the entire operation had been run by British colonials, but World War II made it imperative to embark on Africanization. The colonial government had to communicate to Africans in their own languages in order to maintain the morale of African troops and their families; moreover, it needed to combat propaganda addressed to Africans from nearby French colonies controlled by Vichy, the collaborationist French government. On the eve of independence, Africans occupied 62 percent of the staff positions, though Britishers still held most of the top administrative jobs, such as director of the service and head of programs.[15]

Independence came in 1957 under the charismatic Kwame Nkrumah, who valued broadcasting for its potential in furthering his Pan-African political movement. In 1961 he inaugurated an ambitious external service beamed not only to all parts of Africa but also to North America and Europe. Nkrumah installed television in 1965, with assistance from the Canadian government. A noncommercial service, like Ghana radio, its goal was to "assist in the socialist transformation of Ghana."[16] But Nkrumah's Soviet-inspired economic schemes bankrupted the country, which had started with a sound economy and substantial cash reserves. He was overthrown in 1966. Soon thereafter, the government introduced

---

*In 1982, 250 wired speakers still existed in the Falklands (BBC, June 1983: 14).

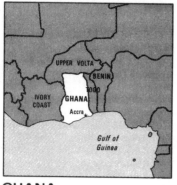

GHANA

commercials into both radio and television, though they have never earned anywhere near enough to make Ghanaian broadcasting self-sustaining.

In 1968 a new law placed all broadcasting under control of the Ghana Broadcasting Corporation (GBC). It was supposed to be an autonomous corporation, insulated from day-to-day politics, on the model of the BBC. However, each new party or army commander in power routinely dismisses the GBC's top administrators and appoints partisan followers in their stead.

Ghana now has two radio services: GBC-1, which feeds the sixty thousand subscribers of the still-operating wired-radio system, mostly in Ghanaian languages; and GBC-2, the commercial service, transmitted mostly in English. The external service closed down in 1979 for lack of funds; though rebuilding began in 1982, it was expected to be a slow process because the personnel skilled in foreign languages had left the country to seek work elsewhere. GBC-TV consists of five stations supplemented by four low-power repeaters, all of which carry the same programs for about six hours each evening.

The North African countries bordering on the Mediterranean—Egypt, Libya, Tunisia, Algeria, and Morocco—have quite different broadcasting histories from the countries of tropical Africa. They had greater exposure to European influences, and they share a common Arab culture that invites broadcasting across borders. This shared culture enabled them to use radio to support each other in their struggles for independence.

Algeria, for example, a French colony since 1830, acquired radio in 1937, television in 1957. The government aimed broadcasting exclusively at French colonists, about 10 percent of the population, plus the few Algerians who had adapted to French culture. Television programming came mostly from France; in fact, other than a daily 15-minute token program, the French allowed no local television material until independence in 1962.[17] Egypt's radio support helped the Algerians in their bitter seven-year war of independence, as did clandestine stations within the country.[18] When the French finally left Algeria in 1962, most broadcasting ceased because no one who remained could run the stations. Though operations resumed in 1963, Algeria still followed the French organizational pattern, and French language and culture continued to exert a strong influence.

Independent Algeria, which became a socialist state with Islamic modifications, has always given high priority to broadcasting as an element in its development planning. The government defrays about 70 percent of the broadcasting budget, and most of the rest comes from

ALGERIA

license fees. Both radio and television reach the entire nation. Algeria set as one priority the installation of a micro-wave relay network to enable interconnection of its television stations; and in 1975 it became the first nation to lease domestic satellite facilities from INTEL-SAT. Algeria also has over-the-horizon terrestrial microwave links (Section 8.4) enabling two-way television communication with France, whose influence remains strong despite an Algerian policy of Arabization. Today its Arabic radio network operates 24 hours a day. Radio networks in French and in Kabyle (language of the indigenous Berbers, representing 18 percent of the population) run for 10 and 14 hours, respectively. Television is on the air 8 hours for four days and 11 hours for three, using Arabic for locally produced material and French for imports.

White South Africa has a highly developed, First World economy, but its apartheid policy keeps its black majority in a position of Third World dependency. Its sophisticated broadcasting system reflects apartheid, with separate services for blacks and whites. South Africa pioneered radio in the early 1920s, later capitalized on FM to provide nationwide segregated FM radio services, as described in Section 8.2. Television, however, did not come until 1976:

> No industrialized nation waited longer or debated at greater length . . . The protracted, 25-year delay was due mainly to the fear within the ruling National Party that the black box would release unsettling forces on what is euphemistically called the "South African way of life." The Calvinistic Afrikaners have long perceived numerous dangers in television. (Hachten, 1979: 62)

Among the anticipated dangers were invasion of foreign-produced programming, exacerbation of black resentment against apartheid, and weakening of domination by the Afrikaner church.

Television began as a nationwide but white-only VHF service, alternating the two official languages of the country, Afrikaans and English, night by night. Later less extensive services for blacks were introduced, one in Zulu and Xhosa and one in the Sotho and Tswana languages. Still later South Africa began introducing localized UHF television in the "tribal homelands," black "nations" within South Africa, putatively independent but not recognized as such by the rest of the world. The first of these, in Bophuthatswana, began broadcasting in English in 1984. The government relayed its UHF signals beyond the homeland borders to large segregated black enclaves of urban workers, such as Soweto, near Johannesburg. When white listeners began buying special antennas to pick up "Bop-TV," the government went to extraordinary lengths to prevent this breach of its apartheid policy. Nevertheless, "viewing figures show that the alternative service is making an increasing impact on those whites who live in the narrow 'spillage' areas" (Sparks, 1984: 2).

Oceania

In both population served and number of receivers, the systems in the Pacific Ocean geographic region constitute the smallest of the regional groupings we are considering. The only large land areas in Oceania are Australia, New Zealand (both discussed in Section 2.2), and Papua New Guinea. The last, which became independent in 1975, occupies the eastern half of the large island of New Guinea, the rest of which forms part of Indonesia. The remaining systems are on widely scattered islands of the Pacific, some with familiar names, such as Guam, Hawaii, Midway, and Tahiti, and some less familiar, such as the republic of Nauru, the federated states of Micronesia, and the kingdom of Tonga. Nauru, an eight-square-mile island east of New Guinea, has the distinction of being the smallest republic in the world. Rich phosphate deposits make its entire population of about eight thousand wealthy by almost any standards. Its broadcasting facilities consist of one 200-watt AM radio station.

More than 20 of these small systems exist in Oceania, many located in dependencies, such as Wallis and Futuna (France), Wake (U.S.), Niue (New Zealand), and Norfolk (Australia). Because of their isolation, the islands of Oceania have a special need for broadcasting, including satellite relays to enable them to get news, sports events, and other timely materials without delay. Ten of them already have television, though on an extremely small scale. The states and dependencies of the region would be prime candidates for a shared television system such as I suggested in the beginning of this chapter.

2▪5 SATELLITES AND BROADCASTING

Technical description of the newer technologies is reserved for Chapter 8, but satellites and cable television need mentioning in this chapter's survey because of their significant international as well as national and regional impacts on conventional broadcasting.

Satellites extend the range and flexibility of conventional broadcasting, but their greatest impact comes from satellite-cable networks. This marriage of two new technologies presents a serious challenge. "The synergistic relationship between cable television and satellites," as one commentator put it, "has been one of the most dramatic and revolutionary developments in the history of television" (Inglis, 1981: 6). Too small individually to make satellite-cable networks cost effective, European nations tend toward multinational ventures in this field. In the early 1980s, such U.S. program providers as the Hollywood production studios and the broadcasting networks began forming consortia with European interests to feed the satellite-cable networks that finally began to emerge in Europe.

Operational communication satellites first became active participants in broadcasting systems in 1965 (see Table 2.2). Within 20 years, they had become a major factor in program distribution and potentially in program delivery. I use the term *distribution* for the network function of carrying program material from centralized points of origination to local outlets. Stations, cable systems, or other local entities *deliver* programs to individual consumers. Satellites, however, can do double duty as distribution-delivery mechanisms. A direct-broadcast satellite (DBS) can send signals directly to consumers instead of going through such intermediate deliverers as stations or cable systems.

Intercontinental Relays

INTELSAT. Although already possessing a highly developed terrestrial system of intercommunication, the United States needed long-distance links to reach its outlying states, Alaska and Hawaii, as well as to relay programs to and from other countries beyond the reach of earthbound microwave and coaxial cable networks. The International Telecommunications Satellite Organization (INTELSAT), which began to relay transatlantic communications in 1965, met these needs. Within four years, INTELSAT had launched additional space vehicles over the Pacific and Indian oceans, enabling worldwide satellite interconnection. The first live telecast between the U.S. mainland and Hawaii occurred in 1966, when INTELSAT relayed the Notre Dame–Michigan State football game to the islands. The most memorable of the early global telecasts, the 1969 *Apollo* moon landing, went to television systems throughout the globe, reaching an estimated one seventh of the world's entire population. In 1976 INTELSAT facilities enabled parts of the Olympic Games to reach more than a billion people.

INTELSAT represents a unique cooperative venture among nations. As of 1983, 109 countries participated as a consortium of investors in the system. Nonmembers can also purchase time, bringing the number of countries with INTELSAT access to 170. Each country has one or more earth stations, giving it access to all the other participating countries via satellite interconnection.

At first, INTELSAT sold access time for television programs by the minute. Only events of unusual importance earned the glamorous caption on television screens, "live via satellite." In 1970 INTELSAT carried slightly more than a thousand hours of television programming; by 1980 the television load had increased nearly tenfold. Not until 1982, however, did INTELSAT offer television users the option of buying full-time instead of by-the-program access. Users could then contract for 24-hour-a-day access. The first customers for such full-time contracts were Australian commercial broadcasters and the U.S. Armed Forces Radio and Television Service. The latter relays stateside programs to overseas military bases.

TABLE 2 ▪ 2 BROADCAST SATELLITE DEVELOPMENTS, 1962–1983

Name of Satellite	Country	Date	Comments
Telstar 1	U.S.	1962	1st transatlantic TV relay Capacity: 1 TV channel
Syncom 2	U.S.	1963	1st geostationary orbit relay
INTELSAT	U.S.	1965	1st commercial communications satellite
Molniya 1	USSR	1965	1st domsat (elliptical orbit)
ATS 1 through 6	U.S.	1966–1974	#6 was used for Indian SITE DBS experiment
INTELSAT	U.S.	1969	Global coverage achieved via satellites over Atlantic, Pacific and Indian Oceans
Intersputnik	USSR	1971	Soviet version of INTELSAT system
Anik 1	Canada	1972	Domsat, 10 TV channels
Molniya S1	USSR	1974	1st USSR geostationary vehicle
Symphonie 1,2	France and West Germany	1974	Cooperative experiment
Westar 1	U.S.	1974	1st U.S. domsat; 12 TV channels
CTS 1	Canada	1976	To cover Northern Territory
PALAPA 1	Indonesia	1976	1st Third World domsat
OTS	Europe	1978	Test satellite owned by consortium of European governments
Yuri	Japan	1978	Dedicated to DBS experimentation
Gorizont	USSR	1979	For DBS experimentation
INTELSAT V	U.S.	1980	50 times the capacity of 1965 version
Anik C3	Canada	1982	Launched from space shuttle vehicle Columbia; borrowed for first U.S. operational DBS service
ECS	Europe	1983	1st European operational satellite

Many countries took advantage of the opportunities INTELSAT offered to obtain daily video newsfeeds for their television stations from major international news agencies. They could also exchange news items among themselves.

Intersputnik. The USSR anticipated the West in establishing domestic satellite relay services but lagged by six years in introducing its own small-scale version of INTELSAT. Called *Intersputnik*, it started in 1981 with relays between the USSR and the East European Communist nations, later extending its range to such client states as Syria and Vietnam. To get satellite access to the non-Communist world, however, the USSR also needs INTELSAT. For example, it buys a daily newsfeed from Visnews, the major agency supplying video news on a global basis, owned by British Commonwealth interests. China used INTELSAT as a nonmember before joining the consortium in 1979. In the same year, Cuba installed an INTELSAT earth station to relay news about a Havana conference of nonaligned states back to the participants' home television systems.

For a quarter century, INTELSAT enjoyed an unchallenged monopoly in the supply of intercontinental relay facilities to Western nations. In the 1980s, however, EUTELSAT, a European consortium of national telecommunication administrations founded in 1977, threatened to challenge INTELSAT's monopoly.

Domestic Satellites

INTELSAT as Domsat. INTELSAT's original goal was to bridge oceans to interconnect existing land-based communication networks. But the system can also act as a national, *internal* relay facility, that is, as a surrogate domestic satellite (domsat). Domsats pick up signals from an originating earth station and then relay them back to one or more receive-only earth stations within the same country. A 1972 experiment demonstrated this possibility when INTELSAT relayed television programs within the state of Alaska. A microwave relay sent television signals originating in Anchorage to a nearby earth station providing an uplink to an INTELSAT vehicle in orbit above the Pacific Ocean. That vehicle relayed the signals back to portable earth stations positioned at six remote locations within Alaska. This was the first use of an INTELSAT vehicle as a domestic rather than international carrier. Now, thanks to other U.S. commercial domsat facilities, Alaska enjoys direct television reception throughout the state, and every settlement of 25 or more persons has telephone service.

In 1975 INTELSAT formalized domsat services by offering member countries the option of using its facilities for internal relays. More than 40 less developed countries took up the offer (see Figure 2.1). These countries made a great leap forward in their domestic telecommunication coverage simply by installing receive-only earth stations at appropriate centers within their territories. Before 1975 they would have

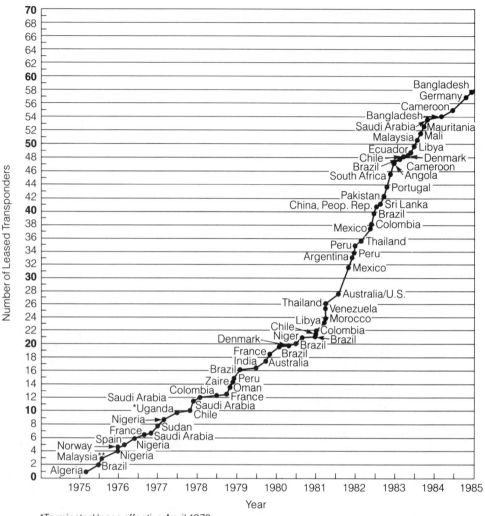

FIGURE 2 ▪ 1 Growth of INTELSAT Use as Domsat. SOURCE: Uplink, "INTELSAT and Developing Countries," 4 Feb. 1984, p. 3.

had little hope of bringing modern telecommunications to their remote regions by conventional microwave relay and coaxial cable networks within the foreseeable future. Such terrestrial systems must construct microwave links to every desired reception point within the national terrain. A satellite-borne transmitter, on the other hand, can reach every point in the terrain at no greater transmission cost than that of reaching a single point.

Developing countries with earth stations linked to INTELSAT use them mostly for telephone and other types of nonbroadcast traffic, but

SUDAN

even a few minutes per day of television access has enabled them for the first time to obtain daily video news from around the world. The Sudan, for example, must cover the largest ground area of any country in Africa. Its population is concentrated along the banks of the Nile and in a few scattered settlements, with vast stretches of desert in between. Almost overnight, the Sudan brought live television to its remote population centers in 1977 by means of 14 earth stations linked to INTELSAT. Mexico, using both INTELSAT and U.S. satellite services, had installed scores of receive-only earth stations by 1982. It expected soon to have 2,000 of them, bringing simultaneous broadcasting to every village in the nation.

Soviet Domsats. Even before INTELSAT made its facilities available for domestic use, the USSR had developed the first domsat as such. It would have taken the Soviets generations to build a ground-based network for distributing simultaneous television throughout its 11 time zones. The cost in both money and time would have been prohibitive. Responding to this special incentive, the USSR concentrated on developing a domsat distribution system. It succeeded in 1965 with the launching of the first in its *Molniya* ("lightning") satellite series. Unlike the INTELSAT vehicles, the *Molniyas* do not maintain a stationary position above their target area but move across the sky, necessitating earth station antennas capable of tracking the moving target. Each satellite remains in view only a third of the time in the course of a single orbit around the earth.

Canada's Domsats. Canada, with coverage problems somewhat similar to those of the USSR (though with 7 rather than 11 time zones), first operated a synchronous orbit domsat. Called *Anik* ("brother" in Eskimo language), it hovers in one place above the target area so that earth stations can remain fixed once they have zeroed in on the satellite's beam. The U.S. recoverable orbiter ("space shuttle") *Columbia* launched a later version, *Anik 3*, in 1982—the first launch of a satellite from a platform in space.

Telesat Canada—a share company half owned by the Canadian government and half by telecommunication authorities of the provincial governments and private shareholders—operates the *Anik* series. Mixed ownership ensures that Telesat Canada will respond to both commercial and public needs. Whereas a purely commercial firm might neglect unprofitable isolated consumers, Telesat Canada assures telephone and television services for even the remotest Indian villages in the northern regions.

U.S. Domsats. Lacking the strong motives for domsat development that impelled the USSR and Canada, the United States lagged behind in that field. Completion of the INTELSAT project had first priority. Congress set up the Communications Satellite Corporation (COMSAT) in 1962 to represent the United States in the INTELSAT consortium and also to develop and operate the system on behalf of the other members. COMSAT works with the National Aeronautics and Space Administration (NASA), which provides technical assistance, including the all-important function of launching the space vehicles.* Members of the public own stock in COMSAT, but its 15 board members (3 appointed by the president of the United States) must abide by the federal Communications Satellite Act of 1962.

In addition to its INTELSAT role, COMSAT developed a subsidiary to own and operate a series of domsats it calls Comstars. Other U.S. companies in the domsat business include Western Union (Westar series) and RCA (Satcom series). The Federal Communications Commission (FCC) stimulated proliferation of domsats by adopting an "open-skies" policy in 1972, liberalizing its licensing procedures to encourage free enterprise in the domsat field. A second facilitating decision came in 1979, when the FCC simplified the licensing of receive-only earth stations. Previously, the rules had required large, expensive receiving antennas costing on the order of $75,000 apiece. With deregulation, cost dropped to about $15,000, enabling hundreds of broadcast stations, cable companies, other businesses, and even private citizens to install their own satellite receivers. This move led to satellite-cable networks and the explosive growth of cable television, quite unlike the situation in other countries, where, until recently, governments tended to insulate satellites, broadcasting stations, and cable companies from the commercial marketplace.

Third World Domsat Ownership. Domsat ownership has a particular appeal for the less developed countries, despite INTELSAT's ability to provide the same services at far less cost. It would be more cost effective for a Third World nation to invest in ground stations to interconnect with INTELSAT vehicles than to buy not only ground stations but also a satellite, launch services, and telemetering facilities to control the satellite. Moreover, INTELSAT, with its backup vehicles both in space and on earth ready for launch, can be far more reliable than a minimal domsat system. But sovereign nations tend to see even greater risks in depending on *another* sovereign nation for vital communication facilities—especially if that other nation happens to be one of the superpowers.

---

*NASA launches vehicles for other countries as well. The only other launcher with foreign clients, Europe's facility in French Guiana, uses the *Ariane* launching rocket. In 1984 INTELSAT employed that facility to launch one of its satellites.

Indonesia, with its thousands of islands stretching across 3,000 miles of Indian Ocean north of Australia qualifies as a developing country with pressing legitimate need for domsat services. It became the first developing nation to have its own domsat when it launched PALAPA in 1976. In 1983 the space shuttle *Columbia* launched PALAPA 3. PALAPA feeds more than a hundred small earth stations for television and still more for other types of communication. Indonesia makes its domsat facilities available to its neighbors, Malaysia, Singapore, and Thailand, so that it qualifies both as a domsat and as a regional satellite facility.*

The NASA shuttle launched India's first successful domsat, INSAT 1B, in 1983 (INSAT 1A had been launched in 1982 but failed).[19] INSAT 1B has two transponders, one devoted to special development programs, the other to relaying regular television. Other Third World nations with large or highly dispersed areas and with well advanced plans for their own domsats included Brazil and Mexico.

Regional Satellite Consortia

In several regions, groups of countries with common interests have developed cooperative plans for launching satellites with multinational coverage patterns. Twenty-two Middle East and North African nations formed ARABSAT, a regional association with plans to launch a satellite system for those countries' collective use. Preparation began in 1976, making ARABSAT the pioneer regional plan among the less developed nations. A contract for two vehicles was signed in 1982, looking toward operations starting in 1984.† According to plans, ARABSAT would relay six television programs, one a common, pan-Arab service. Five Scandinavian countries began discussing a regional system called NORDSAT in the same year that the Arab states began their plan, but in 1984 it was still in the discussion stage.

Further along with experimentation and plans were several other groupings of European states, led by the European Space Agency (ESA), a consortium of 12 states including one non-European nation, Canada. Starting in 1978, the agency launched a series of vehicles called OTS (Orbital Test Satellite) to experiment with delivering television and other services throughout Europe. ESA followed with ECS (European Communications Satellite), a series of operational vehicles. It launched the

---

*Though PALAPA has the earmarks of a shining example of how modern technology can truly serve Third World needs, a contrary opinion holds that it represents exploitation by foreign multinational corporations that covet Indonesia's natural resources and by compliant politicians and ambitious military leaders (Lent, 1982: 172–173).

†ARABSAT's first vehicle was scheduled to be launched in 1984 by *Ariane*, Europe's launch facility, the second by the U.S. space shuttle in the same year. Congress at first opposed selling space on the NASA shuttle for launching ARABSAT because Libya and the PLO are members of the consortium.

first, ECS-1, in 1983, carrying nine transponders—two each allotted to the UK and West Germany, one each to Belgium, France, Italy, Netherlands, Norway, and Sweden.

A 1982 European experiment, Eurikon, used OTS-2 to relay programs to 15 countries, five of which took turns in originating programs a week at a time. Each originating country tried a different approach in dealing with the language problem. The satellite had multiple audio channels, enabling the use of five different languages simultaneously—Dutch, English, French, German, and Italian. Invited groups in the participating countries saw the seven months of test transmissions.*

The first operational European satellite cable television delivery system, Satellite TV (SATV), began feeding programs to cable headends in 1982, using a European Orbital Test Satellite. By 1984 SATV beamed scrambled signals to cable systems in eight countries and expected to be within reach of over two million cable subscribers by the end of the year. Financed by commercials and offered initially free to the cable companies, SATV is owned by a multinational group of investors, headed by the Australian newspaper tycoon, Rupert Murdoch. Delivery to 40,000 British subscribers on three cable systems began in 1984 under the name Sky Channel. Programming consisted of feature films, music, sports features, and light entertainment.

The French, ever sensitive about the status of their language and culture, mounted a Francophone satellite-cable network to counter the English SATV. Three French broadcast television networks and two other European French speaking sources, parts of the Belgian and Swiss systems, combined forces in 1984 to form TV-5. Each program source contributed to TV-5's schedule. A European community satellite relayed the programs to cable headends in the participating nations. The French also planned a joint satellite venture with Germany, a follow-up to their binational 1974–1975 *Symphonie* experimental satellite.

Direct Broadcast Satellites (DBSs)

Experiments with satellites receivable by either small community antennas or individual home antennas began as early as the mid-1970s. Canada, Japan, the United States, the USSR, and a French-German partnership carried out such experiments (see Table 2.2). A Japanese experimental DBS vehicle, *Yuri*, launched in 1978, is credited with being the first "dedicated" broadcast satellite, that is, the first to be designed and launched solely for use in broadcasting.

Best known among the early experiments was the 1975–1976 SITE (Satellite Instructional Television Experiment) in India, which used a

---

*Wright, 1983. European nations planned to follow Eurikon with EPS (European Program on Satellite) as an operational service, using L-Sat.

U.S. vehicle designed especially to carry out DBS trials at home and abroad. NASA shifted the vehicle, known as Applications Technology Satellite Number 6 (ATS-6), into orbit above the Indian Ocean, from which it broadcast adult educational material dealing with health, hygiene, and agriculture to more than two thousand Indian villages, using four different languages. Aside from building and launching the satellite itself, Indian manufacturers and agencies prepared all the hardware and software for this massive educational experiment. Some villages received the instructional programs directly in community centers. Ten-foot earth station antennas, built of chicken wire and other simple materials, picked up the signals from the ATS-6. Other villages received the programs via small local television transmitters fed by similar but larger homemade antennas. The experiment was pronounced a success, with the ATS-6 proving reliable 99 percent of the time and the reception facilities, 80 percent.[20] On the strength of this test, India went ahead with plans for its own domsat, as previously mentioned.

The prospect of foreign direct-broadcast satellites (DBSs), receivable directly by consumers with their own small antennas, raised touchy questions of national sovereignty. Initial planning, therefore, emphasized DBS facilities designed exclusively to serve audiences in the originating nation. A 1977 DBS International Telecommunication Union World Administrative Radio Conference (WARC) on DBS adopted this national focus. WARC '77 set up rules for channel and orbital slot position allotments for the nations of Africa, Asia, and Europe. Each European nation received allotments of five channels. Nations of the ITU's North American region opted to delay setting DBS standards, preferring to wait for a later regional conference. In the meantime, several U.S. companies went ahead with national DBS plans, and the first experimental telecasts started in 1983.

Withdrawal of the United States and Canada from the 1977 ITU conference seems to have been wise in light of subsequent European developments. Nations worry about invasions by television programs from space over which they have no control and which might violate laws governing their own domestic services. Yet where small countries crowd together, as in Europe, satellite footprints cannot be strictly confined to any one territory. Indeed, it has been calculated that it would be possible to pick up a planned French DBS as far away as New York and a British DBS as far away as Chicago. More recent European thinking, therefore, has veered toward cooperative DBS ventures, in keeping with the regional distribution systems discussed in the preceding section.

Companies planning the first DBS services in the United States thought in terms of footprints covering the country in three different zonal patterns. In 1982 COMSAT, which had formed a DBS subsidiary, pressed the Federal Communications Commission to issue rules for licensing DBS operations. The commission awarded construction permits to eight DBS applicants in the fall of that year. The applicants expected that operational (as contrasted with experimental) DBS vehicles would go into orbit near the end of the decade. Experimental direct broadcasts at first used a Canadian *Anik* pending launch of operational American DBS vehicles.

A significant British study of DBS potentialities published in 1981 led to the announcement of plans for launching a vehicle capable of delivering two television channels to the United Kingdom subscribers.[21] It would possibly also relay several radio channels. According to the plan, one television channel would offer repeats of top-flight programs previously aired by the BBC. It would be available at no further cost to those who invested in personal earth stations. The second channel, also controlled by the BBC, would offer a premium subscription service drawn from domestic and foreign program sources. It was thought that this channel would appeal to foreign audiences within the spillover fringes of the coverage area. Later, the British government also authorized the Independent Broadcasting Authority to consider getting into DBS operations. However, by 1984 both authorities began to have second thoughts because of the high cost of DBS. Satellite delivery of programs to networks of cable systems began to seem like a more cost effective option. Cable companies could afford larger receiving antennas and hence cheaper satellites (because of lower power requirements).

The European Space Agency planned to launch an experimental DBS in 1986. It was designed to transmit on higher power than previous satellites so that earth station antennas small enough to be affordable by the average consumer and mountable on the average house could be used. Called *L-Sat*, this DBS vehicle was to be financed a third each by the United Kingdom, Italy, and a combination of six other countries.

The Japanese commercial and public television companies combined to finance a pay-television satellite, BS-3, scheduled for launch in 1989. Meanwhile, in 1982 a Japanese satellite began feeding NHK (public television) signals directly to homes beyond the reach of ordinary television station reception. Homeowners had to purchase a relatively simple one-meter dish antenna to receive the service, which was expected to develop into the world's first DBS service receivable nationally.

2 ▪ 6 **CABLE TELEVISION**

Background

Nowhere else has cable television flourished with such exuberance as it has in North America. As a luxury adjunct to broadcasting that few nations can afford, cable television exists in only about a score of the more highly developed countries. Even in Australia, the minister of industry and commerce could remark that for his country the economics of cable were "ludicrous."[22] Most nations able to afford cable weighed it down with regulations, limiting its growth in order to protect the monopolistic position of traditional broadcasting. But by about 1980, the industrialized countries had concluded that their future economic wel-

BELGIUM

fare required aggressive exploitation of the new information technologies. This change of policy left traditional broadcasting organizations vulnerable. As one observer put it, "The monolithic public service stations of Europe are no longer sure of themselves. They cannot for certain count on continued government pampering and protection. They see themselves as potential victims of technology that's developing faster than protective legislation can accommodate" (Watkins, 1982).

In Europe, cable has succeeded best in small countries bordering on larger nations. Unable to afford elaborate television services of their own, these countries have found it convenient to rely on their neighbors for variety in programming. Thus Belgium, the Netherlands, and Denmark lead the rest of Europe in cable penetration, each with more than 50 percent of its television homes served by cable.*

Belgium, with the highest cable penetration, in addition to being small must mount completely separate program services in Dutch and French. Each linguistic group operates its own external service as well as its own domestic radio and television networks. Each runs two television networks, though the second stays on the air only five hours per day, five days per week. Belgian cable companies pick up programs from over a dozen outside sources—four British, three French, three German, two Dutch, and one Luxembourgian. The law forbids commercials, but cable companies do not bother to delete them from foreign programs.[23]

Canada, though by no means small, faces somewhat the same situation as Belgium: the need to program in two languages and the presence of a wealth of foreign program sources just across the border. But while the Belgians seem to have resigned themselves to a very high percentage of imported programming, Canadians fight grimly to maintain their cultural identity and the economic viability of their own entertainment industry. Canada began importing television via cable as early as 1950, two years before its own television service went on the air. By 1982 Canada's cable penetration had reached about 60 percent, nearly twice that of the United States.

Take Calgary, 140 miles north of the border separating Montana from Alberta province, as an example. Calgary carries all the Canadian national broadcast services, the four U.S. networks and a U.S.

---

*Syfret, 1983, gives 1981 European data and forecasts for 1985 and 1990. Countries with the least cable penetration were Greece, Italy, Portugal, Spain, and Sweden. West Germany, though with only 4 percent penetration in 1981, was on the eve of major expansion.

independent station, and several specialized cable services such as the one carrying the Alberta legislative sessions. Three quarters of Calgary households buy the entire package at a cost of $7.50 per month. Higher subscription rates in the United States have attracted Canadian investors to transfer their cable know-how across the border. Their investments in U.S. cable systems have been controversial because Canada imposes restrictions on similar investments by U.S. firms in their country. American broadcasters also object to the fact that Canada will not allow its advertisers the same tax deductions for the purchase of commercial time on U.S. stations that they get when they purchase time on Canadian stations.[24]

Wired-Radio Precedent

An analogous radio technology, known as wired wireless or wired radio, influenced cable television developments in Europe. As mentioned earlier, Communist broadcasters use this technology more than anyone else (see Section 2.3). The British call these installations "relay exchanges" and the system itself, "rediffusion"—a name adopted by the leading British commercial purveyor of wired wireless. Rediffusion, Ltd., invested in a number of colonial wired-radio systems and is now active in Britain as a cable television supplier.*

The British Broadcasting Corporation regarded rediffusion as a potential threat to its monopoly in the 1930s, when wired radio began to flourish. The BBC yearbooks of the time revealingly express the nature of its concern. The 1933 edition, for example, points out that the rediffusion system

> *contains within it forces which if uncontrolled might be disruptive of the spirit and intention of the B.B.C.'s charter. The persons in charge [of rediffusion companies] can transmit amusing items from the [BBC] programs and replace talks and other matter of an informative or experimental value by amusing items in programmes from abroad and so debase their programmes to a level of amusement interest only. (BBC Yearbook, 1933: 72)*

Restrictive regulations forced British rediffusion companies to carry BBC radio, denying them the right to originate their own programs—a sharp contrast with the practice of the USSR and China, where the opportunity to insert local materials on a closed-circuit basis is regarded as a major advantage of wired wireless.

Some 13 percent of the world's radio receivers still consist of wired speaker boxes, as shown in Table 2.3. Most operate in Communist countries, but a few wired-radio services still exist in Western Europe, Tropical Africa, and the West Indies. In their simplest form, wired

---

*Rediffusion founded Hong Kong's Asia Television, Ltd., which operates two cable channels there. The parent Rediffusion company in England, purchased by British Electric Traction in 1963, still operates major radio and television wired systems in Britain.

TABLE 2 ■ 3 WIRED-RADIO (REDIFFUSION) USAGE

Region	Number of Wired Speakers (thousands)	As Percentage of All Receivers in Region
Asia and Far East	154,144	33
USSR and Eastern Europe	91,160	39
Western Europe	949	*
Tropical Africa	118	*
West Indies	25	*
Latin America	3	*
Middle East	—	—
North America	—	—
Oceania	—	—
Total	246,400	14

* = less than 1 percent
SOURCE: Based on data in BBC External Services, "World Radio and Television Receivers" (BBC, London, June 1983).

speakers deliver only one program, leaving subscribers with "on" or "off" as their only options. More sophisticated systems give subscribers a choice of several programs. Switzerland's wired system feeds nearly half a million homes with a choice of six high-fidelity audio programs— one for each of the three language groups that operate the national broadcasting system (German, French, and Italian), two exclusively for music, and one that picks up a selection of spoken-word programs from neighboring broadcasting systems.[25]

Wired radio has several attractive features in specific situations:

- In poorer countries, wired services enable people who cannot afford to buy and maintain receivers a chance to share in the national radio service for only a few cents per month. Demand for Ghana's wired service, started by a colonial governor in 1935, still remains high (see Section 2.4). As recently as 1983, Bangladesh announced plans for installing a new radio rediffusion service.[26]

- Rediffusion guarantees high-fidelity, interference-free listening in Switzerland, where rugged terrain and a crowded spectrum make clear over-the-air reception difficult.

- Wherever governments prefer to control what people can hear, wired speakers prevent audiences from tuning to foreign stations.

- Governments that rely on radio for social control find it useful to add local materials at rediffusion headends to reinforce messages coming from distant regional or national origination centers.

- In times of emergency, wire systems are immune from jamming or other enemy interference or manipulation. Further, they cannot be used as homing beacons for aircraft or missiles as can broadcast transmitters.

Cable TV Developments

Britain. British wired-radio companies gained a new lease on life when television began. As in the United States, over-the-air television transmitters in Britain at first left substantial areas of the country without service, creating a demand for cable to fill the vacuum. Regulation, however, limited the potential for cable's commercial growth. Must-carry rules were imposed on behalf of the BBC's two networks and one commercial regional service, with neither advertising nor local origination allowed. In any event, the demand for cable fell off as additional broadcast transmitters improved over-the-air coverage. By 1982 only 13 or 14 percent of British households had cable television. When such a falloff occurred in the United States, cable firms compensated by adding attractive new program services not previously available to their subscribers. The technology of British cable systems, however, limits them to only four to six channels, leaving no room for substantial program augmentation beyond the must-carry package.* Cable firms must face the fact that people already pay receiver license fees. Firms have difficulty in persuading potential subscribers to spend still more on cable services if cable does little to expand viewing options.

In 1982 a committee appointed by the home secretary released a report recommending expansion of cable television in relation to broadcasting. Known as the Hunt Report, it proposed ten-year franchises for cable companies, which would be allowed to carry advertising but not pay-cable services. Other proposed rules included (1) no licensing of religious or political groups, (2) must-carry rules with respect to broadcast programming, and (3) no requirement for local access channels.[27] These proposals were incorporated in the Cable and Broadcasting Act of 1984, which established both a Cable Authority and a Satellite Broadcasting Board. The former functions as a licensing authority for private cable systems, while the latter supplies DBS facilities and contracts with program suppliers, assuring DBS services "of high quality (both as to the transmission and as to the matter transmitted) for the United Kingdom" (Great Britain, 1984: 36).

Continental Europe. Cable on the Continent during the 1970s, though, as noted above, received in many homes, bore no resemblance

---

*Modern cable operators get around this limitation by helping subscribers to improve their antennas so that they can pick up over-the-air signals directly, relieving the cable operator of must-carry obligations.

to the more advanced systems of the United States, with their dozens of channels, satellite relays, and overlays of special pay-cable services. Many European installations passing for cable television would in the United States be called MATV (Master Antenna Television) installations. Such an installation simply employs a central antenna delivering programs to households within an apartment complex or other type of multiple-family housing facility. Subscriber lists amounted to three hundred dwelling units at the most, and fees ranged in 1983 from $1.50 to $11.00 per month, with an average of $5.00 for ten-channel systems.[28]

Numerous small-scale hookups of this kind emerged in part because so many municipalities and housing associations operated their own systems. In the Netherlands, for example, municipalities owned more than half the cable systems, with only 13 percent operated as private commercial ventures. Officials in European towns, objecting to ugly forests of television antennas on their rooftops, will not allow stringing cables on poles, the common practice in the United States outside the metropolitan centers. Thus one reason that municipalities got into cable was aesthetic.* The high cost of cable rights-of-way, along with restrictive must-carry and no-advertising rules, discouraged commercial investors.

In the United States, although FCC regulations restrained cable growth to protect broadcast television, entrepreneurs felt relatively free to invest in cable television on a market-by-market basis, responding in free-enterprise fashion to consumer demands. Europe generally took a more centralized approach, stemming the cable tide while parliaments debated national cable policy, delaying full-scale cable installations pending the outcomes of cautious, officially sanctioned experiments.

Cable television had an early but temporary vogue in Italy starting in 1971, when a tiny system opened without benefit of authorization in Biella, a city in the northern region. Tele Biella became famous throughout Europe as the pioneer test case challenging a national broadcasting monopoly (as in much of Europe, in Italy cable is considered a form of broadcasting). Tele Biella inspired cable companies to spring up all over northern Italy (described in Section 4.4). A lower court ruled against private cable television systems like Tele Biella, but in 1974 the Italian Constitutional Court ruled in favor of them. The 1974 ruling also specified that private operators had the right to *broadcast locally*. Because a broadcast station costs far less to set up than a cable installation, the 1974 ruling undermined the burgeoning private cable television movement in Italy. Soon private broadcasting flourished in its stead.

France lagged in cable development until 1982, when it finally adopted a comprehensive cable law authorizing the PTT (the national telecommunication authority) to cable the nation with fiber-optic links.

---

*U.S. city ordinances requiring that homeowners get clearance on the "visual impact" of DBS antennas suggest similar aesthetic sensibility.

The law empowered municipalities to establish local cable companies responsible for headends and programming. Private investors could hold only minority interests. These companies advanced part of the cable installation costs to the PTT, paying back the rest over a period of years. The law permitted local origination, subject to approval of the High Authority, the central body supervising broadcasting.

West Germany, too, accepted cable slowly, introducing local experimental installations in 1984 after several years of planning. Ludwigshaven, the first of four communities authorized to experiment, started with 19 channels. Like the French PTT, the German *Bundespost* planned eventually to install cable throughout the country, a project expected to take decades. In the same year, Sweden also authorized cable experiments, allotting public housing authorities the task of conducting them. Thus, belatedly, uncabled and undercabled parts of Europe began to move into the new field in a systematic way in the early 1980s.

Despite its generally high achievements in communication technology, Japan likewise delayed cable development. Though the islands had thousands of small systems in place in 1983, 99 percent had five hundred or fewer subscribers. No cable networks existed, and only 77 systems originated any programs. Cable still performed the original "community antenna" function, filling in blanks in the over-the-air coverage of regular broadcasting networks. By 1983, however, several companies outside the communication field had announced plans to start modern, broadband cable television services.

Second and Third Worlds. Elsewhere, cable television had made little progress by 1984. High cable costs, low priorities on luxury consumer goods, paucity of ideologically acceptable programs, lack of consumer purchasing power to pay additional fees—all militated against government-sponsored cable development. East Germany appeared to be the leader among Communist countries, with more than two million homes cabled by 1984. The USSR had only a few thousand cable subscribers, though it had announced ambitious plans to cable the entire country. The Soviets had the wherewithal to develop the new technologies as fast or faster than other countries. In fact, they pioneered in the development of satellites for broadcast relays. As an observer long resident in Moscow explained, the apparent lack of interest does not indicate lack of resources: "Rather, the Soviet Union prefers to maintain a centralized communications system that allows a unified approach to the presentation of information. In that way the elites can influence people's tastes and inclinations from above" (Shahzad, 1984: 24).

In the Third World, economics rather than ideology held back adoption of the new technologies. Thailand, a relatively affluent developing country, was exceptional in organizing some small-scale cable installations as early as 1984. They operated without benefit of official authorization in the absence of any relevant statute.[29]

Pay Cable

Naturally, if most countries lagged in developing basic cable television, they fell even further behind in adopting the more costly and demanding technology of pay cable, the introduction of which projected U.S. cable beyond the cottage industry stage. A small system in Helsinki, Finland, pioneered European pay cable in 1978. The pay option occupied one of the system's six channels, in 1982 supplying 30 hours of American and British film entertainment per week. In addition to the pay channel, the Helsinki system supplied basic services consisting of an advertising-supported entertainment channel a few hours per day, a 24-hour information channel, the two Finnish television networks, and a Russian service from Tallinn, an Estonian city just across the Gulf of Finland, in the USSR.[30]

In 1983 the British Home Office granted 11 pay-cable franchises. Collectively they had the potential to reach a million homes. They were to provide 16 to 32 channels. To meet the prospectively huge demand for more programs, British suppliers formed consortia with major U.S. program companies. Britain also had more ambitious plans for cable, however—a nationwide fiber-optic network capable of delivering 30 channels with interactive (two-way) capabilities. According to estimates, this network would cost on the order of $4.5 billion—a daunting investment for a country plagued by unemployment and a depressed economy. As noted earlier, France started its satellite-distributed pay-cable service, TV-5, in 1984. It started with a potential subscribership of about 1.5 million, offering three hours of programming per day.[31] Switzerland began local pay-cable experiments in 1981, followed in 1982 by Europe's first regular pay-cable service, Rediffusion AG (Redi), a cooperative organized as early as 1931. Redi started using the Swiss channel on ECS-1, Europe's operational regional satellite, to deliver pay-cable programs in 1984, calling the service Pay-Sat. At the same time the French-speaking regions formed a pay company to feed programs over a terrestrial cable hookup installed by the Swiss PTT.[32] West Germany, too, planned to feed pay programs to its cable systems via ECS-1.

In 1983 the Netherlands government announced tentative plans for licensing an unusual form of pay cable. Suppliers of cable facilities would rent them to program suppliers on a common carrier basis. No advertising would be allowed, at least at first (in deference to press opposition). The government foresaw the possibility of pay-cable networks, connected by either microwave or satellite relays. The U.S. experience suggested that only by such means could cable achieve the economies of scale needed for commercial success.

Despite its generally prompt acceptance and deployment of new communication technologies, Canada too held back on pay cable, fearing that it would open the way to further domination by American programming. Finally, in 1982 the Canadian Radio-Television and Telecommunications Commission licensed six pay-cable companies, two national in scope and four regional. The commission imposed strict import quotas to ensure that Canadian producers would be well represented in the program offerings. Later, however, the commission lightened these restrictions, having realized that Canadians would resort to their own satellite antennas to pick up U.S. programs (like the United States, Canada had deregulated receive-only satellite earth stations, making them readily available to individual users).

SUMMARY

Each geopolitical region of the world has adapted broadcasting to conform with its own economic, political, and social needs. The First (Western) World generally tends toward pluralistic systems operating competitively, usually in terms of noncommercial government or public corporation services competing with commercial private services. In the Second (Communist) World, monolithic systems prevail, with no opportunity for competition. Broadcasting in the Third (developing) World tends to reflect the influence of the developed countries, with monolithic systems the norm but with countries in the U.S. sphere of influence tending toward pluralistic systems.

Satellites profoundly influence broadcasting in all three worlds, but cable television and pay cable are confined almost entirely to the First World. Most First World countries entered the 1980s planning to invest heavily in the newest communication technologies in order to protect their economic futures. They announced ambitious national cable, direct-broadcast satellite, and programming plans. Because of their small individual size, however, European countries leaned toward multinational satellite-cable and DBS services. Existing cable installations in Europe tend to be small though numerous. Larger installations with many channels began to emerge only in the early 1980s, as did satellite-cable networks.

NOTES

[1]Banks, 1982.

[2]Noriega & Leach, 1979: 22, 51.

[3]Bautista, 1982: 21.

[4]Banks, 1982: 35.

[5]Hollie, 1981.

[6]Mhumbira, 1981; *Combroad*, Dec. 1982: 50.

[7]Troyer, 1983.

[8]Population versus television set figures from BBC estimates as of the end of 1982 (BBC, June 1983).

[9]Howkins, 1977: 7.

[10]O'Callaghan, 1983.

[11]Howkins, 1982b: 111.

[12]*Broadcasting*, 13 June 1983.

[13]Statistics on Latin American television based on data in *Variety*, 30 March 1983.

[14]Katz & Wedell, 1977: 43.

[15]Head, 1979: 46.

[16]See Kugblenu, 1974, for details of Nkrumah's television plans.

[17]Pilsworth, 1982: 172.

[18]For some details on radio's role in Algeria's war of independence, see Elgabri, 1974.

[19]Traub, 1984.

[20]For details on the SITE project, see Chander & Karnik, 1976; Gore, 1983; Agrawal, 1984.

[21]Howkins summarizes the recommendations, 1982c: 17–23. The proposed DBS is called Unisat.

[22]*Combroad*, June 1983.

[23]Fauconnier, 1984.

[24]Banker, 1980; *Broadcasting*, 8 Feb. 1982: 103.

[25]Sandford, 1976: 170–180.

[26]Ansah, 1979: 11; *Asian Broadcasting*, August 1983.

[27]Great Britain, 1982.

[28]*EBU Review*, Jan. 1984.

[29]Waltham, 1984.

[30]Soramäki, 1982.

[31]Peyre, 1984.

[32]*Television Age International*, Oct. 1984; Rostan, 1984.

POLITICS OF BROADCAST OWNERSHIP

A s the overview of the previous chapter shows, each government has shaped its national broadcasting system in keeping with its own nature, especially its political nature. The political implications of ownership patterns and the terms on which political figures gain access to the medium are the subjects of this chapter.

3 ▪ 1 ORIGINS OF POLITICAL CONTROLS

Most pioneer broadcasting stations of the 1920s belonged to private owners rather than to governments. In fact, the government department concerned, usually the PTT (Post, Telegraph, and Telephone administration), often actually opposed the introduction of broadcasting. PTT officials resented diverting attention from serious communications toward what they considered the frivolous use of valuable spectrum space for mere entertainment. They had been trained to foster personal rather than public messages, point-to-point communication rather than the aimless scattering of messages. The British postmaster-general, for example, "hedged round with every kind of irksome qualification" the first permit he issued for broadcasting in the United Kingdom. Transmissions could take place for only one hour a day, either between 11:00 A.M. and noon or between 2:00 and 4:00 P.M. At the end of every seven minutes of broadcasting, the station operator had to stop transmitting to listen for official messages—none of which ever came.[1]

Electrical manufacturers often gave the earliest impetus to broadcasting, as in the case of Westinghouse in the United States, which started KDKA in Pittsburgh in 1920. In the United Kingdom, the Marconi Company joined five other large manufacturers to form the British Broadcasting Company in 1922. In colonial territories, some years later, innovative settlers and civil servants sometimes imported broadcasting, forming clubs to experiment with the new medium. In the USSR, on the other hand, a government that was newly embarked on a far-reaching social revolution recognized broadcasting as an important propaganda tool from the outset. There the impetus came from the top political authority.

Though business people and the general public grasped the meaning of broadcasting more quickly than the bureaucrats, eventual government intervention was inevitable. Mutual technical interference among stations began to destroy the usefulness of unregulated broadcasting. Moreover, governments feared the power of broadcasting to reach and influence entire populations. This new means of public communication had the potential to stir up powerful political undercurrents that could either bolster or undermine political systems, depending on the terms under which the government allowed broadcasting to operate. Political authorities dared not let these forces run loose in the land. They realized, as one observer put it, that "broadcasting confers upon its ostensible or concealed masters a social power which, when not actually wielded by the political authorities, must to some extent be regulated by them if they are not to lose their grip on the levers of power" (Namurois, 1972: 104–105).

The U.S. Radio Act of 1927 designated broadcasting a subject of federal control but left ownership to private, primarily local and commercial, interests. In the same year, King George V signed a royal charter (originating in Parliament) creating the British Broadcasting *Corporation* (BBC) to supersede the manufacturer's British Broadcasting *Company*. The charter established a nonprofit, public corporation to provide broadcasting throughout the United Kingdom "as a public service." The U.S. Radio Act made no statement about financing the new medium, taking for granted that most private licensees would aim at making a profit and that advertising would be their major source of revenue. The BBC's license forbade advertising and provided for funding from fees paid by the users of receiving sets. The licensing of receiving sets had already been mandated by the 1904 Wireless Telegraphy Act.*

Thus the two most closely related of the leading Western democracies established quite different styles of ownership and legal oversight of their national broadcasting systems. In the USSR, meanwhile, a third pattern had emerged. A joint stock company formed in 1924 supervised Soviet broadcasting. Shares were issued in the names of trade union and educational authorities. Because such organizations were in fact arms of

---

*The phrase "without prior approval of the Secretary of State" precedes the stipulation against advertising in the current BBC license. Thus the BBC conceivably could sell commercials at some future time, providing that the government approved. The present law imposing license fees on receivers is found in the Wireless Telegraphy Act of 1949.

the government, however, in effect the government itself retained ownership of broadcasting facilities. In a few years, the fiction of independent ownership disappeared and Soviet broadcasting became a government operation in name as well as in fact.

These three widely imitated models for ownership of broadcasting facilities emerged during the first seven years of the medium's existence. The U.S. model left station ownership and operation open to free enterprise; the BBC model awarded monopoly ownership and operational control of all stations in the nation to a public corporation, insulated from direct government intervention in day-to-day operations; and the USSR model retained ownership and control within the machinery of the central government.

To characterize each in a word, the U.S. system might be called *permissive*, the British system *paternalistic*, and the Soviet system *authoritarian*. Permissiveness implies "voting with the dial"—consumer autonomy, emphasizing what people *want* rather than what some may think they need; it relies on market forces more than on government supervision to control the system. Paternalism means considering needs as well as wants and curbing market forces. Sir Brian Young, former director-general of the Independent Broadcasting Authority, characterized paternalism in British broadcasting as having the following attributes: it makes services generally available, paid for equally by all consumers; not all programs pay their way; the system is used impartially, "exercising some control over what may give offence"; it encourages native writers and producers; it prevents domination by either government or advertisers; and it regulates both the amount and the content of advertising.[2] Authoritarian broadcasting implies still more insulation from both consumer preferences and market forces, with arbitrary government regulation exercised in the name of the people but with little concern for individual preferences that do not coincide with official doctrines.

In practice, each country tends to select elements from various models, evolving a composite system of its own. Even among the Communist systems of Eastern Europe, distinctive national differences arose. But on the whole, most systems can be viewed as falling basically into one of the three political styles.

3 ▪ 2 GOVERNMENT MONOPOLY

As Table 3.1 shows, governments monopolize the great majority of broadcasting systems in the world. Typically authoritarian, one-party regimes permit no private ownership or operation of broadcasting. Marxist governments adopt this policy on ideological grounds, contending that government ownership really means ownership by the masses. Many Third World nations use authoritarian methods comparable to those of the Marxist countries, though usually more for pragmatic than for ideological reasons. In countries where only the state can fund

TABLE **3 ▪ 1** OWNERSHIP OF WORLD BROADCASTING SYSTEMS

Type of Ownership	Radio		Television	
	Number	Percent	Number	Percent
Government	91	49	63	48
Public corporation	38	21	29	22
Private, commercial	36	21	21	16
Combinations of the above	19	10	18	14

COMMENTARY: Percentages rounded to nearest whole number. "Public corporation" refers to ownership by a nonprofit corporation. The largest percentage, nearly half, of both radio and television systems are entirely government owned. The proportions of public corporate and private ownerships are about equal. Television has a lower percentage of commercial systems but a higher percentage of combination systems. Note that the number of commercially owned systems does not reveal the full number that sell advertisements, as many government and public systems depend on advertising for part of their income.
SOURCE: Adapted from late 1970s data in UNESCO, Statistical Yearbook, 1982, tables 11.1 and 11.3. ©UNESCO 1982. Used by permission. The tables omit some countries and count the Panama Canal Zone, the U.S. Virgin Islands, and Puerto Rico as separate systems.

broadcasting, the state becomes the owner willy-nilly. In addition, many Third World governments are too impatient with criticism or dissent to allow private ownership on terms that most investors would accept.

Government ownership and more or less direct control of the national broadcasting system occurs outside the Communist and Third World spheres as well. Some Western-style democracies still have difficulty in resolving the political issues that push and pull broadcasting policy in contrary directions. Faced with constant agitation for more private input, most such countries have begun authorizing privately owned local stations. In Italy, for example, private stations have emerged as a major force.

The USSR

The State Committee for Television and Radio Broadcasting controls Soviet radio and television. Reporting to the highest executive authority of the nation, the Council of Ministers, the committee oversees the "all-union," or nationwide, broadcasting services. Several hundred similar committees supervise broadcasting at lower administrative levels, which originate local or regional programs and retransmit the all-union services.*

---

*Paulu counted a total of 300 provincial broadcasting committees, at levels ranging from the 15 union republics down to individual cities (1974: 54–55).

The Communist party cements the broadcasting system into a consistent whole. Though representing only about 10 percent of the population, the party effectively controls the political system. Its members occupy all the key broadcasting posts, and the party often issues broadcasting policy directives to the State Committee.

Marxist-Leninist ideology dictates policy. It sees the communications media as essential tools for "re-education of the masses."* Private ownership, whether by individuals or corporations, would mean subversion of the media to serve capitalist, bourgeois exploitation of the masses. Only state ownership, on behalf of the masses, can guarantee that the media will genuinely serve the interests of all the people rather than those of capitalist owners and their class.

Viewed from this perspective, Western television seems just as propagandistic as Communist television seems to a Westerner. A Russian commentator writes:

> For all their differences in the structure, the nature of subordination to the government, the sources of financing, etc., [Western] TV services are all important components of the bourgeois propaganda machine and as such their ideological activities are designed to defend the pillars of capitalism. . . . No matter what methods are employed to mould public opinion, bourgeois television is in essence anti-popular and anti-human inasmuch as it is called upon to defend an unjust, exploiting system. (Biryukov, 1981: 87, 107)

China

China organizes broadcasting in a similar manner—it is a state-owned operation, highly centralized as to policy and control, that necessarily delegates a great deal of responsibility to provincial authorities. The central broadcasting services in Beijing (Peking), formerly under the Propaganda Committee of the top Communist party executive committee, come under the Broadcasting and Television Ministry.† The Chinese use the familiar three-tier organizational pattern:

> The first level is the Central People's Broadcasting Station (also the China Central Television, CCTV), which carries government policies through to the masses. . . . The second layer is the regional broadcasting, consisting of

---

*Communist doctrines about the political role of the media developed long before broadcasting and so were based entirely upon the experience of early Communist leaders with the newspapers of their day. So ingrained is that way of thinking that Communist media doctrines still tend to be expressed primarily in terms of the print media. Communist broadcast news continued to sound like a talking newspaper long after Western broadcasters had developed a distinctive broadcast style of newswriting and presentation. To this day, Soviet writers often seem to think of broadcasting as simply a branch of "journalism."

†Like Australia, China uses the English word *broadcasting* to mean radio only.

provincial, autonomous, regional, and municipal networks. Then comes the third layer, which is local (grass roots) broadcasting, comprising wired radio stations in counties, communes, and in big factories, plants, schools, and other work units. In every county seat (China has 2,128 counties) there is a radio station which monitors programs from Beijing and each provincial capital. From county seats wired transmissions are connected to communes, villages, marketplaces, fields, and homes with loudspeakers mounted on walls, poles, or roofs. . . . About 93 percent of the nation's production teams (the lowest work unit) enjoy broadcasting and about 70 percent of farming families have been equipped with loudspeakers in homes. (Li, 1983: 9–10)

The Third World

Most Third World governments own their broadcasting systems, usually ruling out private ownership entirely. Because of U.S. influence, Latin America is a major exception to this generalization. Shortly before granting independence in some of its colonies, Great Britain created statutory corporations on the model of the BBC in an attempt to insulate broadcasting from direct government control. Some of these corporate structures still survive, but in name only. Others were promptly dismantled by incoming independent governments. In Kenya, for instance, two years before independence, an unusual partnership between government and private enterprise had set up the Kenya Broadcasting Corporation (KBC). Its board had equal representation from government, the general public, and an operating contractor. The contracting firm incorporated American, Canadian, British, and East African investors. The year after Kenya became independent in 1963, the new government dissolved the KBC, turning the operation over to the Ministry of Information and Broadcasting, which renamed it the Voice of Kenya.[3]

In still other Third World countries, broadcasting started as a private enterprise, but expropriation later made it a state monopoly. This happened in Cuba, which had a flourishing privately owned broadcasting industry prior to the Castro revolution. In 1959 Castro seized the facilities, now operated by the government Institute of Radio and Television. In Iran a favored private entrepreneur who had the Pepsi Cola and RCA concessions in the country introduced television in 1958. His service, Television of Iran (TVI), proved popular, relying heavily on American program imports. In 1966, however, the shah's government decided to start its own television service. The ambitious young executives who ran it, wanting to break away from dependence on foreign programming and harness broadcasting to national development, refused to schedule popular syndicated programming and even rejected the U.S. 525-line technical standard already in use by TVI. The government system, called National Iranian Television (NIT), operating on the European 625-line system and scheduling programs lacking in mass appeal, ran a poor second to the private service. In 1969 the government nationalized the private company. Seemingly less militant after the removal of its adversary, the NIT management began to schedule more popular programming.*

Most broadcasting leaders in developing countries believe that the special economic, political, and social problems they face mandate government ownership of the medium. The authors of a comprehensive study of Third World broadcasting noted "the virtual abandonment, throughout the developing world, of Western patterns of broadcasting in which, however defined, the broadcasting system has some element of autonomy from the government of the day" (Katz & Wedell, 1977: 212). In a 1981 meeting of Commonwealth broadcasting authorities in the Pacific region participants discussed the proposal of a Canadian company to start a private radio station in the kingdom of Tonga, an isolated island group with a population of about a hundred thousand Polynesians. It has a single 10-kw. AM station operated by a BBC-type statutory body. The meeting participants adopted a resolution opposing the private station, incorporating typical Third World arguments in favor of government ownership:

National broadcasting services have far-reaching responsibilities for information, education and entertainment and specific roles in fostering national unity and assisting development.

Competition from private commercial stations with different objectives diminishes the status of the national service, limits its effectiveness in meeting its national responsibilities, creates undue competition for physical and financial resources and impedes the development of the creative possibilities of radio. (Combroad, Dec. 1981: 44)

France

European systems generally come under the rubric of "public corporation" in Table 3.1, meaning considerable isolation from direct government control but nevertheless more government control than in the United States. French broadcasting has differed from the usual European model. France originally had a mixed private-government system, but resentment against private stations that had collaborated with the Nazis during the German occupation led to nationalization of the entire system following World War II. French broadcasting has been subjected to periodic shakeups ever since. New political administrations introduced their own structural changes, but all firmly retained a political stranglehold. In 1982 yet another new law, replacing that of 1974, implemented the ideas of the Socialist party, which had promised broadcast reforms in the 1980 election.[4] (Figure 5.1 charts the components of the complex new broadcasting law that followed in 1982.) The new law

---

*Katz & Wedell, 1977: 94–95. After the 1979 revolution, the new government changed the name to Islamic Republic of Iran Television.

retained existing state-owned domestic broadcasting companies, including the following:

- *Télédiffusion de France* (TDF), the central technical agency responsible for all transmission facilities.

- Three television networks, *Télévision Français 1* (TF1), *Antenne 2* (A2), and *France Régions 3* (FR3).

- *Radio France,* comprising three radio networks, *France-Inter, France-Culture,* and *France-Musique.*

- SFP (*Société Française de Production*), a television production company serving all three networks (described in Section 8.1).

- An archival, training, and research unit.

Additional units created in 1982 included the following:

- An Audiovisual Communications Authority (*Haute Autorité*), which appoints the presidents of the national services, issues licenses, and has general responsibility for maintaining fairness and balance in programming. The French president appoints three of the authority's nine members, the heads of the two legislative chambers, three members each.

- A new class of privately operated, low-power, noncommercial local stations (a significant breach in the government programming monopoly, described in Section 4.4).

- A company to program stations in overseas territories, *Radio Télévision Française d'Outre-Mer (RFO),* primarily using rebroadcasts of programs selected from the domestic networks.

- A National Audiovisual Communications Council to advise on broadcasting operations.

France also receives service from a group of commercial "peripheral" stations—so called because their transmitters are sited near the French borders (see Section 11.5)—not subject to the new broadcasting authority. The French government owns major shares of the stock in these stations, whose degree of commercialism would not be tolerated even on those official French services that sell advertising.

France's 1982 statute aimed at achieving three major reforms: making broadcasting more accessible to the people, decentralizing it, and insulating it from politics. It also took cognizance of cable television and direct-broadcast satellites. Will the new law succeed any better than previous reforms? A French broadcasting executive summarized public reactions to the new law:

> *The new Act opens the door to the freedom of communications, though doubtless with some supervision and regulation, which has not prevented the*

Communist Party from finding it "foolhardy"—because it gives access to private interests—and therefore not voting for it.

The opposition look on it as a "patching-up job," because the state remains in charge either directly or through the authority, with the concept of "public service" replacing that of "monopoly." (Ridoux, 1982: 13)

Spain

The Spanish broadcasting statute classifies television as a "state prerogative" but allows private radio ownership. The law permits treating television as a government monopoly. However, private owners control about 180 of the nation's radio stations, the government only about 70. "Spanish radio networks are exceptionally complex, with the state, churches, trade unions and private companies operating large [facilities] each with a slightly different relationship to the state-run *Radio Nacional* and to each other" (Howkins, 1983: 22).

A would-be private operator challenged the state television monopoly, arguing that television's status was not only inconsistent with that of radio but also violated constitutionally guaranteed freedom of speech and press. A lower court rejected this argument, but on appeal the Spanish Constitutional Court reversed the lower tribunal. The high court said that the constitutional guarantee did in fact override the broadcasting statute. However, the court left the door to private television ownership only slightly ajar, stating that only the legislature could evaluate the practical considerations involved. In short, authorization of private television stations remained a political decision even though not constitutionally forbidden.[5]

Lebanon

Some countries found it expedient to move in the opposite direction. Prior to the 1975 civil war, Lebanon had an official monopoly on radio but granted a television license to a consortium of Beirut business venturers. In 1959 the investors built the first privately owned, commercially operated television station in the Arab world. A second private commercial station, originally financed in part by the American ABC network, was authorized in 1962. But, finding that Lebanon had too little advertising business to support two fully competitive stations, the two companies worked cooperatively, combining some of their operations on a noncompetitive basis. The Lebanese government kept a close watch on programs, especially news. Government officials sealed international news agency films upon their arrival at the airport, for example, releasing them to the stations only after previewing by official censors. Far from objecting to this encroachment on their programming autonomy, the stations were happy to be relieved of the thankless job of tailoring the news to fit official policies.[6]

New Zealand

Amateur broadcasters started radio in New Zealand as early as 1922, but Socialist governments of the 1930s began bringing all broadcasting under government control. In an unusual move, the government elevated the medium to ministerial level by creating the post of minister of broadcasting. The prime minister himself first held the post—an indication of the significant role broadcasting played in that isolated

NEW ZEALAND

nation. Since 1961 the New Zealand Broadcasting Corporation (NZBC) has supplied radio and television services. The government appoints the NZBC board. By the late 1960s, offshore pirate stations began to woo listeners away from the stodgy NZBC programming, forcing the government to make some changes. In 1968 it set up the New Zealand Broadcasting Authority as a licensing and advisory body. One of the authority's missions was to moderate the government monopoly by licensing private radio station owners. Such authorizations came slowly, however; by 1982 New Zealand still had only 17 private radio stations owned by a dozen licensees. The authority did not allow them to form a network. Meanwhile, NZBC operated two radio networks with a total of some 60 stations, about half of them run on a profit-oriented commercial basis.

The NZBC introduced television belatedly in 1960. It operates two networks, with a single program controller. The networks operate noncompetitively as an article of faith; however, they have a strong commercial orientation, relying on advertising for 85 percent of their budget.

In 1981 the conservative National party won control of the government, reviving long-repressed demands for privately owned television. Newspaper interests proposed starting a third network. The NZBC countered by offering to lease morning hours on its second network to private commercial interests. Proponents of state operation argue that in such a small country, dividing limited resources between public and private sectors could seriously damage the quality of the service. Private commercial stations, they say, tend to be mere parasites, capitalizing on the groundwork laid by the public corporation but failing to make commensurate original contributions of their own. As the chairman of the NZBC put it in a series of rhetorical questions:

> *What has private radio done with its money earned in its flush years? What has it built on the foundation of initial audience interest and support? What contribution to the identification [of] and service to community needs . . . ? What programme ideas and execution? What training for industry? What new wave of broadcasters, equipped for the communication needs of New Zealand in the 80s, has it produced? (Cross, 1982: 14)*

Nevertheless, in 1984 the government announced plans to authorize a third television service within about a year. It was to be privately owned but divided among regional companies, apparently in the manner of the IBA's ITV contractors, with a jointly operated national news unit capable of competing with the news on the government networks.

3 ▪ 3 PRIVATE OWNERSHIP

In the previous section I gave some examples of monopolistic systems in Western Europe that have come under successful attack from interests wishing to introduce privately owned services. In contrast, some nations that initially allowed private enterprise to flourish later began to impose more state controls on private operators and also to set up competing government stations. The reasons for these contradictory trends will be explored in this chapter and the next. About a fifth of all systems fall into the private, commercially operated category (Table 3.1).

The United States

Few countries have broadcasting systems operated solely by private owners. Even in the United States, the archetypical case of a system based primarily upon private ownership and commercial financial support, some licensees are neither private nor commercial. Originally, all U.S. broadcasting licenses permitted commercial operation, but some stations with educational or religious affiliations chose not to sell advertising. Some, like New York City's WNYC, were licensed to municipal governments. Later, the Federal Communications Commission (FCC) created a special class of noncommercial, educational licenses, setting aside channels especially for that class in the FM band (1938) and the television band (1952). Government entities own a number of stations licensed in this category, albeit below the federal level. For example, several states have set up educational television authorities that serve as licensees of statewide networks of stations. It is worth noting that while in America commercial services preceded alternative public broadcasting, in Britain the opposite happened—the British Broadcasting Corporation's noncommercial monopoly preceded alternative commercial services. Such *pluralistic* trends have become increasingly evident in all countries where the political climate allows alternative voices to be heard.

Latin America

Influenced by the U.S. private, free-enterprise model, Latin American countries such as Costa Rica, the Dominican Republic, Ecuador, Guatemala, Honduras, Nicaragua, and Panama started with privately operated systems. In time, however, their governments began operating at least token public service components as well. Such nations tend to have more stations than those where government ownership has been the norm from the outset.

Mexico. As the Latin American country most directly exposed to U.S. influence, Mexico serves as a leading exemplar of adapting the private ownership model to the circumstances of a developing country. As a byproduct of U.S. influence, Mexico ranked among the first nations to initiate broadcasting—radio in 1923 and television in 1950. However, Mexico by no means followed the U.S. model in all details. "Superficially, the Mexican system may appear to parallel or imitate systems of other countries. This superficial resemblance is deceptive. Mexican broadcasting was born in chaos and grew under peculiarly idiosyncratic social, economic and political pressures which have given it its essential form" (Noriega & Leach, 1979: 81).

The Mexican government operates less than 4 percent of the country's more than nine hundred stations, most of the official outlets being television. In 1959 the government authorized the National Polytechnic Institute to offer a noncommercial television service on channel 11 in Mexico City. It specializes in educational and cultural programming but has had only limited impact because of inadequate financing.[7]

Mexico's major state investment in television came about in 1972 as a result of the bankruptcy of the commercial licensee of channel 13 in Mexico City. Having made loans to the private operator, the government took over the station to save its investment. After buying up 16 other stations in the provinces, the government formed the Mexican Television Cultural Network, which also feeds 20 repeater stations. Although it operated the cultural network commercially from the outset, the government did not begin aggressive sale of advertising until 1977, when it decided that the network should become self-sustaining. But like the educational service on channel 11, the government cultural network offers only weak competition against the commercial stations.

A third government television service, *Television de la Republica Mexico (TRM)*, came into being by presidential decree when the state took over channel 13 in 1972. TRM strives to serve remoter areas of the country (Mexico is nearly three times the size of Texas, with many areas isolated from the mainstream of national life). An ambitious plan for installing microwave and satellite relays aims at ensuring services to every settlement of twenty-five hundred or more inhabitants. TRM functions as a delivery service, relying entirely on prerecorded programs obtained from the other government services (channels 11 and 13) and from commercial stations. Educational material forms the largest program category, though more than half of all programming comes from commercial sources.* The agreement by which TRM obtains programs from

---

*In the late 1970s, TRM devoted 24 percent of its time to education (Noriega & Leach, 1979: 70).

MEXICO

commercial sources includes the stipulation that they will be broadcast in their entirety without editing. Thus the rural service, though intended to be noncommercial, actually carries a good deal of advertising.

The salient features of Mexico's government services typify such operations in developing countries where private ownership dominates: (1) government intervenes in order to compensate for the omissions of commercial broadcasting; (2) it supplies services to remote areas neglected by private enterprise because they cannot afford to support commercial stations; and (3) it attempts to broaden the program options by supplying cultural and educational materials that private broadcasters find unprofitable. Third World countries see these moves as vital ways to further national integration and improve the condition of farmers in areas otherwise cut off from participation in the nation's economic, social, and cultural evolution. Unfortunately, these well-meaning government enterprises usually suffer from inadequate budgets and otherwise lack resources to lure substantial audiences away from private stations.* Mexico was no exception. For this reason, the Mexican government created a system of mandated access to the facilities of private broadcasters (discussed in Section 4.2). Thus the government will always be able to reach the mass public without having to compete with private broadcasters in areas served by commercial operations.

Peru. Peru took more sweeping measures to compensate for the distortions that resulted from private ownership. In 1968, when the armed forces took over the government, the state owned only 5 of the 222 radio stations in the country. The private stations clustered together in the main population centers on the coast, neglecting the mountainous interior. As for television, before the 1968 revolution, five wealthy families controlled 13 of the 19 stations then in operation, as well as some 30 of the private radio stations.

In 1971 the military government adopted a new telecommunications law expropriating a share of the ownership in some stations, including a 51 percent interest in all television stations. The new law also mandated

*Colombia deals with this problem in a novel way: although the government owns all television stations, it leases most of their prime-time hours to private entrepreneurs for commercial use (Pierce, 1979: 236–237). Bulk sale of time for subsequent resale to advertisers in this manner is known as *brokerage* in U.S. broadcasting.

reduction of imported programs and of advertising time, elimination of foreign ownership, and expansion of programs concerned with Peruvian culture and education. The ambitious goals of this wholesale renovation included "the fight against illiteracy, linguistic diversity, and regionalism in order to forge a shared national identity, a higher standard of living, and high standards of social justice" (Katz & Wedell, 1977: 33).

Peruvian broadcasting has apparently made little contribution toward achieving these goals. Though foreign ownership has been reduced and advertising excesses curtailed, foreign imports still dominate programming on Peruvian stations (Mattos, 1981: 62).

3·4 BBC: PUBLIC SERVICE CORPORATION MODEL

Between the extremes of predominantly government and predominantly private ownership fall systems that seek the best of both worlds by combining elements of each, but with well-defined limitations on areas in which government may exert control. Most of these systems started with some form of public corporation, operated solely on a noncommercial basis. Only later came service categories that involved private or semiprivate ownership and commercial operation. About a fifth of the world's systems remained public corporations, without taking the further step of adding commercial components (Table 3.1).

As the leading example of the independent public corporation, the British Broadcasting Corporation (BBC) deserves special attention. It furnished the model most widely admired and imitated throughout the world, even though the United States leads in the sheer quantity and popularity of its exported programs and in its influence on commercial operations. As a parliamentary democracy, Britain needed to ensure that broadcasting would respond to the demand for political information without also inviting unfair exploitation of the medium by one political party or another. The party in power had to be prevented from dominating the political uses of broadcasting to consolidate its position. At the same time, means had to be found to prevent a party not in power from demagogic exploitation of broadcasting to overthrow the incumbent party. The paternalistic class structure of Britain, with its tradition of *noblesse oblige*, also had a role in shaping the BBC.

The Royal Charter

In 1925 Parliament appointed a committee of distinguished citizens to consider the future of broadcasting in the United Kingdom.[8] It had to consider whether the corporation formed in 1922 by the radio manufacturers should continue to furnish the radio broadcasting service, and if not, what should take its place. The committee rejected the options of both government and private ownership, recommending instead a pub-

UNITED KINGDOM

lic corporation that, although ultimately subject to parliamentary control, would nevertheless "be invested with the maximum freedom which Parliament is prepared to concede."

Accepting the committee's recommendation, Parliament chose to authorize the new corporation by means of a Royal Charter. This relatively unusual means of authorizing a corporation meant that the BBC would have maximum autonomy and a certain status by virtue of its association with the throne (even though Parliament was the actual grantor). No exact corporate parallel can be found under United States law:

> It is difficult for Americans to understand the relationship between the BBC and the British government. The Tennessee Valley Authority is roughly similar, although its periodic involvement in politics represents a marked departure from the British pattern. The Red Cross, chartered by Congress but independently run by its own Board of Trustees, is perhaps America's nearest equivalent. (Paulu, 1981: 28)

The original charter ran from 1927 to 1936. It has been renewed six times (the latest covering the years 1981–1996) with only slight modifications. A committee study on the future of broadcasting preceded each renewal. These studies differ markedly from the FCC and congressional hearings that precede changes in U.S. broadcasting laws. The committees consist of distinguished citizens, appointed on an ad hoc basis for this particular purpose. They produce extremely thoughtful, even philosophical, documents that become invaluable repositories of serious thinking about the nature of broadcasting.* Parliament may reject committee recommendations, a likely outcome if the majority party changes between the time the committee is appointed and the time its recommendations are considered. By and large, however, these committees have had a decisive influence on the evolution of British broadcasting.

License and Agreement

The BBC charter establishes the corporation, defines its goals, and outlines its constitution. A second legal instrument, the License and Agreement, spells out in more detail the BBC's relation to Parliament. The responsible cabinet minister, now the secretary of state for the

---

*The last such study (the "Annan Report"), published in 1977, is frequently cited in this book (Great Britain, 1977).

Home Office (home secretary, for short) grants the license.* This document spells out the technical regulations and the extent to which the government may control BBC finances and programs. Technical regulations, imposed on all users of the radio spectrum by the Wireless Telegraphy Act of 1949, concern transmitter power, frequency, location, signal quality, and the like. In the United States, the FCC similarly regulates technical aspects of transmission; but whereas the FCC licenses each and every transmitter individually, the home secretary licenses the BBC's hundreds of transmitters collectively, in consultation with the corporation's engineering staff.

Parliament's Reserve Powers. The license and agreement reserves for the government, represented by the home secretary, broad powers over what must be and what may not be broadcast by the BBC. For example, the home secretary may notify the BBC in writing "to refrain at any specified time or at all times from sending any matter or matters of any class specified in such notice." Such sweeping "reserve powers," as they are called, have normally remained just that—powers held in reserve. The government sent down only five formal directives on programming in 50 years, and of these, only two remain in effect. One forbids the BBC from editorializing (a rule that dates back to 1927); the other forbids subliminal messages. The rescinded directives restricted broadcasts dealing with controversial subjects, with matters currently being debated in Parliament, and with partisan speeches by representatives of political parties.

The most recent committee on the future, the Annan Committee, while confessing that it might seem paradoxical to do so, recommended retaining the home secretary's veto power over BBC programming plans. The committee reasoned that:

> In the last analysis, the Government alone can judge and decide whether a programme . . . constitutes a threat to national security, or is likely to lead to riots or other grave disorder. If that responsibility is taken from the Government, it must be transferred to the Broadcasting Authorities: and how much easier it will be for a Minister to paint a picture of the devastating consequences, and how much more difficult for the [BBC] to stand out against his judgement. In the present system, a Minister can state his grave objections: the Broadcasting Authority can then reject these objections and can inform the Minister that under his powers he is at liberty to ban the programme: but if he does, they will tell the public that he has done so. We believe that this is the best way of reconciling the freedom of the broadcasters with the legitimate concern of the Government and of placing the responsibility for prohibiting programmes in the national interest precisely where it belongs. (Great Britain, 1977: 45)

---

*Originally, the postmaster-general issued the license. The annual BBC handbooks reproduce both the charter and the license and agreement in full.

An annex to the license and agreement reiterates assurances first given in a letter from the governors to the postmaster-general in 1964. These assurances represented BBC responses to specific issues that had arisen in the past. The BBC regards them as self-imposed restraints. The annex states that "as far as possible," BBC programs should not "offend against good taste or decency or be likely to encourage or incite crime or lead to disorder, or be offensive to public feeling." On first reading, this expansive disclaimer might seem to put the BBC in the untenable position of promising to live up to a series of undefined, even undefinable, standards. Actually, however, the statement effectively defuses in advance possible criticisms that the BBC has violated those very standards. The board promises nothing more than vigilance and good faith.

Fiscal Controls. Perhaps potentially more dangerous to the BBC's independence, Parliament controls the purse strings and can remove members of the BBC Board of Governors from office at will.

The proceeds of the receiver license fee collections do not automatically go to the BBC. Parliament must authorize both the level of the fees and their payment to the BBC. Nowadays, the BBC gets the license revenue minus the costs of collection by the post office; however, the Treasury may retain part of the net revenue, as it did during the early days of both radio and television. The potential for fiscal blackmail seems to exist, but the leading American student of British broadcasting, Burton Paulu, concluded after exhaustive study, "There is no evidence, . . . nor has it ever been charged, that the government has actually used its financial prerogatives to influence or control the BBC's programme policies or output" (Paulu, 1981: 111–112).

Board of Governors

The government has never used its power to remove a member of the BBC governing board. To an outsider, it seems astonishing that the British system of insulating broadcasting from government, as exemplified in the BBC arrangements, actually works. In almost any other national setting, one suspects, a government with that much latitude to interfere would succumb to temptation. One reason that did not happen in Britain may have been the extraordinary quality of the people who stood between the corporation and government officials—the board of governors and the director-general. The monarch "in council" appoints the 12 members of the board to five-year terms—again a possible temptation for wheeling and dealing. Unlike appointees to the FCC, the BBC governors do not have to be chosen with a view to balancing political affiliations. It is taken for granted that they will act on behalf of the public as a whole, without political partisanship. Board members have usually not been broadcasters but persons with wide experience in public affairs. At least one member must come from each of the fields of diplomacy, finance, education, and trade unions. The board has always included a sprinkling of titled eminences and has sometimes been criticized as being too conservative. In fact, the Annan Committee expressed the hope that "from the list sometimes referred to as 'the Great and the Good,' " the government might occasionally select some of the "Lesser and Better."*

The governors determine policy for the corporation and act as a lightning rod to protect the staff from the more highly charged bolts of criticism from Parliament and the public. They take no part in day-to-day operations, which they leave to their appointee, the director-general. The latter heads the BBC Board of Management, which includes senior officials responsible respectively for television, radio, external (international) services, finance, news, personnel, engineering, public affairs, and relations with the United States.

The Director-General

The brunt of day-to-day criticism falls more on the director-general than on the governors. The very first director-general proved to be a towering though strangely flawed figure. For the first dozen years of the corporation's life, John Reith *was* the BBC. The manufacturers had selected him in 1922 as managing director of the original company, and he simply changed title when the company became the corporation in 1927. A mechanical engineer by training, Reith soon adapted himself to the role of social engineer, becoming an unyielding champion of public service broadcasting. As much as possible, he kept the BBC free from direct government control, yet he remained unswervingly loyal to the democratic system itself (in Britain "the government" refers to the executives representing the party that has at the moment a parliamentary majority, not the underlying system). Though by today's standards an authoritarian and a martinet, Reith had an abiding, fundamental belief in democracy, and that belief animated his broadcasting philosophy: "Most of the good things of this world are badly distributed and most people have to go without them. Wireless is a good thing, but it may be shared by all alike, for the same outlay, and to the same extent. . . . It is no respecter of persons" (quoted in Smith, 1974: 14).

Reith faced perhaps his severest test even before he took office as director-general on 1 January 1927. In 1926 a general strike paralyzed Britain, creating a social crisis of unprecedented proportions. The government wanted to use the BBC (then still a company) as a weapon against the strikers (all newspapers had been shut down by striking printers). Reith's position was highly vulnerable because the BBC charter had not yet been finally approved. The institution's future hung in the balance. Nevertheless, Reith defied the government's wishes, thereby earning the permanent enmity of Winston Churchill, then chancellor

---

*Great Britain, 1977: 48. A study of the 85 governors that served the BBC in its first 50 years can be found in Briggs, 1979b.

of the Exchequer. The BBC did not come out entirely unscathed. Reith bent a little by refusing time to some speakers whose views the government opposed. For example, the archbishop of Canterbury, representing the established church of the nation, wanted to broadcast an appeal urging compromise between the strikers and the government. Although the prime minister had a legal right to do so, he did not order the BBC to refuse the archbishop's request. He merely let it be known that he opposed the speech. This left Reith on the horns of a dilemma, forced to choose (as he described it) between "Premier and Primate" (Briggs, 1961: 379). Reith chose to satisfy the premier. He was doubtless wise to compromise a little to avoid a showdown. But his temporizing gave English historian A. J. P. Taylor an excuse for the waspish remark that "the vaunted independence of the BBC was secure so long as it was not exercised" (Taylor, 1965: 246).[9] Asa Briggs, in his authoritative BBC history, called the turndown of the archbishop the "low-water mark of the power and influence of the BBC" (1961: 379).

There have been only occasional crises of confidence since then, such as during the 1956 Suez crisis when the government claimed wartime powers and threatened to take over the BBC. During the Falklands War of 1982, government leaders severely criticized the BBC for its handling of news. Some critics objected to references to "British ships" instead of "*our* ships." Both the prime minister and the foreign secretary attacked the BBC for being "unacceptably evenhanded" in its treatment of Argentina—an Orwellian phrase for "too objective." The general public disagreed. In an independent public opinion survey commissioned by the BBC, four fifths of the respondents supported the corporation's evenhandedness.[10]

As the cornerstone of his philosophy, Reith adopted the principle of "giving a lead" to popular taste. Broadcasting, he thought, should not cater exclusively to the lowest common denominator (the inevitable tendency in commercially supported systems) but should "carry into the greatest number of homes everything that was best in every department of human knowledge, endeavour and achievement; and to avoid whatever was or might be hurtful" (Reith, 1949: 101). In pursuing this goal, he often seemed to his critics too paternalistic and overbearing. Implicitly defending himself from such charges, some years after leaving the corporation, he wrote:

> The BBC might be considered autocratic or arbitrary in attitude and procedure. It had the courage of its convictions; it did what it believed was in the public interest. Ought that not to apply to anybody vested with authority and responsibility? There was no electoral process anywhere in BBC constitution and procedure. The governing body was nominated, not elected; the programmes were compiled not to meet but to ante-date the popular vote. One knew of what sort they would otherwise have been. (Reith, 1949: 170)

Reith served the BBC only from 1927 to 1938, yet his personal style and uncompromising policies lingered long after he resigned. Though widely honored (he became Lord Reith in 1940), he achieved nothing of note in his subsequent public career. Not only had he antagonized Churchill, he had also developed a crusty manner that served him well in championing the BBC against politicians and bureaucrats but served him badly when he sought to join their ranks. He died in 1971 at the age of 72.

BBC Influence

Wherever a broadcasting system claims the status of an "independent statutory corporation," or words to that effect, it is probably BBC-inspired, though perhaps only indirectly. As recently as 1980, Radio and Television Singapore, a department within the Ministry of Culture, won independence as the Singapore Broadcasting Corporation. A former British crown colony, Singapore is a city-state at the southernmost tip of the Malay Peninsula. It obtained internal self-government in 1959 and independence in 1965 after two years as part of the short-lived federation of Malaysia. Singapore changed to corporate status "to provide for a greater degree of financial autonomy and greater flexibility in such matters as recruitment, salary scales, promotions and development of the broadcasting services" (Fatt, 1980: 6).

Even more recently, Malaysia announced plans for converting Radio Television Malaysia (RTM) into a corporation, citing its problems with the civil service and financial constraints. Although RTM earns more than twice as much from advertising as it does from license fees, revenue from commercial sales goes directly to the state treasury, and RTM operates on a fixed budgetary allotment like any other government bureaucracy. Corporate status was expected to enable more flexible budgeting and personnel policies.

Corporate status along BBC lines appeals to broadcast professionals because the medium always suffers when subjected to government bureaucratic controls. Rigid rules about hiring and firing, budgeting, and making contracts with suppliers rob broadcasters of the essential latitude needed to respond swiftly to technological changes, program trends, and the like. Staff members protected by civil service rules grow lax. Commercially operated services lose a highly effective incentive when staff members know that the revenue they earn goes to the treasury department instead of toward paying for their salaries, supplies, and equipment. Other avenues of BBC influence, some discussed in appropriate contexts elsewhere, include the following:

- Specific influence on West German broadcasting stemming from British post–World War II occupation of parts of Germany

- Training of foreign broadcasters

- Sending of staff members abroad as consultants (for which Reith himself set a precedent) and as supervisors of training

- The practical example set by the BBC External Services Programs, whose formats and styles are widely imitated

- The sale and gift of recorded programs to foreign countries, as well as the rebroadcasting of External Services news programs

- The Commonwealth Broadcasting Association, whose meetings and training sessions serve some 50 broadcasting administrations throughout the world

Evolution of BBC Services

The BBC now offers four national radio networks, designated Radios 1, 2, 3, and 4. Until the late 1960s, British listeners had no local radio services, though the networks did offer some regionalized programming. Parliament authorized the BBC to begin remedying this neglect of local radio, typical of European broadcasting generally, in 1967 when it introduced its first local stations.

Until 1964, when it inaugurated BBC-2, the BBC supplied viewers with only one television service. In the meantime, commercial independent television (ITV) had begun broadcasting in 1955, though the full national network did not come on-line until 1962. The corporation designed BBC-2 as a clearcut alternative to BBC-1 and ITV. Prior to the start of Channel 4 in 1982, BBC-1 and ITV accounted for more than 90 percent of the television audience, leaving only 10 percent for BBC-2. A national network attracting less than 10 percent of the potential audience would hardly be considered cost effective in free-enterprise broadcasting terms. The British believe, however, that their national system should serve not only mass audience tastes but also the tastes of intellectual as well as ethnic minorities.

In addition to its domestic radio and television networks and local radio stations, the BBC operates a prestigious worldwide external (international) service and a flourishing publishing and program syndicating business. It also had plans in the early 1980s to participate in future pay-cable and DBS developments in Britain.

3 ▪ 5 IBA AND CONTROLLED COMMERCIALISM

In 1952 Parliament took up a bill to authorize a competitive, commercially supported television service in Britain. Appalled by the prospect of commercial broadcasting, Lord Reith denounced the bill in the House of Lords, likening it to the bubonic plague.[11] But in 1954 the bill passed, and broadcast advertising began the next year.

The 1954 law created a second broadcasting corporation in Britain, the Independent Broadcasting Authority (IBA).* Like the BBC, the IBA operates as a nonprofit corporation; unlike the BBC, it derives its funds

---

*Originally the Independent *Television* Authority but changed to *Broadcasting* in 1972 when the authority took on responsibility for local commercial radio as well as television.

indirectly from commercials in the form of transmitter rental fees paid by the commercial programming companies. IBA facilities permit national television network coverage comparable to that of the BBC. In fact, the BBC and the IBA share many antenna sites.

Politics of Commercial Broadcasting

No widespread popular demand for commercial broadcasting seems to have arisen in Britain during the period when the BBC monopolized programming. True, some thought the BBC had become rather stodgy, and some opposed the BBC's undemocratic monopoly in principle. Reith had always argued that only through what he called the monopoly's "brute force" had the BBC become a model system.* Those who defended the monopoly used as a favorite argument the *Gresham's Law analogy*. Gresham's Law, named for a sixteenth-century financier, says that when both sound money and debased money coexist in the marketplace, people will hoard the "good" money, leaving only the "bad" in circulation. For example, in 1950 the BBC concluded a statement to a parliamentary committee with the assertion that "because competition in broadcasting must in the long run descend to a fight for the greatest possible number of listeners, it would be the lower forms of mass appetite which would more and more be catered for in programmes."[12] This argument will be recognized as one often directed against the kind of service that results from all-out competition for high ratings among national networks in the United States.

Opposition to the BBC's monopoly would have been futile without support from business interests that favored commercial broadcasting. The question rose to the level of a major partisan political issue. The Labour party opposed commercialization of broadcasting, while the Conservative party supported it. Indeed, it can be said that whenever broadcasting policy becomes a political issue in nations that have free elections, the conservatives (Tories, Republicans, and so on) nearly always take the side of a free-enterprise commercial system, while the

---

*Strictly speaking, the BBC never succeeded in totally excluding alternative programming, despite its strenuous efforts to do so. British audiences could receive programs from international commercial stations on the Continent, such as Radio Luxembourg, from the American armed forces stations during World War II, and from offshore pirates. The British Isles even house a commercial station that neither the BBC nor the IBA controls. The Isle of Man, a dependency of the Crown not subject to Parliament, overcame official opposition in 1964 to found Radio Manx, its own commercial radio operation. As the island lies in the Irish Sea midway between England and Northern Ireland, the British authorities suspected that the island's primary motive for founding Radio Manx was to capitalize on advertising addressed to the mainland (Great Britain, 1962: 297–298). The island government owns the service, but a commercial company operates it under contract. Radio Manx's present 10-kw. AM transmitter can reach only limited parts of the mainland.

liberals (Democrats, Laborites, Social Democrats, and so on) take the side of a nonprofit public service system.

Though broadcasting policy does not emerge as so crucial a political issue in the United States as it does elsewhere, American parties also follow the typical conservative-versus-liberal pattern when broadcasting issues do arise. When the Republicans came to power in Washington in 1980, they cut back on federal support of the noncommercial public broadcasting service and either repealed or weakened many curbs that had previously been imposed on commercial broadcasters.

In Britain, the Conservative party's victory of 1952 provided the opportunity for those who favored privately owned, commercially supported television to have their way. Change did not come easily, however. The procommercial forces succeeded only by virtue of "a sustained campaign of propaganda and persuasion conducted by a group of Tory MPs and businessmen" (Shulman, 1973: 14).* The Broadcasting Act of 1954 finally passed by a vote of 296 to 269.

Independent Broadcasting Authority (IBA) Constitution

Unique among broadcasting institutions, the Independent Broadcasting Authority (IBA) administers and regulates the entire British commercial system. It owns and operates all the commercial television transmitter facilities but does not itself provide any program services or derive any commercial profit.

Comparison with BBC. Like the BBC, the IBA is a public corporation without stockholders that is ruled by a government-appointed board. But whereas the BBC's Royal Charter confers on it the right to do anything not expressly forbidden in that charter, the IBA's parliamentary authorization via statute imposes more explicit restraints. However, nearly identical restraints on programming apply to both corporations.

Again like the BBC, the IBA receives its warrant for limited periods (originally for ten years but recently for longer), after which renewal may or may not occur, with whatever modifications Parliament desires. Over the years, such modifications have more than doubled the length of the act, subjecting the IBA to increasingly detailed and explicit regulations. The latest version, the Broadcasting Act of 1981, extended the life of the IBA to 1996.[13] The most important change in the latest version gave the IBA control over Britain's newly authorized fourth national network, Channel 4 (described later in this section).

An 11-member board governs the IBA. The home secretary appoints the members and may dismiss them at will, just as he may the BBC

---

*Some even alleged a virtual conspiracy by a small group of business leaders, abetted by U.S. advertising agency interests, to force commercial broadcasting on a reluctant British public (Wilson, 1961). For the overall history of the emergence of independent television in Britain, see Sendall, 1982, 1983.

governors. The first IBA chairman, art historian Kenneth Clark, became widely known and acclaimed for his television series *Civilisation*, produced by the BBC after he retired from the IBA. The board includes representatives from Northern Ireland, Scotland, and Wales, each with "special competence" in those parts of the United Kingdom. A director-general heads the executive affairs of the authority, supervising a staff of about fifteen hundred employees.*

The TV Program Companies. The IBA owns and operates television transmitters sited throughout the United Kingdom so as to enable national network coverage (it opened its one thousandth transmitter in 1983). Programming and advertising, however, are the business of private commercial firms. The IBA first contracted with a group of 15 regional program companies, known collectively as Independent Television (ITV), which won their franchises on the basis of competitive applications. A franchisee receives a temporary contract (currently for eight years, dating from 1 January 1982) to broadcast to 1 of 14 specified regions of the nation. Fifteen companies serve only 14 regions because the IBA divided the huge London metropolitan region into 2 franchise components: one licensee (London Weekend Television) broadcasts only on Saturdays and Sundays; the other (Thames Television) broadcasts only on weekdays. Otherwise, a single London region franchisee would have dominated the entire system.

The "big five" ITV companies include, in addition to the two in London, those in the Midlands (ATV Network), the northwest (Granada Television), and the east (Yorkshire Television). These help support the smaller companies by providing most of the national ITV network programs.

The IBA may refuse to renew franchises. For example, when the first occasion for renewal came in 1967, the IBA allowed only 11 of the 15 existing ITV companies to continue in business. The authority cited program quality as the primary basis for awarding or denying renewals. Each company pays the IBA a rental fee for the use of the transmission facilities covering its region. The IBA bases rentals not on actual transmission costs but on each regional company's ability to pay. Annual transmission charges range from a high of about $11 million for London's weekday service to a low of only $18 thousand for the Channel Islands service.

This divorcement of transmission costs from user charges would be impossible if the marketplace regulated rates. It costs far more to cover a small rural population dispersed over a mountainous terrain than to cover a large urban population concentrated in a metropolitan area. Market considerations alone would justify little or no service for the

---

*IBA, 1983: 203. At that time, the commercial companies supervised by the IBA employed about 17,250 persons.

rural region but a great many services for the rich metropolitan region. Such inequitable distribution of services is commonplace in the United States and in other countries where commercial incentives determine where stations will be located. In the United Kingdom, however, the BBC and IBA, as nonprofit public corporations, can afford to provide all regions with essentially identical services, irrespective of their differences as markets.

It could of course be argued that money does in fact motivate the IBA, because its financial health depends upon the success of the commercial companies. Indeed, in its earlier years, the IBA was accused of being too subservient to commercial interests. However, tightening of the broadcasting law on the basis of successive recommendations by committees on the future of broadcasting have ensured an arm's-length relationship between the IBA and commercial interests. The law obliges the authority to put the public interest above that of the commercial companies it authorizes and supervises.

Rental fees charged by the IBA for transmitter services cover all the authority's expenses. It has no other income. In turn, the ITV program companies derive their revenue from the sale of advertising (98 percent), supplemented by such auxiliary enterprises as the sale of programs to foreign broadcasters. After recouping their startup losses, the major companies became so profitable that the government imposed a special *levy* on them, over and above normal business taxes.

Regionalization of franchises by the IBA prevents any one company from dominating the rest while simultaneously ensuring that regional interests will be catered for. But the commercial system also needs to offer a national network service in order to compete effectively with the BBC. The IBA therefore allows the companies to pool their resources to form a national network most of the time. In practice, regional programming accounts for only about 8 percent of the Independent Television schedule. The average ITV program schedule in 1982 broke down about as follows:[14]

Network programs from the "big five" ITV companies	49%
Network programs from outside sources	28%
Network programs from the remaining ten companies	9%
Centrally produced national news programs	7%
Regional programs	8%

National and international news programming does not lend itself to regional pooling as do other types of content. In this instance, the ITV companies abandon their regionalism in favor of a centralized national organization, Independent Television News (ITN). The companies all contribute to the financial support of ITN, which they own as a nonprofit-making subsidiary. ITN supplies the network with three daily newsfeeds and special news features.

Other IBA-Controlled Services

In addition to being responsible for the ITV companies, the IBA supervises several other commercial services: a fourth network, a morning television service, and local commercial radio stations. Figure 3.1 shows how these functions compare with those of the BBC.

Channel Four. United Kingdom spectrum allotments in the UHF television band had long made it possible to authorize enough transmitters for a fourth national network—that is, one more in addition to BBC-1, BBC-2, and the independent commercial network under IBA. How to organize this potential fourth network, or "fourth channel" as the British called it, became a subject of intense and prolonged debate in the 1970s. The IBA argued that it should control another network to match the BBC's two networks. The Annan Committee considered this and many other proposals. In its 1977 report, the committee recommended creating an entirely new broadcasting entity, the Open Broadcasting Authority. The new fourth-channel authority would open it to innovative program ideas and independent program producers hitherto excluded from the existing networks. "Not only could it be a nursery for new forms and new methods of presenting ideas," said the Annan Committee, "it could also open the door to a new kind of broadcast publishing" (Great Britain, 1977: 235).

At a critical moment in the fourth-channel debate, in 1981 the Conservative party came to power. Parliament rejected the idea of a new authority, assigning responsibility for the fourth network to the IBA. However, Parliament did retain the goal of making the new service as innovative as possible. Channel Four, as it came to be called, went on the air in the fall of 1982, financed by funds advanced by the existing IBA program companies. The IBA obliged each company to subscribe 4 percent of its revenue for the first year, with sharp increases in subsequent years. The companies were to recoup this investment from the sale of commercials they inserted into Channel Four programming, each in its own region—without, however, having any control over the new network's programming.

To run the new network, the IBA created a wholly owned subsidiary, Channel Four Television Company, Ltd. It thus differs from the ITV companies, which are independent firms having only contractual relationships with the IBA. Channel Four creates no programming of its own (outside of a weekly viewer "answer-back" show). It either commissions or buys ready-made programs for its entire schedule of 60 hours per week (the initial level, half the length of the ITV company average).* ITN, the regional ITV companies' news subsidiary, supplies most of Channel Four's news. The network's initial offerings included a

---

*The Welsh transmitters are programmed separately (see Section 4.5).

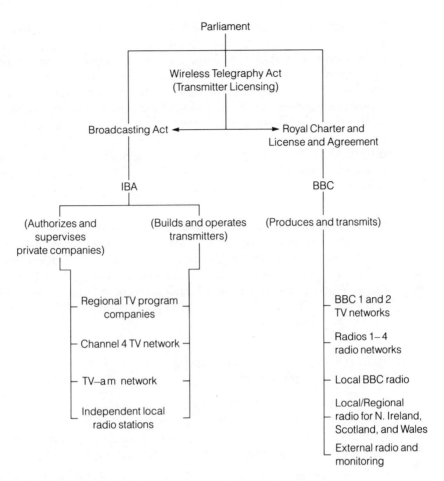

FIGURE 3 ▪ 1 Chief IBA and BBC Broadcast Functions Compared

miniseries based on a successful stage play, *Nicholas Nickleby*, and the American professional football classic, "Superbowl XVII."[15]

Breakfast-Time TV. Prior to 1983, neither the BBC nor the IBA scheduled early morning television, except for certain instructional programs. Authorization to remedy this omission came to both services at about the same time. To produce its commercial morning television show, IBA contracted with a new company, TV-am, Ltd. It has national scope, though it picks up some regionally originated material, and it uses the same transmission network as the 15 ITV companies. Commercial regulations that govern the ITV regional companies also govern TV-am, except for some relaxation of limitations on frequency of commercial breaks.

One of its chief investors, David Frost, well known as a television personality in the United States, acted as one of the hosts on TV-am.

On opening day, Jane Pauley, of NBC's 30-year-old breakfast-time program *Today*, visited her counterpart in London. The program ran daily from 6:00 to 9:15 A.M., broken into three segments: an opening 45 minutes of news, weather, and public service features; a 15-minute children's program; and a final magazine program segment on which David Frost appeared. The insertion of a children's program in the midst of the morning show makes a significant commentary on the philosophical differences between the U.S. and British systems. For NBC to interrupt its *Today* show for a kids' segment would be considered commercial suicide. After a somewhat rocky start, TV-am began to achieve a modest success by 1984.*

Independent Local Radio. In 1972 Parliament authorized the IBA to franchise commercial companies to develop local radio services, following the precedent of the BBC, which had started local stations six years earlier. The first outlet in the Independent Local Radio (ILR) service, London Broadcasting Company (LBC), went on the air in 1973 (see Section 4.5). The IBA has been authorized to supply ILR coverage to a total of 69 communities.

3▪6 SWEDEN'S "PARTNERSHIP IN THE PUBLIC INTEREST"

Many variations on the BBC public corporation ownership model exist. Sweden, for example, puts the corporation in private hands, with shares held not by individuals but by representative social groups. This variation has been called a *partnership in the public interest:*

> Government agencies may be established, altered or dissolved by a unilateral decision of the government; in the case of partnerships in the public interest, the private shareholders have the initiative in framing or amending the articles of association. However, the public authorities must approve them either at the outset or at the time when they take a hand in the activities of the company. (Namurois, 1972: 125)

Britain overcame the disadvantages of monopoly by licensing competitive commercial services. Sweden, on the other hand, sought to enhance competition among the units within the noncommercial national monopoly. The Swedish government owns and controls the physical transmission facilities but turns programming and production over to a private nonprofit corporation, the *Sveriges Radio AB* (Swedish Broadcasting Corporation, or SBC). The SBC's stock belongs to electronics manufacturers (20 percent), publishers (20 percent), and "national popular movements" (60 percent). The popular movements consist of

---

*Revisions included shifting to 6:25–9:25 A.M., with the children's slot at the end (see Table 9.2). For TV–am's history, see Leapman, 1984.

voluntary associations formed by people with common interests, such as trade unionists, consumers, business people, athletes, farmers, landlords, tenants, church members, and teetotallers. In other national contexts, it might seem strange for such partisan groups to play a corporate role in controlling a social institution, but not in Sweden. Such organized groups have played roles in Swedish political and social life for more than a century.

The SBC Board of Governors consists of 13 persons, the majority of whom are nongovernment appointees. The government designates the chairman and appoints five members, another five represent the general public, and two represent the broadcast employees' union. The government makes no programming decisions but does have power over funding. Revenue comes from television receiver license fees that are collected by the Telecommunications Administration and forwarded to the SBC only upon legislative action (as is the case with the BBC's license fee funds). Thus the government retains ultimate control of the purse strings and has at times expressed its disapproval of certain broadcasts by cutting back on SBC funding. A reduction of 15 percent occurred in the early 1970s, for example, in the aftermath of a protracted row over left-wing programs critical of well-known labor union leaders.[16] On the whole, however, the government has used its power with restraint. Indeed, government-appointed members of the SBC board have been less inclined than the private board members to interfere with broadcasting freedom; "representatives of the popular movements are usually more troublesome sources of pressure than are politicians as far as day-to-day programme matters are concerned" (Ortmark, 1979: 156).

The SBC functions as an umbrella organization, allotting funds and determining overall program schedules for five operational companies. These autonomous units make the day-to-day programming decisions for their respective services. They divide responsibilities as follows: (1) domestic network radio (three networks), (2) domestic "local" radio (actually regional services, about 25 in number), (3) external (international) radio, (4) television (two national networks), and (5) educational broadcasting. The so-called local radio services and the educational radio and television services have no transmitters assigned for their exclusive use; instead, they preempt national network facilities at designated hours. In addition, Sweden has authorized experimental low-power ministations on a true local basis, free of supervision by either the established national/regional production companies or the SBC (see Section 4.5 for details).

Regional and local radio programming and heightened competition between the two television networks have somewhat defused criticism of the Swedish system's high degree of centralization. Monopoly nevertheless remains, leaving the Swedish system vulnerable to criticism. However exemplary for its sense of social responsibility, the Swedish system's lack of commercial competition allows it to continue a paternalism that some of its audience find increasingly dated. Licensing of the community ministations was one attempt to diffuse such criticism.

3▪7 MIXED SYSTEMS

About 10 percent of the world's radio systems and somewhat more of its television systems combine two or three of the basic ownership types (Table 3.1). The United States furnishes the leading example of a tripartite system, incorporating government, public, and private ownership. The government component consists of state and municipal stations, the public component, of educational stations. The private, commercial stations outweigh the others by far.* Most other *mixed systems* that reflect U.S. influence can be found in Latin America, the Philippines, South Korea, and Japan.

The term *mixed system* applies best to one that matches two or more types of ownership relatively evenly. Australia, Canada, and Japan make such a division between public and private ownership. All three, although heavily influenced in their public component by the BBC, also have flourishing private enterprise components. Great Britain's system does not qualify as "mixed" in the same sense as these three, because nonprofit corporate authorities control *both* the public and private components of its system, so the profit motive has less freedom to find its own level.

Australia

The underlying concepts of the Australian Broadcasting Corporation (ABC) have much in common with the BBC.† The ABC operates under a government-appointed board but is ostensibly exempt from direct political control. It derives its funds from license fees but must rely on Parliament for annual transfer of funds. Like the BBC, the ABC grew somewhat complacent by the 1960s, losing audience members to Australia's more lively, private, commercially operated stations. However, commercial broadcasting existed in Australia side by side with noncommercial public broadcasting almost from the beginning, not as a later innovation, as in Britain. Political debates in Australia about setting up the noncommercial component as a state-operated service went on for a decade before the ABC finally came into being in 1932 as the public agency responsible for conducting noncommercial public broadcasting.‡ Commercial broadcasters control about 140 radio and 50 television stations, while the ABC controls 110 radio and 87 primary television outlets.

---

*The federal government owns and operates external services aimed at foreign audiences and U.S. Armed Forces stations aimed at service personnel overseas (see Section 11.2).

†The name was changed from Australian Broadcasting *Commission* in 1983.

‡The BBC's first director-general, John Reith, warned Australian officials in 1935 against letting private stations get out of control. As a later general manager of

Canada

Canada has much in common with Australia—a one-time British colony, vast in
size but with its population concentrated in a relatively small strip of its
territory, influenced by the BBC example in the public component of its system but more freewheeling than Britain
in its commercial component. "The
'mixed' broadcasting system in Canada,
which encompasses the elements of
public broadcasting and private broad-

AUSTRALIA

casting, can be appropriately viewed as a compromise between the
American commercial model and the British public-authority model"
(Lee, 1979: 116).

Whereas Australia suffers from isolation, Canada suffers from proximity—the overwhelming presence of the United States on the border,
along which most Canadians reside. This proximity and the presence of
a substantial linguistic minority, the French-speaking residents of
Quebec province, have made broadcasting a subject of intense political
concern in Canada. Broadcasting has been subjected to so many earnest
inquiries in Canada that one commentator called it "the most thor-
oughly scrutinized sector of cultural life" (Lee, 1979: 117).

The Canadian Broadcasting Corporation (CBC), a BBC-like public
body, was founded in 1936. Just as does Australia's ABC, the CBC takes
primary responsibility for national network services covering the remoter areas that cannot support commercial services. These areas include isolated Eskimo settlements in the far north—unlikely targets for
advertising. The CBC's radio networks operate noncommercially, but its
television networks depend on commercials for part of their budget.
Depending on parliamentary grants for 70 percent of its income, the
CBC lacks the sense of independence that the BBC and ABC enjoy
because of their exclusive reliance on license fee revenues. Some Canadian observers would like to ban advertising on the CBC networks
altogether, arguing that the need to please advertisers causes them to
use too many U.S. programs. The CBC also differs from the other major
mixed systems in its reliance on private stations for many of its network
outlets.

CBC radio's English and French networks comprise 42 main stations
plus more than 500 small relay transmitters and about 100 privately

---

the ABC admitted, "What Reith said about public service broadcasting was
listened to in Australia and was highly persuasive in policy formulation in the
early years" (Duckmanton, 1975: 12).

CANADA

owned affiliates. Its English and French television networks consist of 27 main stations plus more than 500 low-power repeaters and about 300 privately owned affiliates. There are more than 900 private radio station owners, some of whom control more than 1 station. Several private television networks exist. The main one, CTV Television, is cooperatively owned by 20 large stations. Supplemented by nonowned affiliates, CTV covers 96 percent of the population. Some television stations affiliate with both CTV and CBC. Altogether, Canada has about 400 privately owned television stations.

Japan

Western observers invariably come away impressed by the achievements of Japan's mixed system—its technical sophistication, its physical coverage, its excellence in news programs, the scope and quality of its educational component. Some foreigners also find the amount of violence and nudity in Japan's mass-appeal programming disconcerting.

Prior to World War II, Japan's broadcasting had been turned over to a public corporation, but during the war, the Japanese Broadcasting Corporation (NHK) became a military propaganda arm. Broadcasting played a critically important role in bringing about Japan's surrender. United States strategists feared that fanatic devotion to the emperor would cause many Japanese to fight on, despite the devastation wrought by atomic bomb attacks on Hiroshima and Nagasaki. But in a precedent-shattering move, the emperor allowed the use of his voice on the radio, ordering the nation to lay down its arms. When General Douglas MacArthur took over the Supreme Command of the Allied Powers (SCAP) following the surrender in 1945, he allowed NHK to stay in place.

Under MacArthur's firm control, SCAP had the mission of dismantling the authoritarian government that had waged the war and substituting a Western-style democratic system. The new constitution, adopted in 1947, awarded high priority to freedom of speech and press. Ironically, though, MacArthur's headquarters at first censored all radio scripts in advance to ensure that nothing critical of the occupation crept into broadcasting. Understandably, Japanese broadcasters found it somewhat puzzling to have to deal with this "new despotic power which had taken the place of the Imperialist Japanese Government" (Uchikawa, 1964: 55). SCAP discontinued censorship in 1949.

MacArthur's staff set up a regulatory body closely modeled on the U.S. Federal Communications Commission. After the occupation ended, however, the Ministry of Posts and Telecommunications absorbed this regulatory agency, where it now has the status of a bureau. It has responsibility for allotting channels, screening applications, and licensing stations.

The Japanese took it for granted that MacArthur would also want to introduce American-style, privately owned commercial broadcasting—something much favored by the Japanese press. In fact, as Japan's first political decision of any note during the occupation, the government offered a plan for the licensing of privately owned stations.[17] Strangely, MacArthur's headquarters stalled in approving this proposal, perhaps because SCAP wanted to deal with a single broadcasting administration rather than with many different station operators.* In any event, in 1950 SCAP approved passage of a new set of broadcasting laws, including provision for licensing privately owned stations. It even arranged to send Japanese communication officials on a tour of broadcasting installations in the United States.[18] In explaining to the legislature its recommendation for a law providing for "civil broadcasters," the Japanese government said that private owners would

> build and elevate broadcasting culture by initiative and invention of individualistic activity. The Bill provides that these two systems [privately owned commercial broadcasting and the NHK] should demonstrate their respective merits, to lead each other and cover respective drawbacks for the ultimate object of enabling the nation to fully receive the benefits of broadcasting. (Quoted in Nomura, 1963: 68)

Some of the anticipated benefits doubtless flowed from ending NHK's monopoly and introducing commercialism. However, in later years after television developed,† some observers thought that Japanese commercial television had experienced the classic Gresham's Law effect, forcing NHK to lower its standards to attract audiences large enough to justify its license fees.[19]

So well did the Japanese absorb the lesson of media freedom that to this day the NHK enjoys more autonomy than any other major public broadcasting corporation. In a rather literal sense, the general public "owns" it by virtue of paying receiver fees. The government cannot veto any program or demand that any program be aired. It leaves the NHK free to set the level of license fees and to do its own fee collecting (which may be why it rates as the richest of the world's fee-supported broadcasting organizations). The legislature does, however, review the corporation's annual budget and license fee proposals. Moreover, the

---

*SCAP became more favorably disposed toward private broadcasting after allegations surfaced that NHK had been infiltrated by Communist sympathizers (Tadokoro, 1978: 64).

†As early as 1948, during the occupation, some American investors proposed setting up television in Japan, but the occupation headquarters disapproved of the scheme. Television actually started after the occupation ended, in 1953 (Nakajima, 1971: 32).

JAPAN

prime minister appoints the NHK Board of Governors, with consent of the legislature. The 12-member board must be representative of Japan's main geographical areas and major occupational groups. Broadcast manufacturers and other media personnel are ineligible.

Under the broadcasting law of 1950, NHK has an obligation to make broadcasting services available to the entire population—no small task, for although Japan's land area about equals that of Montana, it consists of hundreds of mountainous islands scattered across more than 2,000 miles of ocean. NHK uses nearly seven thousand small repeater stations (and in some areas also cable television) to ensure total coverage of its scattered and rugged terrain.

As in most mixed systems, the authorities encourage private operators to do local programming, leaving national coverage to the noncommercial services. Private stations receive licenses for three-year terms, but challenges to renewal do not arise as they do in the United States. The commercial firms, mostly newspaper owners, have an effective self-governing organization that seems to keep them out of difficulties with the broadcast bureau of the Ministry of Posts and Telecommunications. NHK radio facilities far exceed those of private broadcasters, but the television facilities are shared about equally. Like NHK, the private broadcasters use a great many repeater stations to maximize coverage of the scattered islands.

3 ▪ 8 PLURALISM IN BROADCASTING SYSTEMS

As the preceding sections show, broadcasting in all but the more authoritarian nations (and also the most deprived, which have little choice in the matter) has evolved toward *pluralistic* configurations. Pluralism as used here refers to the existence of multiple *motives* as driving forces within a national system, usually the profit motive (commercial component of the system) and the public service motive (noncommercial component).*

---

*Writers on broadcasting use the term *pluralism* to characterize a number of other variables. Namurois, for example, writes of political and denominational pluralism, linguistic and cultural pluralism, financial pluralism, and technical pluralism (1972: 84 ff.). Homet refers to competition between cable and broadcast television as "video pluralism." I use the term in this book rather narrowly to mean national systems that have competing services whose programming philosophies differ because two or more distinctly different motivations govern their operations, such as profit and public service.

Inasmuch as major components of any system necessarily compete for the attention of individuals in the same national audience pool, pluralism includes by definition an element of *competition*. This generalization holds true even though particular units (networks, stations, cable channels) may offer services aimed at narrowly defined audience segments. In the final analysis, all audiences must be drawn from the same finite population; and, whether large or small, each subaudience captured by one service becomes, momentarily at least, unavailable to other services.

Pluralism in Britain: BBC-ITV Competition

The impact of the ITV on the BBC in the 1960s (it took nearly a decade after the 1954 act for the IBA to fully implement its network) furnishes a classic test of competition's role in fostering a diverse national broadcasting system. Monopoly, no matter how benign, inevitably breeds a degree of complacency and a lack of responsiveness to audience demands. The repetitive routines of day-in, day-out broadcast operations tend to stultify creativeness. The spur of competition constantly restimulates creativity.

Reith's successor as BBC director-general, Sir Frederick Ogilvie, acknowledges a still deeper malaise created by a lack of competition. In a 1946 letter to the London *Times*, written several years after he left the BBC, Ogilvie said flatly,

> *Monopoly of broadcasting is inevitably the negation of freedom, no matter how efficiently it is run, or how wise and kindly the boards or committees in charge of it. It denies freedom of choice to listeners. It denies freedom of employment to speakers, musicians, writers, actors, and all who seek their chance on the air. (quoted in Smith, 1974: 85)*

Its staff's high standards of professional competence prevented the BBC from descending to the lackluster level of performance found in most monopolistic systems. Nevertheless, by the 1950s the corporation had earned the condescending nickname "Auntie," projecting a stuffy, old-maidish image and a complacent tone of benign superiority. Moreover, critics said, the BBC remained too narrowly focused on London.

All that began to change once its hitherto captive audience started opting for the livelier programming of the ITV companies. Stimulated by the challenge, the BBC went through a remarkable rejuvenation in the 1960s. To be sure, not everyone agreed that ITV competition alone caused the change. One dissenter called it "naive, implausible, and impertinent" to credit competition with the improvements. He attributed them instead to a new director-general, Hugh Greene, and his "determination to sweep away the musty traditions of Reithian orthodoxy and enlarge the range of BBC broadcasting" (Shulman, 1973: 140).[20]

Most commentators, however, remain convinced that although Greene deserved high marks for his creative achievements, ITV competition had a great deal to do with generating the atmosphere that made them possible. Anthony Smith concluded:

> For many in the BBC competition brought enormous creative opportunities. Under the leadership of Sir Hugh Greene, the BBC responded to the competitive situation not by adopting the programmes or criteria of the commercial system but by acquiring a new impetus of its own. Producers within the BBC were more often conscious of an internal competition between the different sections of the BBC, producing an enormous flowering of talent and inventiveness which became characteristic of the broadcasting in the first half of the 1960s; the coming of commercial television had undoubtedly produced a mood of competitiveness, but the changes which occurred within the BBC were not to any great extent imitative of independent television. (Smith, 1974: 126–127)

Burton Paulu reached a similar conclusion after many years of study and observation from the U.S. vantage point:

> Competition had proved an incentive to the BBC at the same time that it enriched the country's programme service. . . . Competition had improved British broadcasting not only because it provided an alternate channel, but also because the Television Act of 1954 set up a system of "controlled commercial television" favourable to the regulating agency. (Paulu, 1981: 45)

Pluralism as Oligopoly

Competition can of course have negative effects as well. In the above statement, Smith carefully emphasized that competition did not spur the BBC merely to imitate, as so often happens when a new and successful player appears upon the broadcast scene. But division of the entire field between two established power centers, to the exclusion of all other possible players, may mean exchanging monopoly for duopoly (or oligopoly, when more than two compete). Is that necessarily undesirable? Roland Homet, an American writer on comparative communication policies, has pointed out that although European national broadcasting systems include two, three, or four different networks, all-out competition does not necessarily result. In some cases, all networks reflect decisions of the same top administrators; even when that is not so, "harmonization measures are taken to enforce diversity of programming even at the cost of decreased viewing audiences for one or another channel. Competition in this context is an instrument of control rather than openness" (Homet, 1979: 7).

Nevertheless, in democratic countries whose systems, though not dominated by private ownership, do include competitive services, policymakers believe it essential to impose some control on competition. Experience as well as economic theory and research[21] show that oligopolistic competition, such as that of the three U.S. television networks, tends to adversely affect program variety. Under conditions of unrestrained oligopolistic competition, the best strategy may be to schedule more of whatever the competition finds successful rather than to counter with some entirely different type of program:

> When television programming is determined by an unregulated market it does not in practice give people the degree of choice they want. The marketplace is not that simple. Other factors are involved, such as the high production costs and elaborate distribution channels of television. They combine so that even a slight slackening of demand for more demanding programmes can mean that they are driven off the screen. Thus, just because less than a "majority" might watch a programme, viewers would find they were deprived of it altogether. Market forces and competition can be in the consumer's interest. But they are not synonymous. (Ehrenberg & Barwise, 1983: 13)

For example, in Taiwan (whose system has been heavily influenced by American precedents), three commercial networks compete fiercely for survival, each jumping on the bandwagon of the latest programming fad. According to one observer, the Taiwan case offers "a vivid empirical illustration of the thesis that oligopolistic competition leads to a content homogeneity (rather than content diversity) and reduces the audience choices" (Lee, 1979: 151). The upshot in this case was the imposition of severely restrictive government regulations on programming decisions—limiting the total number of allowable serial episodes, for instance, as well as the number of episodes that could be scheduled in a single evening.

Highly developed nations with oligopolistic systems usually anticipate such problems, regulating competition to prevent negative results. The British dual system of financing (receiver license fees for the BBC, advertising for ITV) builds in an element of self-regulation: the BBC could hardly continue to justify collection of receiver license fees from the public if it offered no alternative to ITV programming; at the same time, the BBC escapes whatever pressures (real or imagined) that the ITV companies may experience from advertisers. Varied restraints—government regulations (both actual and potential), codes (both voluntary and mandatory), advisory committees, and required consultations with the general public on such matters as the balance, scheduling, and content of programs—prevent competition between the two corporations from becoming destructive.

Excessive Competition

Dog-eat-dog competition occurs when a market contains more competitors than its economy can readily support. Failing stations or services, struggling desperately to survive, begin to cut corners and resort to substandard (if not downright illegal) practices in order to keep from going under. Even the more successful stations in the market may be forced to lower their standards simply to meet the competition.

In the United States, the free-enterprise philosophy dictates that if this downward spiral occurs, its end result will be elimination of the weak and survival of the strong, with consequent public benefit. The FCC does not take prospective economic injury to existing stations into account when licensing new stations.* Most countries that have adopted the U.S. laissez-faire approach to licensing of stations experience the adverse effects of excessive competition. Weak enforcement of regulations, or even virtual absence of regulations, often makes the results worse elsewhere than in the United States.

In Mexico, destructive competition among private broadcasters brought the threat of government intervention. Officials objected to increased sensationalism in programs as rival networks fought to win larger and larger audiences. Bidding for popular stars and top technicians caused salaries to spiral upward, causing ever more frantic audience-building efforts. Thus a vicious cycle set in as Gresham's Law began to take effect. Finally, a merger broke the cycle, bringing the competing networks under a single umbrella, that of the conglomerate Televisa. With four major stations in Mexico City, each heading its own network, Televisa obtained a virtual monopoly over private broadcasting. It adopted what came to be known as "the Mexican Formula," under which the monopoly continued to maintain rival networks but quelled destructive competition by programming each to a different demographic segment of the potential audience.†

Australia prevents overloading of markets by limiting the number of stations allowed in any one city. There, government-operated networks provide national services, while private stations primarily furnish local and regional services. Australians reasoned that regional interests would be "better served by one single prosperous station rather than by competition between two impoverished stations" (Breen, 1980: 191).

Though they vary in the kinds and extent of competition they allow, most major broadcasting systems of the non-Communist world have adopted pluralistic features. Some, such as Australia, Canada, Great Britain, Japan, and the United States, have well-established pluralistic systems in which commercial and noncommercial services compete for audience attention. Others, though declining to surrender traditional centralized controls, respond to insistent public demands for decentralization by trying to enhance internal competition and by experimenting with such alternative sources of programs as community stations. These alternatives form one of the subjects of the next chapter.

---

*"Economic injury" arose as an issue in the 1930s. The Supreme Court ruled in 1940 that the FCC needn't consider economic injury to existing stations when licensing a new station *unless* such injury would adversely affect the public interest (309 U.S. 470, 25 March 1940).

†Mahan, 1982: 98. Under the Mexican Formula, the government demands free time on private facilities (statutory time), as described in Section 4.2.

SUMMARY

Ownership, more than any other single factor, determines the type of programming that emerges from a broadcasting system. Three basic patterns of ownership are government, private, and public (nonprofit) corporation. Communist and Third World systems are usually government owned; Western systems usually have mixed ownership, combining two or more components. Such pluralistic systems benefit from competition, which tends to make broadcasting more creative and more responsive to audiences than monolithic systems. Competition carried to extremes, however, can backfire by reducing rather than expanding audience options.

NOTES

[1]Briggs, 1961: 72–73.

[2]Young, 1983.

[3]Roberts, 1974: 56.

[4]Kuhn, 1983.

[5]Pol, 1982.

[6]Boyd, 1982: 70.

[7]Noriega & Leach, 1979: 68.

[8]Great Britain, 1926 (the "Crawford Report").

[9]For further unfavorable opinion of the BBC's independence from government influence, see Burns, 1977.

[10]Protheroe, 1982.

[11]Quoted in Briggs, 1979a: 883, more fully in Smith, 1974: 103.

[12]Quoted in Paulu, 1981: 17. Paulu succinctly summarizes both how the BBC monopoly developed and the pros and cons in the debate that it precipitated, pp. 13–20.

[13]Great Britain, 1981.

[14]IBA, 1982: 18.

[15]For details on the Fourth Network, see Lambert, 1982.

[16]Ortmark, 1979: 170–171.

[17]Uchikawa, 1964: 57.

[18]Kato, 1978: 22.

[19]Smith, 1973: 260.

[20]For another dissenter, see Wedell, 1968: 47–50.

[21]See Owen et al., 1974: 103–111.

CHAPTER 4

POLITICS OF ACCESS

In the previous chapter I dealt with the critical importance of facilities ownership in determining the kinds of services broadcasting systems deliver. Ownership determines who will have access to broadcasting, but of course facilities provide only an avenue to the real goal, access to *audiences*. Access seekers sometimes overlook this seemingly obvious point. They forget that even if one can enforce a right of access, one gains no corresponding right to be listened to.

In practice, owners rely primarily on others to furnish program content. It follows, therefore, that the terms under which nonowners gain access to facilities affect the nature of any broadcasting system.

4 ■ 1 EVOLUTION OF ACCESS CONCEPTS

The Right to Communicate

For its first few decades, broadcasting experienced little trouble with demands for access to its microphones and cameras by nonprofessionals, aside from those complaining of unfair treatment. Once broadcasting had been established, people soon took it for granted that only three classes of speakers had any legitimate business on the air: *professional broadcasters* (announcers, news reporters, performers, and so on), supplemented by people temporarily in the news (interviewees, for example), *politicians*, first as candidates, then as office holders; and *experts*—subject matter specialists, usually controlled by broadcast professionals who imposed standard formats such as interviews and discussions. Nonprofessionals and nonexperts became broadcasters only briefly as amateur performers in quiz or game shows or as victims of newsworthy disasters.

During the consciousness-raising ferment of the 1960s, however, people began with increasing militancy to question professionals' exclusive control of access. The concept of an *individual right of access* emerged. Theorists cited the United Nations' Universal Declaration of Human Rights and its promise of the right to "seek, receive, and *impart*" information. They pointed out that to impart information in the electronic age, one needs access to broadcasting, the most universal means of reaching persons beyond the range of the unaided voice.[1]

Access seekers base their claims on arguments such as the following:

- Broadcasting, as a form of communication sanctioned and regulated by government and dependent on a universal natural resource for its operation (the electromagnetic spectrum), should be a public forum open to all.

- Traditional broadcasting has become too centralized, too depersonalized, too mass oriented, too professionalized, and too stereotyped to serve the full range of individual needs.

- Advances in technology, notably cable television, have loosened the restraints on access once imposed by the limited number of stations that could operate without causing interference. In 1975, UNESCO published a study of ways in which new technologies could facilitate access.[2]

- More generally, the contemporary urge for mechanization and bigness tends to intimidate many people. In particular, some feel threatened by the impending global reach of direct-broadcast satellites. They want to restore technology to human scale ("small is beautiful") and revive the sense of belonging—not to a "global village" but to a genuine neighborhood. They see local participatory broadcasting as one means to that end.

The Annan Committee's report on the future of broadcasting in Britain gives an insight into the pros and cons of access demands as voiced by Europeans in the 1970s. The report's testimony came from political parties, religious groups, arts councils, minorities, youth, moral reformers, educators, labor unions, and other access seekers. Said the committee:

> It has been put to us that broadcasting should be "opened up." At present, so it is argued, the broadcasters have become an overmighty subject, an unelected elite, more interested in preserving their own organisation intact than in enriching the nation's culture. Dedicated to the outworn concepts of balance and impartiality, how can the broadcasters reflect the multitude of opinions in our pluralist society? Their obsession with obtaining as large a mass audience as possible, so the argument runs, contorts the scheduling of programmes and constricts the creativity of the producers. (Great Britain, 1977: 16)

Demands for access come from many segments of a population. Politicians, especially those outside the mainline parties, want more opportunities to present their platforms to the public. Local merchants everywhere want to advertise their goods and services only in their own limited market areas—impossible even under systems that permit advertising if the broadcasting is primarily national in scope, which is traditionally the case in Europe. Minorities of all kinds want a chance to use broadcasting to preserve their cultures and promote their viewpoints; ethnic minorities in particular perceive broadcasting as vital for the survival of their languages. Social reformers want to use broadcasting to promote their goals; teachers, to make education more widely available; and creative artists, to express themselves to new audiences and in new ways.

New Access Mechanisms

Most democratic systems long ago adopted rules to give politicians controlled access. For those not so privileged, established broadcast services allow limited amounts of access via special program formats, such as the telephone-talk show. More elaborate "open-door" formats allow groups of nonprofessionals to produce their own segments on access program series.

Broadcasters necessarily limit personal access to centralized national networks more stringently than to small, local stations. Winning the right to set up *localized* services therefore became a primary goal of the access movement. In response to this demand, the monolithic European national systems began introducing community stations; some even permitted private groups to open their own local stations or cable systems, independent of the national broadcasting authorities. In the United States, this movement took the form of liberalized technical standards, allowing the shoe-horning of many new small stations into the tables of assignment. LPTV (Low Power Television) is an example.

In a few instances, national systems have experimented with roving mobile broadcast stations that briefly give local communities a station of their own. Ireland's "Nationwide Community Radio," for example, began touring the countryside in 1974, setting up shop in villages for one- or two-week periods. "A key feature of the experiment is that RTE [the Irish national system] provides the studio and technical staff and gives programme and production advice, but the programming selection, production and presentation are entirely the work of the local community" (Fisher, 1978: 56–57).* The BBC set up a similar service, "Neighborhood Radio," in Wales.[3]

WRTH lists this service as operating on both AM and FM "at various locations during special events." It gives as the usual operating hours 1130–1330 and 1630–1830 on weekdays (*WRTH*, 1984: 101).

Most of these concessions came only after great numbers of clandestine and pirate stations had gone on the air, defying authorities and disrupting authorized services. These interlopers came in two waves, first external and then internal. External pirates operated from ships and islands outside their target countries' territorial waters. After governments passed special laws to cope with the intrusion, a wave of domestic pirates swept across Europe and many other parts of the world. "Free" broadcasting became an organized movement with hundreds of stations, its own publications, and international conferences. The demand for new forms of access became so widespread and intense that democratically elected officials had to change their national systems to accommodate some of the previously outlawed services.

Abhorrent Vacuums

The history of the access movement, along with other evidence, suggests that in broadcasting, as in the physical world, "Nature abhors a vacuum." *Human* nature, it appears, abhors a *broadcasting* vacuum. Wherever broadcasting authorities thwart public demands for a particular kind of broadcasting service, methods of satisfying that demand almost always emerge. They may be legal, as in such external international services as the Voice of America and such spillover services as those between East and West Germany. They may be illegal, as in the case of the seaborne and domestic pirates. Some take the form of broadcasting substitutes—audio and video cassette recordings.* Sometimes clandestine services fill broadcast vacuums, as when Poland's dissident labor union, Solidarity, used underground radio to get messages to its followers in 1982.

People's immediate motive for jumping the traces varies. They may simply desire to receive color television when their home system supplies only black-and-white, as happened in Italy prior to 1977. They may want to learn what is going on when they know or suspect that their home broadcasters suppress or fabricate the news. Or they may want more racy programs when their own system imposes puritanical standards. Local merchants and performers may desire a local electronic platform. Or people may react to the denial of political access or simply to the total lack of a desired service, as when people in countries with no domestic television erect high antennas to pick up signals from abroad; they may even install earth station dishes to pirate signals from satellites.

---

*"To find TV programmes and films that are more entertaining than those offered by Islamic broadcasting Iranians have taken refuge in tapes and video cassettes, as have similar groups in Saudi Arabia and other rich petroleum exporting countries. In Iran, this tactic is basically a post-revolutionary occurrence, repeatedly banned by the government authorities but to no avail" (Tehranian, 1982: 44).

Law-abiding citizens sometimes conspire with illegal operators in order to fill an abhorred vacuum. For example, in 1981 a pirate television station in the Danish town of Randers began playing recordings of programs picked up from West German and Swedish stations. Judging from sale of the required antennas, many thousands of Randers' approximately sixty thousand citizens patronized the pirate outlet. Additionally, anyone spotting a government detection vehicle in the area would warn the pirate operators, enabling them to go off the air before the authorities could zero in on their location and seize their equipment.[4] Many such instances of complicity with pirates have been reported—more evidence of the abhorrent vacuum law at work.

4 ▪ 2 POLITICAL ACCESS

Access for politicians came first. As rule makers, they had the earliest opportunity to set up access machinery for their own benefit.

Authoritarian Systems

Leaders in Communist and in most Third World countries enjoy access limited only by their own appetites for public appearances. Because most have insatiable appetites, newscasts invariably start with an item about the head of state, whether or not he or she participated in what others would regard as a newsworthy event. Official pronouncements and ritualistic occasions take up hours of air time. In some developing countries, covering the movements of the head of state virtually monopolizes the entire mobile equipment of the national television system. Leaders exploit broadcasting to create personality cults, magnifying their images to heroic if not supernatural dimensions. The president of Zaïre (formerly the Belgian Congo), not content to be the subject of the lead story in every newscast, also had himself depicted in the opening footage descending from the clouds upon his country like a god:

> The television screen fills with an image of heavenly clouds. A choir of voices swells in the background. The music grows louder, and as the clouds drift apart there emerges the face of a man. . . . The camera zooms in and holds for what seems like a very long time on the face. It speaks of strength, compassion, wisdom, though no words are uttered. . . . This is the start of the eight o'clock TV news in Kinshasa. (Lamb, 1982: 43)

The shah of Iran used television similarly, though on a more sophisticated level. In glorifying his regime and his person, television drew heavily on ancient and colorful Persian history. As one observer put it at the time, "The television conception of Iranian tradition appears to resemble a Cecil B. De Mille movie in which the part of the Shah is played by the Shah" (Tunstall, 1977: 247). Dissident elements learned the lesson well—after the revolution, the austere image of the bearded Ayatollah Khomeini replaced the glamorized image of the shah.

Unlimited access on their own terms gives leaders with a flair for broadcasting unique opportunities to rule personally and directly, bypassing their own governments when they so desire. Cuba's Fidel Castro has been called the "first modern revolutionary leader to use television as a major instrument of influence and control" (Dizard, 1966: 133). Clandestine radio, an important resource of revolutionary movements, taught Castro the power of broadcasting. As one of his first actions on coming to power in Cuba in 1959, he expropriated the country's well-developed broadcasting system. With unlimited access (stations abruptly interrupted regular programs whenever Castro wanted to go on the air), he quickly became a virtuoso television performer. During the early years of his rule, he broadcast almost daily, mesmerizing huge, enthusiastic crowds for hours on end with displays of revolutionary rhetoric, sometimes first announcing important government decisions in the course of these performances.*

When leaders monopolize access, they of course deny it to their opponents. Nevertheless, Marxist ideology maintains exactly the opposite view. Lenin said that whereas the capitalist press of his day gave access only to the rich, the Soviet press would guarantee freedom of expression to "a very much broader number of citizens, say, to every group collecting a certain number of subscriptions" (quoted in Hopkins, 1970: 31). Yet the right of Poland's Solidarity movement to use television became a major issue in its struggle with the government. After a brief relaxation, the government reasserted its exclusive right, banning Solidarity from further access.†

Democratic Systems

Of course, elected leaders in democratic systems are not above exploiting broadcasting for their own ends. Instead of simply ordering coverage by government-controlled media, however, they must use the arts of public relations to contrive voluntary coverage, for example, by staging tempting "photo opportunities" for the cameras. Those running for office, having far less clout with the media than incumbents, count on regulations to assure them fair access to broadcasting.

Candidates for Office. In political situations where candidates of more than one party contend for voter approval, ensuring that all candidates get fair access to broadcasting presents problems. The public interest requires that parties and their nominees have a chance to put

---

*Dizard discusses Castro along with France's Charles de Gaulle and Egypt's Gamal Abdel Nasser as notable examples of charismatic television performers (1966: 132–154).

†Steiner, 1981; Niemczyk, 1983. As usually happens in such situations, the dissidents then resorted to clandestine broadcasting.

their platforms and themselves before the public; but uncontrolled access risks the possibility that some parties or candidates will gain an unfair advantage. The first U.S. broadcasting statute, adopted in 1927, laid down the rule, still in effect, that "equal opportunities" for *all* candidates for a given office must be offered as soon as any one of the candidates uses broadcasting. Opportunities must be equal in terms of charges for time (if any) as well as amount and quality of time. This solution ignores the relative size of a candidate's support—a representative of the smallest splinter party has the same entitlement as majority party candidates. This can saddle broadcasters with demands from swarms of minor candidates, especially in presidential campaigns.* Most democracies differ from U.S. practice. They usually prorate access time for candidates according to strength evidenced in previous voting records, although Holland, like the United States, gives each party the same amount of time, regardless of its numerical strength.

That political candidates can buy time has greatly increased the cost of campaigning for major U.S. elective offices. Again, other democracies differ: most do not allow candidates to buy time for political campaigning. Britain approaches these dilemmas conservatively, yet it imposes no hard-and-fast rule such as the U.S. equal opportunities law. Instead, the two broadcasting authorities (BBC and IBA) confer with the major party leaders prior to a general election to work out a schedule of broadcasts on behalf of each party. They allot time to parties rather than to individual candidates. The amount of access time awarded each party varies in accordance with the number of votes it drew in the preceding election. Typically, the leading parties get only five or six ten-minute and two five-minute telecasts, along with nine five-minute radio segments. Smaller parties having at least 50 candidates nationwide get one five-minute telecast each. The parties pay nothing for time, which the broadcasters schedule simultaneously on all television (but not radio) networks.

These limitations do not apply to candidate appearances in broadcaster-controlled news, interview, and public affairs programs. All candidates and issues get a thorough airing in Britain through these types of programs. In a curious variation of the general practice in English-speaking countries, Australian law imposes a complete blackout of any broadcast mention of political candidates for the two days preceding an election and on the election day itself. The blackout applies to news and news-related programs as well as to advertisements. Adopted in 1942, this heavy-handed rule reflected an exaggerated fear that voters

---

*In fact, Congress amended the law to exempt broadcasters from the equal opportunities rule in the case of presidential candidates under certain circumstances; this exemption enabled broadcasts of debates between the leading candidates for president without affording time for all the minor candidates as well.

would be stampeded by "false and fictitious claims and by dangerous and unsubstantiated charges." Australian broadcasters have mounted a vigorous campaign to repeal the blackout rule.*

U.S law provides that appearances by political candidates in bona fide news and public affairs programs do not activate the equal opportunities rule. Britain has far more complex fairness rules for appearances by candidates on the air within their own voting districts. Special rules then come into effect, based in part on an election law, the Representation of the People Act of 1969. Roughly summarized, the law requires that a candidate actively participating in a broadcast program within his or her own district may debate with other candidates for the same office only if *all* candidates for that office participate.[5]

Japan has an unusual but logical arrangement: ever since the post–World War II broadcasting laws went into effect in 1950 (see Section 3.7), the Home Office has reimbursed broadcasters for the production costs of political candidates' appearances. In the case of commercial stations (as distinguished from NHK, the public service component of the Japanese system), the Home Office also pays for the time candidates use. Only *local* candidates may use commercial stations, however, because the NHK has a monopoly on national network coverage.

Japanese election laws strictly limit the format that may be used and the amount of time each candidate may have. Prior to television, each candidate had a short biographical sketch read by a radio announcer and then delivered a five-minute speech. In 1963 a new television election law forbade NHK to allow candidates to express their opinions, limiting political broadcasts to biographical sketches of candidates. Six years later, candidates recovered the right to speak on both NHK television and commercial television. Each candidate may make six appearances on radio and television, each broadcast five and a half minutes in length.

Because of a change in the method of electing national candidates, a new election law in 1982 eliminated personal appearances in favor of "party election broadcasts" along the lines of the BBC (because these are national offices, the new rule applies only to NHK). Each party receives a series of time slots, the number depending upon how many candidates each party has on the ballot. Parties with 25 or more candidates receive eight television and four radio time segments of up to 14 minutes each. The parties have not responded favorably to this new arrangement, and changes are expected for the 1986 elections.†

Officeholders. Incumbent candidates have significant advantages over their future opponents. When the head of state, for example, gains

---

*The Federation of Australian Radio Broadcasters has proposed repeal. Virtually all Australian journalistic interests support repeal (FARB, 1981: 3).

†I am indebted to Izumi Tadokoro, Development Department director, Japan Newspaper Publishers and Editors Association, for an analysis of Japanese election broadcast regulations upon which this description is based.

access to address the nation on matters of public concern, the temptation to score political points is virtually irresistible.

The U.S. *fairness doctrine* applies to this situation, giving access to *ideas* rather than to particular proponents of ideas. The doctrine instructs stations to devote part of their time to discussions of "controversial issues of public importance" in their communities of license. After introducing one point of view on such a subject, licensees incur an obligation to allow reasonable opportunities for the expression of opposing views. When the president addresses the nation in a partisan way, political opponents may ask for a chance to reply. The station or stations concerned are free to choose a specific spokesperson from the opposition.

Most other democratic systems regulate access by officeholders more explicitly. The British divide between-elections national political access into three categories:

- "Party political broadcasts" refer to annual presentations by the parties between general elections (in Britain, national elections take place at irregular intervals, not on schedule as in the United States). The broadcasting authorities allot program time according to the number of votes received in the previous election, just as with party election broadcasts.

- "Ministerial broadcasts" refer to official presentations by the prime minister or chief cabinet officers. They trigger no right of reply if they merely explain actions already taken by Parliament or ask for public cooperation on noncontroversial matters. If, however, such broadcasts contain elements of controversy or partisanship, they trigger an unconditional right of reply by the chief opposition party. A third program follows, giving smaller parties a chance to participate. The broadcasting authorities alone decide whether a ministerial broadcast warrants a reply because of partisan content.

- "Budget broadcasts" refer to traditional presentations of the annual national budget plan by the chancellor of the Exchequer. A budget speech automatically gives the chief opposition party the right to reply on the following evening.

The laws and customs of some other European countries insulate their broadcast systems from partisanship less effectively. In France, for example, broadcasting has traditionally been regarded as one of the spoils of office. Unable to curb the criticism of newspapers, parties in power curbed broadcasters. A former minister of information illustrated the subservient position of French broadcasters by the following anecdote: upon assuming office, someone briefed him on the array of call buttons on his desk; this one summoned his reception clerk, this one his private secretary, and these the heads of the government-operated broadcasting services.[6]

Germany and Austria took a different route toward squaring political access with political fairness. There, political authorities appoint the executives of some of the government broadcast services, scrupulously affording proportional representation in accordance with party affiliation. Known as *Proporz*, this system ensures the counterbalancing of each appointee from one party by appointment of his or her deputy from the opposing party. According to one commentator, *Proporz* "can involve much wrangling and sometimes bitterness, and extends to virtually all levels of administration and programme production: everywhere within the organization the balance of attitudes must reflect that found in the [state] parliaments" (Sandford, 1976: 79).

Statutory Time

All governments reserve the ultimate right to demand access to all stations in times of emergency. Under U.S. law, the president has broad powers to use private broadcasting facilities in case of war.* In Great Britain, the two broadcasting authorities must send government messages on request even under nonemergency conditions. In Australia, the government may require up to 30 minutes of free time per day for "items of national interest."

In Third World countries where private owners dominate the national broadcasting system, governments often have a statutory right to use substantial amounts of time on privately owned facilities without paying any compensation to the owners. Mexico's broadcasting and tax laws make several rulings that obligate private stations to surrender time to the state:

- Stations must give 30 minutes per day for public service announcements furnished by government agencies. The time may be either used as a single block or broken into separate shorter segments. Typically, the government fills the time with "social advertising"— spot announcements urging good health practices and the like.

- Stations must make network facilities simultaneously available for the delivery of messages deemed important by the president's office.

- Emergency bulletins must be aired on request.

- Finally, stations must make available 12.5 percent of their total daily air time for government programming. This levy, known as *fiscal time*, originated as a compromise measure after the government demanded that all private stations either give the state a 49 percent interest in their property or else pay a 25 percent tax on total

---

*Section 606 of the Communications Act of 1934 gives the U.S. president virtually unlimited powers over all forms of wire and wireless communication in a war emergency (47 USC 606).

revenues. Broadcasters finally negotiated these confiscatory demands down to what amounts to a barter arrangement—the option
of paying the tax in the form of free time instead of cash. Fiscal time,
which the government uses for educational and cultural materials,
need not be prime time and cannot be accumulated.

These mandatory concessions could give the Mexican government
up to three and a half hours of free time on privately owned stations
every day (depending on the number of hours a station stays on the air).
Fortunately for the viability of private broadcasting in Mexico, the government actually uses less than half the fiscal time concession. What
started as a devastating assault became in the end a slap on the wrist:

> *The strong bargaining position of the broadcast industry in this matter
> certainly can be attributed to the economic and political connections of its
> leaders. However, it can also be related to a consideration which both the state
> and the private industry must be aware of: the state relies on the private
> broadcasting system to disseminate the majority of its messages to the Mex-
> ican people. (Mahan, 1982: 139)*

Other Latin American countries also provide for statutory time.
Argentina's Ministry of Education and Culture claims 7 percent of private stations' time each day. Peru levies 60 minutes daily. In Brazil,
radio stations must carry *A Voz do Brasil* at 7:00 P.M. each evening, an
hour-long program during which the president, the ministers, the legislature, and law courts each gets some time. Known in Brazil as "the
hour of silence," it has been described as "a badly produced propaganda
program touting the 'miracle' of the country's advance as a major power" (Wicklein, 1981: 233). All stations must also carry a half hour of
government-produced educational programming following *A Voz*.

By and large, government efforts to capitalize on the ability of private
enterprise to furnish ready-made audiences have not lived up to expectations. Though the goals may be laudatory, government broadcasting too often lacks credibility. It tends to leave an "abhorrent vacuum,"
impelling audiences to turn to programs from other sources—to spillover services from neighboring countries, pirate stations, foreign external services, and recordings from abroad.

Partisan Political Stations: Chile

From the standpoint of parliamentary democracy, the most damaging
type of political access results from ownership by political partisans who
have no regard for fairness, balance, objectivity, or the right of reply to
personal attacks. Chile furnished a cautionary example of the wholesale
conversion of broadcasting to partisan political ends. Private owners
control nearly all of Chile's 160-odd radio stations, while the government owns most of its 30-odd primary television stations. Television
started as an educational innovation at the Catholic University of Chile
(1958) and the University of Chile (1960). The present government

television network came into being a decade later as a deliberate act of political reprisal.

During the 1960s, the ruling Christian Democratic party in Chile (supported by the Catholic church) engaged in a passionate battle with a rising Socialist party. When Communists infiltrated the university stations, the incumbent Christian Democratic government set up a state television network to counter their political influence. The legislature rigged the new television law so that Christian Democrats could retain control of the network's regulatory board, even if they should lose the presidency, as seemed probable when the law went into effect in 1969.

The next year, Socialist party leader Salvador Allende won the presidential election, setting in motion a fateful struggle in which the United States played a clandestine role,* ending three years later with Allende's death and a right wing military dictatorship.

Allende's victory at the polls in 1970 signaled an all-out fight for mastery of the media:

> The [Socialists], knowing that broadcasting would affect the masses far more than print journalism, directed most of their energies to solidifying control in this field. They had a large head start when they came to power, because both television and radio in Chile had long put political function above commercialism. . . . Struggles by each side to gain internal control of the broadcast media took the form largely of continued infiltration of staffs, counter measures by owners and managers, founding and licensing of new stations, cancellation and reassignment of frequencies, and purchase of existing stations. (Pierce, 1979: 63–64)

One of Allende's stratagems in the bizarre media battles of 1970–1973 took advantage of the president's legal right to require private radio stations to link up and make time available for the president to address the nation. Allende simply kept the stations tied up with programming from the presidential palace, effectively excluding the opposition from the air at crucial times. The University of Chile, unable to dislodge the Marxist personnel who had "kidnapped" its television station, started up a second station. As the moves and countermoves escalated, violent confrontations occurred, with frequent demonstrations, station seizures, and bombings.[7]

After the coup, the military junta found itself burdened with a collection of expropriated radio stations as well as the state-owned

---

*According to a U.S. Senate subcommittee report, the CIA spent more than $3 million to support the Christian Democrats in their battle against Allende and the Socialist party. For example, as far back as 1964, in one June week "a CIA-funded propaganda group produced twenty radio spots per day in Santiago [the capital] and on 44 provincial stations; twelve-minute news broadcasts five time[s] daily on three Santiago stations and 24 provincial outlets. . . . By the end of June, the group produced 24 daily newscasts in Santiago and the provinces [and] 26 weekly 'commentary' programs" (U.S. Senate, 1975: 15).

television network. With radical parties banned and others suspended, political broadcasting subsided and the broadcasting industry returned to the business of entertainment and advertising. The junta discontinued the television network's government grants and told its managers to make the operation self-supporting. In consequence, the state network turned to mass-appeal programming and all-out advertising, taking on all the worst traits of private commercial broadcasting without providing the compensating services expected of government stations. The government's radio network of 70 stations covers the entire country and can force private stations to join the network for "important events and speeches" (Knight, 1982: 215).

4 ▪ 3 GROUP ACCESS: THE NETHERLANDS

Access for nongovernment users creates more potential demands than most systems can satisfy—even assuming that it would be in the public interest to turn over all or most of the available time on the air to private, personal uses. The Netherlands adopted a novel way of dealing with this dilemma, alloting segments of time to representative *groups* of users in amounts proportionate to their size. The groups themselves decide which individuals should be given access. As Anthony Smith put it, the Dutch system "enshrines the grassroots political aspirations of its time in a way which gives them a status in national life in Holland which they do not yet possess elsewhere. It enabled every group of discontented or inspired individuals to propagate its beliefs on its own terms" (1973: 273). He refers to 1965, when in response to widespread discontent, Holland passed a new broadcasting law extending and codifying an access practice that in principle had animated Dutch broadcasting from its beginnings (and the Dutch pioneered broadcasting as early as 1919).

Pillarized Broadcasting

Nineteenth-century religious rivalries in Holland had led Dutch groups with common interests to reinforce their separate identities by developing separate, group-related institutions within the larger national framework. Each group set up its own schools, hospitals, trade unions, newspapers, recreational clubs, and so on. The Dutch carried group chauvinism, a trait common to all pluralistic societies, to its logical extreme.* Known as *pillarization,* this vertical structuring applies to Dutch broadcasting as well as to other institutions. Eight major and many

---

*Religious groups such as American fundamentalists exhibit comparable tendencies. "Born-again" Christians seek to preserve and transmit their beliefs not only by sending their children to their own fundamentalist Bible schools but also by operating their own publishing houses, broadcasting stations, networks, and entertainment enterprises. Some have even issued trade directories designed to dissuade their members from dealing with any but born-again merchants.

NETHERLANDS

minor groups, having organized their own broadcasting associations, divide air time on the national radio and television networks. Three of the eight major associations have religious orientations (Catholic, fundamentalist, and mainline Protestant), one is political (Socialist), one cultural-progressive, and three are neutral. A decline in rigid pillarization accounts for the ideologically neutral groups. Broadcasting itself has been at least partly responsible for this shift: "Television was bound to have a tremendous influence in a country where not only the doors of the living room were closed to strangers but also the doors of school-rooms, union meetings, youth hostels, football grounds and dancing schools" (Wigbold, 1979: 201).

The eight major broadcasting associations receive licenses to broadcast and annual time allotments on the national facilities in accordance with a classification system based on how many members they have been able to recruit. Minimums range from 450,000 members for the largest category to 150,000 for the smallest. Groups able to muster 60,000 members can qualify for a temporary "candidate" category, pending an increase in membership to the minimum level for permanent status. The law also requires allotment of time to churches for conducting services on the air, to political parties, and indeed to any organization whose needs the established associations fail to serve.

A central organization, NOS (*Nederlandse Omroep Stichting*), furnishes production facilities for all users and coordinates assignment of studios and personnel to the access groups. NOS also retains about a fifth of the total air time for its own programs on subjects of broad national interest, such as general news bulletins, major sports events, and Eurovision features (the program exchanges of the European Broadcasting Union, an association of the national broadcasting authorities of the region).*

The minister of Welfare, National Health and Culture controls assignment of time to both NOS and the associations. However, the minister has no prior control of what goes over the air. Only after a broadcast can the minister take action against associations for violating the law by airing unauthorized advertising or threatening public order, decency, or the safety of the state.

Programs of the broadcast associations are supposed to serve "cultural, religious, or spirtual needs" of their memberships. The associations

---

*In 1984 the Netherlands government announced plans to divide NOS into three separate units, one to do programs, another to handle centralized production facilities, and a third to handle administrative functions (Nuyl, 1984).

exist to present their own views; therefore, they have no obligation to balance their views with those of other groups. The system counts on the very fact that every group has a chance to express itself to assure fairness in the long run. This expectation comports with U.S. First Amendment theory, even though the Dutch do not employ an equivalent of the fairness doctrine.

System financing depends primarily on receiver license fees, which contribute about three quarters of the operational budget. The rest comes from advertising; however, the associations do not sell commercial time. A government-appointed agency called STER handles all advertising, which appears only in three blocks of time adjacent to newscasts.

Each association receives a government grant to help defray its broadcast expenses; in addition, the groups collect funds from their members through subscriptions to the program guides they publish to promote their own program segments. These guides also earn advertising income for the groups, and subscriptions serve as an official membership count for purposes of certificating broadcast groups.

Trossification

Ideal though the Dutch pillarized system may seem as a practical application of the access principle, it has its drawbacks. Some access groups have tended to undermine the goals of the system, complying with the letter of the law while violating it in spirit. The group known as TROS (*Televisie Radio Omroep Stichting*), originally a pirate television station operated from an offshore artificial island, became the second largest of Holland's "big eight" by abandoning the motive of commonly held political or religious beliefs. Instead, TROS recruited members of *all* persuasions, united only in their desire for neutral, noncommital entertainment. Using American methods of aggressive promotion and mass taste appeals, TROS gives no time to controversy and other types of off-putting seriousness.

Other associations became alarmed when they began losing members to TROS (remember that the amount of air time an association receives depends on the size of its membership). In a classic example of Gresham's Law at work, they began competing with TROS on its own terms, imitating its mass-appeal methods in self-defense by, for example, purchasing American syndicated shows. A new word came into being to describe this process—*trossification*. It refers to the lowering of standards that results when competition gets out of hand, subordinating all program judgments to the test of audience size alone. "The openness of the Dutch system led to anarchy," wrote a Dutch commentator (Wigbold, 1979: 226).

Susceptibility to trossification must be counted as an inherent weakness of large-scale public access of the kind developed in Holland. It harks back to the Annan Committee's comment that the right to speak confers no corresponding right to be listened to. Before trossification had reached an advanced stage, Anthony Smith wrote, "An air of earnest dullness surrounds the entire output" (p. 276). This solemn atmosphere created a vacuum that the TROS style of upbeat entertainment readily filled—mostly with imported syndicated shows.

Despite trossification, however, the Dutch attempt to solve the access problem deserves notice as a bold and innovative experiment. Smith concluded his critique of the system by saying:

> The pillars of [the Dutch system] may be crushed by the harsh cultural realities of mass society in the long run. Nonetheless the Dutch experience shows that programme diversity can be achieved without monopoly in broadcasting, that a modern society can survive without "objectivity" in all its broadcasting and that [editorial] power can be successfully devolved within a determinedly pluralistic nation. (1973: 278)

4▪4 ILLEGAL ACCESS: PIRATE STATIONS

When frustrated by an established system, the desire for access ultimately inspires illegal "pirate" operations. These can originate either from external locations (typically from ships in waters beyond the territorial limits of the target countries) or from domestic locations, in which case they operate either openly or clandestinely, depending on government policies.

Most receivers can tune to more channels than those occupied by the locally receivable licensed stations. Unlicensed stations can therefore "pirate" unoccupied channels with assurance that most set owners will be able to pick them up. The miniaturization of equipment and the development of video as well as audio home recorders made it possible to assemble low-power pirate stations at moderate cost and with only moderate technical know-how. "Free" radio advocates in Europe exchange how-to-do-it information by means of newsletters and international conferences. They have published many books on the history, philosophy, and strategies of the movement.[8]

Electronic Graffiti

The United States makes such varied opportunities for access available that people have little serious incentive to set up pirate stations. Radio rebels nevertheless crop up, interested in defiance for its own sake. Their illegal transmissions might be compared to graffiti on public property, carried out on a more sophisticated level. The Federal Communications Commission is relatively tolerant of pirates if they do not cause serious interference to licensed services, though it can recommend up to $10,000 in fines and a year in jail for violators. A would-be disc jockey who operated "WBUZ-FM" on Long Island reported that the FCC closed him down twice and assessed a $750 fine—which he failed to pay.

"WFAT" operated intermittently from a public housing development in New York before being tracked down by FCC monitors. The youthful operators used a phone-in format and the motto "FAT is where it's at." The first reported instance of a pirate television station in the United States may have been an operation that went on the air in 1978 as "Lucky Seven" on channel 7 in the Syracuse University area. It appeared only briefly, featuring pornographic movies and commentary by an announcer wearing a gas mask disguise.[9]

Even in authoritarian states such as the USSR, such youthful defiance occurs. Russian newspapers often report the prosecution of "radio hooligans," but the authorities usually treat them leniently if their transmissions contain no outright subversion. In other parts of the world, however, pirate broadcasters, both domestic and external, often have more serious goals in mind. They have profoundly affected the centralized national systems whose monopolies they challenged. They not only forced programming changes but sometimes also precipitated political crises.

External Pirates

Inroads by pirate stations began in 1958 with the first appearance of ship-borne stations operating in international waters. Most of them broadcast from the North Sea and adjacent areas, off the coasts of Britain, Belgium, Holland, France, Germany, and the Scandinavian countries. Pirates have gone as far afield as New Zealand and Africa.

Mounted on small coastal ships or artificial islands left over from World War II offshore forts, the stations claimed immunity from national broadcasting statutes because they operated outside national territorial limits. They appealed strongly to a neglected but commercially significant minority—the teenage devotees of pop music. Such musical interests had been largely ignored by the established systems of Europe, with their goals of raising rather than pandering to untutored musical tastes. Paul Harris, a historian of the pirate movement, summarized their view of the BBC in these unflattering terms:

In its self-appointed and wholly artificial role as an organ of edification and culture [the BBC] always sought to evade its clear duty to cater for popular tastes. The effectiveness of this missionary role was shattered by the offshore broadcasters who brought the pleasure of unpretentious listening to millions. No longer could tastes and attitudes be forced into one uniform mould by the Corporation as a system of independent radio emerged. The brainwashing became less effective and the imposition of its own culture and attitudes more difficult. (Harris, 1970: 203)

Pirate stations drew heavily on U.S. investments and expertise. Not only did they use American program formats, sales methods, and promotional gimmicks, some also used ships and on-board installations that originated in U.S. ports. One of the best-known pirate ships, broadcasting to British audiences as *Radio Caroline* (named after President John F. Kennedy's daughter), was outfitted in Galveston, for example.

Pirates found advertisers interested in the youth market absurdly easy to recruit. The established commercial broadcasting systems had left themselves wide open to such invasions. They declined to play the kind of music teenagers wanted, disdained to hire American-style DJs who knew how to present it, and would not stay on the air for the late-night shows that made the best showcases.*

Leading pirate stations built up huge and passionately loyal followings. When the government closed down the *Radio London* ship, hoards of fans met the train on which its broadcast staff came to London, completely taking over the Liverpool Street station in a tumultuous welcome. Paul Harris attributed the rise of British pop music, London's 1960s' reputation as a "swinging town," and the rise of specialized pop music record labels (which went from 2 percent to 20 percent of the market for recordings within three years) to the influence of the pirates.

Oddly, the major advertisers on pirate stations included evangelistic Christian ministers. Turned down by established national systems because of strict rules on fundraising and policies against religious proselytizing, the fundamentalists resorted to illegal means to reach young Europeans. In fact, religious time buyers apparently kept some pirates afloat at a time when government harassment of regular commercial clients threatened to dry up their normal advertising market. One minister even planned to recommission a retired pirate ship to evangelize the Italians.†

Aside from venturing into commercialized religious broadcasting, however, the pirates generally steered clear of overt ideological program content. A British law in effect since 1949 forbids parliamentary candidates from resorting to foreign stations in political campaigns. Only one instance of attempted interference in a British election was reported, an occasion when a pirate tried to lend support to a candidate who favored a lenient policy toward pirate broadcasters.

Wallowing dangerously under their top-heavy radio masts, frequently caught in vicious North Sea gales, occasionally even boarded by armed raiding parties from rival ships, the pirates led a stormy though briefly profitable career. Onshore authorities harassed them because they not only broadcast without benefit of licenses, they also interfered with legitimate radio traffic and violated copyright and musical perfor-

---

*The BBC was hampered, however, by the severe limits on "needle time" (that is, the number of hours of recorded music they could play) imposed by the phonograph industry. British copyright law (unlike U.S. law) gives rights to recording manufacturers in addition to composers, authors, publishers, and performers. See Browne, 1971.

†Brazer, 1970. Garner Ted Armstrong bought time on six pirate stations, and Seventh Day Adventists invested heavily in them, according to Harris (1970: 55).

mance laws every time they played a recording. In 1965 the Council of Europe adopted a treaty resolution urging member nations to take coordinated legal action against the outlaws. Given the popularity of the pirates, this action was not always politically feasible. Britain finally passed a comprehensive antipirate statute in 1967, making it a punishable offense for anyone to participate in any way in operating offshore or airborne stations, to supply or equip such stations, or to buy advertising from them.*

In any event, by then liberalization of national program policies had begun to dilute the pirates' appeal. Some examples of such pirate-motivated changes include the following:

- Prior to passage of the British antipirate statute, the BBC restructured its radio networks, creating Radio 1 as a popular music network; it even hired some of the ex-pirate disc jockeys, who had huge followings, to preside over new music shows.

- Holland started a new program service aimed at the youth market and eventually accepted two former pirate organizations as legitimate onshore broadcasting associations.

- Sweden adopted a light entertainment and news format in response to pirates that broadcast from ships in the Baltic Sea.

- Israel added a special pop music program to its radio offerings to counteract the lure of the *Voice of Peace*, a pirate ship that started cruising up and down the coasts of Lebanon and Israel in 1973. When owner Abe Nathan had to bring his aging vessel into an Israeli port, he petitioned to be allowed to continue broadcasting from the ship, either moored in the harbor or beached somewhere along the coast. Supporters made a serious but futile effort to get the legislature to amend the Israeli broadcasting law to except Nathan's station from its ban on private stations.†

- Thousands of miles away, cruising in the Tasman Sea, pirates won such a large following in 1967 that the government of New Zealand felt obliged to modify its broadcasting policies.‡

But broadcasting authorities did not match these adjustments in programming with corresponding liberalization of commercial policies.

---

*Smith reproduced both the Council of Europe resolution and the British statute (1974: 153–155). The British government spent thousands of dollars for space in *Time* and other U.S. publications to announce passage of the new law, suggesting the importance of American business interests in the pirate movement.

†Nathan was an idealist in quest of peace, not merely a commercial broadcaster in quest of profits (Chamish, 1982).

‡Toogood, 1978a: 291–292. The present Radio Hauraki, a 24-hour music station in Auckland, originated as a pirate operation. It came ashore as a licensed private station in 1970.

Perhaps for this reason, in the early 1980s, pirate ships began to reappear on their old cruising grounds. Some even bore the old names, such as *Radio Caroline.*[10]

Domestic Pirates

The external pirates represented a response to the hitherto neglected youth market, fueled by the desire of advertisers to reach that market. But demands for access and for localized broadcast services remained unsatisfied, leading to a new wave of pirates, this time domestic. Though commercial interests played a large part in this movement, idealism played a part as well. People with common interests formed cooperatives to run domestic pirate operations. Numerous disaffected and offbeat groups reveled in the chance to air their points of view. It was access in its purest form. "Free broadcasting" became a symbolic act of disobedience that challenged monopolistic state broadcasting laws deemed unjust if not actually unconstitutional.

Italy. Private cable and broadcasting operations in Italy pioneered this movement as a protest against the official monopoly broadcaster, *RAI-Radiotelevisione Italiana.* The Italian pirates became at once the admired vanguard of the free broadcasting movements and the deplored example of the chaos that ensues when national broadcasting laws break down.

A government corporation owns more than 99 percent of the RAI stock company. Second in size in Europe only to the BBC, the RAI derives its funds from license fees (about three quarters of the total) and from advertising. In terms of numbers of transmitters per thousand population, Italy has the most densely concentrated facilities in the world, surpassing even the United States. One reason for the large number of transmitters is mountainous terrain. RAI uses nearly eighteen hundred television repeater stations to achieve full national coverage.

The Italian constitution mandates RAI impartiality, but for years the ruling Christian Democratic party used it as a political arm. To be sure, the law gave all political candidates equal access, but the party in power appointed all key RAI personnel. A 1975 reform law attempted to divorce the RAI from politics, but it seems only to have divided the spoils a little more evenly among the main parties without eliminating the practice of basing appointments on political affiliation:

> *Every problem and every undertaking was treated in terms of political categories. . . . Personal independence, freedom of opinion and respect for the public—values which ought to have taken precedence—had little chance of gaining currency. Efficiency and professionalism suffered too. In order to be accepted, all plans and projects needed a political or ideological justification.*
>
> *Thus the administration of RAI became the scene for continuous political skirmishing among directors, producers and journalists who often called on their external patrons to help them. (Cavazza, 1979: 96)*

ITALY

Naturally, the RAI lost credibility, even though the artistic level of Italian programs was high. RAI's failure to convert to color television when other major European systems made the change also caused alienation. Again, politics was at the root. Unable to decide between the SECAM color standard (vigorously promoted by the French and Russians) and the PAL standard (used by most other countries in Europe), the politicians kept putting off the painful decision. Not until 1977 did RAI finally begin colorcasting, using PAL. In the meantime, hundreds of thousands of Italian viewers had already begun to receive color from foreign sources.

Programs from abroad started to fill the vacuum created by RAI's shortcomings. Within convenient reach, suppliers in France, Yugoslavia, Monte Carlo, and Switzerland beamed signals into Italy. Television originating in these countries blanketed northern Italy, distributed to local cable systems by microwave relays. The demand for alternative programs can be judged by the fact that more than two thousand such relays were built, many with the help of local citizens. Manufacturers of color television sets also invested in relays to enhance the market for receivers.

The next move to fill the vacuum left by RAI came with the unauthorized installations of domestic, private cable television. A venturesome resident of Biella, a textile town in the Piedmont region, set up a small cable system in 1971, in defiance of RAI, which claimed that its broadcasting monopoly extended to cable distribution. Others quickly followed Tele Biella's example. Wrote an Italian commentator:

> It is difficult to convey to a foreign reader the enthusiasm which greeted these first experiments in cable television in Italy. The most emphatic and superlative language was used to describe them. The weekly magazines were full of articles which succeeded in giving one over-riding impression: that very soon Italy would be covered in cables, with hundreds upon hundreds of stations. . . . The desire to demolish RAI's monopoly [was] like a latter-day Bastille. (Cavazza, 1979: 102)

Tele Biella became famous all over Europe as a David challenging the RAI Goliath. It unleashed a decade of frenetic private station and network activity that finally broke the RAI monopoly and forever changed the shape of Italian broadcasting.

The chaotic events of the ensuing decade can be summarized briefly in terms of the following legal highlights:

- 1971—Tele Biella opens, inaugurating both a rush to install private cable systems and a suit by RAI.

- 1973—A court orders Tele Biella to disconnect its fifteen hundred subscribers because it violates RAI's monopoly.

- 1974—The Constitutional Court reverses the lower court, giving private cable systems and, implicitly, private broadcast stations the right to exist as long as they remain local in scope and do not cause interference. Importation of foreign programs and their distribution by relays are also constitutionally protected. Giving the green light to private local broadcasters effectively puts an end to the private cable land rush. In its place, a stampede into broadcasting begins, because over-the-air facilities require less capital investment than cable installations.

- 1975—The legislature passes a new law, formally ending the RAI monopoly except for *national* services; it permits local private broadcast and cable operations but not private *simultaneous* (that is, interconnected) network broadcasting. Networking thus remains an exclusive RAI prerogative. The new law directs the RAI to take steps to ensure access to its facilities by all major social groups.

- 1976—The Constitutional Court confirms RAI's legal right to retain its monopoly on national network broadcasting and the ban on interconnected networks of private stations.

- 1981—The Constitutional Court reaffirms its 1976 ruling against private interconnected networks.*

Following the 1974 decision legalizing private broadcasting, stations went on the air so fast and in such numbers that no one could keep count. At the height of the movement, perhaps 2,000-plus private radio and 450 private television stations were on the air. The majority had commercial motives, finding it easy to sell time, partly because of RAI's highly restrictive policy of lumping all commercials together in limited blocks of time. Moreover, RAI subsidiary SIPRA had a monopoly on time sales. SIPRA often forced time buyers to either purchase space in favored publications or stop buying space in publications associated with opposition political interests. Advertisers tolerated these practices only because they had no choice: RAI originally ran the only game in town.

Station proliferation naturally set off a mad scramble for program materials. Few private operators could afford anything but the most elementary production facilities for preparing local programs, though the movement claimed localism as a primary goal. By 1979, as the realities of broadcast economics caught up with the movement, the inevitable answer to program shortages began to emerge—the sharing

---

*In mid-1984, long-delayed new broadcast legislation—aimed at bringing the private Italian stations under supervision of an IBA-type agency and authorizing them to form networks—was still under consideration (Humi, 1984).

of programs by networks. The law against interconnected, or "hard," networks, as they are called, was ignored until reaffirmed by the high court in 1981, and even then it was not universally observed. A variety of noninterconnected, or "soft," networks evolved.* Leading private "networks" contracted with the major U.S. television networks for exchange of programs and know-how. By 1981 they were able to challenge RAI in both audience size and advertising volume.

RAI completely misread the meaning of the pirate stations. It dismissed them at first as "cheap and often sordid local operations, highlighted by late night programs, erotic 'C' grade movies used by local advertisers to attract viewers who wanted a change from the highly politicized, staid, and puritanical programs dished out by RAI" (Humi, 1982). Though many of the private stations undoubtedly deserved this description, not all did. RAI failed to discern the deeper meaning of these stations in terms of the access movement.

In sum, within the space of a decade, Italian broadcasting recapitulated the entire history of the medium's evolution. It illustrated the growth of access demands, the ways in which both internal and external forces tend to fill a broadcasting vacuum, the weaknesses of politicized government monopolies, and network growth as one answer to program shortage problems.

France. Though organized very differently from that of Italy, France's official broadcasting monopoly experienced the same problems of politicization (the system is described in Section 3.2). Inspired by the Italian example, hundreds of illegal stations opened in France in the late 1970s. The French government tended to be more adamant than most others in repressing pirates. It sent in police with tear gas to overcome defenders, often confiscated equipment, and resorted to electronic jamming to prevent audiences from listening to stations whose cases were on appeal.[11] In 1978, when the lower courts began finding in favor of pirate stations, the legislature amended the broadcasting law, strengthening the government's ability to impose fines and jail terms.

The French author of *Can You Guess Who's Speaking Tonight?*, a history of free radio, opens his book with an anecdote about *Radio Verte Paris*, an ecologically oriented pirate station that went on the air in 1977. One of the government television networks invited a leader of the ecological movement to participate in a panel discussing the outcome of the 1977 French elections. In the midst of the program, the ecologist suddenly thrust an FM receiver tuned to the pirate station before the television microphone. "Some millions of Frenchmen were able to hear a free radio

---

*Silj describes the various types of networks developed by Italian broadcasters (1981). He wrote the first comprehensive description in English of the conflict between private broadcasters and the RAI, based on a 1980 joint research project of the International Institute of Communications and a German foundation. For a more recent study, see Gurian, 1984.

station for the first time, thanks to the fantastic publicity coup of [the ecologist], who announced, 'Now you can hear *Radio Verte Paris* on such-and-such days and times and on such-and-such frequency' " (Bombled, 1981: 13). The free radio movement's seriousness can be judged by the fact that François Mitterrand, the Socialist elected president of France in 1981, put himself in the position of being arrested in 1979 for participating in illegal *Radio Riposte* broadcasts.

In the following year, the new Socialist government did indeed take steps toward liberalizing French broadcasting. The broadcasting authority licensed 88 private stations in the Paris region alone, nearly 1,000 in the country as a whole. Though authorized to operate only noncommercially, many nevertheless sold advertising. It was expected that eventually commercial operations would be formally permitted. "Surveying everything from religious sermons to gay rights, the raucous newcomers have provided a voice for all manner of minority interests. More important, they have set the stage for a comparable expansion of France's tightly state-controlled television system" (*Time*, 21 May 1984).

Great Britain. Even in the less regulated climate of Britain, domestic pirates crop up. In 1984 the home secretary announced plans for suppressing some 40 illegal domestic radio stations. Even pirate television operators existed, using BBC-2's London channel after signoff to furnish illicit all-night programs.[12]

Cable Pirates. In the early 1980s, Netherlands pirates began beaming signals to cable headend antennas late at night, after authorized Dutch cable television programming had ended (24-hour cable schedules were unknown in Europe). Pirates would feed unauthorized commercial programs, some of them pornographic, to cable subscribers all over Holland. Of course, authorized cable operators must have connived in the piracy. They benefited because longer and more varied programming attracted new subscribers at no cost to them.

The cable pirates stole program materials from various foreign sources. They even pulled in signals from a Russian satellite. They set up their own private regulations to share the profits, using gangster-style "enforcers" to discourage those who became too greedy. According to a Dutch writer,

> In no time at all these illegal late shows have become immensely popular, their very illegality enhancing their attractiveness for Amsterdammers. Indeed, everything here is illegal: the unlicensed [cablecasting], the commercials, the videotaping and broadcasting of films without the consent of the copyright owners, the breaking in to the cable system and maybe also the broadcasting of pornography. (Jehoram, 1982: 340)

These illegal operators even published a program guide, *The Pirate*, which printed not only the schedules of pirated programs but also the copyrighted details of the legitimate Dutch broadcasting schedules. Those whose rights the pirates infringed had no immediate recourse under the Dutch broadcasting laws, which had not anticipated the need to deal with such outlandish violations. Moreover, because broadcasting raises such controversial political issues, the government seemed unable to expeditiously amend the statutes to deal with the problem. In the meantime, the pirates' victims (including major U.S. film distributors) found the copyright laws their best ally in repressing the thefts.

Domestic cable pirates have flourished elsewhere as well. In Taiwan, for example, fly-by-night operators set up cable minisystems reaching from a few dozen to a few hundred subscribers, usually confined to a single housing development. They fed Japanese programs (banned by the Taiwan government because of Japan's recognition of mainland China) and pornographic shows. By charging a substantial installation fee (about $50), investors could make a quick killing. Like the Dutch pirates, those in Taiwan also attracted viewers by feeding programs after regular television stations went off the air.

4 ▪ 5 LOCALISM

The community urge to control local broadcast facilities recurs as a running theme in the preceding section on pirates. Most of the world's centralized, network-oriented systems eventually recognized the need for regionalized services but were slower to bring broadcasting down to the community level. Even regionalization sometimes came only belatedly. Italy, for example, introduced regionalized television programming in 1979 on RAI's TV-3, too late to stem the tide of private broadcasting.

Regionalized broadcasting often occurs for only an hour or two per day, when individual stations cut away from national networks. The British refer to "opting out"—giving certain stations the option of dropping off the network and inserting regional or local programs. Such limited concessions to the localization principle have been the usual practice. Opting out bears little resemblance to true localism, which implies the existence of stations able to supply continuous services that enter intimately into community life. The access movement dramatized the need for this type of dedicated local service.

Resistance to localism came from several directions. Central broadcasting authorities often opposed the loss of budget and control that having local stations could entail. Authorities also felt that in paying national receiver license fees, the public earns the right to a universal service, available on equal terms to all. Provincial newspapers feared competition from broadcasting. Shortage of standard (medium-wave) channels, especially in Europe, argued against squandering such precious resources on small coverage areas (FM, however, by supplying a new range of frequencies and by virtue of its inherently limited coverage area, largely removed this difficulty).

United States

Americans find it difficult to appreciate the intense hunger that people elsewhere sometimes feel for broadcast localism. After all, U.S. law recognized the value of localism from the outset. Americans therefore take for granted the existence of local stations and a certain amount of local programs on network stations. Elsewhere, however, true local stations are a relatively new feature of even highly developed broadcasting systems.

When radio broadcasting emerged in the 1920s, U.S. policymakers saw it as a promising way of reviving grassroots democracy by creating "town meetings of the air." Accordingly, Congress framed the broadcasting law to encourage licensing stations in every town, no matter how small—at least to the extent that free-enterprise economics and channel availability allowed. The states' rights principle also favored localism. Though accepting the constitutional necessity for federal control of broadcasting, the states nevertheless wanted to make sure that facilities would be parceled out fairly.

Thus arose a tradition of localism in American broadcasting, reinforced over the years by many rulings of the Federal Communications Commission. For example, the FCC favors local ownership over absentee ownership and requires applicants and licensees to show how they plan to deal with explicit local problems in their programming. The FCC expects all network affiliates to do some local programming, even those owned outright by the networks. In contrast, affiliates in other countries often function merely as passive repeaters of programs coming from the network headquarters station, originating no local programming on their own.

To cover a nation in the prodigal U.S. manner, however, uses up huge numbers of channels and transmitters. The overkill of 30 or 40 stations licensed to serve a single metropolitan area is one price that Americans pay for localism. But for the localism goal, fewer but more powerful regional stations would be far more efficient. Other countries tend to license the fewest possible stations needed for national coverage by two or three national network services.

Television lends itself less readily than radio to localism, because of both its high capital and programming costs and its shortage of channels. These drawbacks may be eased somewhat in the United States by the LPTV (Low Power Television) class of outlets, which the FCC authorized explicitly to make local television more readily available. And, of course, cable television offers an alternative type of video service that (for a price) surmounts the problem of broadcast channel shortages, at least in areas of high population density, which cable needs for cost effectiveness.

True, in practice the economics of programming and advertising tend to favor centralization over localism, especially since the advent of relays and syndicated radio formats. Cynics therefore dismiss the localism ideal in U.S. broadcasting as a mere fiction. In comparison with much of the world, however, localism in American broadcasting is alive and fairly well, even though not as healthy as originally expected.

Emergent Localism: Radio

Following are some examples of measures taken by established systems to introduce legally approved local radio stations.

Great Britain. The BBC responded earlier than most major European systems to needs for regional and local services. Northern Ireland, Scotland, and Wales received considerable autonomy early in the history of radio. However, localism did not come generally in the United Kingdom until the late 1960s.

In a study of local radio's role in democratic political processes, a Birmingham University researcher summarized the potential values of such a service:

> Ordinary citizens would acquire a new and effective channel for their views, demands and grievances. Their elected representatives . . . would become more available and more accountable. Local public officials would be flushed out to explain and answer for administrative action and inaction. Pressure groups would have a new platform on which to make their case and win support. The stream of local news would keep people informed about the issues and policies affecting their lives, supplemented by special investigations into particular matters of local concern. There would be a permanent arena for discussion and debate about local issues. It was thus possible to interpret the official phrases in concrete programming terms which made it plausible to claim for local radio a central place in a revitalized democracy. (Wright, 1979–1980: 2)

Given this activist agenda, little wonder that political establishments are not always eager to embrace localism!

The BBC introduced the first 8 of its low-power local radio stations in 1967–1968. Eventually about 50 are envisaged, subject to availability of funds. Each serves a single city and its immediate environs. BBC local stations can use any program they wish from any of the four BBC networks; in practice, however, they originate most of their own programming, as indicated by their average staff size of 30.

The Independent Broadcasting Authority received parliamentary permission to start franchising local commercial radio stations in 1972. The IBA uses local ownership as one criterion in choosing applicants. The first of these ILR (Independent Local Radio) stations, London's LBC, went on the air in 1973. It has a news and information format, the first station in Britain to employ so specialized a program schedule. During the startup phase, LBC personnel visited U.S. all-news stations to study their strategies. As in the case of its commercial television franchises, the IBA authorized two ILR stations to serve London. The second London outlet, Capital Radio, opened with a general entertainment format a few days after LBC in 1973. A total of 69 areas have been designated to receive ILR services (in some cases, two or more areas may combine resources to support a single station). In areas where listeners can receive both BBC and IBA local stations, ILR stations draw an average of a third of the potential audience (the rest of the audience is divided among BBC network and local services).

Proponents of what some British critics call "alternative radio" remain dissatisfied with the BBC and ILR brands of localism. They argue that in large cities these stations serve audiences in the hundreds of thousands and so cannot be truly local. Moreover, they inherit from their parent bodies an official viewpoint and a kind of professionalism that act as a straitjacket. Alternative radio advocates want small, essentially unregulated stations, operated with a great deal of informality and spontaneity. So far, the government has shown little inclination to move in that direction. It feels that proponents have failed to produce convincing evidence that alternative radio's output would differ significantly from that of existing local stations.[13]

Australia. Australia has a class of local radio outlets called Public Broadcasting Service, consisting of more than 30 low-powered outlets, mostly FM, operated by educational institutions and community associations. This service should not be confused with the publicly owned stations of the Australian Broadcasting Commission that supply the major national network services.

Ireland. Some 70 pirate radio stations operated in Ireland as of 1983, in competition with Radio Telefis Eireann (RTE), the government-operated system. Weak laws against unauthorized broadcasting, coupled with lack of political will to adopt severer penalties, allowed pirates to continue without serious checks. Finally, in 1983 the government introduced a law permitting the licensing of up to 30 privately owned radio stations, ending the RTE monopoly. Unlike such laws in other countries, Irish law permits the country's official service to hold shares in private stations (though only up to 25 percent). Existing pirates could apply for licenses, as could newspapers (the latter limited to a maximum of 49 percent ownership).[14]

Sweden. Sweden calls one of its five independent broadcasting companies, started in 1977, *Sveriges Lokal Radio AB* (Swedish Local Radio Corporation). Despite its name, this service seems more regional than local in orientation. It borrows "opt-out" transmitter time from the national radio networks to provide an hour or two of programming per day to designated provincial and metropolitan regions.

However, in 1978 Sweden also began experimenting with what it calls *närradio* (neighborhood radio). *När* stations operate independently of the regular national system and are open to groups "engaged in non-profit, charitable, political, union or confessional activity." Interest in local service was so intense that the licensing commission received 538 applications, from which it selected only 15 for the initial test. Licensees rent 10-watt FM transmitters from the Swedish Telecommunications Administration for about $1,500 per year. Licensee organizations include representatives of such groups as churches, political parties, labor unions, sports clubs, temperance societies, and motor clubs. Many such groups share in the operation of a single outlet. For example, a hundred groups jointly program two community stations in the Stockholm area.[15]

The commission responsible for recommending the test of this "infra-local" class of stations reasoned that modern communication technology tends to enable persons or organizations with ample funding to gain undue social control. "It is of great importance to democracy," said the commission, "that many small local groups have great influence on the media development and that a counter movement is formed against the tendencies toward the concentration of power" (quoted in Svard, 1982: 30). The Swedish telecommunication authorities foresee licensing two to three hundred of the *när* stations without causing harmful interference to the national network system, should the government decide that the experiment justifies all-out expansion of the new service.

The Netherlands. Access has been a central concern of the official Dutch broadcasting system. Its main component, the "pillarized" broadcasting associations, represents an institutionalized form of group access. In addition, the Dutch experimented with localized access via cable television, discussed later in this chapter.

France. The Socialists, who came to power in France in 1981 promising to reform the broadcasting system, adopted a new statute in 1982 authorizing local privately owned stations and cable services, with the state owning the transmission facilities.* As previously noted, the authorities licensed about a thousand former *radio libres*, all in the FM band.

Switzerland. In 1982, when the Swiss federal government invited local groups to apply for licenses to experiment with small radio or television stations, it received 269 applications—200 for radio, 17 for

---

*A few official experimental regional and local radio stations had been authorized in the late 1970s, but they were regarded as temporary, with no explicit statutory basis for existence (Toledano, 1983). The comprehensive law of 1982 (see Figure 5.1) confirmed an earlier statute, passed late in 1981, that authorized licenses for "free" or "associative," that is, private, stations (Ridoux, 1982: 12).

television, and 52 for pay-television schemes. The experiment aimed at nonprofit operation, with a limited amount of advertising permitted on radio but not on video programs. In the fall of 1983, the Federal Council granted 36 radio applications (plus 4 very low power proposals) and 7 television applications, postponing decisions on the pay-television applications.[16]

Emergent Localism: Television

The Swiss option for local television as well as radio was unusual. Localized television presents more difficult financial and programming problems than radio. Cable—with its potentially large number of channels and its tolerance (if need be) for sub-broadcast-quality productions confined to access channels—offers an alternative to local broadcasting. In fact, access advocates were among the earliest enthusiasts for cable television. In the United States, they persuaded the Federal Communications Commission, when it adopted comprehensive cable regulations in 1972, to require that cable companies make access channels available at no cost to users. It seemed that access programming might blossom profusely; with few exceptions, however, U.S. access programming failed to fulfill its initial promise, though it may yet revive.

With deregulation of cable a few years later, the FCC dropped its access rules, leaving municipalities to negotiate with franchise applicants as they wished. Franchise agreements continue to include provisions for access channels, but cable companies found that most subscribers want professional entertainment more than local access.

Notwithstanding the discouraging U.S. experience with local access cable channels, as well as some equally negative results in other countries, Europeans continue to hold out hope for them. Europe experiences much more difficulty with broadcast television channel shortages than does the United States; and because most stations function as parts of national or regional networks, they offer no opportunities for purely local access. Under such circumstances, cable often seems the only medium feasible for localism in television.

Great Britain. Although the British ITV companies are regional in scope, they cover large regions and most of their programming is in fact networked nationally. It remained for cable to offer the option of local television. In 1972 the British government licensed five experimental local cable services to provide community programming (the numerous existing cable companies in Britain originated no programming of their own, delivering only broadcast station programs). The experimental licenses required that grantees supply programs "designed to appeal specifically to the local community." Not allowed to sell advertising, the services soon found it impossible to stay in business on subscription fees alone. The government changed the license terms in 1975 to permit advertising, too late to save three of the firms.[17] Only one of the experiments, known as Swindon Viewpoint, appeared to qualify as a true local access operation according to the Annan Committee. As the committee put it, "If people can walk into their local [cable company premises], borrow equipment and use it as a means of talking to their neighbours, this is real access broadcasting. The station staff then become professional advisers to the community rather than programme makers" (Great Britain, 1977: 222). The committee recommended that cable television's future role in Britain should be primarily as an access medium. Later, more ambitious plans for a national, large-capacity cable network fed by satellite (see Section 2.6) put the future of these projects in doubt.

Australia. In 1980 the Australian Special Broadcasting Service (SBS) began offering multicultural television programs in Sydney and Melbourne. Designed to serve Australia's growing (and hitherto neglected) minority groups, SBS telecast in 30 foreign languages, primarily using imported programs but devoting a quarter of the air time to locally produced materials. The latter included "S*C*O*O*P" ("Significant Community Observations of People"), a local public affairs series featuring achievements of minority group members. Subtitling of SBS foreign language programs made them generally accessible to Australians. SBS also assists Australia's two ethnic radio stations.

The Netherlands. The Dutch Ministry of Culture began underwriting six local cable experiments in 1974. Later, the ministry phased out its support, expecting local city authorities to take over the responsibility. The cities failed to respond, and with the sale of advertising denied them, the experiments languished for lack of funds. In addition, it appears that some of the experimental operations failed to live up to localism goals, becoming simply small-scale versions of the national service and acting as mouthpieces for local officials.[18]

Despite these setbacks, in 1983 the Dutch government gave localism a new lease on life. A representative cultural organization in any community may apply for a license to originate its own programs and give access to any local person, group, or institution that wants to have a community voice. These organizations will normally use cable television but may use broadcast channels where cable may be impractical. Local governments must underwrite these local access projects, which may not use advertising as a means of support. However, traditional opposition to local advertising, based on concern for the viability of provincial newspapers, may be weakening. The Netherlands Scientific Council for Government Policy concluded that

> local television will only come about if advertising is permitted as a source of revenue. . . . Local industry and commerce—especially small businesses— would be clearly interested in the ability which they lack at present to advertise on television in the area in which they operate. (Netherlands, 1983: 35)

SUMMARY

Determining who should gain access to the medium and on what terms presents one of broadcasting's key political issues. It creates a dilemma, for camera and microphone cannot be made available to literally everyone. In the 1960s, a movement emerged whose members sought to broaden the right of access beyond the traditional users—professionals, experts, politicians, and people in the news. Frustrated would-be users resorted to various kinds of broadcast piracy to gain unauthorized access. Responding to these extralegal operations, many traditional, centralized broadcasting systems liberalized their programming and station-licensing practices to respond more sensitively to access demands. Local or community radio stations, representing a significant aspect of access, are becoming more common. Community television stations are not often practical, but access channels on cable systems offer an alternative.

NOTES

[1] For a discussion of the theory underlying the right-to-communicate movement, see Fisher & Harms, 1983.

[2] Webster, 1975. UNESCO followed with a volume of case histories detailing access experiments in the United States, Canada, and Europe (Berrigan, 1977).

[3] Howell, 1982: 48.

[4] *World Broadcast News,* October 1981.

[5] For details and a critique of these rules, see Smith, 1978: 99–105; Paulu, 1981: 224–236.

[6] Peyrefitte, 1981: 59. For details on the evolution of political broadcasting in France, see Thomas, 1977: 126 ff.

[7] For details of these unusual happenings in the annals of broadcasting, see Pierce, 1979: 62–77.

[8] See, for example, Bombled, 1981.

[9] Barron, 1982; Clines, 1979; *New York Times,* 21 April 1978.

[10] *TV/RAI,* January 190; *Broadcasting,* 2 Nov. 1981.

[11] See *TV/RAI,* Jan. 1980, for a roundup of the legal maneuvers against pirate broadcasters. Flichy, 1978, gives an early analysis of the free radio movement in France.

[12] *EBU Review,* March 1984: 56; *Asian Broadcasting,* 1984.

[13] Higham, 1982; Local Radio Workshop, 1983.

[14] MacSweeney, 1983.

[15] Browne, 1984.

[16] Audience estimates based on Joint Industry Committee Radio Audience Research data for spring 1982 (IBA, 1982: 208).

[17] See Lewis (1978) for details on British cable projects of this era.

[18] Hofstede & Kemme, 1979: 67.

CHAPTER 5

BROADCASTING LAWS

$\mathbf{M}$ ost people once took regulation of broadcasting for granted as a practical and ethical necessity. Even where constitutions forbade government interference with public communication, the law recognized that broadcasting differed from older media. That difference, policymakers thought, justified government intrusion.

However, with the rise of such challenges to the established order as pirate stations and the free radio movement, some questioned the inevitability of current forms of regulation. Moreover, when new but related forms of communication such as cable television and satellite relays came into widespread use, existing laws often proved inadequate to deal with the novel problems the new technologies introduced. Some governments reacted with even more regulation. The United States, however, moved toward *deregulation*. Advocates of deregulation argued that, given the new program delivery systems and the consequent broadening of choices for some consumers, market competition could serve the public interest better than regulations imposed by governmental fiat.

5•1 JUSTIFICATION FOR LEGAL CONTROLS

A few years after the introduction of scheduled radio broadcasting in the 1920s, governments began enacting statutory controls. They had four basic goals: (1) preventing technical interference among stations; (2) conserving channels because of spectrum scarcity; (3) treating the spectrum as a valuable national resource, dedicated to serving the entire people; and (4) preventing misuse of broadcasting's potential for influencing society. In fact, all but the last of these regulatory motives had already been recognized during the radiotelegraphy era. Regulated use of wireless had proved itself by saving lives and property in times of emergency at sea.

Broadcasting, however, brought new urgency to the need for regulation. It tremendously increased the number of stations on the air, each demanding the right to continue transmissions for many hours on end without interruption. Such extended usage contrasted sharply with the intermittent exchange of brief messages between a few coastal stations and ships at sea, the type of traffic that the first laws had been designed to regulate.

Need For Technical Controls

The potential for destructive interference among radio signals makes legislation essential to enable regulating technical aspects of radio communication. For example, rules must govern which services may use which parts of the frequency spectrum, control the siting of transmitters and antennas, and limit the amounts of power that each type of transmitter may use.* The advent of satellites made such needs even more urgent, on an international scale at that. New bands of frequencies suitable for satellites had to be allocated, and orbital positions had to be allotted. The need to standardize technical specifications to make items of equipment compatible and therefore able to work together also arises, although nationalistic political and economic rivalries sometimes interfere with standardization. Ideally, any television receiver would work equally well anywhere in the world; however, nations developed three rival color systems, along with other, more justifiable differences in standards. Where television services employing more than one technical standard can be received, viewers must buy converters if they want to enjoy all the available services.

Scarcity Factor

Another pragmatic justification for the government regulation of frequency use arises from the finite nature of the spectrum. Throughout the history of radio, but especially since the advent of broadcasting, the demand for frequencies has constantly increased. New services continually emerge, creating needs for new frequency allocations. Improved technology helps to make spectrum use more efficient, but acute shortages continue. With satellites has come scarcity of positions in the equatorial orbit, where satellites must be positioned to synchronize with the earth's rotation and so maintain a stationary position relative to their target areas on the earth's surface.

Scarcity has been the rationale most used to justify regulation of broadcasting on legal grounds, even when such regulation would not be legally defensible if applied to other modes of communication. This was

---

*Some deregulation enthusiasts, however, advocate complete liberation of at least some services, relegating them to "anarchy" or "bedlam" bands. Citizens' Band (CB) radio in the United States has already been deregulated to this extent.

the case in the United States, where the courts sanctioned FCC regulation of some aspects of program content, despite the First Amendment's command that "Congress shall make no law . . . abridging the freedom of speech, or of the press. . . ." The courts concluded that channel scarcity justified congressional limitation on the freedom of those lucky enough to own broadcasting stations, despite the First Amendment's prohibition. Regulation to ensure that frequencies would be used in the public interest, not merely in the personal interests of licensees, the courts concluded, served the larger purpose of the First Amendment.

Responsibility for Spectrum Management

The International Telecommunication Union characterizes as "natural resources" both the frequency spectrum and that imaginary circle in space 22,300 miles above the equator that defines the equatorial satellite orbit. Most countries agree on treating them as invaluable elements of their national patrimony. In this perspective, governments have a fundamental duty to protect such precious resources from abuse and to ensure that they will benefit the nation as a whole, now and in the future.

Neither the frequency spectrum nor the geostationary orbital circle is a real object, however; unlike a national park, a waterway, or a historic building, they are mere abstractions. The frequencies and orbital positions exist not as collections of entities but as descriptions of potentials, never realized until someone constructs a transmitter and begins to radiate energy. Does a musical scale exist if no one plays any music? Does the composer of a symphony in F major acquire any property rights to the key of F major? The radio spectrum, like the musical spectrum, can be precisely defined but remains intangible.

> *It cannot be exhausted (like fossil fuels) or temporarily or even permanently damaged (as the sea and the land). But it can be used or misused—used too much, when the result is interference, or used too little, and wasted. More than any other resource, perhaps, the spectrum requires careful management. It requires it on a global scale, yet to a fine degree. The mechanisms and the results of this management are often couched in engineering terms and calculations of esoteric meaning. (Howkins, 1979: 11)*

By what rules should such an elusive yet precious public good be managed? The rules that apply to other goods seem inappropriate. Until recently, the spectrum was almost universally considered exempt from the general rules applicable to economic goods.*

---

*In the 1960s, a pioneer dissenter from this view, R. H. Coase, began advocating "spectrum fees" for the right to use broadcast channels (Coase, 1966). Spectrum fees should be distinguished from "cost of regulation" fees. The FCC briefly collected cost of regulation fees to help recoup its operating expenses, but it suspended collection when legal technicalities arose concerning the scale of charges it imposed.

Potential for Social Control

Researchers on media effects have not agreed on the extent to which broadcasting actually realizes its potential for controlling society as a result of its widespread influence on human behavior. Even such a seemingly elementary question as how television violence affects real-life behavior remains a subject of debate among social scientists. Governments nevertheless tend to assume that broadcasting has tangible social effects. Television heightened concern about such effects, causing increased regulatory intervention. Governments now almost universally regard violence in television as likely to encourage aggressive behavior in real-life situations, and they regulate programs accordingly.

Second World governments take it for granted that media exert social control and seek to capitalize on that power. "Media in the Communist world have always been seen by their shapers as primarily tools of persuasion and education, and only secondarily as transmitters of information" (Mills, 1983: 167). Third World countries, often relatively permissive during the radio-only days, became more interventionist after television came on the scene. Though they regard broadcasting as an ally in social and economic development projects, they also view it as a possible threat to social stability. "The fear of broadcasting as a potentially disruptive factor," wrote Katz and Wedell in their survey of Third World broadcasting, "seems to occupy policymakers even more than its potentially positive role" (1977: 213).

Western democratic governments also fear that broadcasting may bypass elected leaders, directly influencing the public on political issues. This apprehension accounts for the otherwise cryptic complaint that broadcasters act as "unelected" spokespersons on political issues. Europe in particular, after its historical experience with demagogues who exploited broadcasting, feels the need to regulate closely the political uses of the medium. "In the main, West European governments are leery of relaxing controls on broadcasting, for fear that television and to a lesser extent radio might usurp the political prerogatives of parliaments in the realms of debate and conciliation. . . . A monopoly under government control is easier to control than a multiplicity of programming groups" (Homet, 1979: 9).

Deregulatory Trend

Economic theorists who began to achieve ascendancy in Washington in the late 1970s, however, argued that to rationalize spectrum usage, rights to it should be traded on the open market. Only then could a true economic value be assigned to broadcast channels and only then could their use respond fully to competitive market forces. Market economics would determine who among those otherwise eligible would be granted licenses to operate commercially valuable stations in any radio service. This *privatization* of the spectrum plays a key role in the ideology of deregulation.

Deregulation proponents assert that the scarcity of frequencies argument is no longer valid. Many channel shortages, they say, are more artificial than real. Engineers, with their professional tendency toward conservative calculation of risks, may have leaned over backward, setting unnecessarily high standards to prevent interference. The U.S. liberalization of channel assignment policies has actually enabled a great increase in the number of stations without corresponding increase in band allocations. Moreover, cable television allows for virtually unlimited channels. To be sure, they are not universally receivable broadcast channels operating in free space but closed-circuit channels operating within the artificial environment of coaxial cables. Nevertheless, their abundance undermines the scarcity argument and, consequently, part of the justification for government regulation.

Deregulators also believe that the marketplace, relying on competition, can standardize a new technology better than a government agency, relying on laboratory tests and a priori judgments. As examples, manufacturers of two incompatible videocassette recorders were allowed to market their products in the United States; broadcasters have been allowed to decide which of four competing AM stereo techniques to adopt, with minimal guidelines to prevent degrading present services; and the FCC authorized more than a dozen companies to go ahead with plans for direct-broadcast satellite services without setting technical standards for the all-important receiving antennas that homeowners will need to buy. Uncertainty about standards caused the United States to lag behind Europe in development of videotext services (see Section 8.5). Some of the more advanced technologies, however, such as high-definition television and digital signal processing, seem to be moving in the direction of early world standardization.

As broadcasting entered the 1980s, the United States stood virtually alone in considering adoption of spectrum privatization as a goal of official government policy. Other countries had been forced to make some accommodations, such as allowing private stations to compete with the hitherto monopolistic government-operated services, as in Italy. But the crowding together of many small nations in Europe creates horrendous interference problems; for these systems, spectrum scarcity remains an ever present reality.

Few objected when Britain renewed the BBC and IBA charters in 1981 on essentially the same terms as before, even though the *Financial Times* complained of the "paternalism and arbitrary authority of the IBA" and argued for "complete deregulation" (*New Statesman*, 16 Jan. 1981). Sweden's conservative response to the changing telecommunications scene typifies that of most West European countries:

> *The extent of the changes is obvious from the reports of three government commissions on different aspects of the new media, totalling 1,600 pages, which were presented to the Minister of Education and Culture in 1981. Their recommendations do not aim at deregulation. Rather, they signify that Sweden ponders a cautious re-regulation on the threshold of an era which is bringing fundamental changes in the media mix. (Svard, 1982: 29)*

As for the promised abundance of cable, Europeans already pay receiver license fees, whether or not they subscribe to cable services. Additional subscription fees for full-scale cable television would impose a further economic burden (and both receiver and subscription fees would still be paid, even for the set that never picked up over-the-air programs). In most of the Third World, government ownership of broadcast facilities and the general public's inability to buy even television receivers, much less to pay either license fees for broadcasting or subscription fees for cable, make discussion of spectrum privatization irrelevant.

Even more important than these practical considerations, however, is the official paternalism that most countries assume with respect to broadcasting. Governments assume a duty to protect the public both from technical interference to the detriment of clear reception and from private exploitation of the medium to the detriment of national culture. In the words of an American commentator on comparative communication policies, European critics tend to see the laissez-faire commercialism of American broadcasting as

> *the give-away of an enormously important social asset to people who fritter it away to make money satisfying the baser human wants. . . . Americans tend to say that the market must be relied on because no government can presume to decide what is in the best interests of the variegated public. But Europeans rejoin that they have pinned their faith on the possibility of getting a better wisdom than that of the marketplace. (Homet, 1979: 98)*

5·2 INTERNATIONAL BROADCASTING LAW

The International Telecommunication Union (ITU) furnishes a world-wide pattern for technical regulation. It covers not only broadcasting but also all other forms of nonmilitary radio as well as transborder wire communication. An agency of the United Nations since 1947, the ITU has a history of international regulation stretching back to 1865. In that year, 20 nations signed its first convention (in the name of the International Telegraph Union) to facilitate transborder telegraphic communication.*

ITU Organization

The ITU added radio to its responsibilities in the early 1900s and broadcasting explicitly in 1927. ITU member nations agree by treaty to abide by the *International Telecommunication Convention*. Signatory nations revise and renew this document at *plenipotentiary* conferences held at five- to

---

*The present ITU name dates from 1932. It became associated with the UN in 1947 (the UN itself having been founded in 1945). A sister organization, the Universal Postal Union, founded in 1874, also became a UN agency in 1947.

ten-year intervals, each in a different country. The convention (meaning in this context the agreement, not an assembly) functions as the *organic law* of the union.

When the sixth plenipotentiary conference took place in Nairobi in 1982, 3 of the 157 member nations—Belize, Grenada, and Zimbabwe—had joined the union only the previous year. Their presence aptly symbolized the shift in balance of power within the ITU away from the industrialized countries. During the single decade of the 1960s, 35 newly emerged Third World countries joined the union.

Between plenipotentiary meetings, the ITU permanent staff of about six hundred works year-round at its headquarters in Geneva. A permanent unit at Geneva of special interest to broadcasters, the *International Frequency Registration Board* (IFRB), keeps track of worldwide short-wave frequency usage. The ITU permanent staff organizes numerous world and regional technical and administrative conferences (WARCs and RARCs) below the plenipotentiary level. Since the first wireless telegraphy conference in 1903, more than 50 such meetings have dealt with regulation of radio communication (the ITU devotes separate conferences to wire communication). The 1982 Nairobi plenipotentiary meeting scheduled a series of 14 specialized conferences to be held throughout the 1980s.

An important World Administrative Radio Conference in 1979 (WARC '79) addressed the basic framework of the radio regulations, last revised in 1959.[1] It, too, scheduled further conferences, six regional and three worldwide. An idea of the complexity of such a conference as WARC '79 can be gleaned from some statistics: more than 200 delegates attended, representing 142 countries; they met for 11 weeks, considered 15,000 proposals (900 from the United States), used up 32 million sheets of paper, of which 1,100 were needed for printing the *Final Acts*. Significant acts affecting broadcasting included decisions to:

- Enlarge the band of frequencies allocated to AM broadcasting

- Enlarge the short-wave broadcasting band by 60 percent (though dissenters largely defeated or delayed implementation of this decision)

- Allocate for exclusive use of broadcast satellites frequencies that had previously been shared with other types of satellites

ITU Functions

Among many other things, the ITU sets up uniform standards to facilitate efficient interchange of telecommunications, regulates the use of the radio frequency spectrum, and gives technical assistance to developing countries. Its *Radio Regulations* standardize definitions of terms, set up a table of frequency allocations, make rules for the registration of frequencies used by member countries, specify measures for preventing interference, and allot alphabet letters for call signs so that each country's stations can be universally recognized. Like the Telecommunication Convention, the Radio Regulations come into effect upon ratification of treaties by member countries. The revised regulations adopted at WARC '79 filled 720 pages, incorporating more than 5,000 rules and 44 appendices.

National broadcasting controls usually work in a similar two-tier fashion: an organic law or group of laws (sometimes simply a decree or series of decrees) sets up a framework. Thereafter, a board, commission, government official or group of officials reduces the general mandates of the statute to operational terms as regulations.

Spectrum Management. The all-important process by which a station obtains the right to use a particular channel usually involves three distinct steps, two taken by the ITU and the third by the member country. First comes *allocation,* in which the ITU sets aside specific bands of frequencies for specific classes of stations. The ITU allocates bands for either exclusive or shared use by one or more services. Broadcasting is only 1 of 37 services enumerated in the regulations. Long-, medium-, and short-wave AM broadcasting all need their own allocations, as do FM radio and VHF and UHF television. In the next step, *allotment,* the ITU designates specific channels in some bands for use by stations within specific countries or regions. Finally, a given country *assigns* its allotted channels to licensed users (stations or broadcasting authorities) within its own territory. Because of their international reach, long-distance short-wave frequencies are an exception. The ITU does not allot these high-frequency (HF) channels to individual nations. Instead, each country selects the channels it plans to use within the allocated bands,* reporting its plans to the IFRB four months in advance; two months later, the IFRB issues a tentative schedule, pointing out any harmful interference that might arise from proposed uses and suggesting ways to avoid the interference. In this parceling out process, countries already well established as international broadcasters and employing high-powered transmitters have an advantage over newcomers to the scene.

Member countries usually find it in their best interest to comply voluntarily with IFRB suggestions; but if members refuse to comply or violate the Radio Regulations outright, the ITU has no means of enforcement or punishment.† External services seriously overcrowd the parts of

---

*Most of the short-wave (high-frequency, or HF) band is allocated to fixed and mobile telecommunication services. Broadcasting uses only a small percentage of the total band, which runs from 3,000 to 30,000 kilohertz (kHz).

†When members disagree with an action taken at an ITU conference, they may record their objections as "reservations" expressed in footnotes to the regulations, signifying their claims or their intention not to abide by specific decisions of the majority. Footnotes litter the Radio Regulations, with as many as 40 clustering below a single item.

the short-wave band used for international broadcasting. More than 40 nations broadcast "out of band," that is, in parts of the short-wave spectrum allocated to nonbroadcast services. The ITU permits out-of-band operation if no harmful interference results; but short-wave interference has reached such a level that international stations can reach their intended audiences only about 25 percent of the time.[2] Many experts agree (according to research conducted by Donald Browne, a leading U.S. student of international broadcasting) that out-of-band broadcasting, combined with the use of extraordinarily high transmitter power, may well cause a "total collapse" of the ITU system of managing the short-wave broadcasting bands during the course of the 1980s.[3]

The ITU allocates medium-wave (AM) broadcasting channels exclusively for domestic use, but nations often deliberately use them for broadcasts to other countries. The Voice of America's Marathon transmitter in the Florida Keys uses medium waves aimed at Cuba, while the Radio Moscow's relay station in Cuba aims medium-wave signals at the United States. East and West Germany also use medium-wave channels contrary to the ITU rules.

Changes in member countries' circumstances occurring between ITU administrative conferences can cause inequities solvable only by unilateral action. Prior to World War II, an ITU conference had allotted Germany 14 channels, the largest number for any European country. In 1948, during the Allied occupation of Germany, a subsequent ITU conference revised broadcasting allotments in the European area. Occupied Germany, barred from attending, ended up with only 8 medium-wave channels, and those few had to be split between East and West Germany. Postwar Germany actually needed many more channels than previously because of both the east-west split and the decentralization of broadcasting in the West. The two Germanies had no recourse but to use channels not allotted to them by the ITU. Similarly, the African colonies that became independent during the 1960s had been represented at the 1959 plenipotentiary conference by the colonial powers and so had no chance to press for spectrum allotments appropriate to their needs as independent nations.

On the whole, however, member nations abide by the ITU's allocation-allotment plans. For example, in 1974–1975 a two-part Regional Administrative Radio Conference (RARC) revised the European long- and medium-wave broadcasting plans. Wholesale changes in the allotment of twenty-seven hundred channels went into effect in 1978, at great expense to the affected countries. In addition, the 1974–1975 RARC narrowed the medium-wave channel spacing from 10 kHz. to 9 kHz., a change that enabled crowding more stations into the allocated band.

Call Signs. Orderly use of the spectrum makes it important that stations be readily identifiable. As an aid to positive identification, the Radio Regulations assign alphabet letters to each member nation to use in constructing call signs. All U.S. broadcasting call letters begin with *K* or *W* because the ITU has assigned to the United States the sequences KAA to KZZ and WAA to WZZ (plus NAA to NZZ and AAA to ALZ, used for nonbroadcast services).

The Radio Regulations do not mandate actual use of call letters on the air, however, and many countries identify stations by other means. Generally speaking, countries such as the United States, in which a great many private stations operate, find call letters useful because the stations could not readily be identified by town or network affiliation alone. The BBC identifies most of its stations in terms of networks— Radios 1 through 4 and BBC-1 and BBC-2 television. It identifies local stations by city or county—Radio Leeds, Radio Lancashire, Radio London, and so on. Some countries use call sign letters to identify stations by type. In New Zealand, for example, a *Z* as the second character in a call sign signifies a commercial station.

Development Aid. Lack of adequate telecommunications infrastructure (such as telegraph and telephone lines, radio communication networks, and broadcast relay facilities) poses a major problem for the less developed countries. The ITU gives technical assistance in these fields, using funds allocated by the World Bank and the United Nations Development Program. The ITU sends experts to assist in telecommunications development, donates equipment, recruits temporary specialized personnel, provides on-the-spot training of indigenous personnel, and supplies fellowships for study abroad. The ITU budgeted $210 million for such services in 1981–1982, the major portion going toward providing expert assistance and gifts of equipment. Africa, the chief beneficiary, received $68 million in assistance, followed by the Middle East, which received $50 million.

ITU Regions

Because of geographical and other differences among the parts of the globe, the ITU divides the world into three regions. Region I comprises Europe (including the USSR) and Africa, Region II, the Americas and some of the Atlantic and Pacific islands, Region III, Asia and the South Pacific. Because the problems of these regions obviously differ widely, for many subjects the ITU finds it expedient to adopt regional rather than universal rules. Some ITU spectrum allocations, for example, differ from one region to another. At the ITU's 1977 WARC for planning broadcast satellite frequency allocations, Regions I and III agreed to allotments of direct-broadcast satellite frequencies and orbital positions, but Region II postponed making decisions until a 1983 regional conference.

The 1981 Region II medium-wave conference discussed a proposal to reduce channel spacing to 9 kHz. Unlike the Europeans in their similar 1974–1975 conference, the Region II nations failed to reach a decision on switching from a 10-kHz. to 9-kHz. channel separation, even though such a switch would have made 12 additional channels available.

At that conference Cuba proposed changing, as a group, 48 of its allotted 180 medium-wave channels, without discussing the changes individually. The United States argued strenuously that this "block move" would cause harmful interference to U.S. stations. Voted down, Cuba withdrew from the conference before it ended and declined to sign the *Final Acts*. It gave as reasons not only the rejection of its block move proposal but also the U.S. plan to set up a station aimed at Cuba called Radio Martí.

Two months before the conference, the United States had announced its intention to launch Radio Martí, using a powerful medium-wave station located in South Florida, designed to tell the Cubans what the American government considered to be the truth about the Communist regime on the island (see Section 11.3 for details). Fidel Castro professed to be especially outraged that the United States had "sullied" the memory of a Cuban patriot in naming the station. Jose Martí, Cuba's most famous writer and the organizer of its war of liberation against Spain, died in battle in 1895.

Within each of its three regions, the ITU delimits a "Tropical Zone," roughly between the latitudes of Rio de Janeiro to the south and Cuba to the north. Static generated by tropical storms seriously affects medium-wave signals in these equatorial latitudes, making low-power domestic AM stations useless. The ITU allows countries in the Tropical Zone to use less affected short-wave frequencies for domestic coverage, thus making an exception to the general rule reserving short waves for international services.*

Is the ITU Obsolete?

For decades the ITU maintained that it concerned itself solely with technological, not political, matters. This ideologically neutral stance became increasingly difficult to sustain as colonialism receded and the Third World became increasingly critical of superpower domination:

> *The ITU has received promptings from many quarters to generate some structural and administrative reforms designed to furnish mechanisms for absorbing and taking into account political inputs. Currently, the ITU has developed neither traditions for dealing with political or ideological concerns nor the necessary administrative circuitry through which such conflicts could be channelled without crippling the ITU in its technical activities. (McPhail, 1981: 157)*

WARC '79, according to predictions, would precipitate a showdown. In the 20 years that had elapsed since the previous comparable world

---

*The Tropical Zone allocations actually straddle the upper end of the medium-frequency and the lower end of the high-frequency bands, between 2,300 and 5,060 kHz. The HF band begins at 3,000 kHz.

administrative conference, WARC '59, ITU membership had grown from 96 to 154. On the UN principle of equal voting rights for each member country, the Third World (often in alliance with the Communist world) could routinely outvote the industrialized nations. With three quarters of the world's population allotted less than 10 percent of the spectrum, Third World delegates felt they had a legitimate complaint about the way the ITU had managed the spectrum in the past.

If allotted greater shares of the spectrum, however, the less developed countries would be in no position to take advantage of most of their new opportunities. Should frequencies and orbital slots remain idle for decades, awaiting the evolution of Third World economies and technical proficiency? If not, would the industrialized nations accept temporary custody of allotments on the understanding that they would have to surrender them on demand at some future date?

The ITU survived WARC '79 with less trauma than had been predicted. The expected showdown did not occur, largely because the meeting postponed many crucial debates to specialized conferences to be held throughout the 1980s.

Sure enough, the confrontation grew more heated at the 1982 plenipotentiary conference in Nairobi. Wandering far afield from sober engineering considerations, the Arab countries attempted to expel Israel from the ITU, narrowly losing the motion by a 61–57 vote. Such provocations caused the U.S. delegation to threaten a walkout more than once. In an attempt to defuse some of the Third World rancor, the United States offered to step up its training assistance to developing countries. This promise resulted in establishment of the Telecommunications Training Institute, a facility headquartered in Washington and jointly sponsored by major U.S. communication firms and the government.

At the same time, however, the U.S. agencies concerned with the ITU's new direction began discussing alternate strategies to invoke in the (still unlikely) event of U.S. withdrawal from the organization. For example, the congressional Office of Technical Assessment reported that "it is conceivable that the United States could abandon ITU and establish a more congenial grouping of developed countries as a forum for coordination to avoid radio interference, and simply ignore other countries" (USOTA, 1982: 19). Alternatively, the office suggested, the ITU's one-country, one-vote formula might be modified to give more weight to the developed countries; or the ITU could extend regionalization so as to limit some decisions to the regions most affected. Despite such pessimism, the 1983 North American Regional Conference on DBS allotments went off without acrimony, leaving the U.S. delegation pleased with having been allotted the lion's share of the region's orbital slots.[4]

Non-ITU Regional Agreements

Nations sometimes make regional broadcasting agreements among themselves outside the auspices of the ITU. For example, the United States, Canada, Cuba, the Dominican Republic, and the Bahamas entered into the North American Regional Broadcasting Agreement (NARBA), negotiated in Havana in 1937. The participants granted each signatory priority in the use of certain medium-wave frequencies (clear channels). In compliance with NARBA, the FCC ordered nearly eight hundred U.S. radio stations to change channels in 1941 so as not to interfere with clear channels allotted to other countries, notably Mexico.

After the Castro revolution of 1959, however, Cuba began ignoring the restraints imposed by NARBA, finally withdrawing from the agreement officially in 1981. Both the Bahamas and the Dominican Republic also violated NARBA, reducing it in effect to a bilateral agreement between Canada and the United States. But in 1981 Canada, too, indicated its unwillingness to continue abiding by the agreement. A separate bilateral Mexican-U.S. agreement remained in effect.[5]

5 ▪ 3 EVOLUTION OF NATIONAL STATUTES

Summarized in broad perspective, national legal controls over broadcasting in Western systems evolved through four stages. The earliest stations came under the jurisdiction of prebroadcasting laws. Post, Telegraph, and Telephone (PTT) authorities adapted statutes originally enacted to govern maritime wireless. Next came the first laws explicitly designed to govern radio broadcasting as such, enacted in the 1920s and 1930s. World War II intervened before the next phase, breaking the continuity of development, especially in the defeated countries. In the postwar period, adaptation to television brought about the third phase during the 1950s. In the fourth phase, starting in the 1970s and continuing into the 1980s, the access movement, cable television, satellite communication, and other innovations presented new regulatory problems, precipitating a ferment of legal renovation (Table 5.1).

Prebroadcast Era

The historic origins of broadcast legislation can still be discerned in countries where the administrations responsible for the older communication services (generally PTT administrations) still play a role in the regulation, and sometimes even in the technical operations, of broadcasting services. West Germany illustrates both this precedent and the newer trend toward separate broadcasting authorities. Following World War II, when the Allied forces occupied Germany, the Western allies took ownership and control of broadcast technical facilities away from the national Post Office, handing them over to the broadcasting organizations of the several West German states. Later, the postal authorities came back into the broadcasting picture as the provider of television transmitter facilities.

The United States never had a centralized PTT as known elsewhere. The postal services, though operated as a government department until 1970, are now run by a self-supporting independent government agency. U.S. telegraphs and telephones have always been privately owned, as were satellite facilities later. The latter have had government aid from NASA (National Aeronautics and Space Administration). COMSAT, which operates INTELSAT on behalf of an international consortium and has domestic satellite subsidiaries, is owned by private stockholders, though the government helped launch it and has minority representation on its board (see Section 2.5).

Thus no centralized U.S. telecommunications authority like a PTT stood ready to take over radio when it emerged in the early 1900s. The Commerce Department administered the Radio Act of 1912, adopted in response to an international conference on the use of radio in emergencies at sea. Accordingly, when U.S. broadcasting began in 1920, the first stations obtained their licenses from the Department of Commerce. A separate federal regulatory law for radio came into being in 1927, predecessor of the present federal statute, the Communications Act of 1934.

As noted in Section 3.1, in Great Britain the postmaster-general severely restricted the first uses of the spectrum for broadcasting. After the BBC became an independent chartered corporation, it still had to secure channel assignments for its stations from the Post Office. Under the Wireless Telegraphy Act of 1949, the Home Office now plays this licensing role. This statutory separation of the licensing authority from the one that governs broadcasting operations is common. The ITU's Radio Regulations call for designating a single national "administration" to implement ITU rules within each member country. This entity concerns itself with technical supervision of all nonmilitary uses of radio within the nation, not just broadcasting. In the United States, the Federal Communications Commission plays this role.*

Sound Broadcasting Era

As Table 5.1 shows, leading countries of the non-Communist world adopted their first major broadcasting statutes between 1925 and 1935. The U.S. statute, the Radio Act of 1927, though not the first to be enacted, was the most comprehensive of the early broadcasting statutes. It created a federal agency to allot frequencies, license stations, and generally regulate all forms of radio communication. Congress replaced the 1927 act with the Communications Act of 1934, bringing together under one statute the federal laws governing both interstate and foreign communication by both wire and radio. The 1934 act, though often amended, remained in 1984 the oldest major broadcasting statute still on the books.

---

*The FCC controls assignment of frequencies to nongovernment stations only. Responsibility for assigning frequencies to government stations lies with the president, who is advised by the National Telecommunications and Information Administration. The State Department appoints U.S. delegates to top-level ITU conferences because agreements to ITU conventions have the status of international treaties.

TABLE 5 ■ 1 PHASES IN DEVELOPMENT OF BROADCAST STATUTES

Country	Radio Law Phase	TV Law Phase	Contem- porary Phase	Comments
Denmark	1925	1959		
Sweden	1925	1953	1979	
United Kingdom	1926	1954	1981, 1984	The BBC charter, issued in 1926, became effective 1 Jan. 1927. The IBA was founded in 1954. The 1981 act does not cover new technology; hence the 1984 act.
Ireland	1926	1960	1976	
United States	1927, 1934			The Communications Act of 1934 reenacted the 1927 law. Starting late in the 1970s, attempts to rewrite the 1934 law began.
Italy	1927	1948	1975	As of 1984 laws governing private broadcasting were still pending.
Netherlands	1930	1967		
Mexico	1931	1960		
Switzerland	1931			The 1931 law deals only with technical regulation; several attempts to pass a federal law covering other aspects failed.
Argentina	1933	1953, 1957		The 1953 law came under Peron, the 1957 law, after his exile.
Australia	1932	1956	1983	
Brazil	1932	1963		
Canada	1932	1952, 1958	1976	
France	1933	1964, 1974	1982	De Gaulle's law came in 1964, d'Estaing's in 1974.

NOTE: In Phase 1, prebroadcast (radiotelegraphy and radiotelephony) laws passed in the early 1900s prevailed; special laws governing radio broadcasting emerged in Phase 2; adaptation to television occurred in Phase 3; currently most nations are attempting to develop Phase 4 laws, integrating regulation of cable TV, satellite broadcasting, videotex, and other such technologies with existing statutes.

Table 5.1 omits broadcasting laws of Austria, Japan, and Germany because World War II interrupted their evolution. One goal of the Allied occupation authorities in those countries was the destruction of the centralized propaganda machines their enemies had assembled. Eastern European systems lost most of their broadcasting facilities during the war. Upon being rebuilt, they came under control of the ruling Communist parties. Also, many colonial territories became independent during the postwar years. These new nations too experienced a break in the continuity of broadcast law when colonial regulation gave way to national autonomy.

Television Era

The advent of television in the early 1950s put a strain on the old radio statutes, introducing new problems not only in the technical sphere but also in terms of finance, programming, and concern for social effects. As Table 5.1 shows, revision of the old radio-only statutes took place in the latter half of the 1950s and the early 1960s. The U.S. act of 1934 stands out as one of the few able to adapt to the television era. Television stimulated a number of amendments to the act but made no change in its basic philosophy of regulation. Congress had ensured flexibility by leaving day-to-day regulation to the Federal Communications Commission (which the act created).

Both the act and the commission have been much criticized, especially since deregulation policies began taking effect in the late 1970s. Yet looked at comparatively, the 1934 act seems a remarkable legislative achievement. For all its shortcomings, it proved able to accommodate the most profound changes, permitting reasonably rapid development of new technologies without allowing them to disrupt completely the older technologies in the rush of new services to gain market footholds.

Era of New Technology

A combination of social changes and technological innovations precipitated the current phase of legal evolution. The Annan Committee on the future of broadcasting in Britain undertook the kind of soul searching that went on in many Western countries at about that time. In its 1977 report, the committee spoke of Britain's altered climate of opinion:

> The ideals of middle class culture, . . . which had created a continuum of taste and opinion, always susceptible to change and able to absorb the avant-garde within its own urban, liberal, flexible principles, found it ever more difficult to accommodate the new expressions of life in the sixties. The new vision of life reflected divisions within society, divisions between classes, the generations and the sexes. . . . Every major broadcasting country in the West felt these tensions, but there was a special reason why British broadcasting was taken by surprise. For years British broadcasting had been able successfully to

create, without alienating Government or the public, interesting and exciting popular network programmes from the world of reality as well as the world of fantasy. . . . These now began to stir up resentment and hostility, and protests against their political and social overtones. (Great Britain, 1977: 14–15)

In the next year came the first of a series of U.S. attempts to wipe the 1934 statute off the books. All across the broadcasting scene, nations began rethinking their telecommunication policies, wrestling with demands for access and localism; with decisions as to how cable television, satellite relays, direct-broadcast satellites, pay television and teletext should be integrated with traditional broadcasting; and with the question of the most desirable mix of private enterprise and public service. In Britain, for example, a research unit composed of representatives from the BBC, the IBA, and the British Film Institute (with financial help from the Markle Foundation of New York) recommended setting up an entirely new authority, the Cable and Satellite Television Authority. Its role would be to award franchises, license program suppliers, control foreign program quotas, and generally supervise the program quality of cable and satellite services.[6] These recommendations were embodied in the Cable and Broadcasting Act of 1984.

The French statute of 1982 (discussed in Sections 3.2 and 4.5) is one example of the new, comprehensive types of laws enacted in the 1980s. The French used the term *audiovisual communications*, under which they combined provisions for state-controlled national, regional, and local broadcasting (with the option of private ownership of some local stations); external services; centralized units for transmission, production, marketing, and advertising agency functions; authorization of cable television; "telematics" (the various forms of electronic text delivery); assignment of frequencies; advisory councils; training; and research. Figure 5.1 shows the complexity of the resulting legal structure. But that was not all: in addition, the French PTT continued to play a role as the authority responsible for installing a nationwide, broadband cable system, programmed in part by PTT itself with teletext materials.

New technologies have thus brought new life to some of the old PTT organizations. Another example is the German *Bundespost*'s plan to install a national cable network during the 1980s. Britain, which pioneered the PTT concept when it awarded the Post Office a monopoly on telecommunications in the nineteenth century, has a similar cable network plan. However, there the postal and wire communication functions have been split into two state-owned corporations. Wire communications come under the wing of British Telecom, which, in a British deregulation initiative, was due to be sold to private investors early in the 1980s. The British planned to create a new technological regulatory agency to oversee private telecommunications operations. In most other countries, however, governments continue to own the national telecommunications facilities, thus exempting them from this FCC type of public regulation:

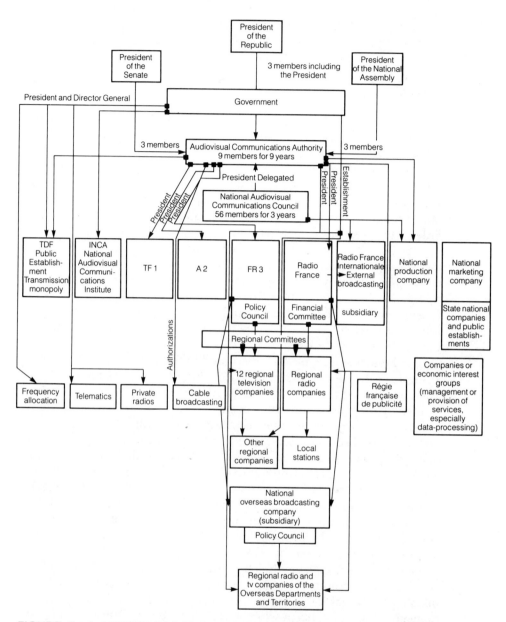

FIGURE 5 ▪ 1 FRENCH BROADCASTING LAW OF 1982. Source: Georges Ridoux,
"Audiovisual Communications in France, Stage 2: The Act of 29 Jan.
1982," EBU Review 33-6 (Nov. 1982), p. 11. Used by permission.

From a North American point of view, perhaps the most notable fact about the
European PTTs is the total absence of any independent regulatory authority.
Rates and service conditions are not subject to the kind of public accountabil-
ity made familiar in the United States and Canada by the FCC and the
[Canadian Radio-Television and Telecommunication Commission]. There is,

moreover, no detached forum for the resolution of inter-industry disputes over the provision of the newer forms of electronic service—broadband cable, for example, or teletext. (Homet, 1979: 16)

Definitions of Terms

As one of its elementary tasks, a broadcasting statute should define *broadcasting* and related terms. Most countries, by virtue of having ratified the ITU's *Radio Regulations*, accept the ITU definitions as basic. However, member countries often add qualifications of their own.

Broadcasting. The ITU *Radio Regulations* define *broadcasting* as only 1 of 37 basic types of radiocommunication services. An adequate definition of any service, therefore, must cover both the generic term *radio* and a specific application. Here are the ITU definitions as they appear in its *Radio Regulations*, followed by the U.S. versions as they appear in the Communications Act of 1934.

> Radiocommunication Service. *A service . . . involving the transmission, emission and/or reception of radio waves for specific telecommunication purposes. (ITU, 1980: 33)*
> Broadcasting Service. *A radiocommunication service in which the transmissions are intended for the direct reception of the general public. The service may include sound transmissions, television transmissions, or other types of transmission. (ITU, 1980: 35)*
> *"Radio Communication" or "communication by radio" means the transmission by radio of writing, signs, signals, pictures, and sounds of all kinds, including all instrumentalities, facilities, apparatus, and services (among other things, the receipt, forwarding, and delivery of communications) incidental to such transmission. [47 USC 153(b)]*
> *"Broadcasting" means the dissemination of radio communications intended to be received by the public, directly or by the intermediary of relay stations. [47 USC 153(o)]*

Common Carriers. A significant line of demarcation separates broadcasting from common carriers. Telegraphs and telephones, the typical common carriers, make their services available to all users on a first-come, first-served basis upon payment of standardized fees. The owners and operators of carriers have no control over who provides the messages or what the messages contain; thus they cannot be held responsible for message content. Broadcasters, in contrast, have the right—and indeed the duty—to choose the users of their facilities and to assume responsibility for meeting content standards. The terms *conduit* and *content* conveniently summarize the difference: common carriers supply only a message conduit, but broadcasters supply both the conduit and the content that flows through the conduit.

Occasionally, broadcasting services cross the line that normally separates them from common carriers by offering limited types of person-to-person message services:

> *A distinctive feature of Austrian radio is the wide use to which the medium is put for passing on various sorts of messages. . . . There are regular announcements about lost or stolen property . . . requests for witnesses to accidents, and personal greetings, for all of which a small fee is payable. Other messages, such as official announcements, SOS messages, and announcements from religious, charitable and educational bodies may be made free of charge. (Sandford, 1976: 147)*

NOS, the umbrella broadcasting organization of the Netherlands, makes its facilities available for urgent messages to tourists who might be unreachable by other means. Australian law permits use of broadcasting for personal messages not only in emergencies but also for "birthday and cheerio calls." Developing countries often press broadcasting into personal use when common carrier services prove inadequate, as in Mexico, where for a small fee broadcast stations in rural areas "carry messages to isolated or remote individuals" (Noriega & Leach, 1979: 42).

Relays. The FCC classifies relay stations as common carriers, defining them as stations "used for the reception and retransmission of the signals of another station or stations." Relays are vitally important to broadcasting because they make possible true networking—that is, the *interconnection* of an originating station with one or more affiliated stations so that all can broadcast the same programs simultaneously. True networks usually lease common carrier wire, cable, microwave, or satellite facilities for interconnection. Of course, noninterconnected groups of stations can also arrange to broadcast the same programs simultaneously by coordinated use of recordings, but such stations constitute only *pseudonetworks* (see the discussion of "hard" and "soft" networks in Section 4.4).

Normally, regular home receivers cannot pick up relay signals. Relaying of a sort can also be done, however, by means of *rebroadcasting*. An affiliate picks up the *broadcast* programs of the originating station or another affiliate, retransmitting them on its own channel. Short-wave international services routinely use rebroadcasting, though it is usually called relaying. The BBC's External Services, for example, send programs overseas via short wave from Daventry and other transmitter sites located within the British Isles. British stations overseas, such as the one on Ascension Island in the South Atlantic, pick up the Daventry signals and rebroadcast them—to Africa and South America in the case of the Ascension Island facilities. However, the Daventry transmitters use frequencies designated for public reception, as do the transmitters on Ascension Island. Neither, therefore, qualifies as a common carrier, but the BBC nevertheless refers to the Ascension Island station as its Atlantic Relay.

Cable TV. Neither the ITU regulations nor most national broadcasting laws had settled the legal status of wired radio and cable television services in relation to broadcasting during the early 1980s. Logically, dependence on physical conduits sets wired radio and cable television apart from broadcasting, the wirelessness of which constitutes one of its unique features. But cable television started as simply a means of extending the reach of broadcasting stations, and in fact most of the world's cable services still have this sole function. As such, they can be viewed in practical terms as integral to the broadcasting services whose signals they deliver. Accordingly, some countries so classify them in their statutes.[7] However, putting cable under existing broadcasting statutes could inhibit its growth because of rivalry between the two methods of program delivery. Consequently, a trend toward new statutes and separate regulatory agencies for cable has emerged.

As it happens, U.S. law makes a sharp distinction between cable and broadcasting but gives the Federal Communications Commission jurisdiction over *both* wire and wireless interstate communication. The "cable" of cable television qualifies as a kind of wire, and its services often involve interstate transmission of program materials. In 1972 the FCC issued the most comprehensive set of cable television regulations ever compiled. Since then, however, deregulation has freed cable of many federal restraints. Surrender of federal jurisdiction enabled states and municipalities to impose restraints of their own, primarily as stipulations in franchises issued to cable operators by local communities. Such deference to local jurisdiction comes as a natural outgrowth of the fact that installation of cable services depends upon the use of physical rights-of-way and public facilities controlled by local or regional political authorities.

Another controversy swirls around the question as to whether cable television should be classed as a common carrier. In practice, most cable operators behave like common carriers much of the time: they supply a conduit but take no part in most decisions about content, relying instead on program originators (television stations or cable program suppliers) to deliver preassembled program services. Some cable operators originate programs themselves, but locally produced content plays only a minor role in the overall menu of program services. As for access channels, by definition accessors, not cable operators, control their own content. Most cable installations enjoy a common carrier–like monopoly within their areas of coverage, either as an explicit stipulation of their franchises or simply as a de facto condition because duplicate cable facilities would be uneconomic.*

These ambiguities arise as typical byproducts of the changing character of communication technology. As a result of the process of technological *convergence*, services once clearly distinguishable from one another now tend to blend and intermingle. Even the press versus broadcasting dichotomy begins to break down with the prospect that

---

*U.S. cable operators call such duplication overbuilding. Only a few communities have dual systems, though most franchises permit overbuilding in principle to avoid conflict with state and federal freedom of expression laws.

newspapers may in the future electronically deliver their content to some readers in their homes, using either the television receiver as a display terminal or a special device to make on-the-spot printed copies.

5·4 FEDERAL VERSUS STATE CONTROL

The selfsame broadcasting outlets can function on either a national or a local-regional level. Depending on how policymakers exploit this distinctive attribute, the medium can serve as either a centripetal, unifying national force or a centrifugal, divisive force. For this reason, political entities that have surrendered part of their autonomy to a central, federal authority find broadcasting an especially sensitive subject. Should jurisdiction over a medium that ignores state boundaries rest with the states or with the federal authority? An ideal system would strike a balance between the needs of the federal government for an all-embracing national voice and the demands of the state governments for preservation of their local rights and cultural identities. National services compensate for local insularity and parochialism; regional and local services prevent the national government from overwhelming the sense of grassroots community.

U.S. Federalism

The U.S. Constitution clearly gives the federal government jurisdiction over interstate and foreign commerce, leaving little room for argument. It remained only to confirm that communication by radio is indeed a form of interstate or international *commerce.* A court decision provided this reassurance shortly after passage of the Radio Act of 1927.* As a counterpoise, the act directs the Federal Communications Commission to distribute licenses, in response to demand, "among the several states and communities [so] as to provide a fair, efficient, and equitable distribution of radio service to each of the same" [47 USC 307(b)]. In the past, the commission has taken this directive to mean that the public interest requires that all stations, including those owned by national networks, *localize* some of their programming so as to serve explicit needs of their communities of license. Accordingly, there has always been an element of localism in the regulation of U.S. broadcasting.

Broadcasting can be more efficiently regulated at the federal level than on a state-by-state basis. Radio transmissions cannot be arbitrarily shut off when they reach state boundaries. Nevertheless, for some countries the importance of local cultural autonomy outweighs the drawbacks of decentralized regulation at the state level. Postwar West Germany, a republic made up of 11 federated states (including the city of West Berlin as one of the states), serves as a key example.

---

*In 1929 a federal court of appeals confirmed that commerce, as constitutionally defined, does in fact include radio communication (31 F. 2d 448).

West Germany

In the aftermath of World War II, the Allies divided Germany into four military occupation zones. The division between the Soviet zone and the three zones of the Western powers eventually hardened into the present wall between East and West Germany. Berlin, the former capital, though likewise divided, remains stranded within the territory of East Germany, a hundred miles from the East-West frontier.

After the German defeat, the Allies restored radio broadcasting without delay. They urgently needed to communicate with the demoralized population so that orders could be issued, food distributed, rumors dispelled, and the routines of daily life restored. But the Allies also wanted to prevent revival of the centralized control over national communication facilities that the Nazis had perfected. Accordingly, the new constitution of West Germany gave the states rather than the federal government jurisdiction over all *cultural* matters—and broadcasting qualified as a cultural rather than a commercial matter.

Under American, British, and French tutelage, each West German state (*Land,* plural *Länder*) could acquire its own regional broadcasting system. Some states, however, opted to combine their resources with others because of geographic and other practical considerations, so the 11 states ended with only 9 regional broadcasting organizations (see Table 5.2).

Each of the Allies promoted a somewhat different broadcasting philosophy, though none favored transferring its own model directly to the German situation. The British public corporation model had the most influence on the system that finally emerged when the Western powers withdrew. According to one historian, "To this day the Federal Republic's broadcasting corporations have more in common with the BBC than with any other broadcasting service" (Sandford, 1976: 71–72). However, remember that the BBC provides *national* services, while the German corporations become national in scope only by means of interstate treaties. Their mode of national network operation somewhat resembles that of the British ITV regional program companies, which combine resources to operate nationally part of the time.

ARD. After several years of negotiation, in 1950 the *Länder* formed a cooperative broadcasting organization known as ARD.* Jointly produced common radio services of ARD (amounting to national network services) include two all-night programs, one light and the other classical music, and special programs in foreign languages for "guest

---

*ARD stands for *Arbeitsgemeinschaft der öffentlich-rechtlichen-Rundfunkanstalten der Bundesrepublik Deutschland.* This unwieldy name "was carefully chosen to denote the relationship that the broadcasting authorities were creating among themselves; the German is so deliberately precise that it defies effective translation." Roughly, it means "Federation of the public broadcasting corporations of the Federal Republic of Germany" (Williams, 1977: 15).

TABLE 5 ▪ 2 WEST GERMAN STATE BROADCASTING
ORGANIZATIONS (ARD)

ARD Member	Headquarters City	Geographical and Political Region	Percentage of ARD TV Network Programming Contributed
WDR	Cologne	West: North Rhein-Westphalia (west-central)	25
NDR	Hamburg	North: Hamburg, Schleswig-Holstein, and Lower Saxony	19
BR	Munich	Southeast: Bavaria	17
SWF	Baden-Baden	Southwest: Baden-Baden segment of Baden-Würtemburg and Rheinland-Palatinate	9
HR	Frankfurt	East-central: Hesse	8
SFB	Berlin	East: City of West Berlin ("Free Berlin Transmitter")	8
SDR	Stuttgart	South-central: Würtemburg segment of Baden-Würtemburg	8
RB	Bremen	North: Bremen (city-state)	3
SR	Saarbrücken	Southwest: The Saar	3

workers." Basically, however, each of the nine state broadcasting organizations produces its own radio programming, which generally consists of three regional services in each *Land*.

The cost of regionalized television on this scale would have been prohibitive, but ARD served as an invaluable ready-made foundation on which to mount a cooperatively programmed national television network. ARD television began operations in 1954 (German postwar television itself began in 1952). All the state broadcasting authorities contribute programs to the national network in amounts proportional to their respective financial standings, as shown in Table 5.2. The largest, WDR (*Westdeutscher Rundfunk*) comprises a quarter of the entire population and contributes 25 percent of the network programs. Each of the smallest units contributes 3 percent of ARD's network schedule.

Despite discrepancies in size, each state broadcasting organization undertakes to produce a full range of program types, with the exception of national news, weather, and sports. NDR (headquartered in Hamburg) specializes in national and international news production for the network, while Hesse (headquartered centrally in Frankfurt) handles national weather reporting. ARD members work together to coproduce sports programs of national interest.

Using a "complex formula and incessant negotiations" among the nine regional organizations, ARD revises its network schedule every six

WEST GERMANY

months (Toogood, 1978b: 84). The states feed their respective contributions to the network through a switching center at ARD's headquarters in Frankfurt. There the member organizations take turns annually as administrators in charge, so that an ARD bureaucracy cannot become so entrenched that the tail begins to wag the dog. Members may opt-out of the ARD network to avoid carrying programs to which they have objections. Network programming begins in the evening at 8:00 P.M.; before that hour, members schedule their own regional programming in their respective areas, using the same transmitters as does the network.

ZDF. West Germany's decentralized system met a crucial test in 1961, when the time came to add a second national network. The federal government, then led by Chancellor Konrad Adenauer, attempted to launch the second network under its own auspices. The *Länder* appealed to the federal Constitutional Court, which ruled that they alone had the authority to set up broadcasting organizations, even though the technical aspect of radio services falls under federal jurisdiction. This decision cleared the way for the states to set up their own second network. ARD had already begun such a second service, but the states wanted to introduce an element of competition rather than merely have the equivalent of a BBC-1 and a BBC-2. Accordingly, the states designed an entirely new organization, ZDF (*Zweites Deutsches Fernsehen*, or Second German Television), which went on the air in 1963.

The second network differs from ARD in major ways without compromising state control. ZDF consists of a single centralized organization solely devoted to programming and producing national network television. It relies on the *Bundespost* (the PTT) for its transmission facilities, in contrast to ARD, which owns its own transmitters. Four major *Länder* cooperate in running ZDF on the basis of a formal treaty among the states.

Two years after the second network began, the basic pattern of West German television services neared completion with initiation of a third network, primarily regional in scope and devoted to elite programming.

Austria: A Contrary Example

West Germany's neighbor, Austria, though also a federal republic (with nine *Länder*), went in the opposite direction. It too underwent four-way occupation by the Allies, each of which installed its own version of broadcasting. Though the Allies advocated decentralized control, as in Germany, the Austrians resisted this trend. Again as in Germany, the issue went to the Constitutional Court, but unlike its West German

SWITZERLAND

counterpart, the Austrian tribunal ruled in 1954 that broadcasting was indeed subject to federal control.

Austria became independent again in 1955, the year television began there. Two years later, the central government placed broadcasting in the hands of a company jointly owned by itself and the states. Under the coalition government then in power, however, the company walked such a tightrope politically that its programs were "reduced to timidity and insipidity as their directors and producers sought desperately to avoid offending each other" (Sandford, 1976: 143).

Dissatisfaction with this state of affairs led to a new federal law in 1976. It retained joint federal-state government ownership of the broadcasting company but also gave assurances of political and financial independence. The Austrian system then came into its own, growing "from one of the most backward to one of the most progressive of the European broadcasting organizations" (Sandford, 1976: 144). The ORF (*Österreichischer Rundfunk*) operates three radio networks and two television networks.

Swiss Federalism

Cultural and linguistic plurality complicate the relations between the Swiss central government and its constituent "states." The Swiss confederation consists of 22 cantons; even below the level of these quite small units, the Swiss insist on governing themselves locally: "Voters are regularly called upon to deliver their verdicts on every conceivable area of civic administration, ranging from the election of nursery school teachers to the widening of a piece of pavement" (Sandford, 1976: 156).

About 73 percent of the population speak dialects of German, 20 percent speak French, and 6 percent Italian. An additional 1 percent speak an ancient Romance language, Romansh. All four languages have official status in Switzerland. The three main language groups control domestic broadcast programming through special associations, some 15 of which form federations in the German, French, and Italian communities. They in turn form the Swiss Broadcasting Corporation (SBC). Organized in 1931, the SBC coordinates use of the federally operated transmitter networks and also supplies a national news service. Each major language group offers a choice of two regional radio network services and a single regional television service. One of the German radio networks carries a few programs in Romansh. To put it mildly, "The organization of Swiss broadcasting is remarkably complex for so small a country"(Sanford, 1976: 183).

The federal government limits itself, perforce, to collecting receiver

YUGOSLAVIA

license fees and operating the transmitter facilities, both done by the PTT. The legal basis for federal jurisdiction over these functions rests on a 1922 telegraph law. Aside from the limited federal oversight by the PTT, the Swiss central government finds itself in the anomalous position of being without a comprehensive national broadcasting law.

The SBC, as a quasi-private corporation, has a "concession" from the central government to coordinate the activities of the local language-oriented broadcasting associations. In 1957 the central government proposed a constitutional amendment, vesting jurisdiction over broadcasting in the Swiss confederation, but the voters turned down the proposal. Subsequent attempts at federalizing control over broadcasting, one as recent as 1982, have likewise failed to win majority support.[8]

Canadian Federalism

Ten provinces and two territories make up the constituents of Canada as a federation. Relations between the provincial legislatures and the central government have often been stormy. In particular, the French-speaking province of Quebec and the oil-rich western provinces have resisted federal domination. The courts have confirmed federal jurisdiction over broadcasting, but cable television has rekindled federal-state rivalries: "Some provinces claim that cable TV takes place entirely within provincial territory and should be under their control. Other provinces have laid claim to all aspects of broadcasting because it is so vital to their cultural life" (Shea, 1981: 128).

Communist Federalism

China comprises 21 provinces and 8 other autonomous units, while the Soviet Union consists of 15 union republics. These countries are so huge and their populations so diversified that they necessarily depend on a certain amount of regional autonomy in their broadcasting systems. The omnipresent Communist cadres, with their tight hierarchical organization, ensure centralized control nonetheless. Regional autonomy may be more genuine in contemporary China than in the USSR, according to reports. One observer of the Soviet scene, for example, reported that although each Soviet republic has its own regional television network, much of the supposedly regional programming actually originates in Moscow. Similarly, although regional programs theoretically use the principal regional languages, in practice those languages may be dubbed over original Russian sound tracks; indeed, sometimes the original track itself is used.[9]

NIGERIA

Unique among the Communist nations, Yugoslavia grants a measure of real autonomy to its six states (called "republics") and two "autonomous provinces." Profound ethnic, linguistic, religious, and historical differences divide these constituent parts of the federal republic. Jealous of their autonomy, they have the power to veto central government initiatives that impinge on their rights. The organization of broadcasting reflects this decentralization. JRT (*Jugoslovenska Radioteleviziya*), the central government broadcasting authority, supervises operations generally, but the eight provincial broadcasting centers own their facilities and enjoy substantial independence. "While choice of programming is made entirely by local stations, major purchases of equipment, and international programs, are pooled through a JRT advisory committee to obtain better prices. Other JRT committees advise on legal matters, technical standards, territorial coverage, etc." (*TV/RAI*, Jan. 1979: A47). Yugoslav stations import a large percentage of their television programming from the West and pursue advertising revenue more vigorously than most other Communist broadcasting services.

Third World

Nigeria. As pointed out earlier, India gained by establishing colonial broadcasting as a central government function, linking together its diverse states and territories under the common rubric of "All India Radio." In Nigeria, however, the British neglected to take the precaution of making broadcasting an exclusively federal matter. This largest of African nations (in terms of population) combines many volatile ethnic elements. The 1954 constitution, under which Nigeria became independent in 1960, permitted both the central federal government and the four regional governments of the time to operate broadcast stations. Political leaders of the regions took advantage of this opportunity. In 1959 the Western Region government opened Tropical Africa's first television station in Ibadan,* followed a year later by the Eastern Region's station in Enugu. Another year went by before the federal Nigerian Broad-

---

*The Western Region's Chief Awolowo started broadcasting because the federal radio network refused him air time to correct some misinformation it had broadcast about his activities in the federal legislature. Overseas Rediffusion, Ltd., which installed Western Region TV, owned 50 percent of the TV station, but the regional government bought out Rediffusion within two years because of disagreements over commercial policies (Egbon, 1983).

casting Corporation (NBC) opened its first television station in Lagos, the capital. The Northern Region followed with its own station in Kaduna in 1962.

According to a former head of the BBC African Service, the coexistence of both federal and regional broadcasting services heightened rivalries within the federation:

> The regional premiers and their ministers used their services for their own purposes, with no regard for the cost. The standard of NBC regional broadcasting tended to decline, and the result was that the divisive influences in Nigeria were allowed to foment ill-feeling through these new regional stations. It is my belief that this step, which undermined the unifying influence of a single Nigerian broadcasting system, played an important part in leading Nigeria to the tragedy of the 1967–70 [Biafran] civil war. (Wilkinson, 1974: 220)

Not all observers credit broadcasting with that much power, but as Nigeria fragmented into more and more states (the original 4 regions eventually broke into 19 separate states), the then military government moved to enhance the role of broadcasting as a unifying national force.

In 1976 the military government took over the ten existing state television stations and the next year placed them under control of the newly decreed Nigerian Television Authority (NTA). Striving for an equilibrium between centralization and regionalism, the government directed the NTA to "ensure that the services which it provides, when considered as a whole, shall reflect the unity of Nigeria as a Federation and, at the same time, give adequate expression to the culture, characteristics, affairs and opinions of each State, Zone or other part of the Federation" (quoted in Folorunso, 1980: 13). The decree divided Nigeria into six zones, each equipped with its own production centers and supervised by a zonal board. NTA set up a federal television station in each of the 19 states.

After enactment of a new constitution in 1978 and the return of civilian rule the following year, the states once more established their own television outlets. By 1983 Nigeria had 32 television stations, more than all the rest of Tropical Africa combined.

Restructuring of radio came in 1978 with abolition of the old NBC in favor of a new organization, the Federal Radio Corporation of Nigeria (FRCN). The federal government allowed the state radio stations to stay in place to cater to specific local needs. The FRCN, however, also provides a second transmitter in each state to disseminate regional and national programs. It divides Nigeria for radio purposes into four linguistic zones. The federal station in each zone has considerable regional autonomy to program appropriately for its own area. Nigerian radio therefore has a three-tier structure: a national service on the federal level whose network news must be carried in all the states; zonal broadcasts along broad regional lines; and local grassroots services from the state stations. In 1983 Nigeria had some 60 medium-wave radio stations, with ownership equally divided between the states and the FRCN.

UNITED ARAB EMIRATES

United Arab Emirates. One of the seven Arab countries known as the Gulf States consists of a federation of small sheikdoms, the United Arab Emirates (UAE). They came together in 1972, when Great Britain withdrew from the Persian Gulf area. One of the seven, Abu Dhabi, serves as the federation capital and as the headquarters for the federal radio and television facilities, known respectively as the Voice of the UAE and the UAE Television Service. The federal system permits individual federation members to have their own facilities. One member, Dubai, concentrates on commercial operations and has developed more elaborate facilities than those of the federal headquarters, ranking as "the most aggressive production and marketing organization for Arabic television programming outside of Egypt" (Boyd, 1982: 158). Meanwhile, Abu Dhabi produces noncommercial programming to serve all seven members of the federation.

European Economic Community

Ten European nations have signed treaties forming the European Economic Community (EEC) to coordinate trade and monetary policies within their region. The EEC does not, of course, meld its members into a single sovereign state as do the federations previously mentioned. Nevertheless, EEC regulations can affect broadcasting insofar as it involves the transfer of "goods." At the start of this section, I made the point that federal jurisdiction over broadcasting in the United States hinges on its being legally classified as a form of "commerce." Italian courts have avoided EEC jurisdiction by regarding broadcasting as a form of "service" rather than as a form of goods. EEC-related legal issues affecting broadcasting that will eventually have to be settled in the European area touch on such areas as copyrights, advertising, and satellite transmissions.[10]

5·5 COPYRIGHT

Many statutes other than those explicitly aimed at broadcasting affect the medium—laws dealing with libel, advertising, and taxation, for example. Of particular significance are laws of copyright, giving authors, composers, publishers, producers, and others the right to prevent performance of their artistic works without license and payment of royalties. Radio's heavy use of recorded copyrighted music has always created problems for broadcasters. In Britain, the music copyright law has been particularly restrictive, at one time limiting BBC radio to only 22 hours of "needle time" (recordings) per week.

The brisk trade in programs and program materials across international borders complicates the problems of copyright enforcement, especially because nations of the world have not been unanimous in their support of universal copyright laws. Both the United States and the USSR declined to sign the first international copyright agreement, the 1887 Berne Convention for the Protection of Literary and Artistic Works. The convention is administered by the World Intellectual Property Organisation (WIPO). The United Nations Educational, Scientific, and Cultural Organization (UNESCO) spearheaded a modern movement to coordinate copyright laws with its Universal Copyright Convention of 1952, one goal of which was to extend the Berne Convention to the Americas. UNESCO also encourages the developed countries to make concessions to the Third World so that copyrighted educational materials can be made available at minimum cost.

New technologies have made it necessary to revise copyright statutes, originally concerned exclusively with printed versions of creative works. Even so recent a statute as the U.S. Copyright Law of 1976 quickly ran into problems of interpretation with regard, for example, to home videocassette recording of broadcast and cable programs and the royalties due broadcasters for their programs distributed by distant cable systems. The 1976 U.S. law introduced the *retransmission rights* concept. It allows copyright holders to demand extra payment for materials delivered by satellite and/or cable into markets not covered by rights purchased by broadcasting stations. This aspect of the new law became highly controversial, because broadcast rights had evolved around the concept of relatively *fixed markets,* defined by station coverage areas. When cable television picks up signals from distant stations for retransmission into areas not covered by the original copyright fee, it undermines the traditional basis for payment. Under the revised law, a cable system incurs an obligation to pay extra fees for retransmission rights.

In a 1948 amendment, the Berne Convention had attempted a similar device to forestall signal piracy, stipulating that authors retained their rights when their works were retransmitted by either wire or broadcast means. However, because of many ambiguities introduced by the various methods of cable and satellite distribution and delivery and their interaction with conventional broadcasting, the law proved difficult to interpret. For example, when a broadcast signal for which copyright royalties have already been paid is retransmitted by cable within the coverage area of the originating station, must additional royalties be paid even though no additional coverage is involved? Or, does a private master broadcast antenna serving a single apartment building and picking up either cable or satellite feeds come under the same copyright restraints as an extended cable system covering many different buildings?[11]

Worldwide syndication of program materials causes international copyright problems because of differing laws from one country to another, difficulties of international enforcement, and emergence of clamorous new markets for copyrighted materials. Copyright disputes hampered cable television development in Europe. It took ten years of negotiation for European continental nations to come to terms on the right to distribute BBC television programs on cable systems. In a test case, Belgium finally reached agreement in 1983, with the Belgian cable operators paying the BBC £5 per year per subscriber.[12]

Worldwide piracy of motion pictures and television programs on videocassettes posed a major problem for program creators, producers, and distributors in the 1980s. A lively demand for videocassette recordings (VCRs) developed as a sudden innovation for which neither control nor licensing mechanisms existed. Piracy problems arose in the Third World as well as in the industrialized countries (but the Communist world apparently escaped because of strict controls over access to all kinds of recording devices). In India, for example, three hundred thousand people had videotape players by 1983. Tapes for them could be obtained in "bookshops, snack bars, grocery stores, and even little betel nut shops" (*Asian Broadcasting*, Aug. 1983). In 1982 the World Forum on Piracy of Sound and Audiovisual Recordings met in Geneva to devise cooperative strategies against some types of pirates.*

SUMMARY

Broadcasting invites legal controls because of the need to prevent interference, to use the spectrum efficiently, to use the medium in the public interest, and to manage its potential for social control. Deregulation, conspicuous in the United States, has so far had less marked effect in other countries. It has affected new technologies more than traditional broadcasting, though the latter will no doubt be profoundly influenced in the long run.

International law rests on individual country treaties with a United Nations agency, the International Telecommunication Union, a main function of which is to allocate frequency bands for the various radio services. National statutes came in four phases—the prebroadcast, radio, television, and new technology phases. Most countries are still trying to cope with the fourth phase. Broadcasting law creates special problems for nations organized on a federal basis because constituent states are jealous of federal encroachments on their rights.

Conspicuous among statutes that affect broadcasting without being unique to the medium are copyright laws. The voracious appetites of broadcasting, cable, and new consumer markets created by home videocassettes have made it necessary to update copyright laws, a com-

---

*After the foregoing was written, an excellent study of international copyright problems came to my attention, a report to Congress by the U.S. Copyright Office, *To Secure Intellectual Property Rights in World Commerce* (Library of Congress, Washington, D.C., 21 Sept. 1984, mimeographed). It traces the history of international copyright agreements and describes contemporary piracy problems and current efforts to deal with them.

plicated problem because of both the novel challenges posed by new technologies and the international character of the market for program materials.

NOTES

[1] U.S. Senate, 1981.

[2] Howkins, 1979: 16.

[3] Browne, 1982: 22.

[4] *Broadcasting*, 25 July 1983.

[5] USDOS, 1982: 1.

[6] Broadcasting Research Unit, 1983.

[7] For a discussion of the arguments for and against classifying wire and cable delivery as forms of broadcasting, see Namurois, 1972: 55–57.

[8] Durrer, 1982.

[9] Niemczyk, 1983: 50.

[10] See Crosby & Tempest, 1983, for an introduction to this complex subject. For EEC studies of copyright and advertising problems, see Dittrich et al., 1983, and Knitel, 1982.

[11] For a survey of leading European court cases dealing with some of these dilemmas, see Speigler, 1984, and Dittrich et al., 1983.

[12] *Professional Video*, Nov. 1983; Verlinde, 1984.

CHAPTER 6

REGULATION

6 ▪ 1 THE REGULATORY PROCESS

$\mathbf{T}$ he organic statutes discussed in the previous chapter remain paper laws until made operational by means of some kind of regulatory machinery. In this chapter I consider the machinery that converts the good intentions of statutes into day-to-day rules for actual broadcasting operations.

Relation of Statutes to Regulations

A wide gulf can exist between what laws say and what regulations actually achieve. The organic laws of broadcasting tend to express idealistic goals that may or may not be achieved (or even achievable). The U.S. 1934 act sets up "public interest, convenience and necessity" as the guiding regulatory principle. It does not, however, say what that phrase means, leaving the Federal Communications Commission to interpret the public interest pragmatically in the course of adopting rules and adjudicating disputes. Beyond that general prescription, the act gives brief, relatively explicit instructions to the FCC. Congress knew that if it allowed the statute's language to become too sweeping, the courts might well declare it unconstitutionally vague. Under the Constitution, laws may not give administrative agencies such imprecise authority that their actions could be legally construed as arbitrary or capricious.

Elements of the Constitution's Bill of Rights sharply curb the FCC's regulatory powers: the First Amendment, guaranteeing freedom of speech and press, and the Fifth and Sixth amendments, guaranteeing due process of law. The First Amendment prevents the FCC from imposing prior restraint on the broadcast of any specific program—"prior" in the sense of restraint that prevents an item from being broadcast. The amendment does not deter the FCC from taking *subsequent* action against a licensee who broadcasts anything contrary to the law. The First Amendment and a specific prohibition against censorship in the act also limit the FCC's ability to make hard-and-fast regulations about program content generally.

The due process clauses ensure that every broadcaster against whom the FCC makes an unfavorable judgment, or whom an FCC rule may adversely affect, has the right to appeal. First, the FCC can be asked to reconsider; next, an appeals court can be asked to reverse the FCC; and, finally, the Supreme Court can be petitioned to overturn a lower court's decision. This elaborate machinery of appeal and counterappeal generates an enormous library of administrative and case law. It also inspires endless litigation, which supports battalions of communications lawyers in Washington, D.C. None of this happens to anything like the same degree in other countries. Opportunities for appeal of administrative decisions usually arise only in rare cases involving major constitutional confrontations. I referred earlier to such watershed cases in Spain (Section 3.2), Italy (Section 4.4), and West Germany (Section 5.4).

In 1980, after five years of debate, Argentina adopted a new broadcasting law that set forth the following goals:

> The broadcasting services should foster the cultural enrichment and raise the moral standards of the public, in keeping with the formative and informative character assigned to these transmissions, aimed at elevating the dignity of mankind, strengthening the respect for the institutions and laws of the republic, affirming the inherent values of family integrity, preserving the historical traditions of the Fatherland and instilling the precepts of Christian morality. [Broadcasts] should "avoid everything which tends to degrade the human condition, affect social solidarity, belittle the sentiments of Argentine patriotism or damage aesthetic values." (Simoncini, 1982: 26)

This language reflects three rather common attributes of organic broadcasting laws: (1) they often express boundless faith in the power of broadcasting to effect all sorts of sweeping social controls; (2) they resort to such broad generalizations that they amount to statements of *policy** rather than solid foundations for regulation; and (3) they often employ vague language, giving administrative agencies or officials a virtual carte blanche to interpret it any way they choose. How, for example, does a bureaucrat define "aesthetic values" and how measure damage to them? It follows that regulatory systems based on such loosely written statutes give great latitude to arbitrary and capricious regulators. Ideally, statutes should impose strict but workable outer limits on the discretion of regulators, leaving them free to adapt to the circumstances of individual cases.

---

*See also the related activity of *policy* formation, discussed in Section 12.2. Policies consist of broadly stated goals, not necessarily accompanied by prescriptions as to how the goals should be reached and not necessarily embodied in formal statutes.

Examples of Administrative Mechanisms

Under authoritarian regimes, of course, the mechanisms rest on the arbitrary power of designated government officials or agencies. The government may encourage a certain amount of public discussion and even criticism in the media, but in the final analysis the government makes the decisions, directly controlling the output. Most democratic regimes, on the other hand, attempt to insulate the regulatory process from direct government intrusion, often also affording some opportunities for appealing major administrative decisions to a higher authority for review. The success with which regulatory mechanisms resist political interference varies, as do the opportunities for appeals to modify or reverse administrative actions.

The Federal Communications Commission (FCC). Few countries have adopted the administrative strategy represented by the U.S. Federal Communications Commission (FCC). It combines under a single agency both wire and wireless communication, both technical regulation (including channel assignments) and program regulation, both station licensing and the hearing of grievances against licensees.

The FCC carries out a delegated constitutional function of the legislature. The executive branch appoints its members, with consent of the legislative branch, as represented by the Senate. It adopts and enforces regulations, an executive function, and it adjudicates disputes in the manner of the judicial branch. Thus the FCC blends (in a way contrary to what American schoolchildren usually learn about the "separation of powers") all three primary government functions—legislative, executive, and judicial.

Nothing quite like this inclusive type of independent federal agency exists elsewhere. Recall (Section 3.7) that under the influence of Allied military occupation authorities, Japan set up an FCC-like regulatory agency following World War II. After the occupation ended, however, the Posts and Telecommunications Ministry absorbed the new agency, reducing its jurisdictional scope much below the level of the FCC's. The Canadian Radio-Television and Telecommunications Commission and the Australian Broadcasting Tribunal somewhat resemble the FCC, but they too differ in the scope of their authority, largely because major elements of the broadcasting systems in those countries approximate the status of governmental services. The following examples of regulatory systems differ still more sharply from the type represented by the FCC.

BBC and IBA. The two authorities responsible respectively for public broadcasting and commercial broadcasting in Great Britain, the BBC and the IBA, enjoy great autonomy within the boundaries set by their respective constitutions (described in Sections 3.4 and 3.5). The BBC combines operational and self-regulatory functions. Within statutory limits, it must go outside its own perimeter only for transmitter licenses, issued by the Home Office. In contrast, the IBA acts more as an external regulator of the ITV companies, though it also has operational responsibility for the transmission facilities of the services it oversees. It exerts virtually unlimited control over the commercial companies that it franchises to carry out programming and advertising operations. It enforces detailed program scheduling, balance, and content regulations as well as strict advertising standards. Moreover, it can cancel existing companies' franchises and choose new companies to replace them. In all this, the companies have no automatic recourse, as do U.S. broadcasters, to judicial appeal processes.

Parliament, once having renewed the BBC charter and reenacted the IBA statute, follows a hands-off policy. Of course, broadcasting periodically comes up for parliamentary debate, especially in connection with approval of the BBC's annual budget (which, though derived from receiver license fees, must nevertheless receive parliamentary endorsement). The major occasion for parliamentary review recurs at about ten-year intervals (longer in recent years), when Parliament considers renewal of the enabling documents. In the meantime, the boards of the two authorities naturally pay close attention to what politicians and bureaucrats say about their operations, but the boards also stoutly resist any direct political intervention.

On paper, the British system appears to leave broadcasting highly vulnerable to political manipulation; no written prohibitions like the First Amendment interpose a protective shield.* In practice, however, traditions of forbearance and free expression fend off political meddling. Should the home secretary use the government's legal right to force the broadcasting authorities either to delete or to add any program materials, the broadcasters have the right to call attention on the air to such government intrusions.† The prospect of having to face public scrutiny of such actions has a wonderfully cooling effect on the passions of the moment.

After many years of studiously monitoring the British system in comparison with the U.S. system, Burton Paulu concluded that "both of Britain's broadcasting organizations enjoy as much freedom from government influence or control as do those in any country in the world, and a good case can be made that they have more freedom than is permitted anywhere else" (1981: 41). The best testimony to the BBC's independence of government domination is that major political figures

---

*Great Britain of course has an ancient tradition of free expression, protected by common law rather than by a written constitution. The explicitly stated Bill of Rights in the U.S. Constitution makes it easier for Americans to bring suits for infringement of their personal freedoms.

†As another example, under Australian broadcasting law, the minister in charge can censor any item or require the broadcast of any item; but the minister must report such action to both houses of Parliament within seven business days.

from both sides often level criticism at the corporation. For example, during the 1982 Falkland Islands War with Argentina, Prime Minister Thatcher and other leaders assailed the BBC for being "unacceptably even-handed" in the way it described events. Its reports of the war never took the "ours" versus "theirs" position demanded by super-patriots, who even objected to photos showing Argentine war widows side by side with British war widows.

Australian Broadcasting Tribunal. Australia makes an effort to insulate privately owned broadcasting from direct government interven-tion by placing it under an independent regulatory body, the Australian Broadcasting Tribunal. The tribunal is much like the FCC but is more powerful, for it can ban specific programs that do not meet its standards. It licenses privately owned stations, regulates their program content and advertising, and advises the government on broadcasting policy.* Although the administration in power appoints tribunal members with-out parliamentary assent, the tribunal functions autonomously.

Israeli Broadcasting Authority (IBA). Though Israel's regulatory system owes a good deal to the British example, it aptly illustrates how new circumstances transform a borrowed structure. Initially, the gov-ernment ran *Kol Israel* (Voice of Israel) as a state monopoly. Prolonged public agitation against political control of broadcasting finally led to the establishment of an independent regulatory agency in 1965, the Israeli Broadcasting Authority (IBA). This move freed the broadcasting services from the need to hire staff through the civil service bureau-cracy and gave broadcasters the right (in theory, at least) to program independently.

The authority follows a three-tier organizational pattern. At the top, a 31-member plenum (council), appointed by the government, establishes general broadcasting policy. Its membership reflects the political com-position of the *Knesset* (parliament); never dominated by a single party, it has always been led by uneasy coalitions among many political splin-ter groups. The government appoints a 7-member management commit-tee from the plenum members to supervise operations. It also appoints the system's operational head, the director-general, after consulting with the plenum. A minority of either the plenum or the management committee can appeal decisions of those bodies to the responsible minis-ter, through whom the government can veto IBA actions.

Clearly, the government still keeps a tight rein on Israeli broadcast-ing, through both its appointment and veto powers. The British govern-ment has never used its "reserve powers" to countermand decisions of

---

*The tribunal has no control over the government-funded services, the Austra-lian Broadcasting Corporation and the Special Broadcasting Service (see Section 2.2), which are licensed by statute.

the BBC Board of Governors; the Israeli government, however, has been less restrained in resorting to similar reserve powers. Yet it would be unrealistic to expect Israeli officials, in the midst of their intense and dangerous political circumstances, to behave with the cool detachment usually displayed by their British counterparts. Television in Israel, as one observer put it, serves as "an instrument for forging a new state and society, which Israelis endlessly define and redefine" (Viorst, 1981–1982: 40).

The most publicized confrontation between government and the broadcasting authority occurred in 1978, when members of the IBA complained to the minister of Education and Culture about a television program that dramatized a published story of Israeli cruelty toward Arab villagers during the independence struggle. Although the script derived from a famous Israeli classic, assigned as a text in the public schools, the minister canceled the telecast. Israel's first publicized instance of outright political censorship of a fictional work set off a furious debate, during which protesting workers blacked out the television screen for 45 minutes.[1] Finally, the IBA allowed the program on the air, but its image as a politically independent body had been damaged. Several years later, the Israeli High Court overturned an IBA management committee order instructing the director-general to ban all television interviews with pro-PLO Palestinians in the occupied zone, a news policy advocated by the Begin government. The committee had to settle for a policy of giving the director-general the authority to ban such interviews on a case-by-case basis if he judges them to constitute "anti-Israeli propaganda" (Goodgame, 1983).

Nevertheless, the IBA can and does assert its independence, more often successfully than otherwise. That most Israeli politicians deeply distrust broadcasting suggests that the IBA does its job of monitoring public affairs independently. Given the constant state of tension in the Middle East and the surrounding examples of total government domination of broadcasting, the IBA stands out as a model of broadcast freedom.

West Germany. Another three-tier regulatory system based on the British example can be found in West Germany, whose decentralized system is described in Section 5.4. The nine *Land* (state) broadcasting organizations vary somewhat among themselves, but each has a broadcasting council to set general policy, an administrative council to supervise operations, and an *Intendant* (equivalent of the BBC director-general) as the chief executive officer. Their jointly operated national television network, ZDF, has a similar three-tier structure.

As representatives of the states' populations, the broadcasting councils reflect the "public interest." State laws specify one of two ways for achieving representativeness in the councils. Council members may be chosen according to recognized interest groups (youth, women, workers, employers, religious sects, for example), in which case each group selects its own representatives; or, council members may be chosen to reflect the political composition of the current state legislature, in which case the legislature ultimately makes the selections.[2]

In addition to setting general policy, the broadcast councils make the key executive appointment, that of the *Intendant*. The administrative council (second tier in the hierarchy) supervises the work of the *Intendant*. The practice of balancing all staff appointments according to political affiliation (*Proporz*) assures political neutrality, but (as indicated in Section 4.2) such contrived equilibrium has its drawbacks. For example, political acceptability far outweighs professional experience in broadcasting as a factor in the selection of *Intendants*.

Mexico. Mexico, a Third World country not imbued with Anglo-Saxon legal traditions, exemplifies a regulatory system designed to accommodate private enterprise as the dominant factor in broadcasting without surrendering the state's right to do its own broadcasting. (In Section 3.3 I described the relationship between the public and private sectors in Mexican broadcasting and how the private services dominate the market.) Two government departments share the major regulatory functions: elements of the Communication and Transportation Ministry assign frequencies and regulate technical matters, while the Interior Ministry monitors programs for compliance with the 1960 Federal Radio and Television Law.*

Private broadcasters must all belong to the National Chamber of the Radio and Television Industry. This organization combines industry public relations and lobbying functions and provides a formal liaison between government and commercial broadcasters as a group. Individual licensees have no official standing before government agencies, as do U.S. licensees before the FCC. They must go through the industry chamber in order to be heard.† The 1960 law and the decree based upon it, along with a number of other legal requirements involving several ministries and government departments, erect an elaborate regulatory structure. However, much of this edifice exists only on paper. In practice, the one dominant private broadcaster in Mexico, Televisa, works out its relationships with government informally, ignoring many legal technicalities. According to an American observer:

> *The formal regulatory structure and process as defined in law do not reflect the day-to-day industry-state relationship. This is most obvious in the case of Televisa, which participates in the regulatory process even though it is not a*

---

*Mexican federal laws come into effect only after implementation by presidential decrees (*reglamentos*). The 1960 organic law received its *reglamento* only in 1973, a lapse of 13 years between the law's passage and its formal implementation.

†Organization of Mexican industries into chambers for purposes of official joint interaction with government is not unique to broadcasting. Such chambers have been operating in many Mexican industries since 1936, in accordance with a law passed in that year.

legally recognized actor. It is also apparent in the uneven enforcement of content regulations intended to assure that broadcast programming serves national development goals and protects cultural values. (Mahan, 1982: 159–160)

The author goes on to explain this apparent weakness as a pragmatic concession, symptomatic of the government's dependence on the private broadcasters both to reach the Mexican people and to earn foreign exchange (Televisa earns substantial income by exporting Spanish-language television programming to the United States). "Broadcast laws are significant, however," concludes Mahan, "not because they ordain what is or should be done, but because they establish a framework which legitimizes the actual push and pull of industry-state interactions" (1982: 160).

In other Third World countries, laws often fall short of implementation simply because of inadequate administrative and enforcement resources. Shortfalls are not, however, confined to the Third World. They also occur in the most advanced industrialized countries, but for lack of will rather than lack of resources. In the United States, the Federal Communications Commission has often failed to live up to the ideals of the Communications Act. Implementation of the statute fluctuates according to swings of the political pendulum. It also varies with the character and quality of the commissioners. Mark Fowler, the Republican commission chairman appointed in 1981, made no bones about his profound lack of sympathy with the philosophy of the statute he was ostensibly appointed to enforce. Calling the commission "the last of the New Deal dinosaurs," Fowler promptly began dismantling its traditional regulatory mechanisms in the name of deregulation.

6 ■ 2 LICENSING CRITERIA

As the preceding section shows, though the machinery of regulation differs considerably from one country to another, the subjects of regulation tend to be similar. In the rest of this chapter, I touch on the major subjects of regulation that occur, in varying forms, almost universally in systems that permit nongovernment or quasi-private ownership of stations. Once again, beneath the individual differences among national broadcasting systems, one finds patterns of uniformity.

Any scheme for regulating nongovernment broadcasting starts with the licensing of stations. According to an ITU regulation, "No transmitting station may be established or operated by a private person or by any enterprise without a license issued in an appropriate form and in conformity with the provisions of these Regulations by the government of the country to which the station in question is subject" (ITU, 1980: 242). The terms on which governments grant, renew, and withdraw licenses (sometimes also called concessions or franchises) determine the effectiveness of regulations as a whole. Revocations (and refusals to renew at the end of a license period) occur rarely, except for cases of outright government seizure of private facilities, as happened in Cuba (see Section 4.2). The FCC refuses few renewal applications and very rarely resorts to outright license revocation. In Britain, the IBA replaced 2 of the 15 independent companies and forced changes in others when the franchises first came up for renewal—drastic actions by the standards of most licensing authorities.* Considerations of citizenship and media monopoly figure among the most widely used criteria in the granting of licenses.

Citizenship

Broadcasting interacts intimately with a nation's entire culture and has a significant national security role in times of war; most nations therefore demand citizenship as a basic qualification for station licensees. Some carry xenophobia even further; Peru, for example, requires that both owners and employees be not only citizens but native-born Peruvians. Third World nations that originally made generous allowances for non-citizen participation in station ownership sometimes found their systems invaded by high-powered foreign investors. Thus, during the 1960s, the major U.S. television networks had extensive interests in Latin American stations, causing the countries concerned to revise their policies. In 1974 the Venezuelan government, for example, tightened citizenship rules, giving the foreign networks only a month to sell their interests. By this time, however, the Americans had already concluded that the expected profits from South American television would not materialize. Venezuela's estimated total advertising revenue potential amounted to $22 million per year, but the three stations in which the U.S. networks had invested cost $24 million per year to operate.[3]

Ironically, Latin American investors have in turn been accused of violating U.S. ownership laws. Televisa, Mexico's dominant private television company, owns a major percentage of the Spanish International Communication Corporation (SICC), which owns five U.S. Spanish-language television stations and controls two others. Moreover, Televisa has a major interest in the Spanish International Network (SIN), a U.S. satellite-connected broadcasting and cable network with more than two hundred affiliates serving the 15 million Hispanics residing in the United States, and in Galavision, a satellite-distributed cable television program service in Spanish. SIN uses Hispanic programs not only from Mexico but also from Argentina, Brazil, Chile, Spain, and Venezuela. An association of U.S. Spanish-language broadcasters charged SICC with being under alien control, and the FCC questioned whether

---

*Only the British Home Office can actually license transmitters, but for all practical purposes the IBA takes on the role of licenser when it selects or rejects program contractors.

the SICC-SIN interlocking ownership might violate other laws. In 1983, after a three-year review, the FCC designated SICC's five stations for a hearing to decide whether the licensee had violated ownership or other laws.[4]

Monopoly

Many national broadcasting statutes take note of the danger of monopolistic concentration of power over broadcasting. They limit ownership accordingly.

Ceiling on Ownership. For decades the FCC limited U.S. owners to a maximum of twenty-one stations, seven in each category (AM, FM, and TV). In 1984 it began deregulating ownership, but Congress opposed lifting of the television station ceiling. Australia permits a maximum of only two television stations and eight radio stations to an owner (but not more than four radio outlets in any one state, only one in a capital city, and no AM-FM combinations). As a contrasting example, Mexican law imposes no limits on media ownership, making it possible for a single company, the aforementioned Televisa, to control four of Mexico City's six television stations, each with its own network.

Cross-Media Ownership. Televisa combines under one conglomerate umbrella dozens of companies, including publishing as well as broadcasting enterprises. Lawmakers in many countries take an interest in such *cross-media ownership,* especially when it involves controlling daily newspapers and broadcasting facilities in the same markets. In many ways, newspapers and broadcast stations complement each other, making ideal corporate bedfellows. However, such pairing can have undesirable consequences. In the United States, for example, First Amendment doctrine stresses the value of *diversity* of ownership in achieving maximum freedom of expression. The more independent voices in the marketplace of ideas, the better. In 1975 the FCC forbade common ownership of a daily newspaper and a broadcasting station in the same market, though most existing cross-ownerships of this type escaped breakup when the FCC adopted the rule—at least until existing owners sell their facilities. Newspaper-broadcasting cross-ownership can also lead to commercial abuses, such as forcing advertisers who want to use only one medium to buy exposure in the sister enterprise and using one enterprise to promote or support the other to the detriment of competing media.

Elsewhere, however, regulatory authorities often permit and even encourage newspaper-broadcasting combinations. The traditional role of newspapers as political party supporters gives them considerable influence in elections in some settings, an influence they can use to persuade legislators to enact laws allowing them to become broadcast licensees. Survival of a viable press serves the public interest. Most

Western European nations fear that local broadcasting competition could ruin provincial newspapers. Accordingly, they either prevent the growth of commercially supported local broadcasting or cushion the blow to newspapers by allowing them to invest in local broadcast stations.

In Britain, the IBA initially encouraged newspaper investment, both in regional commercial television and in local commercial radio. However, Britain, like the United States, also recognized, as the Annan Committee put it, "an editorial danger if the same men own both the main media for news and political expression" (Great Britain, 1977: 198). Later on, Parliament imposed ceilings on such investments. For example, the Thomson Organization newspaper chain, which originally owned 80 percent of Scottish Television (one of the ITV program companies), had to reduce its holdings to a quarter of the voting stock. Press interests hold minority shares in most of both the ITV program companies and the independent local radio stations.*

As a cautionary example of the dangers inherent in newspaper-broadcasting combinations, the Annan Committee cited the case of Australia, where domination over private broadcasting by three large publishing conglomerates has had "very sharp repercussions upon political expression and news" (p. 198). Australian newspaper-broadcasting owners had been accused of discriminating against competing stations in news coverage and of exerting "blatant pressure on TV critics" (Green, 1972: 239). In 1981 a Broadcasting Act amendment gave the Australian Broadcasting Tribunal the right to take concentration of media ownership into account in awarding licenses, but the amendment did not affect existing licensees.

Other countries where newspapers play a substantial role in the privately owned component of national broadcasting systems include Japan, Italy, and Latin America generally. Argentina's 1980 law, however, expressly ruled out broadcast licenses for anyone with press or news agency connections. This prohibition proved unexpectedly disadvantageous. When the Argentine government began seeking bidders to buy back the major television station properties that had been bought out by the Peron regime, the first auctions failed to attract offers: with the most likely bidders for these expensive and risky properties barred, no prospective buyers came forward.

Limitations on Networks. Though not necessarily involving common ownership, groups of stations tied together as networks can raise questions of monopoly power. The FCC's network broadcasting

---

*The Annan Committee listed all these newspaper holdings in Appendix D of its report (Great Britain, 1977: 511–522). The 1981 Broadcasting Act authorizes the IBA to consider whether newspaper shareholding by its contractors is in the public interest.

regulations, including the prime-time access rule, seek to prevent national networks (especially television) both from unduly dominating the national program market and from compromising their affiliates' freedom to make their own decisions locally.

Elsewhere, network-affiliate relations tend to follow different patterns. In Europe and in most authoritarian states, national networks usually own all or most of their affiliates and have monopoly status. I pointed out in Chapter 4 how such monopolies tend to generate public dissatisfaction, inviting challenges from unlicensed broadcasters. In Australia and Italy, and to a large extent in Canada and Japan, national networking remains a monopoly of the public service broadcasting stations, with the privately owned stations legally inhibited from mounting full-scale, interconnected national networks.* Other patterns have emerged in Latin American countries: Mexico's private Televisa network dominates the entire system, yet Argentinian law forbids such networks on a regular basis.

6·3 THE REGULATION OF FAIRNESS

Of all the regulations governing content, the most troublesome seem to be those concerned with *fairness*—fairness to audience members as individuals or groups, to the nation as a whole, to the owners and managers of stations. The concept of fairness has many facets, expressed in such terms as freedom of speech, censorship, impartiality, objectivity, neutrality, bias, balance, and accountability. Special attributes of broadcasting—its ubiquity, its accessibility, its role as a home medium, its potential for exerting social control, its status as a government-licensed medium—heighten the sensitivity and complexity of fairness regulations.

Censorship

Most constitutions, even those of authoritarian regimes, claim to protect their citizens' freedom both to communicate and to receive communications. The U.S. Constitution flatly forbids Congress to make any laws "abridging the freedom of speech, or of the press." Most others, however, follow up such ringing statements with explicit escape clauses. The USSR, for example, assures its citizens of the freedom to communicate as long as they avoid "slanderous fabrications which defame the Soviet state and social system and "propaganda . . . arousing hostility or

---

*Both program and financial considerations urge broadcasters toward networking so strongly that private broadcasters constantly seek ways to get around restrictive laws that reserve networking for the public service component of mixed systems.

dissension of races or nationalities" or "subverting or weakening Soviet authority." Such provisos

> leave wide scope for the punishment of those making public statements deemed hostile to the regime. Article 125 of the Constitution, pertaining to freedom of speech, provides little defense, since it guarantees freedom of expression only in "conformity with the interests of the working people, and in order to strengthen the socialist system," qualifications which the party and the government may define as they wish. (Paulu, 1974: 45–46)*

Such administrator-oriented provisos appear in non-Marxist constitutions as well. Mexico's, for example, speaks of the "right to information and to the free expression of ideas, except when such expression offends morality, impinges upon the rights of third parties, provokes criminal acts, or disturbs the public order" (quoted in Mahan, 1982: 55). Brazil guarantees its citizens freedom of thought and expression, "except with respect to public entertainment and performances . . . propaganda for war, for subversion of order, or for discrimination based upon religion, race, or class, and publications whose content is opposed to morality and good manners shall not be tolerated" (quoted in Wicklein, 1981: 224).

Even so liberal a democracy as Sweden, whose law forbids imposing any prior restraints on communications, bends its strict rules against censorship when the issue is as fundamental as the choice between democracy and dictatorship.† Americans will recognize in this kind of exception echoes of arguments familiar in the United States, where people otherwise supportive of First Amendment rights sometimes violently oppose freedom of speech for Nazi sympathizers, for Ku Klux Klanners, for scientists who argue that intelligence is correlated with race, and for right-wing speakers at university commencements. The First Amendment demands a high degree of faith in citizens' ability to withstand the expression of ideas that most of them deem hateful and subversive. It demands taking the risk of granting those who seek to bring the country down the same constitutional freedoms as the best of patriots. Not everyone has enough faith to agree with Supreme Court Justice William O. Douglas, who said that, under the Constitution, "We have deemed it more costly to liberty to suppress a despised minority than to let them vent their spleen."

The following examples illustrate the widespread use of prior restraint (that is, censorship in its classic form) in broadcasting:

---

*The 1977 Constitution changed this article number to 50.

†In a similar vein, the BBC has said that "impartiality does not imply an Olympian neutrality or detachment from those basic moral and constitutional beliefs on which the nation's life is founded. The BBC does not feel obliged for example to appear neutral as between truth and untruth, justice and injustice, freedom and slavery, compassion and cruelty, tolerance and intolerance (including racial intolerance)" (*BBC 1983 Annual Report*, 1982: 141).

Australia and New Zealand. These two isolated cultures retain a degree of Victorian prudery, despite their general adherence to liberal Western democratic ideals. New Zealand customs agents censor objectionable content in imported videocassettes at points of entry, and Australia's film censorship board has the power to exclude films from television.

Brazil. In the late 1970s, television stations in Brazil had to submit *novelas* (soap operas) to the censors 20 episodes at a time, and stations had to show the *Censura Federal* certificate on the screen before every program. According to a Brazilian television producer, "The slightest attention in a novela to political, religious, sexual, racial or economic problems is definitely forbidden" (*New York Times*, 5 June 1978). In answer to a question by a scholarly investigator, a spokesperson for *Rede Globo*, Brazil's largest television conglomerate, said that "television is a government concern. At any time, they can end the concession. We must be more cautious than the newspapers. . . . One *novela* on youth problems was vetoed because the government did not want to acknowledge that there *were* youth problems" (quoted in Wicklein, 1981: 227). Asked why censorship had been lifted for newspapers but not for television, a Brazilian editor explained that the 10 percent of the people who read newspapers already oppose the government; so newspaper censorship would serve no purpose. But the mass of the people, who depend on television for information rather than on newspapers, could be persuaded either way; so the government has to protect itself by censoring television, even at the expense of consistency.[5]

Ireland. Broadcasting law in Ireland bans news interviews or reports with representatives of organizations listed as subversive. This ban put Irish broadcasters in the curious position of not being able to interview a member of the British Parliament because he happened to belong to an organization on the banned list, the Provisional Sinn Fein (political wing of the Irish Republican Army).

Great Britain. In an unusual instance of prior restraint imposed by a court, a British sugar producer obtained an injunction against the showing of a film about its operations in South Africa, scheduled to be telecast by one of the independent television companies. In the United States, the First Amendment would prevent issuance of such an injunction.[6] Even less conceivable in the United States would be FCC examination of scripts, ordering of changes prior to broadcast, and outright banning of broadcasts—all routine acts of Britain's Independent Broadcasting Authority. True, the IBA does not function directly in a governmental capacity, as does the FCC (bearing in mind that the First Amendment applies to *government*, not private, actions), but the British Parliament nevertheless passed the law giving the IBA sweeping powers to regulate content. The Annan Committee deplored the frequency of IBA intervention, saying that the authority "should censure, not censor" (Great Britain, 1977: 39).

Third World. Newly independent countries do not hesitate to censor both entertainment and news when they consider the welfare of the nation to be at stake. Tom Mboya, a major political figure in Kenya prior to his assassination in 1969, wrote, "Freedom of the press in a new country has . . . got to be limited: not so much restricted by legislation, but rather deliberately guided; for its main functions include not only giving the news but also taking part in the national effort and contributing towards the building of a nation" (Mboya, 1963: 101). Because newly independent nations operate broadcasting as an arm of government, imposition of this philosophy of news functions comes easily.

Neutrality

"The Corporation shall broadcast an impartial account day by day prepared by professional reporters of the proceedings in both Houses of the United Kingdom Parliament." This sentence in the BBC's License and Agreement, their only affirmative program requirement, evidences the high priority most systems award to *neutrality* as the hallmark of professional broadcast journalism. The U.S. Communications Act makes no such demand. The FCC and the courts greatly rely on the "editorial discretion" of journalists. In case of abuse of that discretion, the fairness doctrine guarantees corrective action, at least in theory—though even that protection may be swept away by deregulation.

The fairness doctrine grew out of a reversal by the FCC of its earlier decision in favor of editorial neutrality on the part of licensees. At first the commission forbade station owners to editorialize over their facilities on grounds that they enjoy an unfair advantage over others in gaining access to the airwaves. Later, the commission decided that the public interest would be better served if licensees could editorialize, providing that their advantage would be offset by assurance that opposing views would have a reasonable opportunity to be heard. Most other democratic systems, however, still ban editorializing by broadcasting organizations—certainly an appropriate rule where monopolies prevail. Neither the BBC nor the IBA contracting companies have the right to editorialize in their own names.

In general, however, democratic systems recognize the value of making broadcasting an arena where opposing ideas have freedom to compete for acceptance. The failure of the 1919–1933 Weimar Republic, Germany's first parliamentary democracy, had momentous consequences, for it opened the way to the eventual ascendancy of the Nazi party. A historian of German-language broadcasting cites the "obsessive neutrality" of radio during the Weimar interlude as a cautionary example. In his view, the democratic experiment failed in part because of radio's failure to deal with public issues:

> *The men behind the early days of German radio were genuinely concerned that the new medium, about whose effects so little was known, should not harm the new Republic, whose fate was even more uncertain. But by keeping from the people the very debates that the Republic should grow on, and leaving the dissemination of political opinion to a press ever more dominated by the economically powerful right wing, they undoubtedly lowered the Germans' resistance to the blandishments of National Socialism and its meretriciously simplistic promises. (Sandford, 1976: 67)*

Nowadays, democratic systems leave listeners and viewers free to draw their own conclusions, based on a reasonably comprehensive sampling of conflicting views on public issues. The Netherlands system, in keeping with its "pillarized" nature, imposes no rules of objectivity, balance, or neutrality on the social groups that have access to the airwaves. Each group may push its own views in its own programs to the exclusion of all others (though each must publish the program schedules of the others in its program guide). Audience members unwilling to be confused by the facts (as the saying goes) may well pay attention only to broadcasts from their own group and so not benefit from diversity of opinion; but others may arrive at independent opinions after sampling the competing views of several groups.

At the opposite extreme, Swedish law requires strict *factuality* and *impartiality* in programs dealing with public controversies. This requirement reflects the fact that *Sveriges Radio*, the public corporation responsible for nearly all Swedish broadcasting, has a virtual monopoly. Though seemingly easy to determine, factuality and impartiality can become slippery concepts. For example, during the Vietnam War, the Swedish Radio Council, which hears complaints about programs, found itself whipsawed by the claims and counterclaims of those who took opposing sides on the war (essentially the left wing versus the right wing). Unable to reach a satisfactory judgment, the council referred the problem to a university research team, which arrived at the following formula for testing compliance with the factuality-impartiality law:

> *Factuality contains an element of* truth, *but obviously one can stockpile true statements without being factual, e.g. by consistently selecting true but one-sided facts. An element of* relevance *is also needed. Similarly, impartiality contains an element of* balance, *which means that all parties involved in a conflict are entitled to give their views or have their views presented. And when presenting these views the program must be neutral: so* neutral presentation *is the fourth element. (Quoted in Soderstrom, 1981: 302)*

Satisfied with this "truth-relevance-balance-neutral presentation" formula, the council decided that *Sveriges Radio* had not violated the law in covering the Vietnam controversy. However, when Sweden initiated local private *Närradio* (see Section 4.5) in 1978, the government exempted it from the factuality-impartiality rule. The primary purpose of these low-power stations is to give social groups at the neighborhood level their own voice—recalling the Dutch model, one might call it "micro-pillarization."*

Accountability

A word not much heard in discussions of American broadcasting, *accountability*, often crops up in connection with other Western-style systems. The Annan Committee said that the greatest volume of criticism of current practices in Britain that it received came "from those who believe that the broadcasters have been insensitive in the past ten years to the views expressed by large sections of the public, and are insufficiently accountable to them" (Great Britain, 1977: 32). The committee received testimony on several different versions of what people meant by accountability. They seemed to boil down to questions of (1) responsiveness of regulatory and programming bodies to public wishes and interests and (2) effectiveness of mechanisms for obtaining satisfaction when members of the public lodge complaints about specific programs.

Responsiveness. Accountability in U.S. broadcasting relies, in theory at least, on two mechanisms: (1) the FCC, as a body appointed to represent the public interest, and (2) constitutional due process rights, as the means of giving citizens access to the regulatory process itself. The law makes the FCC responsible for ensuring that broadcasters operate in the public interest, but nothing in the law ensures that the five (formerly seven) commissioners will in fact reflect the actual public. As political appointees drawn mostly from the middle ranks of Washington bureaucrats, they can hardly be considered especially qualified to assess grassroots public needs and wants.

The second avenue to accountability, access to the regulatory machinery, gives private individuals (or, more typically, spokespersons for consumer interest groups) a chance to participate, within limits, in the FCC's rule-making and adjudicatory hearings. Consumer groups had some success during the 1960s and early 1970s in opposing renewal of licensees for stations that they felt had failed to serve the public interest. However, the failure of a well-planned attempt by a group advocating closer regulation of children's programs represented the more typical outcome of efforts to obtain accountability through the due process route.†

---

*Letting down the fairness barriers resulted in some embarrassing excesses, however. One *Närradio* group suggested sending immigrant southern Europeans, Africans, and Arabs back to their countries of origin, where they could "swing in the trees" or "bask in the sun" instead of "contaminating" Swedish society (Browne, 1984: 47).

†In 1970 Action for Children's Television (ACT) petitioned the FCC to adopt rules requiring adequate programs for young children, free of advertiser exploitation. The commission issued a policy statement agreeing to part of ACT's proposal in

Most other advanced Western systems rely on broadly representative citizen advisory councils to sensitize broadcasters and regulatory agencies to public wants and needs. By law, both the BBC and IBA, for example, consult with numerous advisory councils and committees specializing in such subjects as education, religion, agriculture, science, social effects, and local radio. The BBC alone has more than 50 such advisory bodies.

In West Germany, the state broadcasting councils, the top tier of its three-tier system (described in the preceding section), represent the general public. Unlike the British advisory committees, they participate directly in regulation of the system, having the power, for example, to approve annual budgets. In the pillarized system of Holland, the broadcasting associations themselves represent social groups.

Donald Browne interviewed members of advisory councils and staff members of producing organizations in Great Britain and on the European continent in the early 1970s, a period when accountability had begun to emerge as a lively issue. He concluded that

> *Few councils hold public meetings; few council members are strongly encouraged to meet with public groups; rarely are council deliberations publicized (and when they are, it is the press that is employed, and not radio or television themselves); and almost never are members of the general public encouraged to make their feelings known to council members. (Browne, 1973: 26)*

Complaints. In short, advisory bodies do not normally deal directly with complaints from the public, a function requiring another type of mechanism. The FCC has a special complaints unit that receives, processes, and reports on the tens of thousands of complaints addressed to it each year. The great majority of faultfinders receive a form letter advising them either that they have asked the FCC to violate the law by interfering with free speech or that their complaints have no factual basis. As an example of the latter, for years the FCC was flooded by literally millions of complaints about a nonexistent plot to put religious programs off the air. This experience reflects an ambiguity about public complaints: their meaning may be distorted by people with axes to grind who mount letter-writing campaigns. Thus a small minority of organized complainants can take on the appearance of widespread public concern. In any event, the FCC has not found a method of winnowing out the few complaints that deserve serious consideration from the many frivolous and form-letter complaints.[7]

Complaint departments in other systems receive only a fraction of the communications that pour in to the FCC. For example, the IBA received a total of only 1,375 complaints in 1981, most dealing with

---

principle, but it declined to adopt explicit rules. Fifteen years later, ACT was still trying to get the FCC to adopt rules to ensure suitable programming for children—rules of a kind that are commonplace in other Western nations.

program schedule matters. The Annan Committee recommended that the separate, self-administered complaint committees of the BBC and IBA should be combined into a single independent body. The Broadcasting Act of 1981 set up such a joint Broadcasting Complaints Commission. Consisting of three or more members appointed by the secretary of state, it began operating in 1981. Members may not have any connection with the broadcasting authorities.They adjudicate allegations of "unjust or unfair treatment" of participants in programs and invasions of privacy in the course of program preparation. The only punishment the commission can mete out consists of requiring a broadcasting organization found guilty of unfairness to publish the commission's findings. In its first year of operation, the commission adjudicated only 6 complaints against the BBC, upholding 2 of them.*

In Sweden, complaints go to the same Radio Council mentioned earlier as having commissioned a university study on how to adjudicate impartiality. Comparable in size though not in function to the FCC, the seven-member, government-appointed council receives a few hundred complaints per year. It cannot give immediate satisfaction to complainants; it simply reports annually to Parliament on how the *Sveriges Radio* program services abide by the broadcasting law. It may recommend to the parliament withdrawal of *Sveriges Radio*'s corporate charter but has never considered taking so drastic a step.

Right-of-reply rules issued in 1983, implementing France's new law of the previous year, allow for a two-minute rebuttal, read by a broadcasting organization staff member within 30 days of the offending broadcast. Commercial companies as well as private individuals can take advantage of the reply rules under French law.

Mandatory Research. One further aspect of accountability deserves mention. Some broadcasting laws require that the broadcasting services under their jurisdiction conduct sociological research in order to determine objectively what audiences think about the programming they receive. Such research goes deeper than the simple head counts (or household counts) used in the ratings research most familiar to American audiences. Japan's public services corporation, NHK, has such a provision in its charter. In Great Britain, the Broadcasting Act of 1981 requires that the IBA "ascertain the state of public opinion concerning the programs and advertisements broadcast by the authority." The BBC's Royal Charter calls for "constant and effective review" from sources outside the corporation to ensure that it receives information on public opinion concerning programs as well as criticisms and suggestions. (Implementation of this requirement is discussed in Section 10.2.)

---

*In 1984 the commission received 228 complaints, accepting only 47 for action. Of these, 11 were upheld against the BBC, 2 against the IBA (Great Britain, 1984b).

Trends. As this brief overview suggests, no entirely satisfactory solution to the problem of making broadcasting both accountable and *perceived* to be accountable has emerged. In the past, most systems fell short in handling public complaints either because the bodies that received the complaints were the very ones complained of or because the independent body that received them had little power to redress grievances. The ubiquity of broadcasting, along with the heterogeneity of its audiences, inevitably causes accountability problems. Programs reach such a variety of consumers that they cannot fail to offend some people some of the time. Even the wisest and most responsive system gives cause for complaint to some of its audience members. Nevertheless, except in the United States, the trend in Western systems has been toward efforts to develop more effective regulatory mechanisms for ensuring accountability. The United States must be counted an exception because the trend of the 1980s was toward *less* government regulation, with more reliance on consumers to influence broadcasters through their pocketbooks.

6▪4 SCHEDULE REGULATION

Many regulatory authorities regard control over the *timing* of programs as important as control over their content. Objects of schedule regulation include the length of the broadcast day, the balance of program types within the day's schedule, the relationship among two or more simultaneous services, and the placement of programs in terms of their accessibility to children.

Schedule Length

The FCC requires that licensees maintain at least minimum schedules but imposes no upper limits except in the case of daytime-only AM stations (limited to broadcasting during local daylight hours so as to avoid causing sky-wave interference at night).* However, commercial stations, having an incentive to stay on the air as long as possible, always exceed the FCC minima. Stations whose financial support comes from receiver license fees have no such incentive, because consumers pay the same fees, irrespective of program schedule lengths.

In Britain, government officials may limit the schedules of both the BBC and IBA services. They did so for several decades; however, starting in 1964 for radio and 1972 for television, the government left broadcasters free to set their own schedules. Occasionally, governments impose schedule limits in order to conserve electrical power, as hap-

---

*FCC radio minima: two thirds of authorized time during the day, two thirds at night; television: after 36 months of operation, at least 2 hours per day and a minimum of 28 hours per week.

pened in Britain in 1973–1974, when both the BBC and IBA had to close down nightly at 10:30 P.M.*

Balance Among Program Types

The ITV companies have far less latitude than the BBC in planning their schedules. They must clear their program plans at quarterly intervals with the IBA. As a result of this close monitoring, the IBA could claim that "over one-third of ITV's programmes are informative in character, a balance exceptional among privately-financed broadcasters anywhere in the world and much better than in many state-financed systems" (IBA, 1978: 8).†ITV companies must schedule at least 2 television dramas per week (not just episodes of serials), 2 current affairs programs per week, and 39 documentaries per year. Children's, religious, in-school, cultural, local, and news programming must also be scheduled in specified amounts. Further, the program companies may not relegate serious programs to a Sunday morning "cultural ghetto," as do the networks and stations in the United States. As a public service oriented broadcaster, the BBC voluntarily follows practices similar to those of the IBA.

Balance Among Services

In the United States, the FCC has no detailed control over the broadcast schedules of competing services. It does limit somewhat the national networks' ability to dominate all the most desirable hours in their affiliates' schedules, but these rules aim simply at maintaining a degree of independent programming responsibility on the part of affiliates. Occasionally, the three networks voluntarily carry a program of special national significance simultaneously. When that happens, some viewers invariably complain at having to sacrifice their accustomed entertainment programs, even for substitutes of transcendental national importance.

Most of the time, though, the U.S. commercial television networks compete for the largest possible audience size, with no thought at all about the range of real audience choices that such competition provides. Under these circumstances, counterprogramming strategies usually fail to proffer meaningful choices because only a very narrow range of

---

*The BBC License and Agreement still contains a clause, Section 14 (1), empowering the secretary of state to set maximum and minimum times on the air by the day, week, or other time period and to set the hours of the day upon which broadcasting may or may not take place (*BBC 1983 Annual Report*, 1982: 158).

†The corresponding percentage for the BBC television networks was 43 percent in 1981–1982, of which educational programming accounted for 21 percent (*BBC 1983 Annual Report*, 1982: 116).

program types can generate the massive national audiences that commercial networks demand in prime time. Thus, as noted in Section 3.7, instead of enhancing program choice, unbridled competition reduces it.

Both paternalistic and authoritarian systems tend to reject this pursuit of audience size. Most systems employ *complementary* network schedules. This means coordinating scheduling so as to ensure variety of program choice at any given time, with occasional deliberate exceptions for programs deemed so vital that all audiences should receive them simultaneously. Britain regards party political broadcasts just prior to elections as having that kind of importance and sees to it that all television networks carry them simultaneously. Viewers must either watch the prescribed programs or turn off their sets. Most of the time, however, the BBC and IBA, though rivals for audience attention, plan the programs of their four networks to avoid objectionable duplication of program types. However, they do not coordinate their offerings formally and systematically as do the ARD and ZDF networks in Germany.

When information competes with entertainment, the availability of alternative programs, so desirable from the audience point of view, can seem disadvantageous to paternalistic and authoritarian broadcasting organizations. Given the choice between complementary programs, audiences tend to evade serious or propaganda-laden programs in favor of lightweight entertainment. Sweden's experience when it introduced its second television network in 1969 illustrates what can happen. At first, *Sveriges Radio* allowed the two networks to counterprogram, one offering entertainment when the other offered news. Although the amount of news on the air doubled as a result of having two networks, the aggregate audience for news went down by half. Research showed that people switched back and forth between networks, pursuing entertainment exclusively in a tuning pattern the Swedes called the "slalom run." Eventually, *Sveriges Radio* changed to a noncomplementary scheduling policy, requiring one channel to offer minority interest programs when the other offered news.*

A contrasting example can be found in New Zealand. Like Sweden, it has two television networks, both under control of a single national body. In 1973, under the guidance of a liberal government, New Zealand pioneered the worldwide trend toward restructuring traditional monolithic systems along more pluralistic lines. Within two years, however, the conservative National party came back to power. It scrapped the previous government's pluralistic strategy, putting the two networks under a single administrator and opting for complementary scheduling. Instead of the paternalism of Sweden, New Zealand adopted a sink-or-swim counterprogramming policy. This meant

---

*Soderstrom, 1981: 307. Authoritarian governments often routinely require that all stations carry the national news simultaneously.

total abandonment of the patronizing stance taken by other broadcasters faced with a similar situation: news must compete against the most frivolous of light entertainment; local programming against the gloss of the imported product. Of all peoples, the New Zealand television viewer with just two channels is now in the best position to make a real choice. It is a great risk of faith in both the quality of local production and the quality of the audience. (Toogood, 1981: 21)

Another variation, a complementary system of programming networks called "coordinated contrast" occurs in West Germany. ARD and ZDF (see Section 5.4) jointly plan their schedules a year in advance, ensuring varied program choices most of the time. They alternate in carrying major special events. However, they also *coschedule* weekly program magazines on political issues that they consider important for all viewers. All this "involves an immense amount of careful planning, particularly on the part of the ARD, which not only has to perform this task on top of the coordination between its nine constituent television [services], but also has to bear in mind the programme schedules of the third television services," that is, the regional programming by the varying combinations of stations within the respective *Länder* (Sandford, 1976: 108).

Family Viewing

In 1973 the FCC reprimanded a New York FM station for using indecent language in an afternoon radio program. The station appealed the FCC's action on First Amendment grounds, but the court upheld the FCC's contention that it had not suggested actually suppressing the language in question, merely moving it to a later time of the day, when children would be less likely to hear it. Later, the FCC persuaded the broadcasting industry to adopt such scheduling tactics in the name of "family viewing standards." This move, too, came under attack as an infringement on First Amendment rights. Other countries, however, take for granted enforcement of stringent family viewing standards. The IBA, for example, describes its family regulatory policy as follows:

The Authority's Family Viewing Policy assumes a progressive decline throughout the evening in the proportion of children present in the audience. It looks for a similar progression in the successive programmes scheduled from early evening until closedown: the earlier in the evening the more suitable; the later in the evening the less suitable. Within the progression, 9 P.M. is fixed as the point up to which the broadcasters will normally regard themselves as responsible for ensuring that nothing is shown that is unsuitable for children. . . .

Among the reasons why a programme may be unsuitable for family viewing are the portrayal of violence, bad language, innuendo, blasphemy, explicit sexual behaviour, and scenes of extreme distress. The IBA's Television Programme Guidelines sets out the principles which should be applied in relation to these matters both in general and with special reference to young viewers. (IBA, 1982: 19)

The BBC follows similar guidelines.

PROGRAM CONTENT REGULATION

Family viewing policies show that in the minds of broadcasting authorities, regulation of entertainment becomes all the more urgent because of the way it enters and becomes part of the home environment. In its report to Parliament, Britain's Annan Committee opened its chapter on program standards by asking rhetorically, "Why have them at all?" Contrary to the answer from U.S. deregulators, the committee members found ample justification for program content regulation, especially because of those attributes of broadcasting that create a unique psychological climate at the point of reception:

> *People watch and listen in the family circle, in their homes, so that violations of the taboos of language and behaviour, which exist in every society, are witnessed by the whole family—parents, children and grandparents—in each other's presence. These violations are more deeply embarrassing and upsetting than if they had occurred in the privacy of a book, or in a club, cinema or theatre. People distinguish between one medium and another. . . . It is not a rebuttal to say that the viewer can press the button and change the channel after he has been grossly offended. The viewer feels himself implicated in the offensive act. The airwaves, unlike the printing presses, are licensed by Parliament. (Great Britain, 1977: 246)*

Viewed from this perspective, subjects of special regulatory concern include vulgarity, violence, sex, crime, religion, and broader aspects of programs that affect a nation's cultural autonomy or integrity, such as the language(s) of broadcasting and the proportion of imported to domestically produced programming.

Self-Regulation

Nongovernment broadcasters usually cooperate with each other to forestall government interference by adopting voluntary program and advertising standards. The U.S. National Association of Broadcasters' (NAB) radio and television codes covered the typical subjects of self-regulation: obligations to the family; responsibilities toward children and community; standards with respect to such sensitive topics as violence, crime, drugs, and sex; treatment of news and public affairs; fairness in dealing with controversies and personal attacks; politics; religion; and advertising.*

---

*The NAB radio and television codes, never rigorously or universally effective, became moot in 1983 when, as a result of a Justice Department suit against the

In the United States, official content regulation stopped short not far above the level of these voluntary codes. Deterred both by the First Amendment and the broadcasting statute's own censorship disclaimer,* the FCC avoids hard-and-fast content rules. The act requires it to ensure operation "in the public interest," under which rubric the FCC issued localism rules, the fairness doctrine, the personal attack rule (an aspect of fairness entitling the target of personal attacks during the airing of controversial subjects a chance to reply), and the prime-time access rule (limiting television network domination of the best evening hours). Licensees generally encounter policy-based initiatives of the commission in the course of obtaining and renewing licenses. But deregulation is eroding even these minimal content regulations. In contrast to this permissiveness, the systems of other industrialized democracies impose many explicit regulatory controls on programming.

Violence and Sex

Though most cultures agree on which subjects deserve content regulation, they differ on where to draw the line. British and American audiences share sensitivities about violence and nudity, for example, but Americans seem more tolerant of broadcast violence, the British more tolerant of broadcast nudity. Observers have often noted that the British accept nudity more readily than Americans when it occurs in a documentary context. Thus the BBC accepted but NBC cut a few seconds of frontal nudity in "The Holocaust," which showed naked victims being driven into gas chambers.

Both the BBC and the IBA have adopted violence codes. In fact, the law requires that the IBA draw up such a code with special reference to children's programs. Many countries that import U.S. syndicated programs censor them for violent episodes and many for physical contacts between the sexes. Singapore Broadcasting Corporation (a BBC type of statutory board, mentioned in Section 3.4) goes so far as to designate Mondays, Tuesdays, and Fridays as violence-free days, enabling parents to ration television viewing to protect their children from exposure to objectionable episodes.[8]

Religion

Sex standards usually involve religious considerations, which have always played a substantial role in the regulation of broadcasting. The

---

commercial restraints of the television code, the association suspended its implementation.

*"Nothing in this act shall be understood or construed to give the Commission the power of censorship . . . and no regulation or condition shall be promulgated or fixed by the Commission which shall interfere with the right of free speech by means of radio communication" (47 USC Section 326).

U.S. Communications Act says nothing on the subject, but the FCC lists religious programs as one of the types normally expected in a comprehensive service.

Great Britain. Although the Church of England enjoys the status of an officially "established" faith, neither the BBC's charter nor its licensing document mentions religion. John Reith, himself a devout Presbyterian, opted for nonsectarian Christianity on the air when the BBC began operations. He "boldly set aside [sectarian] shades of difference, convinced that it would be scandalous and wrong to allow religious sects time to advertise them on the air" (Boyle, 1972: 175). Originally, Reith closed down the BBC during Sunday church service hours; beginning in 1933, he allowed it to stay on the air during services but only with suitably sober programs.*

Not until 1957 did the BBC abandon its "Reithean Sunday" policy of avoiding competition with church attendance. Paulu concluded that "the British went too far in paternalistically protecting the churches from the competition of television" (1981: 282).

The mainline churches in Britain opposed the IBA, fearing the materialistic influence of broadcast advertising. However, the ITV companies made their peace with the churches, showing imagination and innovative daring in their religious programming. In particular, they introduced more non-Christian religious groups to the air, reflecting Britain's growing cultural diversity.

Like U.S. broadcasters, the BBC chose to avoid religious controversy by giving time only to the main church groups. In the United States, this limitation led evangelical sects and other small churches to resort to purchasing time and founding their own stations in order to get on the air. Small religious groups cannot use this tactic in Britain, for both BBC and IBA rules strictly forbid the use of broadcasting for making sectarian appeals for money. They even enjoin the use of broadcasting for such nonsectarian religious advertising as spot announcements urging listeners or viewers to "attend the church of your choice." Thus the commercialization of the "electronic church" that marks contemporary American broadcasting has no counterpart in Britain or, for that matter, in Europe generally.

Denied the use of established broadcasting outlets, evangelical groups bought time from European pirate broadcasters (see Section 4.4)

---

*Reith's Sunday blackouts of entertainment led to the early success in Britain of foreign commercial stations, such as Radio Normandy in France, which in the 1930s attracted nearly 90 percent of the BBC's audience in the south of England to its Sunday programs. Routine, enforced religiously oriented broadcasting, wherever it happens, generally has depressing effects on audience size. More recently in Malaysia, for example, the evening Quran readings drew less than a hundred thousand television viewers, but the immediately ensuing episodes of *Return of the Saint* attracted more than a million (Lent, 1982, quoting B. Newman: 175).

or from international commercial stations. They even built international stations of their own (see Section 11.6). In Sweden and Norway, evangelical churches took full advantage of the opportunities those countries gave local groups to establish permissively regulated neighborhood stations (see Section 4.5).

Islam. In every country where Islam ranks as the dominant faith, it functions as the state religion, making broadcasting automatically an avenue of religious example and teaching. Earlier I mentioned how the very admittance of broadcasting to Saudi Arabia hinged on finding divine sanction for it in the Quran (see Section 2.4). The fundamentalist Wahabi sect of Saudi Arabia sets the religious tone for Arab broadcasting content standards generally in the Middle East.

In Muslim countries, each schedule not only starts and ends with religious observances, the entire intervening program content reflects the Islamic view of life. Every item broadcast must meet the test of religious acceptability. Saudi broadcasting guidelines explicitly prohibit the following: scenes liable to arouse sexual excitement; women dancing, making love, dressed "indecently," or participating in athletic events; anything connected with alcohol and its consumption; derogatory references to the "Heavenly Religions"; praise, satire, or contempt aimed at other countries; any reference to Zionism; anything derogatory of monarchy; references to betting or gambling; excessive violence.[9] Representatives of foreign firms attempting to sell programs in the Middle East find Saudi Arabia their toughest customer. Even a whisky bottle in the background of a setting, a skimpy bathing suit in a *Love Boat* scene, or innocent physical contact between the sexes can render an entire episode unsalable.[10]

Communist Nations. At the other religious extreme fall the Communist countries. They too tend to be prudish about sex, but most of them forbid religious programs altogether. East Germany permits some religious broadcasts, and in Poland, grudging relaxation of the ban on broadcast religion marked the 1979 visit of Polish-born Pope John Paul II. The national government network carried arrival and departure scenes, but only local stations broadcast ceremonial events within the country. The government issued orders to broadcasters "not to show the enormous throngs that greeted the Pope everywhere he went. It was the first time the Mass had ever been broadcast on television in this overwhelmingly Catholic country" (Niemczyk, 1983: 54). Still more such broadcasts occurred during the Pope's 1983 visit to Poland.

Dress Symbolism

The images of broadcasting carry pervasive cultural overtones. Every gesture and every item of dress can take on unexpected meanings when a program migrates from one culture to another. Thus, to continue with the Saudi Arabian example, once religious objections to creating television images had been overcome, still another problem arose—the appearance of females among those images. Broadcasting opened up a new and unprecedentedly public occupation for women, who

> *were only gradually allowed to be seen on television, and there remains a kind of double standard on the national channel. Western women are considered to be properly attired when their arms are covered and their skirts are not above the knees. On the other hand, Arab women are usually more conservatively dressed, with at least a scarf covering the hair. (Boyd, 1982: 136–137)*

Dress codes have great cultural significance, and television tends to magnify symbolic meanings. Under the shah, Iranian television presenters wore smartly tailored suits and fashionable frocks. As soon as Khomeini assumed control, a dramatic change took place: "The men no longer wear coat and tie but revolutionary fatigues or open neck shirts, and the women have replaced the latest Parisian fashions with modest clothing and an Islamic headcover" (Tehranian, 1982: 42). In Malaysia, the government issued a set of mimeographed drawings stipulating permissible hair length for actors appearing in television commercials.[11]

6·6 LANGUAGE REGULATION

Every aspect of broadcasting has its impact on culture, but none more powerfully than language, which affects radio (the predominant medium in much of the world) even more than television. For many broadcasting systems, therefore, language policy becomes the most intractable and explosive of issues. The peoples of the world use some twenty-eight hundred living languages,[12] without even counting the additional thousands of dialects. Broadcasting's audiovisual nature makes it hospitable to unwritten languages, and the medium speaks directly to the millions who understand written languages but cannot read. Thus broadcasting reaches vast numbers of people never touched by the press.*

Language Chauvinism

English-speaking countries have an advantage in the world program market not only because so many have adopted English as a second language but also because of the similarity between written and spoken English. Some languages, notably Arabic, have spoken forms that differ markedly from the written form. One cannot assume that all

---

*I have not seen a recent broadcast-versus-press language count. A hint may be gleaned from a 1960 report that Africa then used 109 radio languages as against 72 newspaper languages. My own count of African radio languages indicated an increase to 196 by 1972 (Head, 1974: 350). By the 1980s, no doubt two or three times as many languages can be heard on radio and television as can be seen in newspapers and magazines.

speakers of colloquial Arabic can fully understand scripts read on the air, though broadcasting has done much to internationalize spoken Arabic by developing a journalistic version less formal than the classical language of the Quran.

Some observers think English the best adapted of all languages for the modern media. A British scholar speaks of its "brevity, terseness, pace and precision." English, he says,

> contains a greater variety of pithy phrases and simple words from which to choose (compared with French for example) and the English-language version is usually shorter than the version in any other language. And English has simpler grammar than possible rival languages such as Russian. English is the language best suited to comic strips, headlines, riveting first sentences, photo captions, dubbing, sub-titling, pop songs, hoardings, disc-jockey banter, news flashes, sung commercials. (Tunstall, 1977: 128)

Other countries resent the invasion of convenient, slangy English words into their language, a tendency greatly stimulated by broadcasting. The French, well known for battling the "pollution" of their language by Americanisms, regulate the wording of broadcast commercials to ensure linguistic correctness. In 1983 the French Ministry of Communication banished scores of occupational "Franglais" words such as *le copy testing* and *le fade-out*. The grammatical errors common in American commercials (deliberately used because copywriters think "tastes good like a cigarette should" not only rhymes but sounds authentic) would never be tolerated in many countries.

Americans tend to take the English language for granted, happily naturalizing immigrant words along with immigrant citizens. As a melting pot civilization, the United States has evolved an eclectic, self-confident culture. Few Americans realize how radically their country differs in this respect from others. Most nations adopt an official language (or languages) in which broadcasting must be conducted, and, as noted, they take great pains to preserve linguistic purity.

As the American melting pot ideal has receded, however, minorities have become assertive about retaining their separateness. In South Florida, for example, the influx of Cubans and other Latins has been so rapid and so massive that many have remained linguistically unassimilated. Formerly, immigrants gave their highest priority to learning English in their struggle to attain the American dream, but South Florida's Latins considered English less vital for survival and even success. Bilingualism therefore became an explosive political issue in South Florida. Many native-born (and indeed even naturalized) Americans began to feel like strangers in their own land, and some lobbied for a law making English the official language of the state.

In 1980 Miamians in fact passed a county referendum measure banning "expenditure of county funds for the purposes of utilizing any language other than English, or promoting any culture other than that of the United States." Interestingly, this bilingual battle was fought on radio: the original stimulus for the referendum campaign came from a talk show host, and Spanish-language radio stations led the fight against the ordinance. The bitterness engendered by the bilingualism issue in South Florida gave some Americans a mild taste of the chauvinistic intensity of language preferences elsewhere. Language choice can literally become a life-and-death issue in places like India, where thousands have died in language riots.

National Linguistic Environments

The language problems that broadcasters face can be roughly divided according to two linguistic environments: (1) basically monolingual societies, usually with substantial minority languages in the background, and (2) polylingual societies, in which no single language assumes the dominant role. A special case is that of Israel, which seeks to bring to life an ancient language long since relegated to liturgical use.

Monolingualism. Few if any countries can be considered purely monolingual. Wars, conquests, annexations, immigration, and the ethnic separatism that has been on the rise since the 1960s increase linguistic fragmentation, though the total number of living languages declines as small aboriginal groups die out. For example, only about fifty thousand pure aborigines survive in Australia, speaking more than two hundred languages.[13]

Most countries with a single official language also broadcast in other languages to satisfy the needs of aborigines, immigrants, and temporary "guest workers" (the German euphemism for imported menial labor). In the United States, upward of 175 radio stations broadcast in Spanish, and an entire Spanish-speaking network of television stations and cable companies exists, as well as a satellite-distributed cable program service in Spanish. The U.S. aborigines, the Indians, get some service in their own languages from stations in the Southwest. Dozens of foreign languages can be heard on stations throughout the United States, serving enclaves of immigrant Americans. This language diversification on the air comes about not because of government planning but in response to market opportunities, plus a certain amount of mild persuasion from the FCC, which prods stations to serve specific local needs and encourages minority station ownership.

Elsewhere, however, foreign-language programs usually come into being as a result of deliberate government policies. Some governments follow a policy of neglect, acting as though minorities did not exist; some actively seek to erase ethnic separatism by using broadcasting to promote use of the national language. The Sudan, whose official language is Arabic, attempts to use that language as a unifying force. But the northern two thirds, where Arabic and Islam dominate, has serious problems maintaining dominance over the southern third of the vast territory. There, Nilotic tribes speak African languages and subscribe to Christian or animist beliefs rather than to Islam. The central government in the north has always been reluctant to allow the southern tribes to control their own radio stations or to broadcast in their own languages. With minor exceptions, it concentrates broadcast facilities in the north and tries to use radio as a means of Arabicization.

Australia offers an opposite example, the affirmative use of broadcasting to furnish special services to minority groups. I have already mentioned its Special Broadcasting Service (see Section 4.5), which broadcasts in 52 languages. Other examples include the following:

- The Italian government pays the state-run RAI to supply special programming for German, Slovene, and French enclaves in Italy, as well as for immigrant workers.

- In the northern tier of African states, bordering on the Mediterranean, substantial numbers of the aboriginal inhabitants have retained their own languages for more than a thousand years since the original Arab invasion of that region. Algeria recognizes Kabyle as a principal language* and devotes part of the time of a special network to that language. Neighboring Morocco broadcasts short programs in Berber and Hassania. Seventy percent of the Pakistanis speak Urdu, which the nation lists as its only principal language. But Pakistan also broadcasts in Baluchi, Balti, Brahvi, Chitrali, English, Punjabi, Pashto, Shenna, Seraiki, and Sindhi. Fifty people died in riots in 1973 when Sindhi speakers tried to make their tongue the official language of the Sind province.

- Most Central and South American countries list only Spanish as their principal language. Many remnants of the pre-Colombian Aztec and other cultures remain, however, retaining their own languages. Indians represent about half the population of Bolivia, which lists Aymara and Quechua as well as Spanish as principal broadcasting languages. Ecuador and Peru broadcast in Quechua, Paraguay in Guarani. The 1967 Paraguayan constitution gives Guarani equal status with Spanish. More than 90 percent of the population speak the Indian language, the most successful instance of survival against the inroads of Spanish. Guarani has no status as a written language, however, remaining almost entirely oral; yet Spanish remains the main language of broadcasting. The prestige of Spanish as a European language remains high, so it dominates broadcasting to the neglect of indigenous languages. Stations run by missionaries such as the Maryknoll Fathers attempt to fill the gap.

- Malaysia has a geolinguistic problem: each of its three parts, one on the Asian mainland and two on the island of Borneo, have different ethnic and hence linguistic compositions. The government radio

---

*The term *principal language* in the present context refers to the listings supplied by the countries in question to the *World Radio TV Handbook* (WRTH, 1983).

organization lists English, Chinese, "Indian," and local dialects as principal languages, along with Bahasa Malaysia. The state would like to use the last as a unifier, and the country's sedition laws classify the primary language as a "sensitive issue" that may not even be discussed.[14]

Polylingualism. Many countries combine under a single political unit (often one drawn arbitrarily by colonial powers indifferent to existing ethnic boundaries) many different linguistic groups, with no single language dominant. In these situations, broadcasting can face an impossible task. Not all demands can be met, and fractionizing the broadcasting services into short programs in minority languages negates one of the medium's chief advantages—its ability to provide a continuous, timely service. Radio can cope with half a dozen or so languages if need be, but television schedules are too short and dubbing/subtitling too expensive to make much multilingualism practical. Because of the political impossibility of elevating any one indigenous vernacular to the status of a national language, ex-colonies face the galling necessity of adopting the language of their erstwhile colonial masters as the only acceptable common ground.

In Africa, only 4 small nations out of nearly 60 nations in and near the continent speak single tongues—Lesotho, Madagascar, Rwanda, and Somalia. Invader and colonizer languages—Arabic, English, French, Italian, Portuguese, and Spanish—have been superimposed over the crazy quilt of indigenous African tongues. In addition, Africa has 18 trade languages, composite tongues that travel easily across political boundaries, such as Swahili in East Africa and Hausa in West Africa.

In Ghana, where no language is shared by as many as half the people, English has perforce become the official language. Ghana's wired-radio service, GBC-1, uses six indigenous vernaculars in addition to English, distributed as to time per week about as follows: English, 24 percent; Akan, 17 percent; Ewe, 12 percent; Ga, 11 percent; Nzema, 9 percent; Dagbani, 8 percent; Hausa 7 percent; miscellaneous (commercials, and so on), 13 percent.* Each language runs for about 15 minutes before another takes over—hardly an adequate service for any of the languages concerned.

South Africa's broadcast-language policy reflects its apartheid politics. In addition to bilingual services in the two official "white" languages, Afrikaans and English, South Africa provides separate services in the main African languages, both in radio and television. Regional FM services are available in nine African tongues, and three television networks each share languages as follows: TV-1, Afrikaans and English; TV-2, Zulu and Xhoso; TV-3, South Sotho, North Sotho, and Tswana.

---

*Use of English in national and international news and in educational programs accounts for the prominence of that language in what purports to be primarily a vernacular service (Head, 1978).

India's constitution recognizes 380 major indigenous languages, 15 of which are listed as principal broadcasting languages. About 30 percent of the population use Hindi as their primary language. Meeting the needs of such a linguistically diverse population defies the best efforts of broadcasters. India deals with the problem of supplying a national service in part by resorting to syndication of scripts: the central programming organization of All India Radio sends out scripts to the regional stations for local translation and production in the appropriate language.[15]

An Indian broadcast technician described the problem as it concerns television:

> Our insistence on retaining our own language and dialect and on propagating our own cultural values [has] led us to establish broadcasting centres all over the country, each centre going through the laborious exercise of producing all the programs it needs in the local dialect. . . . Doordarshan (India Television) inherited this philosophy from its parent organisation, All India Radio, and is continuing with it. But the television production processes are more complex and expensive. One finds television centres producing different programmes in as many as four languages and, in some cases, six. Notwithstanding this, the programme exchange between various television centres is minimal because of the language barrier. (Sadhu, 1981: 7)

He proposed cutting back on this wasteful repetition by using small segments of the television channel not otherwise engaged in signal carriage to carry six sound tracks. Teletext has demonstrated the feasibility of this technology. A program as it left the network headquarters would have six sound tracks in as many languages. The affiliates would select the appropriate track for their audiences before radiating the signal over their respective coverage areas.

Not all polylingual problems arise in the Third World, of course. I have already mentioned Canada, which maintains complete national services in English and French (see Section 2.2), and Switzerland, where four different language groups actually operate the broadcasting system (see Section 5.4). Belgium, with a population of less than 10 million, maintains two entirely independent, coequal sets of broadcasting services (each including radio, television, *and* external services), one in Flemish (a form of Dutch) and one in French. The Belgians also operate a small radio service in German. All this puts such an unreasonable strain on the resources of a small country that the Belgian services suffer a perpetual shortage of funds. Audiences rely heavily on spillover programs from neighboring countries to supplement their rather meager home-grown resources.

The Soviets wisely placated regional feelings by allowing and even encouraging the constituent republics of the USSR to retain their native languages. As a result, the Soviets have more official languages than any other country—16 in number, ranging from Armenian to Ukrainian. In addition, more than 60 of the more than 100 other languages spoken in the Soviet territories have air time.

Language Revival. A more daunting language problem than the one that faced the *Kol Israel* ("Voice of Israel") can hardly be imagined. The new state chose to revive ancient Hebrew as its official language—a language used liturgically but not employed in everyday affairs for more than two thousand years. It had to become the common medium for people ingathered from all points of the compass, bringing with them numerous foreign languages and Jewish dialects such as Yiddish, Ladino, and Mograbi.

As a matter of practical necessity, *Kol Israel* lists Arabic as a second principal language, but it also broadcasts in English, French, Georgian, Hungarian, Ladino, Mograbi, Romanian, Russian, and Spanish. Most important, it also uses a simplified form of Hebrew as part of the drive to create a common language for the new state. Israeli television employs only Hebrew and Arabic.

Nationalists in Wales would like to use broadcasting to encourage the survival and growth of Welsh, a remnant of the Celtic language that once served all of western Europe. In their long rearguard action to preserve their language and culture, Welsh nationalists blamed the BBC and ITV for luring their countrymen into reliance on English instead of Welsh. Not content with the 13 hours per week in Welsh received from the BBC and HTV (the ITV company serving Wales), the nationalists demanded that the new British network, Channel Four, provide a service exclusively in Welsh. After years of debate, the British government agreed to this demand, only to reverse itself later. This betrayal caused such outrage among the Welsh nationalists that they bombed transmitters, refused to pay their receiver license fees, and threw eggs at the queen. To cap it all, Gwynfor Evans, a venerable and highly respected leader of the language movement, threatened to go on a hunger strike to the death if the British government did not reverse its stand.[16]

As it finally worked out, when Channel Four began operating in 1982 (as related in Section 3.5), the transmitters covering Wales broke off as a special Welsh regional service called S4C (*Sianel Pedwar Cymru*). The service is run by the Welsh Broadcasting Authority; it programs 22 hours per week in Welsh, filling out the rest of its schedule with the regular national programming of the Channel Four network. The BBC and ITV transmitters serving Wales no longer carry programming in Welsh. Not all Welshmen applaud the outcome. Some resent missing out on the regular Channel Four programming during the Welsh-language segments, which, of course, come during prime time. On the other hand, supporters of the Welsh language fear that confining it to a single channel may ghettoize it, hastening its decline rather than reviving it.

Pockets of the ancient Celtic language of Europe also survive in France, and people receive programs in their version of that language, Breton, on a station of *France-Régions 3*, which operates part of the time as a national network but breaks up into a series of regional stations at other times. The Spanish Basques of the mountainous northern province near the French border maintain a unique culture and language. The Franco dictatorship forbade Basques to use their language outside the home, but after Franco's death, the new Spanish government granted the province broadcasting autonomy. The Basques now have their own service in their own language, resulting in the odd circumstance of their television programs being dubbed in Basque but subtitled in Spanish.[17] Catalan speakers of the Barcelona area expect to employ broadcasting similarly to help preserve and extend their language.

6 ▪ 7 REGULATION OF PROGRAM IMPORTS

On the average, about a third of most countries' television programs come from foreign sources. At the high end, in 1983, Brunei, Ecuador, Iceland, New Zealand, and Singapore all imported more than 60 percent (with New Zealand as high as 71 percent, apparently because of its strong emphasis on earning commercial revenue). At the other end of the scale, the United States imported only 2 percent, and China, Cuba, India, and the USSR less than 10 percent.* Most nations worry about the impact of foreign-language programs on their own culture and language, and they require that such programs be dubbed into the national language or at least subtitled—processes that add to the cost of television imports. As an exception, Sweden, which imports about a third of its programs, broadcasts the original sound tracks, usually English. "Youngsters are so 'tuned in to' English that the teachers of Swedish language and history are worried that in a generation or two the mother tongue might vanish" (Soderstrom, 1981: 306).

Changing a program's language, however, does not change its basic style and content. Broadcast programs project not merely words and images but points of view, lifestyles, and philosophies, all of which may be contrary to the ideology of an importing country. Entertainment programs create a reality of their own, especially for young audience members. Fiction draws upon the capacity of audiences to live out imaginary events vicariously and to identify emotionally with protagonists, who often become influential role models. These potentials of entertainment make authorities especially critical of programs that they think depict socially undesirable lifestyles, inappropriate solutions to human problems, and heroes or heroines unworthy of emulation.

Import Quotas

The usual response to this challenge to cultural autonomy is the imposition of *quotas* on imports. Even most of the relatively self-sufficient industrialized societies set ceilings on the amount of foreign material permissible in proportion to indigenous material in their broadcasting menus.

---

*Data on imports are based on a 1983 two-week survey among a sample of countries drawn from all continents, reported by Varis, 1984.

Great Britain. In the annex to its license and agreement (see Section 3.4), the BBC notes "the need to ensure that proper proportions of the recorded and other matter included in the Corporation's programmes are of British origin and British performance" (*BBC 1983 Annual Report*, 1982: 161). An identical provision appears in the IBA's enabling law of 1981. Thus the law leaves the two British authorities free to determine the appropriate ceiling. By mutual agreement they have set the foreign quota at 14 percent of their television output—a curb aimed essentially at U.S. imports.

Most countries need to import far more than that. Britain, after all, ranks second to the United States as a program *exporter*. Allowable quotas of foreign programs run as high as 60 percent and even higher. Of course, a flat percentage has little meaning unless qualified by time of day; in the worst case, local programming could all be relegated to the least desirable hours. As the president of the Canadian Broadcasting Corporation put it,

> The current regulations are such that Canadian content can be packed into low viewing hours during the day and into low viewing seasons. That liberates the broadcaster to pack more foreign programming into high viewing times and seasons and still meet the apparently respectable percentage [of] Canadian content requirements. (Johnson, 1982: 2)

Coproduction deals and other devices can be used to evade the spirit while obeying the letter of quota limitations.

In assessing the significance of quota percentages, one should keep in mind that it would be self-defeatingly chauvinistic to set import quotas unreasonably low. Broadcasting *should* use foreign program materials, both in its educational role and in its more general role as an enlarger of audience horizons. The IBA recognized this point in 1983, when in order to ease somewhat the programming supply problems of the Channel Four network, it ruled that the 14 percent quota need not count educational matter and old films that have historical as well as entertainment values. Japan, one of the few countries to import only 10 percent of its programming, probably needs at least that much for a balanced television diet. The United States imports even less and could be said to be downright insular in its television programming. In the 1980s, however, the growth of cable television created demands for new "product" that ensured increased commercial use of imported material (the noncommercial service had paved the way with its highly successful use of imported British fare).

Australia. Isolated Australia feels a special need to protect indigenous production from foreign competition. It has perhaps the most elaborate quota system in the world, one that tries to anticipate the many ways in which broadcasters evade simple quantitative ceilings. Stations must earn a minimum number of "points" awarded by the regulatory body, the Australian Broadcasting Tribunal (ABT). The ABT awards credits for many aspects of programs, including points:

for type of program, for the scale of the production; for employment of Australians in such diverse fields as writing and acting the scripts, or composing and playing background music; for the hour of the telecast, for catering to special interests such as children and education. There are also requirements for telecasting first-release Australian drama in prime time and for offering annually four big-budget specials. . . . It is an imaginative and successful system that ensures an abundance of quality Australian product. (Toogood, 1983: 87)

ABC, Australia's public service television, planned to increase its minimum indigenous content from 60 to 70 percent in 1984.

Canada. As previously related (see Section 2.2), Canada's proximity to the United States, abetted by the concentration of its urban population along the U.S. border, creates an insatiable demand for American programming. Over the years, Canada has attempted to limit imports to a maximum of 40 percent of all programming.[18] By 1989 the public service CBC was expected to reach 80 percent Canadian content. However, Canadian officials recognized that setting import quotas means nothing if domestic production cannot fill its share of the schedule to the satisfaction of audiences. It announced a new initiative in 1983 to assist financially in the Canadianization of its programming. Under the terms of new regulations authorizing pay-television companies, the government imposed a 6 percent surcharge on both pay-cable and subscription television subscriber fees. The income goes to the Canadian Broadcast Program Development Fund. Administered by TeleFilm Canada (formerly Canadian Film Development Corporation), the fund was expected to grow from an initial $35 million annually to $60 million by the end of the decade. Canadian television program producers can apply for matching grants of one dollar from the fund for every two dollars raised from other sources.[19]

In 1984 the Canadian Radio-Television and Telecommunications Commission issued new rules for calculating quotas, using a point system similar to that of the Australians. To qualify as a Canadian production, a program must earn six points. A Canadian writer and director each counts for two points; one point each can be earned by a Canadian leading or second performer, art department head, photography director, music composer, and editor. Other requirements concern how production money is spent.[20]

The Canadian case brings to the fore another aspect of quotas that must be weighed in assessing their value. Though defended rather loftily in terms of cultural autonomy, quota regulations have obvious economic implications as well. Among the most dedicated supporters of quotas are the talent and craft unions and the domestic producers whose livelihoods are affected by program importation. Chin-Chuan Lee, in a study comparing several national quota systems, pointed out that Canada does not in fact have a distinctive English-language culture to protect. He concluded that "the Canadian government's media policy has been directed primarily toward economics, although it has claimed culture as the ultimate objective" (Lee, 1979: 134).

6▪8 REGULATION OF ADVERTISING

Referring to European attitudes toward broadcast advertising, Roland Homet remarked that "fear of commercial distortion is every bit as strong and pervasive as is, in the United States, the fear of government intervention" (1979: 6). Most countries impose detailed regulations on advertising of a type that if attempted in the United States would collide head on with freedom of press laws. Moreover, because most commercial broadcasters outside the U.S. sphere of influence depend on advertising revenue for only a relatively small part of their budgets, they can afford to adopt a more lofty attitude than can organizations that live solely on commercial earnings.

In accordance with traditional Marxist theory, Communist nations reject advertising as practiced in the West. They see it as a futile capitalist ploy to solve inevitable overproduction.

> *Marx called advertising "parasitic," while Lenin rejected it as a drain on the economy. Both believed advertising was not needed in the socialist world, where careful planning would turn out just the right amount of commodities to meet the needs of the consumers. Their attitude toward advertising can be summed up in one [Lenin] statement: Advertising is an "unproductive exploitation." (Chu, 1982: 40)*

In practice, however, Communist countries today find that advertising serves useful purposes even in planned economies, though they avoid using the irrational appeals of much Western advertising. Marlboro cigarette advertisers do not invite Chinese smokers to "come to where the flavor is"; they simply tell them that the brand is "now available at selected hotels" (Chu, 1982: 44).[21]

The objections most countries have against all-out commercialization of broadcasting found eloquent and influential expression in the Pilkington Committee report, predecessor to the Annan Committee's report on the future of British broadcasting. Arguing for more stringent controls by the IBA over the commercial television program companies in Britain, the Pilkington Committee warned:

> *The social consequences of advertisements shown on television are, because of the unique capacity of the medium to prompt a desired response, likely to be profound. It is not enough therefore to adopt standards which suffice for advertising in other media. Television is intimate, peculiarly dramatic, compelling and available to people of all ages in relaxed and receptive moods; it can use at one and the same time the devices of moving pictures, music and speech. (Great Britain, 1962: 77)*

Note how the unique attributes of broadcasting once again come to the fore in this context.

Commercial Codes

The revised broadcasting law that followed the Pilkington Report transformed the IBA's voluntary advertising code into official regulations. The act instructs the authority not only to adopt a code but, in doing so, to consult an advisory advertising committee, a medical advisory panel, and the home secretary. The resulting code goes much further than did the (now suspended) NAB codes in the United States, which relied entirely on voluntary compliance and expressed most standards as recommendations rather than as binding rules. Most important, of course, the NAB codes had no formal sanction in the law. The IBA can claim, with justification, that Britain's regulatory controls over broadcast advertising

> are among the most comprehensive in the world. The frequency, amount and nature of the advertisements must be in accordance with the Broadcasting Act and the extensive rules and principles laid down by the Authority. There must be a total distinction between programmes and advertisements. The frequency and duration of advertising intervals are strictly regulated by the IBA to ensure that they do not detract from the value of programmes as a medium of information, education and entertainment. (IBA, 1982: 191)

To obtain IBA approval, commercials in Britain first go to the copy clearance departments of the television and radio companies' trade associations. They check on substantiation of any claims the copy may make and on compliance with the code generally. Thus, when the commercial copy reaches the IBA for official clearance, it has already received a basic screening. Nevertheless, in 1981–1982 about a fifth of the commercials submitted to the IBA had to be revised before going into production. The IBA again clears the finished commercials before releasing them to the television and radio companies for airing.[22]

Britain deliberately imposes stricter standards on advertising than on programs, arguing that programs have a "social purpose" that differentiates them from advertising. Audience members can more easily avoid programs they dislike or find offensive than they can advertisements, which take the listener or viewer by surprise. Moreover, the insistent repetition of advertising spots makes anything offensive in them more obtrusive than the appearance of an offensive episode in a one-time program.

Most countries have both industry voluntary codes and officially imposed codes. A survey found that about 70 percent of the countries responding practiced some form of advertising self-regulation. Those that did not were all less developed countries.*

The efficiency and scope of both voluntary and mandatory regulations vary widely from one country to another. In Japan, for example,

---

*The researchers sent questionnaires to 70 non-Communist countries, receiving a 70 percent return (Neelankavil & Stridsberg, 1980).

the government imposes relatively little regulation on commercial broadcasters, yet they have a comprehensive and relatively effective system of self-imposed regulation. Third World countries sometimes set up mandatory advertising codes but lack the administrative machinery to put them into effect.

Subjects of Regulation

Typically, advertising codes set up standards for honesty, taste, and acceptability of products. Certain areas occasion special concern. For example, the IBA code has special sections devoted to advertising as it relates to medicine, financial offers, and children. Cultures differ in their priorities, but most countries feel a strong obligation to protect children from undue exploitation by advertisers. The FCC's refusal to regulate children's advertising stands out as exceptional. By contrast, the IBA code goes into great detail on the subject. It forbids advertisers to urge children to buy things or to urge others to buy or even to make inquiries; further, commercials may not cause children to think that "if they do not own the product advertised, they will be inferior in some way to other children or that they are liable to be held in contempt or ridicule for not owning it" (quoted in Paulu, 1981: 73). Advertisers must take great care to avoid showing children doing anything that in real life could be dangerous to them. The Annan Committee thought that advertising to children should be eliminated entirely. In fact, the Canadian province of Quebec actually banned all advertising addressed to children under 13.*

Aside from general content standards of the kinds just mentioned, the typical limitations on advertising concern (1) the quantity of advertising time relative to program time, (2) the places where advertising messages may be inserted in the program schedule, (3) the broadcast times and services open to advertising, (4) the identification of advertisers with specific programs (sponsorship), (5) the production of commercials, (6) prohibited subjects, (7) the right to sell broadcast advertising, and (8) the percentage of revenue that may be derived from advertising (as against revenue from license fees or government grants). The suspended NAB codes dealt with some of these subjects, though usually in a milder form than elsewhere; some, however, are unknown to American broadcasting.

Quantity Limits. A major function of the NAB codes was to impose limits on the amount of time devoted to advertising. The codes used complex formulas, stipulating a low of 9.5 minutes per hour (for television network affiliates in prime time) to a high of 18 minutes (for radio

---

*The Quebec ban created the anomaly of advertisements in children's programs addressed exclusively to adults. The Canadian distributor of Atari products, the first to be prosecuted under the law, challenged its constitutionality in 1983 (Lippman, 1983).

stations), though escape clauses enabled allotting much more commercial time in specific situations. Most other systems allow far less time for commercials. The IBA, for example, permits an average of 6 minutes per hour for television and 9 minutes for radio. According to a 1983 *Variety* survey, European countries averaged only about half the IBA allowance for television. Heaviest advertising saturation occurred in Luxembourg, Greece, Portugal, and Britain.*

Japanese commercial broadcasters get around time limitations by broadcasting many short programs. Industry rules call for a maximum of 6 commercial minutes for a 60-minute program; but because each 5-minute program may contain a 1-minute commercial, an hour of 5-minute programs permits 12 commercial minutes.

Commercial Placement. Low time allowances for commercials can be ascribed in part to the fact that in many countries, spot announcements occur only in a few fixed blocks of time instead of being scattered throughout the day's program schedule. The U.S. method is to place commercials both between and within programs. This method is known as *trafficking* commercials because station and network traffic departments are responsible for scheduling the announcements. Trafficking of commercials appeals to advertisers because it enables waylaying audiences just when their attention has been heightened by program content.

In contrast, block scheduling makes a clean break between program and commercial time, ruling out both interruptions of program flow by internal commercial breaks and commercial breaks between programs. Commercial blocks usually occur adjacent to news programs several times each evening, each block lasting about five minutes.

Segregation of advertisements in their own little "commercial ghettos" appears to depress effectiveness less than might be expected. Audiences rather enjoy the advertising interludes, which are entertainingly produced, often with clever animated transitional sequences. The circumstances of presentation force advertisers and their agencies to make their commercials as attractive as possible. Loud, repetitive, hard-sell commercials would probably fare badly in this environment. One of Holland's program organizations gave Dutch televiewers a taste of American-style trafficked commercials in a program billed as typical of a day's viewing in the United States. Dutch viewers seemed to tolerate the increase in the number of commercials with equanimity, but 84 percent of the viewers surveyed objected to the intrusive advertising that interrupted programs internally.[23]

The IBA permits a modified form of trafficked commercial placement. Spots may be inserted within programs only at *natural breaks,* such as the

---

*The survey expressed maximum permitted advertising time in minutes per day, ranging from 90 minutes for Portugal and Great Britain down to 15 minutes for the Netherlands (*Variety*, 20 April 1983: 38).

intervals between games in a tennis match or acts in a variety show. The arbitrary chopping up of a feature film to create breaks for spots, common in American television, would not be permitted by the IBA. It allows no internal commercials in "half-hour documentaries; programmes for schools; half-hour adult education programmes; religious services and devotional programmes; half-hour children's programmes; some half-hour plays; formal Royal ceremonies or occasions; Parliamentary broadcasts; and any programme lasting less than 20 minutes" (IBA, 1982: 192). Other European services using trafficked commercial scheduling include those of Greece, Ireland, Italy, Luxembourg, and Portugal.

Advertising-Free Days and Services. A genuine mixed system such as Britain's provides audiences with a real choice between advertising-free and advertising-supported services. Some systems offer such choices on a more limited scale, blacking out advertising on certain days or on certain services. Israel schedules no commercials on the Sabbath, many European systems, none on Sundays and religious or civic holidays. Until recently, New Zealand allowed commercials only five days per week, despite the fact that its government-operated system is highly commercialized. Until 1966, the Swiss blacked out advertising on Tuesdays as well as on Sundays and holidays.

Alternatively, some systems explicitly identify certain of their networks as commercial, others as noncommercial. Examples include Portugal, which identifies two of its four radio services as *Radio Commercial* (AM) and *Radio Commercial Estereo* (FM). Tanzanian radio offers in addition to its noncommercial "Home Service" and "Schools Service" an evening commercial service, both on its most powerful medium-wave transmitter and on a special short-wave transmitter. Using Swahili, the official language of Tanzania and a lingua franca widely understood throughout East Africa, the commercial service extends to nearby countries such as Kenya and Uganda. Ghana's GBC-1, its "Home Service," broadcasts in local languages with no commercials, but the English-language GBC-2 is called the "Commercial Service." Austria carries advertising on only one of its two television channels, while Germany's ARD carries none on its third channel. Some authorities allow advertising on their national services but not on their regional or local services, as in Papua New Guinea, Italy, and Switzerland. France's FR-3 (*France-Régions 3*) went commercial only in 1983. Some systems advertise on television but not on radio.

Indonesia imposes what may be a unique set of restraints on private commercial broadcasting: stations that run commercials are supposed to use transmitters of no more than 500 watts on medium-wave channels only and to operate no more than nine hours per day between designated times.[24]

Advertising-free services operating side by side with commercial services have several functions. They give those opposed to advertising a chance to enjoy broadcasting without having to endure commercials, thereby diffusing somewhat opposition to commercialism. They furnish an opportunity for scheduling programs unattractive to advertisers and therefore sure to be neglected in a purely commercial setting. Regional noncommercial services, in particular, represent a concession to provincial newspapers that might be put out of business if nearby stations began competing for local or regional advertising revenue.

Sponsorship. Opponents of advertising-supported broadcasting have traditionally aimed their most telling criticism at commercial program *sponsorship*—the practice of allowing advertisers to supply, or to have a hand in the production of, specific programs. This practice, opponents believe, inevitably causes bias in program selection and production. Advertiser influence favors light, noncontroversial entertainment to the detriment of more serious programming, such as news, documentaries, discussions, and the classics of music and theater. After the advent of television, the sponsorship issue gradually receded because fewer and fewer advertisers could afford to sponsor entire programs as production and time costs rose. (Nowadays, many different advertisers typically buy spots within and around a program.) With single advertisers no longer in immediate control, broadcasters themselves played a more decisive role in programming. This change did not, of course, eliminate advertising influence; it merely diffused it.

Interest in sponsorship revived in the 1970s on a modified basis. The FCC began allowing noncommercial (public) television to accept money from commercial firms to *underwrite* production of specific programs, for which the firms receive brief acknowledgment of their contribution. This practice has been criticized as having a similar limiting effect on program choice as regular sponsorship. The Mobil Corporation, while happy to underwrite dramatic entertainment such as *Masterpiece Theatre*, has little interest in paying for hard-hitting documentaries.

In Britain, the 1981 Broadcasting Act allows the IBA to make provision for the underwriting type of sponsorship, which particularly suits the programming policy of Channel Four (see Section 3.5).* The law anticipates the problem encountered by U.S. public broadcasting by requiring that such programs be produced specifically for use on independent television and consist of factual portrayals of "doings, happenings, places and things" that the IBA judges to be of intrinsic interest and without undue commercialization. "When a programme contains an acknowledgement to a funder no advertisement incorporating the funder's name is allowed in or around that programme" (IBA, 1982: 191).[25]

Australia considered adopting similar sponsorship rules in the hope

---

*France allows its fourth channel, *Canal Plus*, to sell time for sponsored programs, contrary to the French general advertising practice.

of raising more funds for indigenously produced television programming. However, in 1982 the government turned down the proposal, fearing that it would threaten the Australian Broadcasting Commission's "editorial independence" and would encourage the ABC "to produce the kind of programming likely to attract support funds, with a consequent distortion of ABC priorities and programme schedules" (Brown, 1982: 21).

India, whose broadcasting services have traditionally downplayed commercialism, introduced sponsorship in 1982 to stimulate lagging television advertising sales. Sponsors who supply a 30-minute program, for example, can reserve 5 minutes for advertising—3 at the opening and 2 at the close of the sponsored program.[26]

Production. Concern for cultural autarchy extends to the sources of commercials. Few sights on Third World television screens can equal the incongruity of a slickly produced commercial for some frivolous consumer product, shot in an elegant London or Paris setting. Peruvian law requires that commercials be locally produced; Malaysia imposes a 50 percent surcharge on imported commercials. In Taiwan, commercials for domestically produced products must be announced by Taiwanese talent, and advertising for imported products must be in "refined" Chinese. Australia forbids the bypassing of local production companies and performers in the preparation of commercials.

Prohibited Subjects. Most European systems prohibit advertising of certain products and services. Commonly singled out are matrimonial agencies, money lenders, tobacco, and sometimes alcoholic drinks. Pharmaceutical products must meet fixed standards, and some systems, such as that of Switzerland, ban medical advertising completely. Germany bans war toys, France jewelry, Italy furs. Religious and political advertising is banned throughout Europe.[27]

Sales Agents. Public service oriented broadcasters tend to regard advertising agencies as the real villains of commercialism, with their single-minded pursuit of customers for their clients. Moreover, the international advertising agency qualifies as a quintessential example of the much mistrusted transnational corporation. With branches all over the world, the big international agencies handle billions of dollars worth of accounts annually. Coca Cola, for example, can be obtained in 135 countries and advertises in more than 80 languages.

The pressure to generate revenue can seduce advertising-dependent broadcasting organizations to adopt the advertising agency frame of mind. For this reason, regulations in some countries separate the selling function from the program function. Thus neither the IBA nor the program companies it regulates may act as their own agents in selling commercials. In Britain, private agencies compete for clients, but most other European countries give a government-appointed agency a monopoly on selling commercials in government-regulated broadcasting services. In the Netherlands, STER performs this role; in Italy, SIPRA acts as the exclusive agent for the RAI networks. The West German *Länder* similarly turn over sales to subsidiary companies with exclusive sales rights.

Maximum commercial income cannot be realized under such noncompetitive sales arrangements. But the services concerned have no need to maximize commercial revenue. Monopoly sales agencies can afford to treat clients in a high-handed manner because the demand for the broadcast advertising they control exceeds the supply. Advertisers must get in line and wait as long as a year to get exposure on RAI—a fact that accelerated the growth of private broadcasting in Italy.

Advertising-Dependency Limits. One reason Italy's SIPRA can treat advertisers so cavalierly is that RAI depends on advertising for only about a fifth of its income. Parliament sets the percentage of its budget RAI may defray from advertising earnings. In 1983 Parliament set the limit at 21.8 percent. Thus, with the bulk of its budget coming from receiver license fees, RAI has no urgent need to maximize advertising profit.

Prior to 1982, French law allowed the government broadcasting companies to earn no more than a quarter of their operating expenses from advertising. The comprehensive new law of 1982 (see Section 5.3) repealed this constraint, substituting a limit on the amount a single advertiser could pay: no more than 7 percent of the revenue of any state broadcasting company may come from any one advertiser.

SUMMARY

Though the extent and severity of regulation varies with the type of system (permissive, paternalistic, or authoritarian), the objects of regulation tend to be fairly uniform throughout the world of broadcasting. Regulations deal with licensing criteria, fairness, operating schedules, program content, language, imported programs, and advertising. Of these, the regulation of fairness causes the most difficult problems. Democracies seek to insulate broadcasting from government control with the aim of ensuring its evenhanded use in elections and preventing its domination by the political party in power. Because of the nature of the medium, however, it is impossible to satisfy everyone as to a system's accountability. Regulation of program imports also poses difficult problems. All systems must supplement indigenous programs with materials from the outside. In the case of very small systems and those of the Third World, however, imports tend to overwhelm indigenous cultures and to deny opportunities to indigenous artists. Regulation attempts to deal with this problem by setting quotas on the permissible amount of foreign material that may be imported.

NOTES

[1]*Time*, 20 Feb. 1978; *New York Times*, 11 Feb. 1978.

[2]See Browne, 1973, for a critique of representative councils.

[3]Green, 1972: 57.

[4]*Broadcasting*, 6 June 1983. For analysis of the convoluted ownership patterns of Televisa, SIN, and SICC, see Gutiérrez, 1981, and Walker, 1983.

[5]Wicklein, 1981: 222.

[6]Hershey, 1977.

[7]For a discussion of complaint-processing problems, see Cole & Oettinger, 1978: 117–130.

[8]Lent, 1982: 175.

[9]Boyd, 1982: 137, quoting A. Shobaili.

[10]Schiffman, 1983: 71; Mullings, 1983.

[11]Glattbach & Balakrishnan, 1978: 148. See Martin & Chaudhary, 1983, for a discussion of comparative content regulation.

[12]The French Academy's estimate is 2,796 (Berlitz, 1982: 1).

[13]Berlitz, 1982: 3.

[14]Glattbach & Balakrishnan, 1978: 154.

[15]Awasthy, 1978: 200.

[16]See Howell, 1981, for details on the long and complex struggle over Welsh-language broadcasting.

[17]Howkins, 1983.

[18]Lee, 1979: 121.

[19]*Broadcasting*, 7 March 1983; Adilman, 1984.

[20]*Variety*, 18 April 1984: 60.

[21]For a study of advertising and socialism generally, see Hanson, 1974.

[22]For more details on IBA procedures in comparison with U.S. practices, see Marting, 1973.

[23]*Broadcasting News from the Netherlands*, June 1980: 12.

[24]*WRTH*, 1984: 214. See also Foster, 1984.

[25]See also Glencross, 1983, for a general comment on underwriting from the European perspective.

[26]Dua, 1983.

[27]*EBU Review*, Sept. 1983: 29; Knitel, 1984.

CHAPTER 7

ECONOMICS OF BROADCASTING

People pay for their broadcasting in three primary ways: through government subvention, drawn from general tax revenues; through license fees, paid for by the users of receivers; and through commercial advertising. Funding sources inevitably affect programs, though many systems try to ensure insulation from direct influence. "Each method of finance," wrote Anthony Smith, "carries with it certain risks—moral, practical, fiscal, political—some of which are worth taking in some societies, but not in others" (1978: 43).

In general, the more authoritarian systems favor government funding; paternalistic systems, license fees; and permissive systems, advertising. Few countries, however, rely exclusively on a single funding source. U.S. broadcasting, for example, relies mainly on advertising revenue, but commercial broadcasters also gain income from the sale of programs and services, while public broadcasting depends on a combination of government subvention (through matching funds administered by the Corporation for Public Broadcasting), foundation grants, school funds, public donations, corporate underwriting, and program sales.

7·1 GOVERNMENT FUNDING

As was shown earlier (Table 3.1), governments own about half the world's broadcast services. Government ownership usually means funding primarily from tax revenues. True, many government-owned and operated systems also impose set license fees, though usually only in token amounts. Some also realize income from advertising, but the very fact of government operation usually detracts from commercial efficiency. Most systems supported primarily by government subvention are those of Marxist or Third World states (sometimes, of course, both).

The former rely on tax support as a matter of political philosophy; the latter, as a matter of economic necessity, irrespective of political philosophy.

According to Marxist logic, government ownership means ownership by the workers—preferable to capitalist exploiters. Marxists see no need to insulate broadcasting from the government; by definition, government ownership and operation serves the people, educating the masses and carrying on class warfare. As for the Third World, a study of 91 developing countries indicated the following funding combinations: government plus advertising—43 percent; government plus advertising plus license fees—35 percent; government plus license fees—8 percent; advertising only—2 percent (Costa Rica and Haiti). None relied on license fees alone or on the combination of license fees and commercials. Only 12 percent operated on government funding alone.[1]

In other words, neither advertising nor receiver licensing can bring in enough revenue to finance broadcasting in the Third World; nor can the two in combination. Most Third World governments prefer allotting tax funds to broadcasting in any event—not for Marxist reasons but because they see the medium as an essential element of nationhood, one needed for social and economic development as well as for political integration.

Though government subvention has the advantage of giving direct control to governments whose political philosophies dispose them in that direction, it has significant disadvantages for the most effective use of broadcasting's potential benefits. Government-run systems have trouble establishing credibility with their audiences (though even the least credible services can attract listeners and viewers in the absence of alternatives.)* Government operation and financing also means that civil service procedures must be followed in personnel recruitment, salaries, promotions, and dismissals. Nothing could be less appropriate for effective broadcasting. Civil service establishments, with their rigid rules of eligibility and seniority, leave little scope for developing and rewarding talent and creativity—or for eliminating mediocrity.

Government-operated systems are also hamstrung by bureaucratic budgeting and fiscal procedures, which keep broadcasting management from taking timely advantage of program opportunities and responding sensitively to changing audience interests and tastes. And when it comes to commercial operations, sales revenue usually goes directly to the central treasury. Because broadcasting employees receive no benefits from vigorous, efficient sales efforts, they feel no personal stake in fulfilling commercial commitments. Finally, government funding usually also means monopoly, which tends to stultify broadcasting. As I pointed out in Section 3.4, many countries with tax-supported, monopolistic systems, but without doctrinal reasons for insisting on government operational control, try to insulate broadcasting from the

---

*See the "abhorrent vacuum principle," Section 4.1.

government bureaucracy. Typically, they set up independent, statutory corporations along the lines of the BBC.

The degree of real independence such corporations achieve usually hinges on their ability to distance themselves from direct government funding. The Canadian Broadcasting Corporation, at one extreme, has maintained a high degree of autonomy despite the fact that three quarters of its television budget and its entire radio budget come from annual parliamentary appropriations. At the other extreme, All India Radio (AIR) has no independent corporate status. It started under colonial auspices (see Section 2.4) with the explicit intent of holding government at arm's length, but after India achieved independence in 1947, AIR became part of a government ministry with all its bureaucratic red tape. A former deputy director-general of AIR describes the frustrations she experienced in the 1970s, typical of a ministry-operated system:

> In the first place, our financial administration is highly centralised and prevents departmental initiative and speedy transaction of work. Furthermore, the entire approach is from the [viewpoint] of accounts and audit and is not liberal enough to ensure that spending is result-oriented. A Government department is more interested in avoiding objections than in achieving results. . . . Even the Director General cannot sanction [minor expenditures] without a reference to the Ministries of [Information and Broadcasting] and Finance. For example, he cannot create any posts except those of clerks and peons; he cannot transfer any but junior officials; he cannot send out an officer on tour for more than 10 days at a time, and he cannot authorise air journeys even when there is no other method of transportation. . . . The Director General's estimates of his needs are first scrutinised and usually pruned by the Ministry of Information and Broadcasting and then by the Ministry of Finance. Such reductions are generally arbitrary and often lose sight of the main purpose for which the funds were demanded. (Masani, 1976: 159–160)

7 ▪ 2   RECEIVER LICENSE FEES

Two thirds of Europe's systems depends primarily on license fees for their revenue. About half the African and Asian systems license receivers (though not all succeed in collecting the fees), but only about 10 percent of the systems of the Americas and the Caribbean do.

China never collected license fees; the USSR discontinued collection in 1961. Most other Communist states of Eastern Europe impose fees, but they charge only about a tenth as much as the Western European countries do—a token payment, too small to relieve governments of allotting tax revenues to cover most of the costs of operating their extensive services.

Origins

British manufacturers asked the Post Office in 1922 for a license to operate a broadcasting service. Even before granting a transmitting license, the postal authorities settled on the idea of licensing receivers.

In the first rush of receiver licensing, great debate arose concerning "experimenters" who built their own sets instead of buying them from the manufacturers. After all, the Marconi Company and the others had started broadcasting in order to sell receivers that they themselves built. For a time, the manufacturers advocated a special, more expensive license for experimenters; but by the end of 1926, when the BBC came into being as a statutory corporation in place of the original commercial company, the manufacturers realized that amateur building would scarcely affect the prospective consumer market for millions of receivers.

Until the end of World War II, British set users paid annual fees of 10 shillings (between 2 and 3 dollars).* But in 1946 radio fees doubled. The newly introduced black-and-white television license cost £2, twice the amount of the new radio license. From then on, the rate continued to rise periodically, reaching £46 at the close of 1981 for color television, £15 for black-and-white (separate radio licenses had been discontinued in 1971). European countries that depend more completely than Britain on revenue from license fees charge more, as shown in Table 7.1.

At first, the number of sets rose yearly, yielding a growing license fee income. As set use approached the saturation point, revenue growth leveled off; expenses, however, continued to rise, especially with the advent of color television and the resulting escalation of production costs. The worldwide recession of the early 1970s made matters worse. By that time, the BBC and similarly funded public services in other countries faced a financial crisis. Some European countries that firmly resisted advertising had to give in, allowing their systems to pay 25 to 50 percent of their budgets from advertising. Those unwilling to accept advertising had to cut back on services.

Despite this experience, a BBC spokesperson testified to the Annan Committee that in Britain the fee system had been "a unique success," pointing out that,

> The licence fee system involves each member of the viewing public—or, at least, each honest set-owning member of it—in the feeling that he is entitled to a direct say in what he gets for his money. At the same time the licence fee system puts the broadcasters in a more direct relationship with the public than any other system of financing would. It reinforces a frame of mind in the BBC which impels us constantly to ask ourselves the question: "What ought we to be doing to serve the public better?" (Great Britain, 1977: 126)

---

*The BBC originally spent domestic funds for the External Services, Britain's official overseas radio voice—the only way to get the foreign service started. During World War II, the government took over all BBC costs, domestic as well as foreign. Since 1947, however, the Foreign Office has given the BBC an annual grant-in-aid to cover External Services costs. In some countries (Japan, the Netherlands, and Switzerland, for example), license fees continue to finance external as well as domestic radio, despite the seeming inequity of burdening the license-fee-paying public with the costs of a government service for foreign audiences.

TABLE 7 ▪ 1 RECEIVER LICENSE FEES (EUROPE AND ENVIRONS)
Approximate Annual Fee per Household (in Dollars)

Country	Color TV Only	Color TV and Radio	Radio Only
Denmark	—	111	15
Finland	98	—	—
Austria	—	96	27
Norway	94	—	—
Iceland	—	88	29
Sweden	85	—	—
Belgium	78	—	13
Switzerland	75	—	37
West Germany	—	70	21
United Kingdom	61	—	—
France	58	—	—
Ireland	57	—	—
Israel	—	56	18
Netherlands	—	50	15
Italy	—	44	2
Jordan	30	—	—
Malta	26	—	2
Portugal	22	—	—
Morocco	12	—	—
Yugoslavia	—	3	—
Turkey	1	—	—

NOTE: The following countries in the EBU roster charged no fees: Lebanon, Libya, Luxembourg, Monaco, Spain, Vatican City. Algeria, Cyprus, Greece and Tunisia charged fees in terms of a markup on electric utility bills.
SOURCE: Based on data in "Radio and Television License Fees, 1984," EBU Review 35-3 (May 1984): 62–63. Used by permission. Amounts based on conversion of Swiss francs to U.S. dollars, rounded to nearest dollar, at rate of 1 franc = $0.43.

After reviewing alternatives and palliatives, such as total or partial government subvention, special forms of taxation, all-out advertising, and advertising limited to sponsorship, the committee concluded that the license fee system should be retained.

Theory of Fee System

Proponents see the license fee method of financial support as preferable to both government subvention and commercial advertising: (1) fees create a mutual sense of responsibility between broadcaster and audience members; (2) fees assign costs directly to the consumers of broadcasting, that is, the set users; and, (3) fees free the broadcaster from having to dance to the tune played either by government or advertisers (assuming, of course, that the government releases the license revenue with no strings attached). On the negative side, systems relying primarily on license fees may become too paternalistic and complacent. As it matured, the BBC fell into these attitudes until jolted out of them by competition from the ITV companies (see Section 3.7).

In explaining the economics of the license fee system, the Annan Committee likened broadcasting to such "public goods" as lighthouses for ship navigation. The warning light shines equally for all—for ships it is designed to serve and for all others as well. It costs no more to serve all than to serve only a designated few, and in fact it would be impossible to charge for each look at the light.

The committee concluded that broadcasting does not, however, qualify as an *essential* public good in the same class as police protection and public schools. Anthony Smith disagrees, arguing that broadcasting has become a necessity, not just an optional luxury. "Until 1960," he wrote, "the licence fee looked like part of a transaction between supplier and client; after 1960, it turned into a poll tax" (1978: 41).*

A French financial expert who wrote a monograph for the European Broadcasting Union on license fees concluded his analysis of their legal status by saying that fees must be regarded as "a tax levied on the strength of the state's monopoly over *telecommunications*" (Pons, 1964: 10). That governments still collect fees, even after installing commercially supported services alongside fee-supported services, reinforces the argument that they should be regarded as a form of taxation. Nevertheless, the BBC spokesperson was no doubt right in testifying that the public *perceives* the fee as giving the individual fee payer a personal stake in the system. Presumably, the attitude of fee payers differs in this respect from that of listeners and viewers in most state-supported systems that depend primarily on tax revenues from the central treasury.

Cable television restores the "transaction between supplier and client" that Smith mentioned. Its subscription fees differ from broadcast license fees in that cable suppliers control who receives the service (the lighthouse operator can charge for each "look" at the light, so to speak). It should be added that license fee countries collect the same fees for sets that receive all their signals via cable.

Mechanics of Fee System

In Britain, the BBC neither sets the license fee levels nor collects the money from set owners. Parliament retains control over the fee level through the Treasury Department, with the BBC making recommenda-

---

*In 1976 the New York State Legislature passed a law classifying television receivers along with furniture and refrigerators as legal necessities, exempt from seizure for the satisfaction of debts (*New York Times,* 24 Feb. 1976).

tions.* Disbursement of the total net fee revenue to the BBC does not occur automatically. Parliament allots the funds (before television expenses skyrocketed, it retained a percentage for other government purposes). During the 1957–1963 period, the government imposed a £1 excise duty on each license.

As the government agency in daily contact with virtually every household, the Post Office does the collecting. In fiscal 1981–82, it took in more than £602 million in fees, retaining about 6 percent of the total to cover collection expenses (including charges for investigating interference complaints by the public).† The BBC allotted about three quarters of its income to television and one quarter to radio.

Since 1961, set dealers and rental agencies in Britain have been required to report the names of set renters and owners to the Post Office, giving it a relatively complete roster of people subject to licensing. About 6 percent of users evade paying license fees. The Post Office pursues them by various means, including the use of vehicles equipped with *goniometers* (detection devices that home in on receivers by picking up their radiations). Elsewhere, the extent of evasion varies widely, depending on the efficiency of the collecting agency (usually the telecommunications administration) and on public attitudes toward civic responsibility. Less developed countries lack any ready-made administrative machinery for efficient collection, and if collection cannot be done efficiently, it soon begins to cost more than the revenue it generates.

Few governments allow the broadcasting organization itself to issue receiver licenses and collect fees. Japan, a conspicuous exception to this rule, relies heavily on the Japanese sense of honor and civic duty. The 1950 broadcasting law construes payments by users as voluntary "contracts" between the public and NHK (*Nippon Hoso Kyokai*), the public service broadcasting corporation. Thousands of fee collectors employed by NHK go from door to door, gently extracting monthly payments while also collecting audience data. Though no threat of penalty exists, virtually all set users pay up—including employees of NHK and, indeed, the emperor himself.[2] NHK also enjoys the privilege of setting the license fee level, subject only to concurrence of the parliament, which also must approve the NHK overall budget.

Norway's NRK (*Norsk Rikskringkasting*), a government organization, is an example of a smaller system that does its own fee collecting. Dealers notify NRK of television set sales, and it bills owners accordingly. NRK has the right to confiscate unlicensed receivers.

---

*A license fee campaign unit in the BBC's public relations operation attempts to "explain to Parliament and the public the reasons why the BBC needs a license fee increase and how it spends the money" (*BBC 1982 Annual Report*, 1981: 38).

†All financial data on BBC operations in this chapter, unless otherwise identified, come from the corporation's annual financial report for 1981–82 (*BBC 1983 Annual Report*, 1982).

Types of Licenses

With the introduction of transistors in the late 1950s and the consequent miniaturization of radio sets, radio licensing became impossible to administer efficiently. Most countries either licensed radio and television in combination or, like Britain, dropped radio licensing altogether. About a third of the nations reported in the European Broadcasting Union's summaries (Table 7.1) still issue radio-only licenses. Licenses for color television cost up to two or three times as much as those for black-and-white (still used more widely abroad than in the United States). Most countries charge higher rates for sets used in public places, usually several times the residential rate. The blind and other handicapped persons and sometimes pensioners may qualify for *concessionary* rates below the normal level. However, as the Annan Committee pointed out, problems of definition and of outright fraud make concessionary rates difficult to administer fairly.[3]

Disposition of Revenue

As the sole noncommercial public broadcasting authority in Britain, the BBC receives the entire revenue from fees, after the Post Office has deducted its administrative expenses. In some countries, however, the net revenue must be divided among several entities. West Germany, for example, has a complex disbursement formula. In 1983 the *Länder* agreed by treaty to set the combined radio-television fee at DM16.25 per month (about $75 per year), to run through 1986. The net revenue must be shared between radio and television, among the nine regional broadcasting organizations, and between the two networks, ARD and ZDF, after deduction of small percentages of the total for special funding to support external broadcasting, pilot cable television projects, extension of television into remote mountainous areas, and new developments in cable and satellite broadcasting.

7·3 ADVERTISING

Once broadcasting had been established, few countries other than the United States and its client nations relied heavily on advertising for financial support. Most nations not opting for government funding agreed with Britain's reliance on receiver license fees. Ireland stood out as a European exception. Desperately short of money, the four-year-old Irish Free State opted to sell commercials when it launched radio as a government service in 1926. The government aimed at minimizing commercial revenue, counting on license fee revenue to assume the main burden eventually. To its embarrassment, however, RTE (*Radio Telefís Eireann*) continued to earn more from commercials than license fees. A spokesperson regretted that RTE held "the unenviable distinction of operating the public broadcasting service with the highest dependence on advertising of all European countries" (quoted in Fisher, 1978: 71).

Initially, Marxist governments opposed advertising on principle, regarding it as a capitalist tool for exploiting the workers. The USSR banned radio advertising entirely from 1935 to 1947. Despite opposition to commercialism from both sides of the East-West political fence, an estimated three quarters of the world's systems carry commercials, at least some of the time and on some of their services. In Western Europe, only Albania, Belgium, and the Scandinavian countries held out against the trend toward accepting advertising. Even one of the latter, Finland, allows a contractor to broker time on its national television system for commercial resale.

Communist World

The historic opposition of communism to commercial advertising did not prevent Eastern Europe from using it to move consumer goods, especially when central planning miscalculated demand, saddling the state warehouses with surpluses.[4] With the exception of Yugoslavia, however, Communist systems use advertising more to inform prospective purchasers than to persuade them or to cultivate brand loyalty.[*] Commercials serve "more as a shopper's service than as a means of increasing the sale of goods" (Paulu, 1974: 57). In 1967 the USSR invited U.S. export firms to advertise in the Soviet media but warned them that "it is most important that you refrain from any hard-sell advertising."[†]

Leaders of China's Cultural Revolution (1966–1977) banned commercial advertising but used its techniques to sell ideas and to promote social change.[5] In 1979, after the end of the Cultural Revolution's austerities, China invited U.S. advertising agencies to visit Peking and Shanghai to advise on the reintroduction of commercial advertising. As related in Section 2.3, broadcast commercials began on Chinese television in that same year. At the time, some of the advertised goods were not yet for sale in China, but advertisers wanted a head start in establishing brand consciousness. Moreover, they knew that Chinese consumers would express brand preferences to family members outside the country, many of whom would then send them the products as gifts.

---

[*]France took a similar view when it reintroduced advertising in 1951, allowing only *generic* advertising—pitches for a product as such, not for its trade names. Brand-name advertising did not begin until 1968 (Thomas, 1977: 111–114).

[†]USSR advertisement in *New York Times*, 16 Jan. 1967: 56–57. "Unlike many European countries," proclaimed the ad, somewhat smugly, "the Soviet Union has no ban on commercial TV and radio" (actually few European systems ban commercials). Announcements, said the ad, would be grouped in 10- to 15-minute blocks, scheduled between 7:00 A.M. and 9:00 A.M. and between 5:00 P.M. and 11:00 P.M.

Third World

Most Third World countries lack the consumer purchasing power needed to support privately operated commercial broadcasting. Moreover, they use broadcasting primarily to further social and economic development goals, a usage at odds with efficient commercial management. However, few have gone so far as Indonesia, which abruptly banned *all* commercial advertising in 1981 to protect rural dwellers from what the government considered the disruptive influence of commercials. All but the more doctrinaire government-operated systems in the Third World continue to earn what little they can from advertising.

According to the Katz and Wedell survey of Third World countries, most of those operating commercial services in the late 1970s realized only about a tenth of their broadcasting budgets from advertising. Algeria, Egypt, Iraq, and Senegal, for example, earned 10 percent, Indonesia, 11 percent. Some devoted advertising solely or primarily to state industries and to social development messages.

All India Radio (AIR), after long clinging to the antiadvertising tradition of the BBC, found itself losing both audiences and prospective revenue to a foreign commercial station. In 1950 Radio Ceylon (located on an island off the southern tip of India, now called Sri Lanka) set up a powerful short-wave transmitter to beam popular film music into India, a type of music AIR had banned. This intrusion motivated AIR to establish its own commercial radio service, *Vividh Bharati*, in 1968, but it reached comparatively few listeners. Income from *Vividh Bharati* went directly to the government treasury; so AIR got no benefit, despite the fact that the stated motive for starting the commercial service had been to improve AIR's finances.[6] Finally, in 1981 India allowed AIR's main radio service to start running a limited number of commercials (no more than 5 percent of air time), concerned primarily with such development-oriented goals as family planning, public health, and agricultural improvement.

On the west coast of Africa, Ghana offers a commercial service, GBC-2, but shortages of consumer goods leave manufacturers and dealers with little incentive to advertise. However, GBC-2 does a lively trade in local funeral announcements. As in most societies, funerals serve as important social occasions. In Ghana, to announce them conspicuously on the air or in the newspaper is "something of a prestige practice and accounts for a good proportion of the advertising earnings of the GBC" (Ansah, 1979: 9).

Europe

As noted earlier in this chapter, fiscal problems put great pressure on European public service systems to supplement their license fee revenue with income from advertising. The decision to accept at least limited commercialism was made easier because audiences had grown accustomed to commercials from sources other than their regular domestic services—cable television from abroad, external and internal pirates, spillover from neighboring domestic services, and peripheral commercial stations.*

The British, however, introduced the commercial component of their system prior to the fiscal crunch of the late 1960s and the 1970s. Official consideration of an alternative to the BBC began early in the 1950s, with the first independent (commercial) television company starting operations in London in 1955. "Nowhere else in the world," wrote Paulu, "is there a system to finance broadcasting like that used for the Independent Broadcasting Authority" (1981: 112). The British system does indeed represent a unique solution to the problem of combining both public service (the BBC) and commercial services (the IBA-supervised companies) into a single national system in which each prospers and retains its identity—pluralism at its best. Despite some initial opposition to ending the BBC monopoly, two decades later the Annan Committee found little evidence of overt opposition to the continuance of advertising-supported broadcasting.[7]

Recall that the IBA, a nonprofit public corporation, owns and operates the transmission facilities of commercial broadcasting. It contracts with private commercial companies to provide programs and sell advertising (see Section 3.5). The IBA depends entirely on revenue from advertising, which it receives in the form of rental fees paid by the commercial contractors for the use of transmission facilities. Unwilling to risk deterioration of services in the event of insufficient commercial revenue, Parliament authorized the IBA to use government loans or grants-in-aid to ensure balanced programming. The IBA drew upon such funds in the startup phase of local independent radio.

Fears that commercial television might fail to generate sufficient funds to underwrite a quality service proved groundless—so much so, in fact, that the profitability of the Independent Television (ITV) companies came to be regarded as a scandal. Even after paying the IBA for transmission services, amortization of loans and capital investments, a reserve fund, and overhead, the main ITV companies became so profitable that Roy Thomson (majority owner of one of the companies) made the famous pronouncement that an ITV franchise amounted to "a license to print your own money."†

Starting in 1963 (activation of all 15 regional ITV companies took from 1955 to 1962), the government imposed a special windfall profits tax that came to be called "the levy." In 1982 the levy amounted to 7 percent of the ITV companies' collective income. The companies paid the IBA £36

---

*The French use the term *périphiques* to describe commercial stations located near the national borders, Radio-Television Luxembourg, for example. I treat this class of commercial station as an aspect of transborder broadcasting in Section 11.5. The Council of Europe has considered the human rights aspects of contemporary advertising in a study by Knitel, 1982.

†Anthony Smith is my authority for ascribing this gnomic phrase to Thomson (1974: 130).

million for its transmission services in 1981–82, most of which the IBA spent in operation, maintenance, and expansion of the transmitter facilities. Each ITV company pays the IBA according to its potential income, not according to the actual cost of transmission in each region. This policy enables the IBA to spend more on reaching homes in thinly populated, mountainous areas than would be warranted on a purely commercial basis. The "big five" of the regional companies reach 67 percent of the national audience, whereas the two smallest (the Channel Islands and Border companies) reach less than 1 percent. Thus the larger, more profitable companies subsidize somewhat the transmission costs of smaller, less profitable ones, ensuring close to 100 percent coverage of all homes.

Keep in mind that under Britain's dual public service–commercial system, receiver license fees as well as advertising enter into the revenue equation. The BBC gets no financing from the commercial operations supervised by the IBA, relying entirely on license fee revenue. In 1982 the BBC received £564 million, while the ITV companies' revenue amounted to £680 million, a predictable difference. Typically, when industrialized countries allow advertising to seek its own level—that is, when they refrain from imposing artificial ceilings on advertising revenue—it always outstrips revenue obtainable from license fees. In Japan, for example, though license fees provide relatively generous support for the NHK, revenue of the private stations amounts to three times that of the NHK. Of course, income could be equalized by raising license fees, but fee levels, like tax levels, are a sensitive public issue and can be raised only at great political risk.

Scandinavia represents the last major European redoubt holding out against commercials in broadcasting. One Scandinavian country, Finland, has broken the Nordic front by allowing advertising on its public service–oriented system without giving up the broadcasting monopoly held by *Oy Yleisradio AB* (YLE), a joint stock company in which the Finnish government holds 99.9 percent of the stock. In 1974 YLE agreed to sell blocks of time on its two television networks to a private commercial company, MTV (*Oy Mainos-TV Reklam AB*). Nearly three hundred firms, including some owned by the Finnish government, own stock in MTV. It purchases some 20 hours of time weekly, programs those hours, and sells commercials between programs (limited to 15 percent of the total time). Rental fees paid for transmission time by MTV amounted to 22 percent of YLE's budget in 1980–81.[8]

Much more than a mere go-between broker, MTV produces programs of its own (for which it also finds a market overseas), though it also imports foreign syndicated shows. It came into its own as a broadcaster in 1981 with relaxation of the rule that originally prevented MTV from doing news programs. Nevertheless, the YLE-MTV arrangement has its contradictory aspects:

The relationship between YLE and MTV is unique. YLE, while acknowledging that "in theory" there is no broadcasting monopoly, holds that "in practice," since YLE has the only licence, YLE is a monopoly. . . . Moreover, YLE's licence talks of MTV as "assisting" YLE. According to this interpretation MTV does not have an independence outside the monopoly. MTV sees things differently. It regards itself as an independent company which "rents about 20 hours a week in programme time from the Finnish Broadcasting Company." (Howkins, 1982a: 52)

Brokerage in broadcasting is not very common, probably because it leaves the broker in a dependent position while putting the facilities supplier in the position of possibly looking bad by contrast. The two compete with each other but not on equal terms. Reference was made earlier to brokerage in Colombia and in New Zealand, where the government offered to lease network time to private commercial operators for an early morning breakfast show (see Section 3.2).

There are signs that the other Scandinavian countries may eventually abandon their no-advertising policy. Norway's 1933 broadcasting law seems due for replacement in 1985, at which time Parliament may authorize some form of broadcast and/or cable advertising. Norwegian newspapers are investing heavily in local cable systems to protect their interests (cable, unlike broadcasting, is open to private investment). According to a national public opinion survey, some 70 percent of the Norwegian people favor broadcasting advertising as long as it is scheduled in blocks rather than throughout the day.*

Intermedia Competition

Historically, governments have often supported newspaper and cinema owners by taking strong measures to limit broadcasting's economic impact. Television in particular drains away audiences, advertisers, and program materials from other media at an alarming rate. Ironically, cable television reversed the tables. Television operators came to fear the economic impact of cable in much the same way that operators of older media once feared broadcasting. Then it was broadcasters' turn to seek protectionist legislation to help fend off cable's depredations.

Newspapers. In the United States, newspaper owners tried to bar radio broadcasters from using the newswire services in competition with the press. Not until the mid-1930s did broadcasters win full access to the sources of news. Later, television camera crews were temporarily frozen out of important news conferences by press reporters who denied that broadcasting was a true journalistic medium. In Britain, newspaper owners fought radio even more strenuously. During 1922–1926, when a predecessor commercial company held the sole license to broadcast in Britain, "it was subject to such severe restrictions on the broadcasting of news and outside events that the ordinary listener had only the remotest

---

*Personal interview with Arve Granlund, Norwegian Broadcasting authority.

idea of what the shape of future broadcasting would be" (Briggs, 1961: 267). In both countries, World War II created a need to reach entire populations as rapidly as possible with current news and information; in fulfilling that mission with distinction, radio journalism came into its own.

Opposition to broadcasting as a news medium had implications that went beyond the simple self-interest of newspapers. To this day, some governments oppose local broadcast advertising because it threatens the viability of provincial newspapers by depriving them of essential advertising support. In the early days of television, several European systems adopted radical measures to protect newspapers. In Switzerland, where both radio and the film industry joined newspaper publishers in opposing introduction of television, the press tried to buy its way out of competition:

> The Swiss newspaper publishers had always been uneasy about broadcasting. . . . They had only reluctantly conceded the right of radio operators to broadcast news reports, and now they saw the prospect of television commercials as another threat. . . . The publishers offered two million francs a year in exchange for an undertaking that commercials would not be broadcast. (Sandford, 1976: 173)

Swiss television started in 1958, financed about equally by license fees, a government loan, and the payments from the newspaper association. In 1961, when license fee revenue reached a previously agreed-upon level, the newspaper subsidy ceased. License fees still did not defray all television costs, however, and advertising began as a supplementary source of revenue in 1965. In order to protect newspapers, television accepted only national advertising and that only for 12 minutes per day (later extended to 20), with none on Sundays and holidays (and no television at all on Tuesdays). In a few years, despite such limitations, Swiss television became prosperous enough to advance funds to another victim of competition, the radio services.

When, after prolonged debate, television advertising finally started in the Netherlands, the Dutch system had to turn over 40 percent of its commercial income to newspapers and magazines to make up for their lost revenue. This arrangement lasted until 1977. In 1965 the German newspaper publishers unsuccessfully proposed a law banning all broadcast advertising. The persistence of opposition to broadcast advertising in Sweden can be traced in part to the fact that about 40 percent of the Swedish provincial newspapers already depend on government subsidies, which began in 1969.* In Britain, the IBA allows local news-

---

*Although direct government subsidy of newspapers would be unthinkable in the United States, the U.S. government has given indirect economic assistance to the press by creating special exceptions to the antitrust laws. The 1970 Newspaper Preservation Act allows competing papers to share certain resources, such as presses, thereby cutting operating expenses (15 USC, Section 1801).

papers that would be adversely affected by the competition of local commercial radio to invest in stations, but newspaper ownership remains a minor factor.

Feature Films. A similar protectionist motive leads exhibitors and regulators to control the release of domestically produced feature films to television, both as to their number and their timing. Too rapid release of feature films undermines their long-term profitability and hence the viability of domestic film industries. Feature films made for theatrical exhibition usually must wait several years—typically three to five—before they become eligible for showing on television (cable television release comes earlier because cable has a smaller audience and pays higher rentals). For example, the British theater film exhibitors association has a policy against releasing English-language theatrical films to television before they have been available to theaters for five years. Violators of the embargo face a possible boycott of their films by exhibitors.

A new phased-release pattern has emerged in the United States that will probably become standard elsewhere: first comes theatrical release, then pay television, then basic cable and broadcast television. At the same time, the interest in feature films as a television program type has stimulated production of made-for-television feature films. This trend has been credited with reviving domestic film production in some countries. For example, the emergence of world-renowned German filmmaker Rainer Fassbinder was ascribed to the fact that television put up the money for his productions when he could find no support through regular theatrical film–underwriting channels.

7 ▪ 4 OTHER REVENUE SOURCES

The chief supplementary or alternative sources of revenue for broadcasting include profits from auxiliary commercial enterprises such as publishing and program sales; surtaxes on receivers; surcharges on home electricity bills; foreign government aid; and private gifts. Paul E. Freed, head of Trans World Radio, one of the major international religious broadcasters, reported the most unusual source of funds. Donations poured in to pay a bank loan on the transmitter he was installing in Monaco, but at the deadline for repayment, he still lacked $3,000. Even as the banker warned him that he faced foreclosure, the telephone rang, bringing news of an anonymously telegraphed amount of exactly $3,000. Freed had a simple explanation: "God sent it" (Freed, 1979: 108).

Auxiliary Enterprises

Although the BBC's charter forbids advertising on the air, it does allow the BBC to sell advertising in other media. In fact, the BBC carries on a lively business in commercial publishing, program sales, and other profit-oriented enterprises.

Publications. In the United Kingdom, as in many countries, broadcasting organizations capitalize on demand for program schedules by copyrighting the details and publishing exclusive program guides for profit. Because newspapers at first refused to publish radio schedules, the BBC's predecessor company founded the *Radio Times* in 1923, its second year of operation. It carried advertising as well as program information, and by the 1950s, it had the largest circulation of any weekly publication in the world. In 1955, however, the ITV companies split the market by starting their own program guide, *TV Times*. The Annan Committee recommended requiring that the two organizations share their program information in a joint guide to spare the public the cost of two different publications (daily newspapers supply summary information, but only for one day at a time).* The proposal was not accepted.

A second BBC periodical, *The Listener*, also carries advertising. It functions as a literary magazine, reprinting selected items from BBC programs. Because virtually all the most distinguished British writers contribute at one time or another to the BBC, *The Listener* has a wealth of first-class material upon which to draw. The BBC also publishes many books, not only about broadcasting but also on topics forming the bases of its programs, including materials to supplement its educational programming.

New Zealand's program guide had the highest circulation of any periodical or newspaper in the country, earning some $12 million in 1981–82.†India's guide, *The Indian Listener*, although highly successful in colonial days, fell on hard times after independence. By the 1970s, less than 1 percent of receiver license holders bought copies, apparently because it gave little more information than readers could glean from the newspapers.[9]

In Holland, program guide publications play an important role not only as a source of income but also as a means of formally authenticating membership in the private broadcasting associations that share time on the national facilities. One of the associations ingeniously capitalized on its program guide as a means of doubling its membership almost overnight. AVRO, an independent (that is, nonsectarian) organization, feared that membership attrition would drop it below the 400,000 level needed to preserve its status as a Class A broadcaster. AVRO merged with a popular illustrated magazine that needed to legitimize its pirated program details. By including its membership fee within the magazine subscription price, AVRO immediately doubled its membership.[10]

---

*Curiously, the committee found the leading U.S. publication, *TV Guide*, "unimpressive and hard to read" (Great Britain, 1977: 466).

†A 1982 amendment to the New Zealand law gave the government minister in charge of broadcasting the right to order release of program details to competing publications, allegedly as a punitive measure against the broadcasting corporation, whose program policies had annoyed the government.

Program Sales. Every broadcasting organization capable of producing programs of more than purely domestic interest engages in some form of program sales to foreign buyers. The widespread availability of audiences that speak Arabic, English, and Spanish gives programs originally recorded in those languages a competitive advantage. Of course, programs can be dubbed or subtitled in foreign languages, but these processes add to program costs and are apt to detract from viewer satisfaction.

A subsidiary company, BBC Enterprises, Ltd., handles foreign sales for the corporation. It grossed £23 million in 1981–82, finding a ready market throughout the world, on both sides of the Iron Curtain and in the Third World. Forty-five systems bought "A Prince for Our Time," the BBC's prenuptial program about Prince Charles and Lady Diana; 38 bought "Television Shakespeare," an ambitious cycle of the entire dramatic output of the Elizabethan playwright. A separate sales organization handles BBC educational and training programs. People all over the world use "English by Radio and Television," including the Chinese, who bought several series to broadcast nationally in 1982.

Other profit-making ventures of the BBC include sale of sound and video recordings, leasing of technical facilities, provision of consultants, merchandising of products based on popular characters in BBC programs, mounting of exhibits, and leasing of data-bank services. All this commercial activity, though generally profitable, earns too little to relieve the BBC's budgetary problems, particularly because the government exacts a 52 percent tax on earnings. On gross revenue of £72 million in 1981–82, various BBC enterprises earned a net income of only £4.7 million.

Inasmuch as the IBA does not itself produce programs, it has no international sales operations as does the BBC. However, the individual companies that operate under IBA franchise have active marketing departments. American viewers have become familiar with a number of ITV productions, such as Granada Television's "Coronation Street," Thames Television's "The Benny Hill Show," and London Weekend Television's "Upstairs, Downstairs."

Occasional Sources

Surcharge on Electricity. Gamal Abdel Nasser, Egypt's president from 1954 to 1970, exploited broadcasting vigorously for political ends. In 1959 he restructured Egypt's system, which had been founded under British influence. He introduced commercial advertising and discontinued the hopeless task of collecting license fees. He substituted a surcharge on all electricity bills, an ingenious way of ensuring payment. It may also have stimulated sale of television receivers, because people who used electricity had to pay the surcharge whether or not they owned a set. Cyprus, Greece, Jordan, and Tunisia also collect revenue from electricity users to support state-owned television systems.

Foreign Aid. Third World countries get some help, especially in defraying capital costs, from foreign aid programs. Bilateral government aid to broadcasting tends to favor gifts of (or low-interest loans for) transmitters, studio equipment, and training. Such projects give visibility to the donor country, advertising to the local population its professions of good will toward the recipient country. Donors hope to reap incidental propaganda and intelligence benefits through their access to and influence upon recipient countries' communication systems. At the very least, committing a recipient country to specific types of transmitters and studio equipment manufactured by the donor country creates future markets for the donor's export trade.

High-powered transmitters often figure as foreign aid items. For example, Czechoslovakia has supplied such transmitters to Egypt, Iraq, the Sudan, Syria, and other developing countries. Though popular because they confer prestige as well as expanded signal coverage, extremely powerful transmitters can create more problems than they solve because of maintenance difficulties and lack of reliable power sources to operate them.[11]

West Germany has been especially active in providing both facilities and training to Third World countries. Most countries channel their aid to the Third World through official government agencies, such as the U.S. Agency for International Development (AID). West Germany does this, but it also gives substantial assistance through private foundations linked to Germany's main political parties. Though not run by the government, these foundations receive government funding. The Friedrich-Ebert-Foundation (FES), largest of such institutions, represents the Social Democratic party. Named in honor of the first president of post–World War I Germany, the FES gives material and training assistance to broadcasting organizations in many parts of the Third World.

Private Investment. Private investors have also participated in the development of broadcasting in Third World countries. Earlier I mentioned the British firm Rediffusion, which founded stations and wire or cable distribution systems in a number of British dependencies (see Section 2.6). In fact, entrepreneurs from all the major colonial powers promoted broadcasting in their dependent territories, often pioneering in the introduction of radio in the 1920s and 1930s and of television in the 1950s and 1960s. For example, scores of foreign merchants and other private entrepreneurs opened small stations in Egypt during the 1920s. In 1931 the Egyptian government (then under British domination) closed down these private stations and awarded an exclusive contract to the British Marconi Company to provide broadcasting services for Egypt. This arrangement lasted until 1947, when the Egyptian government canceled the Marconi contract and itself took over the operation. Egypt completed the process of nationalization of broadcasting with the revolution of 1952. Seven years later, when President Nasser wanted to start television, the Egyptian government contracted with RCA to install the system, which went on the air in 1960.[12]

U.S. investors have been the most active entrepreneurs international-ly, launching numerous projects on every continent but especially in Central and South America. Two of the most ambitious American ven-turers, Worldvision and Time-Life, had ties with stations in Bermuda, Japan, the Middle East, Holland, Germany, Sweden, Britain, and the Pacific, as well as in the Americas. The eagerness with which the U.S. networks and manufacturers moved in on domestic broadcasting in other countries led to much adverse comment on Yankee imperialism. As a matter of fact, most of these projects failed, and none paid off in a big way.[13] The syndication of television programs proved to be a more lasting and profitable form of commercial participation by American firms.

The advent of ambitious plans for cable-television networks and direct-broadcast satellite services in Europe once more stimulated U.S. business venturers to go on the road in quest of foreign broadcasting investments. Now, however, they target the developed rather than the developing world. For example, in 1983 a consortium consisting of CBS, Columbia Pictures, Home Box Office, 20th Century Fox, and major British firms announced plans to form a company to supply the United Kingdom with pay-television programming and other services.[14]

Miscellaneous Sources. Irish broadcasting gets about 15 percent of its revenue from government-operated cable television. Audience dona-tions and voluntary subscriptions help finance listener-supported radio and public television in the United States and Canada. Other occasional sources include taxes on private broadcasting to support public broad-casting and excise taxes on the sales of receivers.

7 ▪ 5   PROGRAM COST SHARING

The most critical aspect of broadcast economics, the high cost of pro-gramming, mandates parsimony in the preparation and use of program materials. The need to minimize production costs enforces the use of parsimonious formats such as the soap opera, whose settings, charac-ters, and basic situations can be used over and over again for periods extending into years. Distributing programs to many users by means of *networks* and *syndication* minimizes the number of new programs needed to fill broadcast schedules. Networks as such are treated in the next chapter as an aspect of facilities (see Section 8.4). Here I focus on sharing costs by distributing them among many networks and other outlets.

Ceiling on National Program Resources

It is commonly taken for granted that only lack of money limits the number and quality of programs a broadcasting system can produce. The fact is, however, that national cultural and talent resources impose a ceiling of their own. We should not be surprised that small but modern nations such as Ireland or New Zealand import some 60 percent of their television programming from the United Kingdom and the United States. Such countries simply do not have the cultural resources to produce enough programming of adequate quality, even if they do have the cash. Many highly developed but small countries such as Belgium, Holland, Sweden, and Switzerland face this problem.

A program shortfall inevitably occurs because of the nature of the medium: its continuous operation eats up material so fast that not even the richest and best-endowed nation can keep up with it. The United States, though it purveys syndicated programs and feature films to the world, itself imports programs in order to fill its many channels. Cable television and, prospectively, direct-broadcast satellites make still more demands on the limited world supply. Some observers find it hard to accept the harsh reality of television supply and demand. Why, they ask, cannot a small nation live within its financial and artistic means, cutting back on production costs? This tidy solution will not work simply because most audiences will not accept inferior production. People throughout the world have become knowledgeable about production quality, and most will not tolerate poor quality just because it comes from a domestic source. Programs must be attractive enough to motivate audience members to invest in receivers. Otherwise, listenership and viewership remain small, license fees and advertising income lag, or government propaganda campaigns have no impact. Thus a chicken-and-egg relationship exists between production/program quality and audience size: without quality productions, broadcasting fails to attract sufficient audience to justify the expense of quality productions.

I must add that not everyone agrees with the argument that a ceiling on programming exists in any given national setting, a ceiling that cannot be immediately lifted by money alone. Roland Homet, for example, an American writer on comparative communication policies, speaks of "the myth of the finite programming pie—the notion that a nation's creative resources are limited and if they are drawn to cable they will be lost to broadcasting" (1979: 49). True enough, creative resources as a whole can probably be considered inexhaustible. One could grind out endless interviews, pose innumerable talking heads in front of the camera, make incessant adaptations from literature, run perpetual amateur hours. But a ceiling does exist on the particular creative resources needed to succeed in broadcasting on a large scale—that is, to attract audiences of sufficient size and with sufficient frequency to make the investment in broadcasting worthwhile for all concerned—the public, the government, the entrepreneur, the advertiser—for whomever foots the bill.

Syndication

The most important conservation principle calls for centralizing production in a few localities where specialized facilities and talent have been concentrated. Production at such centers achieves efficiency and high technical quality. There producers can find the most experienced technicians and a large pool of talent in all the arts and crafts of production. The price of this abundance comes high, but networking and syndication bring costs down to a reasonable level for the individual station or cable system. Typically, national domestic distribution relies on interconnected networks, using as relays wire, cable, microwaves, or satellites. International distribution, though also possible on an interconnected basis, usually relies on syndication—the sending of programs on tape or film to individual outlets or networks that contract to lease them for a stipulated number of plays over a limited time period.

"Shareability." Syndication hinges on what might be called the cultural "shareability" of program material. Each culture has its unique features and may therefore devise some programs of purely parochial interest. At the same time, all cultures share common human traits that make for shareability of programs. Commonality of language carries with it a degree of cultural commonality; therefore, programs usually cross cultural boundaries with ease when the same language prevails on both sides of the border. Programs produced in France find a ready acceptance in Canada's Quebec province; those produced in Brazil find acceptance in Portugal. Certainly the English language helps sell U.S. programs in many parts of the world. Some commentators believe, too, that America's multicultural character lends itself ideally to shareability of its popular arts: "American mass media during the first third of the twentieth century invested themselves with a bland ideology compatible with various cultures. Thus they were being well prepared, albeit unwittingly so, to venture into foreign countries" (Read, 1977: 12).

Total shareability does not exist, even between closely linked societies with a common language. The transfer of program concepts instead of ready-made programs can be especially revealing. In the course of its transformation into *All in the Family,* the BBC's *Till Death Do Us Part* suffered a sea change, with considerable softening of the harsh edge of its original satire. But satire seems to make American audiences uneasy. At least broadcasters always temper and even sentimentalize it to suit what they perceive to be the American taste.

Dallas received the highest ratings in Britain and West Germany but rated poorly in Japan. In fact, in mid-1983 no American program ranked among the top 20 programs in Japanese television. Generally, however, American syndicated programming succeeds wherever it plays, albeit often censored for violence and sometimes for sex. Richard Reeves put it that "the films and television series of Hollywood and the Holiday Inns . . . the Nashville sound, and the sounds of the English language, Coca Cola, blue jeans, sweatshirts, shaking hands, majority rule, and freedom of the press seem to appeal to something essential in men and women" (1982: 81).

Reeves quotes a former chairman of Warner Brothers as saying "because we are almost always trying to reach *all* the people, we have found common denominator values that no other society can match" (p. 131).

This may be the true source of the extraordinary shareability of American syndicated programs—the fact that they exploit such fundamental dramatic values, appeal to such basic human emotions, and use such universal modes of expression. I was amazed upon observing the first exposure of Africans who knew no English to undubbed American television shows. They had an uncanny ability to follow even fairly complex stories simply by interpreting actions, gestures, facial expressions, and tones of voice.

Program Costs. The two BBC national networks produce more than 80 percent of their programming in their own studios, spending an average of more than £11,000 per program hour. BBC radio network and local station program costs average about £1,500 per hour.* Unlike the BBC, the three U.S. television networks contract with independent companies for production of their major entertainment programs. Collectively, the networks use more than three thousand hours of prime-time programs per year, much of which eventually winds up on the syndication market. On the average, prime-time entertainment programs cost the networks $650,000 per hour in 1983. After the networks have run them the number of times stipulated in their contracts, these programs revert to their producers, who then put them on the syndication market. A prior successful network run gives such "off-network" programs an advantage over "first-run" syndicated shows, those made for direct sale to the syndication market.

Through the process of syndication, such costly program materials eventually become available at prices as low as $60 per hour. As Table 7.2 shows, a small country can obtain a half-hour television episode for $30, while broadcasting organizations in a major market like that of the United Kingdom must pay as much as $10,000. In other words, prices in the syndication market bear little relationship to original production costs, which in the case of programs made for domestic networks have already been paid; instead, prices for the same programs vary over an extraordinary range, based on the size and prosperousness of the user's audience. Some critics of the U.S. regard the low prices charged to the Third World as "dumping"—deliberate below-cost selling by syndicators to undermine local, indigenous television so as to perpetuate Third World dependency. Defenders of U.S. media see the low prices as the normal give and take of syndication economics, which bases value on the program-audience combination, not on programs in the abstract.

The Swedish Broadcasting Commission, in a report proposing developments for broadcasting in Sweden for 1978–1985, calculated the

---

*Average hourly costs of BBC programs are based on data in the BBC annual fiscal report for 1981–82 (*BBC 1983 Annual Report*, 1982: 97, 115, 117). The averages do not include programs produced for the Open University and the External Services; the BBC receives grants-in-aid to cover costs of these two program categories.

TABLE 7 ▪ 2 COSTS OF U.S. SYNDICATED PROGRAMS IN SELECTED COUNTRIES

Country	Range in Cost for Half-hour Television Episode (in Dollars)	Feature Film (in Dollars)
Haiti	30–50	100–200
Syria	70–90	150–300
Nigeria	100–150	300–1,000
Chile	200–250	750–2,000
Egypt	350–525	1,500–2,000
New Zealand	400–475	1,500–2,000
East Germany	500–1,000	5,000–7,000
Belgium	1,000–1,500	4,000–6,000
South Africa	1,250–1,800	5,000–7,500
Brazil	4,000–6,000	15,000–30,000
France	8,500–10,000	30,000–40,000
United Kingdom	9,000–10,000	60,000–500,000

NOTE: In comparing half-hour episodes with feature film prices, bear in mind that feature films provide three or four half hours of programming, sometimes more.
SOURCE: Based on data in listing by _Variety,_ 21 April 1982: 4. Used by permission.

hourly costs of domestically produced programs of various types as contrasted with the costs of equivalent imported programs, that is, syndicated programs. The results, shown in Table 7.3, indicate that on the average domestically produced programs cost eight times as much as syndicated programs. It also shows that syndicated programs cost about the same, irrespective of program type, whereas home-produced program costs vary widely according to category.

Countries of Origin. For several reasons, the United States at first enjoyed a near monopoly on international syndication of television programs. America had developed television early and so had time to build up a backlog of material before most services began operating. Because of its size and its policy of localism, the United States always had a lively internal market for syndicated shows of its own. The competitiveness of the three national networks drove them toward entertainment programming of a type that had the widest possible mass appeal—an appeal that generally survived transplantation to different cultures. The U.S. motion picture industry had already been selling its products abroad for many years, so well-established marketing mechanisms and sales experience already existed. Finally, the simple fact that

TABLE 7 ▪ 3 RELATIVE COSTS OF SWEDISH DOMESTIC VERSUS SYNDICATED PROGRAMS BY TYPE

| | Index of Costs | |
Program Category	Domestic Production	Syndicated
Drama	100	3
Entertainment	30	3
Music	21	4
Children's programs	20	3
Documentaries	19	3
News and commentary	14	—
Sports	5	4
Average (10 categories)	24	3

NOTE: Read as follows: an amount of drama that cost $100 to produce domestically was obtained for $3 from syndicated sources. Based on 1976—77 actual costs, not counting general administrative costs. Overall average cost for domestically produced programs was SCr.200,000 (U.S. $44,600) per hour; for syndicated programs SCr.20,000 (U.S. $4,460) per hour. News programs, though home produced, usually contain a great deal of syndicated material from foreign news agencies as well as material gathered locally and nationally by domestic news agencies and media reporters.
SOURCE: Based on data in Table 6.1 of Swedish Broadcasting Commission, Proposals, Abridged Version (Ministry of Education and Cultural Affairs, Stockholm, 1977), p. 70.

American programs use English gives them an immediate entree not only to such English-speaking Commonwealth countries as Australia, Canada, and the United Kingdom but also to scores of other countries where English serves as a second language or a lingua franca. Critics add that U.S. syndicators gain an added (and unfair) advantage from the international ramifications of the American military-industrial complex.

American hegemony in the syndication field, so complete at first, actually began to weaken as other centers of production emerged to claim a share of the market. By the late 1970s, the major Western nations and many Third World nations were also marketing programs abroad. The pattern of imports by Sweden in 1978 serves as an example. In that year Sweden bought more than a thousand hours of syndicated programs, distributed as to sources as follows: United Kingdom, 28 percent; United States, 24 percent; France, 10 percent; West Germany, 7 percent; Canada, 4 percent; and others (mostly Nordic countries), 27 percent.[15] Countries outside Western Europe had more limited options for obtaining culturally relevant material, though they are beginning to have wider choices as production centers in the Middle East, Latin America, and Asia develop.

Spain and Spanish-speaking countries of the Americas form a huge common market for programs appealing to shared language and cultural values. Spain annually exports nearly a thousand hours of programming to the Americas, selling large amounts to Colombia, Mexico, Peru, the United States, and Venezuela. Mexico's leading private network, Televisa, dominates the large Spanish-speaking market within the United States. It owns substantial parts of SIN (Spanish International Network) and Galavision (a Spanish-language satellite-cable network), both of which depend heavily on programs produced by Televisa. In 1983 Televisa was even exporting *telenovelas* to the United States, *dubbed in English*.

However, the biggest Latin American producer of syndicated material, Portuguese-speaking Brazil, has to dub Spanish onto its sound tracks. Brazil's equivalent of Mexico's Televisa, *Rede Globo*, probably ranks as the fifth largest network in the world. It finds a ready market for its programs in Portugal, which imported Brazilian *telenovelas* for years before finally getting around to making one of its own. Peru had great success exporting a *telenovela* called *Simplemente Maria* until censorship that followed the 1975 revolution forced a cutback in production.[16]

In the Arab world, as previously noted, Egypt heads the list of syndicators, with substantial sales in the United Arab Emirates (its best customer), Kuwait, Qatar, Saudi Arabia, and the Sudan. Greece has developed into a convenient neutral ground for production of Arab syndicated shows. In the Far East, the British colony of Hong Kong serves as a production center for action dramas in Chinese, which it distributes throughout Asia for widely dispersed Chinese-speaking immigrant populations. Taiwan, the island off the coast of China to which the Chinese Nationalist forces withdrew after World War II, produces thousands of hours of Chinese programming annually, again finding markets throughout the Far East and even among Chinese-speaking residents of the United States.

Language Conversion. Most countries demand presentation of imported programs in their own languages. This means either *dubbing* a new dialogue track or superimposing written *subtitles* on the pictures. A tedious and time-consuming business, dubbing requires that performers read a translation of the original dialogue as they record the dub track while watching the screen and attempting to match their words with the facial movements of the original actors. Dubbers never achieve a perfect match and in any event often lack the acting skills of the screen performers. Some countries prefer subtitling. Taiwan, for example, switched from dubbed U.S. programs to subtitles because viewers found the absurdity of pure Mandarin Chinese issuing from the lips of American cowboys too distracting.

Dubbing, usually a responsibility of the distributor of syndicated programs, adds considerably to program costs. Some countries save money by accepting undubbed material and improvising their own language conversion. Thailand, for example, developed "dubbing troupes"—teams of skilled linguists to ad-lib live dialogue as a film progressed—to convert feature films. Television used these dubbing troupes as well.[17]

Subtitling, too, was a tedious process, involving superimposition of written translations photographically at the bottom of the screen. Television, however, has developed means of generating alphabets and imposing titles electronically. Douglas Boyd describes a field expedient he observed in Jordan, where much of the dubbing and titling in Arabic for the Middle East takes place:

> When the foreign program is aired, the subtitling is done by a machine that uses a monochrome camera with the polarity reversed, so that the black letters ultimately appear white when superimposed or keyed over the picture. An operator sits in a special booth during the broadcast, listens to the soundtrack, and advances the subtitles on the scroll according to the prepared script. This procedure, because of the human factor, produces erratic results, but it saves the enormous expense of dubbing programs onto video tape or of subtitling films. (Boyd, 1982: 93)

In contrast, Kuwait's luxurious production facilities include sophisticated bilingual character generators designed for efficient electronic titling of foreign programs in Arabic.*

Australia's Special Broadcasting Service, which offers television programs in foreign languages to minority viewers, has a subtitling unit capable of preparing English translations of sound tracks in 25 languages. The unit employs 25 full-time subtitlers plus many part-timers. It takes 20 hours to prepare the subtitle script for a 1-hour program.

Marketing Mechanisms. Most countries set up a single sales organization to represent products of their national broadcasting services in the international syndication market, but hundreds of private entrepreneurs also produce and sell programs for international distribution. *Broadcasting-Cablecasting Yearbook 1983* lists about 350 international producers and distributors, not counting U.S. firms. The United Kingdom, Canada, France, and West Germany had the longest lists of firms, but smaller countries such as Belgium, Greece, the Netherlands, and Sweden also appear in the list.

Buyers and sellers can meet to bargain over programs for the coming

---

*A sidelight on the problem of language conversion: syndicators wait for a sale before actually going to the expense of dubbing, which means that buyers must be able to screen programs in the original language. German buyers sent an eight-man team of English-speaking screeners to the United States to preview 359 episodes of *Bonanza*. The previewers had to work full time for an entire month. (Kowet, 1977: 14) season at international trade fairs. The best known, MIP-TV (*Marché International des Programmes de Télévision*), began in 1960. More than four thousand representatives from more than a hundred countries attended MIP-TV's 1983 market in Cannes. In the United States, foreign syndicators attend the annual meetings of the National Association of Television Program Executives (NATPE), whose exhibitions are the U.S. national equivalent of the MIP-TV. The 1983 NATPE exhibit attracted 18 foreign syndicators hoping to sell programs to U.S. clients. They included companies from Brazil and Japan as well as from Europe.

Radio programs also figure in international syndication. U.S. music programs and syndicated radio formats have great popularity abroad, but the BBC must be considered the leading distributor of radio programs internationally. Its Transcription Services sell programs on discs and tapes to more than a hundred countries. A series called *Topical Tapes* has special appeal in the Third World because the programs deal with such practical subjects as tropical medicine and agriculture. Worldwide interest in the English language assures sales of numerous program series produced under the general title *English by Radio and Television*.

News Syndication. Though not usually lumped together with syndicated entertainment programs, news agencies represent the classic (and pioneer) use of the syndication principle. Every nation of any size has one or more national news agencies; several operate on an international scale. Altogether, more than a hundred national and regional news agencies exist.[18]

The major international news agencies spend huge sums on maintaining news-gathering facilities throughout the globe, central offices for editing and retransmission, and wire and radio networks to feed news to their thousands of clients. News syndication, which divides costs among thousands of stations, networks, newspapers, and other users, makes the massive operation economically feasible. Such is the cost, however, that only a few competitors can survive in the international field as full-service agencies. Four agencies dominate the international field (see Section 9.6).

Supplementary Ways of Program Sharing

Most program sharing comes about through syndication, but economies can also be realized through regional exchanges, coproduction agreements, and cultural agreements.

Regional Exchanges. Broadcasters in each region of the world have formed what they call *unions*. These have nothing to do with trade, craft, or professional unions, consisting instead of associations of broadcasting authorities with common regional or sociopolitical interests. A dozen such unions exist, including regional groups in Eastern and

Western Europe, the Asia-Pacific region, Africa, the Arab world, the Caribbean, North America, and the Americas collectively.[19] One function of these unions is to ease program shortages by exchanging programs among themselves. A few of these regional unions are discussed below:

- The European Broadcasting Union (EBU), oldest and most productive of the regional unions, has active organizations in 31 member nations, including several adjacent to but not part of Europe—Algeria, Israel, Jordan, Morocco, and Tunisia. It has associate members in 47 other countries, ranging from Argentina to Zimbabwe. The U.S. national television networks belong, as does the U.S. Information Agency. Unlike the International Telecommunication Union, the EBU is a nongovernment organization, although governments own many of the systems that belong to it.

  The EBU has a technical headquarters in Brussels and administrative headquarters in Geneva. It publishes a journal from each headquarters, the *EBU Review*. The union also publishes monographs, does legal research, and plays an active role in European satellite planning.

  European television program exchanges started when five Western European nations cooperated in coverage of Queen Elizabeth's coronation in 1953. The next year, EBU formed *Eurovision*, which pools materials from member countries and distributes programs to their broadcasting systems. It feeds three newscasts per day to its members as well as sports, cultural programs, and other types of material. The Brussels office coordinates the exchanges, converting signals from one standard to another as required. Eurovision has access to fifteen thousand transmitters with a potential audience of 400 million, using more than 16,000 kilometers of land lines, and satellite links with Arab, Asian, and Pacific broadcasting unions.[20]

- Originally, a pan-European union existed, dating back to 1925, but in 1949 it broke into east-west components. The eastern component became the OIRT (*Organisation Internationale de Radiodiffusion et Télévision*). Much smaller than the EBU, it consists of Communist and Communist-oriented states, with heavy input from the USSR. OIRT has its own version of Eurovision, called Intervision. The two link up for interregional program exchanges.[21]

- The Arab States Broadcasting Union (ASBU) also links up with Eurovision for daily newsfeeds, which Jordan coordinates for the ASBU members involved. A smaller group within the Arab states, the seven nations bordering on the Persian Gulf, formed Gulfvision in 1977, with headquarters in Saudi Arabia. It has ambitious plans, including a colossal series on Islamic civilization, planned to include 156 episodes. Members of the gulf states group cooperated in the production of an Arabic version of *Sesame Street*, called *Iftah ya Simsim* ("Open, Sesame!"):

The result is a visually impressive and extremely popular 130-program series, which was taped in the modern Kuwait television production center. . . . The production is so superior to the various children's programs done by individual stations that it has set a new standard for children's programming. As with the initial reaction to "Sesame Street" in the United States, some of the most ardent fans of the program are parents who watch it with their children. The reaction to the program in Saudi Arabia was so enthusiastic that the government suspended the production of locally produced programs for young children. (Boyd, 1982: 168)

- Broadcasting organizations in some 50 entities formerly linked with the British Empire, including 19 dependencies still under British rule, form the Commonwealth Broadcasting Association (three former Commonwealth members withdrew—Ireland in 1949, South Africa in 1961, and Pakistan in 1972).* The association meets every two years to exchange information and plan training projects and program exchanges. It publishes a journal of news and commentary called *Combroad*.

Coproduction. Another conservation measure brings broadcasting organizations from different countries together to share in the production costs (and sometimes labor) of programs or series. The motion picture industry pioneered *coproduction* as a means of achieving tax and production expense economies. Television coproductions have been particularly popular in France, Italy, and Spain, whose cultural similarities favor such sharing.†They have also made some strange bedfellows, such as Israel and Egypt, which cooperated in *Shalom-Salaam*, a program celebrating the return of the Sinai to Egypt. The USSR has entered into coproduction agreements with Italy, the United States, and West Germany as well as with Eastern European countries. Government propaganda agencies can use coproduction to obtain a backdoor entree to the domestic broadcasting systems of target countries. The U.S. Information Agency (USIA), parent organization of the Voice of America, for example, enters into coproduction agreements with organizations in foreign countries. As a U.S. government report noted, coproduction is "the most promising way of getting on overseas television" (USACPD, 1982: 30).

Even in the absence of coproduction agreements, however, government information agencies such as the USIA stand ready to supply program material to the broadcasting systems of host countries. Material

---

*The British Commonwealth of nations was formed by the Statute of Westminster in 1931 as an association for mutual economic aid and counsel. Its members range from very large states such as Canada and India down to very small ones, such as Tonga and Tuvalu.

†Porter makes the point that coproductions served as "a defensive strategy against the mid-Atlantic–WASP hegemony of Western culture" (1979: 264).

broadcast in this way tends to have more credibility than material broadcast by the Voice of America or other external services, which are more likely to be discounted as propaganda. Moreover, until direct-broadcast satellites become operative internationally, national information agencies have no way to transmit television over long distances to foreign countries in the way they transmit short-wave radio.

Cultural Agreements. Another way of "getting on overseas television" arises from bilateral cultural agreements between countries. Often when a head of state visits a foreign country, the final joint communiqué mentions cultural exchanges between the two countries, which may include the exchange of television programs representative of the two cultures.

SUMMARY

The two most critical economic factors for broadcasting systems are the source(s) of their financial support and the high cost of television programs. Broadcasting systems rely primarily on three basic sources of revenue: government subvention, receiver license fees, and advertising. Additional domestic sources sometimes employed include profits from auxiliary enterprises, such as publishing and program sales, and surcharges on electricity bills.

Government subvention and advertising tend to narrow the choice of programming unless programmers can be insulated from government and advertiser influence. Receiver license fees have the advantage that they somewhat protect noncommercial (or only partly commercial) broadcasting organizations from government fiscal interference. Once set saturation reaches a maximum level, however, income from fees levels off while costs of operation continue to rise.

Because both cultural and economic ceilings on national resources limit the amount of programming a system can generate domestically, program resources must be shared internationally. Syndication, the primary mechanism for international sharing, enables the making of very expensive programs at highly specialized production centers, with costs spread among many users. Syndicated program prices vary less according to production costs than to users' ability to pay, which in turn depends on the size and prosperity of the available audience. The need to provide programs in the language of user countries constitutes one of the expenses of international syndication. Producers that work in a widely spoken language such as English therefore have an economic advantage.

Although the United States was initially the main supplier of syndicated programming, other sources have since come on-line. Buyers can look at program wares from many different countries at trade fairs such as MIP-TV, the annual program fair in Cannes. News as well as entertainment depends on syndication. The expense of international news syndication is so great that only a few news agencies can maintain the necessary worldwide facilities. Secondary means of reducing program costs include coproduction, regional program exchanges, and intergovernmental exchanges.

NOTES

[1]Katz & Wedell, 1977: Table A.2.

[2]A success rate of 96.5 percent has been reported (Ito, 1978: 76).

[3]Great Britain, 1977: 137–139.

[4]Hanson, 1974: 55.

[5]Anderson, 1981: 12.

[6]Masani, 1976: 26.

[7]Great Britain, 1977: 163.

[8]Howkins, 1982a.

[9]Masani, 1976: 147.

[10]Wigbold, 1979: 222.

[11]Boyd, 1982: 53 *et passim*. For details on government aid to African and Asian systems, see Head, 1974, and Lent, 1978.

[12]Boyd, 1982: 14–15, 33–34.

[13]For details on the extent and fate of some of these investment projects, see Read, 1977: 77–95.

[14]Pitman, 1983: 1.

[15]Soderstrom, 1981: 305.

[16]Pierce, 1979: 130.

[17]Katz & Wedell, 1977: 198.

[18]Kurian, 1982: 1134–1137.

[19]See *WRTH* for details about most of these unions as well as other major international broadcasting associations (1984: 60–66).

[20]See Fisher, 1980, for a concise description of EBU and Eurovision.

[21]Eugster, 1983, describes both EBU and OIRT exchanges in detail.

CHAPTER 8

FACILITIES

T he physical facilities of broadcasting consist of the means of program (1) *production*, (2) *delivery*, (3) *distribution*, and (4) *reception*. In addition, broadcasting relies on the support of an underlying physical and organizational *infrastructure* that supplies telecommunication facilities, electrical power, manufacturing resources, trained personnel, and so on. For now, we can also consider the electromagnetic spectrum and satellite orbital space, together with the international regulations controlling their use, as part of the broadcasting infrastructure.

An ideal system would have not only modern, efficient studios but also equipment for picking up programs in the field. It would deploy various types of transmitters to enable national, regional, and local coverage, with network transmitters duplicated to give audiences a simultaneous choice of two or more national programs. It would use relays to distribute programs simultaneously to network outlets throughout the entire country, as well as recording facilities to compensate for time-zone differences and to enable reuse of programs at distant times and places. An ideal system would ensure maximum availability of receivers and the means of maintaining them. It would encourage infrastructural developments to make available (to the extent practicable) locally manufactured hardware and locally produced software, an effective telephone network, and training resources for administrative, production, and technical personnel.

8 ▪ 1 PRODUCTION

In the United States, because of localism in licensing, the *station* forms the basic unit of the domestic broadcasting system. Normally each station is a free-standing entity, combining facilities for both production and transmission under a single management. One expects a station to be equipped with studios, with the gear for doing out-of-studio programs (*remotes*, usually referred to in Europe as *outside broadcasts*), and with a transmitter, to which it feeds programs produced by means of these facilities, along with programs derived from other sources (networks, syndicators). When AM, FM, and television stations fall under common ownership, each is licensed and treated as a separate station.

The U.S. organizational pattern has the advantage that it encourages every station in the system, whether a network affiliate or not, to produce some of its own programs. Each station thus functions at least part of the time as a local outlet, as required by regulation. As noted in Section 4.5, most European systems began providing localized programming only after public pressure forced authorization of community stations as a new class designed expressly for local programming.

Many programs originate outside the station, coming from specialized production sources. Some broadcasting systems carry this separation of functions to the point of segregating programming-production completely from transmission; some also separate production from programming. A "station" may be reduced to the status of a mere transmitter, an anonymous part of an entire network of transmitters. Following are some of the organizational variations that occur:

- In Britain, total separation of transmission from programming-production is represented by the IBA and the ITV commercial program companies. This division ensures that transmission facilities will be so deployed as to give maximum national coverage, avoiding the inequities that arise when commercial motives determine the placement of transmitters.

- A similar separation of functions occurs in many developing countries, but for a different reason: often the national telecommunications administration has the only technically trained personnel and physical resources for maintaining and operating broadcast transmitters. Such division of responsibility and authority can impair the efficiency of broadcasting operations, especially if telecommunications personnel operate production as well as transmitter equipment.[1]

- The IBA's Channel Four company is confined essentially to the programming function: it relies on the IBA for its transmitter network, and it has no production facilities of any consequence because, by design, it functions entirely as an outlet for independent producers and other external suppliers.

- In contrast to the IBA companies, the BBC fully integrates programming-production functions with transmission and network functions. Because the BBC produces programming for two television and four national radio networks, it has a tremendous array of production facilities, probably the most extensive in the world.

- France's complex broadcasting law divides functions among several separate corporations. TDF (*Télédiffusion de France*) has the sole job of handling transmission. Another government corporation, SFP (*Société Française de Production et de Création Audiovisuelles*) creates and sells programs on contract to the French television networks. SFP has extensive production facilities, including 15 studios in Paris and 15 mobile units, operated by a staff of twenty-five hundred. It also does dubbing and subtitling and produces commercials. The French networks use their own limited production facilities mainly for routine news and minor sports coverage, relying on SFP for major public affairs and sports on-the-spot productions. Networks may, however, rent additional studio space and other facilities from SFP. They may also contract with private companies for production of programs. SFP sells some of its productions abroad, but the networks retain resale rights to those produced on their behalf by SFP.[2]

- After Peru's 1968 revolution, the military government introduced broadcasting reforms aimed at ending foreign influences and ensuring programming responsive to Peruvian needs and culture. In 1974 the government took control of programming by creating a central television production unit, *Telecentro*, two thirds of it government owned. This move left Peruvian stations with little to do other than to operate transmitters and sell commercials (*Telecentro* took 60 percent of the stations' commercial income in exchange for its programs).[3]

- Telecom, Australia's national telecommunications authority, installed the Australian Broadcasting Corporation's transmitters and operated them on ABC's behalf for more than half a century. In 1983 a new broadcasting law gave ABC legal control over its own transmitters, but by that time, they had become so intertwined with Telecom's other facilities that they could not be conveniently separated. Under agreement with ABC, Telecom continues to operate the transmitters, though ABC can legally make other arrangements.

- Among networks that produce their own programs, the Japanese public broadcasting corporation, NHK, reputedly has the world's most efficiently organized production system. Relying heavily on automation to carry out most routine operations, it uses a computerized facility called TOPICS (Total On-Line Program and Information Control System). TOPICS monitors and facilitates every aspect of program creation and production, from the first plans to the final taping, scheduling both the human and physical resources needed by each program. Indeed, TOPICS so dominates the production process that Japanese critics have complained that it curbs artistic freedom.[4] According to a British observer,

The studio operation is run by four men and a computer; all the programmes, recorded and stored on tapes, are fed automatically to the transmitters; the complex operations of the studio side of the news bulletins are similarly automated, with virtually no opportunity for human error, as each of the dozens of news items is slotted into the flow of the bulletins. (Smith, 1973: 261)

8 ▪ 2 DELIVERY

How many and what kinds of transmitters does a broadcasting delivery system need, and how should they be deployed? Most developed countries have at least three national radio and two national television networks,* plus a variety of transmitters to supply local, regional, and special services. They employ both AM and FM radio and supplement their main television transmitters with repeaters. Geographical, linguistic, and political variables determine the number of transmitters a nation needs.

When public noncommercial services exist side by side with private commercial services, responsibility for national networking usually falls to the public sector, as illustrated variously by the cases of Australia, Canada, Japan, and the United Kingdom. Private entrepreneurship tends to maximize station numbers because investors continue to found new outlets as long as they believe profits can be made. Government-operated and BBC-type public corporate services rely on fewer but more powerful transmitters, strategically located for efficient national coverage. Table 8.1 indicates the extraordinary transmitter density reached when freewheeling commercial ownership has been the rule, even in underdeveloped countries.

Propagation of Radio Energy

In order to appreciate the factors affecting choice and deployment of transmitter types, it helps to understand some basic facts about the propagation of radio energy. Radio signals travel by several different paths toward their destinations and react in various ways to the objects they meet along the way. These behaviors depend primarily on three variables: the *frequency* of the radio waves employed, the *power* used by the transmitter in launching them, and the *geography* of the terrain over which the signals travel. I will discuss briefly the first two of these factors before considering the several types of transmission. Then, with the types of transmission as background, I will discuss geographical factors.

Role of Frequency. How radio energy behaves after it leaves the transmitting antenna depends fundamentally on its *frequency*, which also can be expressed as *wavelength* (see Table 8.2). Thus a national

---

*In evaluating network claims, remember that some sets of transmitters do double duty as regional outlets part of the time and national networks the rest of the time.

TABLE 8 ▪ 1 TRANSMITTER DENSITY (SELECTED COUNTRIES)

| Country | Area and Population per Transmitter | |
	Population in Thousands	Area in Square Kilometers
India	3,789	16,421
Australia	162	22,691
Mexico	93	2,583
Dominican Republic	32	259
Costa Rica	30	637
United Kingdom	27	116
United States	24	972
Nicaragua	22	1,222
Panama	15	568

NOTE: India represents a developing country in which broadcasting is a government function; Australia, a developed country with a mixed system and large unpopulated areas. Private commercial broadcasting dominates in the rest of the developing countries in the table; some exceed even the United States in transmitter density.
SOURCE: Based on data in Central Intelligence Agency, The World Factbook, 1982 (Government Printing Office, Washington, D.C., 1982).

system's strategies for obtaining the best possible coverage depend heavily upon frequency considerations. One can make the following broad generalizations about frequency in relation to wave behavior, assuming that other variables remain stable:

- The higher the frequency (that is, the shorter the wavelength) of radio energy, the more it behaves like light. As their frequency increases, waves become more directional, more easily reflected, more subject to blockage by objects in their path. Waves in the UHF (ultrahigh frequency) television service can be blocked by tree foliage; those of still higher frequencies can be blocked by objects as small as raindrops.

- The higher the frequency, the more power a transmitter needs. At a frequency of 500 kilohertz (kHz.), a 100-kilowatt (kw.) transmitter will propagate a reliable signal about 140 kilometers (km.). Using the same power but doubling the frequency to 1,000 kHz. causes the propagation distance to drop to 90 km. Similarly, the more information a transmitter must handle, the more power it needs. The video section of a television station transmitter, for example, uses several times as much power as its audio section.

- Transmitters using frequencies located in the medium and the high ranges produce *sky waves* that can travel long distances, bouncing back and forth between the earth's surface and the ionosphere (layers of thin atmosphere at high elevation carrying electrical charges induced by the action of the sun). At medium frequencies, sky waves can be used only at night. However, the ionosphere reflects HF (high-frequency) waves both day and night.

- Energy at low and medium frequencies (long and medium wavelengths) produces *ground waves* that travel along the earth's surface; if sufficiently strong, they follow its curvature, reaching beyond the horizon. Factors affecting their coverage ability include transmitter power and conductivity of the soil or water through which the energy travels.

- VHF (very high frequency) waves, such as those used for television and FM radio, travel in straight lines as *direct waves*. They normally reach only to the horizon, as determined by the heights of transmitting and receiving antennas. For wide-area FM radio and television coverage, engineers therefore site antennas on high, unobstructed mountaintops or on tall supporting towers.

- For efficient propagation, the radiating elements of transmitter antennas must have a mathematical relationship to the length of the waves they radiate. The entire tower of a long- or medium-wave antenna radiates energy, but the tower of a television station merely supports the radiating elements; in keeping with the shorter wavelengths used by television, the radiators need be only a few feet long.

Practical implications of these general rules of propagation in relation to wavelength or frequency in the descriptions of the specific services that follow will emerge later in this chapter.

Role of Power. Transmitter power varies from the 1 or 2 watts of local minitransmitters to the millions of watts used by huge, superpower transmitters. Efficiency calls for using the lowest possible wattage while still obtaining the desired coverage and reliability. Some users, however, want superpower more for its symbolic than its practical value.

In general, high power overcomes interference and reaches longer distances, but a lot depends on the frequencies of the waves involved, the terrain, and nearness to the equator. High power cannot solve all propagation problems, and often it improves coverage only marginally. Most medium-wave stations use 10,000 watts of power or less. In the world as a whole, about seven hundred stations in the low- and medium-frequency bands operate at 100,000 watts or more, 10 percent of those being superpower stations at 900,000 watts and above.[5]

In evaluating a nation's broadcasting facilities, mere numbers, such as transmitter power ratings, can be misleading. As Katz and Wedell remark in their book on Third World broadcasting, "Time and again in our country studies we have come across broadcasting systems that on paper looked comprehensive and effective, but a single spot check, whether of production, transmission, or reception facilities, has shown the system to be seriously defective" (1977: 41). Third World countries tend to seek high-power transmitters, but they often lack both reliable energy sources to feed these monsters and skilled transmitter engineers to keep them in operation—not to speak of hard currency to pay for replacement parts. Extremely high power transmitters are temperamental and require scrupulous maintenance to operate continuously at top power. Unsure technical personnel sometimes avoid the embarrassment of outages simply by operating transmitters at well below their rated power.

Power has an important bearing on ground-wave and sky-wave propagation over long distances. Superpower therefore has special significance for long-, medium-, and short-wave transmitters. Direct-wave propagation, used by FM radio and by television, does not reach much beyond the horizon even with superpower.* However, the horizon can be stretched considerably if the transmitter antenna has great height. Then high power assures strong reception on the fringes of the coverage area as well as immunity from interference. Power ratings of FM and television transmitters range almost as widely as for ground- and sky-wave transmitters, which are rated in terms of *effective radiated power* (ERP). Engineers design television antennas to cut off upward radiation, concentrating the energy in a flat directional pattern angled downward toward the area between the antenna and the horizon. This concentration of the radiated energy increases the effectiveness of power input—hence the concept of ERP. The ERP of television stations is usually given in terms of the power radiated by the video transmitter, which amounts to several times that of the audio transmitter.

Sound Broadcasting

Radio broadcasting uses parts of four different bands of the frequency spectrum, as defined by the ITU: LF (low frequency), MF (medium frequency), HF (high frequency), and VHF (very high frequency). Europeans often refer to the first three of these in terms of their corresponding wavelengths—long waves for LF, medium waves for MF, and short waves for HF (see Table 8.2).

Long Waves. Only 15 channels have been allocated for long-wave radio transmitters (as opposed to more than a hundred each for MF and VHF), and only a score of countries use them. Existing transmitters use

---

*A part of the ionosphere called the Sporadic E Layer can cause abnormal sky-wave behavior during certain phases of the 11-year sunspot cycles. Television signals reflected by this layer have been known to travel a thousand miles and more. Another abnormal condition, called *ducting*, occurs when radio energy gets trapped between atmospheric layers of varying temperatures. Under such conditions, which tend to occur particularly in the Middle East, television signals travel far beyond the horizon. These long-distance phenomena happen too infrequently and unpredictably to serve any useful purpose, however.

TABLE 8 ▪ 2 FREQUENCY SPECTRUM BANDS AS DESIGNATED BY ITU

Band Number	Name of Band	Frequency Range	Wavelength Range (in Meters)
4	Very Low Frequency (VLF)	3–30 kilohertz	300,000–30,000
5	Low Frequency (LF)	30–300 kilohertz	30,000–3,000
6	Medium Frequency (MF)	300–3,000 kilohertz	3,000–300
7	High Frequency (HF)	3–30 megahertz	300–30
8	Very High Frequency (VHF)	30–300 megahertz	30–3
9	Ultra High Frequency (UHF)	300–3,000 megahertz	3–.3
10	Super High Frequency (SHF)	3–30 gigahertz	.3–.03
11	Extremely High Frequency (EHF)	30–300 gigahertz	.03–.003

NOTE: Frequency is measured in cycles per second. A hertz = 1 cycle per second (cps); a kHz = 1,000 cps; a MHz = 1 million cps; and a GHz = 1 billion cps. No frequencies below Band 4 have been allocated to telecommunications. Broadcasting is allocated only portions of these bands.

SOURCE: Based on data in ITU, Final Acts of the World Administrative Radio Conference, Geneva, 1979 (ITU, Geneva, 1980), p. 49.

---

frequencies between 155 and 281 kHz. (medium-wave channels begin at 526 kHz.).[6] Long-wave transmitters generate wide-area ground-wave coverage, day and night, using high power—as high as 2 million watts (40 times the wattage of the most powerful U.S. AM or "standard" broadcasting stations). Most are found in Europe and the USSR. Algeria and Morocco each have one in North Africa, and Turkey has two. None exists in the Americas and the Far East.

Historically, the BBC introduced regular use of long waves in 1925 from its Daventry transmitter site, on a centrally located plateau not far from Stratford-upon-Avon. The BBC still uses the site for external short-wave transmitters. In 1925 the single 25-kw., long-wave Daventry transmitter could reach 85 percent of the United Kingdom's population.[7] Today the BBC uses a long-wave channel at 200 kHz. for part of Radio 4's national coverage. Listeners in Europe recognize 236 kHz. as the long-wave frequency of Radio Luxembourg, a popular commercial station (one of the peripherals) whose 2,000 kw. of power push its signal as far as Ireland in the west and the Communist nations in the east. The USSR by far outstrips all other users of LW frequencies, relying heavily on them for its main transmissions from Moscow.

Medium Waves. What Americans call standard or AM radio, Europeans call *medium-wave* (MW) radio. As it happens, the medium frequencies fall in this region of the spectrum, so AM stations can be called either medium wave or medium frequency. The part of the MF band allocated to broadcasting runs from 526 kHz. to 1606 kHz., with some regional variations within these limits. Medium-wave transmitters provided the first regular broadcasting services, and more nations use these frequencies than any others. They have an advantage for Third World countries, for simple MW-only receivers can be manufactured at minimum cost.

Medium-wave transmitters give reliable ground-wave service day and night but suffer heavy atmospheric interference in the equatorial latitudes. In areas of high station density, their nighttime coverage may shrink because of interference from sky waves. In the United Kingdom, for example, some MW transmitters that reach nearly 98 percent of the population in the daytime reach only about 65 percent at night. On the other hand, sky-wave services of powerful MW stations, if protected from cochannel interference, can cover very great distances. To minimize interference, most countries limit MW power to 50 kw., as do the United States and Canada. The great majority of the world's MW stations have only 10 kw. of power or less. Of the more than eleven thousand MW stations in the world, less than 50 use 100 kw. of power or more.[8]

VHF Waves. Europeans refer to FM (frequency modulation) radio as *VHF radio,* identifying it with the frequency band it uses rather than with its method of modulation. In the United States, the FM band runs from 88 to 108 megahertz (the VHF band as a whole runs from 30 to 300 MHz.). Most other countries assigned some of the VHF frequencies to other services before FM broadcasting came along. They are now correcting their resulting FM radio channel shortages. The United Kingdom, for example, has only 88–97.6 MHz. for VHF broadcasting, though it will eventually extend the band to full limits by reassigning other services.

Cultures whose music has great dynamic range and tonal subtlety welcomed FM for its high fidelity, but it was also valued because it eased the radio channel shortage. Although invented in the early 1930s, FM radio made little headway against AM until after World War II, when overcrowding of the spectrum in Europe created an urgent demand for alternatives to low- and medium-wave channels. Germany pioneered in FM development because of post-World War II channel shortages. It started FM in 1949 and had more than a hundred stations on the air before the BBC began its FM services in 1955. U.S. broadcasters were authorized to use FM as early as 1939, but major growth did not begin until 1958. Today FM surpasses AM in number of U.S. stations on the air.

Only about 20 nations have developed FM extensively, most of them in Europe, where FM comprises more than three quarters of all radio

SOUTH AFRICA

stations. Denmark, Italy, Norway, and Sweden rely on FM for more than 90 percent of their transmitters. Denmark, for example, has only 1 long-wave and 1 medium-wave station but more than 40 FM stations.

The more isolated and poorer countries use little FM. The former face no problem of interference from neighbors; the latter want to take advantage of AM's nighttime sky waves. Both Australia and New Zealand lagged behind other developed countries in their use of FM. About a third of Japan's NHK transmitters but less than 10 percent of the privately owned outlets use FM. According to a 1977 count, only 9 percent of the Third World's transmitters used FM at that time.[9]

South Africa is the one large country outside of Europe and North America to have converted most of its radio system to FM. Nowhere in Africa has the ITU allotted enough MW channels to enable comprehensive national coverage. Most African countries, however, have not developed their broadcasting systems to the point of filling even the limited number of available AM channels. South Africa had both money and motive for increasing the number of its stations far beyond the limits of the available AM channels. It aimed at complete services in all the major African languages within its borders as well as in the two official languages, Afrikaans and English. It embarked in 1961 on what may be a unique example of a highly rationalized, preplanned project for achieving total FM coverage of a large national territory.*

In 1983 FM services could be received within South Africa proper in Afrikaans, English, and seven African languages. Four of the "black homelands" (Bophuthatswana, Ciskei, Transkei, and Venda) had their own FM services in appropriate local languages. In addition, the UN mandate territory of South West Africa (Namibia) had its own system operating 32 FM transmitters, carrying Afrikaans, English, and German (it was formerly a German colony), plus other FM stations that program in four local languages.

Short Waves. The ITU has allocated to broadcasting about 10 percent of the short-wave (high-frequency, or HF) band, running from 3 to 30 megahertz. However, the ITU makes no specific allotments of HF channels to individual countries as it does in the other broadcast services. As

---

*Some details on this project can be found in Orlik, 1974: 143–144. See also Collett (1964), Mills (1964), and Stevens (1964) for a technical account. It has been suggested that South Africa's adoption of FM was also motivated by the desire to make it harder for Africans to listen to foreign broadcasts, which would not be available in FM.

TABLE 8 ▪ 3 SHORT-WAVE (HF) BROADCAST BANDS
AND THEIR USAGE

| Allocation | Band Designation | | Usage (In Daily |
| | | | |
In Kilohertz	(In Megahertz)	(In Meters)	Frequency-Hours)
5,950–6,200	6	49	7,000
7,100–7,300	7	41	3,500
9,500–9,775	9	31	5,300
11,700–11,975	11	25	4,000
15,100–15,450	15	19	3,000
17,700–17,900	17	16	1,300
21,450–21,750	21	13	800
25,600–26,100	26	11	200

NOTE: The 1979 ITU World Administrative Radio Conference agreed on expansion of the 9-, 11-, 15-, 17-, and 21-MHz bands, contraction of the 26-MHz band, and an additional band in the 21-MHz region, for a total increase of 780 kHz. or 33 percent, but these changes awaited decisions by further HF broadcasting conferences in 1984 and 1986.
SOURCE: Based on data in George Jacobs, "High Frequency Broadcast Reception Conditions Expected During 1983" (World Radio TV Handbook, 1983), pp. 52–56. Used by permission.

previously related (see Section 5.2), each administration wishing to use a short-wave channel registers it with the ITU's International Frequency Registration Board (IFRB), which advises whether that use will cause objectionable interference and, if so, how best to avoid it.

High-frequency spectrum blocks allocated to broadcasting fall in various parts of the band, as shown in Table 8.3, ranging from a low in the vicinity of 6 MHz. (referred to in wavelength terms as the 49-meter band) to a high in the 25-MHz. region (11-meter band). This scattering of the assignments enables short-wave broadcasters to change frequency throughout the day as the characteristics of the ionosphere alter during the cycles of sunlight and darkness.

Short-wave radio has the unique advantage of enabling transmission to distant targets, sometimes thousands of miles from the originating transmitter site. But the broadcaster pays a penalty for this advantage in lower sound quality and less reliable service. Subject to fading and interference, sky waves can never be counted on for consistent, high-quality service. Furthermore, not all listeners will put up with the inconvenience of having to retune receivers every hour or two to keep up with the frequency adjustments to changing conditions of the ionosphere.

The majority of SW transmitters are devoted to external services (treated in Section 11.2); here I consider their use for domestic services, which occurs in some 90 countries.[10] Domestic use of HF is common in very large countries that cannot reach all their citizens by means of shorter-range medium-frequency and FM transmitters and that lack sufficient microwave or other relay circuits. High-frequency channels are also used for domestic services because atmospheric noise in equatorial regions makes low- or medium-power MF broadcasting impractical, especially during September to February. As noted in Section 5.2, the ITU has allocated a special group of channels straddling the upper end of the MF band and the lower end of the HF band (2,300–5,050 kHz.) for domestic use by countries located in the tropics.

Indonesia, for example, whose scattered land mass lies within 10 degrees north and south of the equator, uses about four times as many short-wave as medium-wave stations, nearly all within the tropical bands. Ghana, which lies between about 5 and 12 degrees north of the equator, uses no medium-wave transmitters at all, relying entirely on short waves, supplemented by a wired-radio service.[11]

Although hardly a tropical country, the USSR uses many short-wave channels domestically. According to *WRTH*, the USSR declines to supply official facts about its short-wave facilities, and "information submitted to the International Frequency Registration Board appears to be largely inaccurate and out-of-date" (*WRTH*, 1983: 139). However, the handbook editors have pieced together evidence from monitoring reports indicating that the Soviets use about a hundred short-wave stations to deliver or distribute domestic programs—by far the largest number of HF transmitters devoted to domestic broadcasting of any nontropical country in the world.

Australia uses about a dozen short-wave transmitters located at four different sites to relay domestic programs to its vast, thinly populated outback. Canada has no pressing need to distribute services by means of short waves (being well supplied with microwave and satellite relay facilities) but does employ a few low-power short-wave stations for direct reception in remote areas. Other countries using many HF channels for domestic purposes include China, Brazil, and India (the latter two because of distance and tropical interference with medium waves).

Television

Sound broadcasting transmitters have uniform standards worldwide, so receivers built in one country work equally well in others. Not so in television. Many major and minor variations in standards have emerged, largely the result of a mixture of politics and economic chauvinism. A dozen sets of signal specifications exist, stipulating such matters as the number of lines per frame, horizontal or vertical polarization of signal, and size of transmission channel.[12] Further, three different color systems divide the world into spheres of influence—American, French, and German.

General TV Standards. The number of picture lines per frame, the primary standard of general interest, is a rough measure of the degree of resolution a video system permits. The British started with a relatively low standard, 405 lines per frame, while the French went to the other extreme with 819 lines. Both standards eventually gave way to a compromise resolution of 625 lines per frame. The United States and countries within its sphere of influence use 525 lines, but the two standards come out about even when one takes frame frequency into account. U.S. electrical house current has a frequency of 60 cycles per second, while Europe's has 50 cps. Because video systems use house current to establish frame frequency standards, the higher European line frequency compensates for its lower number of frames per second. In practice, this means that the observer sees about the same amount of detail in European as in U.S. television pictures.

Initially, television employed parts of the VHF band, the same band used by FM radio. However, demand for channels soon outran the available frequencies in that band, leading to allocation of more television channels in the next higher band, UHF (ultrahigh frequency).* Given a choice, broadcasters prefer VHF channels because (with a given amount of power) they yield better coverage than UHF channels, but whenever a service needs a large number of channels, it has to move to the UHF band. The first national network to be established in a country usually used VHF, the second and subsequent networks moving up to UHF. Thus BBC-1, the old 405-line British monochrome system, due to be phased out by 1986, employed VHF channels. UHF came into general use in Britain with the introduction of color on BBC-2 in 1967.†

Color Standards. As of 1982, the three rival color systems divided the world of color television as follows: PAL (German method), 49 percent of the systems; NTSC (U.S. method), 24 percent; SECAM (French method), 27 percent.‡ (NTSC comes from "National Television Standards Committee," PAL from "Phase Alternate Line," and SECAM from "*Séquence Couleur à Mémoire*.") Though each color standard claims some advantage over the others, to the layman they seem about equal. Viewers wishing to pick up color programs in more than one system can equip their sets with adapters, as do viewers in East Germany (SECAM) and West Germany (PAL).

During the period when nations had to decide which color system to adopt, proponents of the three contenders indulged in an orgy of promotional efforts and political lobbying. For example, representatives of

---

*Designation of channels differs somewhat from one country to another. WRTH lists both VHF and UHF channels by country and according to the various numbering systems, 1984: 396–397.

†British setowners in areas where signals on both standards can be received use receivers with built-in adapters for both 405- and 625-line signals.

‡Luxembourg and Monaco use both PAL and SECAM in order to be able to reach both France and other nearby European targets with international commercial program services. Saudi Arabia uses SECAM for its domestic viewers and PAL to reach other nations on the Persian Gulf.

all three systems made strong bids for acceptance by China. It seemed as though the plum would surely fall to France, for the USSR (which uses a version of SECAM) aided China in the introduction of television. Before the color decision came, however, the two giants broke off relations, and China finally opted for PAL. However, the French succeeded in Saudi Arabia, whose close relations with the United States would seem to have given NTSC the inside track. But PAL would have been the logical choice, because it is used by nearly all the other countries of the Middle East. In fact, the Saudis hired an American consulting firm to advise on the choice between PAL and SECAM. The firm recommended PAL, but the French had been so persuasive at the highest political levels that Saudi Araba opted for SECAM. The choice paid off handsomely for the French, who shortly thereafter sold the Saudis a color television center characterized as the "most technically advanced in the Arab world."[13]

USSR influence caused Eastern European states to choose SECAM, except for maverick Yugoslavia, which adopted PAL. The only other European country to use SECAM exclusively, aside from France itself, is Greece (though peripheral stations in Luxembourg and Monaco use both SECAM and PAL to broaden their coverage).* U.S. influence outside the Americas caused Japan, the Philippines, South Korea, and Taiwan to choose NTSC. Within the Americas, U.S. influence ensured the choice of NTSC except in the French island dependencies of St. Pierre et Miquelon, Guadeloupe, and Martinique, and in four South American neighbors—Argentina, Brazil, Paraguay, and Uruguay—which use PAL.

Cuba's extensive television system predates Castro and was of course based on American standards. The color issue, however, arose after the revolution. As a Soviet client state, Cuba was a natural candidate for SECAM, which it considered adopting in 1975. The next year, however, it chose NTSC. The U.S. trade embargo made it difficult for Cuba to obtain 525-line receivers. Japan, the only other major producer of the sets, reportedly ceased dealing with Cuba because of unpaid bills. Finally, the USSR set up an assembly line especially to meet Cuba's need for 525-line sets, at greatly inflated prices.[14]

The official go-ahead for NTSC color came in the United States in 1954, but conversion came slowly. Color began to gain ground in the mid-1960s, at which time other leading television systems began to convert. The BBC began colorcasting on its second network in 1967, followed by BBC-1's UHF transmitters and the IBA network in 1969 (BBC's old 405-line transmitters remained monochrome). Canada began colorcasting in 1966; the USSR, in 1967.

Conversion to color is costly not only in capital equipment but in

---

*In 1984 Laos reportedly used both SECAM and PAL, the latter for the short term because existing sets in Laos had been acquired to pick up neighboring Thai programs, the former for the long term because of Soviet influence.

recurrent production expenses. Many countries put off color as long as they could stave off public pressure. Israel, for example, wanted to avoid the expense of color conversion, but the availability of color pictures from Jordan, whose program schedules the Israeli papers printed, forced the government's hand. The political dilemmas of having to opt for one or another of the three systems could also cause delays, as related earlier in the case of Italy, whose politicians waffled until they finally settled on PAL in 1977 (see Section 4.4). Australia held off until 1975, thereupon selling as many sets in two years as the United States sold in its first ten years of color. Countries that delayed television itself until the 1970s, such as Zanzibar (1973) and South Africa (1976), started up immediately with color.

Countries that counted television itself as an expensive luxury could ill afford to spend still more on converting to color. Some, like Israel, actually banned its use for several years during the early 1970s but finally had to give in—not only because of public and political pressures but also because manufacturers of primary television equipment began phasing out black-and-white production, forcing all to join the color parade in the long run.

Most countries dependent on receiver license fees for television budgets set higher fees for color—as much as three times the black-and-white fee but usually about half again as much (see Table 7.1). Upon introducing a separate color fee in 1968, Britain charged £10, twice the monochrome fee. The fee adopted at the close of 1981 set £46 as the color rate, a little more than three times the monochrome rate.*

Economic chauvinism may eventually give way to standardization with the coming of direct-broadcast satellites (DBS). Considerable interest has been shown in a new digital method of signal processing developed by IBA engineers especially for satellite use. Called MAC (for Multiplexed Analogue Component), it has its own color system, independent of existing standards, and incorporates two stereophonic sound channels. Europe's Orbital Test Satellite experimented with MAC in 1982. The British government adopted it as a standard, and it has aroused interest among U.S. DBS planners.[15] The Japanese high-definition standard, if adopted, would also eliminate color incompatibilities.

Repeaters. Television signals normally travel line-of-sight paths between transmitter and receiving antennas. Irregularities in terrain create "shadow" areas not covered by signals. *Repeaters,* small self-operated transmitters used to fill in these voids, often outnumber primary

---

*Not all countries differentiate between color and black-and-white fees, however. Of the 21 European and nearby services listed by the EBU in a 1984 license fee report, 6 had a single rate—Austria, West Germany, Israel, Switzerland, Turkey, and Yugoslavia (*EBU Review*, May 1984).

SRI LANKA

transmitters. The United States has eleven hundred primary television transmitters but more than forty-five hundred repeaters to improve their coverage. This four-to-one ratio of primary to repeater transmitters applies generally to the highly developed systems of the world.

Repeaters simply pick up the originating station's signal (using a relay or an antenna outside the shadowed area, of course) and rebroadcast to a small specific area, such as an upland valley between two mountain ridges. Repeaters usually shift the signal from its original channel to another channel to prevent the signals of the originating station and the repeater from interfering with each other. Repeaters that change frequency in this way are called *translators* or (in Europe) *transposers*.

Broadcasting services legally obligated to reach the entire population may employ very large numbers of translators. Japan's NHK has more than sixty-five hundred. To reach the last 2 percent of a population after 98 percent coverage has been achieved can be extraordinarily expensive. For example, West German experience indicated that it would cost as much to reach the last 2 percent as to cover the first 98 percent. In Britain, the Annan Committee estimated that it might cost a million pounds to serve only eight thousand people in a remote area of the United Kingdom.[16]

The new Low Power Television (LPTV) service authorized by the Federal Communications Commission for the United States in the early 1980s uses repeater-type stations that have the right to originate their own programming. As of 1984, the FCC had authorized several hundred LPTV stations and expected eventually to license thousands. Other countries appear less interested in the possibilities of LPTV, though some have authorized experiments, as detailed in Section 4.5.

Subscription Television

Over-the-air pay television, or subscription television (STV), requires payment of a subscription fee to descramble the picture. In a sense, STV already exists wherever receiver license fees must be paid, though it does not exist widely as an added-cost supplement to regular television. First World STV operates mainly in the United States, though France started a national STV network service in 1984 (see Section 9.1). In the Second and Third Worlds, STV's high cost to subscribers prevents its adoption. The comments of a Nigerian Television Authority official represent a typical Third World reaction to the prospect of any kind of extra-pay service, such as STV or cable television:

ICELAND

The complex technology involved including the satellite, whether "rented" or "launched," makes pay-television virtually impossible in developing countries. Furthermore, since television in developing countries is essentially funded by government, it would be socially indefensible to spend so much government revenue for providing a service which would only be available to a small minority of the population. It is my view that pay or subscription television will have no place in the developing countries for a long time to come, and justifiably so.
(Ugwu, 1980: 15)

Geography and Propagation

How many and what kind of transmitters will be needed to cover a given national territory depends on the size, shape, distribution, and roughness of the terrain. Hypothetically, a transmitter propagates a circular coverage pattern around its antenna. In practice, the pattern may be radically altered, both by geographical influences and by directional antennas.

Shape of Terrain. Ideally, designers of broadcasting systems would prefer to mount FM and television antennas on a high elevation at the center of a round island with an unobstructed view of the rest of the island and with good ground conductivity throughout to maximize the effectiveness of medium-wave transmitters. An island site would be preferable to minimize interference and competition from neighboring country spillover signals.

Few national territories come near to meeting these ideal criteria, though the pear-shaped island of Sri Lanka (formerly Ceylon) comes close. Its central mountains rise to more than 8,000 feet, looking out to the flat shores of the island at the farthest about 160 miles away, in most directions less than a hundred. Three television stations suffice to cover the island, the main one located on the highest peak, Pidurutalagala, at an elevation of 8,281 feet.

Iceland, an egg-shaped island somewhat larger than Sri Lanka, has a central mass of uninhabited glaciers and volcanic peaks. Icelandic villages dot the fringes of the island, often deeply hidden in fiords and therefore cut off by high cliffs from neighboring villages. This terrain calls for many small stations, each covering an isolated village. Iceland uses many very low-power FM and AM stations, some as low as only 2 watts. Television, too, relies on low-power repeater stations to reach villages cut off by the rugged terrain from the possibility of picking up signals from powerful, centrally located stations like the one on Pidurutalagala.

Most countries have odd-shaped land masses, not well suited to circular coverage patterns, while others have land masses fragmented into many islands, separated from each other by wide stretches of ocean. Some examples:

- Chile extends for some 2,650 miles down the west coast of South America, yet it averages only about 100 miles in width. This long, ribbonlike territory has about 150 medium-wave stations, identified in a unique way by both frequency and region—north, central, south, or Antarctic. The last happens to include the world's southernmost city, Punta Arenas, which has a 10-kw. government MW station and a 10-kw. privately owned MW station called *Radio Polar*. The latter's call sign, CD96, identifies it as Chilean, located in Zone D, and assigned to the frequency 960 kHz. Most MW stations have power of only 1,000 watts, but Chile also has a score of domestic short-wave stations for long-distance reception, also with low power except for the *Radio Nacional de Chile* station, which has 100 kw. Italy's similar long narrow shape, much broken by mountains, accounts for its having one of the highest station densities in the world (see Section 4.4).

- The Anglophone West African nation of the Gambia, an even more extreme example of a ribbonlike shape, consists of a narrow, 200-mile-long strip on either bank of the river that gives the country its name. Never more than 20 miles wide, Gambian territory extends into the body of Francophone Senegal, with which the Gambia is loosely federated. Senegal completely surrounds it except for the river's outlet into the Atlantic. Radio Gambia's transmitters inevitably cover more Senegalese territory than Gambian.

- Indonesia, cited in Section 2.5 as a Third World country with an urgent need for domestic satellite interconnection, must cover a territory of some six thousand islands, scattered in archipelagoes across 3,000 miles of Indian Ocean. Its main islands include Sumatra, Java, Madura, most of Borneo, the Celebes, the Moluccas, and Bali. The central and regional governments run nearly two hundred short-wave stations, mostly in the tropical bands. These HF stations function as relays to bring national programs to outlying local outlets. As indicated earlier, the television service, a government operation, relies on the PALAPA domsat for distribution (see Section 2.5). Indonesia had 10 main television transmitters in 1983, supplemented by 21 high-power and 179 low-power repeaters. Other countries with problems of widely dispersed terrain include Japan (Section 3.7) and Malaysia (Section 2.5).

Size. Six nations have land masses of 3 million square miles or more: the USSR (8.6 million, much the largest), Canada (3.8), China (3.7), the

CHILE

United States (3.5), Brazil (3.3), and Australia (3). Each of these nations counts on satellites to obtain simultaneous national coverage.

The Soviet Union's vast territory stretches more than 4,000 miles east to west, crossing 11 different time zones. In the United States, a network football game starting at 2:00 P.M. on the East Coast would be seen live at 11:00 A.M. on the West Coast. A similar live event occurring at 2:00 P.M. on the east coast of the USSR would be seen on its western borders at 1:00 A.M.

Delineation of time zones starts from the prime meridian, or zero degrees longitude, arbitrarily established as passing through an observatory at Greenwich, on the outskirts of London. GMT (Greenwich Mean Time) refers to the time at Greenwich. Nowadays, the ITU uses a geographically neutral equivalent, UTC (Coordinated Universal Time). With GMT or UTC as a reference point, local time can be indicated uniformly for any place on the globe.

Each zone to the west of Greenwich subtracts an hour from GMT; each zone to the east adds an hour. *World Radio TV Handbook* listings indicate the local time of each system in terms of UTC. Minus hours (UTC −) identify time zones of nations located west of Greenwich, plus hours (UTC +) indicate those to the east. Thus U.S. Eastern Standard Time becomes UTC −5; Pacific Time, UTC −8. Local times in the USSR, which lies east of Greenwich, are expressed by plus values: UTC +3 for Moscow, UTC +13 for Anadyr, a Russian city near Alaska. A Japanese commercial television station once dramatized time-zone differences by showing sunrise on New Year's day occurring successively in 15 different zones, starting with New Zealand (GMT +12, that is, the opposite side of the earth from Greenwich). At that time, it was 1:00 A.M. in Japan (GMT +9).*

Some large countries arbitrarily broaden time zones so as to create uniform, nationwide clock time; China, for example, considers itself entirely within the GMT +8 time zone, though its actual territory stretches over several zones. Other countries of large east-west

---

InterMedia, May 1982. Note that in using schedule information from *WRTH*, one must translate UTC into local time. Thus when *WRTH* lists New Zealand as operating on UTC +12 and scheduling daily television programs from 2200 to 1100 hours, one must add 12 hours to these times, converting them to the local time of 1000–2300, that is, from 10:00 A.M. to 11:00 P.M.

THE GAMBIA

dimension include Brazil (3 zones), Canada (4½ zones), Indonesia (3 zones), and Mexico (4 zones).

In the days before videotape became available for high-quality recording of programs for later broadcast, the U.S. networks had to produce repeat live performances of programs such as the evening news; otherwise, the 7:00 P.M. news in New York would have aired at the unsuitable time of 4:00 P.M. in San Francisco. How much greater a problem was this for the USSR, with its 11 time zones to take into account!* Thus time-zone considerations affect the program planning and facilities needs of large countries.

Population Distribution. Coverage patterns depend not only on the shape and size of national terrain but also on population distribution. Examples of populations concentrated in small areas of the national terrain have already been noted, such as Australia (Section 3.7), Canada (Section 2.2), and the Sudan (Section 2.5). Sometimes settlements cluster on coastal fringes, with sparse population in the interior regions, as in the case of Brazil, Peru, and the Maghreb (North Africa). As an added problem, inhabitants of the remote interior areas usually represent remnants of the aboriginal inhabitants, as do the Berbers of North Africa, the aborigines of Australia, the Eskimos of Canada, and the Lapps of Scandinavia. These cultural enclaves impose special demands upon broadcasting systems to provide services in minority languages.

Proximity. Geographic proximity often influences broadcast facilities. The nearness of Europe to Tangier, the Moroccan city only 10 miles across the Strait of Gibraltar from southern Spain, has always attracted broadcasting entrepreneurs wishing to reach European audiences without having to abide by European rules. That Tangier had the status of an internationally controlled free port from the 1920s until its return to Moroccan control in 1956 abetted these opportunistic moves:

> As early as 1937, in spite of French opposition, private entrepreneurs and hostile nations . . . had moved in. A first local station was soon taken over by French interests, then by the state. In 1939, Spaniards built a station . . . but in 1947 it was taken over by Radio Africa, whose principal owner was a Frenchman linked to Radio Andorre. A year earlier, an American had launched Radio Tanger of which 49% was owned by Spaniards, 33% by Americans. (Bertrand, 1982: 199–200)

---

*In practice the Soviets program their services in only 5 time-zone segments.

USSR

To this day, the Voice of America has a Moroccan government contract allowing the United States to operate a relay station in Tangier. Morocco holds a 51 percent interest in an international commercial station, *Radio Méditerranée International,* programming in French to Europe and in Arabic to North Africa.

Geographical proximity accounts for spillover services, previously mentioned in the cases of countries such as Belgium, Canada, and Switzerland. Irish broadcasting has had difficulties because of unevenly distributed spillover. Residents in half the country receive British television (both BBC and ITV), either directly or via local cable services. However, mountains as well as distance cut off inhabitants of the west and south coasts of the island from enjoyment of these supplementary services. This disparity caused controversy as to the need for and the content of a second network for *Radio Telefís Eireann* (RTE). Language policy also became an issue, for some forty-five thousand people in the more remote communities of the west cling to the Irish language and wanted broadcasting services in that language (compare the controversy over broadcasting of Welsh, mentioned in Section 4.5). In the end, Ireland built a second television network, despite its inability to program it fully (the broadcasting authority allows RTE 2 to import 80 percent of its programming). Although the new network "created more viewing options and nearly doubled RTE's airtime total for television, it was done at the expense of home production in general and Irish language content in particular" (Howell, 1982: 45).

Deployment Criteria

Ideally, facilities planners would deploy transmitters so as to achieve the best possible coverage of the national terrain and population, but extraneous factors often influence transmitter placement. From a purely engineering point of view, deployment may be controlled by the desire to position transmitters suitably for use as rebroadcast relays. Thus South Africa designed a grid for positioning its national network of FM transmitters (as described earlier in this section), spacing them not only to achieve national coverage but also to enable rebroadcasting, eliminating the need for a separate relay network.

In commercial settings, siting of transmitters often depends primarily on market dictates, resulting in more stations than needed in urban areas and less than needed in rural areas. Table 8.1 indicates the degree of overkill that can result. Note, however, that when Britain authorized

MOROCCO

commercial television, it forestalled this outcome by removing transmitter control from commercial interests, giving it instead to an independent public service agency, the IBA.

In the developing world, the choice of transmitter sites can become a political rather than an engineering or commercial decision. A broadcasting station can be regarded as a prestigious civic amenity, and towns vie for the distinction of becoming the seat for a unit of the national broadcasting system. Authorizing a station can become a political reward to loyal followers. On the other hand, shaky regimes often centralize transmission facilities where they can be closely guarded, even if that means shortchanging citizens in more remote parts of the nation. Revolutionaries always make the broadcasting station one of their first targets so that they can present their case directly to the people and issue orders to them over the heads of existing authorities.

8▪3 RECEPTION

As I pointed out earlier, one of broadcasting's unique attributes is that the general public invests personally in the hardware of the medium by purchasing receivers. Policymakers in developing countries sometimes underestimate the importance of this factor, taking it for granted that as long as the state invests in transmission facilities, reception facilities will take care of themselves. They often treat broadcast receivers as luxuries, imposing heavy excise and sales taxes. Katz and Wedell found reception facilities the "weakest link" in Third World broadcasting technology, and one likely to remain so for a long time (1977: 63).

Radio Receivers

The advent of transistor radios in 1962 made sets far cheaper, lighter, and more convenient, tremendously accelerating the growth of set ownership. It also freed them from mains electrical supplies or heavy, expensive wet batteries. Nevertheless, the penetration of radio receivers in the regions of the world remains very uneven. Countries with the highest set penetration include the United States (tops, with 1,982 radio sets per thousand population), Canada (1,125), Australia (1,034), the United Kingdom (931), and Japan (763). Countries with the lowest penetration include Upper Volta (30), Ethiopia (33), Bangladesh (33), and Yemen (43).*

---

*The sets-per-thousand concept originated in the 1960s, when UNESCO set as goals for the developing countries 50 radio and 20 TV receivers per thousand

The cost of multiband sets (those able to tune in two or more of the four radio services—long wave, medium wave, short wave, and VHF (FM)—dropped sharply in the late 1970s, increasing the audience for international short-wave programs and making domestic short-wave services more accessible. Although the United States has no domestic short-wave stations, many U.S. listeners own sets that can tune to foreign short-wave and U.S. external broadcasts. Reportedly, some 18 million Americans bought sets with short-wave capabilities during 1972–1981.*

As noted, consumers in many countries need multiband receivers in order to pick up all available domestic services. In India, for example, more than half the stations use short-wave transmitters. According to UNESCO, in 1980 Indian set penetration amounted to only 45 per thousand population. An Indian researcher pointed out that people in rural areas simply cannot afford to buy even simple, low-cost transistor receivers. "We should be proud that we have first-grade transmission facilities throughout the country," he wrote. "However, there exists a wide unbridged communication gap between the broadcaster and the audience mainly in the rural areas, because the most essential link—the radio receiver—is missing in many households" (Rao, 1977: 29). Rao estimated that it would take a tenth of an agricultural worker's average annual income to buy a simple radio receiver at prices prevailing in 1977. Removal of the excise levy, sales tax, and license fee, however, could reduce the price of a set by 34 percent.

Further reception problems arise in Third World and even some Second World countries because of inadequate repair facilities and lack of replacement batteries. As much as 40 percent of the receivers in developing countries may be inoperative at any one time.[17] Difficult reception conditions, sometimes made worse by substandard transmitter operation, cause set owners to turn up the volume to the maximum, thereby rapidly depleting their hard-to-replace batteries.[18]

Television Receivers

If cost limits radio set penetration, it limits television set penetration far more radically. In some African countries, the number of sets per thousand inhabitants amounts to less than one, and even the most

---

population. Data used here are based on end-of-1981 estimates (admittedly only approximations in many cases) in the annual survey issued by the BBC External Services research division (BBC, June 1982).

*Clarke, 1981. A Gallup poll commissioned in the mid-1970s by the Canadian government indicated that 11 percent of a representative sample of Americans owned short-wave radios (Gallup, 1975: 3). The Voice of America estimated (perhaps optimistically) that in 1982 half of adult Europeans had access to the most popular short-wave bands (25–49 meters) and from a third to a half had access in other parts of the world, other than the United States.

affluent countries have far fewer television than radio sets. Some specific penetration figures: as of 1984, the United States had 612 television receivers per thousand population; Canada, 458; Australia, 395; United Kingdom, 359; Japan, 250; and Argentina, 204. Oil-rich Kuwait, with a little more than a million people, had 337 sets per thousand population—highest in the Middle East.[19]

In Third World countries, television receivers, much more than radios, are often regarded as luxury items. In anticipation of the 1982 Asian Games, the Indian government decided to allow its television service, Doordarshan, to convert to color. Originally, the government had imposed a 320 percent import duty on color television sets, but in order to build up the audience for color programs so as to capitalize on their advertising potential, the government reduced the duty to a mere 190 percent![20]

No television equivalent of the transistor revolution that made radio sets so portable and affordable has occurred. Cathode-ray tubes (the "picture tubes" of television receivers) require such high levels of power that battery receivers of reasonable size remain expensive and cumbersome. Normal home receivers still need mains power to be widely practical. Battery-operated receivers have been used in special situations, such as in the national educational television project in the Ivory Coast (see Section 9.7). They proved very costly, however, and required a level of supervision and maintenance that the ordinary householder could not supply.

In addition to reducing taxes on receivers and their components, the responsible national authorities could do more to encourage the growth of television audiences—assuming they really want to maximize the reach of their television services. Governments could remove receiver taxes, set up low-interest time payment plans, and encourage rental of receivers (in the United Kingdom, rental agencies account for more than 60 percent of the television sets in use).

Facilities of private teleclubs or public community viewing centers can be used. However, except for highly structured viewing situations, such as adult education projects, community viewing seems no more than a stopgap measure. The small screen of the ordinary television set lends itself best to individual and small-group viewing, only second best to motion picture projection for large-group viewing. There appears to be no evidence that community viewing provides a satisfying substitute for home viewing when consumers have any choice. Although China organized community viewing very widely and systematically, the desire of the Chinese for home reception appears merely to have been held in abeyance. As soon as the government made receivers available and allowed villagers in production brigades to earn spare money from entrepreneurial sidelines, television receivers rose high on the villagers' list of purchasing priorities. In 1983 came news reports of the Wuzhuang Production Brigade, whose hamlet became known as TV Village because every single family bought a television set.[21]

Conceivably, of course, large-screen, high-definition receivers could make television a more effective medium for public exhibition in the future. Japanese engineers have been working since 1970 on high-definition television (HDTV). They even experimented with satellite transmission of HDTV in 1980, using their experimental DBS vehicle, Yuri. The standard advocated by Japan surpasses the quality of professional theatrical motion pictures, using 1,124 lines per frame and a wide-screen format. HDTV frames contain five times the picture detail of sets using the current 525- and 625-line standards.

The major disadvantage of HDTV—that it requires a much wider channel for each transmitter than do current television standards—means that its widespread adoption will probably be delayed for many years. Nevertheless, the Japanese hope to go ahead with it in their own country, using sophisticated methods of band compression. They advocate eventual use of the 22-GHz. band for satellite distribution of HDTV—higher frequencies than those currently used or contemplated for either relay or DBS satellites.

In the United States, CBS developed a less ambitious experimental HDTV design with 1,050 lines per frame, utilizing two standard 525-line television channels. The CBS HDTV standard achieves compatibility with the older standard by splitting the signal, feeding only one of the two channels to conventional 525-line receivers, which require a converter to pick up the HDTV signal.

8 ▪ 4 DISTRIBUTION

Were it not for the technologies that make it possible to distribute programs far and wide in both space and time, all programming would be limited to small amounts of locally produced materials. Thus limited, the broadcasting medium would be entirely different from the one we actually know, of very little consequence as a source of information or of anything else.

Reproduction

The phonograph flourished before broadcasting came on the scene and immediately became a source of program material when the new medium emerged. But the old needle-in-the-groove technology was too inflexible and crude to meet the reproduction needs of broadcasting. Audio magnetic tape-recording came on the market after World War II, based on German wire recorders developed during the war. Videotape came a decade later. Still later came improvements in small-format, professional videotape recorders that enabled development of ENG (electronic news gathering).

The flexibility and economy of tape-recording enhanced broadcasting resources in several ways. Tape profoundly altered production techniques for both syndicated programming and daily news coverage. It made prerecorded program materials easier to adapt to local needs by simplifying the processes of re-editing and subtitling. And it eased the problem of network-delayed broadcasts for equalizing time-zone differences.

Network Interconnection

Networks equal recordings in importance as a means of sharing broadcast program resources. They depend on expensive technology for the relay of programs from points of origin to affiliated stations or, in the case of cable television, to affiliated cable systems. Many different configurations of program suppliers and stations claim the right to be called networks. Not all meet ideal or indeed even legal criteria for a true network, however.*

True Networks. A national broadcasting network consists of one or more headquarter locations or origination points, *linked by means of relay facilities* to a number of transmitters so positioned around the national terrain as to cover close to the entire population. U.S. television networks supply affiliates with a comprehensive program service. They also provide ancillary services, such as making the interconnection arrangements, conducting national audience research, promoting the network program lineup, and (in the case of commercial networks) selling affiliates' time. Network headquarters usually consult with affiliates to ensure that programming satisfies the wishes of local audiences. From time to time, U.S. television networks pick up news items or other program material from affiliates that happen to be in a position to contribute to the national program schedule.

The U.S. television network pattern has the advantage that affiliates function as complete stations, not merely as transmitters for distributing centrally produced programming. Affiliates are obligated to produce local programs part of the time (even if only a small part), thus enhancing the flexibility of the system. In most countries, local network outlets have no such obligation, though in some cases affiliates may "opt-out" of the network for part of the day to originate regional or local programs.

U.S. radio networks have been reduced to relaying, by wire or satellite, intermittent news summaries, features, and sports events. The bulk of radio programming comes from syndicated and local material put together by the stations. In the rest of the world, radio networks

---

*Some systems use the terms *channel* and *program* as the equivalent of *network*. Thus Britain's Channel Four is a national television network, and the USSR refers to its radio networks as Program 1, Program 2, and so on. To compound the confusion, Europeans often speak of a local cable system as a cable network, whereas in U.S. parlance a cable network is a group of cable systems linked by satellite to a common program source.

generally retain their former character as suppliers of most if not all of affiliates' programming. Indeed, the term *affiliate* hardly applies because the local outlets usually simply relay network fare.

Many variations on the television network pattern exist. In Britain, for example, the ITV companies furnish national television programming, with no single origination point as *the* network headquarters, and each program company represents an entire region rather than the local coverage area of an individual transmitter. On the other hand, the BBC operates both radio and television national networks, with various opt-out arrangements for regional originations. The U.S. public broadcasting network originates no programs of its own, obtaining them from affiliates and other outside producers. Britain's Channel Four similarly relies on outside producers. In Japan, private network organizations may not own any affiliates, all of which must produce 10 percent of their programming locally.

Pseudonetworks. Because the term *network* carries with it a certain aura of prestige and serves as a useful catchall word for various aggregates of stations, one often finds it applied to *pseudonetworks*. These are station groups that certainly have some common bond, but they lack the distinctive network bond of electronic interconnection. Such is the case legally of the private "networks" in Italy, where as a matter of law only RAI, the official government service, may operate true networks (see Section 4.4).

Pseudonetworks distribute programs on tape or film rather than by direct relay. They can, of course, simulate true networks by scheduling identical programs simultaneously. It takes time to ship programs, however, so pseudonetworks lack the unique attribute of feeding timely programs to affiliates both simultaneously *and* instantaneously.

Terrestrial Relays

It follows, therefore, that true networks require some electronic means of relaying signals to affiliates. Normally, networks use nonbroadcast, common carrier facilities that form part of a country's telecommunications infrastructure. Sometimes networks build their own relay facilities, but they usually find it more cost effective to share in the use of common carriers.

Rebroadcasting. In a pinch, broadcast stations can both deliver programs to audiences and distribute them to other stations for redelivery to other audiences. In this case, an affiliate picks up from another affiliate the same signal as that received by the general public, retransmitting the signal to its own audience. Known as *rebroadcasting*, this method of relaying has its drawbacks. The distances between population centers may be too great to permit the over-the-air signal to carry well from one station to the next. At best, broadcast signals suffer some loss of quality, especially when picked up on the fringe of a transmitter's service area, as would most likely be the case when a station rebroadcasts. Thus both coverage and quality usually suffer when networks rely on rebroadcasting as a means of signal distribution.

Developing countries, often lacking relay facilities, must sometimes depend on rebroadcasting in order to have radio networks at all. Because long distances must usually be covered, they use short-wave broadcast transmitters for this relay function—an unfortunate compromise, because sky waves suffer much fading and interference. Television requires special wide-band relay facilities and so cannot use the short-wave relays of sound radio. Many developing countries lack sufficient relay facilities capable of distributing television signals throughout the national territory.

Common Carriers. Radio networks came into being easily enough in countries that already had well-developed telephone facilities. Ordinary telephone lines can be adapted to provide adequate radio interconnection, though not to relay the high-quality sound that later came to be the hallmark of FM radio. Television, however, needs too wide a band of frequencies to pass through ordinary telephone wires for any great distance. It therefore had to wait on development of a special wide-band wire, coaxial cable, before networking could begin. Later, microwave relays replaced coaxial cable for most long-haul, overland interconnection. Today, a new means of extremely wide-band relay has started to come into use, fiber-optic cable employing laser light instead of radio frequency energy.*

A supplementary terrestrial relay system, *tropospheric scatter*, enables transmission across bodies of water for distances up to about 200 miles. The first such installation relayed television from Florida to Cuba in 1954, a distance of 185 miles. Later, France used the same over-the-horizon method to reach across the Mediterranean to its colony, Algeria. About a score of developing countries use tropospheric scatter relays today, mostly for general telecommunications.

Terrestrial relay facilities cost so much to install and operate that in most cases broadcasting alone could not support them. Microwave networks and the like become cost effective only when carrying large volumes of traffic. Thus relay networks normally serve a variety of telecommunications purposes in addition to broadcasting. Many developing countries generate insufficient traffic and have too few active communication centers to support full-scale coaxial and microwave

---

*A fiber-optic transatlantic submarine cable, due for installation by 1985, could serve for relaying television between continents. Older submarine cables, in use since the nineteenth century for relay of telegraph and telephone traffic, lack the wide-band capacity needed for television.

national relay networks. Lack of this infrastructural feature has been the most serious deterrent to national broadcasting development in the Third World.

Airborne Relays. As alternatives to the slow buildup of expensive terrestrial relay systems, relay transmitters have sometimes been installed in circling airplanes and suspended from tethered balloons. Westinghouse experimented at length with airborne relays in the 1950s. In 1954 a relay transmitter installed in an airplane sent a live television program from Cuba to the United States.[22] In 1974 a repeater suspended from a tethered balloon relayed U.S. television signals to the island of Grand Bahama, a distance of 110 miles from the Florida coast.[23] Nigeria planned at one time to employ tethered balloons to relay television to its six regional zones, but the scheme failed to get off the ground (so to speak).

The U.S. government introduced television to South Vietnam by airborne relay—a strange introduction not only because of the relay method but also because television came to the country in the very midst of war:

> *On 7 February 1966, a U.S. Navy Super Constellation (C-121) rolled down the runway of the Saigon airport, climbed to 10,500 feet—reaching a spot about 20 miles southeast of Saigon—and banked into an oval pattern. . . . Inside, there were three 2–5 kw. transmitters, two videotape machines, audio control panels and sets of 16mm. telecine equipment, a studio about the size of a large clothes closet. . . . At 7:30 that evening, the first [Vietnamese] program was broadcast on Channel 9, featuring a newscast, May Day parade film, comedy skit, short film showing prospective Vietnamese pilots in training, and a brief introduction by Prime Minister Nguyen Ky and U.S. Ambassador Henry Cabot Lodge. (Hoffer & Lichty, 1978: 99)*

Space Relays

Airborne relays served merely as a transitional step toward the ultimate solution—relay transmitters operating from space. Developing countries found that they could bypass the slow buildup of coaxial-microwave relay facilities by moving directly into the space age. To be sure, satellite relay facilities also cost a great deal, but costs can be shared among many users, as INTELSAT convincingly demonstrated.

The ITU differentiates between two types of satellites of interest to broadcasters—Fixed Satellite Services (FSS) and Broadcast Satellite Services (BSS). The former pertain primarily to relays, that is, distribution, the latter primarily to direct broadcasting by satellite, that is, delivery.

Fixed Satellite Services. Design strategy for relay satellites put the main burden on the earth stations, where great size and weight can be tolerated. Thus designers could pare down the combined mass of satellite receivers/transmitters (transponders), their antennas, and associated hardware to launchable weight. As satellite launch technology* improved, it became possible to send up heavier vehicles capable of assuming a larger share of the power burden. Even so, transponders (receive-transmit units) on FSS vehicles in the early 1980s still had only 5–8 watts of power—less than a bathroom nightlight.

The weak signals of satellite transponders can punch through the earth's atmospheric envelope because they look nearly straight down. For most of their 22,300-mile journeys, up and down, the signals pass through the vacuum of space; only for the last few miles must they encounter the absorptive barrier of the atmosphere. In contrast, terrestrial microwave relay signals travel continuously through the atmosphere and therefore must be reamplified every few miles to compensate for absorption.

Shifting more power responsibility to the satellite had an important bearing on the growth of satellite services. Only after the size and cost of earth stations came down could they be widely afforded. Originally, most nations participating in the INTELSAT consortium installed only one large earth station to serve the entire country. Later, after satellites grew more powerful and earth stations less costly, some countries could eventually afford hundreds of reception terminals. In 1983 some five thousand U.S. cable systems had their own relatively small earth stations for picking up satellite-distributed programs, as did hundreds of television and radio stations. From the economic viewpoint, this increase in the potential customers for satellite services had great importance, making the ever increasing costs of the satellites tolerable by dividing them among more and more users. In the early 1980s, it was estimated that operational satellites powerful enough to make direct-broadcast reception by consumers feasible would cost on the order of $1 billion apiece. Moreover, to ensure continuity of service, each operational satellite needs several others to back it up both in space and on the ground.

Geosynchronous Orbit. Nearly all FSS and BSS satellites occupy positions in an orbit some 22,300 miles directly above the equator. ITU agreements allot orbital positions in terms of degrees of a circle—0 to 180 degrees east and 0 to 180 degrees west, starting from the prime meridian, the line that runs from one pole to the other, passing through Greenwich in London. These orbital positions correspond to degrees of

---

*Satellite-launching services can be bought from only two sources, the U.S. National Aeronautics and Space Administration (NASA) and the European launch facility, located in French Guiana, a small dependency on the northeast coast of South America. Other nations, such as the USSR and Japan, can launch their own vehicles but do not make their facilities available commercially. The NASA and European facilities book up customers years in advance of actual launch dates.

longitude on earth. Each degree of longitude on the earth's surface represents a distance of about 70 miles, but each degree of the stationary orbit represents 470 miles.

Satellites positioned at the correct distance above the equator revolve in step with the earth's rotation—hence the term *geosynchronous* to describe their orbit.* They stay in place because at that height the downward pull of gravity and the outward pull of centrifugal force reach an equilibrium.

Maintaining this fixed position relative to the earth has two important advantages: earth station receiving antennas, once pointed at a geosynchronous satellite, can remain in that position; such fixed antennas are simpler and cheaper than those requiring precise controls for tracking satellites as they move across the sky. Secondly, signals from geosynchronous satellites can be received 24 hours per day because of their fixed position; nonsynchronous satellites, in contrast, move across the sky, rising above and falling below the horizon like the sun or moon.

When the Soviets initiated the first space relays for domestic television with their *Molniya* series (see Section 2.5), they opted for a nonsynchronous orbit. To visualize the reason for this choice, picture yourself looking up at a satellite. If you stood on the equator at the same longitude as that of the satellite, it would be directly overhead. But as you moved north or south away from the equator, the satellite would appear lower and lower in the sky, approaching the horizon. If you stood on a Soviet island in the Arctic Ocean at 80 degrees north latitude, you would see a geosynchronous satellite only 13 degrees above the horizon. This would mean that its weak signals would have to pass through too much of the earth's atmosphere to be receivable in the far north. The Soviets therefore positioned their Molniyas in a nonequatorial (that is, nonsynchronous) orbit, such that they would pass over central Russia and thus be able to reach the far north. In that orbit, the Molniyas move across the sky for about nine hours, then disappear below the horizon. In other words, a Molniya satellite can see its target area only about a third of the time. Three Molniya satellites, each orbiting several hours behind the next, must therefore be used to provide 24-hour relay service.

8 ▪ 5 ALTERNATIVE DELIVERY METHODS

The main alternatives to conventional broadcasting for delivering program materials to consumers include wire or cable systems, direct-broadcast satellites, videocassette players, and teletext services.

---

*The ITU defines a geosynchronous satellite as "an earth satellite whose period of revolution is equal to the period of rotation of the Earth." One can also use the term *geostationary satellite*, defined by the ITU as one "whose circular and direct orbit lies in the plane of the Earth's equator and which thus remains fixed relative to the Earth" (ITU, 1980: 47).

Cable

As related in Section 2.6, wired radio, or rediffusion, furnished a precedent for cable television. Wired-radio systems pick up broadcast radio signals at central headends and "rediffuse" them by means of wires to loudspeakers located in homes or public places. The headend usually includes a small studio from which local closed-circuit program material can be added to the broadcasts—what came to be called "local origination" with the advent of cable television.

Europe's pre-1980s cable television technology, based upon the wired-radio precedent, differed from that used in the United States. In Britain, "twisted pairs" of ordinary wire served to connect most homes to cable systems, one pair of wires for each channel. The distinctive feature of cable as it developed in the United States—the large number of channels made possible by wide-band coaxial cable—did not emerge in most of Europe until the 1980s. European systems furnished only half a dozen channels, if that many. They also lacked the varied program resources made possible by linking cable systems into satellite "networks."*

Rediffusion Consumer Electronics, the leading company in the development of both wired radio and cable television in Britain, has long advocated a method of cable program delivery different from the U.S. method. The latter, known as the "tree and branch" method, delivers to subscriber terminals the *entire package* of 12, 30, or whatever number of programs the particular cable system furnishes. The subscriber selects from the package, usually by means of a keypad that causes a tuner to single out a particular channel for display on the receiver.

Rediffusion considers it wasteful to deliver many programs all the way to the receiver when only one can be used at a time. It advocates a "switched star" configuration, which delivers the full package of channels via trunk cables to only a limited number of *program exchanges.* Single two-way circuits link a program exchange to each subscriber in its particular group. Using a selector switch, the subscriber sends an electronic order to the program exchange, requesting a particular channel. Only that program goes from the exchange to the subscriber's receiver. Even though the switched star method requires two-way cable linkage between subscribers and program exchanges, the wiring between the exchange and the homes it feeds can be relatively simple and inexpensive, because it needs to carry only one program at a time. Rediffusion had plans in the early 1980s to install a 30-channel interactive cable system in Britain, using the switched star system, which it believes has

---

*Cable "satellite channels," such as Cable News Network, Cable Satellite Public Affairs Network, and USA Cable Network, qualify as networks in the sense that many different cable systems receive programs from a single supplier simultaneously by means of relays; but they lack the complex interactive relationships that exist between U.S. television broadcast affiliates and their networks.

advantages not only for interactive operations but also for eventual changeover to fiber-optic cable.

A 1982 report by the British government's Information Technology Advisory Panel recommended use of the switched system in licensing a new generation of sophisticated cable services in Britain:

> The main trunk lines (probably optic fibres) would deliver all the channels to a local switching point . . . which would serve 50–100 households. From then on, the cables to each subscriber would be smaller (probably coaxial cable, not optical) and capable of carrying only 30–40 MHz instead of the 350 MHz carried on the trunk cables. (Howkins, 1982c: 37)

Most advanced planning for modernization of European cable systems in the 1980s also envisioned using satellite relays to distribute programs to the headends of the new cable services—the aforementioned "cable networks" that became common in the United States during the 1970s.

Direct-Broadcast Satellites

As a BBC research engineer remarked, "Direct broadcasting by satellite surely comes closer to the ideal concept of broadcasting than any other method. There is an elegant simplicity, at least in concept, in a single transmitter of about 200 watts being able to provide a television service to almost every home in the country" (Ratliff, 1982: 37). It seemed possible in the early years of the 1980s, however, that delivery by satellite relays to cable networks would undercut the development of DBS delivery directly to homes.

Each delivery method has its pluses and minuses. Cable television costs the subscriber less (initially, at least), has the potential for virtually unlimited numbers of channels, and can provide locally relevant programming. DBS has the potential for only five channels (according to current standards) but can benefit from economies of scale, which enable purchasing extremely high cost programming for entire nations and even for groups of nations. And it reaches subscribers in areas that cannot be economically cabled.

Introduction of operational DBS services, scheduled for the 1980s, hinged basically on development of small, low-cost receiving antennas and amplifiers that ordinary citizens could mount on rooftops as easily as conventional outside television antennas.

> [Satellite services] intended for individual reception [and] using relatively cheap receiving equipment require very large transmitted powers from the satellite (of the order of several thousand times more effective radiated power than a typical fixed service transmission of similar bandwidth). These high powers pose a potential interference problem to other satellite services and require careful choice of frequency, orbital position and antenna characteristics to minimise the interference effects. (UNESCO, Feb. 1982b: 110–111)

In addition to higher input power, DBS satellites need narrow-beam transmitting antennas to deliver concentrated, high-gain signals. Canada and the United States planned to cover their east-west dimensions with four high-gain regional DBS footprints, though a single satellite could easily cover their entire width with a single lower-gain footprint.* Designers expect to shrink DBS receiving antennas to a diameter of between two and three feet. This size allows reception in the primary service area of the beam; larger dishes would be able to pick up signals over a wider service area, as shown in Figure 8.1.

At WARC 1977, the ITU alloted channels and DBS orbital slots to Regions I and III (Africa, Asia, and Europe).† European nations each received an orbital position separated by 6 degrees from its neighbors and located between 5 degrees east and 37 degrees west. The United Kingdom, for example, received the orbital position of 31 degrees west, a location above the Atlantic off the coast of Africa. From the equator, satellites look down toward their target areas at an angle, creating elliptical footprints, as shown in Figure 8.1. A regional ITU conference, RARC 1983, later allotted DBS orbital slots to Region II (the Americas), ranging from 44 to 175 degrees west. For example, the Caribbean islands received, as a group, a single slot located at 92.5 degrees west, roughly above the Galapagos Islands in the Pacific off the coast of South America.‡ The United States was allotted eight orbital slots, able to accommodate 256 channels. The first operational U.S. DBS service, that of the United Satellite Corporation, began late in 1983, temporarily using Canada's *Anik* satellite. Several other U.S. companies expected to start beaming down programs in 1984–1985.

Cassette Recording

Audiocassettes and videocassettes made recording and playback such simple operations that they can be done by a child. This "deprofessionalization" of recording technology had little effect at first, but by the end of 1982, a boom in cassette recorder sales began creating a host of novel problems. In a neat demonstration of the "abhorrent vacuum" principle (discussed in Section 4.1), consumers began using videocassette recorders (VCRs) to overcome sources of consumer frustration—

---

*Note that the footprint of a geostationary communication satellite *without* directional antenna can cover nearly a third of the world's surface, except for the extreme north and south latitudes beyond 76 degrees. Thus three INTELSAT satellites, one each located above the Atlantic, Indian, and Pacific oceans, can relay signals throughout the world except to the polar regions.

†*WRTH* lists the 40 channels allocated by the ITU, which are located from 11.7 to 12.5 Gigahertz, along with the European channel allotments (1984: 397). See also Howkins, 1981: 19.

‡Formal incorporation of the 1983 allotments into the ITU Radio Regulations had to await the 1985 World Radio Conference on the space orbit.

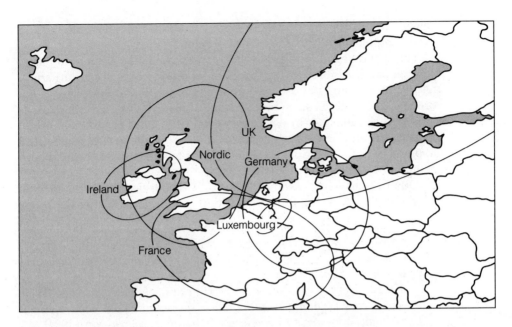

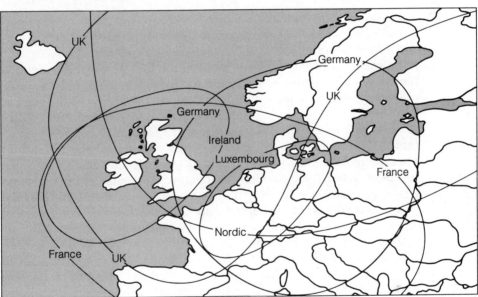

FIGURE 8 ▪ 1 DBS SATELLITE FOOTPRINTS. The upper map shows the hypo-
thetical footprints of European national DBS satellites receivable on
.9-meter antennas for individual homes. The lower map shows the
larger footprints of the same satellites receivable by 2-meter community antennas whose signal would be distributed to homes by cable.
These projections are based on standards adopted by the 1977 WARC.

censorship, prudishness, lack of variety, commercial interruptions, and even complete absence of television services.

This trend began in the early 1970s among the very affluent in places such as Saudi Arabia, where the government imposes strict puritanical television standards and bans public exhibition of motion pictures entirely. The Middle East, in fact, became a major home video market, as indicated in Table 8.4. In 1982 the Persian Gulf states absorbed a fifth of Japan's output of recorder-playback units.* Those who could not afford to buy a VCR for personal use joined clubs to share the expense of both equipment and taped programs.

Other places where extensive use of VCRs has been reported include China, India, Malaysia, Singapore, South Africa, and Sweden.

> *India has advanced a claim that perhaps no other nation would have thought to make—that it has the largest fleet of video-equipped buses in the world. . . . Many restaurants offer the same amenity, though the food is usually a pretext for the film.*
>
> *The video library has also become a fixture in all of India's big cities. Palika Bazaar in New Delhi has an entire row of shops renting out films in Hindi, English, and a few regional languages.* (Channels, March–April 1984)

The Malaysian government ascribed loss of audience for its noncommercial service to the widespread use of personal recorders, giving that as one reason for inaugurating a commercial television service.

In some countries, political motives for VCR use can also be discerned. Audiocassettes made by the Ayatollah Khomeini from his exile in France helped lay the groundwork for the overthrow of the shah of Iran. Khomeini's revolutionary Iranian government found itself in turn under attack in secretly circulated recordings. Iran thereupon banned cassette recorders altogether. In the USSR, cassettes have taken their place alongside handwritten and photocopied documents as part of the corpus of *samizdat*, the clandestine literature that circulates underground within the Soviet Union. Imported recorders there cost as much as ten times what they do in the United States. In 1982 the USSR concluded an arrangement with a Japanese firm to manufacture them at home.[24]

According to a 1983 estimate, as many as a million VCRs had been sold in Latin America, half of them in Brazil. "From Guadalajara to Patagonia, video cassettes increasingly are used to pierce state censorship, to break down isolation in remote areas and to keep expatriates

---

Time, 13 Dec. 1982. According to Boyd, even the controversial program "Death of a Princess," a British-U.S. coproduced program purporting to show how the Saudis put to death a princess of its royal family and her lover as punishment for adultery, turned up on cassettes in Saudi Arabia itself the morning after being shown. The Saudi government bitterly opposed showing of the documentary and tried through diplomatic channels to have it suppressed in foreign countries.

TABLE 8 ▪ 4 HOME VIDEOCASSETTE RECORDER PENETRATION, LEADING COUNTRIES

Country	Recorders as Percentage of TV Households	Country	Recorders (Thousands)
Kuwait	80	U.S.A.	5,250
Panama	68	Japan	3,420
United Arab Emirates	65	West Germany	2,650
Qatar	58	France	1,000
Oman	50	Australia	605
Bahrain	35	Taiwan	525
Singapore	32	Canada	500
Philippines	23	Sweden	500
Malaysia	20	Saudi Arabia	450
United Kingdom	20	Spain	280

NOTE: The first column shows how deeply videocassette recorders had penetrated as of 1982 in developing countries with relatively few TV-equipped households; the second column shows the leading countries in terms of the absolute numbers of VCRs in use. The high percentage of TV households with VCRs in the United Kingdom apparently reflects the decline of the British film industry.
SOURCE: Based on data in InterMedia, "Videocassette Recorders: National Figures, July–Sept. 1983, p. 39. Used by permission.

in touch with home. The 'democratization' of video is bringing new voices to closed societies" (Brooke, 1983).

The unexpected world demand for VCRs created a corresponding demand for taped motion pictures and television programs to play on them, but no ready-made mechanisms existed for serving this new market. Moreover, the very legality of home recording and playing back of materials seen publicly on television came into question. As a result, a huge global black market in pirated tapes emerged. This illegal market caused far more damage to intellectual property rights than did the pirate broadcast stations described in Section 4.4. Some of the legal ramifications of this problem are discussed in Section 5.5.

Videotex

Some commentators regard the various forms of *videotex* as the most innovative of the new communication technologies. Videotex combines television display with the printed word in a new form, differing from both conventional video pictures and the printed page. The generic term for this hybrid form, *videotex*, covers two branches of the technology: *videotext*, which uses cable or wire and allows for two-way (interactive) communication between the source and consumers, and *teletext,* which broadcasts one-way textual matter over conventional television stations.

A number of European countries began developing these technologies in the mid-1970s. European PTTs and telecommunications administrations, perceiving videotext as a means of increasing the earning power of their wire networks, vigorously exploited this new medium. The British Post Office led the way with *Prestel,* the first commercially operative videotext system. Installations based on Prestel have been made in a dozen countries. Other videotext methods include those of Canada (*Telidon*), France (*ANTIOPE*), Japan (*CAPTAIN*), and West Germany (*Bildschirmtext*).*

Britain also pioneered teletext, led by the BBC's *Ceefax* ("see facts") system in 1974. The IBA quickly followed with *ORACLE* ("Optional Reception of Announcements by Coded Line Electronics"), the first advertising-supported teletext system. Teletext uses a part of the television station's frequency band that lies dormant during the vertical blanking period. During this interval at the end of each television picture field, the screen remains momentarily blank for the equivalent time of 21 picture-scanning lines. This pause allows the electron beam that "paints" the picture information on the screen to return to the top of the next field. (The blanking interval lines can be seen as a heavy black band at the bottom of the picture, visible when the picture rolls over.) The time occupied by only 2 of these vertical blanking lines suffices to send the comparatively crude images contained in a teletext frame, or "page." Each page can display only about 150 readable words, so teletext lends itself best to short lists, very brief sentences, and simple maps or diagrams.†

Televiewers in Britain pay no additional fee for Ceefax and ORACLE but must obtain a converter, either as an add-on device or as a built-in component of the television receiver. A keypad calls up indexes of the numbered pages of textual or graphic materials that the service provides. Subscribers then punch in the page numbers of the material they want to see displayed on their television screens. Pages might consist of weather reports, news headlines, transportation schedules, entertainment guides, food prices, games such as simple crossword puzzles, broadcast program schedules, menus, food recipes, and the like—plus advertising in the case of ORACLE. Each of the two BBC networks offers several hundred pages of teletext material, as does the ITV network. By 1983 more than a million sets had been converted to receive the service

---

*Telidon stands for "I perceive at a distance"; ANTIOPE, for *"Acquisition Numérique et Télévisualization d'Images Organisées en Pages d'Écriture"*; CAPTAIN, for "Character and Pattern Telephone Access Network"; *Bildschirmtext,* for "television screen newspaper."

†The Japanese version of high-definition television, though, enables a single frame to carry an entire normally printed page.

in Britain (note the teletext schedules listed in British and French television programs Tables 9.3 and 9.4).

As an important side benefit, teletext has the potential for subtitling (teletext images can either replace the regular television images currently on the screen or be superimposed over them). U.S. networks use a version of teletext for a service for the hearing impaired, "closed captioning," so called because the captions can be seen only with the aid of an adapter. The BBC subtitled 35 hours of programming per week in 1983 and had begun experimenting with captioning even live sports programs.

Videotext, because it uses the full capacity of wire or cable circuits, can offer virtually unlimited numbers of pages. It also allows viewers to respond, so it can be used for taking surveys, feeding back student responses to lectures and demonstrations, giving examinations, placing orders with shops, doing banking transactions, and so on. Videotext also has the technical advantage over teletext of being adaptable to digital forms of signal processing, the method of the future. The reflections or "ghosts" incidental to over-the-air television propagation, however, break up digitized signals.

8 ▪ 6 INFRASTRUCTURE

The best facilities in the world can produce only a mediocre broadcasting service without a supporting infrastructure. An effective system needs the support of (1) reliable and stable electrical power throughout its areas of coverage; (2) a national network of dependable telecommunication facilities (telegraphs, telephones, microwave relays, and access to an international satellite relay service); (3) internal manufacturing plants making the hardware needed by the system, to the extent practicable; (4) the means for training personnel; and, finally, (5) adequate frequency allotments from the ITU and the ability to pursue the nation's interests vigorously and effectively at ITU administrative and plenipotentiary conferences. In this section I discuss the first three of these requisites, focusing primarily on the unavoidable deficiencies of broadcasting in developing countries resulting from infrastructural limitations.

Electrification

Broadcasting in many countries suffers frequent interruption because of breakdowns in the public power supply; indeed, deliberate power cuts at regular intervals to enable maintenance work are common. Transmitters must often operate in areas without central power, necessitating use of diesel generators; but these in turn depend on a steady supply of fuel, not always available in developing countries.

Research has been going on for years to develop receivers and transmitters operated by solar or wind power. No major breakthrough has been made, though experimental units are in operation. In 1981 Britain's IBA built a 150-watt television repeater transmitter powered by a combination of sun, wind, and standby storage batteries. It served an isolated community of three hundred in Cornwall. Even if successful, however, such units would be suitable only for supplementary coverage unless some new method of economically generating high power emerges.

Lack of rural electrification as well as lack of money prevents the spread of television beyond major cities in many Third World countries. Though satellites can solve the problem of program distribution to remote areas, the problem of electrical power for reception facilities remains. Ironically, television, the medium offering the most promise for bringing education, agricultural information, and health guidance to rural areas, finds its primary audience in urban settings, where the residents use it mainly for entertainment.

Telecommunication Networks

Full development of broadcasting needs the support of national networks of common carrier facilities. Colonial telegraphs and telephones linked the capitals of the colonies with London or Paris but made little provision for communication in the hinterlands or between neighboring colonies. After independence, people in adjacent African states found they could not telephone each other without going through Europe. Foreign correspondents covering a 1978 nonaligned conference in Zambia found cables to their headquarters being routed through South Africa; calls to neighboring African countries had to go first to London.[25]

News-gathering and program personnel in developed countries take telephone services for granted. Those who have not experienced it can hardly imagine the frustration of spending hours to put through a single local telephone call or waiting days to make long-distance calls because they must be booked long in advance. Such delays make timely program and production operations impossible.

Manufacturing

Few countries have the industrial base for manufacturing major electronic components such as transmitters. The 25 leading manufacturers of electronic equipment are found in only six countries, with 17 of them located in the United States. Four of the top manufacturers are in Japan, with 1 each in France, the Netherlands, the United Kingdom, and West Germany. It would, of course, be unreasonable to expect scores of countries to manufacture their own transmitters, color cameras, professional tape recorders, and studio control consoles when only a very limited world market exists for such sophisticated equipment. But because of strings attached to foreign aid,* because purchase orders must usually be put out to bid, and because of the desire not to become dependent on only a single supplier, developing countries often end up with a bewildering collection of hardware from disparate sources, not all items completely compatible with the rest. Katz and Wedell cite the case of Indonesia, whose 126 government radio transmitters came from various manufacturers—64 from the U.S., 11 from the Netherlands, and the rest from companies in other countries. These circumstances, say the authors, go "some way toward explaining why 80 percent of the transmitters are operating at less than 60 percent efficiency" (1977: 58, 60).

Cuba finds itself in the awkward position of being cut off from the U.S. suppliers to which it originally committed itself:

> A Cuban broadcasting official claims that Cuban television equipment is the oldest in operation in the world. When Cuban television started in 1952, second-hand equipment from the United States was used. That same basic equipment, supplemented with a patchwork of replacement parts and new equipment, was still in use in 1981. (Nichols, 1982a: 79–80)

Nevertheless, Castro is reluctant to switch over to Soviet-style equipment. It would be incompatible both with Cuba's existing equipment and with that of other Latin American and Caribbean systems.

Some major manufacturers afford partial (though not always satisfactory) independence for Third World countries by supplying guidance in setting up local factories for assembling receivers. These manufacturers supply prefabricated parts that workers with relatively little training can put together on simple assembly lines requiring no great capital investment.

SUMMARY

Evaluating a system's physical facilities involves considering program production, delivery, distribution, and reception, along with such infrastructural underpinnings as electrical power, manufacturing, and training resources. Systems vary in how they integrate programming, production, and delivery. Some, as in the United States, combine all three under a single management, but in many countries different organizations handle each function. Commonly, the organization supplying transmission and interconnection facilities differs from the one supplying production and programming facilities.

Several variables—economics, politics, and geography as well as technology—govern the numbers, types, and locations of transmitters a

---

*Under the terms of the usual bilateral foreign aid agreement, the recipient country must accept hardware manufactured by the donor country, even though it may be either incompatible with hardware already available in the country or ill adapted for use in that country.

system employs. The effectiveness of transmission facilities depends upon widespread distribution of receivers. While in highly developed countries virtually every household has one or more radio and television sets, in many countries relatively few people have access to radio and far fewer to television. Of the limited number of receivers available in developing countries, many may be inoperative for want of repair facilities or replacement batteries.

Program economics demands facilities for storage-reproduction and distribution. Magnetic tape recorders and satellite relays perform these functions with increased efficiency and flexibility. Cable television, satellite relays, direct satellite broadcasts, cassette recorders, and videotex provide alternate or supplementary distribution and delivery methods now in the process of finding their role in the media mix of the marketplace.

NOTES

[1]Elsewhere I have noted the practical problems for production that arise from such divided authority, using the case of Ethiopia (Head, 1974: 41–43).

[2]Garratt, 1982.

[3]Katz & Wedell, 1977: 74.

[4]Green, 1972: 228.

[5]Menzel, 1983: 40.

[6]WRTH lists existing LW stations, 1984: 443.

[7]Briggs, 1961: 224.

[8]Based on data in Menzel, 1983.

[9]Katz & Wedell, 1977: 59.

[10]Codding, 1983: 11.

[11]Reasons for this unusual situation are explored in Head, Sept. 1979.

[12]WRTH carries details of the various world television standards, 1984: 396–397.

[13]Boyd, 1982: 132. See Crane, 1979, for a study of economic chauvinism in television technology subtitled "France and the Color TV War."

[14]Nichols, 1979: 94.

[15]Johnson, 1983.

[16]Krath, 1982: 565; Great Britain, 1977: 374.

[17]Katz & Wedell, 1977: 113.

[18]Amunugama, 1982: 136.

[19]TV set penetration estimates from *Television Age International*, April 1984: 156–158.

[20]*Asian Broadcasting*, Dec. 1982.

[21]*Asian Broadcasting*, Aug. 1983.

[22]*New York Times*, 14 Nov. 1955.

[23]*Time*, 23 Sept. 1974: 71.

[24]*Time*, 13 Dec. 1982. Still other motives for using VCRs emerge from a 37-country survey made by *InterMedia* (July–Sept. 1983).

[25]Pool & Dizard, 1978: 15. Hachten gives some background on colonial communication arrangements, 1971: 57–58.

CHAPTER 9

PROGRAMS AND PROGRAMMING

P *rogramming* refers to the way broadcasters select and combine individual programs or program elements into continuous broadcast services. Not only the selection of individual items but also their sequencing and integration into daily, weekly, and seasonal schedules play important roles in determining the nature of program services. Each program occurs in a programming environment as well as in the social and physical environment that circumscribes reception.

9•1 PROGRAM SERVICES

Ideally, programming gives audiences simultaneous choices among alternative services at national, regional, and local levels. Schedules allow listeners and viewers to make choices at their convenience and in keeping with their needs and interests, throughout a continuous broadcast day. In practice, few systems attain this programming ideal. Choices, if any, usually involve two or three national networks. With the exception of the United States and systems within its sphere of influence, most systems scheduling regional and local services offer only one of each in any given locality. The trend, however, is toward offering more choices at each level. Countries with only two or three network services strive to add a third or fourth; those with no regional or local services strive to create new classes of stations to offer such programs.

Broad-band (many-channeled) cable television can of course increase choices dramatically, as happened in the United States with the growth of satellite-cable networks in the 1970s. Such innovations emerged more slowly and in less abundance in other countries. They come at such high cost that only some people in some countries can afford them. For most of the world, conventional broadcasting remains the only universal source of programming, now and for the immediate future.

The new technologies create a policy dilemma for traditional public service oriented broadcasting, which is committed to making its services available to all at modest cost. Such systems must try to preserve comprehensive, low-cost, universal services in the face of technologies that offer more numerous but more expensive services to a few while at the same time threatening to corner the market for the most attractive programs.

National Programming

Radio. Until the early 1960s, U.S. commercial radio offered only four full-service national networks. With the changes forced by television competition and later by satellite relays, the number of national networks increased, but at the same time the extent of their services decreased. By the 1980s, U.S. radio stations could choose to affiliate with some 20 different national networks; however, affiliates received not full-scale services but brief news bulletins and sports features at intervals throughout the day. A certain dwindling of network radio has occurred everywhere since television arrived but not always as radically as in the United States.

> The BBC continues to broadcast many radio plays . . . as do the West Germany ARD stations, France-Culture, some other West European stations, CBC in Canada, the ABC in Australia, and increasingly, National Public Radio in the United States. Most West European stations also have their own symphony orchestras and commission a number of original works each year. (Browne, 1983b: 193)

About half the European systems offer listeners a choice of three radio networks ("channels," "programs"), with about a fifth offering four. Most of these systems ensure genuine audience choices by giving each network a distinctive character and preventing or discouraging coscheduling of similar programs. Usually, the chronologically "first" network furnishes general interest programs aimed at the mass audience, while subsequent networks offer more specialized fare for smaller audiences. For example, in 1946 the BBC introduced its "Third Programme," an elite service designed for the intellectual minority (the name took on a generic meaning applicable to any service aimed at an intellectual elite). Now called Radio 3, it consumes nearly a fifth of the BBC radio budget while reaching only about 1 percent of the audience.[1]

I have already described present-day British radio networks (Radios 1 through 4) in Section 3.4. Here are some examples of varied radio network arrangements:

- Algeria has three radio networks, one for the main indigenous language (Arabic), one for the former colonial language (French), and one for the language of the aboriginal Berber inhabitants (Kabyle). Arabic programs occupy 17 of the 23 domestic transmitters, 24 hours per day. French and Kabyle divide the remaining outlets on intermittent schedules.

■ Egypt transmits an especially intricate array of services, using 30 medium-wave and 3 short-wave transmitters. That some transmitters aim services such as the Middle East Commercial Program and the Voice of the Arabs to both internal and external audiences complicates the coverage pattern. Altogether, Egypt lists a dozen "programs," only one of which operates nationally 24 hours per day, the General Arabic Program.

■ In the USSR, Moscow originates four services. Only three appear to qualify as "all-union," or national, networks (the Soviets decline to release detailed information about their broadcasting system). The First Program, carrying news and information, is repeated at different hours for distant regions reached by terrestrial and satellite relays. The Second Program (called *Mayak*, lighthouse), the primary mass audience program, featuring music, sports, and news, is the only domestic service on the air 24 hours per day. The Third Program operates 12 hours per day, broadcasting educational and cultural material; it is repeated at appropriate hours in two versions for other time zones. Each constituent republic has its own regional services, one of which mainly rebroadcasts material from Moscow's First Program.

Television. In the United States, full-service, national, over-the-air television networks still number only four—three commercial and one noncommercial. However, they offer less than four genuine choices. The three commercial networks confine their programming to a narrow range of types, so viewers often find similar programs on all three at the same time. Systems with a stronger public service commitment usually aim at *complementary* scheduling, giving viewers a choice of as many different program types as there are networks (see Section 6.4). Three fifths of the European systems offer only two national television networks. Britain had three until Channel Four went on the air in 1982, making Britain the first European nation to offer as many as four national television services. Some examples of other television network arrangements follow:

■ China has a single national television service, which originates at the China Central Television Station (CCTV) in Beijing and is distributed to the main provincial cities. CCTV also has responsibility for a second network, which supplies some centrally produced programs to regional stations.

■ France has three national television networks, *Télévision Française 1* (TF1), *Antenne 2* (A2), and *France Régions 3* (FR3). FR3 is used partly for regional programs on an opt-out basis. The French started a fourth network, *Canal Plus,* in 1984, using the old 819-line network facilities, which closed down for modernization in 1983. *Canal Plus* carries subscription television.

- Hong Kong's 400-square-mile area receives four services—two over-the-air channels, one in Chinese and one in English, and two cable channels, also in English and Chinese.

- Available sources give somewhat conflicting information about Soviet television schedules. According to *WRTH*,[2] in 1983 only one television service reached the entire nation, the First Program, on the air ten hours per day in two segments, the shorter morning segment repeating some programs from the preceding evening. The six-hour Second Program served the Moscow region. A short Third Program in Moscow featured educational programming, and the Fourth Program, also limited in coverage, featured sports. Composite versions of these four services, called respectively Double 2, 3, and 4, were rebroadcast at appropriate hours to three different time zones by means of the *Orbita* satellite relay system. Plans existed for adding Double 1 to cover a remaining time zone by 1985.

Regional Programming

Increased interest in regional programming parallels the worldwide growth of ethnic self-consciousness. So widespread has the interest in broadcast regionalism become that in 1983 the first European Congress on Regional Television Stations took place in Lille, France, site of the first regional station established under the French broadcasting law of 1982.

The extent to which systems schedule regional programming depends, of course, on the size of the territory they must cover as well as on the nation's ethnic and historical diversity. Homogeneous nations and physically small states have little or no need for regional programming. "Sweden with its eight million inhabitants is a national state with very few traits [of] federalism, and this national unity is reflected in its radio and television. . . . Only 2.5 hours per week are regional transmissions" (Soderstrom, 1981: 304). Swedes agitated for *localism* rather than for regionalism (Section 4.5). In contrast, India did not even introduce significant national television programming until 1982, when it began a 90-minute all-India service. The new programs quickly precipitated street demonstrations and parliamentary objections because the national material intruded on preferred regional programs.[3]

Yet even in relatively homogeneous nations such as the United Kingdom, intense regional sentiments affect broadcasting arrangements. The BBC devotes regional services not only to Northern Ireland, Scotland, and Wales but also to the Midlands, North of England, and West of England. Regional differences exist in the United States, of course, but are taken comparatively lightly as far as broadcasting is concerned. The principle of localism in station licensing (Section 4.5) tends to satisfy whatever ardor for regional program services may exist. Many listeners and viewers probably remain unaware that the United States never-theless has a score of regional television networks and a hundred re-gional radio networks (many of them merely part-time arrange-ments, it is true).

In Section 6.6 I mentioned examples of regionalism based on lan-guage differences, perhaps the most powerfully divisive factor political-ly. In Section 5.4 I gave several examples of broadcast regionalism based upon political federalism. Here are some further examples of regional-ism in varied settings:

- China has radio stations at the provincial level and special services aimed at the islands of Taiwan, Quemoy, and Matsu (the latter two lie between mainland China and Taiwan). Ordinarily, these would be called external services, but China claims the three islands as integral parts of the Chinese People's Republic. Special radio ser-vices are also supplied to China's many ethnic minorities. Regional television stations originate programs in local languages as well as carrying centrally produced programs from Beijing.

- France's broadcasting law of 1982 encouraged regional television, authorizing 12 regional companies, with still others projected for the future.

- In the USSR, each of 15 constituent republics has two regional radio services, one repeating some programs from Moscow as well as producing its own programs in local languages; the other uses the main language of the province in which the outlet is situated. Similarly, two regional television services supply programs in local languages, combining centrally and locally produced materials.

Local Programming

National, regional, and *local* are, of course, relative terms. A single service might qualify as all three on a small island, while a regional service in the USSR compares in scope to a national service in a smaller country. Even urban local services can be subdivided into citywide versus com-munity stations (see Section 4.5). American city dwellers take for granted numerous services at various levels—not only national and regional network outlets but also independent (nonnetwork) stations of varying reach and local access cable channels. Many offer similar pro-grams, but a wide range of choices still exists. Choices for audiences in most parts of the world are limited to three or four domestic radio programs and a couple of domestic television programs. These services usually come from centralized origination points, with little if any local input.

European audiences (in particular) can count on adding to their choices by tuning to three sources originating beyond their own borders: spillover from domestic stations of neighboring states, interna-tional commercial stations, and official international stations (external services). Program guides published locally routinely carry information about the first two of these sources.

In recent years, the more highly developed systems have begun responding to insistent public demand by providing for community stations, as related in Section 4.5. In the Third World, broadcasting tends to remain more centralized in the capital cities. International and bilateral sources of aid have, to a limited extent, introduced more localized, rural services. For example, Kenya's Homa Bay project, aided by UNESCO and two European assistance agencies, provides an experimental rural radio service. Homa Bay is located on Lake Victoria, on Kenya's western border. In addition to rebroadcasting programs from the national service originating in Nairobi, the Homa Bay station produces two hours per day of local programs in Dholuo, a local vernacular not included in the dozen languages broadcast by the Voice of Kenya. The project makes receivers available at prices subsistence farmers can afford.[4]

9·2 SCHEDULES

Continuity of Service

Both technical and audience considerations encourage maintaining uninterrupted broadcasting schedules. Manufacturers design broadcasting equipment to work continuously. Frequent switching off and on and periods of idleness are hard on transmitters. Only with continuous service can broadcasters capitalize fully on the *compatibility principle,* the medium's unique ability to time programs so that they are compatible with audience activities throughout the cycle of daily life.*

Ideally, broadcasting schedules would run continuously. Depending on local lifestyles, schedules would last anywhere from about 16 hours to 24 hours per day. The idea of uninterrupted service did not emerge at first, however. Until 1939 the BBC even observed a few minutes of silence between *each program,* on the assumption that listeners tuning in to hear a particular program would be annoyed at having to listen to the tail end of the preceding one.[5]

Typically, early radio stations went on the air for only an hour or two in the evenings; later, they expanded into midday segments and finally into morning segments. Originally, intermittent morning-noon-and-night scheduling apparently reflected an unstated belief that women at home neither needed nor deserved broadcasting services; schedules ran according to men's working hours rather than women's. Morning-noon-and-night segmenting, with breaks at midmorning and midafternoon,

---

*See Section 7.5 for a discussion of the pros and cons of continuous operation from the economic viewpoint.

still characterizes many noncommercial services. Stations primarily dependent on advertising income, on the other hand, tend toward continuous schedules for commercial reasons, if for no other.

Of course, not every system can afford continuous operation. In agrarian cultures where both men and women work in the fields and the hours of sleep correspond roughly with the hours of darkness, intermittent scheduling is justified. But where economically feasible and culturally appropriate, the world trend is toward longer hours of service and fewer interruptions (see Section 6.4).*

Television, because it costs so much more than radio to operate, employs shorter schedules than radio in most countries. Third World stations usually sign on for only four or five hours in the evening (see Table 9.1 for an example). When the African country of Mali began telecasting in 1983, it ran only two hours per day, and when the Indian Ocean island country of the Seychelles went on the air in the same year, it telecast only six hours per week—two hours each on Fridays, Saturdays, and Sundays.

Elsewhere, noon is the usual startup time except for instructional programs. Early morning television, initiated in the United States as long ago as 1952, was adopted in Australia, Canada, and Japan but remained rare until the 1980s. West Germany began an early morning program in 1981, consisting of repeat performances of selected programs from the preceding day's ARD and ZDF offerings. "Breakfast television" began in Britain in 1983 (an earlier BBC experiment had been abandoned). Table 9.2 shows a comparison of the early morning offerings of the BBC and a rival IBA commercial company, TV-am.

Third World systems that must accommodate several languages have no real opportunity to capitalize on the compatibility principle. Unable to devote a complete separate service to each language, they must switch from one to another. No sooner has audience rapport been established in one language than it must be broken to cater for a different group. For example, Ghana's GBC-1 (mainly wired speakers) uses six indigenous languages as well as English. In the course of the day, no language remains on the air for more than 15 to 20 minutes at a time.[6]

Systems sometimes interrupt their services in ways that seem curious—from a strictly commercial viewpoint, even suicidal. In 1979 Sri Lanka started blacking out its television for a half hour at 9:00 P.M. Officials said this hiatus was intended to prevent television from tempting listeners to ignore the prime-time national radio news and from

---

*Some systems economize by combining services to fill in the late-night hours when audiences are smallest. West Germany's regional ARD radio companies, for example, take turns in operating common national services that furnish popular and classical music formats from 11:30 P.M. to 6:00 A.M.; Greece has a special night program on an Athens transmitter from 1:00 A.M. to 6:00 A.M.; Italy's RAI runs "Notturno Italiana" from 12:30 A.M. to 6:00 A.M.; and South Africa combines several of its networks into a special midnight to 5:00 A.M. program.

TABLE 9 ▪ 1 A WEEK OF PLATEAU TV IN JOS, NIGERIA   (JULY–SEPT. 1983)

P.M.	Saturday	Sunday	Monday	Tuesday
4:30	S Sport			
5:00		S Children		
5:30		S Sport		
6:00			L Children	S Children
6:30	L News (Engl.)	L News (Engl.)	L News (Engl.)	L News (Engl.)
7:00	S Protectors/ Harold Lloyd	S Star Parade	L Hot Seat	S Sha-Na-Na
7:30	L Tin City Showcase	L Calling All Christians		L Medical Magazine
8:00	L News (Hausa)	L News (Hausa)	L News (Hausa)	L News (Hausa)
8:30	L Viewers' Request	L Drama	L Ladies World	L You Can Do It
9:00		S Faces of Woman/She	S Soul Train	S Tales of the Unexpected
9:30	L Panorama			L Don Manoma
10:00	S Feature Films	S Banachek	S Hawaii Five O	S Battlestar Galactica
10:50			L News Summary (Engl.)	L News Summary (Engl.)
11:00				
11:10		L News Summary (Engl.)		

NOTE: S = Syndicated (38 percent of programs); L = Local (62 percent of programs)
SOURCE: Personal communication from Dr. Girgis Salama, managing director, Plateau Television Corporation.

luring students away from their homework. In the same year, Thailand stopped telecasting from 6:30 to 8:00 P.M. to cut down on electrical consumption. In the earlier days of television, some systems saved money by closing down completely one day per week. West Germany's third channel (regional programs) simply went on vacation for the summer. Iceland's television service does not broadcast on Thursdays and until 1983 closed down annually for the entire month of July. Hungarian television goes off the air on Monday evenings.

Wednesday	Thursday	Friday
L Lokachin Yara (Children)	S Children	S Children
L News (Engl.)	L News (Engl.)	L News (Engl.)
S Comedy	S Wild Life	S Littlest Hobo
L Raye Rayen Mu	L Students' Panorama	L Islam Half Hour
L News (Hausa)	L News (Hausa)	L News (Hausa)
L Public Utilities	L Guest on 29	L Career Guidance
S Bob Newhart	S Sound Stage	S We're Moving
L You & the Law		L Democracy Today
S Dynasty	S It Takes a Thief	S New Avengers
L News Summary (Engl.)	L News Summary (Engl.)	L News Summary (Engl.)

Comprehensive Versus Generic Scheduling

John Reith, in keeping with his policy of using broadcasting to "give a lead" to popular taste, always insisted that each BBC domestic radio service should offer a balanced program service—a mix of information, entertainment, and education. Following World War II, BBC radio expanded its single Home Service into three comprehensive networks: the Light Program, the Home Service, and the Third Program. They

TABLE 9 ▪ 2 BREAKFAST TV IN BRITAIN (25 JULY 1983)

TV-am: Good Morning Britain		BBC: Breakfast Time	
6:25	Weather	6:30	News
6:30	News	6:31	Weather
6:35	Farming	6:42	Sport
6:45	Sport	6:45	Headlines, regional news,
6:58	Weather		weather, traffic, Getting
7:00	News		Britain Fit, Family Finance
7:05	Today's Papers	7:00	News
7:10	Diet	7:15	Headlines, regional news,
7:25	Competition Time		weather, traffic, Tonight's
7:28	Weather		TV, Sport
7:30	News	7:30	News
7:45	Sport	7:32	Review of the Papers
7:55	Pop Video	7:45	Headlines, regional news,
7:58	Weather		weather, traffic
8:00	News	7:57	Weather
8:05	Star Romance	8:00	News
8:25	Competition Time	8:15	Headlines, regional news,
8:28	Weather		weather, traffic
8:30	News	8:18	Sport
8:35	Today's Telly	8:27	Weather
8:50	Mad Lizzie (keep fit)	8:30	News, Your Stars
8:58	News		(horoscopes), Review of the
9:00	Rat on the Road		Papers
	(fun and cartoons)	8:45	Headlines, Food and Cooking
9:25	Closedown	9:00	Closedown

SOURCE: Adapted from James Bredin, "Breakfast Television in Britain," EBU Review 34-5, September 1983, p. 16. Used by permission.

represented a range of tastes, running from the popular through a middle ground to the elite.

This threefold pattern of BBC services held for more than 20 years, despite changing public tastes. Several influences combined to outmode the traditional network programming patterns, among them the advent of television, the rise of youth culture, and the influence of pirate broadcasting. After much soul searching, the BBC responded by issuing a watershed self-analysis, *Broadcasting in the Seventies.*[7] It announced a policy of moving yet further from Reithian comprehensive radio scheduling by approaching *generic* scheduling—in American terms, formula radio. This report, said the Annan Committee, "provoked a public row of splendid proportions"; despite bitter opposition from those who clung to Reith's philosophy, the BBC transformed its three radio networks into four somewhat more specialized services, roughly characterized as featuring (1) pop music; (2) light music, information, and sports; (3) serious music daytimes, a mix of speech (drama and talks) and music evenings; and (4) news, current affairs, and the spoken word. These networks do not, however, adhere to as rigid a generic formula as do most American radio stations. Meanwhile, the two BBC television networks retained their comprehensive character. BBC-2, initiated in 1964, appealed to a somewhat more selective audience than BBC-1, which competed with independent (commercial) television for the mass audience.

Generic scheduling tends to flourish in permissive settings whose economies allow for many competing services. Paternalistic and authoritarian systems favor comprehensive scheduling. Authoritarian systems avoid complementary scheduling in order to force audience attention. They ensure that especially mandated programs start at the same time on all networks, thus preventing "slalom run" audience behavior (see Section 6.4).

Prime-Time Concept

In accordance with the compatibility principle, broadcasters in all systems recognize that in the course of the day, a period comes when both audience size potential and receptivity reach their maximum. As a writer on German broadcasting put it,

> Television programming schedules in West Germany have always been worked out on the assumption that there is some sacred hour at which it is right and proper for the main evening viewing—the "Hauptabendprogramm"—to begin. Traditionally the witching hour has been 8 P.M., when ARD broadcasts its first major news programme, the "Tagesschau." The 8 P.M. tradition . . . goes back to the 8 P.M. opening of the very first regular German radio service in 1923. (Sandford, 1976: 110)

This is not a phenomenon peculiar to West German broadcasting; it refers to the *prime-time* concept, which exists in one form or another everywhere, though its parameters change with cultures. U.S. prime time varies even within the country—7:00–11:00 P.M. on the East and West coasts but 6:00–10:00 P.M. in the central and mountain time zones. In Japan, prime time runs 7:00–11:30 P.M.; in Canada, 6:00 P.M.–midnight; in Spain, 10 P.M.–11:30 P.M.; in Britain, 6:30–10:30 P.M.

Within the prime-time brackets, the placement of a television service's main evening national news program always ranks as a critical programming decision. Again, preferences vary with cultures: prime-time U.S. news on the East Coast runs within the 6:30–7:30 P.M. hour; in the USSR and Israel, it comes at 9:00 P.M.; in Libya and Nigeria, at 10:00 P.M.; in Spain, at 9:00 and 9:30 P.M. In Britain, the BBC runs its main news at 9:00 P.M., while the ITV network runs its news at 10 P.M. to avoid overlap.

TABLE 9 ▪ 3 A DAY'S TV IN LONDON, 3 OCT. 1983

	British Broadcasting Corporation	
	BBC-1	BBC-2

A.M.

6–7	6:00 Ceefax	
	6:30 "Breakfast Time"	6:30 Open University
7–8		
8–9		
9–10	9:30 Labour Party Conference (live)	9:15 "Daytime on Two" (educational)
10–11	10:30 Children's shows	
11–12		

P.M.

12–1	12:30 News	
1–2	1:00 Travelogue	
2–3	2:00 Labour Party Conference (live)	
3–4	3:53 Regional news (not London) 3:55 Children's shows	3:50 Labour Party Conference (live)
4–5		
5–6	5:40 News	5:00 Sign off 5:40 Sports
6–7	6:30 Interview 6:40 Game show	6:10 Documentary (museum) 6:40 Documentary (political)
7–8	7:10 Documentary (Botany) 7:40 Comedy series	7:05 Interviews 7:35 Cooking
8–9	8:10 News Magazine	8:00 Feature Film (U.S.)
9–10	9:00 News 9:25 Sports	9:30 Documentary (medical)
10–11	10:45 Documentary (cinema)	10:30 Documentary (history)
11–12	11:15 Documentary (politics) 11:40 News headlines	11:00 News and comment
12–1		12:05 Sign off

Independent Television TV-am and Thames Television	Channel 4

TV-am
  6:25 "Good Morning Britain"

Thames Television

9:25 News	9:30 Labour Party
9:30 Children's shows	Conference
	(live)

12:30 Consumer program
      (autos)
1:00 News
1:20 London News
1:30 Interview
2:00 Film play
2:30 Sports
3:30 Children's Shows

	5:00 Game show
5:45 News	5:30 Hobbies
6:00 London news	6:00 Comedy series
6:25 Consumer news	6:30 How-to-do-it show
6:35 Soap opera	
7:00 Game show	7:00 News
7:30 Comedy series	7:50 Comment
8:00 Feature Film	8:00 Sport
	9:00 Documentary
	(The Celts)
10:00 News	10:00 Drama series
10:30 Sport	
	11:00 Documentary
	(Ireland)
12:15 Commentary	1:00 Sign off

TABLE 9 ▪ 4 A DAY'S TV IN PARIS, 6 DECEMBER 1983

Télévision Française 1 (TFI)		Antenne 2 (A2)	
A.M.		A.M.	
10:00	School program	10:30	Teletext transmission
12:00	Interview and weather	12:00	News
P.M.		P.M.	
12:30	Chat show	12:10	Variety
1:00	News	12:45	News
1:45	Program for deaf	1:35	Drama series
2:05	School program	1:50	Interview
2:25	Drama series	2:55	Drama series (U.S.)
3:25	Science	3:45	"Treasure Hunt"
4:20	Documentary	4:45	Magazine
5:30	Documentary	5:45	Children's show
6:00	Candid Camera (U.S.)	6:30	Program for deaf
6:15	Children's show	6:50	Game show
6:40	Variety show	7:15	Regional news
6:55	News briefs	7:40	Experimental theatre
7:00	Weather	8:00	Main news program
7:15	Regional news	8:30	Consumer program
7:40	Game show	8:40	Feature film and discussion
8:00	Main news program	11:15	News
8:30	Consumer program	11:25	Sign off
8:35	Stage drama		
10:10	Art Exhibit review		
10:40	Sports		
11:10	News		
11:25	Sign off		

NOTE: Most starting times are only approximate; note the relative lack of junction points.
SOURCE: Personal communication from Arthur Garratt.

Commercial Influences

U.S. audiences have become accustomed to precise program timing, with station breaks and commercials at fixed intervals. Writers and producers tailor their products to fit this rigid schedule. A program must build to a suspenseful climax before the commercial break to hold audiences through the interruption. Commercial practices can thus severely limit artistic freedom. In systems that bunch advertisements into commercial blocks, writers have more freedom to develop scripts according to the requirements of art rather than of commerce.

To give viewers a reasonable opportunity to make informed choices,

France Régions 3 (FR3)

A.M.

P.M.
5:00   (Regional programs from 12 different pro-
        vincial cities between about 5:00 P.M.
        and 7:30 P.M.)
7:50   Cartoon
8:00   Game show
8:30   Consumer program
8:35   Variety show, including feature film (U.S.)
11:10   News magazine
11:30   Feature film (U.S.)
A.M.
1:20   Sign off

networks need to agree on "common junctions"—moments in their respective schedules when all networks change programs simultaneously. In the United States, common junctions occur automatically because of uniform timing.* In Britain, as in many other countries, unless deliberately contrived, common junctions may not occur at

---

*Note, however, that U.S. television programs end up with uneven lengths when stripped of their commercials. Typically, a 30-minute program minus commercials runs only 22.5 minutes and a 60-minute program only 48.5 minutes.

all in the course of an evening (see Tables 9.3 and 9.4). But common junctions are desirable to enable noncompetitive networks to "cross-trail," that is, give promotional announcements for each other's programs.

9•3 GOALS

How a system programs its services depends ultimately on the goals it seeks to attain. Programs have a purpose, even those that merely seem designed to while away the time.

Generic Goals

The most widely quoted official statement about primary domestic broadcasting goals occurs in the BBC Royal Charter. Its preamble speaks of the great value of the service as a "means of disseminating *information, education* and *entertainment.*"[8] Doubtless the order in which the drafters of the preamble put the three goals reflected their view that entertainment should not be considered the primary one. "That broadcasting should be merely a vehicle of light entertainment," wrote Director-General John Reith in describing the BBC's early days, "was a limitation of its function which we declined to accept. It has been our endeavour to give a conscious, social purpose to the exploitation of this medium" (1949: 116).*

Many current broadcasting charters and statutes repeat the famous "information, education, and entertainment" phrase, even though it fails to mention a major role of broadcasting—that of *persuading* or *inspiring,* upon which the effectiveness of advertising, propaganda, religious proselytism, and self-improvement programs depend. One could list still other roles. The Annan Committee, for example, argued for the addition of "enrichment" as a function of broadcasting: "To enlarge people's interests, to convey to them new choices and possibilities in life, this is what broadcasting ought to try to achieve" (Great Britain, 1977: 27).

All systems seek in varying degrees to inform, educate, entertain, and persuade; they differ, however, in the relative emphasis they put on each category of programs as well as in the emphasis within programs. Broadly speaking, authoritarian systems lean toward persuasion and education.† They see broadcasting as a means of systematically

---

*The British have since moderated this overtly manipulative goal. For example, the Annan Committee said, "We do not accept that it is part of the broadcasters' function to act as arbiters of morals or manners, or set themselves up as social engineers" (Great Britain, 1977: 26).

†According to the *Great Soviet Encyclopedia*, the role of television is "to disseminate information, propaganda, and education and to organize people's leisure time" (Lapin, 1973: 484).

shaping the public's perceptions of the world and of moving people in predefined directions. Paternalistic systems emphasize information and education but usually eschew outright persuasion. Permissive systems give primacy to entertainment but favor the use of persuasion for commercial, religious, political, and other purposes; otherwise, they remain relatively neutral toward content as long as it consistently draws large audiences.

In practice, programs always perform multiple functions. Even the flimsiest entertainment may convey information and implicit endorsement of values. The profoundest educational subjects can be presented entertainingly. Information can be used to educate, persuade, and entertain as well as to inform. Which function comes to the fore depends in the short run on intent, treatment, and audience response; in the long run, it depends on the political context in which the system operates.

Confidence in broadcasting's effectiveness in attaining desired goals also tends to vary with type of regime. Permissive systems are skeptical about the medium's power to achieve profound effects but have great confidence in its ability to achieve superficial effects, such as persuading audiences to switch from one brand of detergent to another. Paternalistic systems, though somewhat more optimistic about broadcasting's ability to bring about change in audiences, do not count on it heavily. Authoritarian systems credit broadcasting with great power to influence the masses for or against official viewpoints. Commenting on Iran's postrevolutionary situation after the overthrow of the shah, an Iranian communications scholar remarked:

> The clerics see themselves as traditional communication professionals, and hope that the mass media (and particularly broadcasting) by the repetition of the God's [sic] message will be able to convert the teeming millions of Muslims to their revolutionary zeal. . . . The Khomeini regime is thus no different from other authoritarian regimes in its illusions about the infinite potency of the mass media. (Tehranian, 1982: 44)

Ironically, Iran's revolutionary zealots had to look no farther than the predecessor regime of the shah for an example of how futile authoritarian manipulation of the media can be.

Practical Goals

In practice, when countries use broadcasting to attain explicit national goals, they combine elements of information, education, entertainment, and persuasion. For example, nations typically use broadcasting to conserve their national cultures and to further political integration. I mention these goals as examples because they illustrate exploitation of the unique ubiquity of broadcasting. Of course, regional and local services have their own more restricted goals as well.

Conservation of Culture. In many countries, broadcasting employs more artists and produces more cultural events than any other agency. I have already mentioned the instances of Australia and New Zealand, where broadcasting plays a central cultural role (see Section 2.2). A British authority has said that broadcasting "can claim to have done more for the artist in Britain than any other agency during the last half-century" (quoted in Paulu, 1981: 339). The BBC alone employs hundreds of musicians and a dozen musical organizations (though these have been cut back somewhat in recent years because of budget problems). The corporation commits itself explicitly to the modification of popular taste through a process that has been aptly described as "making good things popular and popular things good." In Britain and most other industrialized countries, more than in the United States, major artists welcome the chance to contribute to broadcasting. Anthony Smith contrasted the U.S. versus the French view of broadcasting's cultural role and the corresponding attitudes toward central control:

> In the United States, broadcasting automatically became an instrument of low culture; the French, with their deeply-held feeling that France had been and should remain the chief receptacle of European civilization, saw that centralised control of broadcasting was the only guarantee that the instrument would be employed to ensure that high culture would prevail. (Smith, 1973: 158–159)

Communist and Third World systems make an even more explicit effort to use broadcasting for cultural goals than do the paternalistic and permissive systems.

Many developing countries, however, find that their paucity of relevant cultural resources, their lack of trained personnel, and the high cost of local television production undermine efforts to put cultural conservation policies into effect. In these situations, importation of foreign programs compounds the problem: indigenous arts not only fail to benefit from broadcasting, they tend to become submerged by alien cultural artifacts—a process referred to as "cultural imperialism" (treated at more length in Section 12.2). On the whole, Third World countries were slow to recognize this problem and to take corrective steps:

> The deliberate decision to use the broadcast media for national cultural development is in most [developing] countries fairly recent. In Latin America it dates from the rise of the populist movements in the late 1960s . . . ; in francophone Africa, from the decision to replace French cultural dominance by a similarly determined propagation of the indigenous culture; in anglophone Africa, from a similar motive, albeit without the same culture conditioning as that bequeathed to the francophone countries. . . .
>
> In the independent countries of Asia also, political pressures have forced governments to intervene more positively in the promotion of local cultures through the broadcasting services. (Katz & Wedell, 1977: 140)

Iran's prerevolutionary national television (see Section 3.2) affords an example of a policy encouraging indigenous arts, even though it imported many programs. Iran has ancient cultural traditions well suited for adaptation to the modern media.[9] Among other things, Iran's broadcasters set up an experimental television theater, a center for preserving traditional music, and an annual arts festival.[10]

Indonesia's unusual colonial broadcasting experience favored development of indigenous arts. While a Dutch colony, Indonesia had privately owned as well as state-owned radio stations. As early as 1937, the private stations banded together to promote indigenous culture. The Dutch accepted this organized effort, as did the Japanese when they overran the islands during World War II—the latter not with any benign intent but to lend support to anticolonial feeling. After the war, the Dutch attempted to reestablish their hegemony, but when Indonesia won independence in 1949, it inherited a broadcasting system already strongly indigenous in flavor.[11] In contrast to the Indonesian experience, most former colonies had to start virtually from scratch in adapting their broadcasting systems to their own artistic traditions.

National Integration. Broadcasting, with its attribute of reaching out to an entire nation with identical programs, can play a role in drawing a country together, especially in times of crisis. Nations made up of many disparate and often mutually hostile elements look to radio and television as means of finding a common ground. Speaking of the USSR, for example, a commentator noted,

> *Television provides the opportunity for a standardized message; it helps to narrow the very real differences among regions, ethnic groups, and between rural and urban populations. Particularly for rural people, isolated as they are and relatively out of touch with modern life, television may present the only effective image of a dynamic, modernizing Soviet political culture. (Mickiewicz, 1981: 38)*

Certain public events that lend themselves ideally to broadcast coverage serve the cause of national integration by giving the widest possible currency to symbols that evoke national pride and the sense of communal identity. Authoritarian leaders use their power over the media for self-aggrandizement, as noted in Section 4.2. In democracies, the media willingly lend themselves to less obsessive cultivation of national symbols, taking advantage of the "photo opportunities," both natural and contrived.

In Britain, the monarchy serves as such a symbol, providing broadcasting with many made-to-order public events. An early highlight for radio came in 1922, when the prince of Wales made the first royal broadcast, a carefully rehearsed address to Boy Scouts throughout the United Kingdom.* King George V inaugurated the Empire Service with a Christmas Day external radio broadcast in 1932. George VI's

---

*His last BBC broadcast came 14 years later under sensational circumstances, when as King Edward VIII, he announced his decision to abdicate.

coronation in 1937 occasioned the first outside (remote) broadcast by BBC television. The royal event that gave early British television its biggest boost came in 1953 with the coronation of Elizabeth II. In 1981 the BBC's sumptuous coverage of the marriage of the prince of Wales to Lady Diana attracted worldwide interest. Referring to this program, the BBC described the integrative role of broadcasting:

> *The BBC has never felt itself a more integral part of the life of the nation it exists to serve than on the day of the Royal Wedding. . . . Television and radio, it seemed to us, played their part to perfection in making this an unforgettable day of national happiness in which all the people of these islands could feel themselves to be personal participants.* (BBC, 1983 Annual Report, 1982: 2)

By the same token, broadcasting can be invoked to hold a nation together in times of crisis by dissipating tensions and relieving public doubts. Such was the case in 1974 when the U.S. House of Representatives Judiciary Committee allowed televised coverage of its impeachment hearings against President Richard M. Nixon. The sober participation of Republican as well as Democratic members of Congress did much to assure the nation that the impeachment threat rose above a mere partisan attack on the President. As a more extreme example, when Abdul Karim Kassem overthrew the Iraq monarchy in 1958, he had the leaders of the old regime tried on television. According to Douglas Boyd, these trials, though conducted in a highly theatrical manner with no observance of normal judicial restraints, provided "an outlet for people's feelings against the old regime and served as a substitute for mob action" (1982: 111).*

In 1978, radio was credited with contributing importantly to national equilibrium in a time of great crisis in Kenya. The sudden death in 1978 of Kenya's first president, the revered Jomo Kenyatta, created a dangerous power vacuum. The Voice of Kenya helped materially to bridge this perilous interval. Officials at the station received word of Kenyatta's death from Government House by telephone. Hastily convening an emergency committee, the station director, James Kangwana, first faced the problem of authenticating the call. He telephoned Government House, and on the strength of recognizing the voices at the other end decided to go ahead with a public announcement. Government House itself was paralyzed for the moment. The VOK staff wrote the announcement and cleared it over the phone. "Radio was in charge," said Kangwana, "The responsibility of handling the delicate assignment gave us a frightening sense of power. We were probably more concerned with the implications of the truth than with the truth itself." Combining

---

*Iraq had initiated television only two years earlier, the first government in the Middle East to do so. Five years after the trials Kassem himself died in a coup. The new regime triumphantly exhibited his body on television.

all the radio services into a single network, and broadcasting only in Swahili (the VOK normally broadcasts also in other Kenyan languages and English), Kangwana put the announcement on the air as though it had originated from Government House. Staff members absent on leave voluntarily returned and worked as many hours as necessary to keep the VOK on the air with reassuring, factual information that effectively counteracted rumors, helping to forestall the possibility of a coup or some other violent reaction.[12]

9 ▪ 4 PROGRAM TYPOLOGY

Programs nearly everywhere fall into fairly well defined types: "As a result of homogeneity of demand—no matter what its source—the content of broadcasting is similar around the world. The same mix of news and entertainment can be seen and heard in the most diverse cultural, ideological, and economic settings" (Katz & Wedell, 1977: 166). Some commentators ascribe this similarity to imitation and cultural imperialism, but it can also be argued that people everywhere enjoy the same kinds of basic broadcast fare, even though the details of program packaging may differ from one cultural milieu to another.

Moreover, research has shown that though national policies may arbitrarily vary the proportions of time devoted to program types, audiences remain consistent in their preferences. For example, audiences actually tune in only a small percentage of cultural material, no matter how much time their services devote to such material.*

In 1971 UNESCO began reporting world statistics on programming in its *Statistical Yearbook*, using a typology based on six functional categories: (1) information, (2) education, (3) culture, (4) religion, (5) entertainment, and (6) advertising.[13] However, not all countries reply to the annual UNESCO questionnaire; the 1982 yearbook contains program statistics for 98 radio systems and 70 television systems. Tables 9.5 (radio) and 9.6 (television) show the percentages of each program type reported by selected countries, with amounts for cultural and entertainment programs combined into a single category, for reasons explained later.

The data indicate considerable uniformity as to the percentage of time devoted to each program type, even among disparate systems. Moreover, radio and television services conform to similar patterns. Marked departures from the norm can be explained on the basis of the character of the countries involved. For example, Saudi Arabia's relatively high percentages of religious programming, as shown in the two tables, can be attributed to its role as conservator of the main holy

---

*Note "slalom run" behavior by audiences evading serious programming, described in Section 6.4.

TABLE 9 ▪ 5 RADIO PROGRAMS BY TYPE, SELECTED COUNTRIES

Country	Entertain-ment	Percentage of Annual Hours on Air Infor-mation	Education	Religion	Advertising
Algeria	68	15	4	7	0
Australia	68	22	1	2	7
Brazil	54	16	4	3	18
Czechoslovakia	65	19	4	0	*
Cuba	63	24	9	0	4
East Germany	72	23	4	0	0
Egypt	57	11	1	20	0
France	80	15	2	*	*
India	61	18	10	*	3
Ireland	65	26	2	2	3
Ivory Coast	39	35	25	1	*
Japan	79	13	6	0	1
Peru	73	6	5	0	15
Saudi Arabia	53	14	2	30	0
Spain	67	20	6	*	8
Sweden	73	13	3	2	0
United Arab Emirates	64	9	5	13	9
United Kingdom	78	13	2	1	6
Yugoslavia	69	18	4	0	6
Average	66	17	5	8	7

NOTE: * = less than 1 percent. Averages for "Religion" and "Advertising" based on countries that broadcast those categories. "Entertainment" includes "Culture" category. Country percentages do not add to 100 percent because "Other" category omitted. Percentages rounded to nearest whole number. Responding countries supply the data, which are accepted on faith by UNESCO and therefore may be somewhat idealized.
SOURCE: Based on data in Table 11.5, Sec. 10, of UNESCO, Statistical Yearbook, 1982 (UNESCO, Paris, 1982). © UNESCO 1982. Used by permission.

places of Islam (Mecca and Medina) and the zeal of its Wahabi sect. All countries use the same broad program types in similar proportions, though their notions of acceptable programs for each category may vary widely.

An alternative typology looks at programs in terms of their intended audiences rather than in terms of function. Thus children's programs constitute a universally recognized type. Other special target audiences include women, farmers, migrant workers, military forces, tourists, and seamen. A private station in Italy addresses itself exclusively to jewelers, confining its programs solely to reports of gold and silver prices. A

TABLE 9 ■ 6 TV PROGRAMS BY TYPE, SELECTED COUNTRIES

| Country | Entertain-ment | Percentage of Annual Hours on Air | | | |
		Infor-mation	Education	Religion	Advertising
Algeria	67	13	13	2	0
Australia	57	16	11	1	11
Brazil	54	13	7	1	16
Canada	60	18	14	6	0
Czechoslovakia	57	27	9	0	2
Cuba	67	18	8	0	6
Egypt	32	15	4	9	2
France	64	18	2	2	3
India	42	18	17	*	9
Ireland	59	18	5	2	6
Saudi Arabia	46	15	6	13	0
Spain	56	31	1	1	3
Sweden	63	27	10	1	0
United Arab Emirates	63	10	3	14	4
United Kingdom	55	19	15	1	3
Yugoslavia	44	37	7	0	5
Average	55	20	8	4	5

NOTE: * = less than 1 percent. Averages for "Religion" and "Advertising" based on countries that broadcast those categories. "Entertainment" includes "Culture" category. Country percentages do not add to 100 percent because "Other" category omitted. Percentages rounded to nearest whole number. Responding countries supply the data, which are accepted on faith by UNESCO and therefore may be somewhat idealized.
SOURCE: Based on data in Table 11.6, Sec. 10, of UNESCO, Statistical Yearbook, 1982 (UNESCO, Paris, 1982). © UNESCO 1982. Used by permission.

former Scandinavian pirate station, Radio Syd, now located in The Gambia, broadcasts part of the time in Swedish, addressing an audience of sun-loving Swedish tourists who favor the mouth of the west African Gambia River as a vacation spot.

In the ensuing sections of this chapter I discuss the UNESCO functional program categories reduced to four groups, as follows: entertainment, information, education, and persuasion.

9 ■ 5   ENTERTAINMENT

Tables 9.5 and 9.6 combine UNESCO's "Culture" and "Entertainment" into a single category. The distinction between the two is highly subjective; many responding countries had difficulty distinguishing between them and reported only "Entertainment." When defined broadly to include both "light" and "serious" content, *entertainment* nearly always fills the largest segment of broadcast schedules. Among the countries sampled in Tables 9.5 and 9.6, entertainment averages 66 percent of radio time and 55 percent of television time.* Japan, which did not report television statistics to UNESCO, has the reputation of going to extremes—highly popular entertainment on commercial stations, strong education and information components on NHK, the public service corporation. In 1983, on NHK's General Service network, news took 35 percent of the time and education 40 percent, despite the fact that NHK devotes its second network entirely to education.[14]

The difference in the average percentages of entertainment between radio and television shown in the tables is due to television's slightly higher averages for information, education, and religion. If television were on the air as many hours as radio, doubtless the two media's entertainment percentages would be about the same.

The same basic entertainment program formats occur universally—music, drama, variety, games, sports, and so on. Music, for example, finds ready audiences in every culture. However, the term *music* embraces many styles, both within a culture and among cultures. Obviously, not everyone likes the same kind of music, though everyone likes music.

Despite its dominance in program schedules, entertainment has been less studied and analyzed by scholars than other forms of programming. Serious researchers have paid far more attention to news, largely because scholarly interest in the mass media started with the study of newspapers.[15] Most scholars who have taken entertainment seriously as an essential component among the needs of humankind see it as a form of "play."[16] They regard play as an essential activity to which media make an important contribution:

> The functions of entertainment, as far as the individual is concerned, are manifold and, when taken together, are at least as important as those of, say, information. For example, human existence without regeneration, which entertainment helps to effect, is as inconceivable as human existence without education. Furthermore, it must be stressed . . . that there is no such thing as "pure entertainment." All entertainment contains messages and values, whether intended or not. (Fischer & Melnik, 1979: xiii–xiv)

The perception that entertainment "contains messages and values" has led to widespread concern about U.S. domination of the world program syndication market. Critics allege that imported programs serve as agents of cultural imperialism (see Section 12.2). According to a

---

*A more recent study of 69 representative countries roughly confirmed the UNESCO television data, entertainment-sports-culture amounting to an average of 51 percent of all programming (Varis, 1984).

Latin American researcher, for example, even seemingly innocuous entertainment such as *Los Picapiedras*, a Spanish version of *The Flintstones*, teaches such lessons as "the only natural course of humanity is capitalism" and "selfish individualism . . . is the best guide to behavior" (Beltran, 1978: 71).

Communist systems share the view that entertainment must be taken seriously because of its social implications, emphasizing culturally up-lifting programs at the expense of the popular, mass-appeal fare typical of U.S. commercial broadcasting. The *Great Soviet Encyclopedia* speaks disparagingly of the Western preference for light entertainment: "Commercial television chiefly offers comedy, detective, western, and variety programs. Low-quality entertainment and scenes of violence and cruelty are common" (Lapin, 1973: 486). It criticizes Western radio programs in the same vein, adding that they "distract working people from current social and political problems and propagate bourgeois ideology" (Mikriukov, 1973: 403). Western observers are struck by the high proportion of classical music, opera, and ballet in Soviet entertainment broadcasting:

> *It is surprising how often a random flip of the switch will bring forth a classic of the Russian or Western stage or an adaptation of a work of literature. Much of the time, it will be superbly acted by the actors who are appearing or have recently appeared in that very same production at some leading Moscow theater. (Austin, 1979)*

Though light entertainment occurs in Soviet broadcasting, an underlying social message always justifies its existence:

> *All the shows, whether explicitly instructional or not, are educational—that is, they have a distinct didactic flavor and are used to help socialize viewers. . . . There is a popular detective series, called "The Experts Investigate," said to be based on material from actual police archives. There is, however, little of the sex and violence that U.S. police stories have; rather, attention is paid to the social origins of criminal deviance. (Mickiewicz, 1981: 20)*

9 ▪ 6 INFORMATION

According to the sampling of UNESCO program data in Tables 9.5 and 9.6, most systems devote about a fifth of their time to *information*, which UNESCO subdivides into news and "other."* All broadcasting systems with any ambition to be taken seriously carry news. The daily prime-time newscast always ranks as one of the high points of the broadcast day, though cultures differ in their perceptions of news values.

---

*The last year in which the FCC issued program analyses of U.S. commercial stations, about 14 percent of their time went to news and public affairs (FCC, 1980).

News in the West

Western systems stress the values of news timeliness, accuracy, fairness, objectivity, professionalism, relevance, human interest, and independence from government control. The BBC gave the following definition to its General Advisory Council:

> *News is new and honestly and accurately reported information which is (a) about current events, of any kind anywhere in the world; (b) set against a background of other honestly and accurately reported information previously gathered as news; (c) selected fairly but without artificial balancing and without political motive or editorial colouring by trained journalists; (d) included in a [newscast] because interesting, significant or relevant to the . . . audience in the eyes of those journalists; and (e) presented fearlessly and objectively but with respect for the law and for the BBC's own rules concerning taste and editorial standards. (Quoted in Great Britain, 1977: 277)*

Competition also has much to do with how Western broadcasters perceive news values. It causes them to emphasize timeliness and popular human interest more than do their counterparts in the Communist states and the Third World. Western broadcasters also value credibility highly—again a byproduct of competition, for competing stations or networks stand ever ready to expose their rivals' lapses. In Communist and most Third World countries, central broadcasting authorities enjoy airwave monopolies. They need not worry about exposure by competing domestic stations; they worry instead about bureaucratic oversight, a less effective spur than competition.

Though convenient for purposes of exposition, subdividing news into First, Second, and Third World categories does not mean that within each of these worlds news is treated in exactly the same way. Differences between U.S. and Western European news styles, for example, invariably impress Americans who have time to look and listen to domestic broadcasts while traveling abroad: "An American watching European news broadcasts can't avoid having his assumptions about the nature of news challenged" (Pease, 1982: 62). Style of presentation differs, with most European systems using news "readers" rather than news personalities. The large number of documentaries and other news-related features is also likely to surprise the American observer.

Communist News Values

Differences in perception of news values allow Communist broadcasters to ignore timeliness and human interest when it suits them. Sometimes the release of even big, fast-breaking stories must await upper-level political decisions on how to "play" the story. Communist policymakers see no virtue in rushing on the air merely to accentuate the negative. "A factory that exceeds its tractor output target is news; a plane crash is not" (Green, 1972: 161). News should be constructive and uplifting, not divisive and depressing, even though a market exists for the latter (an argument one sometimes hears from Western audiences as well):*

> The communist media play down many kinds of "bad" news items precisely because people have such an "unhealthy" interest in them—not only disasters, fires and crashes, but comparisons of citizens' incomes and retail prices, reports on increased living standards in non-communist countries, the salaries of communist party and government workers, food shortages and the jamming of foreign radios. (Tunstall, 1977: 227)

Soviet broadcasters regard news air time as too important to be wasted on trivia and irrelevancies. They select stories that glorify achievements of workers and the Socialist state, give behavioral models for viewers to follow, emphasize brotherly relationships among Socialist countries, and point out the fatal flaws of democracies.

Dwelling on self-congratulatory news does not, however, entirely rule out investigative reporting of domestic shortcomings. Criticism (samokritika) is "constructive." Its ultimate aim must be to further the goals and policies of the Communist party. In his book on Eastern European broadcasting, Paulu cites several instances of Soviet broadcast samokritika: "Television newscasts show uncompleted buildings, leaky roofs, or falling tiles, while the announcer indicts the agency or individuals allegedly responsible for the failure." Among other examples of indictable failures mentioned by the author: delays in delivery of essential equipment, failure to supply coat racks in new apartments, a mixup in labeling that made fertilizer appear to be coffee beans (Paulu, 1974: 116–117).

Notwithstanding such instances of candor, Communist broadcasting tends to lack credibility among its own audiences. Experience teaches them to discount automatically the official versions of events and to seek correctives elsewhere. Consequently the USSR spends immense sums on jamming in an attempt to prevent audiences from listening to foreign sources.

News personnel in Communist systems need no elaborate lists of "do's and do not's" to tell them whether a criticism qualifies as sufficiently constructive or whether a story should be ignored, played up, or given only brief mention. Personnel become adept at anticipating the official viewpoint and acting accordingly. "Today's television journalists have learned that self-censorship is necessary if they expect to keep their jobs. The limits of 'what is permitted' never need be codified, for fear dictates its own immutable guidelines" (Novak, 1983: 52). Of course, self-censorship can also proceed from personal conviction rather than from the threat of reprisal. Whatever the motive, however, it leads to

---

*Occasionally, U.S. media experiment with upbeat news policies, giving less (or no) space to negative stories. Such experiments always seem to fail in the marketplace.

timidity and consequent insipidity. Indeed, Communist party officials periodically berate the media for their lack of dynamism.

Vremya ("time"), the major Soviet national prime-time newscast, comes on at 9:00 P.M. Domestic news takes up about two thirds of the 35-minute program, delivered by two rather solemn announcers, a man and a woman. Sports and weather items cap the national and regional news items, with a short segment of foreign items at the close.

China's main television newscast was transformed in 1979 by the addition of a ten-minute international news segment relayed from a Western source, Visnews, via INTELSAT. Each segment has its own woman announcer.

> *Before, the evening news had been largely a turgid rehash of stories from the* People's Daily, *plus some dreary homemade features on the latest improvement in machine tool production. But now, in living color, without censorship, Chinese could watch the Pope touring Africa, Ronald Reagan winning the U.S. presidential election, political terrorism in Italy, and even stock-car races in North Carolina and surfing in Hawaii.* (Butterfield, 1982: 398)

A typical 25-minute program, as described by a Western observer, devoted the first segment to low-key domestic stories: leading politicians greeting each other, arrival of a visiting head of state, visiting U.S. newswriters interviewing the Chinese premier, three other delegations meeting with the premier, a feature on how factory hands cut pollution by growing flowers and trees, the latest tea crop statistics, and a martial arts display. These domestic stories differed significantly from the nine Visnews clips of foreign events in the 10-minute segment that followed. The latter included items on the sale of U.S. helicopters to China, U.S. presidential campaign speeches, the Iranian hostage crisis, West German demonstrations against nuclear energy, an attack on the Iraqi Embassy in Rome, and two sports stories, one on tennis from France, one on horse racing from England. The dynamism of these events contrasts significantly with the placidity of the domestic stories. "Only contending forces are pictured on international news; no issues are discussed which could explain the often violent disagreements" (Robinson, 1981: 68–69).

Third World News

In Third World countries whose governments monopolize broadcasting, news controls resemble those in the Communist systems—preoccupation with upbeat, positive news, suppression of the negative (unless about "neoimperialism"), little concern for timeliness, human interest, or credibility. However, unless a Third World country expressly subscribes to Socialist doctrines, its sense of what constitutes news arises more from pragmatic considerations than political theory. Preoccupation with national economic development and antipathy toward stellar broadcast personalities (political leaders tend to regard star broadcasters with strong followings as a threat) combine to exert a depressing effect on programming—at least from a Westerner's perspective. A not very sympathetic American who lived in India several months wrote an article for *TV Guide* describing India's television information programming as

> *a plethora of turgid documentaries that tell the thrilling story of how soybean production has been improved in Uttar Pradesh, or that take them on a scenic tour of all of India's major hydroelectric plants; news programs (in the 14 major languages, plus English) conducted by similar-looking dyspeptic commentators, heads bent down, reading news copy as they sit at bare desks.* (Manning, 1979: 28–29)

A harsh judgment, but it points up the excruciating dilemma of Third World information broadcasting. Developing countries need "development journalism"—ideally the product of writers, producers, presenters, and other personnel trained in the difficult art of transforming dull statistics and unglamorous facts about development projects into interesting, entertaining, and informative broadcast programs—a daunting task for the best-trained and most talented personnel! For undertrained personnel with little natural aptitude for the task, the job often becomes impossible. Civil service regulations make no provision for adequately rewarding creative talent or for encouraging outstanding broadcast personalities; people with the potential for such achievements therefore avoid employment in government ministries, gravitating instead toward advertising and public relations in the private sector.

News Agencies

News was the first type of media content to be syndicated, long before broadcasting began. About 175 such *news agencies* exist, most of them limited to domestic reporting. Eight qualify as major international agencies: AFP (*Agence France Presse*), ANSA (Italy's *Agenzia Nazionale Stampa Associate*), AP (Associated Press), DPA (West Germany's *Deutsche Presse-Agentur*), Reuters (British), TASS (USSR's *Telegrafnoe Agentstvo Sovietskovo Soyuza*), UPI (United Press International), and XINHUA (China).[17] Of these, the Big Four—AFP, AP, Reuters, and UPI—have the largest numbers of subscribers. These international services must remain relatively objective in order to win acceptance among hundreds of clients representing every political hue. Often domestic, that is, national, agencies tend to be more parochial if not downright biased in their treatment of news about their own countries.

Television created a demand for a type of material not purveyed by the traditional news agencies—video reporting. The chief agency devoted to this aspect of news gathering, Visnews, started in 1959. Reuters and the BBC own three quarters of its stock, the other quarter being divided among the public broadcasting organizations of Australia, Canada, and New Zealand. Since 1976 Visnews has offered its worldwide clients daily satellite feeds of pictorial material. In 1983 Visnews served 270 broadcasting organizations located in a hundred countries, sending them up to a hundred minutes of pictorial news per week.[18] Other suppliers of video material include UPITN, a joint venture of UPI and ITN, the British commercial television companies' national news supplier; CBS-Newsfilm; and a West German agency, DPA-ETES.

Many Third World critics, seconded by the Communists, feel that the reporting of the Western agencies betrays insufficient sensitivity toward Third World cultures. They also complain that the Big Four underreport events in the developing world. In an effort to redress the imbalance, Third World national news agencies have formed several regional cooperatives. In addition, Tanjug, the Yugoslavian national news agency, acts as a clearinghouse for the exchange of news among Third World national agencies. These efforts all suffer from the same drawback: dependence on official government agencies undermines credibility for all but politically neutral news—and few subjects of news escape political coloration.

In the ongoing East-West struggle to influence Third World news media, government-owned international agencies (notably the USSR's TASS) enjoy the advantage of being able to offer their newswire services free as a friendly gesture toward developing countries. Agencies operating commercially under private ownership cannot offer their services on the same terms.

Official news agencies often serve as a convenient mechanism for exerting government control over broadcast news. Many broadcasting services have no news-gathering facilities of their own, depending entirely on their national news agency for domestic news and on foreign agencies for news beyond their borders. Broadcasters in this situation are often denied the right to contract with outside news sources; instead, the government domestic agency subscribes to foreign sources on behalf of all media in the country. Thus the national agency can act as filter, controlling content of both the national and international newsfiles relayed to broadcast newsrooms, where broadcasters merely rewrite the stories to fit them into newscasts.

Argentina's former military government adopted an ingenious way of encouraging dependence on the official news agency, Telam, without actually forbidding the use of foreign sources. Telam bought out a small, private advertising agency, thereby linking the use of the government's news handouts with the awarding of government advertising contracts (publicly owned industries and official messages combined to make up a quarter of the nation's advertising outlay). "The generally accepted maxim is that the more an editor chooses Telam stories, the faster government advertising will come" (Pierce, 1979: 15).

9 ▪ 7 EDUCATION

Tables 9.5 and 9.6 indicate that explicitly educational materials amount to less than 10 percent of all programming. Such materials fall roughly into four subcategories: preschool, in-school, home study, and adult education. "Home study" refers to formal schooling conducted in whole or in part by means of radio and television; "adult education" refers to training programs, usually less formal than home study, aimed at a broad range of adult interests.

Though in-school programs generally find time on regular general service networks and stations, a good many systems have special facilities dedicated entirely to educational uses. These, of course, carry adult and other types of educational material as well as in-school programs. Public broadcasting stations and their networks in the United States are a case in point. Legally classified as "noncommercial, educational" facilities, they come under a different set of regulations than commercial broadcasting.

The radio and television educational networks operated by Japan's NHK are outstanding examples of such facilities. One observer credited Japan with being "the first country in the world that has fully integrated television into its educational structure from kindergarten to university-level studies" (Dizard, 1966: 223). Educational programs formed part of NHK's services from its inception. Several national television systems, such as those of India, Israel, Peru, and Senegal, started as exclusively educational ventures. In each case, however, they eventually expanded into general entertainment broadcasting as well.

Preschool Programs

No area of programming more strikingly brings to the fore the differences between permissive and paternalistic/authoritarian policies than children's programming. In both Western and Eastern Europe, broadcast authorities take their responsibilities to children very seriously, assigning some of their most creative personnel to produce children's programs.[19] The U.S. National Citizens Committee for Broadcasting made a comparative study of the differences between U.S. children's program policies and those of 12 West European countries, Australia, and Japan.[20] The committee found that the European systems, for example, allowed no commercial sponsorship of children's programs, with the sole exception of Britain's ITV. Even in that case, the IBA stringently regulates advertising with a code requiring, among other things, treatment of children "with respect and without condescension." As might be expected of systems with the explicit goal of transforming society, Communist broadcasters pay a great deal of attention to children's programs and have been credited with doing them extremely well.[21]

The best-known preschool children's program internationally, *Sesame Street*, a Children's Television Workshop (CTW) production, has been used in scores of countries.[22] In English-speaking countries it may be run in its original form, but in others it has been extensively adapted, both culturally and linguistically, with the cooperation of CTW. I mentioned the successful Arabic adaptation in Section 7.5.

Sesame Street became the first American educational series used in the Communist world when Poland and Yugoslavia bought it in 1963.

The Soviets, however, condemned it as capitalistic propaganda, reprinting a magazine attack from a Mexican publication. This critique and other Marxist attacks published in Latin America alleged, for example, that presentation of the alphabet in the guise of "sponsored" letters teaches children to accept commercials on television; the way *Sesame Street* teaches numbers inculcates capitalistic ideology; the social setting portrays U.S. middle-class values that are at odds with those of developing countries; the series uses proprietors as protagonists without showing how proprietors exploit the workers; the series depicts women as submissive and playing secondary roles.[23]

Notwithstanding such strictures, in 1973 the Mexican commercial network Televisa launched a Spanish-language adaptation, *"Plaza Sesamo"* (in the course of adaptation, Big Bird was transformed into an alligator). Xerox sponsored the Mexican series (support from a multinational capitalist corporation counted as yet another mark against the series in the eyes of Marxist critics). A decade later, Televisa again cooperated with CTW in producing a *"Plaza Sesamo"* series, this time sponsored by Coca-Cola. Nearly a score of other Latin American countries have also used the Spanish-language version. Israel began a Hebrew version in 1983, *"Rehov Sumsum,"* featuring a six-foot porcupine in place of Big Bird.

In-School Broadcasts

Use of broadcasting to supplement formal schoolwork within the classroom began almost as soon as radio itself. Britain pioneered in-school radio as early as 1924, three years before the BBC as a public corporation even began. As the general audience grew, so did the number of students receiving programs in British schools. The BBC has had considerable success with what it calls Radiovision—oral instructional materials received by radio and coordinated in the schools visually with filmstrips produced and sold by the BBC.[24]

Broadcasting seemed to be the perfect answer to the dire need of Third World countries for rapid improvement and extension of their educational systems. The United Nations Educational, Scientific and Cultural Organization (UNESCO), along with many individual donor countries, has invested millions of dollars in experimental educational broadcasting projects. Pioneer television experiments took place in American Samoa, El Salvador, Ivory Coast, Niger, and Senegal. In most cases, the results were disappointing if not downright disastrous.[25]

American Samoa's educational television project furnishes a classic example. It had all the advantages of American money, know-how, and expert personnel, yet it failed almost totally.[26] The U.S. Interior Department administers the small group of Pacific islands known as American Samoa (the rest of the group constitutes independent Western Samoa). At the time the project started in 1966, American Samoa's public education system, consisting of about 50 schools and fewer than six thousand students, was a shambles. The years of neglect ended with a Kennedy administration inspired plan to modernize and transform the system, structuring it around teaching by television.

The National Association of Educational Broadcasters (NAEB) undertook the project, basing its approach on a recently emerged doctrine that educational television worked best when it functioned at the very core of the educational system instead of being tacked on as an added frill. "To make it work," wrote Schramm and his colleagues, the NAEB was "willing to multiply by six the average annual expenditure per student and to spend more on the physical plant and equipment of the schools than had been spent in the *entire history* of Samoan public education" (p. 43, emphasis added). The first year's budget ran to nearly $2.5 million. As an example of the NAEB's all-out approach, it built a mile-long elevated tramway across Pago Pago Harbor to enable using a precipitous volcanic peak as the antenna site.

Within five years of the 1966 start, the elaborate teaching-by-television system had been almost completely abandoned, the splendid facilities turned over to regular home entertainment. By 1980 Samoan television featured wrestling, *Love Boat*, sports, and game shows, as well as the usual PBS evening schedule. As so often happens with such projects, much of the failure could be traced to want of the proverbial horseshoe nail, despite the ample budget. Some of the shortfalls noted in the Schramm report follow:

- So much time went into producing the television lessons that not enough remained for pretesting and remaking faulty programs.

- Instructions on how to use the televised lessons arrived at schools too late to be used by the classroom teachers.

- Most teachers failed to send in the evaluation reports the producers needed in order to improve the televised lessons; when reports did arrive, they came too late.

- Administrators failed to involve adult Samoan leaders sufficiently in the system's initial planning and in its adaptation to Samoan needs as it evolved.

- Once entertainment programs were introduced (originally as a come-on for adult education programs), it proved impossible to stem the tide.

Many of these weaknesses amounted to no more than simple failures of timing and logistics. They are exactly the types of problems that have dogged every Third World project of this kind. The Samoan scheme had much more money and expert help than most such projects and still failed. Any large-scale educational broadcasting project requires a high degree of coordination among many disparate activities—first, generating public support, then, planning, teaching, school administration, program writing, production, graphics design, technical operations, printing, transportation, evaluation research, record keeping, transmission and reception engineering, and so on. When any link in the complex chain fails, it endangers the entire enterprise. All the good will and noble intentions in the world cannot compensate for lack of coordination.

The Ivory Coast, a former French colony in Africa, furnishes an example of a more complex undertaking than the Samoan scheme, involving the educational system of an independent nation larger than New Mexico, with a population of about 8 million. The scheme involved an initial budget of $24 million, with help from the World Bank, UNESCO, and several donor nations. Only a third of the schools had electrical power when the project started in 1969; the rest had to run their receivers on power supplied by 32 automobile-type storage batteries at each reception site.[27] In addition to in-school teaching, the project provided home-study and adult education elements.

Like the Samoan project, however, the Ivory Coast scheme came to naught. Among the reasons advanced for its failure were: inability of the government to take over the full cost of the project in 1981, when foreign aid ran out, especially because the Ivory Coast faced an austerity budget; a perception of the project among Ivoiriens as an international experiment conducted by foreigners at the educational expense of their children; and opposition from parents and teachers, some of whom objected to television's emphasis on oral rather than written skills in French.[28]

Home-Study Courses

Broadcasting has long been used in both the developed and developing worlds to provide home-study courses for dropouts unable to pursue regular schooling to the level of their innate abilities. Home study (or group study, as it must be in countries with insufficient home receivers) leading to a formal college-level degree is relatively new, however. A leader in this field has been the Open University (OU) in Great Britain. Though not the first, it is probably the most far-reaching and fully developed university for "distance learning."

Open University started in 1969, after several years of preparatory groundwork, as an independent, degree-granting university, presenting most of its classwork via radio and television. The OU soon became the largest university in Britain. The BBC furnishes a production staff of more than 350 at the OU's special facility in Milton Keynes, about 50 miles from London. The OU's reimbursement to the BBC for these services amounted to £9.5 million in 1982. Programs were aired 50 hours per week on BBC radio and television. Several thousand part-time tutors meet students at more than three hundred existing educational centers for consultations. Registrants take final examinations, which they must attend in person. OU's success inspired similar high-level educational projects elsewhere. In fact, the Open University has a subsidiary corporation that distributes its educational materials throughout the world.

China established its open university in 1979. It graduated 78,000 students in 1982 and planned on having 2 million registrants by 1990. It began with specializations in science, engineering, and Chinese, with future plans for expansion into business administration, law, and liberal arts. Japan and Thailand also started open universities in 1979, Taiwan in 1983.

Adult Education

Third World countries with a special need for training adults in literacy, health, agriculture, family planning, and the like find broadcasting an ideal medium, though not a panacea. Much study and experimentation went into assessing the effectiveness of the media in such fields, leading to the conclusion that radio and television cannot do the job alone. They need the support of traditional face-to-face communication to succeed.[29]

A technique known as the *radio forum* serves to illustrate the concepts involved. A radio forum has been described as

> *a small listening and discussion group that meets regularly in order to receive a special radio program, which the members then discuss. On the basis of the program and discussion, they decide what types of relevant action to take. . . .*
>
> *The basic elements of most radio forum systems are:*
> 1. *Organizers who establish the forums and help service them.*
> 2. *Written discussion guides that contain information and discussion questions that are distributed to forum leaders.*
> 3. *Regularly scheduled radio programs beamed at forum members who gather in a home or a public place to hear the broadcast and then discuss its contents.*
> 4. *Regular feedback reports (a) of decisions by the forum members, and (b) of questions of clarification to the broadcast programmers. (Rogers & Braun, 1977: 361–362)*

It is important to note the extent to which the participants themselves should enter into the planning and decision making.

Though far less ambitious than the American Samoa classroom teaching project previously described, the typical radio forum demands the same kind of precise coordination of many elements: discussion guides must be written and delivered on time; receiving sets must be maintained in working order; participants must be reminded to gather in time; feedback must be collected and delivered to the producers fast enough for them to answer questions and make changes in future productions in keeping with the needs of the forum members. Because all this demands close and willing cooperation among different government agencies, misunderstandings and jealousies all too often frustrate even the most dedicated organizers.[30]

Many countries use radio and television for language teaching. Outside the United States, foreign-language mastery is so highly prized that a great deal of effort goes into broadcast courses. China, for example, purchased BBC English-language courses in 1982. Zheng Peidi, a young woman teacher from Beijing University, is said to have become the first modern TV celebrity in China on the strength of English lessons she gave on television.[31]

The BBC introduced computer literacy courses on television in 1982, supporting them with a textbook, software, and a home computer. People taking the course could buy the book and software through the BBC. The corporation licensed the commercial manufacture of the BBC Microcomputer, designed by its own engineers. Regular dealers handling computer sales expected twelve thousand orders but were flooded with some thirty thousand.[32]

9·8 PERSUASION

Under the heading "persuasion" I include advertising, religious proselytizing, and other programs that consciously seek to motivate listeners and viewers to direct action. Advertising and religion of all types account for 15 percent of the radio and 9 percent of the television program time of the systems sampled in Tables 9.5 and 9.6.

Advertising

Much commercial advertising comes from multinational corporations, with a few international agencies handling most of the multinationals' accounts.* These common antecedents help give advertising an international character. The ubiquity of Coca-Cola advertising led to the coinage of a new term—*coca-colanization*, referring to the transnationals' invasion of Third World markets.

Whether or not they carry commercial advertising, most broadcasting services broadcast announcements for nonprofit organizations, referred to in the United States as *public service announcements* (PSAs). In many Communist and Third World systems, PSAs take the form of "social advertising"—announcements designed to influence listeners and viewers to move in what governments regard as socially or politically desirable directions. Authoritarian countries can use broadcasting efficiently for such purposes:

> *Once the government decides on a goal, whether it be mass literacy or hygiene education, it can pursue it single-mindedly in a way no pluralistic system can. There are no publicly dissenting views as to the wisdom or the methods of*

---

*According to *Advertising Age*'s annual directory of world advertising agencies, each of the top ten handles gross business of more than a billion dollars per year. The company ranked as number one, Interpublic Group (a holding company for McCann Erickson Worldwide and other subsidiaries), billed $3.6 billion and earned more than half a billion in 1982 (*Advertising Age*, 18 April 1983).

the campaign. Media can command the services of the education establishment or the health establishment because they, like media, are arms of a single government apparatus. (Mills, 1983: 185)

China staged broadcast campaigns urging audience members to use courtesy, help the aged, protect the environment, wait patiently in queues, and generally to conform to good standards of "Socialist behavior."

Media research tells us that good behavior cannot be merchandised as readily as razor blades or soap, but in China such campaigns succeed because they reinforce insistent messages conveyed personally as well as through the media:

The mass media and the interpersonal networks are used in parallel, the one reinforcing the other. . . .

The press, radio, television, street signs, posters in factories and shop windows, blackboards and public address systems carried the same messages that [Communist] cadres and school teachers were promulgating by word of mouth. (Sommerlad, 1981: 27)

Third World broadcasting, though no less authoritarian, generally lacks the highly organized interpersonal support essential to the success of sloganeering. In Ghana, such television messages as "Ostentation ruins national effort" and "Hands are for work, work, work" provoked amusement more than unpretentiousness or diligence.*

Persuasive Entertainment

Social messages are frequently incorporated in entertainment programs. Third World systems often use the serial drama (soap opera or *telenovela*) in this manner, sometimes with the help of international aid. The U.S. Agency for International Development (AID), for example, held seminars for writers, producers, and performers to hone their skills in creating *telenovelas* to convey messages on such topics as hygiene, family planning, and childrearing.

Examples of persuasive campaigns in entertainment format follow:

▪ Social messages imparted via broadcasting seem to get results best when used as motivators to stimulate audiences to enter into face-to-face situations for the actual learning process. In Mexico, Televisa, the dominant commercial television network, produced a daily half-hour serial containing messages designed to motivate nonreaders to enroll in literacy centers. Enrollments tripled, apparently largely because of the persuasive power of the serial. Televisa also

---

*In 1984, a newly installed Nigerian military government used broadcast spots in a "war against indiscipline" (May 1984).

produced a similar series containing motivational messages on family planning. Again, researchers credited the programs with positive results.[33]

- Radio Bangladesh has a "Population Planning Cell," a special unit within the broadcasting organization for promoting family planning. It produced a six-days-per-week, 20-minute serial called "Happy Family," scheduled during the early evening. It motivated listeners to consult family-planning clinics—a particularly difficult task in a Muslim country. The planning unit produced two daytime programs as well, bringing Radio Bangladesh's daily schedule of family-planning material to 70 minutes.[34]

Religious Proselytizing

The percentage of time devoted to religion varies widely from country to country, as shown in Tables 9.5 and 9.6. Amounts range from zero in most Communist countries to as much as 30 percent of Saudi Arabian radio. The Saudis devote two entire services to religion, aimed at both domestic and external audiences.

By no means does all material classed as religion consist of hortatory content, however. The Saudi broadcasts, for example, include not only explicitly religious material but also interpretations of Islam designed to correct misunderstandings among foreigners and to explain Saudi government policies. Its Voice of Islam employs a staff of five hundred production personnel, apart from the Ministry of Information staff responsible for secular broadcasting. It produces programs not only in Arabic but in Bengali, English, Farsi (Persian), French, Korean,* Malay, Somali, Swahili, Turkish, and Urdu.

By way of contrast, Nepal's entire religious broadcasting staff consists of two persons. Nearly 90 percent of the Nepalese are Hindus, and their Himalayan kingdom is the only nation in the world to adopt Hinduism as its state religion. The daily 50-minute religious program, said to be very popular, includes readings not only from the Hindu scriptures but also from those of Islam, Judaism, and Christianity, for Hinduism is an eclectic religion recognizing merit in other faiths.[35]

The most aggressive proselytizing via broadcasting comes from Christianity, particularly from Fundamentalist groups. Many evangelizers zealously follow the precept given to the disciples at the close of the Gospel of St. Matthew, "Go ye therefore, and teach all nations, baptizing them in the name of the Father, and of the Son, and of the Holy Ghost," a command known as the "Great Commission." Broadcasting permits a wonderful fulfillment of this command in the eyes of evangelists, for it enables them to penetrate all corners of the earth with the

---

*Korea is not, of course, an Islamic country, but many Koreans work in the Persian Gulf States, and some have converted to Islam (Roberts, 1982).

"good news" of their faith, giving them access to places that would be closed to personal teaching of Christian fundamentalism.

As a result, there has been tremendous growth in the purchase of time for religious programs as well as in the establishment of stations with missionary goals. Religious stations flourish particularly in the United States, Latin America, and the Philippines. Wherever national policies prevent radio ministries from broadcasting—as in most of Europe and the Communist countries—ministries seek to set up international stations to overcome these barriers.

Two schools of thought divide evangelistic broadcasters aiming messages at Third World countries. Some believe that it suffices to propagate the message of salvation; others believe that they should supplement spiritual messages to serve the "whole person"—that is, religious exhortation should be balanced with education and practical information.

Some examples of religiously oriented stations in the Third World follow:

- The Sudan Interior Mission operates a radio complex called ELWA ("Eternal Love Winning Africa") in Monrovia, Liberia, on the west coast of Africa. Though it also broadcasts on short waves to the rest of Africa, ELWA provides a domestic service to Liberia more comprehensive than the Liberian government's own radio service. It broadcasts in ten Liberian languages as well as in English, providing information and education as well as religion. ELWA also involves itself directly in social services by providing a hospital and various educational and training facilities to Liberians in the Monrovia area. "It would be difficult," declared one observer, "for any other Christian broadcasting operation to match this implementation of the whole man concept" (Cook, 1979: 6).[36]

- Canadian Baptists support *Radio Cruz del Sur* (Southern Cross Radio) in Bolivia. Most Bolivian stations operate commercially in Spanish, despite the fact that more than half the Bolivians are Quechua and Aymara speakers, descendants of the pre-Colombian Indian inhabitants of the region. Southern Cross Radio uses these indigenous languages exclusively, stressing programs on agriculture, health, and education. Though a Protestant station operating in a Catholic nation, it "enjoys absolute religious freedom" (Schey, 1982).

- Protestant broadcasting also flourishes in the Philippines, where Catholics constitute more than 80 percent of the population. The oldest Christian station in the islands belongs to the Far East Broadcasting Company (FEBC), a wide-ranging evangelistic operation with stations in Korea, the Mariana Islands, the Seychelles (off the east coast of Africa), and the United States. FEBC-Philippines uses high-power transmitters to reach not only the islands but the rest of Asia as well. Its programming is dominated by evangelistic messages aimed at Christian minorities.[37]

- West German Roman Catholics help support *Radio Veritas,* whose transmitters in the Philippines reach most of Asia. The station is associated with the Philippine Federation of Catholic Broadcasters, whose membership includes a score of commercial and noncommercial broadcasting outlets. Profits from the commercial operations go to welfare funds.[38]

- In warring Lebanon, a dozen religious factions operate their own stations, with or without government authority. Among the unauthorized stations, one of the oddest is the Voice of Hope. Started by American and Canadian donors, it was operated by High Adventure Ministries, a small, California-based Fundamentalist group. It programmed a blend of country-and-western music, gospel songs, "God's commercials" (60-second Bible readings), and the "shrill, right-wing messages" of Major Saad Haddad.[39] Until his death in 1984, Haddad led the militia of a southern Lebanon Christian minority whose domain borders on Israel (the station is located 2 miles from the Israeli border and ships in its supplies through Israeli ports). He and the station appeared to regard the terrain occupied by the Haddad forces as an independent state, the "Republic of Free Lebanon," much to the annoyance of both the Lebanese and U.S. governments. The Voice of Hope had two sister outlets—the King of Hope, a short-wave station broadcasting fundamentalism "in a great variety of native languages," and the Star of Hope, characterized as "the first Christian color television station in the Middle East."[40] However, finding itself unable to finance the television operation, High Adventure Ministries turned the Star of Hope over to CBN, a U.S. religious network. CBN renamed the station Middle East Television, programming it to attract Christians, Israelis, and Moslems alike with such theologically neutral features as U.S. professional basketball.[41]

SUMMARY

In evaluating the output of a broadcasting system, one should pay attention to program schedules as well as to programs. Ideally, schedules run continuously, with audiences given a choice of local, regional, and national services to the extent that the size, ethnic diversity, and cultural complexity of the nation warrants.

Programs consist generically of entertainment, information, education, and persuasion. The proportions of these types are roughly similar in schedules throughout the world, with the highest percentage of time allotted to entertainment and the second highest to information. The First, Second, and Third Worlds differ in their emphasis within types.

How a regime treats broadcasting depends somewhat on its view of the social effects of the medium. The more authoritarian the regime, the more effective it regards broadcasting as an agent of social change. This expectation may be fulfilled when the regime uses broadcasting to supplement highly organized face-to-face campaigns. Thus broadcasting can be used to motivate people to participate in face-to-face learning situations.

NOTES

[1]Paulu, 1981: 160.

[2]Data on Soviet TV schedules are based on *WRTH*, 1984: 410.

[3]*Asian Broadcasting*, June 1983.

[4]Akenga, 1982: 30.

[5]Briggs, 1965: 74.

[6]Head & Kugblenu, 1978: 128–129. GBC-1 is described in Section 2.4.

[7]BBC, 1969.

[8]*BBC, 1983 Annual Report*, 1982: 144, emphasis added.

[9]See, for example, Motamed-Nejad on traditional Iranian storytelling and the mass media (1979).

[10]Katz & Wedell, 1977: 141.

[11]Katz & Wedell, 1977: 139. The authors give many examples of cultural adaptation by Third World systems, pp. 149–207.

[12]Personal interview with James Kangwana, Dubrovnik, September, 1978.

[13]For an analysis of the first year's data, see Head & Gordon, 1976.

[14]*Time*, 1 Aug. 1983.

[15]For a summary of the reasons for scholarly neglect of entertainment, see Fischer, 1979.

[16]For the leading exposition of this viewpoint, see Stephenson, 1967.

[17]Data on news agencies are based on listing in Kurian, 1982: 1134–1137.

[18]Quinn, 1982.

[19]See Braithwaite & Rustin, 1983.

[20]Fleiss & Ambrosino, 1971.

[21]Niemczyk, 1983.

[22]Palmer et al., 1976.

[23]Beltran, 1978: 74.

[24]*BBC, 1983 Annual Report*, 1982: 23–24.

[25]See Katz & Wedell, 1977: 120–123.

[26]Wilbur Schramm and other experts published a candid analysis of the project, 1981.

[27]Grant, 1974.

[28]Personal communication from Tony Kaye, senior lecturer at Britain's Open University.

[29]For a survey of such research, see Rogers, 1983.

[30]For examples of other types of Third World adult education broadcast projects, see the World Bank case histories edited by Spain et al., 1977, and an earlier three-volume collection by UNESCO-IIEP, 1967.

[31]Butterfield, 1982: 399.

[32]*BBC, 1983 Annual Report*, 1982: 2, 26, 29. See also Radcliffe and Salkeld, 1983.

[33]Poindexter, 1982.

[34]Ali, 1982.

[35]Adhikary, 1982.

[36]See also Robertson, 1974: 204–210.

[37]Browne, 1978: 335. See also Bernardez & Haney, 1978: 340.

[38]Bernardez & Haney, 1978: 341–342.

[39]So characterized by Jack Anderson, whose syndicated column carried an exposé of the operation (16 Oct. 1982). See also Wren, 1980.

[40]High Adventure Broadcasting Network, 1982: 3.

[41]Talen, 1984.

CHAPTER 10

AUDIENCE RESEARCH

B roadcasting stands in special need of systematic audience research. The intangible nature of its product, the fact that consumption typically takes place in private, and the utter freedom of audience members to tune in or out at will—all conspire to hide the facts of listening and viewing. Broadcasters therefore urgently need objective, scientific, continuing research to disclose the results of their efforts to entertain, inform, educate, and inspire or persuade.

Unfortunately, early in its development broadcasting became stereotyped as a "one-way" medium, a simplistic concept that accounts for much of its misuse. "Broadcasting is *not*," wrote the BBC to the Annan Committee, "a one-way process in which broadcasters are sending messages to society at large. At its best and most creative it is a relationship. . . . The real standards of broadcasting are a kind of bargain struck between the professional makers of programmes and the public" (Great Britain, 1977: 80–81, emphasis added). Audience research provides the vital return circuit implementing the "bargain" between audience and broadcaster. Even in the absence of research (and many systems have yet to develop systematic, objective, continuing audience measurements), policymakers and programmers receive feedback from family and friends, if not from the public at large. Such ad hominem feedback may be grossly misleading, but it nevertheless influences program and management decisions.

10 · 1 SET PENETRATION

The number of receivers available relative to population constitutes the most basic audience statistic, referred to as *set penetration*. Approximate set penetration data can be derived from license fee records, import and sales figures, and the like.

Official figures can be misleading, however, both because smuggling accounts for a large percentage of imports in many countries and because officials sometimes exaggerate receiver data for reasons of national pride. Table 10.1 indicates that, according to estimates, on the average about every 2.55 people in the world have a radio set and about every 7 have a television set (note that these averages are based on individuals, not families). Averages conceal vast differences between the most and the least developed systems. A few systems can boast of having more radio sets than people—those of the United States (.45 people per set), Guam (.73), Canada (.81), Sweden (.83), and American Samoa (.87). Close behind them, with about 1 person per radio receiver, come the United Kingdom, Bermuda, and New Zealand. No system has a television set for each member of the population. Guam leads the world with 1.37 people per television set, followed by the United States (1.43), Bermuda (1.4), Sweden (1.85), Canada (1.87), Denmark (2.06), and West Germany (2.06). At the other extreme, Mozambique has an estimated 245 people per radio set and 2,450 per television set.[1]

In short, while broadcasting exists to some extent in every part of the world, its actual availability to audiences varies over a wide spectrum, with close to total penetration in the most advanced countries of the West down to very low penetration in the least developed countries, especially with regard to television. Even so, receivers are the most widely distributed modern convenience, far surpassing such amenities as bathtubs, indoor toilets, refrigerators, telephones, and automobiles.

Determining how many and what kinds of people tune in and (sometimes) how they feel about the programs they receive is the province of audience research. The BBC's experience, typical of highly developed Western systems, indicates that some 80 percent of the population, on the average, tunes in to one or more television services daily; the comparable figure for radio is about 48 percent (see Table 10.2). The *cumulative* tune-in over a period of weeks represents essentially the entire population.

10 ▪ 2 EVOLUTION OF AUDIENCE RESEARCH

United States

Systematic research on audience size began in the United States with the Cooperative Analysis of Broadcasting (CAB) in 1929, at the time when network advertising began its first growth. The radio networks originated the CAB, which used the telephone recall method, asking people in a scientifically chosen sample of telephone homes about listening on the previous day. In 1934 CAB gave way to "Hooperatings," which used the coincidental telephone method (asking respondents what they were listening to at the time of the telephone call, thereby eliminating reliance

TABLE 10 ▪ 1   RECEIVER PENETRATION BY WORLD REGIONS

Region	Number of Persons per Receiver	
	Radio	Television
North America	0.47	1.46
Australasia and Other Ocean Territories	1.21	3.33
Western Europe	1.46	2.82
USSR and European Communist Group	1.65	3.39
West Indies	1.81	5.55
Latin America	3.17	8.08
Middle East	4.38	13.64
Asia and Far East	5.29	23.00
Africa (excluding North Africa)	8.16	36.57
World Total	2.58	7.25

SOURCE: Based on data in BBC External Services, "World Radio and Television Receivers" (BBC, London, June 1983).

on memory of past listening except for nighttime hours). A. C. Nielsen introduced a rating service using a third method of gathering data in 1942—automatic metering devices attached to receivers to keep continuous records of set use. Nielsen adapted these devices, which he called *Audimeters*, to television in the early 1950s.

Eventually, competition in the field of U.S. national television audience measurement reduced the main contenders to two—A. C. Nielsen, using Audimeters supplemented with diaries for data about demographic characteristics of viewers, and Arbitron, using diaries. Both firms employ meters for overnight measurement in a few of the largest cities. Nielsen does market-by-market television surveys, and Arbitron does market-by-market surveys for radio. Another firm does national network radio surveys, using a method based on telephone interviews, with special attention given to out-of-home listening. Still other firms offer various specialized research services, and networks and some stations do research on their own.

The following characteristics typify research in the highly commercialized U.S. system: (1) competing commercial companies, separate from the broadcasters, vie for acceptance in the field; (2) purchase of research reports by advertising agencies, station sales representatives, networks, and stations defrays the relatively high costs of research; and (3) the surveys produce quantitative rather than qualitative measurements, with emphasis on ratings and competitive audience shares.

TABLE 10 ▪ 2 DAILY AUDIENCE FOR BROADCASTING
IN THE UNITED KINGDOM

Television Service	Percentage of Population Patronizing Daily	Radio Service	Percentage of Population Patronizing Daily
BBC 1	58	Radio 1	16
BBC 2	22	Radio 2	15
Independent TV	52	Radio 3	1
Total TV	80	Radio 4	9
		Regional Services	1
		BBC Local	4
		Independent Local	8
		Total Radio	48

NOTE: Patronage = average percentage of total population over five years old; percentages rounded to nearest whole number. The sum of individual services add to more than the totals because audiences may tune to more than one service.
SOURCE: Based on data in Helen Fenton, "Viewing and Listening in the UK in 1980, Annual Review of BBC Broadcasting Research Findings, No. 7, 1980 (BBC, London, 1981), pp. 14, 17.

Great Britain

Elsewhere, research evolved more slowly, often with emphasis on qualitative as well as quantitative measurements.

BBC. For decades the BBC did its own research, finally joining ranks with the IBA commercial television companies in the task of audience measurement in 1981. BBC research deserves special notice for several reasons: it contrasts sharply in many ways with the methods used in the United States; it grew into the world's largest in-house broadcasting research organization; and, unlike many such organizations, it has been relatively unsecretive about its work. Documentation includes scores of published reports, an annual review of research findings, and a book by its first director, Robert Silvey, about its origins and development.[2]

Until 1936 Britain had no systematic audience research, relying entirely on voluntary letters from listeners—later acknowledged as a highly unrepresentative source of information. Most BBC program executives and producers loftily assumed that they already knew how to broadcast effectively without the aid of research. To cite a minor example of how misleading this attitude could be, for years BBC executives took it for granted that "nobody dines before 8"; after research began, they "were staggered to learn that most people had finished their evening meal before 7:00 P.M." (Silvey, 1974: 65).

Adult educational program producers at the BBC began agitating for audience studies as early as 1929. Seven years later, the corporation established a small research unit, headed by Silvey. He came from a major London advertising agency, where he had studied the audience of continental stations that were taking advantage of the BBC's conservative Sunday program policy (see Section 6.5) and the ban against advertising. He also had some background in statistics but, beyond that, no special training for the job—indeed, no such training could be had in England at the time.

Throughout his 32-year career, Silvey maintained an amateur (though by no means *amateurish*) approach to audience research, stoutly resisting the professional jargon that had overtaken broadcast researchers in the United States. Amusing evidence of his low-key approach comes from his reaction to a 1955 visit to England by A. C. Nielsen in a bid to get a research contract with the emerging IBA commercial television companies. Nielsen staged what Americans would call a "presentation" at a posh luncheon in a famed London hotel. Wrote Silvey,

> *Nielsen's case was essentially simple and could have been effectively deployed in at most twenty minutes. It lasted fifty, though it seemed longer. Its protraction was achieved by the use of what I suppose would now be called a teaching-aid. By his side was a set of display cards on an easel. Each card bore one or two words—very occasionally three—presumably intended to drive home the Message. If my memory serves me, one bore the word, say, EFFICIENT, another SWIFT, another ECONOMICAL. . . . A deferential aide stood by to whisk away each card as Nielsen's elephantine exposition disposed of its point. (Silvey, 1974: 175–176)*

Unimpressed, the British commercial broadcasters chose a rival system. Nielsen nevertheless operated in Britain for a time, but eventually the commercial broadcasters formed JICTAR (Joint Independent Committee on Television Audience Research), which appointed a British firm to conduct its ratings research, using methods similar to Nielsen's. Today Nielsen has foreign audience research operations in Belgium, Canada, and Japan.

Silvey started his new job by asking BBC listeners over the air to volunteer as research respondents. To his astonishment, he received twenty-eight thousand applications. From these he chose at random a panel of two thousand to produce what he called a "listening barometer." In 1939 he set up the Continuous Survey of Listening, based on aided-recall personal interviews about the previous day's listening. At first he contracted out the job of data gathering to a commercial firm, but starting in 1943 the BBC recruited its own interviewers, mostly housewives, using quota sampling and in-person interviews.

Initial BBC television research started in 1948, but the Continuous Survey of Listening and Viewing did not emerge until 1952. In addition to this survey, which gathered data on all programs, Silvey set up a network of volunteer "Honorary Local Correspondents" who answered periodic questionnaires on their reactions to selected individual programs and groups of programs. The BBC's relatively simple and inexpensive method of enrolling panels of volunteer listeners or viewers to act as audience samples has been widely used throughout the world.

Silvey always downplayed audience size (that is, *quantitative*) measurements as compared to audience opinion (*qualitative*) measurements. The latter he converted into what he called an Appreciation Index, a term and concept still in use at the BBC. Levels of appreciation do not necessarily coincide with audience size measurements. A program may attract a very large audience, even though most of its members find the program only moderately enjoyable; another program may attract only a small audience, but one that finds it intensely enjoyable.

Silvey scrupulously avoided using the term *rating*, refusing to issue lists of the Top 20 programs, as did the ITV companies. Such listings, in Silvey's opinion, "encouraged an entirely fallacious impression of the real significance of audience size: that every broadcast had the same target—the entire population—and that they were therefore all to be judged by the extent to which their audiences approached that goal" (1974: 185). This outlook characterizes BBC program philosophy to this day, justifying expensive but small-audience services such as BBC-2 and Radio 3.* A similar concept animates many systems outside the U.S. sphere of influence.

BARB. For 20 years, the BBC and ITCA (Independent Television Companies Association) went their separate ways, each producing its own estimates of domestic television audience size. (They tried a joint research operation in 1975, but it failed to take hold.) They usually disagreed as to absolute numbers, though tending to coincide on long-term trends. Their discrepancies, though embarrassing, were inevitable, given that the BBC relied on interviews and counted people, while ITCA relied on meters and counted sets. In response to prodding by the Annan Committee, in 1978 the two groups agreed to set up a common system.† It took three years of negotiations, but in 1980 they finally formed a subsidiary, Broadcasters Audience Research Bureau (BARB), to oversee the joint operation. The BBC and JICTAR each nominate three members of BARB's board. It supervises production of two types

---

*Silvey pointed out that although only 5 percent of the population patronized the Third Program, not all listeners came from the same class; moreover, those who never listened to it felt no resentment—indeed, were pleased with relegation of highbrow stuff to a separate program (1974: 147–148).

†The committee discussed audience research in some detail. While not recommending any particular method, it urged that a single independent entity should measure audiences of both the BBC and the commercial companies (Great Britain, 1977: 450–458).

of periodic reports on both radio and television, one on audience size and composition, one on audience reactions.

BARB contracted with a commercial research company to produce the television audience size reports, starting in 1981, using a combination of meters and diaries. The firm, AGB Research, is the same one formerly used by JICTAR independently. Its national sample consists of twenty-nine hundred metered television households. Individuals in the same households fill out viewing diaries based on usage of each set by each family member aged four and up.

The BBC, under contract to BARB, assumed responsibility for the television Appreciation Index in 1982. This qualitative report is based on in-home interviews supplemented by a five-day mail-in diary left by interviewers at sample homes. The Appreciation Index's daily sample of one thousand viewers answers the question: "How interesting or enjoyable did you find program X?" Respondents rate each program on a six-point scale that ranges from "Extremely interesting or enjoyable" to "Not at all interesting and/or enjoyable." Answers are reduced to an index number for each program, ranging from zero to one hundred. Statistically meaningful results for any program that has a million or more in its audience can be derived.

As to radio, the BBC conducts audience size measurements on behalf of BARB, using a modification of its traditional Daily Survey. Interviewers talk to a thousand people daily, selected according to a quota method designed to obtain a representative national sample. Using an aided-recall technique, house-to-house interviewers ask respondents what they listened to the previous day. Reports on each day's listening to both the BBC services and Independent Local Radio are issued monthly.[3] Because the Daily Survey samples too few to measure *individual* local radio station audiences, the BBC and the Joint Industries Committee for Radio Audience Research each conducts its own local radio measurements.

Meanwhile, the BBC continues to do in-house studies to help in planning future programs, to improve research methods, and to investigate broad social questions, such as the impact of television violence. Many of these special studies appear in the aforementioned annual reviews of research findings.

IBA. According to the Broadcasting Act of 1981, the IBA must "ascertain the state of public opinion" on the programs and advertisements that its contractors broadcast. It therefore conducts its own research program, separate from that of BARB. The authority makes a weekly regional survey based on five hundred diaries, from which it derives its own Appreciation Index. It also does annual surveys using a sample of one thousand respondents, aimed at larger questions, such as the public's assessment of the impartiality of the commercial companies' programs and their general quality.[4]

Research Elsewhere

All well-developed broadcasting systems conduct intensive audience research, especially those heavily dependent on advertising.

Researchers from most Western European and even from some Eastern European systems belong to the Group of European Audience Researchers (GEAR), which meets annually to exchange information and discuss common problems. GEAR found that its member organizations spent an average of less than a half of one percent of their budgets on audience research—a modest investment considering the value of the information derived.[5]

The growth of Italy's private television to the point where it challenged the official service, RAI, for supremacy led to a battle over ratings methods far more raucous than that of the BBC and IBA. After months of wrangling during which each side published audience figures widely at variance with each other, the two sides finally agreed in 1984 to set up a new ratings service, Auditel. It was to be owned equally by RAI, private broadcasters, and advertisers, and was expected to employ meters. Meanwhile, until Auditel began producing ratings in 1985, all parties agreed to accept the findings of Istel, a system developed by Italian public opinion research organizations using diaries and telephone interviews. RAI nevertheless planned to continue experimenting with a wired meter system developed by AGB Research (the company used by BARB in Great Britain) that not only records tuning but allows viewers to register their reactions by pushing buttons on a keypad at home.[6]

Many charters require that broadcasting authorities make enquiries as to how the public reacts to their output, as in the case of the BBC charter and the IBA statute. Japan's NHK, spurred on by such an obligation, pioneered in systematic research. Its license fee collection mechanism, detailed in Section 7.2, provides an ideal opportunity for face-to-face data gathering. Fee collectors began asking questions about audience opinions as early as 1925. In 1932 NHK did a massive study of audience opinion, based on a complete census of more than a million receiver licensees. The more scientific method of sampling surveys came into use as a result of American influence during the Allied occupation after World War II.[7] In 1946 NHK established a Radio and Television Cultural Research Institute aimed at developing guidelines for program improvement. The institute's Theoretical Research Center has published a series of studies on broadcasting.[8] Today, NHK and the Japanese commercial broadcasters use highly sophisticated research methods, in keeping with Japan's leadership in electronic technology. NHK research puts more emphasis on qualitative investigation than does that of the Japanese commercial broadcasters. Japan's commercial interests have employed A.C. Nielsen to conduct surveys since 1961.

China uses a method of research made possible by its tightly organized interpersonal political network. The young people trained to operate the thousands of local wired-radio centers (see Section 2.3) also conduct face-to-face interviews to gather listener reactions:

> They are in their early twenties and hold high-school diplomas. After completing the specialized training, they are assigned to work at a unit in their home county. Besides assuming regular duties at the unit, each young broadcaster has to participate in farm work and call on listeners, particularly old people. Each broadcaster has a circle of "listener-friends," whom he contacts every fortnight or month for suggestions. (Chu, 1978: 39)

China's first survey using scientific sampling assisted by computers took place as recently as 1983.[9]

10 ▪ 3 ATTITUDES TOWARD RESEARCH

Though plainly needed, broadcasting research does not inspire equal respect in all quarters. Attitudes toward it vary widely according to the type of broadcasting system involved, the circumstances under which the system operates, and the system's general philosophy.

Commercial Services

Wherever the sale of commercials plays a significant role, advertiser pressure demands quantitative audience measurements. Advertisers want to know how many and what kinds of people hear or see their messages. Audience opinions of programs matter to them less than audience exposure to commercials.

Media competition makes advertisers and their agencies suspicious of in-house research conducted by broadcasting services themselves; therefore, commercially inspired studies usually come from specialized research companies, separate from both advertisers and media. Again, because of competition, commercial firms that contract for proprietary research usually resist disclosure of full details. Such concealment contradicts a basic principle of scientific research, namely, that methods and results should be freely open to inspection by other researchers.

Research in the Third World

Conducting scientifically based research in the Third World presents the investigator with many intractable problems. Illiteracy, lack of telephones, and limits on funding make it impossible to use the Western data-gathering methods—telephone interviews, diary keeping, and set metering. In-person interviews can be employed, but people unused to being questioned by strangers and suspicious of government intrusion prove uncooperative. In many countries, custom forbids interviewing women, even by other women. The very language of research, the familiar jargon of polling and opinion scaling that Western publics have long since learned to take for granted, may be missing, making it exceedingly difficult to phrase questions to elicit valid responses.

Third World systems depend primarily on letters from the audience for feedback. A British researcher who conducted extensive surveys of audiences in Africa points out how especially misleading letters can be in countries where only a minority of the people can read and write. A popular Tanzanian radio music-request program, for example, reflected only urban tastes in music, for most of the letters came from the capital and a few other major cities; yet most listeners lived in the country and had traditional rather than modern tastes in music. Moreover, most of the comments on the conduct of the service, upon which the staff relied for popular guidance, originated from these same nontypical urban writers.[10]

The secretary-general of the Asian Mass Communication Research and Information Center pointed out that in the early days, Asian broadcasters grew accustomed to dealing with a small urban audience and failed to adjust their sights when sets penetrated into the interior, changing the character of the majority audience:

> Since their earlier clientele came from smaller, easily identifiable elitist social groups, programme personnel in Asian broadcasting tend to place greater credence on "feedback" such as listeners' requests, postcards, radio clubs, letters of commendation or complaint and newspaper comments than on objective research. . . .
> The new audience demands a different approach to listener research. Samples have to be drawn from a much larger "universe" and have to be stratified on the basis of variables which were not considered significant earlier. (Amunugama, 1982: 136)

Policymakers in authoritarian systems do not always find such arguments persuasive. Accustomed to thinking of broadcasting as one-way rather than two-way communication, they have no concept of *feedback—return information that is needed by the system as a guide to modification of its own output*. Politicians use the medium to instruct, command, and exhort, not to carry on a dialogue. Thus authoritarian leaders fall into the trap of overestimating the power of the media. Speaking of the situation in Iran, a former official of the broadcasting service there wrote, "In the absence of feedback and supportive interpersonal or organisational systems the messages of mass communication may fall on deaf [or] incredulous ears. . . . The more centralised the power, the less the feedback and the two-way communication, the greater the illusions of communication and power" (Tehranian, 1982: 44).

Even in the less authoritarian environment of India, as a one-time deputy director-general of AIR expressed it, "Audience research sometimes reveals awkward facts which run counter to the prejudices and predilections of those in authority." Indeed, at one point the government decided that it already "knew what the Indian listener wanted and there was no need for audience research!" (Masani, 1976: 145). AIR was subsequently allowed to revive research, but it still had little effect because executives and producers focused more on pleasing their superiors than on pleasing their audiences. Besides, AIR kept the results of research secret, even from most of its own staff. Masani questioned, moreover, whether research findings would command much authority as long as AIR itself conducted the investigations as an in-house undertaking.

The head of research for the Ghana Broadcasting Corporation complained that the status of research in some developing countries suffers from

> the unhealthy attitude of some broadcasting managements, programme planners and producers. . . . Very often programme evaluation reports dutifully gathered by research personnel are left unread [in] the files of programme planners and producers. Suggestions which are aimed specifically at assisting broadcasting managements to re-think their goals and develop new and more effective policies are ignored or resisted because suggestions run counter to the ideas of managements. (Blankson-Mills, 1982: 28)*

Though disregard of research findings occurs more often and more blatantly under authoritarian types of management, the Third World has no monopoly. Despite the proven value of research, some broadcasters continue to think they know the answers to questions before the questions have been asked. The Annan Committee faulted the BBC because "there is a barrier of considerable suspicion and some ignorance between audience researchers and those in the front line of programme production" (Great Britain, 1977: 456).

Research in the USSR

For decades Communists declined as a matter of policy to engage in scientific audience research. Sociological studies in general had a bad name, but the Soviets eventually concluded that finding out how messages fared after leaving the transmitter could help them achieve their objectives. East Germany, Hungary, and Poland began regular audience research in the 1960s. In one of the few sources of information on the subject of audience research in the Soviet Union readily available in English, Mickiewicz appraised the results of research undertaken in the 1970s. According to the author, the Soviets "no longer assumed that just because a message has been broadcast . . . it has been received,

---

*As an example of excessive secrecy, when I asked Blankson-Mills to talk about GBC research in my class in broadcasting at the University of Ghana, I suggested that she bring examples of the questionnaires she sent out to listening panels (in the manner of the BBC). She turned up without the questionnaires, saying that her superiors forebade their disclosure because they considered them classified information.

understood, and assimilated" (Mickiewicz, 1981: 6). The Soviets now use essentially the same techniques as U.S. investigators and have the same theoretical research interests, though they avoid investigating political questions directly and tend to put more emphasis on qualitative measurements than do researchers in the United States.

Comparing Soviet television audiences with those of the United States in the light of research findings, Mickiewicz observed striking similarities despite the great differences in the policies and goals of the two systems:

- The youth of both cultures watch less than either children or older people.

- In both countries, entertainment draws the largest audiences, with stress on movies, variety, and sports. By the same token, high culture, adult education, and programs about economic questions draw the smallest audiences (with the exception noted below).

- However, a higher proportion of Soviet than U.S. viewers watch opera and ballet.

- In both cultures, the amount of viewing decreases with increasing levels of education.

- As in the United States, viewers in the USSR tend to *say* that they prefer more prestigious program types but actually view more of the lower-level, mass-appeal programs: "In all the polls, Russians consistently say, regardless of age, occupation, and education, that the most important function of television is to acquaint its audience with political events. . . . But people tend to use television primarily for entertainment and relaxation" (Mickiewicz, 1981: 28).

- U.S. viewers watch somewhat more than their Soviet counterparts—an expected difference, considering that U.S. viewers have more choices of programs and their stations stay on the air longer.

- A higher proportion of Soviet than American women work outside the home, making the Soviet daytime audience proportionately smaller than in the United States.

Mandate or Guide?

In stressing the importance of research for facilitating two-way communication between broadcasters and their audiences, I do not mean to imply that broadcasting should be completely subservient to audience preferences. Indeed, one of the most vexing questions of program policy, one on which systems vary widely in their conclusions, is how audience research results should be used. Should research supply a mandate, automatically determining programming decisions? Or should it serve as one factor among several?

Permissive services, notably those of the United States and the countries it influences, tend to regard research results as furnishing a virtual mandate. Deregulatory theory gives intellectual support to this view. The formula runs: people have a right to receive what they want, and quantitative research reveals their program preferences; therefore, programmers should act accordingly. Both paternalistic and authoritarian broadcasters reject this formula. They point out first that audience size research tells only what people watched or listened to *in the past*, offering only the option of imitation for the future. Secondly, because audience size does not necessarily reveal the intensity of audience preferences, merely quantitative findings are an incomplete guide for programmers. Thirdly, unquestioning deference to audience *wants* rather than *needs* results in an unbalanced program mix favoring light entertainment to the relative neglect of culture, information, and education.

Typical of the noncommercial, public service oriented approach is that of Sweden, where broadcasting authorities decline to allot time to preferred program types in proportion to the audience size they draw. According to a Swedish official, though audiences devoted 34 percent of their actual viewing to light entertainment, only 19 percent of the overall program schedule fell into this category. A quarter of all Swedish programming drew only 4 percent or less of the potential audience. This refusal to conform unquestioningly to audience wants "is possibly the most important difference between a commercial and a noncommercial system: the noncommercial system tends to promote a slightly more intellectual ideology in 'good taste,' current affairs, culture and religion, lectures and serious music, whereas what the public wants is entertainment, light music and sport" (Soderstrom, 1981: 304).

Sweden's approach will be recognized as equivalent to Reith's "giving a lead" policy—the theory that if program fare keeps slightly ahead of audience tastes, it will eventually raise those tastes to a higher level (see Section 3.4). So far, however, no convincing evidence that this amelioration actually takes place has emerged. As Paulu put it in discussing British audience research data:

> *A country's intellectual and cultural level is the result of a great many interacting factors, of which broadcasting is only one. Fundamental are historical, educational, racial, and cultural traditions. These are affected by the output of the schools, churches, newspapers, broadcasting, and other means of information, education, and communication, always operating within the current social, economic, and political setting. Therefore it is impossible to evaluate broadcasting by itself, nor is it reasonable to expect it alone to bring about a millennium. (Paulu, 1981: 364)*

SUMMARY

Ideally, broadcasting should be treated as a two-way medium, with objective, scientifically based audience research providing the feedback by which programmers adjust their output in terms of audience comprehension, interests, desires, and needs. The chief methods of gathering data on audiences include interviews (in person or by telephone), diary keeping, set metering, and mail questionnaires answered by panels of listeners and viewers. Quantitative audience research furnishes estimates of the numbers and characteristics of audience members; qualitative research probes into the opinions of audience members concerning the programs they choose. Commercial interests rely primarily on quantitative data, while public service oriented systems demand both qualitative and quantitative data.

The extent to which research feedback governs program policies varies from one system to another. Under permissive systems, quantitative audience data become virtual mandates in making program decisions. Paternalistic and authoritarian systems tend to use audience data in combination with other considerations, weighing what are perceived as audience needs against audience wants as revealed by research.

Authoritarian administrations tend to treat broadcasting as a one-way system for commanding and exhorting, paying little if any attention to audience interests as revealed by research. However, even authoritarian administrations eventually come to realize that audience research can help them achieve their goals. Paternalistic systems hope that by keeping the level of programming slightly ahead of popular taste, mass tastes will be gradually elevated. So far, evidence in support of this theory has not emerged.

NOTES

[1] Set penetration figures based on BBC External Services estimates for December 1982 (BBC, June 1983).

[2] BBC, 1974; Silvey, 1974.

[3] See Reiss, 1983, for details of BARB procedures.

[4] IBA, 1982: 206–207.

[5] Menneer, 1984: 40.

[6] Humi, Oct. 1984.

[7] Okabe, 1963: 19.

[8] NHK, 1963 ff.

[9] *Asian Broadcasting*, August 1983.

[10] Mytton, 1983: 113.

CHAPTER 11

TRANSBORDER BROADCASTING

I n previous chapters I have dealt with *domestic* broadcasting services. I have grouped *external* services separately in order to highlight their special characteristics. The ability of broadcast signals to pass freely across political boundaries gives the medium a unique role in international communication. One can identify seven categories of transborder services, as follows: (1) spillover signals, both domestic and military; (2) official external services; (3) surrogate domestic services; (4) unofficial political services, including clandestine stations and borrowed facilities; (5) military services; (6) external commercial stations, including peripheral, long-distance, and pirate stations; and (7) religious stations. These seven types will be explored in the present chapter.

11 ▪ 1 SPILLOVER SIGNALS

Any station near a border, even if equipped with a directional antenna, will inadvertently spill some of its signal over into the neighboring territory. The ITU recognizes spillover as technically unavoidable. Satellite signals are especially susceptible to spillover. A satellite footprint can never be shaped to match its intended coverage area precisely. For example, any European satellite intended for domestic direct-broadcast service will unavoidably become available to more foreign nationals than to people within its home territory.

Domestic Spillover

By virtue of their location, certain countries experience more transborder spillover than others. Turkey, known historically as a crossroads of commerce and war, is also an electronic crossroads: parts of Turkey can receive spillover programs from Bulgaria, Cyprus, Iran, Iraq, Lebanon, Romania, Syria, and the USSR. In Western Europe, Belgium occupies a similar crossroad for international traffic.

In parts of West Germany, a score of foreign television programs can be seen; in centrally located Cologne, program guide magazines carry, in addition to West German television schedules, listings for two services each from Belgium, East Germany, and the Netherlands, three services from France, and one each from the British Armed Forces and Luxembourg. Tuning to spillover services occurs with particular intensity when neighboring countries happen to have the same language, in part or as a whole, as in East and West Germany, the United States and Canada (see Section 2.2), Ireland and the United Kingdom (see Section 8.2), Spanish-language radio in Miami and Cuba, and China and Hong Kong, to name only a few such cases.

Spillover creates many ironies and rivalries, examples of which follow:

- Four-fifths of the East Germans can pick up West German television. The deprived remaining fifth came to be called *westblind*. After vainly trying various methods of preventing its citizens from tuning to West German broadcasts, the East Germans finally gave up in 1972 and now even print their neighbor's schedules in the newspapers. Partly because of this contact and the spirit of competition it engenders, East Germany reputedly has achieved the best television production quality among the Communist states.[1]

- Jordan's color television signals and its U.S. television program imports proved highly attractive to Israeli viewers, whose austere service eschewed imports and stayed with black-and-white television long after its neighbor went to color. As a result, many Israeli viewers purchased color sets before their own system could supply them with color, and the Israeli papers published the Jordan schedules. Strikes by Israeli broadcasters in 1984 stimulated consumption of foreign programs, including, in some parts of the country, transmissions from Egypt and Syria.

- The proximity of Finland to the USSR made it possible for Soviet viewers in Estonia to enjoy *Charlie's Angels*, a type of imported program never seen on Soviet television. By the same token, Finland's Helsinki cable subscribers can receive a Russian television station.

- Spillover reception of foreign programs sometimes frustrates domestic policies against advertising and exposes the weaknesses of monopolistic domestic programming. During the 1970s, Thailand's radio service failed to cover its southernmost provinces. Thais in that area tuned to neighboring Malaysian radio. Even where Thai radio could be received, listeners preferred Malaysian programs because they found them less long-winded and boring.[2]

TURKEY

▪ Costa Rican officials worried about the fact that their own services did not reach their northern borders when Nicaraguan Sandinista stations did. The Sandinistas, aided by Cuba and East Germany, greatly increased the power and stridency of their stations. Their broadcasts introduced an alien, politically charged atmosphere into what Costa Ricans normally regarded as simple entertainment. One official remarked that children exposed to the Sandinista broadcasts began playing revolutionaries and counterrevolutionaries instead of cops and robbers.[3]

▪ Canada had 140,000 television receivers before it had any television stations because spillover from the United States stimulated set purchasing. Later, cable television increased the flow of programming across the border. Canada was inundated not only by American programs but also by American advertising. The issue heated up in the 1970s to the extent that some Canadian provinces retaliated by deleting commercials from American programs, inspiring a lawsuit on the part of American advertisers and hearings in the American Congress.[4]

▪ Sri Lankan television lured Indian viewers away from their own domestic services because "Indian programming goes in for heavy intellectual slots such as classical music, cultural documentaries and development programs, while Sri Lanka feeds her national beam with a weather eye for entertainment in programs such as pop music, feature films and comedy series" (Wijesekera, 1983: 7).

Military Spillover

Stations designed to serve military personnel stationed on foreign soil represent a special case of spillover. The U.S. Armed Forces Radio and Television Service (AFRTS) has some 100 stations on military outposts in 15 countries. Designed to cover only military installations, most AFRTS stations have very low power. For example, the U.S. Air Force has two 10-watt AM stations on bases in Turkey. However, the U.S. European Armed Forces Network headquarters in Frankfurt, West Germany, has a 150-kw. AM transmitter. It feeds 28 other AMs that range in power from 10 kw. down to .03 kw. AFRTS German facilities also include 12 FM and 8 television stations, the latter supplemented by many small repeaters. AFRTS has 50-kw. medium-wave and 10-kw. short-wave outlets at the Tokyo headquarters of its Far East Network. The short-wave station relays programs to outposts in Japan, Korea, Okinawa, and Taiwan.

AFRTS stations carry sports, entertainment, and news programs from the U.S. domestic networks (minus their commercials), delivered overseas by means of VOA short-wave transmitters. They also carry military news gathered by AFRTS correspondents and produce programs locally. These materials, though intended only for U.S. military personnel, spill over to surrounding civilian populations, giving them an intriguing sample of American domestic programming.

Other major nations also operate overseas armed services facilities. The British, Canadian, and French forces all have stations in West Germany, for example. In East Germany, the USSR has a 200-kw. long-wave station, Radio Volga, which in addition to producing programming locally relays Moscow home service programs.

11 ▪ 2   OFFICIAL EXTERNAL SERVICES

By "official external services" I mean those conducted by governments in their own names (often so identified in titles such as Voice of America, Radio Moscow, and *Deutsche Welle*). Openly aimed at foreign countries, they function as an arm of diplomacy, usually employing short waves to reach distant targets but sometimes also using long- and medium-wave transmitters. The short range of over-the-air television limits its usefulness for external services to foreign countries willing to accept tapes or films for transmission over their own domestic facilities. External broadcasters call this type of release "local placement."

More than 80 countries operate official external services, representing a vast output in a babel of languages.* Table 11.1 shows the ten leading external broadcasters, as measured by their hours on the air. As the composition of the top ten suggests, Cold War rivalry between East and West motivates most large-scale official transborder broadcasting.

The ten leading external broadcasters include three developing countries—Albania, Cuba, and North Korea. Their presence in the big ten can be ascribed to the Cold War. Enjoying far more powerful external facilities than they could afford from their own resources, these Communist client states have foreign sources to thank for their expensive installations. Further evidence of the role the Cold War plays in big-power external broadcasting comes from the statistics on U.S. external broadcasting: a quarter of the Voice of America's audience lives in the Communist world; Radio Free Europe and Radio Liberty (representing more than half of total official U.S. external air time) devote most of their

---

*BBC 1983 Annual Report, 1982: 60. It is difficult to pin down the exact number of external services because some countries, such as Egypt, operate powerful transmitters that serve both domestic and external audiences. Moreover, semiofficial agencies sometimes operate transborder services side by side with official agencies. One authoritative source estimates that 131 countries broadcast to other countries in one form or another (Codding, 1983: 11).

TABLE 11 ▪ 1 TEN LEADING EXTERNAL SERVICES

Service	Radio Hours per Week
1. Soviet Union	2,114
2. United States	
Voice of America (935)	
Radio Free Europe (555)	
Radio Liberty (469)	
Total	1,959
3. China	1,304
4. West Germany	786
5. United Kingdom	741
6. North Korea	581
7. Albania	567
8. Egypt	518
9. Cuba	459
10. East Germany	427

SOURCE: BBC Annual Report and Handbook, 1983 (BBC, London, 1982), p. 59.

efforts to anti-Communist broadcasts; and the Central Intelligence Agency clandestinely supports an additional unknown though doubtless substantial anti-Communist output.

Transmission

HF Propagation. Long-distance radio transmission relies on HF waves bounced back and forth between the earth's surface and the ionosphere, as described in Section 8.2. To exploit the ionosphere effectively, frequency managers of major external services must juggle many variables, including time of day, season, geographical location, levels of solar activity, and interference from other stations (both inadvertent and deliberate). They change frequencies four times per year, in keeping with systematic changes in the characteristics of the ionosphere. The ITU's International Frequency Registration Board (IFRB) keeps track of frequency usage and attempts to minimize interference. In addition, American, British, Canadian, Dutch, and German external services coordinate their plans to avoid conflicting with each other. A great deal of interference nevertheless occurs, as noted in Section 8.2, and many external services operate "out of band," that is, outside the designated international HF bands.

In order to alleviate interference, the ITU is even considering changing to the single sideband (SSB) mode of transmission, a method that reduces the size of the channel for each station by half. However, this would be highly disruptive, for it would entail scrapping millions of the less expensive types of short-wave receivers.

Each major broadcaster uses scores of frequencies in the HF band, changing not only seasonally but also during the course of the day. Frequencies that work well over a given path in the morning will be useless by evening. Transmitters switch to different antennas when they change frequency; thus each short-wave transmitter site must be equipped with a large array of antennas. HF antennas are directional so that transmissions can be directed toward a designated target area. Thus an external service will use many more frequencies than it has transmitters. Canada, for example, has one 50-kw. and five 250-kw. transmitters at Sackville, on the Atlantic Coast. These six transmitters operate, at various times, on 29 different frequencies using as many different antennas. External service transmitters use very high power in order to overcome interference. More than five hundred transmitters use 200 kw. or more of power, in comparison to the 50-kw. maximum usual for domestic transmitters.

External broadcasting transmitter installations occupy a great deal of real estate because of the large size and number of the antennas they employ. The VOA's major domestic installation in Greenville, North Carolina, consists of three separate sites totaling more than six thousand acres. One site provides facilities for microwave reception of programs, all of which come from Washington, D.C. Sixty-eight short-wave transmitting antennas occupy the other two sites, fed by a total of 16 transmitters ranging in power from 50 to 500 kw. The Greenville complex, known as the Edward R. Murrow Transmitting Station, went on the air in 1963 at a capital cost of $25 million.

Relay Stations. Although Greenville's transmitters can be picked up all over the world, the VOA, like other major external services, also uses additional relay transmitters closer to its target areas (see Fig. 11.1).* Most listeners have only small inexpensive receivers that can more readily pick up relayed signals from nearby transmitters than from distant short-wave stations. Even long- and medium-wave relay transmitters can be used from sites adjacent to target areas. For example, the VOA uses medium-wave relay transmitters in Antigua, Greece, the Philippines, and Thailand. The USSR uses fewer relay stations than Western external broadcasters, presumably because it has fewer opportunities than the West to obtain the use of desirable transmitter locations. It does have relays in Bulgaria, Cuba, and East Germany and

---

*However, because of the "skip-distance" of HF waves as they bounce back and forth between earth and ionosphere, short-wave transmitters must be positioned at considerable distances from their target areas.

positions external transmitters near its eastern and western borders to give better access to target areas.

Originally, overseas relay stations had to depend on picking up over-the-air short-wave signals from the originating country.* This meant, of course, that the original signal lost quality in the process of reaching the relay station. Nowadays, the major external services rely more and more on satellites to reach their relay stations (see Figure 11.1). The VOA, for example, leases 18 full-time satellite relay links. Britain, the Netherlands, West Germany, and the USSR also use satellite relays.

Eventually, perhaps, external radio services will be able to use direct-broadcast satellites, eliminating dependence on the cumbersome and unreliable HF system. External broadcasters are also intrigued by the possibility of adding long-distance DBS television to their external services. DBS services would be virtually immune from jamming and clearly receivable throughout large target areas. However, DBS reception of external services would require very simple, inexpensive receivers of a type not likely to be available in the near future. Presumably, conspicuous outdoor antennas would be necessary, making clandestine reception impossible. Also essential would be agreement among ITU members on the allocation of channels and orbital slots for external DBS services, a type of allocation most members oppose.

In the meantime, finding suitable overseas terrestrial relay sites is not easy. Host countries demand substantial payments, in cash or in kind, for the use of transmitter sites, and at best the relationship remains a delicate one. An external service may be constrained to make political concessions to avoid antagonizing the host government so as not to lose a valued relay site. This is said to have happened in the case of the U.S. government in its relationships with a dictatorial regime in Greece, for example.†

The VOA usually signs a memorandum of understanding with host governments for the use of relay sites for fixed periods. For example, Antigua gets $12,000 per year from the VOA for the use of a medium-wave site on that Caribbean island. In exchange for the use of sites in Thailand, Botswana, Greece, and Morocco, the VOA provides substantial amounts of transmitter time to the host countries. In Sri Lanka, the government broadcasting organization owns the transmitters, leasing time to the VOA; the Sri Lanka government retains the right to approve schedules and program content. In Liberia, the VOA agreed to provide

---

*Sometimes submarine cable is also used, as in the case of Canada's linkage to its United Kingdom relay transmitter.

†Browne, 1982: 107. Browne also reports a 1974 conversation with a Cyprus broadcasting official who complained that the way the Greeks used the VOA Rhodes transmitter exacerbated Greek-Turkish tension in Cyprus; open conflict erupted later that year (p. 128).

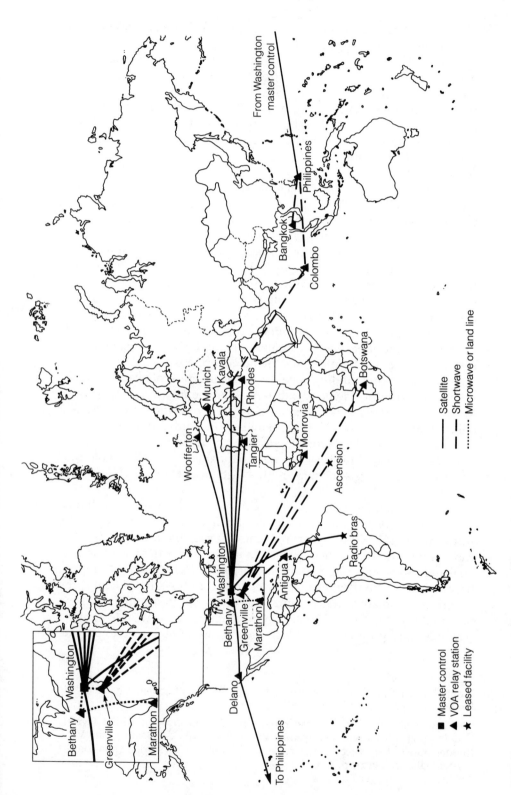

FIGURE 11 ▪ 1 VOA RELAY CIRCUITS <u>Source</u>: **Voice of America**

transmitter training to Liberian citizens. Upon termination of the contract with Morocco, its government will retain ownership of the VOA facilities in Tangier.*

History

Origins. Experiments with HF propagation enabled the start of transborder broadcasting within the first decade of radio. At the height of their strength, during the 1920s, colonial powers wanted to keep in direct contact with their nationals residing in distant overseas territories. The Netherlands initiated the first regularly scheduled external service in 1927 (initially operated privately), directed toward the Dutch East Indies. Germany followed in 1929, France in 1931, and Great Britain in 1932. These countries broadcast in their own languages to reach their own citizens overseas, ignoring the local, indigenous peoples.

With the rise of Hitler and the outbreak of World War II in the late 1930s came foreign-language external broadcasting (including the languages of the indigenous peoples of the colonies). War also brought the deceptive use of radio for propaganda and intelligence purposes. But the idea of external radio simply as a peaceful means of keeping in touch with one's own nationals beyond one's borders persisted. Neutral Switzerland, for example, started an external service for that purpose in 1935. Many small external services today exist primarily to maintain contact with nationals who have migrated to foreign countries in search of work and education.

BBC External Services. The BBC began experimental long-distance HF transmissions in 1927, leading to formal establishment of the Empire Service in 1932. Director-General Reith wrote that the inaugural broadcast, featuring an address by King George V, was

> the most spectacular success in BBC history thus far. The King had been heard all over the world with surprising clarity. . . . . It was sensationally starred in foreign countries; the New York Times in large type: "Distant Lands Thrill to His 'God Bless You' "; two thousand leading articles were counted in Broadcasting House. (Reith, 1949: 169)

At first these external services, operating at BBC expense (that is, on domestic license fee income), consisted simply of selected programs repeated from the domestic radio service. Not until 1934 did the Empire Service set up its own news department.

Big-power rivalry in the Middle East led the West to start foreign-language broadcasting, the distinctive feature of modern external

---

*Terms of agreement for the use of foreign sites can be found in Department of State, *United States Treaties and Other International Agreements* (Government Printing Office, Washington, D.C.).

services. In 1935 Italy began transmitting in Arabic from a station in Bari, a town on the Adriatic coast near the heel of the Italian boot (Italy had a North African, Arabic-speaking colony, Libya). Britain countered with its own Arabic service three years later.[5] It took that long for the government and the BBC to decide who should be responsible for what. As it worked out, the British Foreign Office retained control over which languages would be used and the hours devoted to each, while the BBC retained control over programming. The Foreign Office assumd financial responsibility.*

Aside from decisions as to languages and hours on the air, the BBC operates the External Services without government supervision, though naturally close liaison had to be maintained with the Foreign Office during World War II. For example, external broadcasts often incorporated coded messages to leaders of resistance movements. Nevertheless, to a remarkable degree, the BBC retained the confidence of its listeners throughout the world, during the war and after, building a unique reputation for accuracy and objectivity in reporting:

> *Accuracy and comprehensiveness were two of the pillars on which the wartime reputation of BBC news was built. A third was consistency. The same truth must be told to everyone. There could be no question of broadcasting different versions of what was taking place to different audiences in different languages, as the Germans did in the mistaken belief that they would not be caught out. . . . As suspicion of propaganda grew, so there was an increasing tendency for listeners who were able to do so to tune in to broadcasts not aimed at them. (Mansell, 1982: 91)*

During the 1982 Falklands War, South American broadcasters relied heavily on the BBC for war news. Even an Argentinian station carried interviews with BBC staff members until stopped by the Argentine government. Uruguay and Chile carried BBC items throughout the hostilities. Though South American broadcasters disagreed with the British government, they apparently trusted British broadcasting.

In 1982 the BBC External Services broadcast in 35 foreign languages. Arabic occupied the most time (63 hours per week), Nepali the least (45 minutes). In addition, the World Service in English ran 24 hours per day. Table 11.2, showing one day of the World Service, gives an idea of the scope of its programming.

Voice of America. External broadcasting, like domestic broadcasting, began in the United States as a private undertaking. Sporadic long-distance transmissions began, mainly as technical experiments, in the 1920s. By the time the United States declared war in 1941, half a

---

*During World War II, the government gave the BBC a subvention to support both domestic and external services. Following the war, domestic programming went back to license fees for support, but the Foreign Office continued to reimburse the corporation for the costs of the External Services.

TABLE 11 ▪ 2 A DAY IN THE BBC'S WORLD SERVICE
(FEB. 3, 10, 17, & 24, 1984)

0000 World News
09 News about Britain
15 Radio Newsreel
30 Radio Theatre 3rd, For Maggie, Betty and Ida; 10th, Royal Necklace; 17th, Anchor And Hope; 24th, A Bid for Happiness
0115 Outlook
45 *Ulster Newsletter
50 *In the Meantime
0200 World News
09 British Press Review
15 *3rd, 10th, Personal Impact; 17th, 24th, I Know It's Here Somewhere
30 Talking about Music
0300 World News
09 News about Britain
15 The World Today
30 *Business Matters
0400 Newsdesk
30 Country Style
45 Financial News
55 Reflections
0500 World News
09 *Twenty-Four Hours: News Summary
30 *After Hours
45 The World Today
0600 Newsdesk
30 *The Tone Poets
0700 World News
09 Twenty-Four Hours: News Summary
30 *Rock Back the Clock
45 *Merchant Navy Programme

0800 World News
09 Reflections
15 The Bach Family
30 Women of the World
0900 World News
09 British Press Review
15 The World Today
30 Financial News
40 Look Ahead
45 Album Time
1015 Merchant Navy Programme
30 Business Matters
1100 World News
09 News about Britain
15 In the Meantime
25 Ulster Newsletter
30 Meridian
1200 Radio Newsreel
15 Jazz for the Asking
45 Sports Round-up
1300 World News
09 Twenty-Four Hours: News Summary
30 Radio Theatre
1415 Letterbox
30 John Peel
1500 Radio Newsreel
15 *Outlook
1600 World News
09 Commentary
15 *Science in Action
45 The World Today

1700 World News
09 *Sarah and Company
40 *Book Choice
45 Sports Round-up
1800 Newsdesk
30 Edward Elgar: The Making of a Composer
1900 Outlook
39 Stock Market Report
43 Look Ahead
45 About Britain
2000 World News
09 Twenty-Four Hours: News Summary
30 Sherlock Holmes
2100 Network U.K.
15 Music Now
45 The Painter of Signs (ex 24th, Mr. Know-All)
2200 World News
09 The World Today
25 Book Choice
30 Financial News
40 Reflections
45 Sports Round-up
2300 World News
09 Commentary
15 From the Weeklies
30 3rd, What is History?; 10th, The Barefoot Microchip; 17th, Protectionism; 24th, The Overcrowded Airwaves

*Regionalized programs in English for Africa and Asia also broadcast at these times.

SOURCE: BBC World Service, London Calling, February 1984, p. 20.

dozen private broadcasters had sketchy external services in place, among them the CBS and NBC networks. The following year, the Office of War Information took over private stations, creating an official government service, the Voice of America (VOA). At this point, the U.S. external service had only 12 short-wave transmitters, as against Germany's 68, but the BBC made facilities available to the Americans, and as the war progressed, the Allies captured important foreign transmitter sites, such as Tunis, Palermo, Bari, and Luxembourg.*

Radio broadcasting came into its own in World War II, both domestically and externally. External services used psychological warfare techniques. In order to maintain their credibility, however, most official external services avoided out-and-out deception. Although the BBC did send coded messages to resistance forces in Europe, it avoided both the deceptive types of material featured by clandestine stations and explicit incitement. Soviet wartime broadcasting used less restraint, being "more hard-hitting and even reckless in terms of urging people in the occupied areas to risk their lives for the overthrow of the Nazis" (Browne, 1982: 226).

When hostilities ceased, the United States disbanded the Office of War Information, leaving the future of the VOA in doubt. Congress had always been uneasy about authorizing an American propaganda agency, fearing that it could be turned against the American people by a determined political party in power. Even during the war, opponents of Franklin D. Roosevelt accused the VOA of covertly furthering his candidacy for an unprecedented fourth presidential term. In the first postwar years, Congress reluctantly voted funds year by year to continue the VOA as an arm of the State Department. Accustomed to private, one-on-one negotiations, however, the State Department had little interest in public diplomacy via the airwaves. In 1953 Congress finally created a separate entity, the United States Information Agency (USIA), to be responsible for the VOA and other such informational activities.†

Whipsawed by the changing political winds from both Congress and the White House, the VOA has remained a constant storm center. An advisory commission on public diplomacy described the competing viewpoints as they strove for dominance under the Republican administration of Ronald Reagan:

Some observers have expressed concern that the integrity of VOA's news programs has been undercut by more strident programming policies and a series of recent senior management changes which have received national media attention. Others have suggested that VOA's coverage of world events is unbalanced and even at times inimical to the best interests of the United

---

*Winkler, 1978: 78. The VOA still contracts with the BBC for the use of transmitters in England.

†From 1977 to 1982, the agency was called the International Communication Agency, which yielded the initials *ICA*—rather too close for comfort to *CIA*.

States. Still others believe that the Voice should be more hard hitting and aggressively propagandistic as a foreign policy instrument. (USACPD, 1982: 17)[6]

The controversy centers mainly on the issue of the programming policy best adapted to achieving the national goals of the U.S. external service: should it function as a public relations–advertising-propaganda medium or as a legitimate news-information medium? Or, to put it in the more colorful terms often employed, should the VOA paint a warts-and-all portrait of the United States, or should it doctor the picture for foreign consumption? The results of scholarly research on communication effects tend to favor truth saying as the most effective policy, but political expediency favors propaganda.

Most rank and file personnel of the agency believe passionately in the need to maintain credibility by sticking to professional news standards. They can hardly help envying the position of their BBC counterparts, who enjoy the luxury of administrative continuity as well as professional independence. The political appointees who come in with each new U.S. president want to make their mark without delay. But as Hugh Greene, one-time BBC director-general, remarked, "The truth is an unexciting weapon and it often works too slowly for those who, naturally enough, are eager to see quick results" (quoted by Hale, 1975: 73–74).

Radio Moscow. Not having to maintain contact with an overseas colonial empire, the Soviet Union started Radio Moscow with motives different from those of most other pioneer external broadcasters. The Soviets wanted to explain their revolution to both sympathizers and opponents in the West. Accordingly, in their transmissions to Europe, they used English, French, and German as well as Russian from the outset. Sporadic transmissions began as early as 1926, but the regular external service of Radio Moscow started in 1929.

The Soviets also differed in their treatment of broadcasting following World War II. While the BBC, the VOA, and other Allied broadcasters cut back on their external services, Radio Moscow helped East European broadcasters to establish (or reestablish) Communist-oriented external services. Choice of languages and hours devoted to them became a barometer of the USSR's increasingly complex international relations as the leader of the Second World. Wherever it faced imminent conflict, as on the Chinese border, and wherever it gained an overseas ideological foothold, as in Cuba, Moscow's languages and hours immediately expanded accordingly.* Radio Moscow grew into the world's most

---

*Western external services eventually began to react similarly. The VOA, for example, seized on the Solidarity crisis in Poland to expand its Polish-language service, leased time from Brazil's state radio to increase its South American coverage during the Falklands War, and started Pashtu broadcasting, the majority Afghan language, when the Soviets invaded Afghanistan.

massive external service. As Donald Browne put it, "The sheer physical power and linguistic scope of Radio Moscow are awesome to behold: millions of kilowatts of transmitter power broadcast to the globe daily in well over 80 languages" (1982: 224).

One of Radio Moscow's strategies has been to use neglected minority languages, such as Quechua and other aboriginal tongues of South America and the local vernaculars of Africa, to reach neglected, disaffected, and downtrodden minorities. In contrast to Radio Moscow's 80-plus languages, the VOA uses only 40-plus.

In addition to the central Radio Moscow service, the USSR permits some of its constituent republics to originate their own external services. That the central authority risks allowing regional authorities to broadcast externally attests to the high degree of control that the Communist party exerts over all phases of Soviet broadcasting. A third source of external programs, Radio Station Peace and Progress, bills itself as the voice of the people, operating under the auspices of the National Union of Journalists and similar organizations but using Radio Moscow transmitters and frequencies. It appears to serve in part as a method of launching trial balloons. According to one commentator, Peace and Progress programs tend to be "more outspoken and often more bitter than Moscow Radio. If other countries take offense, the Communist Party and the government can hide behind the shield of 'public opinion,' over which they have 'no control' " (Hale, 1975: 17).*

External Programming

A well-designed external service harnesses all four basic generic program types—information, entertainment, education, and persuasion—to national foreign policy goals. As one might expect, external programming places much less emphasis on entertainment than does domestic programming. The VOA, for example, broke its 1983 program content down as follows: information and editorials, 61 percent; features (science, arts, Americana), 27 percent; music, 12 percent. Information and information-related programs form the core of an external service, with other types of programs serving primarily to attract audiences and put them in a receptive frame of mind.

After nearly 20 years of listening to the Voice of Moscow, Donald Browne says he became aware of insistent underlying themes woven into an unvarying "credo":

> One of the strongest elements in this credo is "the workers and peasants are the foundation of the Soviet Union and of any true socialist state." . . .

---

*In comparing U.S. external broadcasting strength with that of the Soviets, one must consider each side's ancillary services. Radio Liberty, Radio Free Europe, and other U.S.-supported services should be added to the VOA's statistics to make a valid comparison (Section 11.3).

> *Other themes are nearly as prominent . . . the importance of young people and women in Soviet society; the economic strength of the USSR; the nation's desire for peace but readiness and ability to defend itself . . . the importance, popularity, and accessibility of culture in the Soviet Union; the high esteem in which the Soviet Union is held by foreign visitors and observers; the inevitable triumph of world Communism, hopefully through peaceful means; the aggressive intentions but increasing weakness (as revealed by strikes, inflation, rising unemployment, etc.) of the capitalist nations. No newscast or feature fails to work in at least some of these themes. (Browne, 1982: 233)*

Not all external services use the public diplomacy of the airwaves in such a disciplined and systematic way. In fact, some of the smaller Third World services seem to play no ascertainable diplomatic role. Confined mainly to routine news reporting, self-serving commentary, and a smattering of cultural features, their main function seems to be to assert that the originating country exists as a nation. External broadcasting may symbolize nationhood without doing much to further foreign policy objectives.

Some external broadcasting initiatives arise primarily to support the personal ambitions of charismatic politicians. Thus Egypt's elaborate external services (see Table 11.1) came into being as an expression of President Gamal Abdel Nasser's ambition to become the leader of both the Arab and African worlds. When Nasser took power after the overthrow of the British-supported King Farouk in 1952, Egypt had no external service and only minimal domestic services. Sensing the potentialities of broadcasting as a personal vehicle, Nasser almost immediately began expanding Egyptian broadcasting facilities, both internal and external. Within a few years, he increased total power by a factor of seven, to a cumulative power of over half a million watts. He created the Voice of the Arabs as a vehicle for pan-Arab agitation throughout the Middle East and North Africa:

> *Nasser himself set the style for the Voice of the Arabs. He had a talent for using the Arabic language effectively and he helped popularize the neoclassical Arabic which is widely used in the mass media. . . . The result was an Arabic which not only could be understood by literate and illiterate alike in most of the Arab World, but which gave the people "an unprecedented kinship with the new leadership." (Boyd, 1975: 646)*

Nasser also mounted special external programs aimed at Tropical Africa, using (like the Soviets) numerous vernacular languages not ordinarily heard on the airwaves.[7]

In peacetime, the more responsible external services refrain from inciting violence and take care not to mislead listeners into expecting the originating country to back up actual rebellion. Nasser, however, characteristically allowed his rambunctious external broadcasts to go overboard:

> *Most of Cairo's broadcasts urged violent solutions: revolution and assassination. Often a voice beamed at one country would be contradicting a*

voice speaking at the same moment to another country. . . . On all wave lengths Englishmen and Frenchmen were either imperialists, bloodsuckers, or colonialism's stooges. . . . Nasser's secret Voice of Free Africa referred to Americans in general as "pythons, white dogs, and pigs." (St. John, 1960: 285)

Egypt's immoderation eventually caused its external services to lose credibility. During the 1967 Israeli War, the Voice of the Arabs poured out extravagant claims of glorious Egyptian victories. Disclosure of Nasser's humiliating defeat made a laughing-stock of his radio services. This experience had such a sobering effect that since then Egyptian external services have been less extreme.[8]

Feedback Stimulation. Well-designed external services use apolitical entertainment, cultural, and educational features to attract listeners and to create a favorable environment for reception of their more politically charged offerings. It is standard practice to stimulate two-way communication by motivating listener mail. Features designed to obtain such feedback include contests, music-request programs, DX clubs, language teaching, new product announcements, and even phone-in talk programs.

The larger external services routinely offer prizes for essays, answers to questions, and even for just asking questions. Prizes might consist of books, radio receivers, or trips to the country of the program's origin. Such contests cultivate good will, focus attention on favorable aspects of the broadcasting country, provide listener satisfaction, and serve the needs of audience research.

Music-request programs represent a popular listener feedback format widely used by external as well as domestic services. All types of music are featured in such programs, from classical to the top pop tunes. They permit mentioning many names on the air, a sure-fire way of pleasing listeners.

A score of external services broadcast DX programs, aimed at broadcast enthusiasts who make a hobby of picking up distant stations and securing written confirmation of their feats of long-distance reception.[9] Major DX clubs broadcast in several languages. Radio Nederland, for example, transmits a DX program in Arabic, English, Portuguese, and Spanish. Some programs provide how-to-do-it instruction to assist DXers in building antennas and components and in learning about radio propagation. External broadcasters find DX listeners especially useful as evidence of receivability in widely scattered areas. Some DXers become so expert on short-wave propagation and reception that they find employment in intelligence and external broadcasting work.

An external service kills several birds with one stone when it offers courses teaching its own language. Language teaching establishes feedback, promotes the culture of the originating country, and provides a useful service to listeners. External services offering language lessons usually provide students with books and tapes. The most highly developed language teaching comes from the BBC, whose *English by Radio and Television* series finds a ready market worldwide, not only because of the popularity of English but also because of the quality of the language teaching. The BBC External Services broadcasts nearly 40 hours per week from these series. "It is remarkable and astonishing," wrote Burton Paulu, "that many East European countries broadcast *English by Television*, since the programmes expound British concepts while teaching the language" (1981: 389). The BBC also sells teaching programs on tape to scores of countries for local broadcast on both radio and television domestic facilities, and it even offers a three-week summer school in England for students of its broadcast language courses.

In one sense, all external broadcasting can be construed as attempting to sell ideas. More literal sales programs designed to encourage enquiries about new products of originating countries also occur. Several major broadcasters, including the BBC, the VOA, and Japan, try to interest potential foreign buyers in newly developed products. Programs designed to promote enquiries about tourism fall in somewhat the same category of feedback programs.

A recently developed type of feedback program is the international telephone call-in show. Radio Nederland initiated *Short-Wave Feedback*, a weekly dial-direct call-in feature, in mid-1982. Listeners from all over the world responded, calling at their own expense to express their views about Dutch programming and to ask questions. Callers had 90 seconds in which to record a statement for the program.[10] More politically oriented was a British call-in program initiated later in 1982. Callers could either write or call in before a scheduled prominent speaker appeared on the program. The BBC telephones the correspondent at its own expense while the show is on the air. Prime Minister Margaret Thatcher was the first national leader in the world to participate in such an international exchange. She had no prior warning as to the nature of the questions she would have to field extemporaneously. Questions came from Barbados (about the U.S. invasion of Grenada), from Nicaragua (about possible U.S. invasion of that country), from the Falkland Islands (about the future of that disputed territory), and from Hong Kong (about the future of *that* disputed territory).[11]

The telephone call-in show represents a logical development from a traditional external service feedback feature, the "mailbag" program. This format, very widely employed on external services, is simply a question-and-answer show, giving an opportunity to inform and persuade listeners in a relatively painless and seemingly unprejudiced way. Radio Moscow, for example, has a lively and entertaining version, *Moscow Mailbag*. Armenian announcer Joe Adamov, one of five English translators on Radio Moscow, has won international recognition for his perfectly idiomatic English and his informal answers on this program.[12] Despite Adamov's apparent informality, the USSR calculates its broadcast responses with care; one can hardly imagine it using as spontaneous a call-in show as the BBC's. Thus the very formats of external broadcasting can make their own political commentary by implication.*

Local Placement

An alternative method of external broadcasting relies on "placement" of programs on a host country's own domestic broadcasting system. This in fact is the only way that external services can deliver television programs to distant targets.

The BBC has been particularly successful in promoting the use of its programs in recorded form by other countries. More than 80 countries use programs from its Transcription Service. More than 50 countries take certain BBC radio programs directly off the air, rebroadcasting them live. A different tack has been taken by the U.S. Information Agency, parent body of the VOA. Capitalizing on new technological resources, USIA's Television and Film Service makes newsworthy materials available to foreign broadcasters to use in their own news programs. USIA's weekly Satellite File goes from the agency's Washington studios to commercial international news services for distribution to stations in 80 countries. The file also goes by hand to foreign news correspondents stationed in Washington.

In 1983 USIA's Television and Film Service also set up satellite teleconferencing links with two-way audio and one-way video feeds between Washington and U.S. embassies overseas. Newsworthy figures in Washington make themselves available for television interviews via satellite with foreign officials and media people. USIA inaugurated this service, which it called Euronet, with a program explaining the U.S. rationale for the invasion of Grenada. An American official and the prime ministers of two other Caribbean islands responded to questions from foreign journalists at five U.S. embassies in Europe. The European Broadcasting Union's full network of 27 countries carried a Euronet program featuring live television interviews by the U.S. president and West Germany's chancellor with Spacelab astronauts in orbit in December 1983. USIA planned to expand Euronet worldwide.[13]

External Audience Research

Researchers cannot normally gain direct access to the external target areas in which they have the greatest interest. Even areas that can be entered for research purposes often pose difficult problems, as noted in the discussion of Third World research (see Section 10.3). Nevertheless,

---

*The relative spontaneity and informality of the phone-in talk show reflect a growing tendency among leading external services to cultivate a relaxed entertainment style. This trend may have been stimulated by the success of colorful DJ personalities and pop music formats featured by the international commercial stations discussed in Section 11.5.

to the extent possible, the leading Western transborder services do conduct formal survey research. They usually contract such investigations out to local or regional commercial research organizations.

In 1983 the VOA summarized the cumulative results of such surveys in 70 countries. In 37 percent of the countries, the BBC had the largest audience, while the VOA led in 23 percent. No other external service ranked as the favorite in more than 2 or 3 countries, and none of these were the services of Communist countries.

Although researchers regard audience mail as having only limited value, external researchers necessarily rely heavily upon it. As previously noted, they often stimulate such feedback by running competitions. Of course, little or no mail response can be expected from closed societies. The BBC and Australia's external services received only a trickle of letters from China during the Cultural Revolution; the moment that China restored relations with the West, however, letters poured in by the thousands. In total, the BBC receives over 300,000 pieces of mail per year, the VOA somewhat less. The latter has been criticized for lacking a coordinated system for handling listener mail efficiently.[14]

Interviews with travelers and refugees provide a third body of information on the effects of external services. Like listener mail, this source has the defect of being unrepresentative of the audience as a whole.*

Despite its obvious importance, research seldom has high priority in the administration of external services. After many interviews with researchers, Donald Browne concluded, "Strong support for audience research from top administrators has been very rare, except for the BBC" (1982: 334–335). An advisory commission faulted the USIA (which conducts research for the VOA) for the paucity of its research activities:

> The Commission notes that the [USIA] Office of Research conducts surveys of VOA listeners in various foreign countries to help determine both audience size and preferences. It has undertaken a study to help determine whether or not medium-wave broadcasts in English to Western Europe would be justified. It also has made studies of communication/media habits in a few key countries that should be of considerable value in developing future program plans. . . . This is all highly useful and commendable, but more should be done. Regrettably, the shortage of staff and funds limits the Agency's research activities. (USACPD, 1982: 34)

Monitoring

One type of audience that research organizations have no need to measure is the listeners who work for the monitoring services operated by external broadcasters. Monitors record and translate programs off the

---

*Browne mentions several other, less routine sources of data: listener panels, content analyses, comprehension studies, analyses of target countries' media reactions to foreign broadcasts, and computer simulation (1982: 319–330).

air with a view to finding out what other countries are saying, both to their own citizens and to external audiences. Whenever a coup occurs in some distant part of the world, radio sources usually supply the first and only news of the event. News organs often rely on official monitoring services to supply this type of information.

> *Though the speed with which news can be reported is a spectacular asset of a monitoring service, its daily round is no less important. The output of all radio channels, domestic and international, when intelligently selected, provides one of the most reliable and complete pictures of the events and policies of a foreign country. In wartime, monitoring reports provide Intelligence services with basic information for assessing an enemy's future moves. It was apparent from this source alone that Germany planned to invade the Soviet Union in the summer of 1942, as there was a growing tendency to renounce the propaganda truce agreed to in the signing of the Nazi-Soviet Pact. (Hale, 1975: 161)*

The United States and Britain collaborate in the endless task of monitoring the world's broadcast output. To monitor everything, of course, would be physically and financially impractical. Monitoring services listen selectively, concentrating on news, commentaries, and editorials. A unit of the Central Intelligence Agency, the Foreign Broadcasting Information Service (FBIS), has the responsibility on the U.S. side; the British rely on the BBC External Services, which houses its monitoring operation in a country estate 40 miles from London. According to the BBC, neither unit would be complete without the other.[15] Between them, CIA and BBC monitors pick up broadcasts from 120 countries in 50 languages. The FBIS publishes world lists of stations on the air as well as monitoring data. The BBC External Services sells subscriptions to its daily *Summary of World Broadcasts* and several other reports, including a teleprinter news file. Subscribers include embassies, government departments, research organizations, and news media. Indeed, when a major international news story is breaking, news media do not always wait for BBC publications but go directly to the monitoring center. For example, as the Iranian hostage crisis reached its climax, "the cameramen of international television companies seemed at times to camp in the Listening Room, filming monitors with their ears glued to Tehran Radio" (*BBC 1982 Annual Report*, 1981: 62).

As an example of monitoring report content, the BBC *Summary of World Broadcasts* carried a long USSR report on the previously described USIA Euronet. Typical of Soviet-style copy, it said, in part:

> *Using modern space communications satellites, the USIA has set itself the aim of pouring by television onto the West European public heaps of slander about the policy of the USSR and lies about the supposed "love of peace" of the Reagan administration; it is far from accidental that the Washington specialists in the field of ideological sabotage chose as the targets for this "brainwashing" above all the countries of Western Europe which the USA is now "endowing" with lethal first-strike nuclear weapons. . . .*

"Euronet," as conceived by the organizers of "psychological warfare" in Washington, is meant, ultimately, to fulfill the functions that are carried out on the air by the Voice of America—one of Washington's main mouthpieces for circulating the anti-Soviet forgeries concocted by the CIA and the Pentagon. (BBC Monitoring Service, 23 Jan. 1984.)

Knowing that monitored information comes forcibly to the attention of a wide spectrum of significant people, some governments deliberately plant stories in their broadcasting services to bring specific matters to the attention of foreign governments. Intelligence and news organizations must, of course, treat monitored reports warily because they may consist of disinformation rather than genuine information.

Jamming

Indirect evidence of the perceived effectiveness of external services comes from the fact that the Soviets and their allies spend huge sums in trying to prevent their citizens from hearing certain broadcasts from the West. This is done primarily by *jamming*—the transmission of interfering signals making it difficult if not impossible to understand an incoming program. It takes three or four jamming transmitters to counteract a single incoming transmission, and even then jamming is only partially effective. Nevertheless, the Soviet Union and its allies consider jamming a worthwhile investment.

Jammers usually ignore broadcasts in the language of the transmitting country, objecting primarily to broadcasts in the language (or languages) of their own country (Israel's broadcasts in Hebrew to the Soviet Union are one exception). Jammers argue that broadcasts in their own language represent intrusion upon their internal affairs, in violation of the Helsinki Agreement.

The unrest in Poland during the Solidarity crisis stimulated the West to increase its broadcasts in Polish and the Soviets to increase their efforts at jamming, which tend to rise and fall with the political temperature of events:

The duel in the airwaves attained unprecedented intensity after the military takeover in Poland in December 1981. . . .

Western radio was subjected to intense jamming. Transmitters in the Soviet Union, Czechoslovakia, East Germany and later Bulgaria joined in a combined effort to interfere with the Polish language broadcasts of Radio Free Europe, the Voice of America and the British Broadcasting Corporation. So fierce was the jamming that nearly half the popular 16-, 19-, and 25-meter shortwave bands were rendered useless in prime evening hours, with meaningless noise drowning out incoming signals. . . .

The estimated cost of the jamming to the Soviet Union exceeds the combined budgets of Radio Free Europe/Radio Liberty and the Voice of America. (BIB, 1983: 1, 3)

Although the Communists do most of the jamming, nearly all major broadcasters have resorted to it at one time or another. Despite having signed ITU agreements to refrain from jamming, most countries seem to feel that if sufficiently provoked, they have the right to violate such agreements. Some examples follow:

- Britain, West Germany, and Norway jammed pirate stations in the North Sea.
- France jammed the Voice of Free Algeria during the Algerian war of independence. More recently, the French domestic broadcasting authority jammed domestic pirate stations.
- During the 1960s, Rhodesia jammed a British station set up in nearby Botswana to oppose the Rhodesian unilateral declaration of independence from Britain.
- Egypt has frequently jammed rival stations in the Middle East.
- Iran, following the takeover by the Khomeini forces, jammed the VOA, the BBC, West Germany, Iraq, Saudi Arabia, and several opposition clandestine transmitters.
- During the Falklands War, Argentina jammed the BBC Latin American service and a special Ascension Island service that the British armed forces aimed at Argentine troops on the Falklands.
- Cuba has jammed Spanish-language U.S. domestic stations that can be heard on the island.

Logically, jamming seems to amount to an admission either that one's own arguments are too weak to withstand the challenge of open debate or that one's own citizens cannot be trusted to make up their own minds. Aside from the logical and legal objections to jamming, it tends to be destructive in other ways. Innocent bystanders usually suffer, both because jamming signals spread to adjacent channels and because the jammee usually responds by using excessive power and an excessive number of frequencies in attempting to overcome the interference. Thus jamming both directly and indirectly exacerbates the overcrowding and degradation of HF broadcasting.

As an alternative to jamming, nations have occasionally tried persuasion or punishment to prevent their citizens from tuning to foreign stations. At one time, East German school officials asked children to sign pledges to ignore West German stations. But repressive measures never seem to work for long. The principle of the abhorrent vacuum (see Section 4.1) intervenes. Some countries have tried pretuned, or fixed-frequency, receivers, as did the Nazis during World War II with their mass-produced People's Receiver. This stratagem also breaks down because of the ease with which tuning can be altered. Governments also try to control incoming signals by offering wired-radio services at a low price, thus discouraging the purchase of tunable receivers.*

Countries that rely on jamming view with alarm the prospect of direct-broadcast satellites. Incoming DBS signals would be immune to conventional types of jamming because satellites use much higher frequencies than terrestrial transmitters. Anticipating this possibility, the USSR and its supporters have sought through international bodies such as the United Nations and the ITU to outlaw external broadcasting by satellite except with permission of the target countries.

11 ▪ 3 SURROGATE DOMESTIC SERVICES

Some officially sponsored transborder stations differ from normal external services by assuming the role of surrogate domestic services in target countries. On the assumption that actual domestic broadcasting conceals the truth from its own audiences, a foreign surrogate service offers substitute, uncensored home news and information. Naturally, the targets of surrogate services question their objectivity, seeing them as an unwarranted interference in the affairs of foreign countries.

RFE and RL

The United States operates the best-known services in this category, Radio Free Europe (RFE) and Radio Liberty (RL). RFE aims at audiences in the USSR's buffer states (Czechoslovakia, Bulgaria, Hungary, Poland, and Romania), while RL aims at audiences in the USSR itself. A presidential study commission described them as "unique in the entire spectrum of international broadcasting." According to the commission, RFE and RL

> differ substantially from the official broadcasts of the United States and Western European nations. They operate essentially as a free press does in the United States. They too bring world news and interpretation into the Soviet sphere, but they devote a substantial portion of their broadcasts to news and essential background information about internal developments in and among the communist states. They correct misinformation or partial information offered by the internal mass media of the Soviet Union and Eastern European countries. (PSCIRB, 1973: 2)

To play the surrogate role, RFE and RL maintain a huge research library on Eastern Europe and the USSR—a massive collection of newspapers, magazines, radio monitoring reports, and samizdat.† This

---

*Note also the allegation that South Africa resorted to FM in part to discourage foreign listening by black Africans (Section 8.2).

†Samizdat, mentioned in Section 8.5, are clandestinely circulated writings and recordings of such items as excerpts from censored books and letters or state-

collection enables writers, reporters, and commentators to act as though they worked within the target country itself. They have a field day whenever the Communist countries withhold news from their own people, who then turn to external sources such as RFE/RL to find out what is going on. RFE/RL's bird's-eye perspective of Eastern Europe as a whole enables the stations to exploit "cross-reporting"—the highlighting of embarrassing inconsistencies in conditions, regulations, and practices between one Communist country and another.

Policy guidelines forbid RFE/RL to use "material which could be reasonably construed as incitement to revolt or support for illegal and violent actions" and "programming that could be construed as encouraging defections" (BIB, 1983: 34). These rules represent a change from the original orientation of the stations, which once quite blatantly urged violent resistance to Communist rule.

The reason for their original subversive style did not emerge publicly for several decades. From their founding soon after World War II to 1967, RFE/RL masqueraded as privately funded operations supported by public donations from freedom-loving Americans. Each year, the Advertising Council designed a promotional campaign to collect money for them. In 1966 news stories revealed that the funding actually came from the Central Intelligence Agency.* During the public debate that followed, some members of Congress argued that the RFE/RL operations were counterproductive, merely exacerbating the Cold War without compensating gains for the West.

In the end, however, Congress decided to fund the services directly, placing them under a Washington-based nonprofit corporation, the Board for International Broadcasting (BIB). The USSR continues to regard the operations as subversive and devotes a great deal of money and effort to jamming them. When Burton Paulu asked Soviet radio officials what they thought of RL, they characterized it as "irresponsible and dishonest."†

The BIB, consisting of nine board members appointed by the president with consent of the Senate, supervises the two services, which have the legal status of a nonprofit corporation. Congress allotted more than $90 million to their operation in 1982 (compared to the VOA

---

ments of protest by suppressed political, ethnic, and religious groups. Nowadays, such materials also appear in recorded form (*magizdat*).

*Conceivably, the CIA itself could have leaked the story (though it never had been a well-kept secret). According to a former CIA agent, agency studies had repeatedly recommended phasing out CIA support, but each time "a few old-timers in the CIA, whose connection with the stations went back to their beginnings, would come up with new and dubious reasons why the radios should be continued" (Marchetti & Marks, 1974: 169).

†Paulu, 1974: 214. The chairman of the BIB suggested at one point that the board would consider giving Communist officials an opportunity to use RFE/RL facilities to reply to "specific complaints which have merit" (BIB, 1978: 3–4).

1982–83 projected budget of $130 million). The stations have operational headquarters in Munich, West Germany, with transmitters not only in Germany but also in Portugal and Spain (locations chosen to obtain suitable sky-wave skip-distance). They use 46 transmitters broadcasting on 80 frequencies.

RFE/RL's 21 languages include some of the regional languages of the Soviet Union, such as Uzbek and Tatar. In order to overcome jamming and the uncertainties of HF propagation, the services build a great deal of redundancy into their schedules. For example, in 1982 the Russian service stayed on the air 24 hours per day but produced only a little more than 6 hours of new programs each day. Strong emphasis is given to news and news-related material, with three quarters of all programming focused on Communist and East-West affairs.

RIAS Berlin

Radio in the American Sector of Berlin (RIAS) has somewhat the same relationship to East Germany that Radio Liberty has to the USSR. In fact, RIAS set the pattern for the surrogate type of operation. A significant difference, however, is that RIAS broadcasts from *within* its target area. Berlin lies inside East Germany, giving stations in West Berlin easy access to surrounding East German audiences. Even short-range FM radio can serve RIAS purposes, though it also uses powerful short- and medium-wave transmitters.

Also unusual is the fact that although the U.S. Information Agency helps fund RIAS, West Germans administer and operate the service. With the easing of relationships between the two Germanies and the increase in the number of externally originated services available to East Germans, RIAS has lost some of its reason for existence. According to Donald Browne, it nevertheless persists because it "stands as a symbolic guarantee of U.S. presence in West Berlin and U.S. interest in East Germany, and its reduction or abolition would doubtless touch off speculation as to U.S. motives" (1982: 135).

Deutschlandfunk

In West Germany, two different external services have evolved, *Deutsche Welle* (German Wave) and *Deutschlandfunk* (Germany Radio). The former plays the role of a conventional external service, broadcasting in many languages and using overseas relay stations. *Deutschlandfunk* broadcasts only in German and other European languages. It bills its German-language programs as a "home" service, yet it appears to function at least partly as a surrogate service aimed at East Germany. It has four very powerful transmitters, two of them on long waves, each having 500 kw. of power. As Browne puts it, "There is a great deal about the two-station system that does not seem terribly rational."[16]

Radio Martí

Radio Martí, a 1984 addition to the U.S. roster of surrogate services, aims programs at Cuba. Radio Martí was a hotly debated innovation of a Republican administration, reflecting its aggressive external broadcasting policies. Originally proposed as an independent service with its own board along the lines of the BIB, Radio Martí was finally authorized by Congress as a special 14-hours-per-day Cuban service within the VOA. However, it remained independent of normal VOA supervision, with its own presidential advisory board. Its medium-wave transmitter on Marathon, an island in the Florida Keys, had previously carried regular VOA programs in Spanish. Radio Martí was due to start broadcasting late in 1984.

The U.S. Advisory Commission on Public Diplomacy deplored the awkward grafting of this surrogate service onto the VOA:

> As the official voice of the U.S. government, VOA's mission historically has differed significantly from the surrogate broadcasting activities of Radio Free Europe and Radio Liberty and the mission for Radio Martí envisaged by President Reagan. Placing Radio Martí within VOA can cast doubt on VOA's most important and fragile asset—its credibility. (USACPD, 1983: 36)

In theory, Radio Martí compensates for the biases and omissions of Cuban domestic news sources. However, critics of the scheme pointed out that Cuba already could receive ample corrective news from the Voice of America, from other official external services, and even from U.S. domestic stations broadcasting in Spanish from south Florida. Tiny Cuba could not possibly furnish sufficient material to mount a full-scale surrogate news service such as the vast territories of Eastern Europe and the USSR make possible for RFE/RL. Critics anticipated that Radio Martí would end up transmitting the same kind of entertainment formerly supplied by the VOA, plus ineffectual propaganda. John S. Nichols, an academic specialist on Cuban media, testified to a congressional committee that he suspected that

> the true mission of Radio Martí has nothing to do with communicating alternative ideas and information to the Cuban people. In my view, the true purpose of Radio Martí is political harassment, and the true audience is President Castro and the Cuban government leadership. . . .
>
> If the Cuban government responds with jamming of foreign radio, the effect of Radio Martí will be to reduce, not increase, the range of ideas and information available to the Cuban people. Second, if the Cubans do not jam, Radio Martí might further discredit the information content of VOA and Miami radio to which many Cubans already listen. (USHR, 1982: 214–215)*

---

*See also Nichols, 1984. Cuban listeners reaped an unanticipated benefit when Castro improved Cuba's domestic services in anticipation of Radio Martí competition (Treaster, 1984).

11 ▪ 4 UNOFFICIAL POLITICAL SERVICES

In addition to official external services as defined in the previous two sections, certain unofficial political services are aimed at the destabilization of existing governments. One group consists of *clandestine* services, often purporting to come from within the target country but actually originating elsewhere. I have included under the clandestine heading some that do originate within the target country, because they function much as they would if hidden in a neighboring country.* A second group of politically motivated services obtains the *loan* of official facilities from sympathetic governments, usually gratis but sometimes on a rental basis.

Clandestine Stations

Clandestine stations have been defined as those that "are not the mouthpieces of governments in power and which play some kind of subversive role by beaming propaganda at a particular localized area for tactical reasons."† In a study of clandestine stations operating during 1981, Soley identified 42 stations aimed at 20 countries.‡ The largest number targeted Iran (8 stations), followed by Cuba (7 stations). Clandestines usually operate only intermittently and on short schedules. They come and go with the changing political fortunes of unstable countries. However, Radio Free Spain, a clandestine service originating in the USSR, ran 80 hours per week for more than three decades. It finally closed down in 1977 after the death of Spain's dictator and the restoration of free elections.

In addition to their role in encouraging resistance against established governments, clandestines, like open external services, also count on being picked up and distributed by official monitoring services, enabling them to bring their causes to the attention of other governments and the press. News media frequently report on statements picked up from clandestine broadcasts.

A classic instance of clandestine broadcasting was the CIA's

---

*The clandestine underground radio operated intermittently by Solidarity in Poland, for example, differed from the classic transborder clandestine. Its primary function seems to have been to enable rapid communication among Solidarity members so that they could act in concert in staging demonstrations or strikes.

†Hale, 1975: 103. *Pirate* stations, though sometimes operated from secret locations, are not considered clandestines because they are not devoted primarily to political propaganda.

‡Soley, 1983. The author based his tabulation on the CIA's Foreign Broadcasting Information Service reports and *FRENDX*, a publication of the North American Shortwave Association, a DX society. *WRTH* does not list clandestine stations, saying "we would never give them a status equal to the official stations by listing them" (1980: 576).

successful destabilization of a left-wing government in Guatemala in the 1950s. The CIA mounted a small, rag-tag invasion force that could not possibly have defeated the Guatemalan forces in open battle. To demoralize the government, the CIA used a clandestine station, the Voice of Liberation, located outside the country but pretending to be operated by patriots within Guatemala.

> The station claimed to be located not too far from Guatemala City. As proof, it would simulate a raid by government officials and return to the air the next day from a fictitious new location. . . . The Voice of Liberation sounded so authentic that many foreign correspondents accepted it as the most accurate source of information. (Immerman, 1982: 164)

The CIA hired private pilots to make showy but not really effective bombing raids. During the so-called raids, the CIA jammed Guatemala's own radio stations, giving the Voice of Liberation free rein to describe devastating but imaginary effects. A defecting Guatemalan pilot recorded an appeal for others to defect. When the Guatemalan president heard the appeal on the clandestine station, he grounded all his planes for fear of further defections. The government might have survived had it not been for the devastating psychological effects of the Voice of Liberation broadcasts.[17]

Clandestines in World War II. Experts on clandestine operations honed their skills during World War II, which afforded the first opportunity for the all-out use of "black" propaganda on the airwaves. More than 60 clandestine stations operated during 1939–1945.

> In the hot-war situation, all kinds of nefarious radio operations got under way, including such hopeful devices as a station covertly sponsored by the Nazis and purporting to be the voice of the "Christian Peace Movement," whose message was to turn the enemy off "ungodly" war and sue for peace. As the war went on, phoney Nazi freedom stations proliferated, from Subhar Chandra Bose's Free India Radio to Radio Mexican and an "Iowan" station called Radio Debunk. (Hale, 1975: 106–107)

American broadcasting executive William Paley, a psychological warfare colonel during World War II, writes of a famous operative in his autobiography:

> One of the best of our black operations was a German radio station—that is, a "German" station broadcasting supposedly in Germany when in fact the entire operation was run by Sefton Delmer, a bearded British news correspondent, from a village outside London. Delmer worked in a closed compound. From the moment one entered the gate, only German could be spoken there. Everything was aimed at creating the illusion that this was a part of Germany. (Paley, 1979: 157)[18]

One Allied ploy was to play back Hitler's promises from off-the-air recordings, juxtaposing them with news of their failure to materialize. On the Soviets' side, a "Comrade Ivan" would lie in wait on the frequency of the main German domestic station, and during pauses in the reading of the German news, he would interject disruptive comments. Thus if the newsreader said, "The victorious German army marches on . . . ," Ivan would add, ". . . to their graves."[19]

One of the most effective of the Allied clandestines, Operation Annie, purported to be an underground station within Germany, run by loyal Germans worried that their compatriots were not getting a true picture of the war. Actually located within Allied-controlled territory, "Annie" broadcast authentic news and gradually built up the image of a reliable source of information about the situation of the German forces— an investment against the day when its credibility could be used against the Germans. The opportunity came at last:

> German troops in the Eifel Mountains were surrounded by Allied forces but still had safe areas for retreat. "Annie," with a reputation for truthfulness firmly established, labeled other areas as safe and led the Germans into an Allied ambush. As Germany's defeat grew near, the propagandists decided that the station had served its purpose. A staged scuffle, broadcast over the air, left "Annie" in ruins. (Winkler, 1978: 128)

Postwar Clandestines. In the immediate postwar era, clandestines virtually disappeared from the airwaves except for the few long-lived stations such as the previously mentioned Radio Free Spain. But the Cold War and colonial liberation movements brought clandestines once more to the fore. It was estimated during the 1970s that clandestine transmissions accounted for 5 to 6 percent of all transborder broadcasting.[20] Some examples follow:

- Among the many anti-Khomeini stations was one set up by the CIA in Egypt, the Free Voice of Iran, during the hostage crisis and prior to Anwar Sadat's assassination.[21]

- French and Italian intellectuals advertised in 1981 for funds to help support Radio Free Afghanistan, a mobile clandestine radio operation opposing the Soviet occupation of Afghanistan.

- During the 1970s, when Thailand imposed strict censorship on radio news, the Voice of Free Thailand from China "sometimes seemed to know more about what was happening in Bangkok than did Radio Thailand itself" (Katz & Wedell, 1977: 174).

- Clandestine radio played an important role in the Sandinista revolt against the Somoza regime in Nicaragua. After the Sandinistas took over, they put the original Radio Sandino transmitter on display in the Museum of the Revolution in the capital.*

---

*Wood, 1983: 604. Radio amateurs within the country supplemented Radio Sandino with their own network, over which they reported government troop movements (p. 605).

- The Sandinistas followed a pattern set by Fidel Castro in Cuba, whose Radio Rebelde, though located within the island and therefore not literally a transborder station, functioned in the manner of a clandestine. The original impetus for using radio came from a key Castro follower, Ché Guevara:

It was set up in the safe location of Fidel's military headquarters at La Plata. On February 24, 1958, preceded by the tune of the "Invaders' Hymn," Radio Rebelde officially went on the air. It was soon powerful enough to broadcast overseas, as well as around the island. The content of the programs was mainly about the war. When other fronts were opened up, each had its own local radio receivers and transmitters. Radio Rebelde proved highly effective in circumventing Batista's press censorship. Fidel first polished his oratorical gifts from the "Territory of Free Cuba in the Sierra Maestra." (Matthews, 1975: 100).

More recently, Cuba has been the target of clandestine broadcasts from various sources, including Miami, Florida. There an anti-Castro station, *Voz de Alpha 66,* operated for some time in defiance of U.S. law against clandestine broadcasting from U.S. soil. In 1982 the FCC sent Alpha 66, a militant anti-Communist group of Cuban exiles, notice of a fine of $750. The station nevertheless continued on the air, possibly from some point outside the United States.*

- Radio Venceremos served the guerrillas of El Salvador. A newswriter pointed out how the rebel station furnished far more interesting copy for the news media than the "dry army press releases listing tallies of dead 'subversives' ":

"We have established contact with our mobile unit in Usulutan," a Venceremos radio announcer excitedly tells listeners in a March 31 broadcast. "Go ahead Usulutan," he shouts into the microphone.

"This mobile unit of Radio Venceremos is right now somewhere in Usulutan," begins a live relay. "This city has been held by [guerrilla] forces for the past six days." (Brooke, 1982)

There followed a vivid account of the clash between guerrilla and government troops.

Borrowed Facilities

Leaders of dissident movements often borrow facilities from neighboring official external services. Borrowing transmitter time avoids the expense and hazards of clandestine station operation, assuring greater

---

*Soley, 1983: 249. An earlier anti-Castro station had been set up by the CIA on the Swan Islands, off the coast of Honduras, to support the Bay of Pigs invasion by Cuban exiles in 1960. Although the CIA-supported attack on Cuba ended in fiasco, Swan broadcast upbeat reports of a nonexistent popular arising against

power and better facilities than clandestine stations normally have. A pattern for this kind of transborder broadcasting originated during World War II, when the BBC External Services made facilities available to the Free French and other governments in exile. Radio Moscow furnished similar services for exiles from various Socialist and Communist regimes.

In the postwar years, Egypt's Nasser welcomed representatives of African liberation movements to Cairo, allowing them to use his extensive external facilities to broadcast back to their homelands.[22] In both Africa and the Middle East, the Palestine Liberation Organization (PLO) has been particularly successful in borrowing facilities regularly from African as well as Arab nations. Such broadcasts, normally lasting only 15 or 30 minutes, are usually too ephemeral to have more than symbolic value, but symbolism is precisely the role of much transborder broadcasting.

11 ▪ 5   TRANSBORDER COMMERCIAL STATIONS

A class of high-powered, commercially motivated stations exists that target programs toward foreign markets. Such stations usually find advertisers and audiences with ease, furnishing programs not available, or available only in limited amounts, on domestic services within the target countries—pop music, advertising, and (sometimes) unbiased news reporting. Three classes of such commercial operations can be distinguished: (1) legally constituted stations sited on or near the borders of target countries (known as *peripherals*); (2) legal stations located at greater distances from their targets and therefore usually dependent on short-wave transmission; and (3) pirate stations, operating without benefit of license from locations outside the territorial waters of target countries.

Peripherals

The French originated the term *stations périphériques*. It refers to a group of stations under the total or partial control of SOFIRAD (*Société Financière de Radiodiffusion*), a holding company owned by the French government. A somewhat shadowy corporate octopus, SOFIRAD has links with dozens of media-related companies.[23] The French government wanted to profit by, and have some say-so regarding, foreign stations that lured a substantial percentage of the national audience away from official French broadcasting services.

Some examples of peripheral stations follow.

Castro (Nichols, 1984: 285).   In 1984, President Ronald Reagan initially appointed a one-time Radio Swan commentator to head the Radio Martí board (Treaster, 1984).

LUXEMBOURG

Luxembourg. A pioneer among the peripherals whose original company dates back to 1929, RTL (Radio-Télé-Luxembourg) has a strategic transmitter location at a point where the borders of Belgium, France, and West Germany intersect. The company has a commercial franchise from the Grand Duchy, which obliges RTL to observe strict neutrality in its treatment of news. Its 2,000-kw. long-wave radio transmitter and powerful medium- and short-wave transmitters enable it to reach not only its immediate neighbors but also England,* Holland, Italy, and even Czechoslovakia and Hungary. RTL has three powerful television transmitters, using both PAL and SECAM color in order to reach its national audiences. RTL maintains sales offices in Brussels, London, and Paris. Most of RTL's programs, however, originate from its Paris studios. France was its principal target, but in 1984 it also began a German service aimed at the Saar. The ITU, at its 1977 DBS conference (see Section 2.5), assigned Luxembourg a satellite channel, and RTL immediately began laying plans to augment its transborder services by means of a DBS satellite, LUXSAT. The neighboring countries drew the line at becoming targets of peripheral satellite services, however, and sought to block RTL's satellite plans.

Monaco. A tiny principality near the border between France and Italy on the Mediterranean, Monaco is known for its Monte Carlo resort. Radio Monte Carlo (RMC) is organized as a private corporation, with most of the stock owned by SOFIRAD. Since RMC's transmitters are now located on French military property, technically it no longer functions as a French peripheral, though it continues as an Italian peripheral. RMC has a 1,400-kw. long-wave transmitter, two very powerful medium-wave transmitters, and five television transmitters using both PAL and SECAM color. The company has a subsidiary on the island of Cyprus, Radio Monte Carlo Middle East, which uses a 600-kw. AM station to broadcast in Arabic and French. The Cyprus location gives the station a commanding signal in parts of North Africa as well as in the Middle East, where it is extremely popular both for its music and its objective news reporting. RMC produces the Middle East programs in Paris and relays them to Monte Carlo by microwave and from there to Cyprus by undersea cable.

---

*The Beatles are said to have derived their earliest musical inspiration from listening to Radio Luxembourg.

MONACO

Morocco. Across the Strait of Gibraltar from Spain, ideally situated to radiate programs both to Europe and neighboring North African countries, Morocco has long attracted peripheral broadcasters (see Section 8.2). *Radio Méditerranée International*—owned 51 percent by the Moroccan government, the rest by SOFIRAD—broadcasts in French and Arabic, using two medium-wave transmitters and a 1,200-kw. long-wave transmitter.

The Saar. SOFIRAD has majority interest in Europe No. 1, a peripheral radio station whose transmitter is located in the Saar, a small West German state south of Luxembourg once administered by France. Europe No. 1, SOFIRAD's biggest earner, took in nearly $16 million in 1980.[24] It has a 2,000-kw. long-wave transmitter and programs in French, with all materials originating in Paris.

Swaziland. Situated on the border between South Africa and Mozambique, Swaziland provides an ideal site for a peripheral station aimed at South Africa. Radio SR, using a 50-kw. medium-wave and a 100-kw. short-wave transmitter, broadcasts to South Africa in English, Indian languages, Portuguese, and Zulu. Americans and South Africans as well as Swazis are involved in the ownership of Radio SR, which has studios in Johannesburg.

Yugoslavia. Studio Koper (in Italian, Radio Capodistra), located in Slovenia just across the border from the Italian city of Trieste, has 100-kw. AM and 400-kw. television transmitters that broadcast in Italian and carry commercials for many Italian advertisers. Koper's location across the Adriatic Sea from Venice gives it excellent propagation conditions for covering the northern portion of the Italian peninsula.[25]

Mexico. A 250-kw. AM station, XERF, covers most of the United States at night from across the Rio Grande from Del Rio, Texas, in the Mexican town of Ciudad Acuna. One of a group of stations known as "border blasters," XERF acquired fame in the early 1960s from its use of a colorful American disc jockey, Wolfman Jack. Border blasters evade U.S. power limits and commercial restraints by operating as peripherals. XERF, though owned by a Mexican company, functions to all intents and purposes as an American operation.

CYPRUS

Pirates

External commercial pirate stations could represent a subclass of peripheral stations in that they site their transmitters just beyond the legal boundaries of their target areas; but they differ from peripherals in operating without benefit of license. A few onshore external pirates have existed in Europe, but most operated offshore, beyond the territorial limits of their target areas. I have already described their operations in discussing access controversies (see Section 4.4). Liberalization of domestic programming policies, combined with strenuous legal efforts to put the pirates out of business, has greatly reduced their number.*

Distant Commercial Stations

Some external commercial stations operate too far from the borders of their target countries to be construed as peripherals. During the early 1920s, the U.S. networks and electronic manufacturers began developing commercial operations using short waves aimed at Europe and South America.[26] As previously related, the U.S. government took over these facilities to create the Voice of America during World War II. As private ventures they had never made a profit and seem to have been undertaken primarily as experiments and as hedges against possible future development of lucrative short-wave salesmanship. After the war, the field was left to a few quasi-commercial international religious broadcasters selling time to religious groups but not to commercial advertisers.

In more recent years, U.S. entrepreneurial interest in the outright commercial use of short-wave international stations has revived. In 1980 the FCC somewhat reluctantly licensed WRNO in New Orleans, a 100-kw. short-wave sister station to WRNO-FM.† The FCC permitted short-wave stations to advertise only products available in the stations' target areas, but it waived this rule for WRNO. This waiver enabled WRNO to

---

*Sometimes illegal domestic stations operating with ideological as well as commercial motives are also referred to as pirates. The term *piracy* is also applied to the unauthorized use of cable and satellite services and the copying of both recorded and broadcast program materials (Section 5.5).

†Garay, 1982. One reason for FCC reluctance was the fact that it costs the U.S. government thousands of dollars each year to negotiate the use of HF frequencies by privately owned short-wave stations at the ITU. Only the designated government unit ("administration") can deal officially with the ITU.

SWAZILAND

simulcast the FM station's local programming, resulting in the somewhat bizarre situation of New Orleans dry cleaners, fast-food outlets, and other local businesses being advertised in communities thousands of miles away. The owner contended that foreign audiences are just as fascinated by American domestic advertising as they are by the rock music featured on WRNO-FM. The station targets Canada and Europe; incidentally, of course, it also reaches most of the eastern and central United States.

A more conventional short-wave commercial station, KYOI, won a license in 1982 to operate in Saipan, an island in the U.S. trust territory of the Mariana Islands, fifteen hundred miles south of Tokyo. An American syndicator, Drake Chenault Enterprises, programs KYOI with a Top-40 format in Japanese, using a 100-kw. short-wave transmitter to reach Japan.

Other short-wave commercial stations have begun to emerge elsewhere in the world. For example, SOFIRAD runs Africa No. 1, a commercial short-wave radio station located in Gabon, a former French colony on the west coast of Africa. Gabon owns a majority share in the station, which has four 500-kw. short-wave transmitters and broadcasts in French and several African languages. Africa No. 1 is extremely popular throughout West Africa.

11 ▪ 6 TRANSBORDER RELIGIOUS STATIONS

International religious broadcasting has had a remarkable growth, making it possible to tune in a spiritual message on the short-wave bands at any hour of the day or night. Some 27 international Christian religious broadcasting organizations exist,[27] some owning their own facilities, others renting time from both religious and lay commercial stations.

Religiously sponsored transborder Christian broadcasting began in 1931, when Guglielmo Marconi gave the Vatican a short-wave transmitter and personally introduced Pope Pius XI on the air to deliver a greeting in Latin.[28] Today Vatican Radio counts as a major international broadcaster, even to the point of being singled out for jamming by the Soviets. The Vatican uses six short-wave transmitters with power up to 500 kw., radiating programs throughout the world in more than 30 languages, including Esperanto and Latin. Radio Vatican's transmitter site on the outskirts of Rome occupies ten times as much space as Vatican City. Unlike other Christian broadcasters, Radio Vatican has government status and as such could be classed as an official external service. Similarly, Islam has official standing in most Muslim states, so services such as Egypt's Holy Quran program and Saudi Arabia's Voice of Islam (see Section 9.8) could also be considered parts of those countries' official external services.

Within months of Vatican Radio's debut, the first Protestant transborder station began, HCJB, the Voice of the Andes, located in Quito, Ecuador. The World Radio Missionary Fellowship, with headquarters in Florida, operates HCJB. It has first-class facilities, including eight shortwave transmitters ranging up to 500 kw. in power and its own hydroelectric power generating system. Religious stations, like official external services, sometimes have to make concessions in order to obtain permission to broadcast from foreign sites. HCJB's agreement with Ecuador includes the obligation "to intensify the cultural, social and touristic propaganda of the nation, to the benefit of its integral development, in all bands of the [radio] system and in diverse idioms" (quoted in Browne, 1982: 302). This requirement proved advantageous to HCJB, making its programming less monotonous than that of most religious transborder stations.

Many religious broadcasters operate from several different sites. Trans World Radio (TWR) owns stations in Monaco, the Netherlands Antilles, Swaziland, and Guam and also rents facilities in Cyprus and Sri Lanka. A nondenominational organization, International Evangelism, operates the TWR empire from headquarters in New Jersey. For programming, it relies on production centers located in or near its target areas. This arrangement, typical of international religious broadcasters, makes it unnecessary to assemble a staff of linguists at transmitter sites.

Some religious broadcasters buy time in blocks from certain commercial stations that thrive on time brokerage. Adventist World Radio, for example, has a European branch that buys time from commercially operated facilities in Portugal and Malta, while the Asian branch buys similarly from Sri Lanka, Macao, and Hong Kong.

Organizations that operate their own stations usually depend for operating income primarily on the sale of time to other religious organizations. The Far East Broadcasting Association, which broadcasts from the Seychelles, a group of islands in the Indian Ocean, says in its statement of programming policies:

> *Because FEBA is a service mission, co-operating programme suppliers are asked to share in the cost of operating the station. Capital for the building and development of the station together with missionary staff allowances are raised separately and are not a charge on programme suppliers.*
>
> *It is policy that the airtime costs of all programmes must be covered either by the supplier or a third party, but FEBA may, at its own discretion, assist suppliers if the situation and programme quality justify it. (FEBA, n.d.: 9)*

FEBA charged £25 for 15 minutes on a single 100-kw. transmitter, £32.50 for 30 minutes. Unlike some religious broadcasters, FEBA allows neither solicitation for donations nor offers of books, recordings, and the like for purchase. FEBA is interdenominational, but programs "must be unreservedly in sympathy with the FEBA doctrinal basis." This means that they must, for example, reflect belief in the Bible, the Trinity, the resurrection, and the essentiality of regeneration of sinful man by the Holy Spirit.

Transborder religious broadcasters survive on minimal budgets by using as staff missionaries and other believers who work at minimum cost, often supported by their own home churches at no expense to the broadcaster. This limitation on the choice of talent, together with the fact that the primary criteria for program acceptance are the ability to pay and doctrinal conformity, means that international religious programs suffer in quality compared with most other transborder broadcasts with equal power. Perhaps for this reason, along with the narrow scope of most programming, transborder religious stations usually fare badly in the survey research studies conducted by official external broadcasters. The stations themselves rely mainly on letters as evidence of listenership, and the major stations receive a great many letters. Donald Browne suggests that lack of money may not be the sole reason for lack of research:

> Certain stations see their work as divinely inspired and guided, so that research is unnecessary, while others seem more interested in providing a transmission facility for still other religious broadcasters, who, if they wish to know more about their listeners, should go to the expense and effort of doing so themselves. (Browne, 1982: 311–312)

SUMMARY

Seven types of transborder broadcasting can be distinguished, the chief type being official external services, supported by governments as a form of public diplomacy. The short-wave bands, upon which external radio services depend for reaching distant target audiences, are seriously overcrowded, making it necessary to use very high power and many different frequencies to ensure effective coverage. Overseas relay stations are also used to improve the coverage of external services. Only the larger countries can afford such redundancies in their facilities. For disseminating television to foreign audiences, external services depend on local placement, that is, persuading the domestic services of target countries to schedule their programs. Special types of political external broadcasting include surrogate domestic services, clandestine stations, and borrowed external facilities. Inadvertent spillover from stations in neighboring states and transborder commercial and religious stations complete the roster of international broadcasters.

NOTES

[1]Kiester, 1977; Marks, 1983; Boyd, 1983; Kleinsteuber, 1983.

[2]Scandlen, 1978: 140.

[3]Christian, 1982.

[4]Lee, 1979: 131.

[5]Browne, 1983a.

[6]For details of the VOA controversy, see the report of a panel discussion hosted by the Media Institute, 1982.

[7]For an appreciation of Nasser's skills in exploiting broadcasting, see Dizard, 1966: 147–153.

[8]Boyd, 1982: 261.

[9]*WRTH* carries a list of DX clubs and programs (1984: 391–395, 569).

[10]Personal communication from W. van der Flut, 25 Aug. 1982.

[11]Personal communication from Graham Mytton, 4 Nov. 1983. The VOA had plans for starting a similar program in 1984.

[12]Klose, 1979; Browne, 1982: 228–229.

[13]*Broadcasting,* 26 March 1984: 65.

[14]USGAO, 1982: 18.

[15]*BBC 1982 Annual Report,* 1981: 61.

[16]Browne examines the rationale of the two services and the differences between their programs in considerable detail (1982: 193).

[17]Immerman, 1982: 168.

[18]Delmer wrote a book about his experiences, *Black Boomerang,* 1962.

[19]Browne, 1982: 225.

[20]Hale, 1975: 104.

[21]Binder, 1980.

[22]For details, see Kushner, 1974, and Browne, 1982.

[23]For analysis of the complex network of SOFIRAD corporate relationships, see Boyd & Benzies, 1983.

[24]Boyd & Benzies, 1983: 61.

[25]*TV/RAI,* Jan. 1979.

[26]For details of these ventures, see Deihl, 1977.

[27]*WRTH* lists religious broadcasting organizations (1984: 68–71).

[28]Onder, 1971.

CHAPTER 12

BROADCASTING AND FREEDOM

In previous chapters the point has often been made that broadcasting naturally lends itself to international communication. Moreover, its voluntary character leads people to expect the kinds of programs they want rather than those an arbitrary authority may regard as proper or suitable. If they cannot get what they want from authorized domestic sources, they seek satisfaction from unauthorized and foreign sources.

In the early days of radio, Swiss newspaper publishers, in their panic at the prospect of broadcast competition, "went so far as to suggest that radio was an inherently communist medium because it addressed itself without distinction to all and sundry" (Sandford, 1976: 173). Nowadays, one would be more inclined to describe it as an inherently *democratic* medium precisely because of its universal availability and because audiences have such complete freedom of choice among available offerings. This freedom does not go unchallenged, however, nor do all broadcasters take full advantage of its democratic potential. The persistent and costly jamming of international programs by Communist nations, for example, illustrates to what length authorities will go to inhibit freedom of choice. Moreover, most systems impose some degree of governmental control on the freedom of domestic broadcasters, preventing them either from ignoring public taste at one extreme or responding to it slavishly at the other.

The issue of broadcasting freedom is caught up in a controversy of global dimensions. It involves all forms of communication, but broadcasting's inherent internationalism, its primacy as a news medium, its ability to reach nonreaders, and the social power these attributes imply bring it to the forefront of the freedom controversy. One camp would allow broadcasting to take fullest advantage of its ability to transcend national borders. The other camp argues for curbing this ability in the interests of preserving national sovereignty and cultural identity. The controversy thus has domestic as well as international dimensions.

12 ▪ 1 FREE FLOW VERSUS A NEW ORDER

Free Flow Doctrine

Advocates of maximum freedom support the *free flow doctrine,* enshrined in the 1946 United Nations Declaration on Freedom of Information:

> *All states should proclaim policies under which the free flow of information, within countries and across frontiers, will be protected. The right to seek and transmit information should be insured in order to enable the public to ascertain facts and appraise events. . . . (Quoted in Gunter et al., 1979: 17)*

The term recurs in the constitution of the United Nations Educational, Scientific and Cultural Organization (UNESCO), a specialized agency of the UN responsible for dealing with communication matters. Article 1, adopted in 1946, states that UNESCO will

> *collaborate in the work of advancing the mutual knowledge and understanding of peoples, through all means of mass communication and to that end, recommend such international agreements as may be necessary to promote the free flow of ideas by word or image. (Quoted in Gunter et al., 1979: 26)*

The free flow doctrine, as embodied in these and other international documents of the 1940s, reflected the communication ideology of the United States and of the West generally. In the earlier years of the UN and UNESCO, the West dominated; the USSR was relatively ineffective at UN parliamentary maneuvering at first, and it actually boycotted UNESCO until the late 1950s. It fell to UNESCO in the 1950s and 1960s to help implement free flow goals by such activities as assisting in the development of Third World media facilities, improving media training resources, and lowering barriers to the exchange of information (by reduced customs, telegraph, and telephone rates, for example). There was apparent agreement that (1) uninhibited circulation of information throughout the world enhanced the chances for preserving peace and that (2) the free flow doctrine offered a logical means of achieving that end.

That this unanimity was more apparent than real, however, became evident as the optimistic postwar euphoria gave way to the harsh rhetoric of the Cold War. As for broadcasting, Communist nations saw in the free flow doctrine a Western excuse for attacking their sovereignty; and as new Third World nations emerged from colonialism, they complained that for them free flow meant in fact *one-way* flow—from the developed countries of the north to the developing nations of the south. Traditional, militaristic colonialism, they felt, merely gave way to "neocolonialism" based on economic and cultural domination, aided and abetted by the free flow doctrine.

Thus the assault on free flow gained strength from the coinciding of East-West political rivalries with North-South cultural-economic tensions. Few developing countries subscribe to Marxism, but the Communists made common cause with the Third World in international forums such as the UN, UNESCO, and the ITU. There the principle of one-nation, one-vote gave their coalition an unbeatable parliamentary advantage over the West.

New World Information Order (NWIO)

Origins. Organized attacks on the free flow doctrine began in the late 1960s in meetings of the Organization of Non-aligned States and in the United Nations and its specialized agencies, such as UNESCO and the ITU. During the early 1970s, the assault coalesced under the banner of a New World Information Order (NWIO) movement.* A Western commentator defined the NWIO as

> an evolutionary process seeking a more just and equitable balance in the flow and content of information, a right to national self-determination of domestic communication policies, and, finally, at the international level, a two-way flow reflecting more accurately the aspirations and activities of the less developed countries. (McPhail, 1981: 14)

Mustapha Masmoudi, a Tunisian official who became one of the chief spokespersons for the NWIO in UNESCO, defined it in part as

> the establishment of a new, open-ended conceptual framework leading to a freer, more efficient, more equitable, better balanced international communication system, one founded on democratic principles and favouring equality in the relations between sovereign states. . . .
>
> It would, above all, allow individuals, communities and nations to make known their aspirations, their concerns and their problems in struggling to shape a better future. This new order would help the cause of liberty and justice, just as it would help to prevent rabble-rousing; end racism, do away with intellectual and ideological hegemony and maintain peace in the world.
>
> The new order must preserve cultural identity and the values of each culture, while promoting knowledge of other cultures and balanced exchanges in the sphere of culture. (Quoted in McPhail, 1981: 237–238)

NWIO goals, expressed in such general terms, sound idealistic and benign. However, this high-sounding language conceals a hidden agenda that becomes evident only when the NWIO is reduced to practical terms. In particular, when rationalized according to Marxist concepts, the NWIO agenda infuriates media leaders of the United States and

---

*As the NWIO movement grew, embracing more and more aspects of communication, some advocates broadened the name to New World Information and Communication Order.

other Western countries. According to this rationale, the free flow doctrine deliberately subverts the freedom and cultural autonomy of developing countries; it amounts to a capitalist plot led by America's multinational corporations. Broadcasting, in particular, serves as an agent of capitalism. It helps extend the power of multinational corporations, which exploit Third World natural resources and incite wasteful consumption and class exploitation. Herbert Schiller, the best-known American exponent of the Marxist NWIO interpretation, has said that "the 'have-not' nations stand practically defenseless before a rampaging Western commercialism. . . . Expectations of new roads to national development which *might* foster motivations and behavior different from contemporary Western styles are being dashed in their infancy" (Schiller, 1969: 107).

The MacBride Report. At the 1976 biennial general meeting of UNESCO, in Nairobi, the West staved off a showdown on an unacceptably strong NWIO resolution by voting to appoint an International Commission for the Study of Communication Problems. Sean MacBride, a distinguished Irish statesman, headed the 16-member commission. The U.S. member was Elie Abel, then dean of the Columbia University School of Journalism. MacBride set forth the goals of the commission as (1) defining a "free and balanced" flow of information, (2) defining the NWIO, (3) studying the newly recognized *right to communicate* (discussed earlier in connection with the concept of access (see Section 4.1), and (4) devising means to ensure media objectivity and freedom from government control.

The MacBride Commission report, which took four years to complete, contained 82 recommendations.[1] Though it avoided explicit endorsement of the more radical NWIO proposals, it still failed to satisfy the West. The following quotations, excerpting recommendations especially relevant to broadcasting, give an idea of the report's tone and its themes:

> 8. *The development of comprehensive national radio networks, capable of reaching remote areas, should take priority over the development of television, which, however, should be encouraged where appropriate. . . .*
> 9. *National capacity for producing broadcast materials is necessary to obviate dependence on external sources over and beyond desirable programme exchange. . . .*
> 14. *Utilization of local radio, low-cost small format television and video systems and other appropriate technologies would facilitate production of programmes relevant to community development efforts, stimulate participation and provide opportunity for diversified cultural expression.*
> 20. *Tariffs for news transmission, telecommunications rates and air mail charges for the dissemination of news . . . and audiovisual materials are one of the main obstacles to a free and balanced flow of information. . . . Profits or revenues should not be the primary aim of such agencies. . . .*

29. *Communication and cultural policies should ensure that creative artists and various grass-roots groups can make their voices heard through the media. . . .*
30. *. . . . Mechanisms such as complaint boards or consumer review committees might be established to afford the public the possibility of reacting against advertising which they feel inappropriate.*
31. *In expanding communication systems, preference should be given to noncommercial forms of mass communication.*
43. *. . . . The adoption of codes of [journalistic] ethics at national and, in some cases, at the regional level is desirable, provided that such codes are prepared and adopted by the profession itself—without governmental interference.*
45. *Conventional standards of news selection and reporting, and many accepted news values, need to be reassessed. . . .*
54. *Communication needs in a democratic society should be met by the extension of specific rights such as the right to be informed, the right to inform, the right to privacy, the right to participate in public communication—all elements of a new concept, the right to communicate. . . .*
58. *Effective legal measures should be designed to . . . reduce the influence of advertising upon editorial policy and broadcast programming. . . .*
63. *. . . . Those in charge of the media should encourage their audiences to play a more active role in communication by allocating more newspaper space, or broadcasting time, for the views of individual members of the public or organized social groups. (UNESCO, 1980: 254–269, passim)*

Most of these themes have emerged in previous chapters, in discussion of, for example, radio's primacy in the Third World, the goal of total coverage, localism, access, accountability, and the right to communicate. New, however, is the MacBride report's recurrent antiadvertising, anti–profit motive emphasis.

U.S. Withdrawal from UNESCO. The MacBride report ranks as a uniquely wide ranging international discussion of global communication issues; but the commission's efforts at soft-pedaling the controversial aspects of NWIO satisfied neither side. The West objected to the report's skepticism about a free market in communication, including its opposition to advertising, for example; many NWIO supporters objected to its downplaying of government controls (for example, its advocacy of self-imposed rather than government codes of ethics for journalists) and its failure to condemn neocolonialism explicitly.

At the close of 1983, the United States gave UNESCO notice of its intent to withdraw from the organization (the rules require that a withdrawal notice be submitted a year in advance). UNESCO, said the State Department, had been hostile toward press freedom and free enterprise; its management had become politically biased and wasteful. Unstated officially but widely discussed were allegations of nepotism and bias on the part of the Senegalese UNESCO director-general, Amadou M'Bow. Several other Western nations and even some Third World countries had similar complaints.

Not everyone concerned agreed with Washington's assessment, which some thought too narrowly focused on communication issues. The U.S. National Commission for UNESCO, a nongovernment organization, recommended continued U.S. participation, pointing to "the tangible benefits of U.S. participation in UNESCO, particularly in the fields of education and the natural sciences." The commission commented on the "widespread misperception in the United States that the U.S. role in UNESCO is primarily that of benefactor, not beneficiary" (USNC, 1982: 1–2).

The United States left the way open for review of its decision should the organization undertake suitable reforms (as indeed had several other UN organizations in response to previous U.S. withdrawal threats). Inasmuch as the United States contributed a quarter of UNESCO's budget, the membership had good reason to take the U.S. threat seriously. Nevertheless, the United States insisted that its withdrawal notice represented more than a pressure tactic, asserting that it could better fulfill UNESCO's role through other UN agencies and through bilateral agreements with individual nations.[2]

12•2 NWIO ISSUES

Withdrawal of the United States from UNESCO would not, of course, eliminate the NWIO movement. Its issues remain, touching on virtually every aspect of every means of communication as practiced in the West. Discussion of NWIO issues that have special relevance to broadcasting follows.

Cultural Imperialism

Syndicated Television Programs. As related in Section 7.5, most countries find it necessary to share program costs by importing syndicated materials. The NWIO critique sees the "dumping" of Western (especially American) syndicated television programs in Third World countries as devastating to their indigenous cultures. Imported programs overwhelm traditional arts and introduce alien value systems. For example, they emphasize materialistic comforts and individualism; they depict the roles of children and of women and the relationships between the rulers and the ruled in ways that local tradition may consider subversive; and they inspire imitation in dress, language, and music among the youth of the country. Moreover, according to many NWIO adherents, imperialistic designs, not simply impersonal economic or technological factors, account for the invasion of destructive foreign programs.

Of course, importers can and do censor foreign programs, as related in Section 6.5. Nevertheless, local cultures undoubtedly do get swamped when nations first introduce television. It takes time to build up a fund of experience and a backlog of locally produced programs.

However, critics who charge cultural imperialism ignore the experience of many countries, which shows that once local producers acquire the skill and the money to adapt local arts to the broadcast media, such programs usually capture more audience attention than do imports.* In the meantime, foreign material, even though not appropriate, can serve a useful interim function by encouraging purchase of receivers and filling out broadcast schedules while local forces generate the funds and know-how to become more self-sufficient.

In *Broadcasting in the Third World*, Katz and Wedell give many examples of successful adaptations of local cultural resources to broadcasting. From another source comes this example, in reference to Malaysia:

> *A current revival in ethnic music owes a great deal to radio-TV exposure, as does appreciation of local textiles, silverware, and painting. Radio and television maintain a 60-piece professional orchestra and regularly hire local dance troupes. Local talent is encouraged through a series of competitions organized by [Radio-TV Malaysia]. The department of broadcasting also publishes books of traditional, modern, and children's songs.* (Glattbach & Balakrishnan, 1978: 150)

Japanese dramas based upon feudal stories of Samurai warriors have had a huge success since 1963.[3] In Latin America, locally produced serial dramas known as *telenovelas* have attained great popularity. Many succeed in international syndication. Joseph Straubhaar has studied the evolution of *telenovelas*, particularly in Brazil, where they constitute "a unique, distinctively Brazilian cultural industry." He presents evidence to show that given a market of significant size, the existence of indigenous producers, government support, and a suitable cultural background, locally produced materials eventually displace imports.[4] Unfortunately, not every country can meet these preconditions, though hardly because of cultural imperialism. Some nations, including highly developed ones, are just too small to enable development of a completely self-sustained television service.

Well, replies the skeptic, why must broadcasting aim for the mass audience? Why not aim for cumulative size by attracting many small audiences? All very well, but small audiences can be served only after mass audiences have been motivated to buy sets. Thus U.S. public and cable television can "narrowcast" to small, specialized audiences because mass-appeal programs have long since stimulated virtually everyone to invest in receivers. Narrowcasting by itself could never have brought about the 95 percent set penetration that makes for near universal "reception readiness."

How about cutting back on air time? Transmitters could be turned on only every other day, for example, and then for only two or three hours.

---

*The "product life-cycle" theory has been advanced to account for this tendency (Straubhaar, 1983).

Again the chicken-and-egg factor: Why should people invest in sets if their system deliberately discards one of the basic advantages that broadcasting offers—its continuous availability? Why should broadcasters or broadcasting authorities invest in expensive production, transmission, and relay equipment—facilities capable of operating efficiently 24 hours per day—only to leave them lying idle and deteriorating 90 percent of the time?[5]

Nations with strong cultural traditions in the performing arts have difficulty enough in generating a major share of their own programming. Those whose cultures give little or no experience to talented artists in occupations analogous to those of actors, dramatists, designers, directors, producers, and composers must embark on television almost totally dependent on foreigners. Japan's rich legacy in the visual and performing arts enabled it to adapt to television as naturally as a duck to water. In contrast, countries of the Middle East, where orthodox Islamic belief condemns as sacrilegious the depiction of living forms, found television not only totally foreign to their cultural tradition but also highly threatening to its survival (note the religious opposition to introduction of even radio broadcasting in Saudi Arabia, discussed in Section 2.4).

Of course, cultures can change, though not overnight. Egypt's long association with the culture of its Western neighbors across the Mediterranean softened Islamic fundamentalism and established cultural precedents. Modern contact with the West began with Napoleon's invasion in 1798. Egypt has a press tradition rooted in the nineteenth century and a motion picture production tradition going back to the early years of the twentieth century. When television arrived in 1960, Egypt already had trained cadres of performers, directors, producers, technicians, writers, editors, composers. Their experience could be adapted to the needs of television. Indeed, driven by high taxes and Arab boycotts (occasioned by the moderation of Egypt's policies toward Israel), Egyptian production crews fanned out to other Arab production centers, such as Jordan and Dubai, as well as to Britain, West Germany, and Greece.

On the other hand, Dubai, one of the tiny United Arab Emirates located on the Persian Gulf, has no cultural background relevant to the needs of television. Yet, with the help of Egyptian, Jordanian, British, and other expatriate workers, it has become a major Arab television production center. Facilities of Dubai's Arabian Gulf Production Company are

> *frequently rented by Egyptian directors and producers who import Egyptian actors to make programs. Egyptian material is still the most popular in the Arab world; moreover, Egyptians who produce and appear in productions not taped in Egypt are not subject to the Arab boycott. The Arabian Gulf Production Company has helped the Egyptian television organization to sell programs taped in Egypt by editing that makes them appear to have been shot*

elsewhere. This highly professional facility includes an adjoining hotel and restaurant that caters exclusively to artists who come to Dubai to undertake television productions. (Boyd, 1982: 158, 160)

Dubai's economic wealth enabled it to establish a production center, but its poverty of experience, talent, and tradition in the relevant arts made it necessary to import all its creative personnel from abroad.

The director-general of television in the Sudan, a country in the interior of Africa, much more remote than Egypt from relevant cultural traditions, said, "We can't broadcast only local programmes because it would be very expensive. For instance, the price of a 60 minute, hired film is about $100. If we wanted to produce the same programme here, it would cost $700" (quoted in Boyd, 1982: 59). This seems like a gross underestimate of local costs for all but the simplest program (compare the data in Table 7.3). In any event, even if the Sudan television service had unlimited funds, it would still not be able to match the cheaper syndicated material for long. It would very soon run out of relevant human and cultural resources.

Cultural Survival. Examples of successful "indigenization" could be multiplied at length, but I must concede that cultures lacking any large heritage of artistic works made possible by an accumulation of written records may soon run short of broadcastable material. Traditional arts have qualities of orality, pageantry, color, symbolism, and ritual that seem made to order for broadcasting. But these arts are firmly attached to real-life events, typically the great rites of passage—birth, coming of age, marriage, death. These rites occur in natural settings and relatively infrequently. Broadcasting chops culture into time-bound segments, transfers it to the artificial environment of a studio, initiates it on cue, and spins it out endlessly to feed the ravenous appetite of the medium. All this can be very destructive to traditional ceremonial arts.*

NWIO ideologues take the romantic view that every culture should and can survive in the modern world and therefore must be protected from the influence of imported technologies and materials. Broadcasting should reflect indigenous culture, not bury it in a tidal wave of alien programming. But when a single country has hundreds of different languages, broadcasting cannot possibly validate all of them. In any event, the inexorable processes of modernization, not merely radio and

---

*As an incidental impediment to the easy adaptation of indigenous arts to broadcasting, performing artists often have very low social status in traditional cultures. Telling of his experience in developing broadcasting in India, Fielden wrote "the worst hurdle was the performers. Music and mummers were matters held in low repute. . . . When I got to India they were almost entirely (the ballet was an exception) in the hands of prostitutes and pimps. No man or woman of the upper or middle classes of India would stoop to the practice of music or acting" (1960: 185).

television, will overwhelm many of them in the long run. As Jeremy Tunstall, an English commentator by no means hostile to many of the NWIO goals, has said, traditional culture is often

> *typically archaic, does not fit with contemporary notions of justice and equality, and depends upon religious beliefs which have long been in decline. Many traditional cultures were primarily carried by a small elite of scholars and priests, who often used languages which few other people understood. Not only Arab and Hindu cultures but many others ascribed a fixed subservient position to women, the young and the occupationally less favoured. It is precisely these unpopular characteristics of much authentic culture which make the imported media culture so popular by contrast. (Tunstall, 1977: 58)*

Indeed, some developing nations "actively seek and welcome the coming of Western mass culture and the end to traditional culture, for they see the old ways as impediments to development and modernization" (Gunter et al., 1979: 75).

Measuring the Influence of Imports. NWIO advocates often seem to regard audience members as so many empty receptacles into which messages can be poured or injected. For example, a Latin American critic of American imported television programs writes of "social vaccination" in describing the presumed effects of such programs on Latin American viewers.[6] Research has explicitly rejected as unrealistic the notion that communication effects are simply "injected." Far from being passive targets, recipients of messages actively participate in the communication process:

> *It does not logically follow—given the ability of American mass media merchants to make their wares near-universally available—that they possess inherent powers of persuasion to bring about the adoption of values contrary to their audiences' true beliefs in a system that benefits the communicator only. (Read, 1977: 181)*

Most research measuring the presumed influence of imported programs tacitly accepted the injection theory of effects by concentrating on the sheer quantity of imported programs, expressed as a percentage of program schedules. By implication, viewers in a country importing 70 percent of its programs would be presumed twice as heavily influenced as those in a country importing only 35 percent. Katz and Liebes asked a more analytic research question: "What actually happens in the minds of viewers exposed to a foreign program?" They showed an episode of *Dallas* to groups of viewers, discussing with them their interpretations of the goings-on in the Ewing family. They talked to ten groups of Israeli viewers from varying ethnic backgrounds, comparing their reactions to those of ten groups of American viewers of comparable social standing.

Though the researchers made no claim to definitive answers to their research question in this preliminary study, their findings clearly showed that foreign audiences interpret in their own terms even so alien a culture as that depicted in *Dallas*.

> *We are impressed by the sophisticated ways in which very common people discuss these stories. . . . Issues discussed include "success," "loyalty," "honour," "money and happiness," sex roles, the functions of children. . . . The social distance between the Ewing family and the rest of the world seems far less important than one might have thought. Unhappiness is the great leveller. (Katz & Liebes, 1984: 32)**

Production Methods. The NWIO critique finds evidence of cultural imperialism in that along with the importation of Western technology come Western methods for using it. "Once RCA has sold you the new technological pill and you've swallowed it, then the rest follows" (Tunstall, 1977: 266). Professional standards for broadcast production and programming, highly regarded in the West, may be inappropriate to the needs of developing countries, inhibiting them from using their own initiative and adopting their own, possibly more appropriate, methods. NWIO critics also claim that foreign advisers and aid projects impose unnecessarily expensive and complex equipment on developing countries. Advisers fail to recommend cheaper, simpler hardware ("appropriate technology") that could do the job because, they say, it would be less profitable to Western exporters.†

However, the leaders of developing countries see little reason why they should be fobbed off with second-best equipment. Moreover, subprofessional broadcasting hardware lacks the ruggedness and reliability essential for continuous operation under conditions of professional use. As to production methods and programming standards, one wonders what would happen should equipment arrive in a developing country without benefit of advice and guidance from experienced professionals. If it survived the period of trial-and-error usage, would not users in developing countries end up with substantially the same standardized production methods and program formats, in keeping with the technological determinism principle discussed in Section 1.3?‡ Despite differences of language and other cultural artifacts, when it comes to broadcasting, people everywhere tend to develop the same fundamental interests and expectations that require the same fundamental methods of production.

---

*Note the relevance of the Katz and Liebes findings to the notion of program "shareability" put forward in Section 7.5.

†In recent years, development aid organizations have turned away from ambitious educational television schemes, such as those in American Samoa and the Ivory Coast (Section 9.7), toward such simpler technologies as audiocassettes, community radio, and satellite teleconferencing.

‡Tunstall points out, however, that the technological determinism argument has been used by both sides of the NWIO controversy (1977: 266–267).

Dominance of Western News

The importation of syndicated news material represents a special case of neocolonialism in the NWIO perspective. Touching as it does sensitive nerves of national pride, news syndication has become an even more pressing issue than that of entertainment and cultural programming.

As related in Section 9.6, the Big Four news agencies—Agence France Presse, Associated Press, Reuters, and United Press International, supplemented with special video material syndicated by Visnews and UPITN—move most of the news from the Third World to the West. Developing countries bitterly complain that these agencies neglect Third World news, and when they cover it at all do so not on Third World terms but in terms of their Western clients' interests. Third World news stories therefore tend to present a distorted picture, stressing violent and bizarre events to the neglect of less picturesque but more positive achievements in economic and cultural development. NWIO reformers want not only a free but also a *balanced* flow of news. By balance they mean both more news about the Third World and a fairer representation of events there.

> *There may be nothing dramatic or sensational about the construction of health centers, schools, and bridges, but these efforts in social and economic development are being made in the face of great odds and deserve to be better publicized than tribal conflicts or abortive coups, which constitute an inordinately large portion of Western media offerings.* (Ansah, 1984: 86)

Some Third World spokespersons propose that governments should have a "right of rectification," giving them free access to the media to correct what they perceive to be false or "unbalanced" reports.

Ironically, the United States once had a similar complaint against the European news agencies. Prior to 1935, the Associated Press belonged to a global cartel that divided the world outside the United States among British, French, and German agencies. U.S. diplomats and business executives objected, with some justification, that the rest of the world saw the United States only through the prejudiced eyes of gatekeeping European newswriters and editors.*

This historical precedent makes a strong point in favor of the Third World argument for a more balanced news flow. However, the argument is weakened in Western eyes by the claim that news should be insulated from the marketplace. For example, Chilean NWIO advocate Juan Somavia has said that "providing information is a social function; it should not be a business transaction" (quoted in Tatarian, 1978: 30). But of course the credibility of the much criticized Big Four news agencies

---

Gatekeeping is a research term for processes such as editing that control the content of news by opening and closing gates in the course of its flow from original reports to final delivery to consumers.

relies on the marketplace. Subscribing news media give the agencies their financial support; judgments of newsworthiness must therefore take the interests of the ultimate consumers into consideration. "The ideological gamut of the thousands of subscribers of each of the major news agencies guards against deliberate bias. No agency that sells the same service to *Maariv* of Israel and *Al Ahram* of Egypt can stray too far from objectivity" (Rosenblum, 1978: 124). Because agencies find most of their consumers in the West, they select and edit the news according to Western interests. The Soviet news agency, TASS, ignores the marketplace, relying on government for its support; but it has no credibility as an independent news source, being regarded as a government mouthpiece. As an African commentator wrote, "It may not be an exaggeration to assert that, all their deficiencies notwithstanding, if the transnational news agencies did not exist it might be necessary to invent them" (Ansah, 1984: 85).

Third World advocates of the NWIO seem rarely to consider the consumer's point of view. They picture news as flowing in only one direction; another African observer said, "There is a tendency to regard the press as a medium through which the government may reach the people rather than one through which the people may reach the government" (Mazrui, 1972: 54). A Third World journalist complained that two thirds of the world's people live in developing countries, but they furnish only one third of the agency news, implying that editors should base news judgments on the numbers of people involved rather than on the significance of events. Another critic objected that the news agencies told him more about the United States president than about the presidents of neighboring countries, implying that every national leader has equal significance as a subject of news. Such comments betray a one-way view of broadcasting, a disregard for news values as defined by audience interest.

The perspective of Western news media on NWIO strictures may be summarized in the words of a well-known foreign correspondent, who wrote that the Third World really wants not news but "boosterism, a style of advocacy journalism that concentrates on the opening of civic centers and ignores the warts. . . . It wants to be covered by historians, not journalists. . . . To write about only what is good does not mean that what is bad will simply evaporate" (Lamb, 1982: 252–253).

Government News Control

Western critics reject the NWIO call for adoption of a universal code of journalistic ethics and a system for licensing news personnel. These measures, they say, would inevitably involve governments in the control of journalists, an idea foreign to Western freedom of information concepts and specifically violative of the U.S. Constitution's First Amendment.

"Development journalism" provided another avenue of government intervention. The Press Foundation of Asia, organized in 1968 with the help of a Ford Foundation grant, embarked on a program to train journalists to report effectively on Third World efforts at economic and social development. Reporters need specialized training in development economics to cover such stories constructively. It is most difficult to explain to people whose ancestral homes must be abandoned to make way for a hydroelectric dam why their personal sacrifice serves the national interest. Development journalism, as originally conceived, would teach reporters how to handle such tasks. They would become expert at analyzing and interpreting the often highly technical details of development projects. Some NWIO advocates, however, sought to convert this specialized application of normal news reporting into the notion that journalists must express only the government point of view on development activities. Reporters would have no right to report objectively on a project if investigation revealed mismanagement, for example.*

Many Third World rulers feel that their fragile control over governments riven by tribalism and weakened by corruption and single-product economies cannot withstand criticisms by uncontrolled news media. They feel that they need a grace period, a moratorium during which the press must forego its watchdog function and simply support the government of the day. Many Western critics have little patience with this rationalization:

> When Third World leaders complain of lack of social cohesion in their countries or express anxieties about their fragile structures they do not realise that it is the absence of a free national press which makes their social orders even more fragile. . . .
>
> The popular argument in the Third World that the press must first learn to be responsible before it can be allowed to operate and develop freely is brazen sophistry. The press cannot be more responsible or conscientious than the community. (Gauhar, 1979: 73)

The author goes on to point out that failure of the domestic media to cover news objectively merely increases the impact of foreign news agencies, making audiences more susceptible to outside influences.

But the hold of most Third World leaders over their one-party regimes is so shaky that one can appreciate their reluctance to grant reporters and editors freedom from all government constraints. Inadequately trained news personnel, infected with the tribalistic prejudices, can pose a real threat to a regime's stability. Third World commentators point out that even in the United States, a "clear and present danger" to the security of the nation has been recognized as justification for hedging on the freedom conferred by the First Amendment.

---

*Note, in contrast, the Soviet practice of *encouraging* reporting of instances of mismanagement (Section 9.6).

National Communication Policies

The NWIO urges nations to articulate national communication policies. UNESCO has published a series of country-by-country studies, the preface to which defines communication policies as "sets of principles and norms established to guide the behavior of communication systems. . . . Emanating from political ideologies, the social and economic conditions of the country and the values on which they are based, they strive to relate these to the real needs for and the prospective opportunities of communication" (Stapleton, 1974: 5). Translated from UNESCOese, national communication policies define priorities and set up guidelines for development. Though on the surface such planning seems eminently desirable, Western critics read into them a hidden agenda for government takeover of communications.

Access to the Spectrum

Another argument against the free flow doctrine arises from the uneven availability of the radio spectrum. Traditionally, the ITU parceled out the spectrum on a first-come, first-served basis. As a result, the Western nations obtained a disproportionate share of frequency allotments. NWIO reformers want to force reallotment to give Third World countries a larger share of the frequencies. Moreover, with respect to newly developed technologies, they advocate advance planning to reserve future access for countries not yet able to take advantage of new opportunities. The United States counters with the argument that advance planning of this kind wastes spectrum resources and inhibits development by imposing unrealistic restrictions on access. At the 1977 WARC on the allotment of direct-broadcast satellite facilities, each country in ITU regions I and III (Africa, Asia, and Europe) received a share of the orbital slots, irrespective of its readiness to use them. The United States, however, refused to go along with this plan, postponing decisions on Region II (the Americas) DBS rules until the 1980s.

Some NWIO supporters advocate assessing the developed countries fees for the use of the spectrum and of satellite orbital slots. Such fees would go into a fund to help developing countries to improve their telecommunications infrastructures. While rejecting this solution, the West acknowledges that the Third World needs and deserves assistance in developing better facilities. Rather than cutting back on the communication capacity of some, argues the West, it would be more constructive to increase the capacity of others.

The United States proposed a clearinghouse for Third World telecommunications assistance projects. After much wrangling, in 1980 Western delegates agreed to establish an International Program for the Development of Communications (IPDC). Over the objections of the United States, it was placed under control of UNESCO. However, the West succeeded in stipulating that funding would be flexible and not fully under UNESCO domination.[7] The IPDC provides aid in the development of Third World communication infrastructure, professional training, and equipment resources. By 1983 the IPDC fund amounted to $3.9 million, of which the United States contributed half a million. In addition, some three hundred private U.S. sources had promised Third World assistance along similar lines.

Satellite Threat to Sovereignty

NWIO critics see direct-broadcast satellites as a potential threat to national sovereignty, even though DBS receivers seem unlikely to be practical for most developing countries for many years to come. The Communist and even some Western countries share concern about DBS. They fear not only the receipt of objectionable political messages but also the invasion of alien cultural values and unwanted advertisements.

This issue emerged at a 1969 meeting of the UN Committee on Peaceful Uses of Outer Space (COPUOS), when the USSR proposed that any country wishing to send direct-broadcast satellite messages to another country should first obtain "prior consent." Because no such regulation governs direct reception of international radio broadcast signals, the United States strongly opposed the motion as a violation of established free flow principles. American delegates took the position that satellite communication should proceed experimentally, without being hampered by a priori regulations. Nevertheless, at a 1982 UN General Assembly meeting, a motion was made to direct COPUOS to draw up regulations covering DBS transmissions. The United States, opposing the motion, failed to recruit a single supporter, finding itself in the embarrassing posture of being on the losing end of a 102 to 1 UN vote.

12 ▪ 3 CONCLUSION

Involvement of East-West political rivalry in the Third World's NWIO struggle makes many of the problems as insoluble as the opposition between Marxism and capitalism. Developing countries are by no means as uniform in their outlook as their apparent unanimity in the NWIO controversy might suggest; but the superpowers curry favor with them, attempting to co-opt their support for one ideology or the other. Thus polarization occurs, and advocates become intransigent in their advocacy of extreme positions. In many cases, if only disputants could forego ideological flag waving, a workable middle ground might be found. Obviously, the United States will not give up its belief in a capitalist, market-oriented approach to communication, any more than the Communists will give up their Marxist-Leninist ideal of government control on behalf of the workers. Insisting, as some NWIO supporters do, that the entire world must subscribe to a uniform set of communication rules ignores underlying political realities.

A primer on the NWIO debate, funded by the U.S. International Communication Agency[8] and prepared for the benefit of "U.S. government and private media leaders," far from dismissing the importance of the movement, concluded that it had considerable validity:

> A prime conclusion which can be derived from a review of the world "information order" debates is that U.S. perceptions of the challenges to the "free flow of information" have been incomplete. American leaders have tended to attribute most of the changed atmosphere to the needs of authoritarian governments to shield their people from the truth, in order to perpetuate their rule. While this motivation is a factor in some East bloc and Third World countries, it does not explain differences between the U.S. and smaller Western nations. It also overlooks the fact that most countries in the world have deep and honest differences with the U.S. regarding the appropriate role of mass media within societies and internationally. (Gunter et al., 1979: 109)

Another reason for the incompleteness of American perceptions is that the Western press, because of its obvious vested interest, has taken the lead in opposing NWIO initiatives. Through the World Press Freedom Committee, other private organizations, and frequent editorials in major newspapers, the Western press has focused attention on those NWIO proposals that most directly affect its interests—licensing of journalists, the right to rectification of inaccurate news stories, opposition to advertising and market-oriented financing, and so on. The press has given less coverage to the more complex issues involving such subjects as transborder data flows, copyright and patent restrictions, spectrum allotment inequities, and the right to communicate.

SUMMARY

Issues of media freedom divide the world into two camps: the supporters of "free flow" versus the advocates of a "New World Information Order." The former include media leaders of the Western democracies, who argue for a government hands-off policy and for a free marketplace. The Communist and many Third World countries argue for government controls, divorcement of public communication from profit considerations, and a more balanced flow of news. The dispute has become politicized by intransigent Cold War attitudes, which make compromise virtually impossible. UNESCO became so deeply embroiled on the NWIO side of the dispute that the United States announced its intention to withdraw from the world body at the end of 1984.

Among the subjects at issue are the alleged cultural imperialism implicit in Western (particularly American) television program syndication, the imposition of inappropriate Western production standards and professional codes on developing countries, the dominance of Western news agencies over the international flow of news, proposals for government licensing of journalists and control over their movements,

Third World access to the electromagnetic spectrum and the equatorial satellite orbit, and regulation of direct satellite broadcasting across national boundaries.

NOTES

[1]UNESCO, 1980.

[2]U.S. Senate, 1984.

[3]Makita, 1979.

[4]Straubhaar, 1982, 1983.

[5]For an argument against the idea of continuous operation, see Wedell, 1968: 170.

[6]Quoted in Beltran, 1978: 72. For evidence of the "passing of the passive audience," see Izcaray & McNelly's discussion of Venezuelan TV (1984).

[7]Harley, 1984; Block, 1984.

[8]Formerly (and now) called the U.S. Information Agency (USIA).

AFTERWORD

W hat of the future? In the preceding chapters I have alluded repeatedly to the changes taking place in the entire telecommunications field. Assaulted by revisionist social outlooks and undermined by new technologies, many of the stable broadcasting institutions of the 1950s and 1960s are fighting for survival, at least in their traditional form, in the 1980s. Here I return chapter-by-chapter to the topics covered in the book and speculate on what the next few years may bring. Such speculation involves a good deal of "on-the-other-handing," for the same stimulus often produces simultaneous opposing effects.

A ▪ 1 THE NATURE OF BROADCASTING

Are the very attributes of broadcasting, as described in Chapter 1, changing? In the main, no. The new technologies in fact enhance most existing attributes. DBS promises to make broadcasting more ubiquitous than ever; proliferation of cable channels increases the medium's voracity by heightening program competition; enhanced program options augment broadcasting's voluntary character; cable delivery, DBS, and equipment miniaturization enhance accessibility; and cable eases interference problems. On the other hand, in the more advanced countries, prosperity and cheaper receivers tend to personalize television, repeating radio history; in those countries, television no longer functions so clearly as a family medium. Thus, for example, a new research method in Italy uses interactive meters, enabling eight *individual* viewers in a single household to record their separate presences in the audience.[1] Recent German research appraises receiver usage not only for television reception but also for teletext and videotext and for connection to video games and personal computers.

Proliferation of program options results from the use of non-broadcast technologies and improved efficiency in the use of the spectrum. Does this mean that the channel scarcity, a feature of the inter-ference-proneness attribute, no longer exists? Despite claims to the contrary, I have argued that channel scarcity remains a factor. Only by ignoring its inherent coverage limitations can one maintain that cable television eliminates channel scarcity as a broadcasting attribute. DBS likewise suffers limitations, both in terms of channel and orbital slot scarcities.

In most parts of the world, broadcasting can probably be expected to survive essentially in its present forms. Remember that most new technology enhances not only program options but also consumer costs, putting much of the new technology beyond the reach of most people. For those who can pay for them, it remains to be seen which of the new options afforded by technology will seem worth the price. In the United States, attempts to establish certain interactive cable services and high-quality satellite-cable arts programs have already demonstrated that not every innovation succeeds. People may climb mountains just because they are there, but they do not necessarily buy innovations just because they become technologically feasible.

A ▪ 2 THE THREE WORLDS OF BROADCASTING

With time, will First, Second, and Third World broadcasting grow more uniform? Structurally, probably not. The economic and political differences among the three worlds militate against the leveling process. The Second and Third Worlds will continue to prefer authoritarian rather than permissive modes of control and will continue to find full exploitation of costly new technologies beyond the means of mass consumers. On the other hand, if DBS and the VCR open them to easier intrusion of foreign programs, authoritarian regimes may have difficulty in keeping audiences satisfied with their traditional domestic fare. Some homogenization of programming may result.

A ▪ 3 OWNERSHIP PATTERNS

Are ownership patterns changing? In the West, yes; elsewhere, no. Localism, cable, and satellites have been chipping away at the old European monopolies. More private ownership can be expected, especially at the local and regional levels. Something like the IBA model of controlled commercial competition among private companies will be widely imitated, increasing pluralism in the advanced Western systems. Monopolies will not simply disappear, but most will broaden into duopolies or oligopolies or else tolerate a limited amount of local competition.

A ▪ 4 ACCESS

Will broadcasting become more accessible to more people? Yes, in all three worlds. Improved relay methods enable more complete national network coverage, while in many countries, local and regional services increasingly supplement national services. Satellite signals (initially often pirated) and VCR technologies increase television program availability in areas not yet fully served. Third World countries are beginning to do more to encourage receiver purchasing—or at least less to discourage it. The high demand for local stations, as an aspect of the access movement, continues, and one can expect to find ever more small-scale FM stations, run informally by local interests, operating with minimal interference from central authorities.

A ▪ 5 NEW STATUTES

The law, one of the more volatile aspects of broadcasting in the 1980s, tends toward new and separate cable television legislation. Satellite transborder broadcasting creates a need for regions to adopt uniform national laws in such areas of common interest as copyright and advertising. The European Broadcasting Union, the Council of Europe, and the European Economic Community have shown a practical interest in such legislation.[2]

International coordination of telecommunication law through the ITU will become more important than ever as transborder flows increase. Doubts about the viability of the international rule of law seem to be fading. Simple self-interest makes it essential. Signs of a new spirit of accommodation emerged at the 1984 WARC on the high-frequency allocation plan.*

A ▪ 6 REGULATION

Regulatory activities will of course reflect changing statutes, though complex interactions among the media and among their technologies will make close supervision increasingly difficult to achieve. Areas in which new regulatory activities can be expected include fairness and accountability, language policies, import quotas, and advertising.

The rest of the world does not, on the whole, share the American enthusiasm for deregulation, viewing control by marketplace competition with skepticism. As a British commentator put it, "American television stands as an awful warning" of what surrender to the market can bring.[3] Although more advertising can be expected, it will be strictly regulated. The pioneer European satellite-distributed cable network service, SATV, set as its initial standard the IBA advertising code; however, it had to adopt even more conservative standards to avoid violating rules in other countries.

Controls over cross-media ownership among media may loosen as

---

Broadcasting headlined a story on the meeting "U.S. Returns from WARC Pleased with Itself and ITU" (20 Feb. 1984). However, the second half of the conference, scheduled for 1986, will present a severer test. It will consider the computer-generated HF allotment plan prepared by the IFRB in the interim.

division of the advertising pie into thinner slices creates financial problems for newspapers and magazines. Having an interest in preserving the viability of independent print media, Western nations, hitherto highly sensitive to the monopoly implications of cross-ownership, may become more tolerant of mergers between privately owned print news media and commercial electronic entertainment media.

A · 7 ECONOMICS

Official enthusiasm for cable television and videotext in Europe arose less from response to public demand for new services than from the perception that these technologies represented a major new industry. Nations wanted to ensure their place in a field that seemed to have great economic potential in terms of jobs and trade, both domestic and export. The traditional PTT ministries, finding much of their former importance eroded by newer means of electronic communication, saw in videotext both a way of augmenting the profitability of their existing wire networks and a justification for enhancing their role by installing broadband fiber-optic networks.

In the future, services dependent on license fees probably will derive higher percentages of their revenue from advertising. As examples, in the mid-1980s the Netherlands planned to double its advertising quota; Denmark planned a second television network partly supported by advertising; West Germany discussed the possibility of private commercial stations; Britain considered partially supporting the BBC from advertising revenue; and Belgium (perhaps the most adamant opponent of advertising in the past) planned to introduce "noncommercial" advertising, the equivalent of paid public service announcements.[4]

Canada may have set an economic precedent when it earmarked part of the profits from pay cable to finance Canadian production. Such *cross-subsidies* among media may become more common, with the feature film industry and newspapers involved as well as broadcasting and cable. At the same time, print media will loom larger in the broadcasting picture as they move to invest in new technologies to compensate for losses of advertising revenue.

A · 8 FACILITIES

Profound changes can be expected in the area of facilities because the new technologies largely represent new configurations of hardware. Though cable installations will go forward in various parts of the world, the greatest area of cable concentration, after North America, will be Europe. But it will be a long time before broad band cable facilities in Europe, as a whole, equal the density of those in the United States. In general, Europe was not expected to reach the 1980 U.S. level of cable penetration until 1990.

Europe's delayed cable development precipitated a race with DBS. The success of one may well doom the other to an inferior role. DBS may prevail because of cable's high cost, slow progress, and uneven distribution (cable is cost ineffective in thinly populated areas). DBS puts all prospective consumers on an even footing, a point much in keeping with the European public service ideal engendered by the receiver fee method of broadcast financing. Observers feel that perhaps the sharp distinction between domsats and DBS will fade, with many of the same satellites performing both relay and direct-broadcast services. On the other hand, by 1984 a slowdown in DBS development occurred, even in the United States, where one of the major companies abandoned its ambitious direct-broadcast plans.

Slow development of cable in Europe can be ascribed to a number of reasons in addition to its high capital costs, among them: limitations on indigenous program resources, which engendered European fears of inundation by American programming and advertising; limits on potential profits because of the lower advertising levels in European countries, as compared to the United States; and the resistance of powerful broadcasting monopolies.

In the Third World, the last bastions of radio-only systems will fall as television completes its global penetration, preceded in some cases by a preliminary invasion of VCRs and satellite relays. In the meantime, the older services still limited to black-and-white pictures will of necessity convert to color as manufacturers phase out monochrome hardware.

A ▪ 9 PROGRAMS

The major changes in programs to expect include (1) increase in "narrowcasting," because of both the growth of local and regional programming and the opportunities for specialized services offered by broadband cable; (2) greater transborder flow of programs, because of syndication and increased reliance on coproduction arrangements; and (3) shaping of many programs to have broad transnational regional appeals for use on multinational DBS systems.

Narrowcasting enables serving locally small audiences (though large when many markets are aggregated) with programming too specialized for the mass market. On the other hand, the high capital investment required by both cable and DBS encourages operators to aim for the largest possible audience on each and every channel, especially those who count on advertising for support. Again, U.S. experience gives some evidence of what to expect: as previously mentioned, several highly touted cable arts channels failed, losing many millions in startup costs, when they proved unable to generate sufficient audience interest. Most narrowcasting may prove workable only for the least expensive types of programs.

Scheduling may decrease in importance because consumers will be able to devise their own program menus, choosing from among many services and using VCRs to "time-shift" programs that arrive at inconvenient times. It is not clear, however, that mass audience members necessarily want to compose their own program schedules. Some U.S.

cable program services have found it expedient to adopt the traditional network practice of tailoring programs to fit the different parts of the day, synchronizing with the changing needs of audiences as the day's activities unfold. It may turn out that most consumers prefer ready-made schedules, finding it a bore constantly to make their own programming decisions.

A ▪ 10 RESEARCH

A corollary of increased dependence on advertising will be increased dependence on audience research. At the same time, researchers face the problem of measuring an ever more fragmented audience. As noted earlier, television audience research can no longer rely on the evidence of simple set tuning to a few broadcast stations; it must also take into account the many channels of cable television, the replay of programs on VCRs, and reception of teletext and videotext. The trend is toward more sophisticated research technology. In 1984, for example, both Malaysia and Thailand were considering abandoning the old diary panel method inherited from the BBC tradition, opting instead for metered receivers. The more advanced countries were considering instantaneous, two-way meter systems that enable direct audience response as well as immediate reporting of tuning data.

A ▪ 11 TRANSBORDER SERVICES

The prospect of international DBS services has interesting but highly ambiguous significance for transborder broadcasting. The peripheral commercial stations pioneered the notion of popular, advertising-supported transborder programming via conventional high-power transmitters. A move into similar services delivered by DBS, though a logical follow-up, raises opposition from even friendly, politically similar target countries. Luxembourg, which offers the most advanced peripheral services, illustrates the ambiguities of the situation. The *Compagnie Luxembourgeoise de Télédiffusion* (CLT), owner of the peripheral RTL stations was an early advocate of DBS. The Luxembourg government was anxious to move ahead with the project, dubbed LUXSAT, but French and Belgian stockholders opposed the satellite. This stalemate led to the emergence of a rival Luxembourg satellite plan, one in which Clay Whitehead, a former U.S. telecommunications official in the Nixon administration, played a key role. Whitehead owned a substantial minority interest in the new company, *Société Luxembourgeoise des Satellites.**

---

*Symptomatic of European reactions was *Variety*'s headline on this deal: "U.S. TV Shows on Euro Satellite: Concept Panics Common Market Politicians" (Monet, 1984).

External services may solve the problem of HF band crowding by going to DBS, but this solution seems remote from both political and engineering viewpoints. There seems little prospect that even radio via DBS will be available without rather expensive, specialized reception facilities, far more costly and complex than a simple short-wave radio. Moreover, as Donald Browne has pointed out, in countries where listening to (or watching) foreign programs can be dangerous, DBS reception facilities will be far more difficult to conceal than short-wave radios.[5] Despite spectrum overcrowding, external services can be expected to continue to expand, encouraged by the wider availability and reduced cost of efficient short-wave receivers.

A ▪ 12 THE NEW WORLD INFORMATION ORDER

Serious concern about media imperialism seems on the wane. Though some cause for complaint may well be justified, evidence of U.S. imperialistic designs in the program field was the product of a temporary situation that has been rapidly changing. More sources of internationally syndicated programming constantly emerge, and the United States itself has increasingly become an importer of foreign programming. Though amounts of imports continue at a relatively high level in most countries, percentages in relation to total programming have tended to decline.

Consciousness of the Western international news agencies has been raised as to sensitivities of Third World countries; the latter, in turn, have begun exchanging more news among themselves. If past experience is any indicator, aid afforded by the IPDC (International Program for the Development of Communications) will have only marginal effect, even with generous funding. Development needs are so massive that such projects only nibble at the problem, while political and bureaucratic restrictions tend to nullify good intentions.

The U.S. withdrawal from UNESCO, even if it turns out to be only temporary, will have a salutary effect. The wholesale exploitation of such international organizations by Third World bureaucratic wheelers and dealers will be reduced, though not entirely eliminated. By sheer weight of numbers, the Third World membership in UNESCO, ITU, and other UN agencies will continue to give them forums in which to air their complaints, both legitimate and contrived. So long as the First and Second Worlds politicize Third World issues, however, the NWIO controversy will go on.

NOTES

[1]Guider, 1984.

[2]Crosby & Tempest discuss the European Economic Community's advertising law initiatives, 1983; Pridgen summarizes steps taken by the Council of Europe, the EBU, and the European Economic Community, 1984: 17–

26. See also Tempest, 1984, and *EBU Review*, Sept. 1983.

[3]Trethowan, 1984: 4.

[4]For the Belgian advertising proposal, see *EBU Review*, March 1984: 44.

[5]Browne, 1982: 348.

GLOSSARY OF ACRONYMS AND SPECIAL USAGES

(Note: Terms printed in **boldface** in the definitions are also found in the glossary/index.)

abhorrent vacuum principle. The concept that in the absence of satisfying program services from authorized sources, unauthorized sources will spring up to fulfill audience desires.

ABT (Australian Broadcasting Tribunal). Australian regulatory agency.

access. The opportunity for individuals and social groups to use broadcasting.

accountability. The concept that a broadcasting service has an obligation to satisfy the wishes of audiences, to practice fairness, and to make corrections when individuals or groups have been treated unfairly.

administration. The government entity "responsible for discharging the obligations undertaken in the Convention of the International Telecommunication Union and the Regulations."

AFRTS (Armed Forces Radio and Television Service). Arm of the U.S. military services responsible for broadcasting stations on overseas military bases.

Agence France Presse. One of the "Big Four" international news agencies.

AIR (All India Radio). India's government-operated radio services.

allocation. In **ITU** regulations, "Entry in the Table of Frequency Allocations of a given frequency band for the purpose of its use by one or more terrestrial or space radiocommunication services . . . under specified conditions." *See also* **allotment** and **assignment.**

allotment. In **ITU** regulations, "Entry of a designated frequency channel in an agreed plan, adopted by a competent conference, for use by one or more administrations for a terrestrial or space radiocommunication service in one or more identified countries or geographical areas and under specified conditions." *See also* **allocation** and **assignment.**

Anik ("brother"). Canadian domestic satellite series.

Annan Committee. Most recent in the series of major government-appointed committees reporting on the future of British broadcasting. It submitted its report to Parliament in 1977.

Antiope (*Acquisition Numérique et Télévisualization d'Images Organisées en Pages d'Ecriture*). French **videotex** and **teletext** system.

AP (Associated Press). One of the "Big Four" international news agencies, headquartered in the United States.

appropriate technology. Technology no more complex and expensive than necessary to accomplish a designated task efficiently in a developing country.

ARABSAT. Regional satellite service planned jointly by Arab states, due for launch in 1985.

ARD (*Arbeitsgemeinschaft der Öffentlich-rechtlichen Rundfunkanstalten der Bundesrepublik Deutschland*). Radio and television program supplier organized jointly by the West German states to operate their regional radio and their first and third TV networks.

Ariane. Satellite rocket launcher developed by a European consortium led by France and operated by Arianespace. Sited at Kourou in French Guiana, on the north coast of South America.

ASBU (Arab States Broadcasting Union). Intergovernmental organization of Arab broadcasting authorities.

Asia-Pacific Broadcasting Union. Association of broadcasting organizations in the Middle East as well as in Asia and the Pacific.

assignment. In ITU regulations, "Authorization by an administration for a radio station to use a radio frequency or radio frequency channel under specified conditions." *See also* **allocation** and **allotment.**

ATS (Application Technology Satellite). Series of U.S. space vehicles used to test direct-broadcast satellite reception. *See also* **SITE.**

A2 (*Antenne 2*). One of the French state-operated television networks.

autarchy. A policy or condition of national self-sufficiency, specifically with reference to the production of cultural artifacts such as broadcast programming.

authoritarianism. Policy of strict government control of broadcasting with little regard for popular taste. *See also* **paternalism** and **permissivism.**

autonomy, corporate. Ideally, independence from government bureaucratic machinery and official intervention resulting from management of broadcasting by a nonprofit public corporation. Refers especially to autonomy in personnel, fiscal, and programming policies. The BBC is a leading example.

auxiliary enterprises. Nonbroadcast activities of a broadcasting authority, such as publications and program sales, usually undertaken for profit.

band. (1) A large group of frequencies representing a segment of the radio frequency spectrum, as defined by **ITU**; for example, the **HF** (high-frequency) band. (2) A smaller group of frequencies allocated by the ITU to a particular use; for example, the **MF** (medium-frequency) broadcast band.

BARB (Broadcast Audience Research Bureau). Joint agency for conducting systematic quantitative and qualitative audience research, controlled equally by the **BBC** and **ITV.**

basic cable. The complement of programs normally delivered by a **cable TV** system without payment of extra subscription fees for **pay-cable** services.

BBC (British Broadcasting Corporation). Nonprofit statutory corporation that conducts Britain's public service broadcasting. Originally, the BBC monopolized **UK** broadcasting, but it now competes with the commercial services supervised by the **IBA.**

BBC-1, BBC-2. Names of the two **BBC** television networks.

Berne Convention. An international copyright agreement for the protection of literary and artistic works, initiated in 1887.

Bildschirmtext (screen text). German interactive **videotex** system.

block scheduling. Practice of scheduling all commercials in groups at a few designated times of day. *See* **trafficking.**

blocktimer. A program for which its sponsor has purchased time. Refers especially to religious programs.

border blasters. Extremely powerful **MF peripheral** stations located in Mexico near the U.S. border.

British Telecom. UK telecommunications authority, originally a government monopoly but due to be sold to private investors during the 1980s.

broadcasting. Communication of sound and pictures to the general public by means of radio waves in space. Sometimes **cable TV** is termed broadcasting though it does not use radio waves in open space as its medium of communication. Distinguished from **common carrier.**

BRT (*Belgische Radio en Televisie*). Dutch-language component of the dual Belgian broadcasting system. *See also* **RTBF.**

BSS (Broadcast Satellite Service). ITU designation for direct-broadcast satellite (**DBS**) service. *See also* **FSS.**

Bundespost. West German **PTT** authority.

cable. *See* **cable TV, coaxial cable, optical fiber.**

cable TV. System for delivering television programs to subscribers over cables rather than by means of over-the-air TV stations. Also referred to simply as "cable."

Canal Plus. French subscription TV network started in 1984, using the old 819-line TV channels and facilities but conforming to current European line standards.

CAPTAIN (Character and Pattern Telephone Access Network). Japanese **videotex** system.

CATV (Community Antenna Television). Term for **cable TV,** now archaic in the United States but still used in Europe. It generally implies a "signal enhancement" service, improving reception of already available over-the-air signals but lacking in special channels carrying nonbroadcast programming.

CBS-Newsfilm. U.S. network-based agency supplying television news pictures internationally. Other networks offer similar services.

CBU (Caribbean Broadcasting Union). Association of broadcasting organizations located in Caribbean area.

CEEFAX ("see facts"). **Teletext** system developed and operated by the **BBC.**

channel. (1) Group of frequencies designated for the use of a single station. (2) The station using a particular channel. (3) The programming available on a particular cable TV channel, as "Sports Channel." (4) A network, as **Channel Four.**

Channel Four. British commercial TV network launched in 1982, a wholly owned subsidiary of the **IBA.** So called because it is Britain's fourth TV network, coming after **BBC-1, BBC-2,** and **ITV.**

circular rediffusion. Translation of Italian term for "broadcasting."

clandestine. Applied to secretive, unauthorized stations having political motives. Distinguished from **pirate** stations, which usually have commercial motives and are not secretive.

closed circuit. Descriptive of a radio or TV service whose components are physically interconnected by wire or cable links, with no "open" (that is, over-the-air) links.

coaxial cable. A metallic conductive medium consisting of a solid central conductor surrounded by a tubelike housing, capable of passing much wider **bands** of frequencies than simple wire conductors.

common carrier. A **telecommunication** facility for hire to all comers on a uniform cost basis. The telephone is the classic example. Distinguished from **broadcasting** in that a common carrier addresses specific recipients, not the general public, and in that the operator assumes no responsibility for content, as does the broadcast operator.

Commonwealth Broadcasting Association. Organization of public broadcasting authorities of Commonwealth countries, numbering about 50. Publishes *Combroad*.

complementarity. A relationship between a system's simultaneous network programs, ensuring that they will be of different types rather than imitative of each other. Characteristic of controlled competition.

comprehensive programming. A service offering a well-rounded mix of program types; contrasts with **generic programming.**

COMSAT (Communication Satellite Corporation). Authorized by the U.S. government, COMSAT operates the **INTELSAT** system on behalf of the international consortium of owners. It also has subsidiary companies, including one that operates the U.S. **domsat** series, *Comstar.*

controller. British term for a high-ranking broadcasting executive in charge of a department.

Coordinated Universal Time. *See* **UTC.**

coproduction. Joint undertaking by producers in two or more countries to share in the production of a film or television program.

COPUOS (Committee on Peaceful Uses of Outer Space). United Nations committee concerned with, among other things, the effects of **DBS** on national sovereignty.

coverage. The reach of a broadcast station's signal, usually measured in terms of signal strength or percentage of homes reached in a designated geographic area. *See also* **penetration.**

cross-reporting. Technique used by **RFE** and **RL** to embarrass Communist states by comparing conditions or events in one nation with those in another, calling attention to inconsistencies in the way the regimes treat their citizens.

cross-trailing. The practice of mutually promoting simultaneous programs on two or more networks; that is, Network A promotes the competing program on Network B and vice versa. Characteristic of **complementary** services.

cultural imperialism. *See* **media imperialism.**

DBS (Direct-Broadcast Satellite). A satellite with sufficient power to be receivable by small antennas suitable for individual home use. The **ITU** defines DBS in terms of both direct individual home reception and community reception by means of retransmission over a small TV station or cable TV system.

delivery. The step in a communication chain that provides material directly to the ultimate consumer. Distinguished from **distribution,**

which refers to prior links in the chain, such as the relay of network programs to stations or cable TV headends.

Deutsche Welle. West Germany's main **external service.**

Deutschlandfunk. West German external service aimed at European listeners.

development journalism. News reporting especially adapted to the coverage of Third World economic and social development projects, sometimes implying subservience of such reporting to government. *See also* **DSC.**

direct relay. *See* **rebroadcasting.**

director-general. British term for top administrator, equivalent to general manager.

disinformation. Deliberately planted false information released in the guise of news.

distribution. *See* **delivery.**

domsat (domestic satellite). A national satellite that relays signals back to points within its own national terrain.

Doordarshan (distance view). India's government-operated TV service.

DPA-ETES. West German supplier of syndicated television news pictures.

DSC (Development Support Communication). A form of **development communication** explicitly designed to further the objectives of development rather than the objectives of journalism as usually understood. DSC plans are built into development projects to facilitate understanding on the part of those affected, to foster participation, and to encourage acceptance of innovations.

ducting. Sporadic long-distance propagation of TV or other signals normally reaching only to the horizon; they reach much farther when trapped between layers of atmosphere acting in the manner of a duct.

DX (distance). Long-distance broadcast reception, with particular reference to the hobby of logging reception of distant stations and obtaining verification from the program sources.

earth station. A terrestrial facility that sends signals to and receives signals from one or more satellites. Those designed for reception only are sometimes called **TVROs.**

EBU (European Broadcasting Union). Association of European and some adjacent public broadcasting organizations. It operates **Eurovision** and publishes *EBU Review.*

ECS (European Communication Satellite). Series of communication satellites belonging to **ESA,** initiated in 1983.

Empire Service. Original name of British External Services, opened by the BBC in 1932.

EPS (European Program on Satellite). Operational regional DBS service planned for 1988, successor to the **Eurikon** experiment, using **L-Sat.**

ESA (European Space Agency). Consortium of European agencies conducting satellite research and development, founded in 1975. Its projects include **Ariane, ECS, L-SAT,** and **OTS.**

Eurikon. Experiment in the satellite distribution of pan-European programming, conducted in 1982. Five **EBU** members took turns in devising the programs, which were privately viewed in 15 countries. *See also* **EPS.**

Euronet. System of internationally televised press conferences using satellite linkage, staged by **USIA** as a means of placing pro-U.S. stories in foreign news media.

Eurovision. International program exchange arranged by **EBU.**

Eutelsat. Consortium of European **PTT** authorities coordinating management of **OTS** and **ECS** satellite series.

external service. A government broadcasting service openly aimed at foreign countries as an official arm of international diplomacy. External services make extensive use of short-wave radio.

farm forum. Type of adult education program for farmers that incorporates systematic feedback from target audiences.

FBIS (Foreign Broadcast Information Service). Monitoring service conducted by the Central Intelligence Agency.

FEBC (Far East Broadcasting Company). Evangelical broadcasting organization with stations in the Philippines, San Francisco, Saipan, the Seychelles, and South Korea.

FES (*Friedrich-Ebert-Stiftung*). West German foundation active in assisting development of broadcasting and other media in the **Third World.**

fiber-optic cable. *See* **optical fiber.**

First World. The industrialized, democratic nations, referred to loosely as "the West." *Compare* **Second World** and **Third World.**

fiscal time. Air time given by private broadcasters to the Mexican government in lieu of taxes. *See also* **statutory time.**

footprint. The area of the earth's surface covered at a designated signal strength by a satellite transmission.

Fourth Network. An IBA subsidiary, the UK's fourth national **network** (the other three being BBC-1, BBC-2, and ITV), called **Channel Four.**

Fourth World. Term sometimes applied collectively to so-called stateless minorities, such as the Welsh in Great Britain.

FR3 (*France Régions 3*). One of the French state-controlled TV networks, supplying both national and regional services.

free flow doctrine. The belief in a policy of encouraging the uninhibited exchange of information within and between nations, without government interference. *See also* **NWIO.**

FSS (Fixed Satellite Service). ITU-defined category of service devoted to **point-to-point** satellite communication. **INTELSAT** is the most notable example. *Compare* **BSS.**

gallery. British term for TV control room, said to derive from the fact that the control room in an early BBC studio in Alexandra Palace was situated in a minstrel's gallery.

GEAR (Group of European Audience Researchers). Association of researchers from both Eastern and Western European broadcasting organizations.

generic programming. Program scheduling aimed at a particular audience or audience interest. *Compare* **comprehensive programming.**

geostationary orbit. A circle 22,300 miles above the equator where satellites remain stationary with respect to the earth because they keep in step with the earth's rotation. A satellite in this orbit remains fixed above its target area 24 hours per day, whereas satellites in nonsynchronous orbit travel across the sky, unable to reach their target areas after they pass below the horizon. Also called geosynchronous orbit.

"giving a lead." Phrase summarizing the philosophy of John Reith, the BBC's first **director-general,** who believed that program quality should remain a little ahead of popular taste.

GMT (Greenwich Mean Time). Mean solar time at 0 degrees latitude, which passes through Greenwich, England. Also called **UTC** (Coordinated Universal Time).

goniometer. Directional sensing device that can be used to locate unlicensed sets by picking up radiations from broadcast receivers.

Gorizont. USSR geostationary satellite series, initiated in 1979.

Gresham's law. The economic doctrine that bad money drives out good, often applied to broadcasting; that is, low program quality in one service tends to drag down all competing services to the same low level.

hard network. An interconnected, or true, network, as contrasted with a noninterconnected or **soft network.**

Haute Authorité (High Authority). The agency with top legal responsibility for broadcasting under the French law of 1982.

HCJB. Pioneer high-power, overseas Christian evangelical station located in Quito, Ecuador.

HDTV (High-Definition TV). Experimental, improved TV standard, greatly increasing the resolution of the TV picture, enabling large-screen, wide-format images.

headend. Cable TV or **wired-radio** installation that picks up programs off the air, receives relayed programs, and (sometimes) originates closed-circuit programs, **rediffusing** them by wire or cable to individual subscribers.

Hermes. Pioneer Canadian experimental **DBS** vehicle launched in 1976.

HF (High Frequency). Short wave, referring to the band used for, among other things, long-distance radio broadcasting.

IBA (Independent Broadcasting Authority). British nonprofit public corporation set up to authorize and supervise commercial radio and television operations. It builds and operates transmitter facilities, renting them to the services it authorizes.

IFRB (International Frequency Registration Board). Permanent ITU headquarters unit in Geneva, responsible for keeping track of frequency usage by member nations and advising them on interference problems.

IIC (International Institute of Communications). Society of communication scholars, executives, and practitioners that studies communication issues, conducts conferences, undertakes consultancies, and issues reports. Publishes the semimonthly journal *InterMedia.*

ILR (Independent Local Radio). British local radio stations operated commercially under supervision of the **IBA.**

Independent Television. Group of UK commercial program companies, private contractors authorized and supervised by the **IBA,** comprising the 15 regional companies and **TV-am,** collectively forming the ITV network. **Channel Four** is not considered part of the group because it is owned by IBA.

infrastructure. Basic national resources, such as power, telecommunications network, manufacturing capacity, and training facilities, that largely determine the kind of broadcasting system a nation can support.

INSAT. India's **domsat,** launched in 1983.

INTELSAT (International Telecommunications Satellite Organization). Consortium of more than a hundred countries organized to operate a worldwide satellite relay system, the most extensive facility of its kind. **COMSAT** operates the system on behalf of the consortium.

Intendant. German term for top broadcasting operational official, equivalent to **director-general.**

interference. In telecommunication services, radio energy that conflicts with intended signals, causing distortion and loss of intelligibility. Conflicts come from other transmitters and from such natural causes as electrical storms. **Jamming** is intentional interference.

International Telecommunication Convention. Document forming the legal basis for the **ITU,** periodically revised and readopted at plenipotentiary sessions of the union.

Intersputnik. Communist equivalent of **INTELSAT.** It has 12 members and uses satellite facilities leased from the USSR.

Intervision. East European program exchange organization, equivalent to the West European **Eurovision.**

IPDC (International Program for the Development of Communications). **UNESCO** project for assisting **Third World** media development, founded in response to **NWIO** pressures.

ITCA (Independent Television Companies Association). Trade association of the British commercial TV companies.

ITN (Independent Television News). Nonprofit subsidiary of British commercial television program companies, supplying national and international news for their networks.

ITU (International Telecommunication Union). United Nations agency formed by most of the world's nations to regulate and facilitate wire and wireless communication and to manage the **spectrum** in the common interest. Its basic statute is the **International Telecommunication Convention,** supplemented by the **Radio Regulations.** *See also* **RARC, WARC.**

ITV. The UK's 15 regional commercial TV program companies and **TV-am,** authorized and supervised by the **IBA.** *See also* **Independent Television.**

jamming. Creation of deliberate **interference** to prevent domestic reception of programs, usually aimed at external services coming from foreign countries.

JICTAR (Joint Industry Committee on Television Audience Research). Association of the British commercial program companies under **IBA** for the purpose of jointly furthering audience research.

junction point. A moment in time at which two or more networks simultaneously change programs, enabling them to **cross-trail** each other's offerings.

Kol Israel (Voice of Israel). Israel's government radio services.

LDC (Less Developed Country). A **Third World** country.

levy, the. A special tax imposed in addition to normal business taxes on British **ITV** companies because of their extraordinary profitability.

license fee, receiver. A fee paid by users for the right to operate receiving sets.

lingua franca. Any hybrid language used as a common tongue in a multilingual society.

local placement. Arrangement by an **external service** to have a program broadcast on the domestic system of a target country.

L-SAT (Large Satellite). High-power, direct-broadcast satellite planned by **ESA.**

LUXSAT. **DBS** satellite proposed by CLT (*Compagnie Luxembourgeoise de Télédiffusion*), the parent company of **RTL,** looking toward multinational commercial programming from Luxembourg.

MAC (Multiplexed Analogue Component). Advanced digital method of TV signal processing developed by **IBA** engineers. It would eliminate differences in color standards.

MacBride Report. Report on **NWIO** goals published in 1980 by **UNESCO,** prepared by a committee headed by an Irish statesman, Sean MacBride.

magizdat. Clandestinely circulated recordings in the USSR. *Compare* **samizdat.**

MATV (Master Antenna Television). Cable TV system based upon subscriber hookups to a single common antenna in a housing complex, usually limited to three hundred or fewer subscribers. Called SMATV when receiving programs by satellite relay.

media imperialism. Alleged cultural domination of Third World countries by Western nations through control over communication media, notably by means of international news agencies and program syndication. *See also* **neocolonialism.**

MF (Medium Frequency). *See* **MW.**

MIP-TV (*Marché Internationale de Programmes de Télévision*). Major international trade fair held annually in Europe for the sale of syndicated programs.

mixed system. A broadcasting system in which two or more entities with contrasting programming motives compete, typically pitting a public service component against a commercial component.

Molniya. Nonsynchronous Soviet satellite series for relay of broadcast signals, started in 1965.

monitoring. Systematic recording and reporting of foreign broadcasts for the purpose of gathering news and intelligence information.

MTV (*Mainos-TV Reklam*). Finnish commercial company that schedules programs and advertisements on time bought from the noncommercial state TV authority (not to be confused with MTV, the U.S. satellite-cable network).

must-carry rules. Rules forcing **cable TV** systems to carry the programs of stipulated broadcast services.

MW (Medium Wave). Adjective often used to designate standard or AM broadcasting.

Närradio (neighborhood radio). In Sweden, a special class of local ministations outside the control of the regular Swedish state radio monopoly and minimally regulated.

narrowcasting. Designing broadcast or cable program services with appeals limited to specialized audiences, counting on the cumulative audiences of many markets to justify expense of the services.

NASA (National Aeronautics and Space Administration). U.S. government agency operating satellite launch facilities used by both U.S. and foreign interests.

NASDA (National Space Development Agency). Japanese equivalent of **NASA,** the third facility (after **NASA** and the USSR) to launch a satellite into geosynchronous orbit.

NATPE (National Association of Television Program Executives). U.S. organization that among other things stages an annual international trade fair for the sale of **syndicated** programs.

needle time. Amount of time that British broadcast stations may devote to recorded music, as limited by copyright holders.

neocolonialism. Alleged successor to militarily enforced colonialism, based on cultural and economic domination of Third World nations by the leading industrialized countries. *See also* **media imperialism.**

network. Group of two or more broadcast stations or cable systems interconnected physically and organizationally so as to broadcast the same program schedule simultaneously. Outside the United States, a local cable TV system is often referred to as a network. *See also* **channel, program,** and **pseudonetwork.**

NHK (*Nippon Hoso Kyokai*). Japan's **public service** broadcasting corporation.

NIIO (New International Information Order). Variation of **NWIO.**

nonaligned nations. Originally a group of 77 (later approximately 100) developing countries that adopted a policy of political independence vis-à-vis both the Western and the Communist blocs.

NORDSAT. Proposed common satellite to service the Nordic (Scandinavian) countries.

NOS (*Nederlandse Omroep Stichting*). Umbrella company responsible for providing production facilities for the Dutch broadcasting organizations, for producing programs of national interest (40 percent of the output), and for certain other general functions.

NTSC (National Television System Committee). Term designating the U.S. color TV system. *See also* **PAL** and **SECAM.**

NWIO (New World Information Order). A set of goals proposed for reforming the global communication system to make it fairer to the **Third World.** In particular, the NWIO opposes the **free flow doctrine** and market-oriented aspects of communication as practiced in the West.

OB (Outside Broadcast). British term for **remote broadcast.**

OIRT (*Organisation Internationale de Radiodiffusion et Télévision*). Communist equivalent of the **EBU.**

open-skies policy. U.S. Federal Communications Commission policy encouraging an uninhibited marketplace for the commercial development of communication satellites.

optical fiber cable. Wide-band transmission medium using a thin bundle of glass filaments to convey a modulated laser light beam. It passes a much broader frequency **band** than **coaxial cable,** potentially sending hundreds of television channels over a single cable.

opt-out. Said of a network affiliate when it leaves its network occasionally, by prearrangement, to broadcast regional or local programs.

ORACLE (Optional Reception of Announcements by Coded Line Electronics). British **teletext** system developed by **IBA** engineers and operated by **ITV**.

orbit. The path followed by a satellite in revolving about the earth. Communication satellites may follow a **geosynchronous orbit** or a nonsynchronous orbit.

Orbita. USSR television relay system for reaching distant areas, utilizing the **Molniya** satellite series.

ORF (*Österreichischer Rundfunk*). The Austrian state broadcasting organization.

OTS (Orbital Test Satellite). Series of experimental European satellites used by **ESA**.

OU (Open University). Degree-granting British university that does much of its teaching by means of radio and television.

out-of-band. Said of broadcast transmissions that use channels other than those authorized by the **ITU**; especially common among shortwave stations.

outside contributor. British term for a creative freelance broadcasting employee.

PAL (Phase Alternate Line). West German color TV system, generally used in Europe. *See also* **NTSC** and **SECAM.**

PALAPA. Indonesian domestic/regional satellite system, first to be developed by a **Third World** nation.

paternalism. A policy halfway between **authoritarianism** and **permissivism,** generally eschewing censorship but not entirely subservient to the lowest common denominator of audience preferences.

pay cable. Cable TV program services costing an additional fee over and above the **basic cable** subscription fee, often distributed by **satellite-cable networks.** *See also* **pay TV** and **STV.**

pay TV. Any TV service supported by subscriber fees, as distinct from services supported by advertising. *See also* **pay cable** and **STV.**

penetration. The extent to which the population within a service area can receive a broadcast signal, or the extent to which receivers in a service area are available. May be measured as a percentage of all households or of the total population. **UNESCO** has used as a penetration measure "sets-per-thousand population."

peripherals. Commercial stations near the borders of a country that beam programs into that country without having to abide by its commercial regulations. Usually located in ministates such as Luxembourg and Monaco.

permissivism. Policy of imposing minimal government controls over the free play of marketplace demands, characteristic of highly commercial broadcast services. Emphasizes audience wants as indicated by tuning behavior. *Compare* **authoritarianism** and **paternalism.**

Pilkington Report. One of the series of reports on the future of British broadcasting, published in 1962, notable for its analysis of commercial television, which had been introduced into Britain in the 1950s. *See also* **Annan Committee.**

pillarization. A characteristic of Netherlands broadcasting, which is conducted primarily by eight major religious/political groups (pillars), in keeping with traditional Dutch deference to democratic principles of group self-government.

piracy. (1) Operation of unauthorized commercial stations, usually in international waters near target regions; pirates violate ITU frequency regulations, copyright laws, and national broadcasting laws. (2) Duplication and sale of program materials, particularly television programs on videotape, in violation of copyright laws. (3) Theft of cable television or satellite signals.

playout center. A TV network producing none of its own programs but acting as an "electronic publisher" of programs produced by others. Britain's **Channel Four** is an example.

pluralism. Condition obtaining when a broadcast system has several competing components animated by differing motivations for programming. *See also* **mixed system.**

point-to-point communication. Transmission of signals from one specific address to another, as distinguished from **broadcast** transmission to the general public. **Relays** are a common example.

Prestel. **Videotext** system developed and operated by the British Post Office.

prime time. The evening segment of the broadcast day when the maximum number of televiewers turn on their sets. Prime time hours vary with national life styles.

prior consent. Term used in connection with **DBS,** referring to the claim that no DBS signals should be directed to a foreign country without first obtaining that country's permission.

privatization. A deregulatory trend toward the transfer of control over matters hitherto under government domination to private hands. Examples of areas subject to privatization in some countries are spectrum use and national telecommunication services.

product life-cycle theory. The theory that audiences prefer their own nationally produced programs to foreign syndicated programs once local production facilities and know-how have evolved.

program. Sometimes used as equivalent to **network.**

program contractor. In Britain, one of the independent companies franchised by the **IBA** to broadcast commercial programming.

program exchange. Regional arrangements for the sharing of programs among a number of countries. **Eurovision** is an example.

program guide. Published details of broadcast program plans, often copyrighted and issued exclusively by broadcasting authorities as money-making ventures.

Proporz (proportional representation). Practice in some German-speaking broadcasting systems of appointing people to key posts in accordance with their political affiliations so as to reproduce the power balance in parliament. Typically, a broadcasting official and that official's deputy represent opposing parties.

pseudonetwork. Two or more stations broadcasting common programs but not interconnected for simultaneous release of those programs. *Compare* **network.**

PTT (Post, Telephone, and Telegraph). A government agency (often a ministry) responsible for national **telecommunications** facilities.

public broadcasting. Not used with uniform meaning in all countries but generally implying services with a strong **public-service broadcasting** orientation, not primarily dependent on advertising.

public-service broadcasting. Broadcasting in which the public interest takes priority over commercial interests. Public service broadcasters carrying advertising usually depend on commercial income for only part of their revenue, thus forestalling undue advertiser influence over programs.

qualitative research. Investigation of the intensity of people's program likes and dislikes. Contrasts with *quantitative* research, which focuses on the sizes of audiences and characteristics such as age and sex of audience members.

quotas. Ceilings on the amount (usually expressed as a percentage of all programming) of programming that broadcasting services are allowed to import from foreign sources.

Radio Caroline. Best known of the offshore **pirate** stations in the North Sea.

Radio France. State company in charge of the several French radio networks, such as *France-Culture, France-Inter, France-Musique.*

Radio Martí. A U.S. **surrogate domestic service** under **VOA** auspices, aimed at Cuba and operating from Marathon, Florida.

Radio Moscow. The USSR's official **external service.**

Radio 1, 2, 3, and 4. The four national radio **networks** in Britain, operated by the **BBC.**

Radio Peace and Progress. An unofficial **external service** of the USSR, ostensibly sponsored by public organizations.

Radio Regulations. The detailed rules of the **EBU,** periodically revised at regional and world conferences. The regulations include the frequency allocation tables.

radiovision. A **BBC** system for marrying radio broadcasts with photographic slides for educational use in the classroom.

RAI ("Italian radio listening"). Italian state-controlled broadcasting service (full name: *RAI-Radiotelevisione Italiana*).

RARC (Regional Administrative Radio Conference). A regional meeting of **ITU** members to adopt regulations covering a specific field of activities. *See also* **WARC.**

rebroadcasting. The broadcast of material picked up directly (that is, off the air) from another broadcasting station.

rectification. The correction of an inaccurate or unfair news story by the offending medium, one of the proposed reforms of the **NWIO.**

Rede Globo. A Brazilian private television network, one of the world's largest.

rediffusion. **Delivery** of programs by means of wire or cable. Sometimes also used to mean **broadcasting** (see, for example, **circular rediffusion).**

relay. The act of passing on a signal from one point to another in the course of **distribution;** or, a facility that does relaying (that is, wire, coaxial cable, microwave links, or satellites). Normally, the general public cannot pick up relay signals. Networks depend on relays to interconnect their affiliated stations. Also loosely used to mean **rebroadcast,** especially by **external services.**

relay exchange. (1) The **headend** of a **rediffusion (wired-radio)** system. (2) An intermediate point in a **switched star** cable TV system where, at the request of subscribers, individual channels are selected for sending to subscribers' terminals.

repeater. A subsidiary transmitter, usually automated and of low power, **rebroadcasting** the signals of a main transmitter.

retransmission right. In copyright law, an additional right of copyright holders to collect fees for the **cable TV** delivery of broadcast programs to distant markets not originally contemplated in the grant of local broadcasting rights.

Reuters. British international news agency, one of the "Big Four."

RFE (Radio Free Europe). U.S. radio **surrogate domestic service** aimed at the Communist countries of Eastern Europe, with the exception of the USSR, headquartered in Munich, West Germany. *See also* **RL.**

RFO (*Radio Télévision Française d'Outre-Mer*). Agency serving the broadcasting needs of French overseas territories.

RIAS (Radio in the American Sector [of Berlin]). **Surrogate domestic service** aimed at East Germany, operated by West Germans but supported in part by **USIA.**

right to communicate. A basic human right, as proposed by NWIO advocates and others, guaranteeing among other things individual and group **access** to the means of communication.

RL (Radio Liberty). A U.S. **surrogate domestic service** aimed at the USSR, operating from Munich,West Germany. It is funded by Congress and supervised by the Board for International Broadcasting, a nonprofit corporation.

RTBF (*Radio-Télévision de la Communauté Française*). Broadcasting service of the French-speaking population in Belgium. *See also* **BRT.**

RTE (*Radio Telefis Eireann*). The public corporation responsible for Irish broadcasting.

samizdat. Covertly circulated documents in the USSR. Used by **RL** as a source for program materials. *See also **magizdat.***

satellite-cable network. A program source feeding scattered cable systems simultaneously by means of satellite relays.

SATV (Satellite TV). A pioneer European international **satellite-cable network,** based in the **UK.**

+SBC (Swiss Broadcasting Corporation). The nonprofit public company responsible for coordinating operations of the several language-based societies that furnish Swiss broadcasting services.

scanner. British term for portable TV field studio.

SECAM (*Séquence Couleur à Mémoire*). French color TV system. *See also* **NTSC** and **PAL.**

secondment. Assignment of an employee to another organization temporarily, typically from a developed broadcasting organization to a developing one.

Second World. The Communist states collectively, especially those of Eastern Europe, as distinguished from "the West" and the **Third World.**

service. The programming of any broadcasting network or station that makes up part of a national broadcasting **system.**

SFP (*Société Française de Production et de Création Audiovisuelle*). State production company at the disposal of the French television networks.

SIPRA (*Societa' Italiana Publicita' per Azioni*). Official advertising agency that handles **RAI** advertising.

SITE (Satellite Instruction Television Experiment). Indian adult education experiment that used **ATS** for direct satellite broadcasting to villagers.

skip-distance. Terrain area missed by a sky-wave signal when it bounces between earth and ionosphere and back.

Sky Channel. Name used for the **SATV satellite-cable network** service when fed to **UK cable TV** systems.

slalom run. Term descriptive of viewing pattern when audiences switch back and forth between TV channels to avoid serious content.

SOFIRAD (*Société Financière de Radiodiffusion*). French holding company that controls several of the major **peripheral** stations broadcasting to France.

soft network. A **pseudonetwork.**

spectrum. Electromagnetic energy as systematically delineated in terms of a range of frequencies or wavelengths.

spectrum management. Regulation of **spectrum** use with the goal of enabling maximum efficient utilization while minimizing destructive interference from other authorized stations.

spillover. Domestic signals that inadvertently cross national boundaries. Sometimes called overspill.

sponsorship. Public identification of an advertiser with a specific program, usually one supplied and controlled by the advertiser. *Compare* **underwriting.**

SSB (single sideband). Method of signal modulation that economizes on band width. Commonly used in radiotelephony, it has been proposed for use in short-wave broadcasting but would outmode most short-wave receivers.

statutory time. Free air time that some governments require private stations to make available by law for government use.

STV (Subscription TV). Coded (scrambled) over-the-air (broadcast) television service for which audiences pay a subscription fee. *Compare* **pay TV.**

subvention. A government grant for the operation of a broadcasting service.

surrogate domestic service. An **external service** that attempts to behave like a domestic service for the target country with a view to "correcting" the information disseminated by the actual domestic services of that country.

switched star. Phrase descriptive of a cable TV connection method that delivers the system's entire package of channels only to **relay exchanges.** Individual subscribers call up one **channel** at a time from their nearest relay exchange by means of a two-way circuit. Contrasts with **tree and branch** cabling, standard in the United States.

Symphonie. Joint French-German experimental satellite series started in 1974.

syndication. Reduction in the expense to individual users of expensive, prepackaged program materials by dividing costs among many users.

system. (1) A nation's broadcasting services and their organizational structure considered in the aggregate. (2) A local **cable TV** installation, comprising a headend, cable links to subscribers, and business arrangements for obtaining programs, collecting subscription payments, and so on under the terms of a franchise or license.

TASS (*Telegrafnoe Agentsvo Sovietskovo Soyuza*). Soviet official news agency.

TDF-1. Satellite planned by *Télédiffusion de France,* as part of a joint French-German DBS project, successor to the *Symphonie* experiment. *See also* **TV-Sat.**

technological determinism. Theory that a system's output is largely controlled by its technology. For example, the concept that the technology of broadcasting largely determines the types of programs a **system** is likely to produce, irrespective of the human factors involved.

Tele Biella. Illegal Italian cable TV system opened in 1971, precipitating a series of court decisions resulting in the legitimization of private broadcasting in Italy.

telecommunication(s). Generically, anything communicated at a distance by wire or radio but usually implying such nonbroadcast communications as telegraph, telephone, and data transmission. *See also* **PTT.**

Télédiffusion de France. Agency responsible for supplying the transmission facilities for French state broadcasting services.

telenovela. A serial drama similar to a soap opera, a popular program format in Latin countries.

Telesat Canada. Corporation under combined public and private ownership, responsible for operation of Canada's **domsat** services.

teletext. One-way transmission of text and graphics by means of television broadcast stations. Often also applied to text transmitted by cable TV systems. *See also* **videotex.**

Televisa. The major private televison network operator in Mexico.

Telidon. Canadian **videotex** and **teletext** system.

TF1 (*Télévision Française 1*). One of the state-owned French TV networks.

Third Program. Historically, a third radio network introduced by the **BBC** to cater to the intellectual elite.

Third World. The less developed countries of the world, numbering about a hundred. *Compare* **First, Second,** and **Fourth Worlds.**

time zones. Areas of the world that operate on different time-of-day standards, such as the U.S. Eastern, Central, Mountain, and Pacific zones, each an hour apart.

TOPICS (Total On-Line Program and Information Control System). Elaborate automated production system used by Japan's **NHK.**

trafficking, commercial. Scheduling commercials throughout the broadcast day, between and within programs. Contrasts with **block scheduling.**

translator. A **repeater** station, usually low power and self-operating, that converts an incoming broadcast signal to a different frequency before **rebroadcasting** it.

transponder. A unit within a satellite that combines the functions of both receiving and retransmitting signals. Normally, each transponder can handle a single television program, and each satellite carries a number of transponders.

transposer. British term for **translator** station.

tree and branch. Phrase descriptive of a method of wiring a cable TV system so that all channels of the system are delivered to each subscriber. Contrasts with **switched star** method.

tropical band. Frequencies, mostly in the **HF** band, **allocated** by the **ITU** especially for domestic use of stations in the tropical latitudes, where static interferes with the **MF** signals normally used for domestic coverage.

tropospheric scatter. A method of relaying **HF** signals beyond the horizon by the reception of scattered rays of energy dispersed by contact with the troposphere, a high layer of atmosphere.

trossification. The tendency for bad programs to drive out good in a competitive situation, so called because the Dutch broadcasting group TROS is alleged to have caused such an effect in the Netherlands.

TV-am. British "breakfast program," offered by a commercial network supervised by the **IBA**.

TV-5. French-language, satellite-distributed TV program service planned by France to counter **SATV**.

TVRO. A receive-only satellite earth terminal, consisting of an antenna and associated signal-processing equipment.

TV-Sat. German DBS vehicle expected to be launched as part of a joint French-German project. *See also* **TDF-1.**

TWR (Trans World Radio). Evangelical broadcasting organization with stations in Cyprus, Guam, Monaco, Netherlands Antilles, Sri Lanka, and Swaziland.

UK (United Kingdom). Stands for the United Kingdom of Great Britain and Northern Ireland, a more inclusive term than *Great Britain*, which includes Scotland and Wales but excludes Northern Ireland.

underwriting. A form of commercial **sponsorship** less compromising than outright sponsorship. Underwriters provide funds for creating broadcast materials in return for a limited mention of their role as program providers.

UNESCO (United Nations Educational, Scientific and Cultural Organization). A United Nations agency in the forefront of the agitation for adoption of the **NWIO** program.

union. A group of national broadcasting authorities organized for mutual benefit, especially for purposes of regulation (for example, **ITU**) or of regional program exchange (for example, **EBU**).

UNISAT. Domestic satellite planned by **UK** for 1986.

Universal Copyright Convention. **UNESCO**-sponsored international copyright agreement extending the **Berne Convention** to the Americas.

UPI (United Press International). One of the two major U.S. international news agencies, a member of the "Big Four."

UPITN. International TV picture news agency combining the resources of **UPI** and **ITN**.

URTNA (Union of National Radio and Television Organizations of Africa). Association of African national broadcasting authorities.

USIA (United States Information Agency). Arm of the U.S. government responsible for international exchange of persons and information. The **VOA** falls under USIA jurisdiction.

UTC. *See* **GMT.**

Vatican Radio. Vatican City religious broadcasting service, mainly **external.**

VCR (Videocassette Recorder). Small-format magnetic TV recorder and playback unit suitable for use by the general public.

VHF broadcasting. FM broadcasting.

video. (1) A **VCR** program for home use. (2) The home VCR business generally. (3) A visual accompaniment for an audio recording. (4) Nonbroadcast TV production generally. (5) The visual component of any TV presentation.

videotex. Generic term for the family of systems for two-way transmission of textual and graphic materials by means of wire or cable connections between the home TV screen and a central office. (In U.S. usage the generic term is *videotext,* with *videotex* meaning a two-way data retrieval system.) Compare **teletext.**

videotext. Interactive (two-way) text displayed on a TV screen, transmitted by telephone wire or cable.

viewdata. Another term for **videotex.**

Visnews. Leading international agency dealing in TV pictorial news material.

VOA (Voice of America). U.S. official **external service,** operated directly by the federal government through **USIA.**

WARC (World Administrative Radio Conference). Meetings held by the **ITU** periodically to update specific aspects of the **Radio Regulations.**

WIPO (World Intellectual Property Organization). Administrative organization of the **Berne Convention.**

wired radio. Method of delivering audio programs from a **headend** by means of wire connections to loudspeakers in the homes of subscribers and in public places. Also called **rediffusion.**

WRTH (*World Radio TV Handbook*). Annual directory of world broadcasting containing detailed information about each national **system** and about international broadcasting organizations.

Yuri. Japan's first broadcast satellite, launched in 1978 under auspices of **NASDA, NHK,** and the Japanese **PTT.**

ZDF (*Zweites Deutsches Fernsehen*). The "Second German Network" (after **ARD**), a cooperative national television network operated on the basis of a treaty among the West German states.

CITATIONS

Abel, John A., et al. 1970. "License Revocations and Denials of Renewal, 1934–1969." *Journal of Broadcasting* 14 (Fall): 411–421.

Adhikary, Dhruba H. 1982. "Nepal, World's Only Hindu State." *BM/E's World Broadcast News* (Dec.–Jan.): 56–58.

Adhikarya, Ronny, et al. 1977. *Broadcasting in Peninsular Malaysia.* IIC Case Studies on Broadcasting Systems. Routledge & Kegan Paul, in association with International Broadcasting Institute, London.

Adilman, Sid. 1984. "Canada Fund an Unexpected Success," *Variety* (18 April): 49.

Advertising Age. 1983. "Foreign Agency Income Profiles" (18 April): Special Insert.

Agrawal, Binod C. 1984. "Satellite Instructional Television: SITE in India." In Gerbner & Siefert: 354–359.

Akenga, Jamen. 1982. "Voice of Kenya—Past and Present." *Combroad* 56 (Sept.): 28–35.

Ali, Syed A. 1982. "Population Planning Broadcasts in Bangladesh." *Combroad* 55 (June): 37–38.

Amunugama, Sarath. 1981. "Open University Method of Politics: Sri Lanka Accepts Television." *Viertel Jahres Berichte* (Bonn) 85 (Sept.): 263–270.

———. 1982. "Broadcasting in Asia: A Sleeping Giant." *Media Asia* 9-3: 132–137.

Anderson, Jack. 1982. "Notorious Major Haddad Retains Israeli Support." United Feature Syndicate, *Miami Herald* (16 Oct.): 31A.

Anderson, Michael H. 1981. "China's 'Great Leap' Toward Madison Avenue." *Journal of Communication* 31-1 (Winter): 10–22.

Ansah, P. A. V. 1979. "Problems of Localising Radio in Ghana." *Gazette* 25-1: 1–16.

———. 1984. "International News: Mutual Responsibilities of Developed and Developing Nations." In Gerbner & Siefert: 83–91.

Asian Broadcasting. 1982. "India Goes Colour" (Dec.): 4–8.

———. 1983. "A Controversial Program" (June): 10.

———. 1983. "Full Penetration in TV Village" (Aug.): 16–17.

———. 1984. "And Now . . . Pirate TV" (April–May): 19.

Austin, Anthony. 1979. "Soviet TV—Better Packaging for the Party Line." *New York Times* (21 Oct.): D-1, D-4.

Awasthy, G. C. 1978. "India." In Lent: 197–211.

Banker, Stephen. 1980. "For Cable TV, It's a One-Way Border." *TV Guide* (Jan. 12): 31.

Banks, Loxley. 1982. "Radio Cayman's First Five Years." *Combroad* 54 (March): 34–36.

Barron, James. 1982. "Illegal Radio Operations Transmitting Regularly." *New York Times* (24 April): 26.

Bautista, Hipolito. 1982. "Expanding Radio in Belize." *Combroad* 54 (March): 18–22.

BBC (British Broadcasting Corporation). Annual. *Annual Report and Handbook.* BBC, London.

———. Monitoring Service. Weekly. "Summary of World Broadcasts." BBC, Caversham Park, Reading.

———. World Service. Monthly. "London Calling." BBC, London.

———. 1933. *Yearbook.* BBC, London.

———. 1969. *Broadcasting in the Seventies: The BBC's Plan for Network Radio and Non-Metropolitan Broadcasting.* BBC, London.

———. 1974. *Annual Review of BBC Audience Research Findings.* No. 1, 1973–74. BBC, London.

———. 1981. *Annual Review of BBC Broadcasting Research Findings.* No. 7, 1980. BBC, London.

———. External Services. 1982. "World Radio and Television Receivers" (June). BBC, London.

———. 1983. *Annual Review of BBC Broadcasting Research Findings.* No. 8, 1981–82. BBC, London.

———. External Services. 1983. "World Radio and Television Receivers" (June). BBC, London.

Beltran, Luis R. 1978. "TV Etchings in the Minds of Latin Americans: Conservatism, Materialism, and Conformism." *Gazette* 24-2: 61–85.

Berlitz, Charles. 1982. *Native Tongues.* Grosset & Dunlap, New York.

Bernardez, Constantino E., & Haney, William E. 1978. "Religious Broadcasting in Asia." In Lent: 338–350.

Berrigan, Francis J., ed. 1977. *Access: Some Western Models of Community Media.* UNESCO, Paris.

Bertrand, Claude-Jean. 1982. "Morocco." In Boyd: 197–216.

BIB (Board for International Broadcasting). Annual. *Annual Report.* GPO, Washington, D.C.

Binder, David. 1980. "U.S. Concedes It Is Behind Anti-Khomeini Broadcasts." *New York Times* (29 June): 3.

Biryukov, N. S. 1981. *Television in the West and Its Doctrines.* Progress Publishers, Moscow.

Blankson-Mills, Maud. 1982. "Audience Research in West Africa." *Combroad* 54 (Jan.–March): 27–29.

Block, Clifford H. 1984. "Instituting the International Program for the Development of Communications." In Gerbner & Siefert: 475–485.

Bombled, Thierry. 1981. *"Devine Qui Va Parler Ce Soir?": Petite Histoire des Radios Libres.* Syros, Paris.

Boyd, Douglas A. 1975. "Development of Egypt's Radio: 'Voice of the Arabs' Under Nasser." *Journalism Quarterly* 52 (Winter): 645–653.

———. 1982. *Broadcasting in the Arab World.* Temple University Press, Philadelphia.

———. 1983. "Broadcasting Between the Two Germanies." *Journalism Quarterly* 60-2 (Summer): 232–239.

Boyd, Douglas A., & Benzies, John Y. 1983. "SOFIRAD: France's International Commercial Media Empire." *Journal of Communication* 33-2 (Spring): 56–69.

Boyle, Andrew. 1972. *Only the Wind Will Listen.* Hutchinson, London.

Braithwaite, Claire, & Rustin, Dan. 1983. "Children's Programming Receiving More Attention in Western Europe than at Any Time in TV's History." *Television/Radio International* (Sept.): 24–34.

Brazer, Joan. 1970. "Last Voyage of a Musical Pirate." *Miami Herald Tropic* (22 Feb.): 15.

Bredin, James. 1983. "Breakfast Television in Britain." *EBU Review* 34-5 (Sept.): 16.

Breen, Myles P. 1980. "Australia: Relay Now or Direct Broadcast Later." *Journal of Communication* 30-2 (Spring): 190–202.

Briggs, Asa. 1961. *The Birth of Broadcasting. The History of Broadcasting in the United Kingdom*, v. 1. Oxford University Press, London.

———. 1965. *The Golden Age of Wireless. The History of Broadcasting in the United Kingdom*, v.2. Oxford University Press, London.

———. 1979a. *Sound and Vision. The History of Broadcasting in the United Kingdom*, v.4. Oxford University Press, Oxford.

———. 1979b. *Governing the BBC*. BBC, London.

Broadcast Communications. 1982. "Cable to Expand in Europe" (Dec.): 10.

Broadcasting. 1981. "Pirate Radio Makes Comeback in England" (2 Nov.): 52.

———. 1982. "Mirror Tax Law Introduced in Senate" (8 Feb.): 103.

———. 1982. "Eyesore Factor" (8 Nov.): 7.

———. 1983. "Canada Eases Programming Restrictions" (7 Mar.): 41–42.

———. 1983. "SIN Licenses Up for Hearing" (6 June): 79.

———. 1983. "CBS's Open Door Policy with China" (13 June): 100–101.

———. 1983. "U.S. Team Back from Geneva, Pleased with Itself" (25 July): 26–27.

———. 1984. "U.S. Returns from WARC Pleased with Itself and ITU" (20 Feb.): 37.

———. 1984. "The Television Future of USIA" (26 March): 65.

Broadcasting-Cablecasting Yearbook, 1983. 1983. Broadcasting Publications, Washington, D.C.

Broadcasting News from the Netherlands. 1980. "A Day American Television" [sic] (June): 12.

Broadcasting Research Unit. 1983. *A Report from the Working Party on the New Technologies*. Broadcasting Research Unit, London.

Brooke, James. 1982. "Guerrilla Broadcasting Aiming for Listeners' Hearts and Minds." *Miami Herald* (9 May): 22A.

———. 1983. "It's 'Viva Video' in Latin America." *Miami Herald* (23 July): 1D.

Brown, Neil. 1982. "New Deal for the ABC in Australia." *Combroad* 56 (Sept.): 17–24.

Browne, Donald R. 1971. "The BBC and the Pirates: A Phase in the Life of a Prolonged Monopoly." *Journalism Quarterly* 48-1 (Spring): 85–99.

———. 1973. "Citizen Involvement in Broadcasting: Some European Experiences." *Public Telecommunications Review* 1-2 (Oct.): 16–28.

———. 1978. "International Broadcasting to Asia." In Lent: 318–338.

———. 1982. *International Radio Broadcasting: The Limits of the Limitless Medium*. Praeger, New York.

———. 1983a. "Going International: How BBC Began Foreign Language Broadcasts." *Journalism Quarterly* 60-3 (Autumn): 423–430.

———. 1983b. "Media Entertainment in the Western World." In Martin & Chaudhary: 187–208.

———. 1984. "Alternatives for Local and Regional Radio: Three Nordic Solutions." *Journal of Communication* 34-2 (Spring): 36–55.

Burns, Tom. 1977. *The BBC: Public Institution and Private World*. Macmillan, London.

Butterfield, Fox. 1982. *China Alive in the Bitter Sea*. New York Times Books, New York.

Cavazza, Fabio L. 1979. "Italy: From Party Occupation to Party Partition." In Smith: 76–113.

Chamish, Barry. 1982. "Israel's 'Voice of Peace' Falls Silent." *World Broadcast News* (June): 6.

Chander, Romesh, & Karnik, Kiran. 1976. *Planning for Satellite Broadcasting: The Indian Instructional Television Experiment*. Reports and Papers on Mass Communication, No. 78. UNESCO, Paris.

Channels. 1984. "The Big Turn-On in India" (March–April): 7–8.

Christian, Shirley. 1982. "Nicaraguan Broadcasts Fill Costa Rican Ears Near Border." *Miami Herald* (2 Nov.): 7A.

Chu, James C. Y. 1978. "People's Republic of China." In Lent: 21–41.

———. 1982. "Advertising in China: Its Policy, Practice and Evolution." *Journalism Quarterly* 59-1 (Spring): 40.

CIA (Central Intelligence Agency). 1982. *The World Factbook, 1982*. GPO, Washington, D.C.

Clarke, Gerald. 1981. "Babel in the Ionosphere." *Time* (12 Jan.): 43.

Clines, Francis X. 1979. "The Sound of Silence on WFAT, Pirate Radio." *New York Times* (21 Apr.): 27.

Coase, R. H. 1966. "The Economics of Broadcasting and Government Policy." *American Economic Review* 56 (May): 440–447.

Codding, George A. 1983. "World Administrative Radio Conference for the Planning of HF Bands Allocated to the Broadcasting Service: A Pre-Conference Briefing Paper" (Nov.). International Institute of Communications, London.

Cole, Barry, & Oettinger, Mal. 1978. *Reluctant Regulators: The FCC and the Broadcast Audience*. Addison-Wesley, Reading, MA.

Collett, H. O. 1964. "VHF/FM Sound Broadcasting in the Republic of South Africa. Part I: General Considerations." *EBU Review* 84A (April): 55–57.

Collins, Larry, & La Pierre, Dominique. 1972. *O Jerusalem*. Simon & Schuster, New York.

Combroad. 1981. "CBA Regional Group Meetings: Pacific . . . Tonga," 53 (Dec.): 42–48.

———. 1982. "TV Plans Shelved in Tanzania," 57 (Dec.): 50.

———. 1983. "Cable TV in Australia Ruled Out," 59 (June): 45.

Cook, Bruce L. 1979. "African Christian Broadcasting: Needs and Trends" (31 Oct.). Paper presented at African Studies Association Annual Meeting, Los Angeles.

Crane, Rhonda J. 1979. *The Politics of International Standards: France and the Color TV War*. Ablex, Norwood, NJ.

Crosby, Scott, & Tempest, Alastair. 1983. "Satellite Lore: Copyright, Advertising, Public Morality and Satellites in EEC Law." *EBU Review* 34-3 (May): 30–38.

Cross, Ian. 1982. "Broadcasting in New Zealand: Need for Political Consensus." *Combroad* 57 (Oct.–Dec.): 12–14.

De Fleur, Melvin L., & Ball-Rokeach, Sandra. 1975. *Theories of Mass Communication*. 3d ed. Longman, New York.

Deihl, E. Roderick. 1977. "South of the Border: The NBC and CBS Radio

Networks and the Latin American Venture, 1930–1942." *Communication Quarterly* 25-4 (Fall): 2–12.

Delmer, Sefton. 1962. *Black Boomerang.* Secher & Warburg, London.

de Silva, M. A., & Siriwardene, Reggie. 1977. *Communications Policies in Sri Lanka.* UNESCO, Paris.

Dittrich, Robert, et al. 1983. *Intellectual Property Rights and Cable Distribution of Television Programs.* Mass Media Files, No. 5. Council of Europe, Strasbourg.

Dizard, Wilson P. 1966. *Television: A World View.* Syracuse University Press, Syracuse, NY.

Domínguez, Jorge I. 1982. *Cuba: Internal and International Affairs.* Sage, Beverly Hills, CA.

Dua, Mulakh. 1983. "Doordarshan Woos Advertisers." *Asian Broadcasting* (Aug.): 90.

Duckmanton, Talbot. 1975. *Public Service Broadcasting: The Australian Experience.* BBC Lunch Time Lectures 10-1 (Oct.). BBC, London.

Durrer, Beat. 1982. "Recent Political and Legal Developments on the Media Front in Switzerland." *EBU Review* 33-5 (Sept.): 17–22.

EBU Review. 1983. "Direct Broadcast Satellites and Television Advertising," 34-5 (Sept.): 25–32.

———. 1984. "An EBU Survey on Cable Television in Europe," 35-1 (Jan.): 31–42.

———. 1984. "Belgium: Noncommercial Advertising and Pay Television at RTBF," 35-2 (March): 44–46.

———. 1984. "UK Action on Pirate Radio," 35-2 (March): 56.

———. 1984. "Radio and Television License Fees," 35-3 (May): 62–63.

Egbon, Mike. 1983. "Western Nigeria Television Service—Oldest in Tropical Africa." *Journalism Quarterly* 60-2 (Summer): 329–334.

Eguchi, H., & Ichinohe, H., eds. 1971. *International Studies of Broadcasting with Special Reference to the Japanese Studies.* NHK, Tokyo.

Ehrenberg, Andrew, & Barwise, Patrick. 1983. "Do We Need to Regulate TV Programmes?" *InterMedia* 11-4/5 (July–Sept.): 12–15.

Elgabri, Ali. 1974. "Algeria." In Head: 31–34.

Emery, Walter B. 1969. *National and International Systems of Broadcasting: Their History, Operation and Control.* Michigan State University Press, East Lansing.

Eugster, Ernest. 1983. *Television Programming Across National Boundaries: The EBU and OIRT Experience.* Artech, Dedham, MA.

F. (*Federal Reporter*). 1929. *U.S.* v. *American Bond & Mortgage.* 31 F. 2d 448.

FARB (Federation of Australian Radio Broadcasters). 1981. "A Proposal to End the Election 'Blackout.'" FARB, Milson's Point, New South Wales.

Fatt, Cheng T. 1980. "Corporation Structure in Singapore." *Combroad* 49 (Dec.): 6–9.

Fauconnier, Guido. 1984. "Serving Two Cultures: Local Media in Belgium." In Gerbner & Siefert: 322–329.

FCC (Federal Communications Commission). 1980. *Annual Programming Report for Commercial Television Stations: 1979.* FCC, Washington, D.C.

FEBA Radio. n.d. "Programming Policies and Guidelines for Programme Producers." FEBA, London.

Fenton, Helen. 1981. "Viewing and Listening in the UK in 1980." In BBC: 13–20.

Fielden, Lionel. 1960. *The Natural Bent*. André Deutsch, London.

Fischer, Heinz-Dietrich. 1979. "Entertainment—An Underestimated Central Function of Communication." In Fischer & Melnik: 2–19.

Fischer, Heinz-Dietrich, & Melnik, Stefan, eds. 1979. *Entertainment: A Cross-Cultural Examination*. Hastings House, New York.

Fisher, Desmond. 1978. *Broadcasting in Ireland*. IIC Case Studies on Broadcasting Systems. Routledge & Kegan Paul, London.

Fisher, Desmond, & Harms, L. S. 1983. *The Right to Communicate: A New Human Right*. Book Press, Dublin.

Fisher, Harold. 1980. "The EBU: Model for Regional Cooperation in Broadcasting." *Journalism Monographs* 68 (May).

Fleiss, David, & Ambrosino, Lillian. 1971. "An International Comparison of Children's Television Programs" (July). National Citizens Committee for Broadcasting, Washington, D.C.

Flichy, Patrice. 1978. "France: 'Parallel' Radio and Program Revitalization." *Journal of Communication* 28-3 (Summer): 68–72.

Folorunso, Isola. 1980. "FRCN Zonal Structure in Nigeria: A New Dimension in Radio Broadcasting." *Combroad* 46 (Jan.–March): 12–13.

Foster, David. 1984. "Indonesian Broadcasting Kaleidoscope." *WRTH*: 599–606.

Freed, Paul E. 1979. *Towers to Eternity*. Sceptre Books, Nashville, TN.

Friedman, Charles. 1959. "Unrest in Cuban TV Studios." *New York Times* (10 May): 59.

Gallup Organization, Inc. 1975. "Short-Wave Listening in the United States," Part 2 (April). Conducted for Radio Canada International. Gallup Organization, Princeton, NJ.

Garay, Ronald. 1982. "WRNO Worldwide: A Case Study in Licensing Private U.S. International Broadcast Stations." *Journal of Broadcasting* 26-3 (Summer): 641–655.

Garratt, Arthur. 1981. "Programming: The French Picture." *Video* (July): 36–37.

———. 1982. "Production International SFP, Paris." *Video* (Jan.): 14–23.

Gauhar, Altaf. 1979. "Free Flow of Information: Myths and Shibboleths." *Third World Quarterly* 1-3 (July): 53–77.

Gerbner, George, & Siefert, Marsha, eds. 1984. *World Communications: A Handbook*. Longman, New York.

Gibbons, R. Arnold. 1974. "Francophone West and Equatorial Africa." In Head: 107–124.

Glattbach, Jack, & Balakrishnan, Ramanujan. 1978. "Malaysia." In Lent: 142–155.

Glencross, David. 1983. "Sponsorship: A New Source of Program Finance?" *EBU Review* 34-3 (May): 12–15.

Goodgame, Dan. 1983. "Israelis Ban Arab News Service, Demand It Apply for State License." *Miami Herald* (27 April): 8A.

Gore, M. S. 1983. *The SITE Experience*. Reports and Papers on Mass Communication, No. 91. UNESCO, Paris.

Grant, Stephen H. 1974. "Case Study: Ivory Coast ETV." In Head: 315–319.

Great Britain. 1926. *Report of the Broadcasting Committee, 1925*. Cmnd. 2599. ("Crawford Report"). Her Majesty's Stationery Office, London.

———. 1962. *Report of the Committee on Broadcasting*. Cmnd. 1753. ("Pilkington Report"). Her Majesty's Stationery Office, London.

———. 1977. *Report of the Committee on the Future of Broadcasting.* Cmnd. 6753. ("Annan Report"). Her Majesty's Stationery Office, London.

———. 1981. *Broadcasting Act of 1981.* Chapter 68. Her Majesty's Stationery Office, London.

———. 1982. "Report of the Inquiry into Cable Expansion and Broadcasting Policy." Cmnd. 8679. Her Majesty's Stationery Office, London.

———. 1984a. *Cable and Broadcasting Act 1984.* Chapter 46. Her Majesty's Stationery Office, London.

———. 1984b. *Report of the Broadcasting Complaints Commission 1984.* Her Majesty's Stationery Office, London.

Great Soviet Encyclopedia. 1973. 3d ed. 31 vols. (from 1970 Russian edition). Macmillan, New York.

Green, Timothy. 1972. *The Universal Eye: The World of Television.* Stein & Day, New York.

Guback, Thomas, H., & Hill, Steven P. 1972. "The Beginnings of Soviet Broadcasting and the Role of V. I. Lenin." *Journalism Monographs* 26 (Dec.).

Guider, Elizabeth. 1984. "RAI Plugs in Italian Meters; Rivals Peeved." *Variety* (28 March): 1.

Gunter, Jonathan F., et al. 1979. *The United States and the Debate on the World "Information Order."* Academy for Educational Development, Washington, D.C.

Gurian, Silvia. 1984. *Les Radios Privées en Italie.* Technique, Media, Société, Paris.

Gutiérrez, Felix F., & Schement, Jorge R. 1981. "Problems of Ownership and Control of Spanish-Language Media in the United States." In McAnany et al.: 181–203.

Hachten, William A. 1971. *Muffled Drums: The News Media in Africa.* Iowa State University Press, Ames.

———. 1979. "Policies and Performance of South African Television." *Journal of Communication* 29-3 (Summer): 62–72.

Hale, Julian. 1975. *Radio Power: Propaganda and International Broadcasting.* Temple University Press, Philadelphia.

Hanson, Philip. 1974. *Advertising and Socialism: A Study of the Nature and Extent of Consumer Advertising in the Soviet Union, Poland, Hungary, and Yugoslavia.* Macmillan, London.

Harley, William G. 1984. "UNESCO and the International Program for the Development of Communications." In Gerbner & Siefert: 467–474.

Harris, Paul. 1970. *When Pirates Ruled the Waves.* 4th pr. Impulse Books, London.

Head, Sydney W., ed. 1974. *Broadcasting in Africa: A Continental Survey of Radio and Television.* Temple University Press, Philadelphia.

———. 1979. "British Colonial Broadcasting Policies: The Case of the Gold Coast." *African Studies Review* 22-2 (Sept.): 39–47.

Head, Sydney W., & Gordon, Thomas F. 1976. "The Structure of World Broadcast Programming: Some Tentative Hypotheses." *Gazette* 22-2: 106–114.

Head, Sydney W., and Kugblenu, John. 1978. "GBC-1: A Survival of Wired Radio in Tropical Africa." *Gazette* 24-2: 121–129.

Hershey, Robert D., Jr. 1977. "British in Rare Ban on TV Film." *New York Times* (15 Dec.): A5.

High Adventure Broadcasting Network. [1982?]. "Information Summary," HBN, Van Nuys, CA.

Higham, Nicholas. 1982. "Demand for 'Alternative Radio' Grows in Britain." *World Broadcast News* (Feb.): 37–40

Hoffer, Thomas W., & Lichty, Lawrence W. 1978. "Republic of Vietnam (South Vietnam)." In Lent: 93–111.

Hofstede, Peter, & Kemme, Geert-Jan. 1979. "The Dynamics of Stagnation: Local Broadcasting in the Netherlands." Paper read at International Institute of Communication Conference, London.

Hollie, Pamela G. 1981. "Life Without Television Is a Pressing Issue in Fiji." *New York Times* (25 Oct.): 16.

Homet, Roland S. 1979. *Politics, Cultures and Communication: European vs. American Approaches to Communications Policymaking.* Praeger, New York.

Hopkins, Mark W. 1970. *Mass Media in the Soviet Union.* Pegasus, New York.

Horton, Philip C., ed. 1978. *The Third World and Press Freedom.* Praeger, New York.

Howell, W. J., Jr. 1981. "Britain's Fourth Television Channel and the Welsh Language Controversy." *Journal of Broadcasting* 25-2 (Spring): 123–137.

———. 1982. "Bilingual Broadcasting and the Survival of Authentic Culture in Wales and Ireland." *Journal of Communication* 32-1 (Autumn): 39–54.

Howkins, John A. 1977. "The Chinese Way of Broadcasting." *InterMedia* 5-2 (April): 6–8.

———. 1979. "The Management of the Spectrum." *InterMedia* 7-5 (Sept.): 10–22.

———. 1981. "The Next Wave of Television." *InterMedia* 9-4 (July): 14–27.

———. 1982a. "Communications in Finland." *InterMedia* 10-4/5 (July–Sept.): 41–60.

———. 1982b. *Mass Communication in China.* Longman, New York.

———. 1982c. *New Technologies, New Policies? A Report for the Broadcasting Research Unit.* British Film Institute, London.

———. 1983. "Basques Use TV to Speak Their Own Language." *InterMedia* 11-3 (May): 20–25.

Humi, Julius. 1982. "RAI-Indie Battle to Have Far-Reaching Effects." *Television/Radio Age International* (Sept.): 50.

———. 1984. "Possible Merger of Big Commercial Italian TV Broadcasters Spells Even More Trouble for RAI." *Television/Radio Age International* (Feb.): 16–30.

———. 1984. "New Rating Service Calms TV Furor in Italy." *Television Age International* (Oct.): 33–36.

IBA (Independent Broadcasting Authority). 1978. *Television & Radio, 1979: IBA Guide to Independent Television and Independent Local Radio.* IBA, London.

———. 1982. *Television and Radio, 1983: IBA Guide to Independent Broadcasting.* IBA, London.

——. 1983. *Television and Radio, 1984: IBA Guide to Independent Broadcasting*. IBA, London.

Immerman, Richard H. 1982. *The CIA in Guatemala: The Foreign Policy of Intervention*. University of Texas Press, Austin.

Inglis, Andrew. 1981. "Satellite Television in the United States." *Combroad* 50 (March): 1–8.

InterMedia. 1982. "Japan Shows a Global Sunrise," 10-3 (May): 46–47.

——. 1983. "Videocassette Recorders: National Figures," 11-4/5 (July–Sept.): 38–39.

Ito, Masami. 1978. *Broadcasting in Japan*. IIC Case Studies on Broadcasting Systems. Routledge & Kegan Paul, London.

ITU (International Telecommunication Union). 1980. *Final Acts of the World Administrative Radio Conference, Geneva, 1979*. ITU, Geneva [as reprinted in U.S. Senate, 1981, q.v.].

Izcaray, Fausto, & McNelly, John T. 1984. "Selective Media Use by Venezuelans: The Passing of the Passive Audience in a Rapidly Developing Society." *Studies in Latin American Popular Culture,*" forthcoming.

Jacobs, George. 1983. "High Frequency Broadcast Reception Conditions Expected During 1983." In *WRTH*: 52–56.

Jehoram, Herman C. 1982. "The Unique Dutch Broadcasting System on the Eve of the Revolution in Teletechnics and the Freedom of Information." In Netherlands Comparative Law Association: 327–343.

Johnson, A. W. 1982. "Canadian Content in Canadian Television." *Combroad* 54 (March): 1–4.

Johnson, Tim. 1983. "Surprise Selection of MAC as Standard for UK DBS Seen as Having Broad Implications Throughout Europe." *Television/Radio Age International* (Feb.): 48.

Katagiri, Akinori, & Motono, Koichi, eds. 1963. *Studies of Broadcasting,* v. 1. NHK, Tokyo.

Kato, Hidetoshi. 1978. *Communication Policies in Japan*. UNESCO, Paris.

Katz, Elihu, & Liebes, Tamar. 1984. "Once Upon a Time in Dallas." *InterMedia* 12-3 (May): 28–32.

Katz, Elihu, & Wedell, George. 1977. *Broadcasting in the Third World: Promise and Performance*. Harvard University Press, Cambridge, MA.

Kiester, Edwin, Jr. 1977. "The Great International Ratings War." *TV Guide* (29 Jan.): 34–41.

Kleinsteuber, Hans J. 1983. "More on the Two Germanies." *Journal of Communication* 33-4 (Autumn): 123–124.

Klose, Kevin. 1979. "Joe Adamov, the 'Moscow Mailbag' Man." *Washington Post* (27 Jan.): D1.

Knight, Robert P. 1982. "Chile." In Kurian: 203–217.

Knitel, H. G. 1982. "Advertising in Radio and Television Broadcasts," Mass Media Files No. 1. Council of Europe, Strasbourg.

Kowet, Don. 1977. "Maybe They Lose Something in Translation." *TV Guide* (10 Dec.): 12–14.

Krath, Herbert. 1982. "Broadcasting Service Coverage in the Federal Republic of Germany." *Telecommunication Journal* 49-9 (Sept.): 562–566.

Krishnatray, Pradeep. 1981. "Radio and Television in India." *Combroad* 51 (June): 36–39.

Kugblenu, John. 1974. "Ghana." In Head: 89–95.

Kuhn, Raymond. 1983. "Broadcasting and Politics in France." *Parliamentary Affairs* 36 (Winter): 67–83.

Kurian, George T., ed. 1982. *World Press Encyclopedia*. 2 vols. Facts on File, New York.

Kushner, James M. 1974. "African Liberation Broadcasting." *Journal of Broadcasting* 18 (Summer): 299–309.

Lamb, David. 1982. *The Africans*. Random House, New York.

Lambert, Stephen. 1982. *Channel Four: Television with a Difference?* British Film Institute, London.

Lapin, S. G. 1973. "Television Broadcasting." In *Great Soviet Encyclopedia*, v. 25: 484–486.

Leapman, Michael. 1984. *Treachery? The Power Struggle for TV-am*. Allen & Unwin, London.

Lee, Chin-Chuan. 1979. *Media Imperialism Reconsidered: The Homogenization of Television Culture*. Sage, Beverly Hills, CA.

Lent, John A. 1978. *Broadcasting in Asia and the Pacific: A Continental Survey of Radio and Television*. Temple University Press, Philadelphia.

———. 1982. "ASEAN Mass Communication and Culture Submission." *Media, Culture and Society* 4: 171–189.

Lewis, Peter M. 1978. *Community Television and Cable in Britain*. British Film Institute, London.

Li, Zhang. 1983. "Unpublished and Unofficial Paper Summarizing Chinese Mass Media Facts."

Lippman, Thomas W. 1983. "French Canada Takes on the Kidvid Jungle." *Miami Herald* (1 May): 1F.

Local Radio Workshop. 1983. *Nothing Local About It: London's Local Radio*. Comedia Series, No. 14. Comedia, London.

Lower, Elmer. 1982. "French TV Under the Socialists: Less Emphasis on Entertainment, Heavier Accent on 'Education.'" *Television/Radio Age International* (Sept.): 35–48.

McAnany, Emile G., et al. 1981. *Communication and Social Structure: Critical Studies in Mass Media Research*. Praeger, New York.

McCavitt, William E., ed. 1981. *Broadcasting Around the World*. TAB Books, Blue Ridge Summit, PA.

McPhail, Thomas L. 1981. *Electronic Colonialism: The Future of International Broadcasting and Communication*. Sage, Beverly Hills, CA.

MacSweeney, Edward F. 1983. "Irish Prepare for Indie Radio Units." *Variety* (24 Aug.): 64.

Mahan, Mary E. 1982. "Commercial Broadcasting Regulation: Structures and Processes in Mexico and the United States." Ph.D. dissertation, University of Texas (Austin).

Makita, Tetsuo. 1979. "Television Drama and Japanese Culture with Special Emphasis on Historical Drama." In Fischer & Melnik: 63–73.

Manning, Jo. 1979. "Doordarshan Knows Best." *TV Guide* (27 Oct.): 28–30.

Mansell, Gerard. 1982. *Let Truth Be Told: 50 Years of BBC External Broadcasting*. Weidenfeld & Nicolson, London.

Marchetti, Victor, & Marks, John D. 1974. *The CIA and the Cult of Intelligence*. Knopf, New York.

Marks, David. 1983. "Broadcasting Across the Wall: The Free Flow of

Information Between East and West Germany." *Journal of Communication* 33-1 (Winter): 46–55.

Martin, L. John, & Chaudhary, Anju G. 1983. *Comparative Mass Media Systems*. Longman, New York.

Marting, Leeda P. 1973. "British Control of Television Advertising." *Journal of Broadcasting* 17-2 (Spring): 159–172.

Masani, Mehra. 1976. *Broadcasting and the People*. National Book Trust, New Delhi.

Matthews, Herbert L. 1975. *Revolution in Cuba: An Essay in Understanding*. Scribner's, New York.

Mattos, Sergio. 1981. *The Development of Communication Policies Under the Peruvian Military Government (1968–1980)*. Klingensmith, Austin, TX.

May, Clifford D. 1984. "Nigeria's 'War Against Indiscipline': The Military is Not Sparing the Rod." *New York Times* (10 Aug.): 6.

Mazrui, Ali A. 1972. *Cultural Engineering and Nation Building in East Africa*. Northwestern University Press, Evanston, IL.

Mboya, Tom. 1963. *Freedom and After*. André Deutsch, London.

Media Institute. 1982. *Voice of America at the Crossroads: A Panel Discussion of the Appropriate Role of the VOA*. The Institute, Washington, D.C.

Meneer, Peter. 1984. "Broadcasting Research: Necessity or Nicety?" *InterMedia* 12-3 (May): 39–42.

Menzel, Willi. 1983. "World Communications Year 1983 and Broadcasting." In *WRTH*: 38–46.

Mhumbira, Ignatius. 1981. "Thirty Years of Broadcasting in Tanzania." *Combroad* 50 (March): 21–24.

Mickiewicz, Ellen P. 1981. *Media and the Russian Public*. Praeger, New York.

Mikriukov, M. P. 1973. "Radio, Art of." In *Great Soviet Encyclopedia*, v. 21: 402–403.

Mills, D. H. 1964. "VHF/FM Sound Broadcasting in the Republic of South Africa, Part III." *EBU Review* 86A (August): 162–168.

Mills, Rilla D. 1983. "Education, Persuasion, and Opinion Making in the Communist World." In Martin & Chaudhary: 167–186.

Monet, Jack. 1984. "U.S. TV Shows on Euro Satellite: Concept Panics Common Market Politicians." *Variety* (30 May): 1.

Motamed-Nejad, Kazem. 1979. "The Story-Teller and the Mass Media in Iran." In Fischer & Melnik: 43–62.

Mullings, Merry. 1983. "Mid East TV Mixes Exotic and Western Styles." *Video Age International* (April): 40–44.

Mytton, Graham. 1983. *Mass Communication in Africa*. Arnold, London.

Nakajima, Iwao. 1971. "The Broadcasting Industry of Japan: Its Historical, Legal, and Economic Aspects." In Eguchi & Ichinohe: 15–68.

Namurois, Albert. 1972. *Structures and Organization of Broadcasting in the Framework of Radiocommunications*. 2d ed. European Broadcasting Union, Geneva.

Neelankavil, James P., & Stridsberg, Albert B. 1980. *Advertising Self-Regulation: A Global Perspective*. Hastings House, New York.

Netherlands Comparative Law Association. 1982. *Netherlands Reports to the Eleventh International Congress of Comparative Law, Caracas, 1982*. Kluver, Deventer.

Netherlands Scientific Council for Government Policy. 1983. *A Coherent*

Media Policy: Summary of the Twenty-Fourth Report to the Government. NSCGP, The Hague.

New Statesman. 1981. "The Right to Print Money" (16 Jan.): 6–7.

New York Times. 1955. "Cuba TV Program Relayed by Plane" (14 Nov.): 52.

———. 1967. "Foreign Trade Is Two-Way Traffic" (16 Jan.): 56–57.

———. 1976. "The Tube" (24 Feb.): 34.

———. 1978. "Israel Moves to Reverse Ban on Controversial Film About Banishing of Arabs" (11 Feb.): C5.

———. 1978. "FCC Hunts an Illicit TV Station That Pirated Some Notable Show" [sic] (19 Apr.): 42.

———. 1978. "On the TV Screen: A Distorted Picture" (5 June): A10.

NHK (Nippon Hoso Kyokai). 1963 ff. *Studies of Broadcasting.* Radio and TV Culture Research Institute, NHK, Tokyo.

Nichols, John S. 1979. "Cuba: Right Arm of Revolution." In Pierce: 80–95.

———. 1982a. "The Mass Media: Their Function in Social Conflict." In Domínguez: 70–111.

———. 1982b. "Republic of Cuba." In Kurian: 257–271.

———. 1982c. "Statement and Testimony." USHR: 205–215.

———. 1984. "When Nobody Listens: Assessing the Political Success of Radio Martí." *Communication Research* 11-2 (April): 281–304.

Niemczyk, Barbara. 1983. "Eastern-Bloc TV Shows Better Picture of Closed Society." *Video Age International* (April): 50–54.

Nomura, Yoshio. 1963. "System of Broadcasting in Japan and Its Characteristics." In Katagiri & Motono: 65–80.

Noriega, Luis A. de, & Leach, Frances. 1979. *Broadcasting in Mexico.* IIC Case Studies on Broadcasting Systems. Routledge & Kegan Paul, London.

Novak, Jan. 1983. "Socialist Realism on the Czech Evening News." *Channels* (Jan.–Feb.): 52–54.

Nuyl, Piet te. 1984. "Sowing the Seeds for Pay-TV." *InterMedia* 12-1 (Jan.): 9–11.

O'Callaghan, Mary L. 1983. "Advanced Colour Centre in Beijing." *Asian Broadcasting* (Aug.): 16.

Okabe, Keizo. 1963. "Broadcasting Research in Post-War Japan." In Katagiri & Motono: 7–47.

Onder, James J. 1971. "The Sad State of Vatican Radio." *Educational Broadcasting Review* 5-4 (Aug.): 43–53.

Orlik, Peter B. 1974. "Radio in the Republic of South Africa." In Head: 140–154.

Ortmark, Ake. 1979. "Sweden: Freedom's Boundaries." In Smith: 142–190.

Owen, Bruce, et al. 1974. *Television Economics.* Lexington Books, Lexington, MA.

Paley, William S. 1979. *As It Happened: A Memoir.* Doubleday, Garden City, NY.

Palmer, Edward L., et al. 1976. "Sesame Street: Patterns of International Adaptation." *Journal of Communication* 26-2 (Spring): 109–123.

Paulu, Burton. 1967. *Radio and Television Broadcasting on the European Continent.* University of Minnesota Press, Minneapolis.

———. 1974. *Radio and Television Broadcasting in Eastern Europe.*, University of Minnesota Press, Minneapolis.

———. 1981. *Television and Radio in the United Kingdom.* University of Minnesota Press, Minneapolis.

Pease, Bill. 1982. ". . . And This Is How They Do the News in Europe." *Channels* (April–May): 62–63.

Peyre, Paul. 1984. "TV5: A French-Language Satellite Television Service." *EBU Review*, 35-3 (May): 22–25.

Peyrefitte, Alain. 1981. *The Trouble With France.* Knopf, New York.

Pierce, Robert N. 1979. *Keeping the Flame: Media and Government in Latin America.* Hastings House, New York.

Pilsworth, Michael. 1982. "Algeria." In Boyd: 170–183.

Pitman, Jack. 1983. "CBS, HBO, Col, Fox, Goldcrest for Brit. Cable." *Variety* (8 June): 1, 46.

Poindexter, David. 1982. "Broadcasting and Population Planning." *Combroad* 55 (June): 34–36.

Pol, Ramon V. 1982. "Spain: Private Television Stations." *EBU Review* 33-5 (Sept.): 34.

Pons, Eugene. 1964. *General Considerations on Licence Fees for Radio and Television Sets.* EBU Legal Monograph, No. 1. European Broadcasting Union, Geneva.

Pool, Ithiel de S., & Dizard, Stephen. 1978. "International Telecommunications and the Requirements of News Services." Murrow Reports, Fletcher School of Law and Diplomacy, Tufts University, Medford, MA.

Porter, Vincent. 1979. "Television and Film Production Strategies in the European Community." In Fischer & Melnik: 258–272.

Pridgen, Dee. 1984. "Commercial Advertising on Television Across National Frontiers: Issues and Strategies for Consumers." National Consumer Council, London.

Professional Video. 1983. "Belgian Cable Operators to Carry BBC Programmes" (Nov.): 10.

———. 1984. "Laos Plan [sic] Both PAL and SECAM Transmissions" (April): 41.

Protheroe, Alan. 1982. "Covering the Event in a Parliamentary Democracy: The British Media in the Falklands Crisis." *EBU Review* 33-6 (Nov.): 14–16.

PSCIRB (Presidential Study Commission on International Radio Broadcasting). 1973. *The Right to Know.* GPO, Washington, D.C.

Quinn, Brian. 1982. "Twenty-Five Years of Visnews." *Combroad* 55 (June): 23–25.

Radcliffe, John, & Salkeld, Roberts, eds. 1983. *Towards Computer Literacy: The BBC Computer Literacy Project, 1979–1983.* BBC, London.

Rao, B. S. 1977. "A Case for Cheaper Radio Sets in India." *Combroad* 35 (June): 29–32.

Ratliff, Paul. 1982. "Satellite Broadcasting and BBC Plans for UK Services." *Combroad* 56 (Sept.): 37–42.

Read, William H. 1977. *America's Mass Media Merchants.* Johns Hopkins University Press, Baltimore, MD.

Reeves, Richard. 1982. *American Journey: Traveling with Tocqueville in Search of Democracy in America.* Simon & Schuster, New York.

Reiss, Pamela. 1983. "Continuous Research for Television and Radio: The 1980s Approach." In BBC: 13–26.

Reith, J. C. W. 1949. *Into the Wind*. Hodder & Stoughton, London.

Ridoux, Georges. 1982. "Audiovisual Communications in France, Stage Two: The Act of 29 July 1982." *EBU Review* 33-6 (Nov.): 6–13.

Roberts, John Stewart. 1974. "Kenya." In Head: 54–61.

Roberts, John Storm. 1982. "Saudi Arabia: Islam's International Voice." *BM/E World Broadcast News* (Dec.–Jan.): 53–54.

Robertson, E. H. 1974. "Christian Broadcasting in and to Africa." In Head: 204–211.

Robinson, Deanna C. 1981. "Changing Functions of Mass Media in the People's Republic of China." *Journal of Communication* 31-4 (Autumn): 55–73.

Rogers, Everett M. 1983. *Diffusion of Innovations*. Free Press/Macmillan, New York.

Rogers, Everett M., & Braun, Juan R. 1977. "Radio Forums: A Strategy for Rural Development." In Spain et al.: II, 361–381.

Rosenblum, Mort. 1978. "The Western Wire Services and the Third World." In Horton: 104–126.

Rostan, Blaise. 1984. "Pay-Television in Switzerland." *EBU Review* 35-2 (March): 33–38.

Sadhu, S. 1981. "Pattern for Multi-lingual Television in India." *Combroad* 51 (June): 7–9.

St. John, Robert. 1960. *The Boss: The Story of Gamal Abdel Nasser*. McGraw-Hill, New York.

Sandford, John. 1976. *The Mass Media of the German-Speaking Countries*. Iowa State University Press, Ames.

Scandlen, Guy B. 1978. "Thailand." In Lent: 123–142.

Schey, Lida von. 1982. "South American Religious Radio Serving All." *BM/E World Broadcast News* (Dec.–Jan.): 58–60.

Schiffman, Steven M. 1983. "Despite Rapid TV Expansion in the Middle East, Western Programming Continues to Be a Tough Sell." *Television/Radio Age International* (April): 71–74.

Schiller, Herbert I. 1969. *Mass Communications and American Empire*. Augustus M. Kelley, New York.

Schramm, Wilbur, et al. 1981. *Bold Experiment: The Story of Educational Television in American Samoa*. Stanford University Press, Stanford, CA.

Sendall, Bernard. 1982. *Independent Television in Britain*. V. 1, *Origin and Foundation*. Macmillan, London.

———. 1983. *Independent Television in Britain*. V. 2, *Expansion and Change 1958–68*. Macmillan, London.

Shahzad, Badhnaseeb. 1984. "TV Is the Opium of the People." *InterMedia* 12-3 (May): 24–25.

Shea, Albert A. 1981. "Broadcasting in Canada." In McCavitt: 120–132.

Shulman, Milton. 1973. *The Least Worst Television in the World*. Barrie & Jenkins, London.

Shummo, Ali. 1974. "The Sudan." In Head: 46–50.

Silj, Alexander. 1981. "Italy's First Few Years of Private Television Broadcasting." *InterMedia* 9-5 (Sept.): 12–25.

Silvey, Robert. 1974. *Who's Listening? The Story of BBC Audience Research*. George Allen & Unwin, London.

Simoncini, Pedro. 1982. "Broadcasting in Argentina: A Search for Balance." *InterMedia* 10-4/5 (July–Sept.): 24–27.

Smith, Anthony. 1973. *The Shadow in the Cave: The Broadcaster, His Audience, and the State.* University of Illinois Press, Urbana.

———. 1974. *British Broadcasting.* David & Charles, Newton Abbot, England.

———. 1978. *The Politics of Information: Problems of Policy in Modern Media.* Macmillan, Atlantic Highlands, N.J.

———. 1979. *Television and Political Life.* St. Martin's Press, New York.

Soderstrom, Herbert. 1981. "Broadcasting in Sweden." In McCavitt: 299–312.

Soley, Laurence C. 1983. "The Political Context of Clandestine Radio Broadcasting in 1981." *Journal of Broadcasting* 27-3 (Summer): 233–250.

Sommerlad, E. Lloyd. 1981. "Communication in the New China." *Media Asia* 8-4: 23–40.

Soramaki, Martti. 1982. "Finland's Experiences with Pay-TV." *InterMedia* 10-2 (March): 27–28.

Spain, Peter L., et al., eds. 1977. *Radio for Education and Development: Case Studies.* World Bank Staff Working Papers, No. 266 (May), 2 vols. World Bank, Washington, D.C.

Sparks, Allister. 1984. "The Call of Bop-TV." *Connections: World Communication Report* (10 Sept.): 1–2.

Speigler, Steve. 1984. "Border Proximity Promotes Piracy All Over Europe." *Television Age International* (April): 21–36.

Stapleton, John. 1974. *Communication Policies in Ireland.* UNESCO, Paris.

Steiner, Rob. 1981. "The Struggle for Poland's Airwaves." *Channels* (Oct.–Nov.): 24.

Stephenson, William. 1967. *The Play Theory of Mass Communication.* University of Chicago Press, Chicago.

Stevens, B. J. 1964. "VHF/FM Sound Broadcasting in the Republic of South Africa. Part II: Network Design." *EBU Review* 84A (April): 58–63.

Straubhaar, Joseph D. 1982. "The Development of the Telenovelas as the Pre-Eminent Form of Popular Culture in Brazil." *Studies in Latin American Popular Culture* 1: 138–150.

———. 1983. "Factors in the Growth of Television Exports from Latin American Countries." Paper delivered at Communication, Mass Media and Development Conference, Northwestern University (13 Oct.).

Svard, Stig. 1982. "Sweden Re-regulates Its Media Mix." *InterMedia* 10-2 (March): 29–31.

Sweden. Swedish Broadcasting Commission. 1977. *Radio & TV 1978–1985: Proposals.* Ministry of Education and Cultural Affairs, Stockholm.

Syfret, Toby, ed. 1983. *Television Today and Television Tomorrow.* J. Walter Thompson-Europe, London.

Tadokoro, Izumi. 1978. "Japan." In Lent: 60–74.

Talen, Julie. 1984. "From the Eye of the Storm." *Channels* (Jan./Feb.): 10.

Tatarian, Roger. 1978. "News Flow in the Third World: An Overview." In Horton: 1–54.

Taylor, A. J. P. 1965. *English History, 1914–1945.* Oxford University Press, New York and Oxford.

Tehranian, Majid. 1982. "Communications Dependency and Dualism in Iran." *InterMedia* 10-3 (May): 40–45.

Television Age International. 1984. "Worldwide TV Set Count" (April): 156–158.

———. 1984. "Cable Takes Root and Prospers in Switzerland" (Oct.): 39–40.

Tempest, Alastair. 1984. "Why We Need Advertising." *InterMedia* 12-2 (March): 14–19.

Thomas, Ruth. 1977. *Broadcasting and Democracy in France.* Temple University Press, Philadelphia.

Time. 1974. "Down-to-Earth Satellite" (23 Sept.): 71.

———. 1978. "Untimely Story: A TV Blackout of History" (20 Feb.): 36.

———. 1982. "VCRs Go on Fast Forward" (13 Dec.): 72.

———. 1983. "Lofty TV Goals" (1 Aug.): 78.

———. 1984. "France: Confrontations with Reality" (21 May): 64–67.

Toledano, Vincent. 1983. "Les Radios Locales du Service Public." *Telerama* [Paris] (1 Jan.): 42.

Toogood, Alexander F. 1978a. "New Zealand." In Lent: 288–298.

———. 1978b. "West Germany: Federal Structure, Political Influence." *Journal of Communication* 28-3 (Summer): 83–89.

———. 1981. "Experiment and Change in New Zealand Broadcasting." In Wedemeyer: A2, 18–22.

———. 1983a. "Broadcasting as a Reflection of the Politicizing of German Culture." Paper presented at Conference on Culture and Communication, Philadelphia (March).

———. 1983b. "Aussie TV: She's a Bewdy Mate." *Television Quarterly* 20-3 (Fall): 81–90.

Traub, James. 1984. "Beaming the World to Andhra Pradesh." *Channels* (May–June): 41–43.

Treaster, Joseph B. 1984. "Cuba Livens Up Its Radio As U.S. Prepares Station." *New York Times* (5 Aug.): 10.

Trethowan, Ian. 1984. "The Next Age of Broadcasting in Britain." *Combroad* 62 (March): 1–6.

Troyer, Warner. 1983. "Television in Sri Lanka." *Combroad* 59 (June): 6–10.

Tunstall, Jeremy. 1977. *The Media Are American.* Columbia University Press, New York.

TV/RAI (Television/Radio Age International). 1979. "Already Broadcasting in Several Languages, Yugoslavia Adds One More—and Conquers Italy" (Jan.): A46–51.

———. 1980. "Broadcast Operations in Europe Heading Toward Independence; Governments Losing Grip" (Jan.): A34–40.

Uchikawa, Yoshimi. 1964. "Process of Establishment of the New System of Broadcasting in Post-War Japan." In NHK: 51–80.

Ugwu, Godwin. 1980. "Managing Television in Developing Countries." *Combroad* 49 (Dec.): 13–17.

UNESCO (United Nations Educational, Scientific and Cultural Organization). 1980. *Many Voices, One World: Towards a New More Just and More Efficient World Information and Communication Order* (MacBride Report). Unipub, New York.

———. 1982a. *Statistical Yearbook, 1982.* UNESCO, Paris.

———. 1982b. *The Use of Satellite Communication for Information Transfer.* PG1-82/WS/5. Prepared by the IIC. UNESCO, Paris.

UNESCO-IIEP (United Nations Educational, Scientific and Cultural Organization and United Nations International Institute for Educational Planning). 1967. *New Educational Media in Action: Case Studies for Planners.* 3 vols. UNESCO/IIEP, Paris.

Uplink. 1984. "Intelsat and Developing Countries: An Interview with Richard Colino," No. 4 (Feb.): 1–3, 12.

U.S. (United States Reports). 309 U.S. 470, 25 March 1940. *FCC v. Sanders Bros.*

USACPD (United States Advisory Commission on Public Diplomacy). Annual. *Report to the Congress and to the President of the United States.* USACPD, Washington, D.C.

USC (United States Code). 1976. GPO, Washington, D.C.

USDOS (United States Department of State). 1982. *Report of the United States Delegation to the Regional Administrative MF Broadcasting Conference (Region 2) Second Session, Rio de Janeiro, Nov. 9–Dec. 19, 1981.* (12 Feb.). Department of State, Washington, D.C.

USGAO (U.S. General Accounting Office). 1982. "The Voice of America Should Address Existing Problems to Ensure High Performance." Report to the Director, U.S. International Communication Agency. GAO/ID-82-37 (29 July). GPO, Washington, D.C.

USHR (U.S. House of Representatives). Committee on Energy and Commerce, Subcommittee on Telecommunications, Consumer Protection and Finance. 1982. *Radio Broadcasting to Cuba.* Hearing on H.R. 5427 (10 May). Ser. No. 97-127. GPO, Washington, D.C.

USNC (U.S. National Commission for UNESCO). 1982. *A Critical Assessment of U.S. Participation in UNESCO.* Special Meeting of the U.S. National Commission for UNESCO, June 1–3, University of South Carolina. GPO, Washington, D.C.

USOTA (U.S. Office of Technical Assessment). 1982. "Radio Frequency Use and Management: Impacts from the World Administrative Radio Conference of 1979." Executive Summary. U.S. Congress, Washington, D.C.

U.S. Senate. Select Committee to Study Governmental Operations with Respect to Intelligence Activities. 1975. *Covert Action in Chile, 1963–1973.* Staff Report. 94th Cong., 1st Sess.

———. 1981. *Radio Regulations (Geneva, 1979) and Final Protocol.* Message from the President of the United States. Treaty Document No. 97-21, 97th Cong., 1st Sess.

———. Committee on Foreign Affairs. 1984. *U.S. Withdrawal from UNESCO.* Committee Print.

Variety. 1982. "Global Prices for TV Films" (21 April): 4.

———. 1983. "Latin American TV at a Glance" (30 March): 64.

———. 1983. "Commercial Television Today" (20 April): 38.

———. 1984. "New Canadian Content Regulations" (18 April): 60.

Varis, Tapio. 1984. "The International Flow of Television Programs." *Journal of Communication* 34-1 (Winter): 143–152.

Verlinde, W. 1984. "Some Comments on the Signing of the Cable Agreement in Belgium." *EBU Review* 35-2 (March): 27–32.

Viorst, Milton. 1981–1982. "The Tug of War in Israeli Television." *Channels* (Dec.–Jan.): 40–42.

Walker, Savannah W. 1983. "In the Grip of SIN." *Channels* (July–Aug.): 46–49.

Waltham, Tony. 1984. "Cable Controls for Thailand?" *Asian Broadcasting* (April–May): 14.

Watkins, Roger. 1982. "Commercial TV Sweeping Across Europe." *Variety* (21 April).

Webster, B. R. 1975. *Access: Technology and Access to Communications Media.* Reports and Papers on Mass Communication, No. 75. UNESCO, Paris.

Wedell, E. G. 1968. *Broadcasting and Public Policy.* Michael Joseph, London.

Wedemeyer, Dan J., ed. 1981. *PTC '81.* Pacific Telecommunications Council, Honolulu.

Weiss, Frederic A., et al. 1980. "Station License Revocations and Denials of Renewal, 1970–78." *Journal of Broadcasting* 24-1 (Winter): 69–77.

Whylie, Dwight. 1975. "The Future of the Jamaican Broadcasting Corporation." *Combroad* 27 (April–June): 13–18.

Wicklein, John. 1981. *Electronic Nightmare: The New Communications and Freedom.* Viking Press, New York.

Wigbold, Herman. 1979. "The Shaky Pillars of Hilversum." In Smith: 191–231.

Wijesekera, Nalin. 1983. "Rupavahim a Threat to Indian TV." *Asian Broadcasting* (Dec.): 7.

Wilkinson, J. F. 1974. "Great Britain." In Head: 216–225.

Williams, Arthur. 1977. *Broadcasting and Democracy in West Germany.* Temple University Press, Philadelphia.

Williams, Raymond. 1975. *Television: Technology and Cultural Form.* Schocken, New York.

Wilson, H. H. 1961. *Pressure Group: The Campaign for Commercial Television in England.* Rutgers University Press, New Brunswick, NJ.

Winkler, Allan M. 1978. *The Politics of Propaganda: The Office of War Information, 1942–1945.* Yale University Press, New Haven, CT.

Wood, George. 1983. "Rock and Revolution—Radio in Nicaragua." In *WRTH:* 604–605.

World Broadcast News. 1981. "Denmark" (Oct.).

Wren, Christopher S. 1980. "Lebanon Hills Echoing with Gospel Tunes." *New York Times* (15 Aug.): A10.

Wright, Anthony. 1979–1980. *Local Radio and Local Democracy: A Study in Political Education.* University of Birmingham, Birmingham, England.

Wright, Marc. 1983. "Urikon Reviewed." *EBU Review* 34-4 (July): 31–38.

WRTH (*World Radio TV Handbook*). Annual. J. M. Frost, ed. Billboard Publications, New York.

Young, Brian. 1983. "Paternalism in British Broadcasting." *Combroad* 59 (June): 36–41.

Index

(Note: f = figure, n = footnote, t = table.)

A

Abhorrent vacuum
   principle, 100–102, 107,
   274
Aborigines, 192, 193, 260,
   321, 360
Abu Dhabi, 158
Access to broadcasting:
   demand for, 44–45, 116,
      119, 141, 145
   future, 397
   group, 109–112
   ideal, 8
   illegal, 112–121
   and localism, 121–127
   mechanisms of, 99–101
   and NWIO, 380–381
   political, 69, 101–109, 116
   as a right, 97–99, 380–381,
      393
Access channels, cable TV,
   126, 149, 287
Access to spectrum, 391–392
Accountability, 8, 174,
   179–182, 397
Action for Children's
   Television, 179n
Adamov, Joe, 355
Adapter. See Converters
Administration, as ITU
   term, 142, 372n
Adult education, 317–318
Advertising:
   and access, 99
   amount, 202–203, 304t,
      305t
   blackouts, 204
   block, 217n, 221
   cable TV, 47, 50, 53, 126,
      127

as career, 311
and children, 179, 185–186
degree of reliance on, 207,
   212, 216–217, 218, 220,
   222
external broadcast, 351
future of, 398
and government
   broadcasting, 209–210,
   312
growth of, 20, 212
influence, 59, 205, 289
newspaper vs. broadcast,
   172–173
opposition to, 188, 200,
   205, 212, 217, 396, 399
pirate, 114, 115, 120
placement of, 203–204
production of, 206
as program type, 318–319
and RAI, 116–119
regulation of, 83, 158, 167,
   200–207, 397–398
as revenue source, 216–223
satellite, 44, 392
schedules, 296–298
social, 106, 217, 218
sponsorship, 205–206
teletext, 278
transborder, 269–273, 369
in USSR, 217
See also: Commercials,
   individual countries and
   regions
Afghanistan, 14
Africa:
   aid to, 138
   broadcast systems of,
      32–36
   culture and broadcasting,
      300

FM, 250
and ITU, 45, 137
pirates, 113
receivers, 263, 327t
satellites, 274
wired radio 48, 49t
See also individual countries
Africanization, 33
African liberation
   broadcasting, 369
Africa No. 1, 373
AGB Research, 331, 332
Agence France Presse (AFP),
   311, 388
Agencies, advertising, 79n,
   111, 145, 206–207, 217,
   318n, 327, 329, 333
Agencies, news, 235,
   311–312, 401. See also
   individual agencies
Agency for International
   Development (AID),
   226, 319
Aid, technical, 135, 138,
   226–227, 281, 319. See
   also individual countries
AIR (All India Radio). See
   India
Albania, 217, 342, 343t
Algeria, 34–35, 40f, 193,
   213t, 268, 305t
Allende, Salvador, 108–109
All in the Family, 229
Allocation, frequency, 135,
   136–137, 274
Allotment:
   frequency, 136, 137, 279
   orbit, 270
Alternative radio, 124. See
   also Community
   broadcasting